FIFTY
CONTEMPORARY
FILMMAKERS

Fifty Contemporary Filmmakers examines the work of some of today's most popular, original and influential cinematic voices. Each entry offers both an overview and a critique of its subject's career and works, looking at the genres in which they work and their relationships to other films and filmmakers. It covers filmmakers drawn from diverse cinematic traditions from around the world. Among those included are:

- Luc Besson
- James Cameron
- David Lynch
- John Woo
- Julie Dash

- Spike Lee
- Joel and Ethan Coen
- Martin Scorsese
- Mira Nair
- Wim Wenders

Each entry is supplemented by a filmography, references and suggestions for further reading, making *Fifty Contemporary Filmamkers* an indispensable guide for anyone interested in contemporary film.

Yvonne Tasker is Senior Lecturer in Film Studies at the University of East Anglia. She is the author of *Spectacular Bodies: Gender, Genre and Action Cinema* and *Working Girls: Gender and Sexuality in Popular Culture*, both published by Routledge.

ROUTLEDGE KEY GUIDES

Routledge Key Guides are accessible, informative and lucid handbooks, which define and discuss the central concepts, thinkers and debates in a broad range of academic disciplines. All are written by noted experts in their respective subjects. Clear, concise exposition of complex and stimulating issues and ideas make *Routledge Key Guides* the ultimate reference resources for students, teachers, researchers and the interested layperson.

FIFTY
CONTEMPORARY
FILMMAKERS

Edited by Yvonne Tasker

London and New York

First published 2002
by Routledge
11 New Fetter Lane, London EC4P 4EE

Simultaneously published in the USA and Canada
by Routledge
29 West 35th Street, New York, NY 10001

Routledge is an imprint of the Taylor & Francis Group

selection and editorial matter © 2002 Yvonne Tasker
individual chapters © 2002 the contributors

Typeset in Times by Taylor & Francis Books Ltd
Printed and bound in Great Britain by TJ International Ltd,
Padstow, Cornwall

British Library Cataloguing in Publication Data
A catalogue record for this book is available from the British Library

Library of Congress Cataloging in Publication Data
Fifty contemporary filmmakers / [edited by] Yvonne Tasker.
(Routledge Key Guides)
Includes bibliographical references and index.
1. Motion picture producers and directors–Biography–Dictionaries. I. Tasker,
Yvonne, 1964– II. Series.

PN1998.2 .F53 2001
791.43′0233′0922–dc21
[B]   2001048281

ISBN 0–415–18973–X (hbk)
ISBN 0–415–18974–8 (pbk)

FOR MICHÈLE SCOTT – THANKS!

CONTENTS

CONTRIBUTORS

Justine Ashby is Lecturer in Television and Film Studies at the University of East Anglia, UK. She has published essays on British cinema of the 1960s, 1980s and 1990s and is co-editor (with Andrew Higson) of *British Cinema, Past and Present* (2000). She is currently writing a book about the British filmmakers Muriel and Betty Box for Manchester University Press.

Anne Ciecko is Assistant Professor in the Department of Communication at the University of Massachusetts-Amherst, USA, where she teaches courses on international and intercultural cinema, gender studies and community arts. Her scholarly work has appeared in many academic journals and anthologies including *Cinema Journal, Journal of Film and Video, Post Script, Velvet Light Trap, Jump Cut, Spectator* and *Asian Cinema*. She has also organized exhibitions and festivals showcasing women film and video artists.

Paul Coates is Reader in Film Studies in the English Department of the University of Aberdeen, Scotland. His books include *The Story of the Lost Reflection: The Alienation of the Image in Western and Polish Cinema* (Verso, 1985), *The Double and the Other* (Macmillan, 1988), *The Gorgon's Gaze: German Cinema, Expressionism and the Image of Horror* (Cambridge University Press, 1991) and *Film at the Intersection of High and Mass Culture* (Cambridge University Press, 1994). He edited *Lucid Dreams*, a collection of essays on Krzysztof Kieślowski, for Flicks Books (1999) and is currently completing (for Ashgate) a book on religion and cinema, which includes several sections on Kieślowski.

Glyn Davis is Lecturer in Screen History and Theory at Edinburgh College of Art, Scotland. His publications include papers on Todd Haynes' *Safe* and on homosexuality in British cinema. He is currently co-editing, with Kay Dickinson, *Teen TV: Identity, Isolation and Inclusion*.

Lesley Deer recently completed a doctoral thesis on the work of Hal Hartley at the University of Newcastle upon Tyne, UK. She has presented papers on both French and American cinemas and is particularly interested in Hartley's adoption of the characteristics of art-house cinema.

Dean DeFino teaches Literature and Film Studies at Iona College, New York, USA. He has published on a wide variety of subjects, from the Salem witchcraft trials and Shakespeare to detective movies and multimedia pedagogy. His current projects include a series of scholarly forums concerning contemporary US culture, essays on Poe, Ken Burns, and the television series *The Sopranos*, and a book-length study of the American detective film between the First and Second World Wars.

Fidelma Farley is Lecturer in Film Studies at the University of Aberdeen, Scotland. She is the author of *Anne Devlin* (Flicks Books, 2000), *This Other Eden* (Cork University Press, forthcoming), and articles on maternity in Irish cinema, masculinity in contemporary Northern Irish films, the Irish in British cinema, and women and nature in Scottish and Irish cinema.

Gwendolyn Audrey Foster is Associate Professor in the Department of English, University of Nebraska, Lincoln, USA, and Editor-in-Chief of *Quarterly Review of Film and Video*. Her most recent books include *Captive Bodies: Postcolonial Subjectivity in Cinema* (State University of New York Press), *The Films of Chantal Akerman* (Flicks Publishing) and *Troping the Body: Etiquette, Conduct and Dialogic Performance* (Southern Illinois University Press).

Martin Fradley is a Ph.D. candidate in the School of English and American Studies, University of East Anglia, UK. His research concerns masculinity, paranoia and contemporary US cinema.

Aaron Gerow is Associate Professor in the International Student Centre at Yokohama National University, Japan, where he lectures on Japanese film and popular culture. He is currently preparing a forthcoming monograph on Kinugasa Teinosuke's *Page of Madness*. Gerow has written numerous articles on Japanese cinema that have appeared in several languages, covering such topics as early censorship, industry history, wartime film reception, and on directors Kitano Takeshi and Miike Takashi. He regularly reviews

Japanese films for the *Daily Yomiuri* newspaper. He also manages the *KineJapan* discussion list and is writing a book on contemporary Japanese film.

Susan Hayward is the Established Chair of French at the University of Exeter, UK. She is the author of *French National Cinema* (1993), *Luc Besson* (1998) and *Cinema Studies: Key Concepts* (2000). She is currently writing a book on Simone Signoret. Hayward is also the general editor of the National Cinema Series (edited by Routledge) and has just launched a new journal on French cinema, entitled *Studies in French Cinema*.

Mette Hjort is Associate Professor of Intercultural Studies at Aalborg University, Denmark, and former Director of Cultural Studies at McGill University. She is the author of *The Strategy of Letters* (Harvard University Press, 1993), the editor of *Rules and Conventions* (Johns Hopkins University Press, 1992), and co-editor of *Emotion and the Arts* (Oxford University Press, 1997), *Cinema and Nation* (Routledge, 2000), *The Danish Directors: Dialogues on a Contemporary National Cinema* (Intellect Press, 2001) and *Re-imagining Belonging: Self and Community in an Age of Nationalism and Postnationality* (University of Minnesota Press, 2001).

Jennifer Holt is a Ph.D. candidate in the Department of Film and Television at UCLA, Los Angeles, USA.

Leon Hunt is Lecturer in Film and Television Studies at Brunel University, UK. He is the author of *British Low Culture: From Safari Suits to Sexploitation* and has published work in *You Tarzan: Masculinity, Movies and Men*, *British Crime Cinema*, *Framework* and *Unruly Pleasures: The Cult Film and its Critics*.

Mark Jancovich is Senior Lecturer and Director of the Institute of Film Studies at the University of Nottingham, UK. He is the author of several books: *Horror* (Batsford, 1992), *The Cultural Politics of the New Criticism* (Cambridge University Press, 1993), *Approaches to Popular Film* (co-edited with Joanne Hollows, Manchester University Press, 1995), *Rational Fears: American Horror in the 1950s* (Manchester University Press, 1996) and *The Film Studies Reader* (co-edited with Joanne Hollows and Peter Hutchings, Arnold, 2000). He is currently editing *Changing Channels: Television in the Digital Age* (BFI Publishing, forthcoming) and *The Horror Film Reader* (Routledge, forthcoming). He is also writing up the results of an AHRB-funded research project as a book, *Film CinemaSpace: Cultural Geographies of Film Consumption* (BFI Publishing). Jancovich is a founder member of *Scope: An Online Journal of Film Studies* and a series editor (with Eric Schaefer) of the Manchester University Press book series, *Inside Popular Film*.

Ros Jennings teaches Film Studies and is Director of Postgraduate Research for Arts and Humanities at Cheltenham and Gloucester College of Higher Education, UK. Her publications indicate a fascination with 'strong women' (Ripley in the *Alien* films and DCI Jane Tennison in Lynda La Plante's *Prime Suspect*), text/audience relationships and cultural identities. Her current research explores questions of identity and cultural exchange in the relationship between Australian films, television programmes and a British viewing context.

Stan Jones is Senior Lecturer in German and Film at the University of Waikato, Hamilton, New Zealand. He teaches German Language, German and European Film and General Film Studies. In 1987 he co-founded the university's Screen and Media programme and was its first convenor. He has published on German Expressionism, Wim Wenders, Marcel Ophüls, and the reception of New Zealand film in Germany. His current interests are national identity in filmmaking, particularly in the European context, Wim Wenders (his current project is a comparison of *Der Himmel über Berlin* and *City of Angels* as an example of cultural transfer in filmmaking) and film synchronization.

Alexandra Keller (BA Harvard University, Ph.D., New York University) is Visiting Assistant Professor in Film Studies at Smith College. She has published essays and articles on silent cinema, avant-garde film, video and radio, popular and postmodern culture and Westerns. Her forthcoming book is entitled *Re-Imagining the Frontier: American Westerns since the Reagan Administration* (Westview Press).

Chuck Kleinhans is Director of Graduate Studies, Radio-Television/ Film Department, Northwestern University, USA, and co-editor of *JUMP CUT: A Review of Contemporary Media*. His current research centres on changing production conditions for US documentary and experimental film and video.

Peter Krämer teaches Film Studies at the University of East Anglia, UK. His essays on US cinema have appeared in *Screen*, *The Velvet*

Light Trap, Theatre History Studies, The Historical Journal of Film, Radio and Television, History Today, Film Studies and numerous edited collections. Together with Alan Lovell, he co-edited *Screen Acting* (Routledge, 1999). He is currently completing *The Big Picture: Hollywood Cinema from Star Wars to Titanic* (BFI Publishing).

George S. Larke is Lecturer in Film at the University of Northumbria, Newcastle, UK. She is currently completing her doctoral thesis on Hollywood gangster films since the 1960s.

Jon Lewis is Professor of English at Oregon State University, USA. His books include *The Road to Romance and Ruin: Teen Films and Youth Culture, Whom God Wishes to Destroy: Francis Coppola and the New Hollywood, Hollywood v. Hard Core: How the Struggle over Censorship Created the Modern Film Industry* and, as editor, *The New American Cinema*.

Sheldon H. Lu teaches Chinese Film, Literature, Art and Cultural Studies at the University of Pittsburgh, USA. He is the editor of *Transnational Chinese Cinemas: Identity, Nationhood, Gender* (1997), and author of *From Historicity to Fictionality: The Chinese Poetics of Narrative* (1994) and *China, Transnational Visuality, Global Postmodernity* (2001).

James Lyons is Lecturer in Film in the School of English at the University of Exeter, UK. He is the author of *Changing Channels: Television in the Digital Age* (edited with Mark Jancovich, BFI Publishing, forthcoming). He is currently researching the evolving role of new media in US urban culture.

Scott MacKenzie is Lecturer in Film Studies in the School of English and American Studies at the University of East Anglia,UK. He is co-editor of *Cinema and Nation* (Routledge, 2000) and author of a forthcoming book on Québécois cinema and national identity. He has taught at McGill University and the University of Glasgow.

Terry Moore is Assistant Professor of Women's Studies at Ohio State University, USA, where she teaches courses in Film, Literature and Lesbian Studies. She is currently completing a book-length study of the lesbian presence in film noir.

Marc O'Day is Associate Dean of Social Studies at Suffolk College, Ipswich, UK, where he teaches on the Media Studies programme. He has published on fiction, film and television, including essays on the early novels of Angela Carter, the adaptation of David Cronenberg's *Crash* from book to film, postmodernism, and television and style in *The Avengers* (in the forthcoming Routledge *Action Television Series* collection, edited by Bill Osgerby and Anna Gough-Yates).

Devin Orgeron is Visiting Professor in the Program in Media Studies at the Catholic University of America, where he teaches courses in Media Studies and Film. His recent publications include articles on British filmmaker Isaac Julien in *Film Quarterly*, postmodernity and *Pulp Fiction* in *Post Script*, the films of Buster Keaton and Charlie Chaplin in a special issue of *College Literature*, and the historical roots of the road film (in the second edition of the book *Travel Culture*, forthcoming). He has also interviewed Isaac Julien for *COIL*.

Mark Peranson is editor and publisher of the Toronto-based film quarterly *Cinema Scope*. His film writing has appeared in *The Globe and Mail*, *The Village Voice*, *Chicago Reader*, *City Pages* (Minneapolis), *indieWIRE*, *CineAction* and *Now* magazine (Toronto), among others. A programming associate for the Vancouver International Film Festival, he is currently writing a book on Steven Soderbergh for publication in 2001 by the University of Illinois Press.

Geoff Pevere is a movie critic for *The Toronto Star*. He is the co-author of the best-selling *Mondo Canuck: A Canadian Pop Culture Odyssey* (Prentice-Hall, 1996), and a former radio host with the Canadian Broadcasting Corporation. He has worked as a programmer with the Toronto International Film Festival, and has written and taught extensively on things best done in the dark. Though a lifelong Canadian, he has never learned to skate.

Phil Powrie is Professor of French Cultural Studies and Director of the Centre for Research into Film and Media (CRIFAM) at the University of Newcastle upon Tyne, UK. He has published widely on French cinema, notably *French Cinema in the 1980s: Nostalgia and the Crisis of Masculinity* (Clarendon Press, 1997) and, as editor, *Contemporary French Cinema: Continuity and Difference* (Oxford University Press, 1999). He has recently completed a book on the films of Jean-Jacques Beineix (Manchester University Press, 2001), and is currently co-authoring a student introduction to French cinema for Arnold. He is directing several research projects for

CRIFAM, notably a study of film adaptations of *Carmen*, masculinities and film, and music and film.

Brigitte Rollet teaches French cinema and language at the University of London Institut Britannique de Paris. She has published widely on French contemporary cinema and on French films by women. The author of a book on Coline Serreau (1998) for a series on French film directors (Manchester University Press), she is currently completing a book on contemporary French women directors, co-authored with Carrie Tarr.

Christopher Sharrett is Professor of Communication at Seton Hall University, USA. He is editor of *Mythologies of Violence in Postmodern Media and Crisis Cinema: The Apocalyptic Idea in Postmodern Narrative Film*. His work has appeared in *Cineaste, Persistence of Vision, Journal of Popular Film and Television, Film Quarterly* and numerous anthologies. He is on the editorial board of *Cinema Journal*.

Ian Haydn Smith is a London-based freelance writer. He studied film at Birkbeck College and the University of Westminster, and is currently writing a book on Ang Lee for the Directors' Cuts series published by Wallflower Press.

Tytti Soila is Associate Professor, Chair of the Department of Cinema Studies and Director of the Swedish Programme at Stockholm University, Sweden. She has published on feminist film theory and film history, is co-author of *Nordic National Cinemas* (Routledge, 1998), and is a contributor to Finnish National Filmography (Filmografia Fennica) and Swedish National Encyclopaedia. She received a Fulbright stipend in 1992 and 1999, and was a fellow at the Bunting Institute at Harvard University, 1998/9.

Julian Stringer is Lecturer in the Institute of Film Studies at the University of Nottingham, UK, and an editorial board member of *Scope: An Online Journal of Film Studies*. He is editor of *Movie Blockbusters* (Routledge, forthcoming).

Carrie Tarr is a Research Fellow at Kingston University, UK. She has published widely on gender and ethnicity in French cinema. Her recent publications include *Diane Kurys* (Manchester University Press, 1999), *Women, Immigration and Identities in France* (co-edited with Jane Freedman, Berg, 2000) and *Cinema and the Second*

Sex: Women's Filmmaking in France in the 1980s and 1990s (with Brigitte Rollet, Continuum, 2001).

Yvonne Tasker is Senior Lecturer in Film Studies at the University of East Anglia, UK. She is the author of *Working Girls: Gender, Sexuality and Popular Cinema* (1998) and *Spectacular Bodies: Gender, Genre and the Action Cinema* (1993).

Sharon Tay is a Ph.D. candidate in the School of English and American Studies, University of East Anglia, UK. She is researching the applicability of Deleuze to feminist film theorizing and the horror film.

Glyn White is a Lecturer in Film and Media Studies at the University of Central Lancashire, UK. He lectures on semiotics and the hybridization of the documentary form in contemporary television, but is currently researching, with much pleasure, British and American versions of the gangster movie.

Tony Williams is Professor and Area Head of Film Studies in the Department of English at Southern Illinois University Carbondale, USA. He is the author of *Jack London: The Movies* (1992), *Hearths of Darkness: The Family in the American Horror Film* (1996), *Larry Cohen: Radical Allegories of an American Filmmaker* (1997) and *Structures of Desire: British Cinema 1939–1955*, and co-editor of *Vietnam War Films* (1994) and *Jack London's The Sea Wolf: A Screenplay by Robert Rossen* (1998). Williams has also written on Hong Kong cinema for *Cinema Journal* and *Quarterly Review of Film and Video*.

Mary Wood is Senior Lecturer in Media Studies at Birkbeck, University of London, UK. She is also Director of Birkbeck's Continuing Education Media programme which offers courses in film, television, screenwriting and journalism to adults in Greater London. Her publications include articles on the cinema of Francesco Rosi, Italian cinema and media industries and a chapter on the actress Anna Magnani in Ulrike Sieglohr's (ed.) *Heroines without Heroes* (Continuum, 2000). She is currently writing a book on contemporary European cinema (Arnold, forthcoming).

Justin Wyatt is a Senior Research Analyst at the entertainment marketing and consulting firm, Frank N. Magid Associates. He is the author of *High Concept: Movies and Marketing in Hollywood* (University of Texas Press) and *Poison* (Flicks Books). Wyatt is also the series editor for *Commerce and Mass Culture* at the University of Minnesota Press.

Zhang Zhen is Assistant Professor in Cinema Studies at New York University, USA. Her scholarly and creative writings have appeared in numerous journals and anthologies. Zhang was the co-organizer of The Urban Generation: Chinese Cinema and Society in Transformation, a film series exhibited at several major public and academic institutions in the US in February–March 2001. She is currently completing a book on early Chinese film culture and the modern experience.

ACKNOWLEDGMENTS

This project has drawn on the time, energy and commitment of numerous people – not least the contributors whose enthusiasm has been invaluable throughout. Editors and others at Routledge have managed to achieve the right combination of patience and persistence, and I thank both Roger Thorp and Rebecca Barden for seeing the book through some difficult patches. I would also like to thank Bob Kolker, Barry Keith Grant, Judith Mayne, Michael Raine, Mark Reid, Jane Gaines, Scott MacKenzie, Kevin Sandler and Ginette Vincendeau for putting me in touch with some excellent contributors. I am also very grateful to colleagues and graduate students in Film Studies at the University of East Anglia, especially Justine Ashby and Jane Bryan for offering moral support, Jayne Morgan for her help in collecting materials and Michael Williams for his invaluable assistance in preparing the manuscript. My own essays on Allison Anders and Kathryn Bigelow were supported by a grant received from the Arts and Humanities Research Board to work on women filmmakers. I would also like to thank Michèle Scott and Jeff Harris for their generosity and friendship. Finally, as ever, I'm grateful to Rachel Hall who has lived with this project rather longer than she might have wished, though she has been too polite to say as much.

NOTES ON THE TEXT

Each essay includes a brief filmography that focuses primarily on directorial work, giving details of English titles where appropriate. Some entries also give information on other roles undertaken – such as writer, author of the screenplay, performer, composer or editor – as well as major television work. In addition to works cited in the footnotes, suggestions for further reading are given at the end of individual essays.

INTRODUCTION

Authorship and contemporary film culture

Yvonne Tasker

Film criticism today is caught in a peculiar dilemma whereby thinking and writing about filmmakers – what we can loosely term ideas of cinematic authorship – is both immensely resonant and yet critically somewhat bereft. Authorship is viewed with scepticism in film studies, despite the continued currency of filmmakers hailed as auteurs in the 1950s and 1960s (for example, Ford, Hitchcock, Hawks, Sirk). Filmmakers (usually, though not always, the director) remain a point of reference for cinemagoers, the film-related popular press and the industry's own marketing. This collection of fifty essays on contemporary filmmakers underlines not only the diversity of contemporary filmmaking but also the continuing significance of the filmmaker as a figure within film culture. Moreover, the essays indicate the quite distinct ideas of authorship that have developed in relation to, say, the international art cinema on the one hand, and US commercial (which is also, in effect, international) cinema on the other.

The filmmakers whose work is explored in this book are drawn from Europe, North America and Asia. They work in very different contexts – national and international: from the European art cinema to commercial filmmaking in the United States or Hong Kong, to television and the festival circuit. Some command vast budgets whilst others pursue state- or television-derived funding for their feature projects. Similarly, their work is *seen* in very different contexts, whether widely available through major cinema chains and video rental and retail outlets, or accessible only within specialist cinemas or through film festivals. It is clear that no one model of authorship is adequate to these different contexts. Unsurprisingly, therefore, the writers in this collection approach their subjects from different perspectives. Some discuss particular films in detail, whilst

1

others interrogate the critical reputation that has built up around an individual. Mark Jancovich and James Lyons, for example, question the division of John Sayles' work into that of a writer for hire and the more prestigious role of writer/director. Peter Krämer explores Spielberg's extraordinary commercial success in terms of continuities with films and filmmakers of the past, whilst Jon Lewis ponders how it is that Joel and Ethan Coen continue to make movies at all given their repeated failure to generate profits. Tytti Soila considers the place of the Kaurismäki brothers in Finnish as well as international film culture, while essays on Abbas Kiarostami (by Sharon Tay) and Zhang Yuan (by Zhang Zhen) comment on the consumption of specific national cinemas within an international frame. Jennifer Holt frames Steven Soderbergh through the rise to prominence of the Sundance Film Festival, while festival success more generally provides a reference point for several of the writers in this volume.

In the 1950s, authorship criticism sprang, as Peter Wollen put it, from a 'conviction that the American cinema was worth studying in depth' and that 'masterpieces were made ... by a whole range of authors, whose work had previously been dismissed and consigned to oblivion.'[1] It also stemmed, as James Naremore emphasizes, from a passionate interest in the cinema.[2] Building on the frequently chaotic *politique des auteurs*, the auteur theory or auteurism flourished in English-language criticism of the 1960s, playing an important part in establishing the academic study of popular cinema, as well as generating passionate and close readings of films in such magazines as *Movie* in Britain and *Film Comment* in the United States. Like the culture of the film festival, which rapidly gained momentum in the post-war period, authorship was always about the cultural status of film – whether reductively in the production of a canon, or polemically in an insistence on the importance of commercial or genre filmmakers such as Howard Hawks or Douglas Sirk. The most positive legacy of both the French *politique* and British and American auteurism was the establishment of a serious interest in the possibilities of popular cinema, in part through the strategic extension of a critical method associated with art cinema to other arenas. In a similar spirit, this collection considers filmmakers from commercial as well as experimental and art cinemas. Not all of the essays focus on directors, although most do (polymath star performer/choreographer/director Jackie Chan and producer Christine Vachon are the key exceptions). Even so, the idea of the filmmaker typically involves more than just the director, suggesting an individual or team involved in a creative vision which includes production, writing, editing and sometimes performing. Over time, teams develop vital formal and informal relationships. And though many of the contributors have pointed to the importance of such collaborations, the length of the essays presented here does not allow for a really developed treatment of this subject.

The limitations of ideas of cinematic authorship are by now familiar: the overly romantic figure of the individual filmmaker in a medium which is not only typically complex and collaborative, but corporate in character; the reductive reading of film as autobiography; the repression of complexity in the desire to identify an overriding stylistic or thematic unity. Thus, for example, Richard Maltby writes that the 'multiple logics and intentions that continue to impinge on the process of production ensure that authorship remains an inadequate explanation of how movies work'.[3] These limitations are very real, as contributors to this volume are acutely aware. What does it mean, for example, to identify an individual as the one responsible for a complex entity like a film? And how might we distinguish between what is obviously a personal film in one context (for instance, Julie Dash's lengthy struggle to get *Daughters of the Dust* to cinemas)[4] from its wider significance, for example. Moreover, as Carrie Tarr demonstrates, a filmmaker such as Diane Kurys both explicitly invites and plays with an autobiographical reading of certain films. In their attention to the institutions within which filmmakers produce and exhibit their films, as well as discussion of the films themselves, the essays in this collection aim to contextualize individual filmmakers and their work, acknowledging the limitations, but also the possibilities of an authorship approach.

It is something of a truism that the filmmaker, groomed, promoted and interviewed, has become a star in his or her own right. A particular director or producer can function as a type of brand name – Ros Jennings points to this effect in relation to producer Christine Vachon, whose association with a project promises a level of provocation and interest. The idea of the filmmaker as an impresario or self-publicist is far from new, accelerating in the American cinema of the post-war period as more directors took on the role of producer.[5] In an interview given in 1975, Victor Perkins spoke (in relation to Hawks) of 'the evasions and the image-mongering of the director, the whole projection business'.[6] What is perhaps distinctive to the contemporary scene is the scale of this phenomenon and its distribution across different sectors. As Todd Solondz notes:

One of the things you've got going for you now is that there's more publicity for low-budget independent directors ... your name as a director is something that you can develop into a certain kind of value, so you can be less dependent on cast. When you buy a book, you look at the author.[7]

This literary analogy returns us to early writings on authorship – Alexandre Astruc's *Caméra Stylo*[8] – in a rather telling way, evoking the director's name as a factor in consumer choice. The film festival, we should recall, revolves around film commerce as much as film culture: effective film criticism must consider both. Equally, whilst it is evident that young (male) filmmakers are hyped as the new voice of independent cinema, this does not mean that the term is simply redundant; rather that we need to understand critically the process that produces some filmmakers (and not others) as star names. Cherry Smyth cites producer Christine Vachon's comment on the marketing of *Poison* and *Swoon* in this context: 'It's just so much easier to position men as the new artistic hot potato to watch.'[9]

Finally, a word on selection. With various filmmakers added and removed at different stages, the choice of subjects has been an ongoing process in the development of this book. The final selection is not offered in a spirit of exclusion or with the intention of designating these fifty (actually fifty-two including siblings) film-makers as the most significant of those working today. Some are already the subject of major critical studies. Others are well-established international auteurs. Yet others are key figures in the popular cinemas of the United States, Europe and Hong Kong. I have not felt obliged to include established figures (Jean-Luc Godard, for example), choosing instead to juxtapose filmmakers who are at very different stages of their careers and who have very different critical reputations (James Cameron as against Steven Soderbergh, for example). Perhaps inevitably, the selection tends towards my own interests in areas such as commercial and independent US cinema, women filmmakers and queer cinema. Nevertheless, the collection aims to provide an introduction to different types of filmmaking and different types of filmmaker. Thus my contention is not that there are few British or Indian filmmakers working today but, more positively, that the essays presented here open up a range of different and complementary issues to do with authorship in contemporary cinema. My guiding principle has been to work across popular and high or established film culture. Rather than a parade of established international auteurs, I hope that the final volume is a genuine engagement with those figures who have shaped, and are shaping, contemporary filmmaking and film culture.

Notes

1 Peter Wollen, 'The Auteur Theory', in Bill Nichols (ed.) *Movies and Methods*, Berkeley, University of California Press, 1976, p. 530.
2 James Naremore, 'Authorship and the Cultural Politics of Film Criticism', *Film Quarterly*, Fall 1990, pp. 14–23.
3 Richard Maltby, *Hollywood Cinema: An Introduction*, Oxford, Blackwell, 1995, p. 33.
4 See Terry Moore's essay in this collection.
5 Maltby writes of Hitchcock as a 'deliberate commercial creation': 'Before Hitchcock the author there was Hitchcock the marketing strategy, promoting the visibly self-conscious presence of Alfred Hitchcock in the movies he directed' (*ibid.*, p. 438).
6 See the extracts from a 1975 *Movie* roundtable in John Caughie (ed.) *Theories of Authorship*, London, Routledge/BFI, 1981, p. 59.
7 'Van-guard Roundtable', *Premiere*, October 1998, p. 88.
8 See Ed Buscombe, 'Ideas of Authorship', in Caughie (ed.). Astruc's 'The Birth of a New Avant-garde: La Caméra-stylo' is translated in Peter Graham (ed.) *The New Wave*, London, Secker & Warburg/BFI, 1968.
9 Cherry Smyth, 'Beyond Queer Cinema: It's in her Kiss', in Liz Gibbs (ed.) *Daring to Dissent: Lesbian Culture from Margin to Mainstream*, London, Cassell, 1994. For an example of the speedy but knowing elevation of the director as star-auteur see Peter Biskind (on Quentin Tarantino), 'An Auteur is Born', *Empire*, November 1994, pp. 94–102.

Further reading

Timothy Corrigan, *A Cinema without Walls: Movies and Culture after Vietnam*, London, Routledge, 1991.
Andy Medhurst, 'That Special Thrill: *Brief Encounter*, Homosexuality and Authorship', *Screen*, vol. 32, no. 2, 1991, pp. 197–208.
V.F. Perkins, 'Film Authorship: The Premature Burial', *CineAction*, no. 21/22, 1990, pp. 57–64.

FIFTY CONTEMPORARY FILMMAKERS

ALLISON ANDERS

One of the few women directors to establish herself as a presence in the male-dominated scene of US independent filmmaking, Allison Anders has redefined the possibilities of the woman's picture. With their multiple protagonists and careful attention to the lives of a diverse range of women, Anders' films are both tough and intimate, humorous yet deeply felt. Anders is no ostentatious stylist, but her films are none the less both innovative and cinematic. Her cinematic influences and sources are diverse: from popular music to the classical woman's film, from Sirkian melodrama to the movies of Scorsese and Wenders. Yet beyond their shared commitment to telling stories from a woman's point of view, her films are not easy to categorize. The critic B. Ruby Rich describes *Gas Food Lodging* as 'one of those rare films that reminds us that there should be whole genres of movies like this instead of a single stand-out specimen'.[1] Or, to put it another way, in redefining the woman's picture to include small-town lives, LA girl gangs and the music business, Anders underlines the potentiality of the form.

An interest in women with responsibilities over angst-ridden male adolescents gives Anders' movies an emotional depth. Her well-received directorial début, *Gas Food Lodging*, follows waitress Nora Evans (Brook Adams) as she struggles to raise her daughters Shade (Fairuza Balk) and Trudi (Ione Skye) whilst attempting to have a life of her own. An elegant travelling shot of the highway, complete with evocative music, opens the film. Yet as the credits end, we turn off the road, to static images of a town that has stopped in its tracks – an isolated trailer, a drained pool. Road imagery, long a feature of romantic rebel male stories (given a queer inflection through 1990s movies such as *The Living End*, *Postcards from America* or *My Own Private Idaho*), is quietly set aside here. *Gas Food Lodging* is an off-the-road movie, leaving us for the majority of the film firmly in the restricted lives of an isolated desert community. However, this is not to say that Anders neglects the poetic beauty of the New Mexico landscape, or even the town's state of aesthetic decay. Indeed, whilst the film is bleak in its determined portrayal of everyday detail (as suggested by the title), it is also romantic: Trudi and her lover Dank (Robert Knepper) in a cave illuminated by ultraviolet; Shade dancing with Javier (Jacob Vargas) and his mother; Shade and Javier lying in the desert ('In his arms I knew who I was', her voice-over tells us). Such moments do not represent a redemptive climax in

Anders' films – their conventional function in many Hollywood narratives – but they are none the less part of her characters' lives.

In one such moment, we learn that the rebellious Trudi was gang raped, an experience she has never before shared but now confides to the stranger Dank. When the seemingly sincere Dank fails to return (we later learn that he has died), Trudi finds she is pregnant. Though her mother comments that she has 'no choice', she opts to go to Dallas to have the baby and to give it up for adoption. After the birth, she swears she will never return to Laramie, although we are left with little optimism that her hopes of a career in modelling will be realized. Against this background, Shade, the film's unconventional adolescent heroine, finds her primary sustenance at the movies, though not the Hollywood variety. She spends her time in the Spanish movie theatre, absorbed by the star presence of Elvia Rivero in elaborate black and white melodramas (shot by Anders). Yet as the film makes clear, the movies are not enough – Shade's developing romance with projectionist Javier suggests her need to move beyond mimicry (her awkward attempt to court her gay best friend Darius by impersonating his icon Olivia Newton John is excruciating).

Shade's movie-inspired quest provides a thread that runs throughout the film, as her introductory voice-over tells us: 'I knew what was missing from my life – a man! Oh no, don't get me wrong. Not a man for me, for my mom. Then we could do all the dumb normal stuff regular families do.' Shade is preoccupied by the image of her father, preserved in a spool of film in a tin under her pillow. By the time we see the film, flickering on the wall of the cinema's projection box, its privileged status has been somewhat undermined. The moment recalls the home movies that detail a lost, happier time in Wim Wenders' *Paris, Texas,* on which Anders worked as a production assistant (by her own account after bombarding the filmmaker with letters). Her admiration for Wenders notwithstanding, Anders crafts a very different tale of fragmented family lives. It is clear that Shade's investment in the image spills over into her romantic quest to find her mother a man/her family a father. Yet whilst this investment in magic shapes Shade's actions to some extent, the narrative as a whole is more sceptical. When she finally meets her father he is, after all, only human.

Mi Vida Loca (*My Crazy Life*) aims to dramatize the lives of Latina gang members in the Echo Park neighbourhood of Los Angeles. Divided into three chapters, each one highlighting different characters within the same group, the film makes creative use of overlapping stories (female and male, different generations). The first concerns Mousie (Seidy Lopez) and Sad Girl (Angel Aviles), once inseparable friends, now enemies who have both had children by the same man, Ernesto (Jacob Vargas again). The second part sets Whisper's (Nelida Lopez) move into dealing against the release from prison of an older, more sanguine Giggles (Marlo Marron). In the final section we meet La Blue Eyes, Sad Girl's sister who falls in love with a prisoner with whom she corresponds; when he is released from prison the letters abruptly stop. The girls arrange for her to meet El Duran at a party, aiming to reveal his true nature; meanwhile the boys vow to kill El Duran. Finally, Ernesto's truck Suavecito (hidden from both Mousie and Sad Girl) links all three sections. In the films closing moments, Big Sleepy's little daughter is shot in revenge for El Duran: hers is the last of the film's three funerals.

Mi Vida Loca combines melodrama with gritty realism, acknowledging the material limitations on the characters' lives. At times fast paced, there are also reflective moments (as Anders has pointed out, it was never intended to be the female gangster movie some critics seemed to want). Multiple voice-overs offer us different angles on living in this difficult world. If Anders' films share one feature – beyond a concern with female experience – it is their careful pacing and structure, slowly elaborating on the lives of multiple protagonists rather than following the goals and desires of one. *Gas Food Lodging*'s threefold character-centred narrative or the overlapping stories of Mousie, Sad Girl, Whisper, Giggles, Ernesto and others in *Mi Vida Loca* produce a complex kind of story-telling. Even *Grace of My Heart*, very much Denise's (Illeana Douglas) story, emphasizes that her personal journey does not make sense without the connections to others that are so important to her.

In interviews, Anders comes across like her films – simultaneously tough and intimate: if the former stems from necessity, the latter is a characteristically personal choice. Her willingness to discuss her personal life and the wide circulation of biographical details in the promotion of *Gas Food Lodging* (according to the press release 'the story ... cuts deeply with the authenticity of her own past, present and future') have contributed to Anders' persona as a passionate and uncompromising filmmaker. Rich's affectionate 1995 profile in *Sight and Sound* magazine sums up her distinctive persona thus: 'She's an anomaly among today's independent US film-makers: a mature woman not a twenty-something prodigy. In a time of aerobicised bodies, she eats as she pleases. In the heyday of Armani

11

chic, she dresses how she likes and happily shows off her tattoos and her children. She's a single mother in a Hollywood obsessed with photo-op matrimony. She's a feminist eternally on the look-out for a man.'[2] Forthright in interviews, Anders talks about her working-class background and the difficult personal experiences (of abuse, rape and mental illness) on which she has drawn in her work. Already a (lone) mother of two when she attended film school at UCLA, she later adopted a third child, the son of a gang girl who died after the filming of *Mi Vida Loca*. As Anders said of Denise Waverley, *Grace of My Heart*'s singer/songwriter protagonist: 'she gets sidetracked all over the place, and if she didn't take those detours, she wouldn't have anything to write about – she wouldn't have her authentic voice'.[3]

The media focus on Anders' personal life speaks volumes about the perceived novelty of a woman filmmaker in the independent sector – or indeed in the public eye. More than one critic interpreted *Mi Vida Loca* as a straightforward projection of the director's concerns onto the lives of the women the film sought to portray. Collaborators are more likely to comment positively on her ability to make the material her own, to inhabit and invest stories with personal significance. Yet Anders has turned this interest to her advantage, emphasizing the personal dimensions of her work in promotional interviews.

After the slow-burning critical success of *Mi Vida Loca*, Anders collaborated with Quentin Tarantino, Alexandre Rockwell and Robert Rodriguez on the Miramax portmanteau project *Four Rooms*. Set in a hotel on New Year's Eve, each filmmaker directed a segment set in one of the rooms. Anders' segment, 'The Missing Ingredient', which opens the film, is a comic piece – farce and slapstick provide the movie's prevailing tone – focusing on a witches' coven gathered together in the honeymoon suite to lift the curse on blonde goddess Diana. In the build-up to its release the filmmakers all received extensive press coverage, although its low-key release was matched by poor reviews. A patchy production with undoubted moments of panache, *Four Rooms* failed to bring the four segments together or to effectively stage any meaningful collaboration between its filmmakers. In any case, Anders had already signed up to Universal for her next project, with Martin Scorsese as executive producer. *Grace of My Heart* is a magnificent piece of period filmmaking, a kind of feminist riposte to music mythology as told in movies like Oliver Stone's *The Doors*. A bigger budget brought Anders the chance to work on a much larger scale, whilst retaining her distinctive sensibility. The film treads a precarious line around its setting, careful (and for the most part successful in its attempt) to avoid succumbing to nostalgia.

A woman's picture in the Hollywood tradition, *Grace of My Heart* tells the story of Edna Buxton (a Pennsylvanian heiress) who becomes Denise Waverley, a songwriter whose friendships, working partnerships and relationships we follow through various musical eras from her championing of the girl group The Luminaries, crafting a tune for closet lesbian Kelly Porter through writing songs for a 1960s' television show (*Where the Action Is!*) to the release of her own album in the singer-songwriter era of the 1970s. She doesn't fit the mould – 'you're either a singer or a songwriter – which is it?' asks Brill Building producer and mentor Joel Milner (John Turturro). For a long time she chooses writing, though the film closes with the triumph of her platinum album *Grace of My Heart* (the rendition of this title song intercut with her mother receiving a copy and seeming to smile to herself).

Grace of My Heart is definitely one woman's story – in contrast to the complex narrative patterning of *Gas Food Lodging* or *Mi Vida Loca*. None the less, it is one woman's story set within a rich context of the major and minor players in her life. Denise is also Anders' first essay with a decidedly middle-class protagonist. Her mother appears only at the beginning and the end of the film (other relations not at all), first rejecting her (summed up in her sweetly delivered line 'The dress fits the occasion – it's you who doesn't fit') and later seeming to approve her daughter's success. Denise collaborates with men and women – including Doris Shelley (Jennifer Leigh Warren) (who she meets backstage at a talent contest – the two swap dresses – and who later leads in The Luminaries) and Cheryl (Patsy Kensit), whose initial rivalry turns to friendship. This sense of collaboration is appropriate, given Anders' open commitment to working partnerships and to mentoring. (In publicity for *Sugar Town*, co-written and directed with Kurt Voss, Anders talked of how 'You recognize your shortcomings when you work with someone else. We really nurtured each other's strengths and concentrated on our own weaknesses.')[4]

Grace of My Heart resists the temptation to trade pop music off against some more authentic mode of expression (though the relationship between white writers/producers and black performers is an important aspect of the first part of the film). While *New York, New York* is an obvious reference point, there is no single equivalent to Robert De Niro's brilliant but self-absorbed jazzman in Anders' film. Howard (Eric Stoltz) starts to go there but is given little credence. The torch of artistic integrity is most obviously carried by Matt Dillon's Jay Phillips. Brought in to produce her solo début, he encourages Denise to produce her own work, though his self-destructive nature makes increasing demands on her.

Anders has spoken regularly of the centrality of music to her visual imagination, as well as the importance of music in her life. Like the later *Sugar Town*, *Grace of My Heart* is as much a musical as it is a melodrama and builds on this fascination with music using carefully integrated numbers that counterpoint Denise's personal journey. In ambitious fashion, Anders and her team commissioned new material, pairing stars of the period with contemporary performers. Burt Bacharach and Elvis Costello's 'God Give Me Strength' is rendered in a powerful studio solo scene that underlines Denise's sense of personal loss, prefiguring the end of the New York phase of her life (and recalling an equally emotionally charged Liza Minnelli solo in Scorsese's *New York, New York*). The Luminaries' controversial song on teen pregnancy ('Unwanted Number') emphasizes the extent to which pop has the capacity to tell stories from a female point of view, not least since co-writer Howard wants to focus on the father's dilemma.

Lisa Ouellette has written that Anders' 'decision to work in the genre she calls "melodrama" is part of a conscious effort to redefine filmmaking from a female perspective'.[5] Her centring on female protagonists certainly puts a different spin on familiar themes and genres (teen angst, gangster, biopic). Speaking about *Gas Food Lodging*, Anders notes how: 'The male actors were constantly asking for one more scene ... and it was always these very heroic scenes. So finally I realized that, oh, my God, they're totally not used to not being the one controlling the action.'[6] If Anders is fairly intolerant when it comes to male narcissism, men are not ogres in her movies, though they may fail the women we are more concerned about – think of John Evans in *Gas Food Lodging*, Ernesto or Big Sleepy in *Mi Vida Loca*, the weak-willed John Murray or the passionate Jay in *Grace of My Heart*. Anders' ability to preserve a strong feminist commitment to women's stories alongside the desire for emotional intimacy and heterosexual love has been one strong mark of her work. Indeed she has defended herself against a perception of indulgence in relation to male characters – her romanticism understood as a potential failing. Manohla Dargis noted in *The Village Voice* 'an almost atavistic interest in the opposite sex', quoting Anders' seemingly defensive comment that 'The men change nothing for these women, they change absolutely nothing.'[7] Perhaps the key lesson that Anders takes from melodrama is that realism does not need to be unrelenting to make its impact.

Biography

Allison Anders was born in Kentucky, USA, in 1954. She worked as an assistant on Wim Wenders' *Paris, Texas* before enrolling at UCLA where she gained attention with her screenplay 'The Lost Highway' and co-directed *Border Radio*, based around the music scene in Los Angeles. *Gas Food Lodging* was awarded the New York Film Critics Circle Award for Best New Director.

Notes

1 B. Ruby Rich, 'Slugging It Out For Survival', *Sight and Sound*, vol. 5, no. 4, 1995, p. 15.
2 *Ibid.*
3 'Shooting Straight from the Heart', *Interview*, September 1996, p. 72.
4 *Screen International*, 15 January 1999, p. 40; Anders' latest feature, *Things Behind the Sun*, was also co-written with Voss.
5 Lisa Ouellette, 'Reel Women: Feminism and Narrative Pleasure in New Women's Cinema', *Independent*, April 1995, p. 30.
6 Noel Black, 'The 1st Annual Directors' Retreat', *Directors Guild of America Magazine*, December 1997–January 1998, p. 53.
7 Manohla Dargis, 'Giving Directions', *The Village Voice*, 18 August 1992, p. 60.

Filmography

(All US productions unless otherwise indicated)

Border Radio (with Kurt Voss, 1988) also co-writer
Gas Food Lodging (1992) also screenplay
Mi Vida Loca / My Crazy Life (UK/USA, 1993) also writer
Four Rooms (segment 'The Missing Ingredient', 1994) also writer
Grace of My Heart (1995) also writer
Sugar Town (UK/US, with Kurt Voss, 1999) also co-writer
Things Behind the Sun (2001) also co-writer

Further reading

Rosa Linda Fregosa, 'Hanging Out with the Homegirls?', *Cineaste*, July 1995, pp. 36–7.
Karen Hollinger, *In the Company of Women: Contemporary Female Friendship Films*, Minneapolis, University of Minnesota Press, 1998.
Maitland McDonagh, 'Sad Girls', *Film Comment*, vol. 30, no. 5, 1994, pp. 75–8.

Andy Medhurst, 'Songs from the Heart', *Sight and Sound*, March 1997, pp. 12–14.

YVONNE TASKER

AOYAMA SHINJI

In *Helpless*, Aoyama Shinji's controversial début film, the shocking moment when Kenji kills the cook and waitress of a diner defies easy explanation. Perhaps it was a matter of mood: the teenage Kenji had witnessed a murder earlier, and had learnt of his father's suicide moments before. At one time, Aoyama himself posited another reason: Kenji, as a member of a generation removed from Japan's crimes during the Second World War, could only recognize such guilt by re-enacting them himself. Such postulations, however, are difficult to ground in a work that offers spectators little access to character psychology. Even if there are motivations for Kenji's actions, they remain beyond the spectator's reach, a point Aoyama stresses.[1] That does not mean, however, that the film refuses the mediation of conceptual discourses. For a director who studied under Japan's foremost film intellectual, Hasumi Shigehiko, at Rikkyō University,[2] and who has continued to write criticism since graduating, writing and viewing have retained a reciprocal relationship that invites us to explore the intertexts to Aoyama's work. Such a process helps us to understand his films as important political interventions in contemporary Japan, ones that call for a rethinking of history and a redefinition of the individual on the basis of an encounter with the Other.

In a manifesto-like essay on Phillipe Garrel, Aoyama offers a political conception of the individual that is crucial to his work. In defining a 'nouvelle vague as a mode of thought' as 'a discourse duelling over the sole point of how to treat the Other from a political perspective, with the individual being the subject in struggle in the end', he stresses that the individual is that 'unitary existence that possesses no meaning and is 'representative of nothing' – is that which 'cannot be generalized or universalized'. To him, then, politics – the true *nouvelle vague* – is the 'struggle to protect the individual as an individual'. Since the Other can also be conceived of as an individual, this is neither a self-centred politics, nor a form of radical individualism,[3] but a politicization of the micro-relationships between Self and Other.[4]

This protection of the individual may imply a disturbing rejection of solidarity politics, but it must be considered in historical and cinematic context. While reflecting the deep distrust towards political narratives that has reigned among young Japanese since the left's internecine killings of the 1970s, it also participates in a resistance against the emperor system (*tennōsei*), a dominant modern discourse which effaces the Other in an all-encompassing national Self located around an often unspoken term, the emperor. In cinema, this effacement is evident, for example, in the humanism of directors like Yamada Yōji, whose nostalgic world promises a unity in which all are good and knowable, or in the aesthetic naturalism of such recent films as Koreeda Hirokazu's *Maborosi* (*Maboroshi no hikari*, 1995) or Oguri Kōhei's *Sleeping Man* (*Nemuru otoko*, 1996). Aoyama has participated in discussions criticizing the latter works both for absorbing the Self in a nature never analysed for its involvement in national ideologies like the emperor system and for privileging beauty and nationalized emotions like 'mono no aware' (the sadness of things) over critique.[5]

Kenji's impenetrability should be considered as a counter to such discourses that could absorb his Otherness in a universalized knowability. On a stylistic level, this countering is effected through Aoyama's strategic use of what I call the 'detached style', a form of distantiation on the level of narration prevalent in 1990s' independent Japanese cinema that utilizes long-shot, long takes, generally avoids close-ups and point-of-view shots, and refrains from analysing the scene psychologically. In films by Aoyama Hashiguchi Ryōsuke and Suwa Nobuhiro, this style can work to detach the Other from the Self, but its aesthetic tendencies – composing beautiful tableaux – can in other texts, like *Sleeping Man* and *Maborosi*, absorb Otherness in a unity of subject and landscape. The fact that such beauty can be a manifestation of subjective character emotion lends credence to Hikoe Tomohiro's argument that these texts exhibit symptoms of Freudian melancholy, where the ego sets up the lost object within the ego in a form of narcissistic identification.[6] Aoyama's films resist such tendencies. The general avoidance of point-of-view shots, coupled with many long-shot, long takes, maintains a distance between the camera and the characters that inhibits spectator efforts to impose meanings on these individuals. At the same time, the abrupt insertion of close-ups works against the impulse to aestheticize. Even when Aoyama returns to his native Kitakyūshū in *Helpless* and *Eureka*, the detached photography deters the nostalgic unity of character and landscape found in *Maborosi*.

Constructing individuals resistant to generalized categories is thus, for Aoyama, a distinctly political issue. But it is also a cinematic one. If an individual is 'a naked state that represents nothing other than itself', then the film presenting the individual should pursue a 'materialistic cinematic practice that conflicts with what is generally called "depicting humanity" or "depicting emotions" '.[7] In practical terms this means a cinema that avoids explanation, that leaves the world and the image equally bare. Aoyama in general refrains from the full explanation of not only characters, but narrative actions (such as Yasuo's 'death' in *Helpless*), and he is not alone in this tendency. While contemporary Japanese television prioritizes clarity and comprehension, directors who work in the detached style prefer ambiguity. This attitude can be considered part of Hasumi's legacy. While famous for advocating cinematic specificity – to study films as films; to make films that rely only on cinematic devices – Hasumi's vision of the motion pictures, as evinced by his work on Ozu Yasujirō,[8] is not one of filmmakers using the infinite means in their toolbox to overcome the limitations of cinema, but of utilizing inherently restricted means to acknowledge those material limits and thus the horizon of film. This perspective constitutes part of the discursive background for both the minimalism of the detached style and the tendency to avoid explanation beyond what 'cinema' is capable of.

Significantly, Aoyama's characters toil against their own limits. Hikoe correctly notes that many of his heroes – Yasuo and Kenji in *Helpless*, Mizoguchi in *WiLd LIFe*, Saga in *An Obsession* – are suffering from losses, with *Eureka* being the most thorough representation of the resulting work of mourning. But whereas characters in melancholic films passively unify with landscape, Aoyama's struggle against their surroundings. His heroes generally refuse to be part of an institution (Michio and Yōichi in *Two Punks* and Hiroki in *WiLd LIFe* all resist the life of the yakuza), or begin to question it and move out on their own (Saga, or Shingo in *Shady Grove*). Yet Aoyama's individuals do not act on the basis of metanarratives like 'humanity' or 'liberty'. Saga, for instance, pursues Shimano and Kimiko not to arrest them or save their lives, but simply to get his gun back. He does afterwards point his gun at the white-clad 'death squads' that punctuate *An Obsession*, but that symbolizes more his 'protection of the individual' than the adoption of a general political narrative.

While some of those who have experienced loss, like Yasuo in *Helpless* or Naoki in *Eureka*, are unable to overcome it and descend into narcissistic acts of killing, Kenji, Saga and Makoto in *Eureka* all ultimately surmount the urge to absorb the Other, and opt to valorize its life (for Kenji, Yasuo's sister; for Saga, his wife Rie; for Makoto, Kozue). Whether the object was lost in romance or violence, Aoyama's characters must overcome the lure of narcissism and recognize the existence of others. Shimano's question to Saga – 'Do you know how love can be proven?' – inquires as to the method for doing that. Shimano's answer, which is in some ways that of Rika and Yoshiki in *EM/Embalming*, is mutual annihilation. Hikoe takes this as proof of Shimano's narcissism, but it is important to note that Saga does not reject this solution either: consenting to die with another out of love is a step beyond solipsism, albeit on the paradoxical level of joining another in nothingness. Saga, however, provides an additional answer: 'live together for the rest of your lives'. It is a logically less clean solution than Shimano's, and offers no incontestable proof of the Other's existence, but it represents both Aoyama's rejection of nihilism and his basic stance that relating to the Other is never a matter of certainty. Rika's and Shingo's union in *Shady Grove*, after all, takes place in a grove that no longer exists. As their dual narration says at the conclusion, their recognition of the Other, and thus confirmation of the Self, is a matter of listening to a voice in the dark, of grasping uncertain hand holds in the void.

This uncertainty is partially a factor of contemporary existence. The act of recognizing the Other has pertinence in late 1990s' Japan, where sensational juvenile crimes have sparked media discourses that maintain that some young Japanese, raised in a virtual reality of video games, mobile phones and manga, have ceased to acknowledge the reality of others. These discourses are important contexts to Aoyama's films, but Aoyama, instead of endorsing their repudiation of the present, works to reconceptualize the relationship between Self and Other in this new age. Mobile phones become not only a means of contact for Rika and Shingo, but also another variable in the complex relationship with others. In *June 12 1998*, Aoyama's documentary of Chris Cutler's improvisational musical performance, Cutler speaks of his association with his mixer and mikes as a relationship with another performer: a complex give and take with a technological Other that creates an order best described by chaos theory. Perhaps, to Aoyama, the relationship with the Other in this technological age must be conceptualized through order in chaos. He, however, does not valorize any technology in this formulation.

An amateur rock guitarist who has scored most of his own films with Yamada Isao, Aoyama has maintained a distinction between computer synthesizers, epitomizing an ordered, universal 'cognition' (*ninshiki*), and the 'self-tuned' guitars of Sonic Youth, with their individual, variable 'existence' (*sonzai*).[9] His cinema, politics and music can all in some way be said to involve this contemporary 'tuning' of 'existence' in opposition to 'cognition'.

One other aspect of this 'chaotic' association with the Other is the issue of representation. One must ask, for instance, how it is possible to recognize the Other given the detachment Aoyama's films evince towards the individual. Many of his commentators have argued that his characters resist the emotionalization of landscape common in contemporary melancholic films by not exhibiting a substantive internality (for example, Saga, who, with a lost lung, is quite literally 'hollow' inside).[10] How then are Aoyama's narratives of romance possible? The answer must consider Aoyama's effort to present the impossible. In underlining the limits of cinema, Hasumi has helped make impossibility a central issue in Japanese discourses on film: whether or not a text challenges cinematic impossibility (*fukanōsei*) while still acknowledging the limits of the medium. Aoyama, Kurosawa Kiyoshi, and others influenced by Hasumi have similarly made the representation of the unrepresentable a central concern in their film practice. Aoyama has termed his 'marriage trilogy' – *WiLd LIFe*, *An Obsession* and *Shady Grove* – his own experiment in 'showing the unseen' – here, love[11] – but his cinema in total can be considered an effort to tread the line between the representable and the unrepresentable. For instance, certain cinematic devices can hint at the internality of characters, yet without denying that the representation of such internality is impossible. Both *Two Punks* and *A Weapon in My Heart* feature camera movements that begin with a character in the present and proceed to show in the same shot a past event that occurred in that location. By externalizing these events, Aoyama avoids the internalization of a traditional flashback structure, yet still allows for – though does not determine – a reading that the character is recalling past events. Similar strategies are evident in the use of false point-of-view shots. While he rarely uses the conventional ABA 'seer-seen-seer' structure, Aoyama can utilize ambiguous eyeline matches (only 'AB' without the second shot of the seer) or even impossible ones (like Kenji's last 'view' of Yasuo's car) to imply perception without completely tying the object to the subjectivity of a character. The internality of the character is thereby connoted without ever being denoted, raising the issue of what the

Other thinks while reminding viewers of the impossibility of indisputably knowing that.

Communication is also subject to this balance of possibility/impossibility. With many of Aoyama's characters having difficulty expressing themselves and some, like Kozue and Naoki in *Eureka*, being unable to speak, true communication seems as impossible as knowledge of the Other. Yet Aoyama's heroes are sometimes quite talkative: witness Shingo's long speech to Rika in *Shady Grove*. In some cases, as with Akihiko (a character in both *Helpless* and *Eureka*), an abundance of words is actually a sign of the inability to communicate, but in others, it can at least represent the material fact of communication. Higuchi Yasuhito has argued that the sudden outflow of words from taciturn characters like Saga is representative of their discontinuous subjectivity, where words are markers of the deaths to which Aoyama's individuals are sometimes suddenly subject.[12] But it is also important to see them as material assertions of existence, where the fact of speech speaks of internality in terms less of providing a window onto the soul, than an opaque marker of intentionality. Aoyama has written that 'the individual is words; the individual is not the image', by which he means the materiality of language that resists the categorizable 'image' (meaning) a person can have.[13] *Eureka* is very much a film about communication, but there the model is Makoto's knocking on walls. Someone answers in the jail, but the film makes no issue of who 'he' is, or of what is being communicated: the fact of communication itself is what matters. The 'extra-perceptual' communication between Kozue and Naoki may appear to contradict these avowed limitations to contact with an Other, but Aoyama in interviews characterizes their conversation as non-linguistic. In some ways, it and the internalities being represented express Aoyama's hopeful assertion of what is possibly behind the wall of impossibility.

It is important to note that communicative acts like Makoto knocking on the wall are usually repeated in Aoyama's work. Beyond underlining that communication is as much a material as a semiotic process, they also participate in a strategy of doubling and repetition which informs Aoyama's conceptions of time and history. Significant narrative actions are often repeated: Saga visits the tunnel and Shingo 'visits' the grove twice each. These certainly add structure to the narrative, but they also echo the doubling of characters. Doubling is effected by different characters engaging in the same action (for example, both Makoto and Naoki drive the bus), as well as cinematic devices (such as cutting between two characters performing similar actions) and objects in common (Saga's gun joins him to Shimano). Couples are frequently mirrored, which suggests that one function of these repetitions and doublings is to establish patterns of comparison and contrast. One of the differences is generational, with Michio and Miya in *Two Punks* and Saga and Rie in *An Obsession* being in their late thirties compared to the twenty-something couples of Yōichi and Yūko and Shimano and Kimiko.

Focusing on generational divisions helps Aoyama depict the emptiness and lack of place young Japanese feel, but the differences are also historicized. Generations are often mapped onto post-war Japanese history. Kenji's father was a member of the old left and Shimano's mother a Hiroshima survivor, yet Kenji can't remember the words to 'The International'. *Helpless* is set in 1989, the year the Berlin Wall fell and the Shōwa Emperor died. The end of this history means a loss of identity for Kenji's father (who commits suicide) and Yasuo (who insists his boss, his emperor, is not dead), but not for the young. They are at once removed from this history and, like the leukaemia in Shimano's body, nevertheless bear its scars. This is particularly because history, even amidst its breaks and disruptions, tends to repeat itself (Daitokuin, in *Embalming*, engages in the human experiments he did in Unit 731). Murders also seem to be serial events that occur again and again. This circular temporality is echoed on the visual register by the circles that pervade the *mise-en-scène*: the wheels on the ever-present bikes, the weathercock in *Two Punks*, or the circle painting in *Embalming*.

The question to Aoyama is how individuals should relate to this circular history. Clearly serial events like murders must be stopped, but breaking the circle is not the only solution: given the choices Makoto gives to Naoki (keep riding around in a circle or stop and kill Kozue), continuing the repetition can sometimes signal an end. None the less, Hiroki's life of repetition in *WiLd LIFe* must stop if he is to unite with Rie. It seems that repetition must be a form of mourning that honestly faces and overcomes the past. Akihiko is in the end unable to continue with Makoto and Kozue on their trip because, unlike them, he has never revisited the site of his own traumatic incident. Mizoguchi in *WiLd LIFe* cannot overcome past scars because the whole episode was hushed up. As with Makoto and his 'other bus', they must return to the scene of the past and start over again. Yet not, however, like Daitokuin and his children, who experiment with a means to 'reset' the human psyche like a video game. That is too reminiscent of, on the one hand, Shimano's nihilistic return to nothingness, and, on the other, the fiction of post-war Japan, which forgot the wartime past in order to begin anew. Aoyama's films thus confront the consequences of modern Japanese amnesia, but not by narrating stories of the Second World War. Aoyama firmly locates himself in his own age, which has suffered breaks and divisions from the past. If the scars still remain, they must be dealt with now on the level of micro-political, personal relations with the Other. To Aoyama, the individual arises from these interstices of History and history,[14] from the negotiations between past and present, the personal and the social.

There seem to be limits, however, to the efforts to mourn and overcome the past. At the end of *An Obsession*, the void inside Saga remains and the death squads, ignoring Saga's gun, continue on their lethal rampage. Saga can start anew, returning to Rie and her family's business, but there is a sense that the circularity surrounding these characters has also ringed them in. One must recall the television show Akihiko tells Kenji about in *Helpless*: it is *The Prisoner*, especially the episode in which Number 6 escapes the Village only to find himself returned there. Like many other Japanese filmmakers, from Kitano Takeshi to Kurosawa Kiyoshi, from Miike Takashi to Zeze Takahisa, who depict characters that desire to escape Japan but cannot, Aoyama conceives of Japan as the Village, as a system which even in the global age entraps the individual. That is one reason why characters like Michio in *Two Punks* run to the beach and die there. It is significant, however, that Makoto and Kozue in *Eureka* turn away from the shore and head for the mountains. To Aoyama, ending the film at the coast would imply an affirmation of Japan's identity as an island system,[15] when what was needed was to 'remain here and eat it away from within'.[16]

Aoyama's form of political filmmaking pursues this stance. Working on the borders between entertainment and art cinema, between American, European and Japanese film styles, between a variety of genres and conventions, Aoyama seeks to strategically work these into an individual cinema which not only resists generalization, but which marks the personal as the starting point for political change from within.

Biography

Aoyama Shinji was born on 13 July 1964 in Kitakyūshū, Fukuoka Prefecture, Kyūshū (Japan's southwestern island), to schoolteacher parents. He attended Rikkyō University in Tokyo from 1984 to 1989, where he majored in American literature. Aoyama took courses from the critic Hasumi Shigehiko while making 8mm films in the Rikkyō film circle. Starting with *The Guard from Underground* (*Jigoku no keibiin*, Kurosawa Kiyoshi, 1991), he worked as an assistant director on numerous films and television programmes, including *The Written Face* (Daniel Schmidt, 1994), *Cold Fever* (Fredrik Thor Fridriksson, 1995), *BeRLin* (Rijū Gō, 1995) and other Kurosawa films. He made his début as director in 1995 with *It's Not in the Textbook!*, a made-for-video film. He has continued to write film criticism while making movies. *Eureka* won the FIPRESCI Prize and the Prize of the Ecumenical Jury at the 2000 Cannes Film Festival. Aoyama's own novelization of *Eureka* won the coveted Mishima Yukio Literature Award in 2001.

Notes

1 Interview with Aoyama Shinji, 7 May 2000, Tokyo. Aoyama's previous remarks were voiced in a personal conversation in September 1997.
2 For an account of his experiences under Hasumi, who has taught such filmmakers as Kurosawa Kiyoshi, Suo Masayuki and Shinozaki Makoto, see the roundtable discussion between Aoyama, Kurosawa, Manda Kunitoshi, Yabe Hiroya and Sekiguchi Ryōichi, ' "Eiga Hyōgenron" kara 25-nen', *Cinetic* 3, 1999, pp. 246–78.
3 The hero in *An Obsession* ultimately rejects individualism.
4 Aoyama Shinji, 'Yo wa ika ni shite Gareru shito ni nari shika', *Cahiers du cinéma Japon* 21, 1997, pp. 166–75.
5 See Aoyama Shinji, Yasui Yutaka and Abe Kazushige, 'Kenzaikasuru "Nihon" to iu jiko', *Cahiers du cinéma Japon* 19, 1996, pp. 84–100.
6 Hikoe Tomohiro, 'Merankorī to hiai – Aoyama Shinji no sakuhin o megutte', *Cahiers du cinéma Japon* 22, 1997, pp. 64–76.
7 Aoyama, 'Yo wa ika ni shite', *op. cit.,* pp. 171, 175.
8 Hasumi Shigehiko, *Kantoku Ozu Yasujirō*, Tokyo, Chikuma Shobō, 1983.
9 Aoyama Shinji and Inagawa Masato, 'Nihon eiga wa naze kiki o kaihisuru no ka', *Yuriika* vol. 29, no. 13, October 1997, pp. 220–1.
10 See, for instance, Hikoe, 'Merankorī to hiai', or Saitō Kōji, 'Shitai no hō e: Aoyama Shinji *EM/Embalming*', *Cahiers du cinéma Japon* 28, 1999, p. 179.
11 Kurosawa Kiyoshi, Aoyama Shinji, Higuchi Yasuhito and Yasui Yutaka, 'Karappo no sekai – Cure o megutte', *Cahiers du cinéma Japon* 22, 1997, pp. 39–40.
12 Higuchi Yashuhito, 'Eiga ni kotoba=shi o!', *Yuriika* vol. 29, no. 13, October 1997, pp. 95–101.
13 Aoyama, 'Yo wa ika ni shite', *op. cit.,* pp. 171–2.
14 Aoyama, interview.
15 *Ibid.*
16 Aoyama, 'Yo wa ika ni shite', *op. cit.,* p. 175.

Filmography

It's Not in the Textbook! / Kyōkasho ni nai! (1995) also screenplay
Helpless (1996) also screenplay, music
1/5 (1996) 8 min. short for the 'Celebrate Cinema 101' compilation
A Weapon in My Heart / Waga mune ni kyōki ari (1996) also screenplay, music
Chinpira / Two Punks (1996)
WiLd LIFe (1997) also screenplay (with Satō Kumi), music
An Obsession / Tsumetai chi (1997) also co-producer, screenplay, music, editing (with Satō Kumi)
Shady Grove (1999) also screenplay (with Satō Kumi), music
EM/Embalming (1999) also screenplay (with Hashimoto Izō), music, editing (with Ueno Sōichi)
June 12 1998 (1999) video documentary
Eureka (2000) also screenplay, music, editing
To the Alley / Roji e: Nakagami Kenji no nokoshita firumu (2000) documentary
Desert Moon / Tsuki no saōaku (2001) also screenplay, editing
Note: all music credits shared with Yamada Isao.

AARON GEROW

GREGG ARAKI

Gregg Araki probably remains best known for *The Living End*, a scruffy, cheaply made film about two HIV-positive lovers (a hustler and an intellectual film critic) on the run from Los Angeles after committing murder. The film attained popular and critical fame and notoriety when it was identified by critic B. Ruby Rich as one of the key texts in the inauguration of the New Queer Cinema 'movement'. Rich saw Araki's film as an exemplar of the 'Homo Pomo' style, an aesthetic supposedly characterized by 'appropriation and pastiche, irony, as well as a reworking of history with social constructionism very much in mind'. New Queer Cinema films, claimed Rich, 'are irreverent, energetic, alternately minimalist and excessive'. She linked Araki's film with, among others, Todd Haynes' *Poison* (grand prize-winner of the 1991 Sundance Film Festival), Christopher Munch's *The Hours and Times* (1991), Tom Kalin's *Swoon* (1992), Laurie Lynd's *R.S.V.P.* (1991) and the Pixelvision videos of Sadie Benning.[1]

In fact, Araki's film fits Rich's description rather well. On the whole, politicized lesbian and gay filmmakers of the 1970s and 1980s had tried to counter the mainstream cinema stereotyping that portrayed queers as repressed, lonely fuck-ups and/or killers with 'gay is good' imagery which propagated the assimilationist view that 'we are just like you, really, so please accept us'. In contrast, queer filmmakers (who tended to believe the assimilationist strategy had failed in its efficacy, and was misguided anyway) reclaimed and revelled in those straight stereotypes. Taking a defiant stance against tedious, restrictive heteronormativity, such filmmakers as Tom Kalin and Araki set their libidinally charged gay killers against crappy and/or oppressive representatives of straight society (police, hetero-sexuals generally). This reclamation/subversion penetrated deeper: Kalin's *Swoon* is a 'properly gay' retelling of the Leopold and Loeb murder case which was the inspiration for Hitchcock's desexualized *Rope* (1948); *The Living End* was one of the first overtly gay road movies; the protagonists in Araki's film are both recognizable gay representational types (identified by Richard Dyer as 'macho' and the 'sad young man').[2] In other words, New Queer Cinema texts would 'take back' materials used by straight cinema – stereotypes, stories, genres – and in an anarchic, subversive spirit, rework them, and thus alter their social and political implications.

Araki's style in *The Living End* is also recognizably queer. The acting is stagy, clumsy, campily theatrical, provoking comparisons with the early films of John Waters; the set design is basic, and often recognizably artificial. That this draws attention to the film's constructed nature would seem to be Araki's intention; his rather heavy-handed referencing of his cinematic heroes (Godard, Bazin) serves the same purpose.

As with many other so-called New Queer Cinema filmmakers, Araki has spent his subsequent career trying to escape the label and its implications. He went on to make a trilogy of films about teenagers – *Totally Fucked Up*, *The Doom Generation* and *Nowhere*. All three suffered from poor distribution in Britain and the US, often relegated to film festival screenings (*Splendor*, Araki's latest feature, was shuffled away in the small-print depths of the London Lesbian and Gay Film Festival). Despite the critical recognition provoked by Rich's essay, Araki's films have often been derided by critics. *The Living End* and *Totally Fucked Up* tended to be lambasted for their cheap aesthetic style and leaden, preachy didacticism (respectively, the messages of these films are: the straight world doesn't care about gay men infected with HIV; and the lack of support for, and recognition of, the queer teen experience leads to inflated levels of lesbian and gay suicide). In contrast, *The Doom Generation* and *Nowhere* have been dismissed for the opposite reason: that is, for being too vacuous. In these latter films, both of which had more substantial budgets, Araki seems to have honed a distinctive cinematic style: speedy, hyperbolic teen-speak; rapid editing; a gaudy colour palette; meticulously designed, abstractly fictitious locations. The suggestion of the critics is that this surface sheen mitigates against any deeper content. For instance, Liese Spencer, commenting on *Nowhere* in *Sight and Sound* magazine, argues that:

> Art-directed to within an inch of its life, *Nowhere* could just as easily be retitled 'Nothing', its failure to engage with any real emotion not so much a comment on air-headed youth as a symptom of it. ... One wouldn't want hectoring, but there's a slightly troubling lack of analysis or depth here.[3]

Putting aside Spencer's (now somewhat anachronistic) apparent implication that all gay directors must use their medium to make a political point, it is of course arguable that a blank style, which may neatly suit the characters and locations depicted, prevents the expression of more profound ideas and concerns. Yet Spencer is not alone in her critique. Geoffrey Macnab, for example, seems unable to see beyond *The Doom Generation*'s garish cartoon stylistics. 'The America it depicts,' he writes, 'a surreal expanse of fast-food outlets, bars and derelict cars, is too kitsch to bear easy comparison with the landscapes of *Natural Born Killers*. If anything, it recalls the hyper-animated world of Jim Carrey.'[4]

Araki's films are far from perfect; indeed, they seem to date rather quickly. However, the dismissive approach to his work taken by many critics is unduly rash, since both his representation of adolescent sexuality and the manner in which he handles the interaction of space and sexual orientation in his depictions of Los Angeles demand attention.

Araki's adolescents – like most average teenagers – are obsessed with sex and relationships. Mel (Rachel True) in *Nowhere*, for instance, thinks that she should spread her love around freely before she gets 'old and ugly'. And while the last two decades (especially) have seen the production of a variety of films concerning teenagers and sex, their tones tend to be those of gross-out comedy (*Porky's*, *American Pie*), saccharine romanticism (*She's All That*), or, occasionally, honesty/exploitation (*kids*), whereas Araki's films veer wildly between alternate modalities. In addition, teen movies almost never confront queer sexualities. There have been occasional attempts to handle queer teens – from *The Fruit Machine* to *Beautiful Thing* – but they are the exception.

Araki, then, is one of a kind: as Robin Wood acknowledges, contrary to almost every other representation of teenagers, Araki seems to know, understand and deeply empathize with his protagonists.[5] And reflected in the circumstances of their existence, he seems to see both the miserable futile position teenagers are in within American society *and* some intimations of a potential utopian future.

In *Totally Fucked Up* we follow the day-to-day experiences of a group of six teenagers (two lesbians, three gay boys, and one boy, Andy, who 'might be bisexual ... Girls are nice and warm ... soft to touch ... I do know that I think butt fucking is totally gross'). After Andy's boyfriend Ian cheats on him, and a subsequent attempt at prostitution goes wrong, Andy commits suicide by drinking bleach and falling into a swimming pool. The message is clear: parents (who are almost entirely absent from Araki's films) and society refuse to acknowledge the existence of teenage homosexuality and lesbianism, thus increasing the isolation and pressures on those adolescents. And yet, as Chris Chang has remarked, the teens in *Totally Fucked Up* are incredibly supportive of each other, forming a proto-family. This dynamic is made particularly explicit in one party scene, in which the two lesbians want to conceive, asking all four boys to donate sperm.[6]

The utopian potential of Araki's queer teens becomes more evident as the trilogy develops and the clear identity categories of *Totally Fucked Up* become more malleable and less important. In *The Doom Generation*, Jordan and his girlfriend Amy pick up an enigmatic drifter, Xavier (or 'X'). After killing a psychotic Korean shopkeeper, they all go on the run. As their journey progresses, Amy sleeps with X, and Jordan does not mind. X teaches Amy to experiment sexually, with tricks and methods which she then tries out on Jordan. Finally, all three have sex together in an abandoned warehouse that contains a conveniently placed mattress. In other words, as the three protagonists escape from conventional society, the ideals of heteropatriarchy (monogamous couples, heterosexuality) break down, and are replaced by a different – polymorphously perverse – libidinal economy. It is, then, perhaps no surprise that the warehouse scene and its sexual idealism is interrupted by fascist rednecks, who murder Jordan with a large pair of shears.

In *Nowhere*, identity categories are hardly even mentioned. Both Dark and his girlfriend Mel are bisexual, yet never identify themselves as such; Lucifer is referred to as a lesbian; and in the film's final scene, Montgomery climbs into bed with Dark, saying 'I'm not gay, but ... '. The adolescents in *Nowhere* are frequently annoying: in their vapid teen lingo and affluent ennui, they are only one step removed from the cast of *Beverly Hills 90210*. And yet, in their refusal to recognize sexual orientation as an important discriminatory variable, they do present a 'perverse' ideal. As with the other two films, *Nowhere* ends violently: the moment of connection between Dark and Montgomery is broken when the latter, who has been abducted by aliens earlier in the narrative, has a gigantic bug burst out of his body.

If the deconstructive approach to sexual identity categories that Araki's teen trilogy incorporates is further indication of his 'Pomo Homo' aesthetic, then the setting of his films in and around Los Angeles is entirely appropriate. Throughout much of the 1980s and 1990s, Los Angeles was seen as the quintessential postmodern city. For the major theorists of postmodernity, Los Angeles exemplified postmodern urbanity; both the shape of the city and the behaviour of its inhabitants were deemed to be perfect, 'logical' expressions of the impact of late capitalism on the urban experience. Here was a city in which wealth was harshly polarized; in which people drove everywhere, including to the gym, where they would pay money to walk on treadmills. Here was a city built on dreams: the dreams of Hollywood, aerospace engineers and Silicon Valley technicians. Here was a city with no recognizable centre; a city in which, as Norman Klein has noted, buildings would be destroyed in one year and were completely forgotten by the inhabitants by the next.[7]

The mythical, fantastic nature of Los Angeles confuses things further. Los Angeles is the city of noir, books and movies; yet it is also located in California, the sunshine state, with its promise of health and revitalization. Los Angeles continually revisits its history (as in *Chinatown*) and projects its own future (as in *Blade Runner*). In fact, the form of the 'real' Los Angeles becomes impossible to discern, lost in a sea of hyperbole: Louis Adamic claimed that 'Los Angeles is America. A jungle'; a character in Bret Easton Ellis' *The Informers* states that there is 'nothing' in LA. Academics also recognize the overstated and paradoxical form of the city: as Mike Davis states, Los Angeles 'has come to play the double role of utopia *and* dystopia for advanced capitalism'.[8]

This fragmented, complicated city provides the site for much queer cinema: as well as Araki, most of Bruce LaBruce's films are set in LA, as is the unintentionally hilarious film by Scott Silver, *Johns* (1995). Does the city – in fiction or reality, although that is obviously a difficult distinction to make – provide a unique space for the expression of queerness? Chris Chang has claimed that:

There is something quintessentially L.A. about an Araki film, but there are no recognizable landmarks. It's all claustrophobic rooms, claustrophobic clubs, storefronts and, most pervasive, an endless array of bottomless parking areas. Everything is surface; the only depth is in receding void space; characters appear as transients walking the edge between facade and abyss. Araki [says]: 'It's my L.A.'[9]

But is it? Does Araki work with or against the dominant tropes of LA's mythical form? It is worth briefly considering three of these elements: apocalypse, simulation and the notion of community.

Los Angeles is the city where the end of the world begins; it is often envisioned as the site of apocalypse, both natural and unnatural. There are repetitive notions of the city burning; earthquakes and smog both intimate apocalypse; in noir films and books, Los Angeles is often supposed to die. Araki's teenagers talk constantly about the end of the world, the coming of the apocalypse and their role in it. At one point in *The Doom Generation*, Amy and Jordan lie in bed together in a motel room. 'I hope we die simultaneously,' says Jordan, 'like in a fiery car wreck or a nuclear bomb blast or something.' 'You're so romantic', replies Amy. For Araki's teens, armageddon is often romanticized or eroticized; scenarios of doom imply a way to experience feelings. And yet this apocalypse is mediated: for the trio in *The Doom Generation*, the signifiers of the end of the world orbit around the car; in *Nowhere*, Dark talks about filming his own death, and when he sees an alien for the first time (in itself, a signifier of science fiction apocalypse), his impulsive response is not to run away, but to record it.

The Doom Generation is also scattered with signifiers of an impending religious apocalypse. Sometimes these are *literally* signs: 'Welcome to Hell' in a club; 'Pray For Your Lost Soul' in a 7–11 store. In every convenience store the trio enter, the cost of the bill is always $6.66. And in the film's finale, the rednecks threaten to rape Amy with a china figurine of the Virgin Mary. Religious messages are also present in *Nowhere*. Alyssa, shortly after telling Montgomery that the rapture is due to happen today, complains that her palm is itchy. Later, while having sex with a man called Elvis, she asks him whether he believes in God, and what he would do if California blew up. Montgomery, for his part, leaves behind his crucifix when he is abducted by aliens; the cross is found by Dark, who presumes Montgomery dead ... only for Montgomery to be resurrected, so that he can spread a message of love. Finally, *Nowhere*'s narrative is shot through with scenes of the rhetoric of a televangelist preacher, a patois so seductive that it results in the elaborately staged suicides of two susceptible teenagers.

Mike Davis extends the concept of LA's apocalypse further, and states that the novels of John Rechy, Joan Didion and Bret Easton Ellis portray the city as the site of a 'moral apocalypse'. Clearly, certain critics would also argue that Araki's films are shallow and vacuous, devoid of morality and emotion. However, there is one crucial difference between Araki and authors like Ellis: Araki's characters do make meaningful connections, sometimes only fleetingly, usually through love, sex and lust.

Los Angeles, as many writers have noted, is a heavily mediated city, a place in which it is nearly impossible to separate myth from reality. Araki's LA is a hyperreal, simulated version of the city. He heightens the intensity of colours and uses filters to alter the hues of buildings and skin tone. In *Nowhere*, the bedrooms of the characters mostly display enormous murals that spread across the ceilings and floors, and match their duvet covers and clothes. Araki knows this landscape is fictitious, but he uses it to reflect his recognition of LA's surface culture, its false sheen. This is made particularly clear by one sequence in *Nowhere*. A young bulimic girl called Egg is picked up by a teen idol from *Baywatch* in her local hangout; he takes her to a ridiculously false alpine location, where a wooden bridge spans a deep blue lake, and verdant hills rise in the background. The idol tells Egg of his romantic desire to run away from it all, and just be in love. He then takes her home, gets her drunk and rapes her. Running away from him, she stumbles bloody-faced and distraught through gridlock. After weaving through the traffic, she runs past a billboard depicting the alpine landscape in which she was sweet-talked. The implication is obvious: just as the idol's handsome, romanticized exterior hid a malevolent nature, so LA's myths of its own beauty are undercut by its snarling carmageddon.

The other main element of Araki's simulated LA is the presence in his narratives of video cameras: his characters are obsessed with recording their own experience, as if this somehow makes it more real. Dark, in *Nowhere*, constantly films his life; and *Totally Fucked Up* contains a lot of home movie footage, of the characters shopping, taking ecstasy in a multi-storey car park, having sex, being interviewed. The complication with this home video material, this simulation of the lives of the characters, is that it is often clichéd, or contains a recognition of its own spurious nature as 'truth'. The trio in *The Doom Generation* treat their car windscreen as a television or cinema screen. And as the only way to get around LA is by car on the freeways, the city appears as a simulation on the windshield.

Finally, we turn to community: Los Angeles is a city with no centre, and this, according to many theorists, including Roland Barthes, prevents the experience of connection between its inhabitants. Is this true? Araki's films would seem to suggest not. The connections made between his characters may only be fleeting, but they are often intensely passionate. For example, Luke tells Jon in *The Living End* that he loves him 'more than life itself'; Andy's relationship with Ian in *Totally Fucked Up* is sexy, exciting and unpredictable; before Montgomery explodes at the end of *Nowhere*, he and Dark truly seem to have found each other. In addition, beyond this sexual level, Araki's protagonists bond through similar experiences of disenfranchisement. In *The Doom Generation*, for instance, Jordan tells Amy he is happy for X to accompany them on their flight from LA because 'he's sort of like us. Lost. Like he doesn't fit in.'

In the lusty linkings of Araki's characters, Robin Wood seems to locate the lost heart and soul of Los Angeles; and in their attempts at bonding through love and friendship, he seems to perceive a quiet revolution being effected. Yet what is fascinating is *where* all this takes place: claustrophobic rooms and clubs, storefronts, motels, warehouses, parking areas, subways, and so on. Araki's queer characters, as befits their position within society, live in and occupy sites of marginality and transience, locations which are largely ignored by straight society, but which hold great potential. Perhaps the true significance of Araki's films – aside from their contributions to debates about adolescence and homosexuality – will prove to be their imagining of spaces in the United States in which tomorrow's generation, in all their flawed glory, attempt to shape their world.

Biography

Gregg Araki was born in 1963, in Santa Barbara, California, USA. He graduated from the USC School of Cinema Television, to which he has returned to teach.

Notes

1 B. Ruby Rich, 'New Queer Cinema', *Sight and Sound*, vol. 2, no. 9, 1992, pp. 30–9, p. 32.

2   Richard Dyer, *The Matter of Images: Essays on Representations*, London, Routledge, 1993.
3   Liese Spencer, 'Nowhere', *Sight and Sound*, vol. 8, no. 6, 1998, pp. 36–7, pp. 52 and 37.
4   Geoffrey Macnab, 'The Doom Generation', *Sight and Sound*, vol. 6, no. 6, 1996, pp. 37–8.
5   Robin Wood, *Sexual Politics and Narrative Film: Hollywood and Beyond*, New York, Columbia University Press, 1998.
6   Chris Chang, 'Absorbing Alternative', *Film Comment*, vol. 30, no. 5, 1994, pp. 47–53.
7   Norman Klein, *The History of Forgetting: Los Angeles and the Erasure of Memory*, London, Verso, 1997.
8   Mike Davis, *City of Quartz: Excavating the Future in Los Angeles*, London, Verso, 1990.
9   Chris Chang, *op. cit.*, pp. 50–3.

Filmography

Three Bewildered People in the Night (1987)
The Long Weekend (O'Despair) (1989)
The Living End (1992)
Totally Fucked Up (1993)
The Doom Generation (1995)
Nowhere (1997)
Splendor (1999)

Further reading

Roy Grundmann, 'The Fantasies We Live By: Bad Boys in *Swoon* and *The Living End*', *Cineaste*, March 1993, p. 18.
Katie Mills, 'Revitalizing the Road Genre: *The Living End* as an AIDS Road Film', in Steven Cohan and Ina Rae Hark (eds) *The Road Movie Book*, London, Routledge, 1997.
James M. Moran, 'Gregg Araki: Guerilla Film-maker for a Queer Generation', *Film Quarterly*, vol. 50, no. 1, 1996.
Raymond Murray, *Images in the Dark: An Encyclopaedia of Gay and Lesbian Film and Video*, London, Plume, 1996.

GLYN DAVIS

JEAN-JACQUES BEINEIX

Beineix is generally seen, with Luc Besson and Leos Carax, as the best example of the *cinéma du look*, a mode defined by Ginette Vincendeau in terms of 'youth-oriented films with high production values'. The 'look', notes Vincendeau, 'refers to the films' high investment in non-naturalistic, self-conscious aesthetics, notably intense colours and lighting effects' with 'spectacular (studio-based) and technically brilliant *mise-en-scène*'.[1] While Besson's films have had box-office success, Beineix's early films are more obviously cult movies. His first short film, *Le Chien de Monsieur Michel*, combined laconic, off-beat humour with an exploration of the individual and his relationship to a community. (The hero invents a pet dog in order that he can eat the butcher's off-cuts for himself. When the imaginary dog takes over his life, he tells his neighbours that the dog is dead. They club together to buy an Alsatian, which terrorizes him.) *37° 2 le matin*, known as *Betty Blue* in the UK and the US, has maintained a cult status with international youth audiences, while *La Lune dans le caniveau* (*The Moon in the Gutter*), savaged by critics on its release, has steadily gained a critical following. *Diva*, Beineix's first feature and the only one to attract considerable critical attention (Jameson termed it the first French postmodern film),[2] combines high culture (opera) and the popular culture of the French police thriller: Jules, a young postman who illicitly records the diva, is pursued by thugs when a tape denouncing the corrupt police chief ends up in his possession.

French critics took a dislike to the supposedly superficial aspects of postmodern style, namely an attachment to objects and to surface effect at the expense of character psychology or moral message. The arguments which raged in *Cahiers du cinéma* came to a head at Cannes, where Beineix showed his second film, *La Lune dans le caniveau*, based on David Goodis' low-life novel, *The Moon in the Gutter*, in which Gérard Depardieu plays a loner obsessed with discovering his sister's rapist. Consciously operatic, with languorous tracking shots, artificial colour schemes and emphatic music, intended to convey the dream-like atmosphere of the novel, the film's high production values were felt to be at odds with the 'low-life' subject matter. The film was booed and publicly repudiated by Depardieu.

Beineix's third feature, *37° 2 le matin*, co-produced by his new company Cargo Films, became an even greater cult film for youth audiences in France and abroad. A tale of mad love between a world-weary man (Zorg) and a rebellious young woman (Betty), the film's success owed much to Djian's novel and to the leads, Béatrice Dalle and Jean-Hugues Anglade, who managed to capture the mixture of masculinity in crisis, rebelliousness, innocence and marginalization which characterized the 1980s' youth *Zeitgeist*.

Beineix's next film, *Roselyne et les lions*, despite a storyline which on paper might seem calculated to please the *cinéma du look*'s youth audience – a young couple seek adventure in the world of the big top by training lions – achieved only average box-office business, perhaps because it was too obviously an allegory about perfecting one's art. Beineix's last feature to date, *IP5*, did somewhat better. It is a narrative of initiation as two streetwise youths go on the road in search of romance, only to meet an old man (Yves Montand in his last role), apparently doing much the same thing. During the 1990s Beineix turned to documentary filmmaking. Like his feature films, the documentaries focus on characters who are socially marginalized, as is the case with Beineix's return to feature filmmaking, *Mortel Transfert*. In this comedy thriller, a psychoanalyst, played by Jean-Hugues Anglade, wakes up after dozing off in a session with a client, to find her murdered.

This brief overview suggests the features which define Beineix's cinema: an emphasis on the comical, although tinged with derision and irony; an attraction to community as a concept, counter-balanced by a strong sense of independence which manifests itself as marginality in his characters. The work also features a strong erotic charge, whether in relation to what his characters do (one thinks of the long opening sequence of *37° 2 le matin* where Zorg and Betty make passionate love), or the way in which his images are frequently calculated to seduce the spectator.

We can see how the scepticism which attaches to the postmodern collapse of 'master narratives' might lead to the melancholic and often bitter rejection of society by Beineix's characters. *Diva*'s opening sequence which mixes shots of the Three Muses on the roof of the Paris Opera with Jules' space-like crash helmet (reminiscent of the closing sequence of Kubrick's *2001: A Space Odyssey*, 1968) is an archetypal postmodern image in this respect, as is *IP5*'s long shot of Tony covering a billboard with a huge city-like graffiti in the middle of a windswept rural landscape. The consequences of divorcing the image from a deep history and from a coherent aesthetic context are that images are bound together by play on the surface of meaning. As Jameson puts it, 'depth is replaced by surface, or multiple surfaces'.[3] Consider the insertion into a film of quotations from other films, or indeed other media, which do not appear to have a clear function other than to perform as quotations: for example, *Diva*'s apparently motiveless quotation from Wilder's *The Seven Year Itch* (1955) where a Monroe lookalike's white dress billows up on the updraft from the metro grill below her.

In France, the establishment view of Beineix focuses particularly on the interrelated issues of technology and surface. In keeping with the position established by *Cahiers du cinéma* during the 1980s, *Le Monde*'s critic uses Beineix as the best example of what he calls 'le Visuel', the abandonment of classic narrative for seduction by the image. This type of cinema, claims Frodon, involves the intervention of technology (very mobile cameras such as the Steadicam and the Louma, as well as Dolby sound), distancing the spectator from 'reality'.[4]

Jullier, too, points out how the track forward, particularly when associated with Dolby surround-sound, can affect the whole body, creating a dizzying feeling of exhilaration. Beineix does not systematically use this effect, although his sweeping lateral tracking shots and excessive camera angles (extreme high or low angle/canted), frequently associated with close-ups, work in the same way. For Jullier such a style projects spectators into the fictional world through sensation rather than reflection, producing a cinema centred less on character than on the spectator. Effects of this type are not confined to the cinema of the 1980s, but critics disliked Beineix's use of them, leading to the view that his cinema, by its predilection for the object, was symptomatic of alienation, and beholden to a style more familiar in advertising and music videos.

The immersion of the spectator, not in some kind of 'depth' but, paradoxically, in an infinite 'surface', is the common factor here. The spectator does not go beyond the surface of the narrative, which functions like a peg on which to hang the coat of style. It is not the psychological complexity of the character which gives pleasure, but the way in which the character behaves. In other words, what matters is what can be seen, what is presented, rather than what can be worked out, or constructed. Given the mistrust of the visual prevalent in much of twentieth-century French intellectual work, it is hardly surprising that French film critics took a dislike to this new style.[5] In 1967, for example, situationist philosopher Guy Debord had analysed the way in which spectacle had become all-powerful, driving out humanity: 'All that was once directly lived has become mere representation.'[6]

It is no surprise perhaps that for writers associated with *Cahiers du cinéma* the postmodern image was linked to advertising. French advertising of the 1980s often foregrounded style over product. The medium became the message, with sophisticated visual and verbal displays showing a level of provocative creativity intended to dazzle. The advertising image can be seen as the perfect postmodern image, with Beineix representing everything which *Cahiers du cinéma* saw as most reprehensible in this new style of filmmaking (this was not helped by the fact that Beineix, like many directors during the 1980s, made a number of television commercials). Beineix was frequently cited by advertising guru Jacques Séguéla, who understood the form as a combination of seduction and derision (encapsulated in his 'three r's', 'rire, rêve, risque' – laughter, dream, risk).

If this cocktail upset the critics, it appealed to a youth audience familiar with advertising images, pop videos and the romantic plots to which Vincendeau draws attention. By incorporating such elements in their films, Beineix (and Besson) ensured a following among youth audiences. As Beineix later wrote, in a provocative defence of the advertising aesthetic:

> Advertising has never invented anything except what artists have invented. On the other hand, it has been able to capture, inflect, parody, imitate. It appropriated the Beautiful which the cinema of the New Wave had rejected, which makes certain ignorant critics say that beautiful equals advertising. It kidnapped colour, which the cinema no longer violated, so preoccupied was it with being true to life, which makes certain cretinous critics say that colour equals advertising. It dispensed with stories, which the narrative cinema was unable to do without, so some stupid critics are saying that a film without a story equals advertising. Finally ... it generally captivated young people, whose aspirations the ageing cinema no longer translated, so that some old critics who are only interested in what's dead and gone, or those who are dead and gone are saying that youth cinema equals advertising.[7]

Beineix's films, like Besson's, managed to reflect the contemporary mood of cynicism and alienation prevalent in the youth class, which felt disenfranchised, as films by the new breed of French filmmakers, for example Kassovitz's *La Haine* (1995), have continued to underline. Beineix's combination of passion and derision, therefore, corresponded with the prevailing mood of youth audiences: 'Romantic and cynical, it's a mixture of both. It's a romanticism you don't really believe in.'[8]

By the end of the decade, the passion raised by postmodern youth cinema had run its course; the *cinéma du look* was revalued as baroque (the term had regularly appeared in reviews of *Diva*). Writing for the *Revue du cinéma* in 1989, Bassan points out (as had Beineix himself) that artists use whatever material is to hand in the world around them, and that therefore it was illogical to criticize Beineix's use of 'low' cultural material. He also points out that Beineix's fetishization of objects extends to locations (such as the loft in *Diva*) nd that the films *construct* a new urban myth, rather than slavishly pastiching advertisements. His major concern, however, is to outline the way in which the *cinéma du look* can be called neo-baroque:

> In art the baroque wants to astonish, touch the senses, dazzle. It does so by using effects which rely on movement and contrast of light, forms which are stretched and strained to the point where perspective is disrupted and mutates into trompe-l'oeil. Architecture, sculpture and painting tend to blend together into a unitary spectacle whose dazzling energy conveys euphoria.[9]

Calabrese's study of the neo-baroque is less about the baroque than about the postmodern as an echo of the baroque, and as such it provides a useful frame for thinking about Beineix's cinema. He explores contemporary culture to isolate what are now considered typical postmodern effects, such as excess, fragmentation, vortical turbulence and metamorphosis, which he links to show how the postmodern seeks to avoid the centre by excessive fragmentation. This creates monstrous forms, in the baroque sense of a combination of the marvellous and the enigmatic.[10] Beineix's excessive camerawork can be explained by this attraction to the metamorphosis of the real into the excessive. Calabrese also invokes figures such as the knot and the labyrinth, forms of 'constructed undecidability'.[11] In this sense, *Diva*, with its double narrative strands which intertwine in a complex puzzle, really is a perfect postmodern film, but the analysis is equally applicable to the darkly operatic *La Lune dans le caniveau* and the glisteningly repetitive and allegorical *Roselyne et les lions*.

Rather like Calabrese's notion of the labyrinth or knot, Deleuze sees the fold as archetypally baroque. Further, Deleuze insists on the spiritual side of the decorative. Beineix's films are vehicles which express not just disillusion with the world as it is, but also aspirations to a better world, a striving for a utopian perfection, so strong that it is analogous to what Deleuze means by the 'spiritual'. Beineix's characters are obsessively passionate, single-mindedly committed to their vision of perfection, whether it be Jules and the perfect sound, Gérard and the perfect world, Betty and the perfect novel, Roselyne and the perfect act, or Tony and the perfect love. They are so single-minded that their mode of operation is a heady mixture of tragedy and melodrama. In this respect the frequent comic interludes in Beineix's films function as necessary releases of tension, which, since they are more often than not associated with secondary characters, serve only to isolate and emphasize the solitude of the hero. The hero is less of a hero than an anti-hero, weak, feminized, marginal, usually derisively self-deprecating, leading to a curious attitude of passionate detachment from his environment. Derision mocks the world because it does not come up to expectations, because it cannot deliver the ideal to which Beineix's characters aspire. His characters are not nihilists, however, since they are implicated totally and obsessively in what they do, and the context in which they do it, while at the same time being distanced from it.

Beineix's films constantly gesture to a utopia formed from an amalgam of passion and emptiness, contradictory positions of total commitment and disgusted resignation and abnegation; as the advertising hoarding of *La Lune dans le caniveau* puts it: 'Try another world'. Beineix's emphatic and baroque use of colour, music and décor, his reliance on luxurious artifice, underline the vacuity of the world and the desire for something better. The characters of Beineix's films have indeed lost their bearings, and find themselves nowhere, in a labyrinth from which there is apparently no escape. The decorative in Beineix's films is, to recall Deleuze, a fabrication expressing the intensity of the spiritual, the urge to make a somewhere of the nowhere. In other words, the baroque of Beineix's films is an attempt to approximate the world of purity which is just beyond reach, as in *La Lune dans le caniveau*, with its operatic blend of dazzling camera effects, emphatic music and colour contrasts.

The bitter arguments in the film press of the 1980s around Beineix's work were in a sense misplaced. Their context is the film establishment's fear of Hollywood, and their insistence that French national cinema is the major cultural export, and as such a key component in the maintenance of French national identity. French critics disliked the postmodern style as exemplified by Beineix for three major reasons: as a vehicle for consumer objects rather than high-cultural objects; because the notion of a postmodern style transcended issues of national specificity; and because it under-mined, as a result, the very French notion of an *auteur*.

There is considerable irony in singling Beineix out here. First because in 1994–5 Beineix was president of the *Association des auteurs, réalisateurs, producteurs*, a particularly vocal association for cinema professionals, and was elected to the committee of Unifrance Film International, an association established to promote French cinema internationally. In these posts, he spent much of his time defending French cinema. Second, because his work is characteristically that of an *auteur*. He has a personal style based on colour, artificial décor, emphatic music and melodramatic romantic plots; he returns obsessively to fetish objects (cars), dialogue (references to Zen) and structures (Oedipal struggles); and, like Hitchcock, he manages to combine the popular with the experimental, and familiar plots with an obsessive personal vision.

What the discussion of baroque and neo-baroque helps us to see, beyond the arid position-taking of the 1980s, is that in Beineix's films we find a heady mixture of passion and derision, the idealism of youth, light, excess, monstrosity, fragmentation and, last but not least, the urge to find the lost centre of a complex labyrinth in which the spectator's body is transformed through pleasure.

Biography

Born in Paris, France, in 1946, Beineix began his career in the cinema in 1969 as a trainee for a long-running television comedy series, *Les Saintes Chéries*, directed by Jean Becker. In the following ten years, he moved up to second assistant director, and then to first assistant director on some fourteen minor films, most of them comedies, working with a number of well-known directors, such as René Clément, Claude Berri and more particularly Claude Zidi, which allowed Beineix to work with well-known comic actors.

Notes

1 Ginette Vincendeau, *The Companion to French Cinema*, London, Cassell/BFI Publishing, 1996, p.50.
2 Fredric Jameson, *Signatures of the Visible*, New York and London, Routledge, 1992, pp. 55–62.
3 Fredric Jameson, 'Postmodernism, or the cultural logic of late capitalism', in Thomas Docherty (ed.) *Postmodernism: A Reader*, New York, London, Toronto, Sydney, Tokyo and Singapore, Harvester Wheatsheaf, 1993, pp. 62–92, p. 70.
4 Jean-Michel Frodon, *L'Age moderne du cinéma français: De la Nouvelle Vague à nos jours*, Paris, Flammarion, 1995, pp. 574–8.
5 Martin Jay, *Downcast Eyes: The Denigration of Vision in Twentieth-century French Thought*, Berkeley and London, University of California Press, 1993.
6 Guy Debord, *The Society of the Spectacle*, New York, Zone Books, 1995, p. 12.

7   Denis Parent, *Jean-Jacques Beineix: Version originale*, Paris, Barrault Studio, 1989, p. 222 and p. 224.
8   Jean-Jacques Beineix, 'Interview', *Séquences*, no. 129, 1987, pp. 40–7, p. 43.
9   Raphaël Bassan, 'Trois néobaroques français', *Revue du cinéma* no. 449, 1989, pp. 44–50, p. 49.
10 Omar Calabrese, *The Neo-Baroque: A Sign of the Times*, Princeton, NJ, Princeton University Press, 1992, pp. 92–3.
11 *Ibid.*, p. 139.

Filmography

Le Chien de Monsieur Michel (1977) short
Diva (1981)
La Lune dans le caniveau / *The Moon in the Gutter* (1983)
37° 2 le matin / *Betty Blue* (1986)
Roselyne et les lions (1989)
IP5 (1992)
Mortel Transfert (2001)

Documentaries

Les Enfants de Roumanie (1992)
Otaku (1993)
Place Clichy … sans complexe (1994)
Assigné à résidence (1997)

Further reading

Guy Austin, *Contemporary French Cinema: An Introduction*, Manchester, Manchester University Press, 1996.
Laurent Jullier, *L'Ecran post-moderne: Un cinéma de l'allusion et du feu d'artifice*, Paris, L'Harmattan, 1997.
Phil Powrie, *Jean-Jacques Beineix*, Manchester, Manchester University Press, 2001.

PHIL POWRIE

BERNARDO BERTOLUCCI IN CONTEXT

The trade press publicity for *Stealing Beauty* quoted the *New York Times* film critic's praise of Bertolucci for retaining 'his extra-ordinary visual edge. Intense and alluring powers of seduction'.[1] Hailed as a cultural event, the film was much heralded as 'Bertolucci's return to Italy', and to small-scale production after three international mega-productions (*The Last Emperor, The*

Sheltering Sky and *Little Buddha*). However, critics who expected to see a return to an engagement with Italian politics, or a many-layered, Freudian-inspired narrative, were disappointed. The film was criticized as sexist and slight – not the work of a director of Bertolucci's stature (a pattern repeated with *Besieged*). Still regarded as an important filmmaker, critics find Bertolucci's later work problematic, to the extent that his survival as a culturally influential director is interesting. His very virtuosity and the visual splendour of his films have ensured that he still manages to make films, even if critics are today ambivalent about that virtuosity.

In the critical discourse surrounding his films, Bertolucci talks prolifically about his work: 'My films are the story of my life – and they are what I've been doing, thinking, feeling, been interested in, all these thirty years – it's my way of working.'[2] His début was certainly due to his personal position in Italian cultural circles as the son of a famous poet, Attilio Bertolucci. Bertolucci's first film, *La commare secca* (*The Grim Reaper*), was made in 1962, when he was only 21 years old, from a subject suggested by Pasolini. It was a moderate financial and great critical success and launched his career.

Bertolucci tends to work for many years with the same people, though the creative team is never precisely the same from one film to the next.[3] Moreover, on a film project he is often involved at several levels – most significantly working on the script and the screenplay. Of course, there are financial reasons for a script credit, but we can see Bertolucci benefiting both from the input of other creative people and from stamping his mark on the final film. Equally, the structures of the art cinema give particular weight to the director (he or she is an important part of the 'package' put together to attract finance, and figures large in the selling and marketing of the film). This is reinforced by the system of recognition at film festivals and by state and other prizes. The Italian film industry is notoriously Byzantine: industry bodies produce exhaustive statistics of box-office returns in order to calculate the track record of the creative team and the possible appeal of a particular subject. A film might be a critical success but unless distributors and producers receive a return, a director's continued employment would be in question.[4] Bertolucci has used the structures of both Italian and international film industries effectively, constituting himself as a 'great director'. What he says about the process of filmmaking, about his ideas and preoccupations, is a factor in the film's journey. To ignore this is to ignore the equally interesting work that Bertolucci as director has to accomplish in order to continue working.

The first main claim which Bertolucci makes is that his work is informed by a Marxist perspective. To a greater or lesser extent, this philosophical position is fundamental to most of Bertolucci's work. *The Grim Reaper*, for example, starts with the dead body of a murdered Roman prostitute, using flashbacks to explore the stories of those who came into contact with her on her last day. A quest narrative, the film uses the familiar device of a death starting an exploration for reasons. The quest allows a milieu to be sketched, that of the poor quarters of Rome; the repeated revisiting of parks, lower-class homes and streets as each character re-enacts his or her contact with the crime, allows an overwhelming impression of authenticity. The characters have no ambitions to make their mark on history, but their lives are shaped by social hierarchies. Long shots show the characters in their social context, while close-ups show emotion and indicate motivation. Characters looking at each other, noticing things, mirror the audience's activity. Through his use of realist cinematic conventions (inherited from post-war neo-realist cinema) and the investigative narrative, Bertolucci is able to suggest that there is truth to be discovered beneath the apparent referent, the impression of authentic, working-class Rome. The narrative concludes with the identification of the murderer, but also with the assertion that there is not one true referent, but multiple referents, multiple explanations. The film also exhibits the interplay between the analysis of events (a desire to know) and an impulse towards composition and aesthetic display. Space is organized both to give a full context to the action and to display the aesthetic qualities of buildings and perspective.

Freudian analysis, with its emphasis on latent and manifest meanings, is equally important. Bertolucci is not only the son of a great man, with whom he has had to come to terms. He shares with his generation a preoccupation with coming to terms with Italian history, particularly its fascist past, and with Italian culture in the unsustainable post-war flowering of anti-fascist, artistic culture in neo-realism. His generation of male, bourgeois, Marxist intellectuals construct their identity against a complex political past. From film to film, Bertolucci gives us varying representations of his generation's difficulty, bringing aspects of his own personal history into his films and the universal, Oedipal, conflict between generations and artists.

Following *The Grim Reaper*, Bertolucci made documentaries for television and two (unsuccessful) feature films – *Prima della rivoluzione* (*Before the Revolution*) and *Partner* – both of which were heavily influenced by the work of Godard. By the late 1960s, he had come to realize that his own style and preoccupations were different, and that he wanted to reach a wider audience. In this, Bertolucci (like others of his generation) was influenced by the work of Antonio Gramsci. Gramsci's ideas appealed because they gave Italian intellectuals the role of making readings of Italian cultural history in order for the *structural* reasons for the left-wing exclusion from power to be visible, and to do this in an accessible language. After *Partner*, Bertolucci therefore determined to move into more mainstream production,[5] taking advantage of Rai television's new cultural agenda of co-producing films with established directors. The budgets were not large,[6] and the subject matter had to have a high cultural (but mass) appeal since the films were publicized as cultural events in Rai scheduling.[7] *The Spider's Stratagem*, made back-to-back with *The Conformist* in 1970 (the same year Bertolucci started psychoanalysis), exemplifies the Rai film genre. A loose adaptation of a novella by cult author Borges, the film explores the betrayal of the intellectual – both past and present. Young Athos Magnani is summoned to the town of Tara by his father's (also Athos Magnani) mistress, Draifa. He is reluctantly charged with discovering who murdered his father (immortalized in sculpture as an anti-fascist hero) in the 1930s. It is another quest narrative, using conversations and testimonies in the present to evoke events in the past; this doubling and repetition presents 'a view of history as a past inaccessible to truth'.[8] The film closes with disappointment as Athos discovers that his father was murdered in order to prevent the discovery of the fact that he had betrayed a plot to murder Mussolini; but the film is prevented from being tainted with this sour emotion by the beautiful, dream-like *mise-en-scène*. Athos discovers the world of his own unconscious, his own identity. The colour tones are particularly sensual – the rich, warm tones of Draifa's house and her flowers; the interplay of green, orange and white on the way to the fascist, Beccaccia's house; and the warm pinks and browns of the salami-taster's home. Considering that this film was made for television, it contains a large number of long shots. Bertolucci is concerned to show his characters in their social setting, but also – by the use of framing devices, such as doors and windows – to suggest a complex, multi-layered reality.

This visual beauty, and complexity of *mise-en-scène* slow the narrative, inviting the spectator both to interpret latent meanings and to admire the director's skill. In the type of Italian auteurist cinema typified by Bertolucci, realism and spectacle form a symbiotic relationship, suggesting the complexity of contemporary reality and of masculine identity. It has been suggested that 'the pleasure of texts involving "spectacle" lies in the images themselves; it is a visual, not a narrative pleasure'.[9] This provides some explanation of why a director such as Bertolucci has been able to move into international co-production. Italian audiences, or audiences with cultural capital,[10] will make more or less informed readings of both narrative and visuals, while the international art cinema audience will be seduced by visual pleasures, complemented by information gleaned from secondary texts surrounding the films.

The critical success of *The Spider's Stratagem* and *The Conformist*, Bertolucci's virtuosity of *mise-en-scène*, his ability to handle complex narratives and an international cast meant that he could now become part of an international production 'package'. At the risk of being schematic, I will just indicate that the enormous financial success of *Last Tango in Paris* moved Bertolucci's worth in the investors' league tables up several notches. In fact, we see him move into the 'quality film', entrusted with big budgets and big international themes.

Novecento is the product of a particular moment of the early 1970s, when the political upheaval of 1968 had caused Gramsci's ideas to be re-evaluated. There is no space here for detailed consideration of how an Italian Marxist managed to make a two-part epic film with the financial assistance of Paramount, United Artists and 20th Century Fox.[11] Its English title, *Nineteen Hundred*, closes off an entire layer of significance; the Italian title signifies both the year 1900 *and* the century – obviously calling a film 'the twentieth century' implies something altogether more grand, more significant, more meaningful and powerful than a single year. It predisposes us to consider the work's epic sweep, that the filmmaker has something to tell us, and above all, that the events described will have a historical basis in fact.

The subject of the film, the rise to political consciousness of the peasants of Emilia Romagna between Summer 1900 and April 1945, is framed by a painting and by the prologue set on Liberation Day, 25 April 1945. The painting shows the purposive movement forward in collective action of peasant figures, setting the style and expectations of the following narrative. Again, Bertolucci's philosophical position informs the most minute artistic choices. He uses the lives of two boys, born on the same day – one into the peasant classes and the other into the landowning classes – to represent class struggle symbolically. The meaning of the story, the truth of class relations and how and why the upper classes supported fascism, is suggested not only by the informative dialogue but by the visual organization and emphasis. The *mise-en-scène* repeatedly draws attention to the fact that the peasants, the Dalcò family, only have *natural* light (they eat quickly because that is all they have). Their collective nature is stressed by their compression into one space, as well as by the heroic figure of Leo Dalcò, who delivers the lesson of family (and metonymically, class) solidarity. By contrast, the landowner's family occupy many rooms and use artificial light. As in all of Bertolucci's films, the exploration of sexual relationships is fundamental to that of social and political relationships; repression associated with political oppression, anality and sodomy used as metaphors for the exploitative, consumerist relations of capitalist society.[12] *Novecento* uses sexual perversion to indicate the decadence and degradation of bourgeois society in the fascist period.

The quest for identity, and to come to terms with parents recurs in *La luna*, made in English with an international cast. Music, as in all Bertolucci's work, suffuses the film and is used to deepen the emotional content and response to the narrative; the words sung (especially opera) have a resonance to the story events. An adolescent American boy, in Italy with his opera singer mother, realizes that his mother's deceased husband was not his father. At the end of the film, against the backdrop of a rehearsal in the Baths of Caracalla, the boy escapes the emotional power of his mother (expressed through the incestuous relationship), and is reunited with his father.

Bertolucci's last Italian film, *La tragedia di un uomo ridiculo* (*The Tragedy of a Ridiculous Man*) (again about fathers and sons, and history), was not very successful. It has been described as his 'anguished response to contemporary Italy',[13] and he determined not to work there in the 1980s. His previous films had shown that he was capable of handling large budget films, with international star casts, hundreds of extras, serious themes and complex plots. His interest in a Marxist view of history and in Freudian analysis also meant the inclusion of the occasional scenes of sex and violence and sexual perversity, always associated with the evils of fascism and capitalism, none of which ever hurt in box-office terms. However, Bertolucci left psychoanalysis in 1984 (although, as he has commented, you never really stop), and the crises of socialism and communism, culminating in the fall of the Berlin Wall, left a great void in his life. From the mid-1980s Bertolucci's films question the values of European society, exploring other cultures and belief systems. His track record means that he is offered large budgets to do this – $25 million for *The Last Emperor* (which won nine Oscars and grossed $93 million) and *The Sheltering Sky*, $33 million for *Little Buddha*. These are sumptuous, widescreen films which seduce us with their striking and sensual use of colour and composition, and interest us in the ideas expressed. Bertolucci has commented that, under the influence of multinational business corporations, and the media which they control, western societies are becoming more mono-cultural; class struggle has been ironed out and most Europeans live in an ideological desert.[14] These films are both quests for personal authenticity, embodied in the non-western Other, and explorations of other sexualities. *The Sheltering Sky* is another adaptation of a cult novel which Bertolucci has broken down in order to explore the complexities of human relationships, and the shock of the meeting of two cultures (North American and North African). A neurotic American couple, Port and Kit Moresby, travel to North Africa to experience a 'more authentic' way of life. They get more than they bargain for. Port dies of typhus, after which Kit wanders off into the desert in a daze. She is taken up by a Bedouin camel train and becomes the sexual slave of its leader, Belqassim. Critics felt very uneasy about the end of this film, remarking on the use of 'son of the sheikh' stereotypes and picture postcard landscapes. The film does not escape the stereotypes of the desert movie and the Western, but, as Geoffrey Nowell-Smith has noted, by presenting North Africa through western eyes, the film does encourage an awareness of the limits of touristic and colonialist understanding.[15] The film oscillates ambivalently between a celebration of personal and sexual confidence embodied in indigenous peoples and alarm at the removal of boundaries to experience. The film is also ambivalent about its own position. Port's and Kit's lives are represented as problematic and inauthentic, yet, as soon as they step outside the civilized coastal fringe of North Africa, they encounter the American Express advert world of danger, dirt and disease associated with dark-skinned Others, whose speech is incomprehensible and whose actions and lifestyles are inexplicable. Many of the characters are represented as sexually ambiguous (Belqassim is stunningly beautiful; the Tuareg boy in the camel train may be a girl; Kit disguises herself as a boy in order to have a sexual relationship with Belqassim) or homosexual (Erick openly; Port is feminized). But the fluidity of sexual identity promises a liberation never quite delivered. Kit develops from a rich, bored and neurotic traveller, towards a sense of her own female identity, but it is uncertain whether she returns strengthened or annihilated. In this respect, these three films of the clash between alien cultures display similar anxieties and preoccupations.

Stealing Beauty has limited locations and costumes, but a star-filled international cast. In a 1996 *Guardian* lecture, Bertolucci claimed that he now feels an outsider in Italy, explaining his interest in the group of British and Irish expatriates which the film is about. His characters are both involved in local matters and (by virtue of their cultural background) outsiders. Their quest for meaning has led them to a farmhouse in Tuscany, and a search for spiritual and creative 'authenticity', yet Alex's death from AIDS and Lucy's personal quest cause them to interrogate their certainties. Lucy, a 19-year-old American, has been sent to Italy by her stepfather after her mother's death. While exploring her mother's identity and seeking her real father, she is also searching for the ideal partner who will take her virginity. Lucy's quest for a sense of identity depends largely on her relationship with men. Through ignorance about her father, Lucy has been denied access to her past, mirroring Bertolucci's contention that the younger generation today has no sense of history.[16] Lucy's search is framed by an anonymous video camera recording of her journey, giving an uneasy sense of male empowerment through access to the world of emotion represented by the feminine. This sense of unease is also generated by *L'Assedio* (*Besieged*), Bertolucci's next film, through the white master's conquest of his young, black servant. He appropriates her sexually, and culturally by compelling her to reveal her story. This may be a metaphor for the colonial situation, but she, like Lucy, remains in a subordinate situation.

Bertolucci has been intermittently working on an Italian-language production, *Heaven and Hell*, a similar mixture of the intimate and the epic. The production company, Mikado, is experienced in the 'selling' of important art cinema directors such as Almodòvar and Bertolucci. It is clear, therefore, that European filmmakers have colonized a space in the market where medium-budget films with serious themes and the stamp of an individual's style can be very profitable, without the risks (and stress) involved in big-budget production.

Both *Stealing Beauty* and *Besieged* are lower-budget co-productions with television companies,[17] and their preoccupation with identity chimes with that of the mass multicultural audience. The sensual appreciation of space and landscape which, in the pre-1981 films, was both an evocation of context or referent and an indication of the presence of the director's hand, have assumed a more postmodern form. Space and architecture formerly signified a particular (usually Italian) social reality. Signifier and referent were in their proper places. Since 1987 the sensuous composition of cinematic space and architecture in spectacular images deflects attention from narrative progression towards other referents: literature, painting, popular culture, the tourist experience. The paucity of dialogue[18] facilitates reading of the connotative cues and/ or enjoyment of the visual virtuosity which is one of his trademarks. Bertolucci is asserting both the fluidity of identity (personal, sexual and national) and the impossibility of the existence of one overarching metanarrative or explanation of the meaning of life. Therein lies the basis of Bertolucci's continued importance in international cinematic culture.

Biography

Bernardo Bertolucci was born in Parma, Italy, on 16 March 1940, the son of the poet and film critic, Attilio Bertolucci. The family moved to Rome when Bertolucci was 13, mixing in cultural and artistic circles which encouraged his experiments with filmmaking. He abandoned his university studies to work as assistant director on Pasolini's *Accatone*, establishing his reputation with the success of his first film in 1962. His ability to present ideas clearly whilst showing his complete technical mastery of the visual and aural possibilities of the medium have enabled Bertolucci to move from the art cinema sector into 'quality cinema' – auteurist, big-budget co-productions with international appeal, shot in English. After 1996, he returned to the exploration of contemporary issues, taking advantage of the global distribution networks of the 'quality' film. He is married to filmmaker Clare Peploe, who has creative involvement in his later films.

Notes

1 *Screen International*, 10 January 1997.
2 *Observer*, 24 April 1994.
3 The well-known editor, Nino Baragli (who had also worked with Pasolini), worked on *La commare secca*. Subsequently, Roberto Perpignani edited the low-budget films up to *The Spider's Stratagem*. This latter film, produced by Bertolucci's brother, Giuseppe, and Rai television, marked the beginning of the director's collaboration with the respected cinematographer Vittorio Storaro (*Apocalypse Now*). Other creative partnerships include the editor Franco (Kim) Arcalli from *The*

Conformist to *1900*, and with Gabriella Cristiani (who is particularly interested in the possibilities of digital editing) from *La luna* onwards.

4 With the deregulation of Italian television in 1976, the picture has become much more complex. Films are now generally made with complex co-production deals with television, with producers selling time-specific rights to exploitation by television, satellite, video cassette, video sales through news kiosks, and DVD. In Bertolucci's case, the 'package' now includes worldwide sales to film distributors, television and satellite operators, etc.

5 Donald Ranvaud and Enzo Ungari, *Bertolucci by Bertolucci*, Milan, Ubulibri, 1987, p. 52.

6 Francesco Pinto, Guido Barlozzetti and Claver Salizzato (eds) *La televisione presenta ... La produzione cinematografica della Rai 1965–1975*, Venice, Marsilio, 1988, p. 70.

7 Aldo Grasso, *Storia della televisione italiana*, Milan, Garzanti, 1992, pp. 234–52.

8 Josefa Loshitzky, *The Radical Faces of Godard and Bertolucci*, Detroit, Wayne State University Press, 1995, p. 57.

9 Nicholas Abercrombie, Scott Lash and Brian Longhurst, 'Popular Representation: Recasting Realism', in Scott Lash and Jonathan Friedman (eds) *Modernity and Identity*, Oxford, Blackwell, 1992, p. 121.

10 Pierre Bourdieu, *The Field of Cultural Production*, Cambridge, Polity Press, 1993, p. 133.

11 Robert Kolker, *Bernardo Bertolucci*, London, BFI Publishing, 1985, pp. 68–77.

12 Josefa Loshitzky, *op.cit.*, p. 188.

13 *The Times*, 28 April 1994.

14 *Guardian* Interview, National Film Theatre, London, 23 August 1996.

15 Geoffrey Nowell-Smith, 'The Sheltering Sky', *Monthly Film Bulletin*, January 1991, p. 26.

16 *Guardian* Interview, *op. cit.*

17 *Stealing Beauty* ($10 million) was a financial and critical success for Fox Searchlight, the studio's prestige art-house division, making and distributing what are regarded as risky films, using internationally known directors but aiming at a successful, worldwide distribution. The company is part of the Murdoch empire, facilitating access to satellite channels. This could almost be a definition of the 'quality' film. *Besieged* cost $3 million and made more than $2 million in the US alone in its first three months of release.

18 Gérard Legrand, 'Beauté volée: innocence du devenir', *Positif*, no. 424, 1996, p. 29.

Filmography

(All Italian productions unless otherwise indicated)

La commare secca / The Grim Reaper (1962)
Prima della rivoluzione / Before the Revolution (1964)
La via del petrolio / The Oil Trail (1966) television documentary
Il canale / The Canal (1966) short documentary

Agonia / *Agony* (1967) episode of *Amore e rabbia*
Partner (1968)
La strategia del ragno / *The Spider's Stratagem* (1970)
Il conformista / *The Conformist* (1970)
La salute è malata or *I poveri muoiono prima* / *Health is Sick* or *The Poor Die Young* (1971) documentary for the Italian Communist Party
Ultimo tango a Parigi / *Last Tango in Paris* (France/Italy/US, 1972)
Novecento / *1900* (1976)
La luna (1979)
La tragedia di un uomo ridiculo / *The Tragedy of a Ridiculous Man* (1981)
The Last Emperor (Italy/Hong Kong/UK, 1987)
The Sheltering Sky (UK/Italy, 1990)
Little Buddha (France/UK, 1993)
Io ballo da sola / *Stealing Beauty* (Italy/France/UK, 1996)
L'Assedio / *Besieged* (1998)

Further reading

Zygmunt Baranski and Robert Lumley (eds) *Culture and Conflict in Postwar Italy*, London, Macmillan/University of Reading, 1990.

Robert Burgoyne, *Bertolucci's 1900: A Narrative and Historical Analysis*, Detroit, MI, Wayne State University Press, 1991.

Angela Dalle Vacche, *The Body in the Mirror*, Princeton, NJ, Princeton University Press, 1992.

T. Jefferson Kline, *Bertolucci's Dream Loom. A Psychoanalytic Study of Cinema*, Amherst, University of Massachusetts Press, 1987.

Mira Liehm, *Passion and Defiance: Film in Italy from 1942 to the Present*, Berkeley, California University Press, 1984.

Millicent Marcus, *Italian Film in the Light of Neorealism*, Princeton, NJ, Princeton University Press, 1986.

John J. Michalczyk, *The Italian Political Filmmakers*, Cranbury, NJ, Associated University Presses, 1986.

David Thompson, *Last Tango in Paris*, London, BFI Publishing, 1998.

MARY WOOD

LUC BESSON

BARD AND FILMMAKER

Luc Besson is a self-made filmmaker. Since his third feature *Le Grand bleu* (*The Big Blue*) his films have regularly attracted large audiences.[1] Besson, then, is a financial success; he has (in French terms at least) beaten the Americans at their own game – or, more precisely, held his own against them.

Besson's breakthrough came in 1981 with his first feature, *Le Dernier combat* (*The Last Battle*), which won the Avoriaz Science Fiction Film Prize (both the Critics and the Special Jury). Various cinema journals saw promise in this young man's film and heralded him as the new hope for French cinema – doubtless seeing in him a renewal of a 'serious' cinema and a return of the 'auteur'. However, this was to misread Besson. He regards himself as neither intellectual nor an 'auteur', seeing himself rather as a bard who tells stories to broad cinema audiences for their pleasure. The paradox is, of course, that Besson is an auteur in the earliest sense of the term: he is a master of visual style, and his style is distinctively his own. He takes astonishing risks, refusing to accept easy solutions in either cinematography or *mise-en-scène*. Furthermore, he either co-scripts or scripts his films based on an original idea that is his own (although pending law suits contest this) and he has overall control of the complete production process, beginning with the budget. In short, he is a major presence at all levels of the production of meaning.

Although Besson is now a very bankable filmmaker, in the early days he had tremendous problems obtaining finance. As a result, he set up his own production company (currently called Leloo Productions) which he uses both to ensure his own projects get off the ground under his control and to help new and struggling filmmakers fulfil their own ambitions (he helped finance Gary Oldman's *Nil by Mouth*). Bankable he may be, popular with audiences and popular film magazines he most certainly is, but liked by the heavyweight critics he is not. There are two interesting exceptions as far as critics are concerned: his first film and his most recent.

Whilst one can well see why *Le Dernier combat* might have appealed to the critics, it is less obvious why *Jeanne d'Arc* (*Joan of Arc*) is not critically dismissed as the rest of his work has been – as style without substance. *Le Dernier Combat* is ground-breaking arguably because it both shows and conceals the paucity of its means of production. Shot in black and white in Cinemascope, bearing the hallmarks of art-house cinema whilst incorporating many of the techniques of the comic strip, the film is a hybrid of popular and high-art sources, something that Jean-Luc Godard, another master of mixing registers, might appreciate. The complete lack of dialogue contrasts with the use of natural sounds and a strong musical sound-track, producing a form of aesthetic counterpoint in which the soundtrack stands as a unit of meaning in its own right against the image. This innovative soundtrack was also the cheapest option at the post-production stage, although the narrative does make clear that everyone has lost the use of their vocal chords as a result of the holocaust that has hit them (one assumes the film is set in a post-nuclear Paris and environs). However, the narrative is deeply conservative, not to say misogynist: through a series of chases, escapes, fights and conquests, the protagonist eventually defeats his enemies and wins the female (the trophy for all his hard work).

Interestingly, the use of point-of-view in *Jeanne d'Arc* serves to distance it somewhat from charges of misogyny through adopting, almost exclusively, that of Jeanne herself. This is particularly striking during the battle scenes where, courtesy of the dazzlingly energetic camerawork, we are carried on horseback with her as she swathes her mighty sword. This is female agency at its most violent, for sure, but refreshing none the less. French critics seem to have overlooked this aspect of the film on the whole and have complimented Besson instead on his refreshing approach to the epic style (a genre rare in French cinema), on his use of stars John Malkovich and Dustin Hoffman, and on his narrative treatment. Besson is unlikely to be moved at once more finding favour with the criterati; his interest lies with pleasing his audiences. Small wonder since they have consistently been his greatest support, saving *Le Grand bleu* from oblivion after the critics had panned it.

Besson has made seven feature films and one sixty-minute 'documentary-opera' about the underwater sea world (*Atlantis*).[2] Though often seen as a youth-oriented filmmaker, his stories are not directed at a single audience. He appeals not only to the predominant cinemagoing public of 15 to 35 year olds, but older generations and much younger audiences (*Le Cinquième élément* [*The Fifth Element*], for example, was a big hit with the under-12s). Thus although hardly family fare, no exclusive generation forms the audience for Besson's movies.

Given the broad appeal of his work, it is difficult not to see Besson as a filmmaker who makes films that are signs of their times. As such his films fulfil a bardic function: he tells stories of individuals who have difficulty in adapting to a society which, in his opinion, has seriously let the family down, creating emotional deprivation in young people. His work, as he sees it, is to reflect that world and to give, if not a solution, then some way of countering the despair felt at an uncaring world. Leaving aside *Jeanne d'Arc*, which represents a shift in genre as well as content, we might say that Besson's films are about youth in crisis, the dysfunctional family, a fractured and alienating society of surveillance and technology.

Although in some ways a transitional film leaning towards the more epic style of *Jeanne d'Arc*, I would still include *Le Cinquième élément* in this domain of preoccupations. As such, Besson qualifies as the new moralist of the 1980s and 1990s; part of this new moralism lies in his representation of consumer commodities as signs of death rather than of well-being, hence the focus on flotsam in his films and the persistent notion of recycling. *Le Cinquième élément* is just as preoccupied with waste and its reuse as *Le Dernier combat*. Even the female lead, Leloo, is recycled, regenerated from burnt body waste.

This moribund worldview goes further than these first signs of death (waste and technology) might suggest, having two major aspects: the death of utopia and the death of the family. By the death of utopia Besson primarily refers to the death of the free spirit and free love of the 1970s. Society is represented in his films as a force that kills love but which sells sex. Sex, for Besson, is everywhere while the concept of pure love is gone. In both *Léon* and *Le Cinquième élément* Besson provides us with examples of what he means by pure love. In the former film Léon ultimately perishes as a chivalric hero to save Nathalie. In the latter, Leloo finally agrees to human love in order to save the planet. Both are fairly selfless acts of love, even though they are not unproblematic in their representation (Nathalie's love for Léon is hard to swallow, while Leloo's acceptance of Korbin Dallas only serves to diminish her power).

The death of the family is a constant thread in Besson's work. The mother is nowhere to be seen. At times she emerges as a proto-mother, a mother-figure, but she is usually depicted as an evil force (Yolande in *Jeanne d'Arc* is no exception to this). As for the true mother, she is either absent (*Nikita*), uncaring (*Léon*), or a demanding presence at the end of a phone-line (*Le Cinquième élément*). The father is almost always absent. In the rare moments that he appears, he is represented as impotent (*Le Grand bleu*). If there is a patriarch around, the real father's absence is substituted for by a father-figure or proto-father, typically represented as dangerous and a potential menace (Bob in *Nikita*). In this dysfunctional or non-existent family, sons are either incapable or unwilling to fulfil an Oedipal trajectory. Indeed, they often perish for their unwillingness and, as such, their behaviour can be read as a resistance to the patriarchal order. Daughters, meanwhile, disappear (Nikita), reproduce in abandonment (Johanna in *Le Grand bleu*), or, in the case of Leloo, exist only as a woman recycled from a piece of waste as a product of male genetic engineering. Such death, or non-being, is prefigured through the death of speech: there is very little talk in a

Besson movie. Part of this could be attributed to the comic strip influence, though it would also be possible to see this lack of language as indicating the lack of a patriarch (a figure so visibly absent from Besson's dysfunctional family).

This, then, is the alienating context in which Besson's heroes and protagonists live. An alienating context that is, literally, enhanced by a society of constraints and surveillance technology. Besson's films speak about the loneliness and suffering of their protagonists, all of whom come from modest backgrounds (which is part of their appeal). Moreover, and here is Besson's message of resistance, all of his protagonists seek solutions to their sense of alienation. This is a second aspect of their immediate appeal, particularly to the younger generations for whom there is no great optimism (25 per cent of the unemployed are under 25 in France). Besson's films suggest that there is a way out. His protagonists seem to find it by fulfilling some self-styled art form, whether in music (Fred in *Subway*), violence (Nikita, Léon), love (Nathalie, Korben Dallas), or diving (Enzo and Jacques in *Le Grand bleu*). However, in each instance the protagonists end up by disappearing, self-erasure or death (even Dallas ends up being rendered invisible in a manmade capsule while being observed fornicating with Leloo). This type of escape, or closure, is deeply ambiguous, for while the act of escape is part of the attraction of the film (feeding into our desire to flee from constraint) it remains deeply problematic. Nikita has to give up her identity (again) in order to escape. But escape to what, with no name and pursued by the state police? In this way, films about love and self-erasure do not seem too far removed from a sort of death wish.

Thus Besson's films seem to offer 'both/and' rather than 'either/or' when it comes to narratives and their closures. They can thus be read as counter-texts to a fractured and alienating society, to a society of constraints, of technics and robots that dispense with man (erase the need for his labour), a society of technology and surveillance that can intrude even into the subject's body (Nikita). They also offer a way out from a morally corrupt society that prohibits all emotional bonds. Hence the undoubted attraction of literal and figurative underworlds in Besson's films (be it the metro, the sea, or the lower regions of cities and buildings). But this underworld, I would argue, is only an anteroom to disappearance (a degree zero 'way out'), a first step towards disappearance, to not being.

Besson has a fairly consistent mode of working. Over the years he has accumulated a regular and expanding team of people with whom he works and whom he refers to as 'la famille'. These working arrangements are based in a fierce kind of loyalty. Besson does not tolerate what he considers to be 'betrayals'; you are either with him or against him in his extremely demanding working practices. Accounts of the shooting of *Jeanne d'Arc* attest to a severe taskmaster and to extremely tough working conditions for all members of the crew.[3] Besson's father Claude is always attached to his son's films in one way or another, either as executive producer or appearing in a small role. Besson shot his first three films with Carlo Varini as director of photography and since then has used Thierry Arbogast. This has led to a noticeable change of style, in particular a greater reliance on natural light and a predilection for the medium shot – which, working as it does in tension with Cinemascope (the widescreen format and the closeness of the medium shot to the subject), creates a certain kind of violence within the frame by drawing attention to the horizontal and vertical reality of the scope format. In terms of music, Eric Serra has been with Besson from the beginning. The bass guitar that we associate with a Besson movie is Serra's own. Much of the scored music, however, is derivative and it is never very difficult to trace the (unacknowledged) source – the most recent example being a slice of Carl Orf's *Carmina Burana* in *Jeanne d'Arc*. Further family associates include favourite actors: Jean Reno, Gary Oldman, Tcheky Karyo, Matthieu Kassovitz and, of course, his female stars who do not return quite so often – not always because of personal reasons (much as the press would like to claim). Certainly, Anne Parillaud more or less walked away from Besson after *Nikita* and they subsequently divorced, but then Milla Jovovich, already divorced from Besson at the time of making *Jeanne d'Arc*, has remained loyal to him.

Besson scripts and produces his own films. He tends to co-script from an original idea, claiming that he does not feel completely assured in that domain.[4] Frequently he already has a new project in mind as he enters the filming stage of the current project. In some instances, as for *Le Grand bleu* and *Le Cinquième élément*, he had the idea written out years before. Occasionally, Besson writes a script with a specific actor in mind (as with *Nikita*, *Jeanne d'Arc* and *Léon*), but he claims to prefer to get the script right first before seeking out people to play the part.[5]

Excess and stylization are the two major hallmarks of Besson's *œuvre*. We are most vividly aware of this in the domain of characterization, décor and genre. Characters are larger than life, often inordinately powerful physically – be they men or women –

much like the comic strip characters to whom their genesis owes a great deal. Although they are larger than life they are, because they are deeply lacking in any psychology or history, often much less than the sum of their bodily parts. Again this brings them close to the comic strip characters they seem so closely to emulate. It should be added that this lack of a history makes Besson's characters emblematic of a certain reading of the postmodern condition whereby the individual exists no more but has become bleached out by technology. In terms of décor, the films are often in excess of their referent to the point of overriding the narrative. Thus scenes/sets such as the metro in *Subway* or space-age New York in *Le Cinquième élément* become more significant than the original to which they refer and because of their excess obtain more signification than the narrative which they are intended to illustrate. They are, in a sense, too dense, more real than real, a kind of hyperreal. Incidentally, this hyper-realization of the décor is not new in French cinema. It can be traced to the 1930s and to the work of, among others, Alexander Trauner who (it should not escape us) was responsible for the décor on Besson's *Subway*. Thus, here we have another example of the mode of production calling attention to itself (as with the use of Cinemascope and medium shots). We can talk of Besson forging a self-referential cinema, but he is producing more than an effect. The excess is one of violence (violent in its excessiveness) pointing to a lack, an emptiness of meaning. Thus, as I have noted, the characters – though larger than life – are in fact empty and ahistorical; similarly, the décors reduce the original topography to which they refer to an ugliness or grandiosity beyond their reality. The outer abundance points horribly to the lack within: characters and décors mirror each other in their excess and their violence until, finally, characters literally become the embodiment of violence (even the heroine of *Jeanne d'Arc* experiences this). We are warned, in Besson's films time and again, of the effects of man's pursuit of technology and his drive to control death through making life (bringing Nikita and Leloo back to life, for example). As we use technology to give birth how can we forget that it will also bring death – ours.

Besson's use of excess and stylization should not be read solely as a metaphor for violence and death. It is also extremely playful. He mixes violence with humour (and did so long before Quentin Tarantino). He blends the intertexts of early cinema with the comic strip for the best entertainment effect. The slapstick and gags of the former sit well with the bare narrative offered by the latter and the combination works to propel the spectator helter-skelter from one instance of full action to the next – the cinema of attractions at its best. Finally, in terms of excess and stylization, Besson's films are a *bricolage* of genres with no clear demarcation lines: musical, comedy, thriller, science fiction can all be rolled into one film and appear as a harmonious whole, that is until the rollercoaster comes to a stop, the film ends and we know we have had a good time even though we might feel breathless.

Biography

Luc Besson was born 18 March 1959, in Paris, France. His original ambition was to be a deep-sea diver, but a diving accident in 1976 put paid to his dreams. In this same year, aged only 17, he quit school and decided to become a filmmaker. His breakthrough film, *Le Dernier combat* (*The Last Battle*, 1982) won the two major Avoriaz Film Festival prizes (Critics and Special Jury). Since that auspicious beginning Besson has gone on to establish his own production companies (Films du Loup, Films du Dauphin, and most recently, Leeloo Productions) with which he produces not only his films but those of young aspirant filmmakers (e.g., Mathieu Kassovitz and Gérard Pirès).

Notes

1 His latest film, *Jeanne d'Arc*, attracted audiences of over three million in France alone.
2 Both documentary and sea opera, the film is stunningly shot and brilliantly edited with an astonishing soundtrack in which Eric Serra mixes standard contemporary French pop and disco with oriental music, cantatas, arias and requiems.
3 The issue of the French popular film review *Cine Live*, no. 29, November 1999, gives some interesting details of Besson's working conditions.
4 *Nikita* was his first solo script. Since then he has alternated between using several scriptwriters to help him and going solo. For more detail see my *Luc Besson*, Manchester University Press, 1998, p. 35.
5 *Ibid.*, pp. 54–5.

Filmography

La P'tite sirène / *The Little Mermaid* (1978) short
Voici / *Here You Are* (1980) music clip
Formule 2 / *Formula 2* (1980) commissioned short
L'Avant-dernier / *Second Last* (1981) short
Le Dernier combat / *The Last Battle* (1983)
Subway (1985)

Le Grand bleu / *The Big Blue* (1988)
Nikita / *La Femme Nikita* (1990)
Atlantis (1991)
Léon / *The Professional* (1994; 'director's cut' released in France 1996)
Le Cinquième élément / *The Fifth Element* (1997)
Jeanne d'Arc / *Joan of Arc* / *The Messenger: The Story of Joan of Arc* (1999)

Further reading

Luc Besson, *L'Histoire de Nikita*, Paris, Bordas et Fils, 1992.
—— *L'Histoire du Cinquième élément*, Paris, Intervista, 1997.
—— *L'Histoire de Jeanne d'Arc*, Paris, Intervista, 2001.
Susan Hayward, *Luc Besson*, Manchester, Manchester University Press, 1998.
—— 'Besson's Mission Elastoplast: *Le Cinquième élément*', in Phil Powrie (ed.) *French Cinema in the 1990s: Continuity and Difference*, Oxford, Oxford University Press, 1999.
—— *Recycled Woman and the Postmodern Aesthetic: Luc Besson's Nikita*, London and New York, Routledge, 2000.

SUSAN HAYWARD

KATHRYN BIGELOW

Since her first commercial success with the film noir/vampire/ Western *Near Dark*, Kathryn Bigelow has steadily developed a cult reputation among audiences and critics. Typically developing her own projects, she has worked with medium to big budgets, star names and popular genres. Though rarely achieving significant box-office success, her films have continually intrigued, shocked and seduced. An art-house-oriented filmmaker who seems to revel in genres conventionally understood as both 'masculine' and artless – whether road movie, teen-pic, horror, cop thriller, action, buddy yarns or science fiction – Bigelow has attracted both curiosity and, more recently, sustained critical interest. *Blue Steel* in particular attracted her a much wider critical audience and an uneasy interest from feminist critics, simultaneously drawn to her compelling scenario of a female police officer and repelled by the movies rape-revenge elements.

Mainstream critical responses to Bigelow's work are typically ambivalent, perturbed perhaps by her use of violent imagery and uncertain as to whether the supposed 'breathless pace' of films like *Point Break*, indeed the high style of her work as a whole, might somehow function as a substitute for content. *Strange Days*, for instance, was read as both astonishingly creative, 'staggeringly ambitious' and basely exploitative. Others wondered of *Strange Days* how a woman could produce scenes such as the horrific sequence of rape and murder (shot *Peeping Tom*-style from the attacker's point of view). A visual, often visceral filmmaker, critics have also found her abilities with plotting and narrative less than convincing. One reviewer, though praising her early works *The Loveless* and *Near Dark*, called *Strange Days* 'grossly inflated visually': 'the film foams at the mouth with ideas but ultimately delivers nothing but mammoth clichés culled from a hundred other movies. The orchestration of them, however, is often quite something.'[1]

Those critics who despair over the lack of narrative coherence and drive in Bigelow's work have a point: such films as *The Loveless* and *Blue Steel* persistently sidetrack the audience into the pleasures of looking, while none of her films could be described as particularly goal-oriented. Bigelow's reputation as an action auteur stems quite particularly from the fantastic set-pieces that regularly appear in her films (the bank robbery in *Point Break*; the convenience store hold-up in *Blue Steel*; the roadhouse massacre in *Near Dark*). While Bigelow might be a great director of action sequences she cannot really be described as an action filmmaker in the contemporary sense – *Point Break* is probably the nearest she has come to a conventional action film. After a break of five years, Bigelow's latest film, *The Weight of Water*, a thriller that juxtaposes a period murder case with a contemporary investigation, suggests another shift of pace.

Writing of *Near Dark*, Pauline Kael comments on Bigelow's 'talent for the uncanny', pointing to her art training and film school background. Bigelow's art background has led critics to describe her work as 'painterly', feeding the notion of an ambivalent action auteur enamoured with the possibilities of the image. To some extent all Bigelow's films can be said to share an uncanny quality, something we might attribute to her peculiar situation as an experimental genre filmmaker. It is Bigelow's art-house approach to genre cinema that is most distinctive. She has spoken not only of her fascination with genre, but her interest in redefining it, creating hybrids that enable the filmmaker 'to invest ... genres with new material'. If the notion of an art-house sensibility might suggest a desire to somehow 'transcend' popular genres, Bigelow both exploits and values the genres within which she works. Moreover, from a feminist perspective, the interest of her work has as much to do with its capacity to underline the limitations of thinking about certain kinds of genres and styles as 'masculine' (what does that really mean after all?) as with their status as competent exercises in once forbidden territory.

The Loveless, Bigelow's stylish first feature, which she termed a 'psychological biker film', co-written and directed with Monty Montgomery, is perhaps the most explicitly art-house project with which she has been involved. A pastiche of 1950s' teen movies, loaded with self-conscious allusions to the 1954 exploitation picture *The Wild One* (not least via Willem Dafoe's central performance), *The Loveless* consistently keeps the spectator at one remove from events even at their most dramatic. Long shots, an often static camera (the film is after all concerned with the perils of being stuck) and elaborate montage all contribute to this feeling of distance, as do the central characters' mannered performances of cool. The soundtrack is used at times to counterpoint the action, occasionally to almost obliterate the dialogue and to create striking effects of noise against silence (as in the final bar scene where the shots that focus on Telena are practically silent, whilst those focusing on the group in the bar are chaotic with laughter and gunfire).

For Bigelow the film functions as playful homage ('very tongue-in-cheek') in its juxtaposition of *The Wild One*, Douglas Sirk's high melodrama *Written on the Wind* (1956) and Kenneth Anger's exercise in fetishistic montage *Scorpio Rising* (1964). Borrowing its basic narrative structure and imagery from *The Wild One* – bikers stop over in a small town bringing the community's latent tensions to the surface – the film takes its tone from the combination of elements rather than any one. More ironic than Bigelow's later work (though her films have remained self-conscious to say the least), *The Loveless* stages a commentary on the moralistic structure through which Brando's inarticulate not-all-bad biker boy learns the value of life from a good girl in a small town. Instead of salvation, Dafoe finds only corruption and an overwhelming sense of boredom. 'If you weren't born here you wouldn't have a whole lot of reason to hang around', a waitress tells him: she later performs an antiseptic striptease in the town's cocktail bar.

The Loveless combines a fetishistic attention to period detail – décor, signs, costume, design – with another sort of visual pleasure, evident in both lingering images and rapid close-ups of motorcycles, cars, leathers, tattoos, belts and bodies. The small town where Vance (Dafoe) and his friends are temporarily stalled is structured around increasingly apparent divisions of black and white, between those who stay and those who go, between adult and teenage worlds. After

Vance sleeps with the boyish Telena (the androgynous female protagonist who pre-figures *Near Dark*'s Mae, *Blue Steel*'s Megan and *Point Break*'s Tyler) her sexual relationship with her corrupt father is revealed. The movie climaxes with Telena shooting her father and then herself, a suicide 'seen' through Vance's seemingly impassive face: only the soundtrack which minutes before replays her words in his head suggests to us that he may have any involvement in the events played out before him.

The townsfolk project both fears and desires onto the wild ones in their midst – some parade themselves whilst others simply snatch a look (the woman whose tyre Vance changes in the opening scene or the garage owner who tells his son: 'They're *animals*. Hell. I'd love to trade places with them for a day or two'). Dafoe's Vance may just be 'a nobody' without his bike as Telena tells him, but the bikers can drive away at the end, just as the camera pulls back from the door of the bar. Telena's transport, a red sports car, is a guilt-inspired gift from her father and thus unlikely to take her anywhere: as if to confirm Telena's lack of mobility he shoots the tyres out on discovering her in a motel with Vance. In another scene the bikers on the road are juxtaposed with Telena and her father wrestling in his car – they crash, her collapse prefiguring her suicide at the film's closure.

Road movie imagery recurs in *Near Dark* in which Caleb (Adrian Pasdar) is initiated by Mae (Jenny Wright) into the world of a vampire 'family' who transport him from the fixed life of the farm and small town into a terrifying but stimulating alternative world. The film revolves around Mae's and Caleb's mutual fascination, a relationship that brings out tensions in the vampire family since Caleb is unable or unwilling to kill, becoming increasingly dependent on Mae's ability to feed him. Alongside its 'B' movie wipes and the spectacle of gore, *Near Dark* deploys grim comedy played out through visual horror and one-liners, whilst offering a stylish and atmospheric vision of the Western landscape. For Wheeler Winston Dixon, the film is 'a trancelike fabric of sleep, slaughter, and survival, an endlessly evolving tapering of thirst and fulfilment underscored by Tangerine Dream's hypnotic, droning electronic music' (once again an evocative soundtrack is central to the film's effect).[2]

As is appropriate for a filmmaker associated so much with visual spectacle and stylish showpieces, the narrative revolves explicitly around the play of light as the band of vampires attempt to feed, move on and evade the sunlight. *Near Dark* uses a tenet of vampire movie mythology – daylight will destroy a vampire – to generate its central visual device. The early scenes in which Caleb first glimpses Mae, is mystified by her and then horrified by his new situation are suffused with blue, a simulation of moonlight that reappears in the rather different twilight world of *Blue Steel*. Daylight and daybreak provide *Near Dark* with its most striking visual effect: the wide open spaces turn deadly as vampire flesh catches fire when struck by beams of light. As in the later *Point Break*, Bigelow here explores the inversion of values through which the criminal/inhuman world holds an appeal unmatched in the everyday world. The scene in *Near Dark* in which Caleb's vampire 'family' encounter his 'real' (that is, biological) family dramatizes both the similarities as much as the difference of normal/monstrous groupings. This is not to say that *Near Dark* is somehow an unusual or atypical horror film: though it is both visually stylish and original in its juxtaposition of horror and Western conventions, the film none the less exploits the existing richness of these forms. Equally, *Point Break* rehearses what are familiar cop/buddy clichés in its constitution of the outlaws as moral centre against the dryness of the FBI. The film's impact lies in the deployment of cinematic spectacle to support that opposition, right down to the final showdown on the beach. Vitality belongs to the bank-robbing/surfer outlaws led by Bodhi (Patrick Swayze) and is enacted through the exhilarating set-piece scenes of surfing (at night in one case), robbery and skydiving.

Of the six features that Bigelow has directed to date, it is *Blue Steel* that has received the widest critical comment, not least since its attempt to put 'a woman at the centre of a movie predominantly occupied by men' formed a timely visual intervention.[3] Co-produced by Oliver Stone, with whom Bigelow later worked on the paranoid television series *Wild Palms*, the film signalled a move into bigger budgets. Once again Bigelow exploits the androgynous appeal of her female lead – here Jamie Lee Curtis as Megan Turner in a charged performance as a rookie cop struggling to produce an identity for herself in a world of shadows. Stylish images, atmospheric lighting and off-centre compositions contribute an uncanny, dream-like quality to the film as we watch the unfolding of serial killer Eugene's (Ron Silver) growing obsession with Turner. Atmospheric and somewhat perverse, *Blue Steel* also plays out its themes of obsession and fetishism visually – lingering over weaponry, uniforms and evocatively lit interiors. Widely – and not entirely accurately, given the evident debt to horror – reviewed as a meeting of action and woman's picture, *Blue Steel* shares the leisurely pace of *The Loveless* rather than the rapid tempo of contemporary urban action films.

The millennial noir/science fiction fantasy *Strange Days* draws on diverse generic reference points including the thriller, film noir and science fiction. The movie's tech-noir imagery and nihilistic urban vision recalls scriptwriter James Cameron's breakthrough low-budget film, *The Terminator* (1984), though one of the film's most self-conscious allusions comes in the opening sequence where Hitchcock's *Vertigo* is evoked in a rooftop chase that ends in death. Preoccupied with questions of vision, voyeurism, spectacle and identity, *Strange Days* has the 'retinal fetish' nightclub as a key setting, following reluctant hero Lenny Nero's obsession with his own romantic past – he 'replays' scenes of flirtation and passion whose brightly lit qualities renders them 'unreal' against the pervasive darkness of the rest of the film. The movie's themes touch on racism, addiction and social decay, before resorting to an unconvincing cheerful ending. For many critics the ending provided an indication of the shortcomings of both Bigelow and Cameron in the attempt to articulate a political sensibility within a generic context.

If films such as *Blue Steel* and *Strange Days* seem (and in many ways are) more respectable than *Near Dark* or *Point Break* – big themes, beautiful images and subsequent critical fascination – they are also exploitative too, featuring an excess all too apparent to reviewers. Audiences meanwhile, end up in a position not too far from the townspeople in *The Loveless*, leaving the high ground to peer in on lives lived on the edge, in the form of the charged but rather seedy existences of Bigelow's protagonists.

Biography

Born in 1952, California, USA. Bigelow studied painting at the San Francisco Art Institute before moving to New York on a scholarship to the Whitney Museum in 1972. Her experiments with film began whilst working as an assistant to Vito Acconci, which led to a period at Columbia's Graduate Film School. Her television work includes *Wild Palms* and the police series *Homicide*.

Notes

1 Derek Malcolm, *Guardian*, 29 February 1996, p. 8.
2 Wheeler Winston Dixon, *The Transparency of Spectacle: Meditations on the Moving Image*, State University of New York Press, 1998, p. 131.

3 'Walk on the Wild Side: An Interview with Kathryn Bigelow', *Monthly Film Bulletin*, November 1991, p. 313.

Filmography

The Loveless (1981) also co-writer/director (with Monty Montgomery)
Near Dark (1987) also co-writer (with Eric Red)
Blue Steel (1990) also co-writer (with Eric Red)
Point Break (1991)
Strange Days (1995)
The Weight of Water (2000)

Further reading

Jim Hillier, *The New Hollywood*, London, Studio Vista, 1992.
Christina Lane, *Feminist Hollywood: From 'Born in Flames' to 'Point Break'*, Detroit, MI, Wayne State University Press, 2000.
Needeya Islam, ' "I Wanted to Shoot People": Genre Gender and Action in the Films of Kathryn Bigelow', in Laleen Jayamanne (ed.) *Kiss Me Deadly: Feminism and Cinema for the Moment*, Sydney, Power Publications, 1995, pp. 91–125.
Kathleen Murphy, 'Black Arts', *Film Comment*, vol. 31, no. 5, 1995, pp. 51–3.
Anna Powell, 'Blood on the Borders – *Near Dark* and *Blue Steel*', *Screen*, vol. 35, no. 2, 1994, pp. 136–56.
Laura Rascaroli, 'Steel in the Gaze: On POV and the Discourse of Vision in Kathryn Bigelow's Cinema, *Screen*, vol. 38, no. 3, 1997, pp. 232–46.
Yvonne Tasker, *Spectacular Bodies: Gender, Genre and the Action Cinema*, London, Routledge, 1993.

YVONNE TASKER

CHARLES BURNETT

Charles Burnett is the writer and director of one widely recognized masterpiece, the neo-realist *Killer of Sheep*, and a major achievement in African-American film, *To Sleep with Anger*. Imbued with a deep humanist vision, a searching concern with characters facing moral and ethical decisions, and a tendency to allegorical expression, Burnett's work has gained critical regard while his career demonstrates the problems of a black American auteur working in the last quarter of the twentieth century. From an initial position as an independent feature writer/director/cameraman, Burnett has sustained his career by working on a number of Hollywood and television projects which range from the accomplished to the banal in direction; of these none has had strong commercial success.

Burnett's position can be usefully compared and contrasted with other African-American directors. Most successfully within traditional Hollywood terms, comic actor/directors such as Eddie Murphy and Keenan Ivory Wayans sustain their efforts in conventional work with crossover in mind. Other black directors within the industry such as Albert and Allen Hughes exploited 'in the hood' and rap/hip hop sensibilities and themes to gain box-office success from the racially and culturally diverse viewers who consume black youth culture. In contrast, Spike Lee (very much a New York, not Hollywood, director) turned himself into a celebrity auteur, maintaining his distinct style and themes through obvious talent, creative versatility and a hard-sell personality.

In contrast to those working in the commercial mainstream, some independent writer/directors, such as Julie Dash and Haile Gerima (*Sankofa*, 1993), mounted dramatic features deeply resonant with African-American history, won a strong critical response, and carefully promoted African-American audience interest. An even wider range of creative work has appeared from directors working in more experimental and documentary modes, often university-based such as the late Marlon Riggs, Zeinabu irene Davis and Ayoke Chenzira, or connected with the art/theatre/music world such as Camille Billops and the late Bill Gunn, or documentary and broadcasting such as Bill Greaves and St Clair Bourne.

Charles Burnett made his first feature drama, *Killer of Sheep*, as his thesis film in the UCLA MFA film programme. An episodic slice of life, the film shows the daily routines of a slaughterhouse worker, Stan, interspersed with views of the Los Angeles black community's residents. Stan suffers insomnia, putting him in a liminal world of reduced affect, an emotional state echoed by exterior shots that reveal an urban landscape filled with demolished sites. Scenes with children playing form a powerful counterpoint to the actions of adults as we see the kids repeating the verbal and physical violence which the adult community exhibits as behaviour and symptom. Stan's work preparing sheep sets up an inescapable parallel – that the children are lambs being led to slaughter.

Particularly poignant moments highlight Stan's inhibited relation with his wife: she urges him to sleep and he cannot. Alone, they dance together to Dinah Washington's slow sad ballad, 'This Bitter Earth', but the tenderness never blossoms into a physical consummation; she tries to entice him, but he is unresponsive and then his young daughter comes over and massages his shoulders – the child taking over an adult role while mother and daughter stare at each other. This dysfunctional social world finds an objective correlative in cars that do not work, keeping the community penned up in the ghetto. In the most memorable scene, Stan and a buddy buy a used engine on pay day to rehabilitate an old car. The optimism is dashed when through their negligence the engine block hits the pavement and cracks.

The soundtrack echoes the screen action with unseen events: a menacing watchdog barking, a car starting with difficulty, police sirens, children's nursery rhymes, the chimes of an ice-cream vendor. A rich music track provides an additional counterpoint, joining commercial blues and soul with classical music and Paul Robeson's performances. Already tinged with a bitter irony for African-Americans, Robeson sings 'What is America to Me?' against images of sheep being moved to slaughter. Later slaughterhouse images play against Dinah Washington's slow love ballad, 'Unforgettable'. Yet the film does not end in naturalist despair. Rather, a bittersweet persistence of hope within this dysfunctional environment appears near the end of the film when an apparently mute young woman shyly but happily reveals to a group of women that she is pregnant. Stan continues to work, to endure, to support his family within a world of diminished opportunity.

Burnett worked on two more films that continue the closely observed study of ghetto masculinity. With *My Brother's Wedding*, another feature-length film, he served again as writer/director/cameraman, and he worked as screenwriter and cameraman on Billy Woodberry's *Bless Their Little Hearts*.[1] These films continued in the mode of production of low-budget independent film. With more critical recognition, Burnett finally directed his screenplay *To Sleep with Anger*, leveraging a larger budget (US $1.5 million) with star Danny Glover's participation. The film changed Burnett's previous pattern of contrasting exterior cityscapes, workplace and the social space of the community to the domestic space of home and family, a contrast so pronounced in *Killer of Sheep*. This time the film is grounded in the house of a lower-middle-class Los Angeles family which becomes infected with a foreign presence, who slowly causes a chaotic crescendo in the family's three generations. Harry (Glover) arrives unexpectedly from 'back home' in the Deep South, is welcomed, and stays on and on. Gradually this trickster figure's presence and actions bring out the social situation's underlying contradictions and tensions until the home seems invaded by his cronies, the patriarch suddenly lies paralyzed in bed, the family garden dries up, and the two adult brothers begin fighting. In the film's dramatic climax, the matriarch intervenes just in time to prevent one son from killing the other.

Harry may have more than a touch of Satan in him (flames appear on his feet at one point), but he is a minor devil at best. He works by finding fault lines which set in motion tremors which can demolish unsteady structures. He is also an engaging rogue, and if our sense of justice is relieved when he dies in an accidental fall, we are also a bit regretful to see him go. Actually, he doesn't go. He dies at the start of a long weekend, and the coroner's office fails to pick up the body in the kitchen, so the family has to eat picnic-style while friends and neighbours come by. Again the mood is bittersweet, with the emphasis on a comedic ending, underlined by the film's buoyant script, excellent acting, slow build-up of a sense of community, and reflections on past and present, country and city, and pretence and realism. Although the film concentrates its visual power by bringing all characters into the house, a key scene resonates with wider social power. Following the brothers' fight, they go to a hospital emergency room where we see the physical toll of community instability.

With Burnett's next feature project, *The Glass Shield*, the writer/director adapted a former cop's account of the Los Angeles police. A black rookie is assigned to an all-white station filled with violence-prone racists; he tries to fit into an ethos of toughness and covering-up police abuse but he comes to question his own position. Finally awakened, with the unit's only woman, he works to expose the corruption, and in the process finds his life in danger from fellow officers. At last, he loses his job. The film is marked by tense dramatic sequences and an effective use of interiors and night scenes with a haunting blue tone to the visuals. The sets lean toward the abstract (for example, silhouetted figures against closed window blinds) while the film bends towards the allegorical. Part of this must be by design, but part by its main actor's limited dramatic range and the script's strong black/white dichotomy in racial depiction.[2] Except for the Jewish female cop and one old jailer, all the white characters are uniformly malevolent racists and all the blacks are model upright minority citizens. The result is an awkward set-up. The hero starts out as terribly naïve; but without any engaging rogues as counter-point, it is hard to understand why he wants to be like the white guys. The problem lies partly in Burnett's adaptation of the story from an autobiographical account which took place many years before, when integration of the police force was still a novel matter. By the time the film appeared, big city police departments were (uneasily) integrated and, clearly, violent and corrupt cops were not just an African-American versus white problem. Psychologically nuanced portraits of cops – black and white, male and female, rookies and veterans, moral and abusive – were widely seen on popular television shows such as *Hill Street Blues, Homicide, Law and Order, NYPD Blue* and part of the popular imagination. Lost in the allegory is Burnett's initial creative strength in relating community settings to social psychology and his probing issues of troubled black masculinity.

Following that last attempt at being a feature dramatic writer/ director, and with his two Hollywood projects not returning their production costs, Burnett has worked only as a director. He shot three juvenile dramas for television aimed at the 'young adult' segment. *Nightjohn* is the most accomplished: set in the 1830s in the plantation slavery South, it portrays the relation between a young slave girl and an older man who teaches her the forbidden knowledge of reading. Well crafted, the film rests on easily understood pathos to make its points. Two more Burnett projects also use dramatic sentimentalism, but far less successfully. *Selma, Lord, Selma* presents two teens who become involved in the famous Civil Rights march. The film suffers badly in comparison with Spike Lee's imaginative documentary examining the same period, *Four Little Girls*. In *Finding Buck McHenry*, children uncover a mystery surrounding a legendary star of the Negro baseball league while clunky plot points, uneven acting and heavy-handed didacticism limit the film's impact. Strong acting and carefully crafted filmmaking mark the television mini-series drama *Oprah Winfrey Presents: The Wedding*, which considers the colour and class line within an upper-class black community in the 1950s. A recent romantic comedy of elders casts James Earl Jones and Vanessa Redgrave as eccentric loners who unexpectedly fall in love. Superbly shot, *The Annihilation of Fish* seems like a play adapted to film, more theatrical than cinematic. Though screened at festivals, it is unlikely to find a commercial release.

Burnett's career is best understood against the backdrop of changes in Hollywood, independent and black filmmaking. When he began studying film in 1967, contemporary black film was just getting started with Blaxploitation yet to emerge. When *Killer of Sheep* appeared a decade later, Hollywood began to consolidate to a dominant model of 'high concept' blockbuster filmmaking, but the independent feature phenomenon known as the Sundance film was still a decade away.[3] In the 1960s and 1970s black artists and intellectuals thought that, given gross misrepresentation by Hollywood, the main task was for blacks to make films about themselves. Burnett's early work fits this pattern with serious dramas set in the inner-city African-American community. But the trade-off for having complete creative control was severely restricted budgets and venues limited to art-house, festival, museum and campus audiences. The temptation of 'going Hollywood' for talented artists is strong but the exchange for getting more resources tends to be working in predictable ways in predictable genres (the ghettocentric action film, the black minstrelsy comedy, etc.) and/or loss of creative control. (How Spike Lee has negotiated this tension for a productive career needs close examination.) With time, as more films starring African-Americans written and directed by African-Americans and aimed at a black audience appeared, especially in the 1990s, it became clear that the 'black audience' was not a unified entity in either sensibility, politics or market. The call to unity that was so forceful in the Civil Rights era as political rhetoric did not have analytic power in the millennium's reality of a consolidating global entertainment marketplace, neo-liberal politics, and a growing gap between inner-city and middle-class African-Americans.

Politically aware African-American filmmakers (as for feminist, Latino and gay media artists) face the dilemma of negotiating mainstream versus independent options. Reflecting on his own experience, Burnett has observed that, 'The situation is such that one is always asked to compromise one's integrity, and if the socially oriented film is finally made, its showing will generally be limited and the very ones that it is made for and about will probably never see it.'[4] In *Redefining Black Film*, Mark Reid comments that:

> production and stylistic freedoms permit black independent filmmakers to experiment with audio, visual, and performance methods that seem unrefined to audiences and film critics reared on Hollywood films. Thus, the use of non-star talent, innovative aural and visual narrative techniques, and abrupt editing (all of which are at odds with the classical Hollywood narrative style) make black independent films different in content and form from studio-distributed black films.[5]

The border between independent vision and mainstream accomplishment has formed a basic controversial topic for African-American filmmakers and critics for the past twenty-five years. For those directors who have had the opportunity to work within Hollywood, the experience has its rough spots. Many of Burnett's supporters charged that *To Sleep with Anger* was sabotaged by bad distribution and publicity. Yet, in discussing the film in *Framing Blackness: The African American Image in Film*, Ed Guerrero remarks on

> the frustrating intersection of independent and mainstream issues debated among black filmmakers. Added to this are the overdetermining, paradoxical problems of winning broad distribution and popular box office support for a film that in its vision and style runs far beyond the colonized appetites of the sex-violence-action trained consumer audience, be it black or white.[6]

In more recent interviews Burnett has spoken of the opportunity to work on larger projects with a professionally skilled creative team and top-notch acting talent, the need to make a living and support a family with one's creative work, and the desire to work regularly. His move into television, like that of Julie Dash (for example, an episode of *Women: Stories of Passion* and a romantic comedy for Black Entertainment Television) and Darnell Martin (*Homicide, ER, Oz*, after her directorial début with *I Like It Like That* in 1994), reflects what is possible in a bottom-line driven industry in which 'film artists' become 'content providers' to transnational corporations. In the current phase, the most commercially successful black films by African-American directors have been projects such as *Waiting to Exhale* (Forest Whitaker), budgeted at US $15 million with a US theatrical return of $66.2 million and $33 million in video rentals, and *Soul Food* (George Tillman Jr), a $43.5 million return on a $7.5 million budget. At present, Bill Duke and Carl Franklin seem to be the most durable directors, balancing serious African-American themes with the need for a respectable box-office return. However, the director who has managed to gain maximum attention, budgets and rewards is actor/writer Eddie Murphy, for such films as *Nutty Professor II: The Klumps* ($123 million domestic gross on $84 million budget), as has writer/director Keenan Ivory Wayans for *Scary Movie* ($157 million domestic gross on $19 million budget).

Characteristically soft-spoken, Charles Burnett has moved through life, creative opportunities and a changing situation for filmmakers with a clear conviction:

it is the little personal things that begin to give a hint of the larger picture. The story has the effect of allowing us to comprehend things we cannot see, namely feelings and relationships. It may not give you answers but it will allow you to appreciate life, and maybe that is the issue, the ability to find life wonderful and mysterious. ... One has to work on how to be good, compassionate. One has to approach it like a job. Until there is a sharing of experiences, every man is an island and the inner city will always be a wasteland.[7]

Biography

Born 13 April 1944, Vicksburg, Mississippi, Burnett grew up in Los Angeles, California, USA. He attended the University of California, Los Angeles (MFA 1977) and received the McArthur Foundation 'genius' award in 1988.

Notes

1 Chuck Kleinhans, 'Realist Melodrama and the African-American Family: Billy Woodberry's *Bless Their Little Hearts*', in Jacky Bratton, Jim Cook and Christine Gledhill (eds) *Melodrama: Stage, Picture, Screen*, London, BFI Publishing, 1994, pp. 157–66.

2 The classic 'rookie exposes corruption' film is Al Pacino in *Serpico* (Lumet, 1973). Burnett's film appeared two years after the notable *Deep Cover*, directed by African-American Bill Duke and starring Laurence Fishburne.

3 For an elaboration see Justin Wyatt, *High Concept: Movies and Marketing in Hollywood*, Austin, University of Texas Press, 1994, and my 'Independent Features: Hopes and Dreams', in Jon Lewis (ed.) *New American Cinema*, Durham, NC: Duke University Press, 1998, pp. 307–27.

4 Jim Pines and Paul Willemen (eds) *'Inner City Blues': Questions of Third Cinema*, London, BFI Publishing, 1989, p. 226.

5 Mark Reid, *Redefining Black Film*, Berkeley, University of California Press, 1993, p. 131.

6 Ed Guerrero, *Framing Blackness: The African American Image in Film*, Philadelphia, PA, Temple University Press, 1993, p. 170.

7 Jim Pines and Paul Willemen, *op. cit.*, p. 226.

Filmography

Several Friends (1969) student film
The Horse (1973) student film
Killer of Sheep (1977) also writer, cinematographer
My Brother's Wedding (1984) also writer, cinematographer

To Sleep with Anger (1990) also writer
America Becoming (1991) TV documentary. Also writer (with producer/
writer Dai Sil Kim-Gibson)
The Glass Shield (1994) also writer
When It Rains (1995) also writer
Nightjohn (1966) Disney cable television
The Wedding / Oprah Winfrey Presents: The Wedding (1998) TV mini-series
Dr. Endesha Ida Mae Holland (1998) documentary
Selma, Lord, Selma (1999) Disney TV
The Annihilation of Fish (1999)
Olivia's Story (1999) (with producer/writer Dai Sil Kim-Gibson)
Finding Buck McHenry (2000)

Further reading

Charles Burnett, 'Charles Burnett: Killer of Sheep', in Phyllis Klotman (ed.)
Screenplays of the African American Experience, Bloomington, Indiana
University Press, 1991, pp. 90–116.
bell hooks, 'A Guiding Light: An Interview with Charles Burnett', in *Reel to
Reel: Race, Sex, and Class at the Movies*, New York, Routledge, 1996, pp.
152–69.
Peter Lev, 'From Blaxploitation to African American Film', in Peter Lev,
American Films of the 70s: Conflicting Visions, Austin, University of Texas
Press, 2000, pp. 127–41.
James Naremore, *More Than Night: Film Noir in its Contexts*, Berkeley,
University of California Press, 1998, pp. 246–9.
Chris Norton (n.d.), *Black Independent Cinema and the Influence of Neo-
realism: Futility, Struggle and Hope in the Face of Reality*, *Images Journal*,
no. 5. Online. Available HTTP: < http://www.imagesjournal.com/issue05/
featues/black.htm> (accessed 28 April 2000).
Bérénice Reynaud, 'An Interview with Charles Burnett', *Black American
Literature Forum*, vol. 25, no. 2, 1991, pp. 323–34.
Almond White, 'Charles Burnett: Sticking to the Soul', *Film Comment*, vol.
33, no. 1, 1997, pp. 38–41.
—— 'To Sleep with Anger', in Armond White (ed.) *The Resistance: Ten
Years of Pop Culture that Shook the World*, Woodstock, NY, Overlook
Press, 1995.

CHUCK KLEINHANS

TIM BURTON

'Eccentric', 'macabre', a 'self-confessed weirdo': Tim Burton and his
movies have often been characterized in similar terms. Specializing
in quirky subjects, off-beat images and the darker side of popular
culture, Burton has established himself as a strong visual stylist,
bringing a fascination for the ghoulish (and the tacky) to the screen

with flair, emotion and a certain sentimentality. Burton sometimes gives the impression of having stumbled into the business of making movies by chance – the result of a childhood spent watching monster movies and experimenting with Super 8, followed by some lucky breaks working at Disney in the studio's period of turmoil following its founder's death. And though his films are off-beat, Burton is very much part of the industry, directing distinctive, commercially successful films including *Beetlejuice*, *Batman* and *Sleepy Hollow*. An unexpected 'player', he has worked as director, producer and consultant across fantasy genres, in animation and live-action, cinema and television. Moreover, Burton has made his mark with both relatively intimate pictures (*Edward Scissorhands* or *Ed Wood*) and blockbusters (*Batman* and the sequel *Batman Returns*). The critical success of *Ed Wood*, on the one hand, and the record-setting *Batman*, on the other, might suggest an opposition between personal and commercial projects – a dichotomy that has, of course, long been played out in writings around Hollywood.

As a highly *visual*, indeed surreal, filmmaker, it is perhaps no surprise that Burton began in animation, or that his time at Disney wasn't the most straightforward. He made two short films there: *Vincent*, which used puppets and stop-motion animation to grotesque effect, and the live-action *Frankenweenie*, in which a boy rewires his dead dog Sparky. Both betray a fascination with horror and fantasy; *Vincent* was narrated by Vincent Prince, whilst *Frankenweenie* reworked James Whale's 1931 *Frankenstein* (both Price, as kindly creator-recluse, and the *Frankenstein* reference reappear in *Edward Scissorhands*). Though not widely seen in theatres, both films made an impact in terms of Burton's career, attracting a small-scale critical buzz and industry interest. The extent to which Burton's visual sensibility is somehow part of, but out of kilter with, conventional expectations – like the perverse Christmas toys gleefully manufactured by the residents of Halloween town in Burton's spectacular holiday fable *Nightmare Before Christmas* (Henry Selick, 1993) – was already evident in these early films. *Frankenweenie* was at one stage intended to accompany the re-release of *Pinocchio*, but these plans were scrapped after the film was rated PG in what was to become a recurrent theme in Burton's career: *Nightmare Before Christmas* was also bizarrely rated PG, whilst *Batman Returns* was criticized as too scary for children (the target audience for merchandizing, if not the film itself). Given this edginess, there was a certain irony in Burton's finding an unlikely home for *Ed Wood*, his biopic of the cult cross-dressing director, with Disney's Touchstone (Columbia apparently weren't happy with the use of black and white). Of course, Burton had already 'returned' to Disney to produce *Nightmare Before Christmas*, an ambitious feature-length stop-motion project based on ideas and images he had initially developed whilst working at the studio (ideas which Disney therefore owned).[1]

Although gaining only limited distribution (Disney later gave it a video release), *Frankenweenie* helped get Burton his first feature: directing *Pee-Wee's Big Adventure* for Warners. A (relatively) low-budget vehicle for Paul Reuben's surreal act, the film was hugely successful commercially (though not with critics). *Pee-Wee's Big Adventure* was in some ways as much a showcase for Burton as its star. Centred on Pee-Wee's child–man persona, the film has trademark gadgets, fantastic sets and comic special effects (with ghostly trucker 'Large Marge' probably the most memorable). For Ken Hanke, Herman was 'the perfect Burton hero', a figure who somehow 'could not be objected to' but was obviously 'neither quite "normal", nor quite "safe" '.[2] Burton followed up with *Beetlejuice*, another fantasy/comedy which employed self-consciously 'cheesy' special effects (delivered on a mini-budget in relative terms) and a wry sense of humour, and was, once again, big box office. The tale follows Adam and Barbara Maitland as they haunt their former dream home, calling on the services of the comically gruesome Betelgeuse (Michael Keaton) to evict the yuppie family with whom they ultimately learn to co-exist. The film's setpieces include a mundane after-life complete with seedy waiting room, a voracious sandworm (*Dune* on a budget) awaiting the Maitlands outside their house, and Betelgeuse himself (the film's make-up team won an Academy Award for their work). Winona Ryder's Lydia Deetz, feeling herself in tune with the macabre, mediates between the film's different worlds. Though her dark sensibility is adolescent posturing to some extent, she is the only one who can see the Maitlands. A child–woman, Lydia is one of a series of transitional figures (almost always male) in Burton's films. The easy use of effects, 'horror', comedy and sentiment – not to mention profits – finally convinced Warners to let Burton direct a major fantasy film in the shape of *Batman* (somewhat controversially with Keaton in the title role), a project he had already been working on for some time (and which had been in development for even longer; the rights had been purchased in 1979).

Even before *Batman*'s status as the event movie of 1989, Burton had acquired a cult critical following, with general and specialist fantasy-film magazines hailing his distinctive style. Of course it is in part because of his background in animation and his immersion in fantasy genres that the design and effects aspects of Tim Burton's films receive as much popular critical attention as themes or stars. This facet of his work seems particularly interesting when set against a prevailing perception of contemporary Hollywood as 'effects-driven' – the supposed triumph of spectacle over thematic complexity or character development. On the one hand, this might be said to tally with Burton's typical operation at one remove from scripting (his contribution certainly includes stories, but can more often be summed up in sketches and visual ideas). Yet it is both the total sense of visual design – the way in which, for example, effects are integrated into the film image – and the plain weirdness of the characters that command attention in the best of his films. From *Vincent* through 'Large Marge' and *Beetlejuice*'s sandworm to the complex characterization seen in *Nightmare Before Christmas*, there is also both a raw quality and a sense of technical experimentation with the possibilities of animation and visual effects.

Moreover, the effects and the imagery are firmly integrated within the fantasy world, as in the comic/grotesque physical transformations of *Beetlejuice* or, rather differently, Ichabod Crane's dreams (which feature the film's most vivid use of colour) in *Sleepy Hollow*. There is a sense of *design* in operation. Some of this is undoubtedly down to ongoing collaborative relationships – not only regular faces such as Johnny Depp or Jeffrey Jones, but also producer Denise Di Novi, costume designer Colleen Atwood, visual effects/production designer Rick Heinrichs and, of course, composer Danny Elfman, who has scored all but one of Burton's features to date.

Batman's tone was markedly darker than the typical late 1980s' blockbuster, with Sam Hamm's screenplay taking its cue from the then relatively recent success of Frank Miller's graphic novel *The Dark Knight Returns*, which emphasized the tormented psychology of the caped crusader. Not that comedy is missing, more that the film carefully avoids either camp or parodic humour (of the kind later to be seen in *Mars Attacks!*). Instead, the film's humour stems primarily from the peculiarities of the scenario and its characters, from the Joker (unsurprisingly) and even from Batman himself: as Burton notes, 'it's a guy dressing up as a bat and no matter what anyone says that's weird'.[3] Keaton's Bruce Wayne is the film's straight man – haunted by the murder of his parents years before, he remains a quietly repressed rather than an extravagantly tormented figure. Disguised in both his personae, he is not an obvious hero in any way (as Kim Basinger's Vicky Vale remarks, 'You're not exactly normal, are you?'). The budget allowed the construction of elaborate sets, used to full effect within the film's overall atmospheric visuals. Gotham's urban space is recognizable yet clearly fantastic in its mix of gothic and modernity – familiar enough and yet weird (that is, uncanny) enough for the version of the comic-book character played out here. Both *Batman* and *Batman Returns* situate Keaton as a misfit rather than conventionally heroic, closer to the enemies he confronts (Joker, Catwoman, Penguin) than to the mainstream world of Gotham society. *Batman Returns* goes further, replacing the Wayne/Vale romance with the highly charged interaction between Wayne/Batman and Selina Kyle/Catwoman – a pair of cross-dressers perversely drawn together. Meanwhile, Danny DeVito's Penguin – abandoned by his parents in the opening scene – is a mutated misfit who explicitly plays to public sentiment about his status as outcast.

Though *Batman Returns* was extremely successful, it was Burton's last outing with the material as director (he was executive producer on *Batman Forever*). Press accounts differed over whether the director himself was no longer interested, or whether Warners simply felt his style was too 'dark and weird' for the franchise – a combination of the two is perhaps more likely. *Batman* was a big movie with a lot at stake; representing a move into filmmaking on a different budgetary scale, its success launched Burton into what was in many ways a more confusing world. It was this success that made funding for a more off-beat project like *Edward Scissorhands* (with Twentieth Century Fox) possible, yet it also generated expectations, particularly in relation to the timing and shape of a sequel. Burton himself moved into production at this time, working with Denise Di Novi on his own films as well as projects such as *Nightmare Before Christmas* and *James and the Giant Peach* (1994, both directed by Henry Selick, whom Burton had first met at Disney).

Mars Attacks!, a science-fiction comedy/disaster movie pastiche based on a series of lurid trading cards from the 1960s, was Burton's return to big-budget filmmaking: an unpredictable convergence with Fox's blockbuster *Independence Day*, indicating just how far removed from the mainstream he could be. Although a hit overseas, the film did not do particularly well at the US box office. Critics pointed to the apparent contradiction of an expensive, star-studded movie that looked so garish. More fundamentally, perhaps, the film's satire looks a little directionless. And while *Mars Attacks!* is very funny, not least in its gleefully vindictive Martians (with Lisa Marie as a Martian in human drag seducing White House aide Martin Short a highpoint), it is also atypically cold. The commercial disappointment of *Mars Attacks!* made things difficult for Burton, who spent over a year trying to develop a Superman project. Andrew Kevin Walker's script for *Sleepy Hollow* provided an opportunity to return to gothic fantasy in a reworking of Washington Irving's 1819 tale. Here the combination of a low-budget sensibility, a strong creative team (including cinematographer Emmanuel Lubezki) and enough money to construct a small town set in Britain is incredibly effective. A hybrid feel of atmospheric location work and evidently stagy sets, stylized action and artful cinematography, humour and gore provides the perfect backdrop for the film's thematic concerns (the gothic and the modern, illusion and reality). Another Oedipal figure, Depp's effete Ichabod Crane, with his 'girlie' screams (he told Mark Salisbury that his performance was a combination of Roddy McDowell, Angela Lansbury and Basil Rathbone 'but a lot more girlie')[4] and peculiar investigative instruments, is also an unconventional hero, an outsider who aims to trust in reason but who is dogged by (and drawn to) the supernatural. Though in many ways a very different sort of film, *Ed Wood* offers a similar, highly polished B-movie feel, right from its elaborately crafted credit sequence, which whisks us through a gothic house, Jeffrey Jones' introduction delivered from a coffin, a graveyard, sea monsters and flying saucers, ending on the famous Hollywood sign and panning down to Wood waiting anxiously for the press to appear for a performance of his new stage show.

Burton has spoken of Vincent Price's iconic horror films as emblematic of his antipathy towards the social: 'Growing up in suburbia, in an atmosphere that was perceived as nice and normal (but which I had other feelings about), those movies were a way to certain feelings, and I related them to the place I was growing up in.'[5] Burton's image as eccentric non-conformist couples an insistent antagonism towards the superficial appearance of normality and respectability with an interest in the freakish and weird in both everyday life and popular culture. In turn his films embrace the truism of horror and fantasy fiction, that villains are typically more interesting – certainly more complex – than clean-cut heroes, bringing out in the process the sinister aspects of what passes for normal and the potential beauty of what gets called weird. These themes are most explicitly visualized in *Edward Scissorhands* and literally embodied in the protagonist, whose half-finished physical state renders him an in-between, transitional figure (after all, like the later *Sleepy Hollow* it is a rites of passage tale of sorts). Here Vincent

Price cameos as a loving (and loved) paternal figure to Edward. Themes of inclusion and exclusion are further mapped through the film's two worlds: suburbia, with its sunshine, colour and social niceties, versus the gothic of Edward's collapsing mansion on the edge of town. This is not the starkly satirical (and more explicitly sexual) vision of suburban America associated with David Lynch's films. In this fable Johnny Depp's Edward is a sensitive outsider (like Pee-Wee, a child–man) who brings funky hairstyles and elaborate topiary to suburbia, where his presence has a magical, transformative effect – at least for a time. His scissor-hands allow Edward to create fantastical shapes, but also render him dangerous; for cheerleader Kim (Winona Ryder, jokily cast here as the ultimate insider), who narrates the story to her own granddaughter, Edward offers a sensitive contrast to her lumpen boyfriend. Ultimately, although the neighbourbood masses on the gothic mansion in anger, the house isn't destroyed. In *Frankenweenie* the community realizes the error of its ways – here it is simply deceived, with Edward and Kim returning to their two separate worlds.

The benign outsider is also central to *Ed Wood*, a character-driven ensemble piece (written by Scott Alexander and Larry Karaszewski) that represented a significant departure for Burton. Structured around the friendship between Ed and the washed-up, drug-addicted horror star Bela Lugosi (Martin Landau), *Ed Wood* celebrates an alternative film community in which social misfits are funny, but not played for laughs. Bill Murray's Bunny Breckinridge, Lisa Marie's Vampira, Jeffrey Jones as Criswell and George 'The Animal' Steele as Tor Johnson are both 'special' and 'tragic' in the intensity of their self-belief (and indeed their belief in Wood). The film functions as an ode not to failure, but to a passionate love of filmmaking – a meditation on the more bizarre aspects of the film industry. Although framed by Wood's cult status as a 'bad' filmmaker, Depp plays Wood as an upbeat, optimistic figure, almost a visionary – his ecstatic face, lit up by the cinema screen or by the act of directing, serving as one of the film's recurrent images. Moreover, Ed's anxieties rarely surface explicitly, just as we see only brief glimpses of the negative or amused responses of others (the executives watching *Glen or Glenda*, say, or Delores/Sarah Jessica Parker's angry outburst at the wrap party for *Bride of the Atom*). Similarly, Wood's cross-dressing is never presented as freakish, despite the fact that his declaration to Kathy (Patricia Arquette) takes place in the darkness of a 'spook house' fairground ride. Instead, the film deals with a marginal showbiz world in which

Wood and his associates form their own society and pursue their own dreams, staging a fantasy meeting between a frustrated Wood and his inspiration, Orson Welles (played here by Vincent D'Onofrio).

Perhaps what stands out most about Burton's films is the combination of technical experimentation and visual innovation with strongly emotive storylines. Sentiment shifts the films away from being exercises in style, whilst attention to design and visual flair prevents them from seeming too self-indulgent in their narratives of troubled male protagonists. Like other filmmakers of his generation, Burton shows himself aware of cinema's past – hence the allusions in films and interviews to Whales' *Frankenstein*, the Poe horror cycle with Vincent Price, to Hammer, monster movies, Fellini, Harryhausen and Expressionist imagery. Yet the films usually manage to avoid getting bogged down in either heavy-handed references or smug irony. Hammer, as Salisbury notes, provides a reference point for *Sleepy Hollow*, a feeling to aim towards rather than a blueprint.[6] While American independent cinema too often seems characterized by a purposeless – or at best nihilistic – irony, Burton's movies are both dark and weird and yet strangely sentimental: exercises in heart-warming horror.

Biography

Born in Burbank, California, in 1958, he attended the California Institute of the Arts before working with Disney and moving on to direct features. His television work includes serving as executive producer on Spielberg's animated *Family Dog* series. In 1997 Burton published an illustrated collection of short stories and poems, *The Melancholy Death of Oyster Boy & Other Stories*.

Notes

1 'I love stop motion,' says Burton. 'There's a certain beauty to it, yet it's unreal at the same time. It has reality. Especially on a project like *Nightmare*, where the characters are so unreal, it makes them more believable, more solid.' Frank Thompson, *Tim Burton's The Nightmare Before Christmas: The Film, the Art, the Vision*, New York, Hyperion, 1993, p. 11.

2 Ken Hanke, 'Tim Burton', *Films in Review* vol. 43, no. 11/12, 1992, p. 380.

3 Mark Salisbury (ed.) *Burton on Burton*, London, Faber and Faber (2nd edition), 2000, p. 75.

4   Mark Salisbury, 'The American Nightmare', *The Guardian*, 1999, 17 December, pp. 2–3.
5   Mark Salisbury, 2000, *op. cit.* p. 4.
6   Mark Salisbury, 1999, *op. cit.*

Filmography

Vincent (1982) short
Frankenweenie (1984) short
Pee-Wee's Big Adventure (1985)
Beetlejuice (1988)
Batman (1989)
Edward Scissorhands (1990) also story, producer
Batman Returns (1992) also producer
Tim Burton's The Nightmare Before Christmas (1993, Henry Selick) as producer
Ed Wood (1994)
Mars Attacks! (1996)
Sleepy Hollow (1999)
Planet of the Apes (2001)

Further reading

Lawrence French, 'Tim Burton's *Ed Wood*', *Cinefantastique*, vols 25 and 26, no. 6/1, 1994/5, pp. 10–18 and 112–20.
Stephen Pizzello, 'Head Trip', *American Cinematographer*, December 1999, pp. 54–9.
J. Hoberman, 'Pax Americana', *Sight and Sound*, vol. 7, no. 2, 1997, pp. 6–9.
Taylor L. White, 'Making of Tim Burton's *Beetlejuice* and his other bizarre gems', *Cinefantastique*, vol. 20, no. 1/2, November 1989, pp. 64–85.

YVONNE TASKER

JAMES CAMERON

> Every time I make a movie, everybody says it's the most expensive film in the film industry.
>
> James Cameron[1]

One may use the designation 'auteur' only in the loosest way with Cameron. In the traditional sense, as initiated in the 1950s by André Bazin and his colleagues at *Cahiers du cinéma*, as subsequently debated in the 1960s in the United States by Andrew Sarris and Pauline Kael, and revised in the 1970s (this time off the Continent) by Peter Wollen, Cameron is only provisionally an artist, and certainly one whose entrance into either the famed Pantheon (Hawks, Ford) or even Sarris' Far Side of Paradise (Sirk) is questionable. Nevertheless, Cameron has a true genius for special effects, technological ingenuity, and an extraordinary knack for giving the spectator a remarkably physical, visceral viewing experience. On the one hand, Cameron is responsible for some of the most innovative techniques and indelible images in contemporary cinema. When *Titanic* called for underwater camera movement impossible with existing equipment, he simply invented what he needed, and there is no doubt that the sight of the Terminator (Arnold Schwarzenegger) removing his own eye has become iconic.

However, on the other hand, Cameron is often legitimately seen as a megalomaniac lurching around a large pit of money, and his films can be not just expensive but offensive. *True Lies*, in which Schwarzenegger plays an American secret agent single-handedly battling hordes of generic, hysterical Arab terrorists offends like few films since *Birth of a Nation* (1915), but with none of the sustaining film historical interest that D.W. Griffith's film offers. (In some respects it is worse – we are supposed to have a significantly shorter fuse concerning racism now than in 1915.) His technological achievements and visual and thematic consistency notwithstanding, Cameron merits consideration for two interrelated reasons. First, he is responsible for many of the most expensive films ever made, as well as the highest grossing film in history, *Titanic*, a film that also tied the record for most Academy Awards won.[2] Second, though Canadian by birth, he may be the most symptomatic director of American mainstream cinema of the last twenty years.

Prior to *Titanic*, it was possible to say that Cameron's genre was science fiction or action (or some combination of the two), but his most recent film, currently holding the world box-office record of over US $1.8 billion in gross receipts appears to be a radical departure.[3] This generic difference makes auteur criticism a useful framework for discussing Cameron as a director. As a set of organizing principles, it helps address how *Titanic*, a film that seems anomalous in the largely sci-fi and action-oriented works of the Cameron *œuvre* is actually very much in the Cameron groove. Increasingly, Cameron's groove has been money itself. Just as John Ford made his mark in the Western and Alfred Hitchcock spoke through the thriller, so Cameron, once called the Cecil B. DeMille of his generation,[4] seems to have gravitated toward the blockbuster, and in so doing has helped redefine radically what that genre is. Not least, he has continually pushed the limits on budgets: *Titanic*, dubbed Cameron's $200-million art film by Fox CEO Bill Mechanic,[5] required the funding of two studios, 20th Century Fox and Paramount, and clinched the proposition that the more money spent on a film, the more it was likely to make – a precedent set by Cameron three times before with *The Abyss, Terminator 2: Judgment Day* and *True Lies*.[6] Atypical of most blockbuster films in that it was neither science fiction nor action, *Titanic*, both the most expensive and the most profitable film of all time, has nevertheless become something of a Golden Mean for blockbuster cinema. In this sense, one may legitimately argue that whatever other themes Cameron concerns himself with from film to film, one of his favourite subjects is the transparent cinematic representation of capital, and his access to and control over it.

In this, among other things, Cameron is a decidedly post-studio director. In other ways he more typifies the patterns of the Classical Hollywood studio system. His favourite film is *The Wizard of Oz* (1939), but the film that sparked his desire to make movies was Stanley Kubrick's *2001: A Space Odyssey* (1969), which he saw ten times on its release. Cameron was born in Canada and raised near Niagara Falls. Frequent trips to the Royal Ontario Museum in Toronto, where he sketched antiquities, helped him become a skilled illustrator.[7] At the age of 17, his family relocated to Los Angeles, where Cameron, after false starts in college majoring in both physics and English literature, became a truck driver. In 1979 he went to work for B-movie king Roger Corman, who also helped jump-start the careers of Martin Scorsese, Francis Ford Coppola, Ron Howard and Jonathan Demme, among others. Here Cameron first began to hone his special effects techniques. Officially, his first directorial effort was *Piranha II: The Spawning*, but Cameron was fired from the project after twelve days, though his name was kept on the film. Cameron himself considers *The Terminator* his directorial debut.

It has been called 'the most important and influential film of the 80s',[8] and *The Terminator* set crucial precedents in Cameron's career. It was the beginning of the collaboration between Cameron and body-builder turned actor Arnold Schwarzenegger, which has so far yielded four films (*The Terminator, Terminator 2, True Lies* and *Terminator 2 3-D: Battle Across Time*), and is likely to produce more.[9] It was also the first time Cameron had complete control over a film from story idea to script to production deal to locations to storyboarding to special effects to editing, a control he has seldom if ever relinquished. *The Terminator* also marks the start of Cameron's fascination with violence, technology, strong women, money, and the nexus of representation and history.

Any one of Cameron's films lends itself easily (some more than others) to readings both progressive and conservative. For example, Cameron seems at once suspicious of both Big Government and Big Business. In film after film he takes a dim view of the power of government and the inevitability of big business to screw things up. In *The Terminator* and *Terminator 2*, government and corporations get into bed together, and the result is nuclear war and a race of genocidal cyborgs. In *The Abyss*, the Navy and a multinational oil company are revealed as morally bankrupt by the extraterrestrials living under the ocean floor. In *True Lies*, Schwarzenegger's government operative actually has to disobey orders to get the job done. And in *Titanic*, it is clear that the corporate-driven desire to bring the ship across the Atlantic in record time leads directly to the disaster.

Yet seen as a group these simultaneous readings are not possible. The more of Cameron's films one sees, the more his conservative ideology comes to the fore, ironically in his apparent attachment to strong women characters set in male-addressed cinema. *Titanic* may be exceptional in Cameron's work for a fan base mainly consisting in teenage, Leonardo DiCaprio-addled girls, but this does not mean that his earlier science fiction and action films, masculinist though they are at a generic level, have not actively invited female spectators.

If Cameron has other consistencies in his films, one of the most important remains his heroic, and very often physically powerful, female protagonists. If *The Terminator*'s Sarah Connor (Linda Hamilton) is the first of these heroines, she is latent until *Terminator 2*, at which point her extremely muscular body competes with Schwarzenegger's for the spectator's attention and admiration. In between, Cameron made *Aliens*, which turned Sigourney Weaver's Ellen Ripley from Ridley Scott's more measured, stately and almost intellectual force in *Alien* (1979) into a contemplatively pumped up rebel who, it happens, has spent some time training at the Yale Drama School. In *The Abyss*, Mary Elizabeth Mastrantonio seems to take an almost existential pleasure in relentlessly being called a bitch – what in Cameron's world you would apparently have to be to design, build, manage and save a colossal oil-rig-cum-deep-sea-exploration-unit. In *True Lies*, even Jamie Lee Curtis' Little Susie Homemaker character, Helen Tasker, is man enough to throw punches not only at the enemy (male and female) but also at her husband, for lying to her so patronizingly all these years.

But Mastrantonio is still a bitch, softening only when her estranged husband (Ed Harris) finally hails her as 'wife' from 20,000 leagues under the sea. Curtis is seen as manly when she strikes, rather than as the gun-toting, helicopter-hopping fury of a woman she becomes. Weaver's major motivation to heroic action is almost exclusively maternal, and she can only dispense with the alien queen when the showdown is framed in mother versus mother terms. And *Terminator 2* sees Hamilton, for all her action hero antics, as nowhere near as good a mother to her son as Schwarzenegger's Terminator. Thus, Cameron's fierce women are always pressed back into the service of patriarchy, pleasantly reaffirming the way things are in a manner equally palatable to both women and men. Time after time, Cameron has his heroines use their spunk and force to maintain the status quo.

In *Titanic*, Kate Winslet's high-spirited heiress, Rose, initially seems to lack the physical force of Cameron's previous heroines (though she has an exemplary turn-of-the-century feminist social stance),[10] but as the ship goes down, she seems as unstoppable as the Terminator in her efforts to free her lover from his watery prison below decks. She is as independent, wilful, smart, sexy and idiosyncratically beautiful[11] as Cameron's previous leading women. And yet again, Rose, a powerful but pleasing figure of the feminine, ultimately serves both patriarchy and the owning classes she appears to spurn in favour of Jack and all he represents. All Cameron films have a kind of bait-and-switch when it comes to their heroines, and ultimately many of Cameron's narratives provide the viewer with the Classical Hollywood closure of the union of the heterosexual couple, as well as the (re)constitution of the nuclear family, though often with a dystopic twist.

In *The Terminator*, love-struck Kyle Reese (Michael Biehn) succeeds in his mission of impregnating Sarah Connor before he is killed. In *The Abyss*, Harris and Mastrantonio are reunited in a finale that seems specifically to be an aquatic response to both *Close Encounters of the Third Kind* (1977) and *E.T. The Extra-Terrestrial* (1982), one which seeks to erase the heartbreak of separation of the latter film. In *Titanic*, Rose and Jack find true love, consummate it, and Jack (like Kyle) sacrifices his life for hers.[12] In *Terminator 2*, Sarah and John Connor and the T-101 (Schwarzenegger) briefly comprise the happy family unit, and again, the sacrificial figure is the father rather than the mother. In *Aliens*, the makeshift family of Ripley, Hicks (Michael Biehn again) and Newt (Carrie Henn) survives, though Hicks has sustained critical injuries to assure that. And in the ultimate happy ending, Schwarzenegger having rescued his daughter from a skyscraper in a military jet, *True Lies'* Helen and

Harry Tasker have their happily-ever-after kiss in front of an atomic mushroom cloud.

In a film in which, Cameron claims, almost everything was supposed to be received tongue-in-cheek ('And you know what?,' he once quipped, 'I'm not a P.C., candy-assed director'),[13] this mushroom cloud kiss instantiates his fascination with the failure or betrayal of state of the art technology, and yet, using state of the art technology – often of his own invention – he neither questions nor problematizes it, or his use of it, to bring this fascination forward. There is good technology and bad technology in Cameron films, and this is distinct from the good and bad people who wield it. (The Terminator is an interesting example of both technology and its user wrapped into one.) Moreover, while much is made of his frequent use of firearms and high body counts, the technology that fascinates Cameron most is not the technology of death, but the technology of representation.

The extent to which Cameron frequently sees representation as more real than the real is the extent to which he often refers (somewhat obliquely) to history and politics as if they are mere accessories. Image in Cameron's films is more real – or more revealing – than reality. This, of course, is a sleight of hand symptomatic of a television-era director, three of whose films have been serials (*The Terminator, Terminator 2, Aliens*).[14] If image says more about reality than reality, then Cameron has it both ways – his metaimages supersede the reality of the films, and yet it is clear that the film as a whole is itself an image which supersedes the reality of the film audience. This particularly postmodern relationship of representation and real is seen in each of his films in a remarkably consistent way.

Among the many other important tropes of a Cameron film, perhaps the most crucial is the notion of prosthetic vision, and its implications. Cameron has never made a film without prosthetic vision. *Titanic* is no exception, and here, where it is least obvious, it might be most important. For in *Titanic*, Cameron's use of prosthetic vision manifests what Robert Burgoyne and Alison Landsburg call 'prosthetic memory' which 'describe[s] the way mass cultural technologies of memory enable individuals to experience, as if they were memories, events through which they themselves did not live'.[15] The implications of *Titanic*'s prosthetic memory may be less dire than Burgoyne's exemplar, *Forrest Gump* (1994), simply because the event itself does not have the import of 'The Sixties'. But the note it strikes is no less false, and may be even more so since it is part of a larger aesthetic tradition presented under the sign of Cameron.[16]

In *The Terminator* we are presented early on with the now famous red field of Schwarzenegger's cyborg vision. All visual information is mediated, and text breaks the world down into data – animal, vegetable, mineral, terminal. It is a method of negotiating the world visually that is distinctly non-human, distinctly technological. In *Aliens*, Ripley sees a great deal of the initial Marine incursion on a number of video screens, which transmit what each soldier sees (as well as the vitals signs of each – *Terminator* redux), as she sits safely inside a protective vehicle. Cameron specifically aligns her view with that of Corporal Hicks' camera, a character with whom she will later form a couple. In *The Abyss*, in a direct precursor to *Titanic*, there are little video camera rovers which swim through the depths of the ocean, moving ahead of divers, a pair of scouting eyes through which Harris and Mastrantonio see both the oceanscape and, at times, each other. In *Terminator 2*, the cybervision is back, but in addition there is also a lengthy scene in which we observe Sarah Connor undergo some slightly sadistic psychiatric testing. Our vision is often mediated by a video screen, which highlights the clinical power and detachment of her doctor, but it also shows us a pathos the doctor cannot see. In addition to all the high-tech, highfalutin night sights befitting a secret agent's mission in *True Lies*, the *Terminator 2* video probe repeats itself as Schwarzenegger anonymously verbally tortures his own wife, who sits behind a two-way mirror. The audience often sees her through a video feed and the glass simultaneously, as well as on a television screen that abstracts her image to highlight heat-emitting areas – predictably, tears. We can go further and include *Strange Days* (1995), the script he wrote and produced for his then-wife Kathryn Bigelow.[17] The film's foundational premise revolves around the ability to 'jack in', or plug other people's visual and sensory experiences, which have been stored in disc, directly into one's own brain, a kind of hyped-up virtual reality complete with snuff films. In all of these films, this prosthetic vision simultaneously, and often paradoxically, both further distances the spectator by adding another layer of vision to the experience of watching a film, and brings her closer, by reminding us through this now-conventional coding that we are, in fact, engaged in the act of watching a movie.

This thematic of mediated vision reappears in *Titanic* as Bill Paxton, captain of the present-day dive crew, cynically delivers a dramatic, made-for-the-Discovery-channel narrative to accompany the roving camera's investigations into the ship. But prosthetic vision in *Titanic* is not just the technological, it is the historiographic as well. The visual aid technologies embodied by the underwater Mir exploration crafts which lead the crew (remaining safe and dry inside their submersible) to the safe in which lies the drawing of young Rose, not only moves the crew (and the spectator) between viewing paradigms, but also between two eras. And this, too, is typical of Cameron.

Why? For one thing, with the exception of *Aliens*, these films all take place in the present, and *Titanic* is no exception. Cameron, whatever else he is, is not a modernist, nor even simply a postmodernist. He is *presentist*, and this is especially evident in *Titanic*, his single period piece, his one and only foray into history and the past. As *New Yorker* critic Anthony Lane pointed out in his review of *Titanic*, the film about a sinking ship was actually more like the two *Terminator* films than it was a 'fresh departure' from them, because in all three, Cameron is 'obsessed by the bending and shaping of time'.[18] And this obsession with time becomes, in the case of *Titanic*, an obsession with history.

This obsession with history brings us back to Cameron's symptomatic nature: the assertions, both visual and thematic, that Cameron makes in his films carry with them their own repudiation or counter-criticism. His heroines are stronger than his heroes, but their strength is used to uphold patriarchy. His assertion that facts are facts is undermined by his repeated use of images that supersede what they represent. And in what may be his most interesting contradiction as a director, his films constantly criticize government and especially big business, and yet this latter is precisely what James Cameron is and does.

Biography

Born Kapuskasing, Ontario, Canada, 16 August 1954, Cameron moved to Los Angeles, USA, in 1971. He was apprenticed with Roger Corman as a set designer, art director, miniature set-builder and process projection supervisor. Cameron made both the first $100-million film (*True Lies*) and the first $200-million film (*Titanic*). He has been married and divorced four times: Sarah Williams (1974–85), Gale Anne Hurd (1985–89, producer of the Cameron projects *The Terminator*, *Aliens*, *The Abyss* and *Terminator 2*), Kathryn Bigelow (1989–91) and Linda Hamilton (1997–99). He is currently involved with actress Suzy Amis, who starred in *Titanic*. He has retained his Canadian citizenship.

Notes

1 Quoted in John H. Richardson, 'Magnificent Obsession', *Premiere*, 1997 (December), pp. 125ff., p. 128.
2 Nominated for fourteen awards, *Titanic* won eleven, including Best Picture.
3 *Titanic* has grossed over $1.8 billion in theatres worldwide, and an additional $3.25 million in US home rentals.
4 Brian D. Johnson, 'Titanic Ambition: A Canadian Sails Hollywood's High Seas', *Maclean's*, 8 December 1997, vol. 110, no. 49, p. 86.
5 Cameron himself has often referred to it as his $200-million 'chick flick'.
6 *Titanic* is often compared to *Gone with the Wind* in its sweeping epic proportions, and to *Cleopatra* in its runaway expense; Cameron himself has repeatedly drawn parallels between himself and *Dr Zhivago* director David Lean. But in 1939 MGM carried the financial burden of *Gone with the Wind* on its own, and co-operated with another studio only to borrow Clark Gable from Columbia.
7 He storyboards most of his films, also sketching the portraits of Rose attributed to artist Jack Dawson in *Titanic*.
8 Sean French, *The Terminator*, London, BFI Publishing, 1996, p. 9. *Esquire* magazine also selected it as its film of the 1980s.
9 Schwarzenegger is the best known, but not the only actor with whom Cameron has worked repeatedly. Others include Michael Biehn, Bill Paxton and, of course, ex-wife Linda Hamilton.
10 This feminist voice is not so difficult for Cameron to accord Rose, since the turn of the century of the film's plot is 100 years before that of the film's release.
11 Cameron has never cast a typically beautiful female star in any of his films. Linda Hamilton, Sigourney Weaver, Mary Elizabeth Mastrantonio, Jamie Lee Curtis and Kate Winslet are, in a variety of ways, gratifyingly wide of the mark of what audiences seem to want in their Hollywood femininity – young, or re-cut and liposuctioned to look it, buxom, and yet stick-thin everywhere else, delicately bobbed nose, and blonde, blonde, blonde.
12 Jack's death is not the tragic ending for Rose that it first appears to be. It is a commonplace of feminist criticism of the film that Rose always knew that Jack would end up disappointing her in the end. As Katha Pollitt asked in *The Nation*, 'How many happy artists' wives do you know?', Katha Pollitt, 'Women and Children First', *The Nation*, 30 March 1998, p. 9.
13 Brian D. Johnson, *op. cit.*, p. 87.
14 A sequel to *True Lies* is reportedly in the works.
15 Robert Burgoyne, *Film Nation: Hollywood Looks to U.S. History*, Minneapolis, University of Minnesota Press, 1997, p. 105. See also Alison Landsburg, 'Prosthetic Memory: *Total Recall* and *Blade Runner*', *Body and Society*, nos 3–4, 1995.

16 Indeed, in *Titanic*, Cameron seems to equate memory, even a fictitious one, with experience. As Cameron stand-in Bill Paxton's contemporary ocean explorer asks the older Rose (Gloria Stewart) in an early scene, 'Are you ready to go back to *Titanic*?'

17 Musing on his four wives: producer Gale Anne Hurd, director Kathryn Bigelow, actress Linda Hamilton, and unknown (to the industry) wife number one – on whom the character of Sarah Connor was based, we must retool that old adage to say that, in Cameron's case, behind every great man there are several great women.

18 Anthony Lane, 'The Shipping News: *Titanic* raises the Stakes of the Spectacular', *The New Yorker*, 15 December 1997, pp. 156–7.

Filmography

Piranha II: The Spawning (1981)
The Terminator (1984) also writer
Aliens (1986) also story and writer
The Abyss (1989) also writer
Terminator 2: Judgment Day (1991) also writer
True Lies (1994) also writer
Terminator 2 3-D: Battle Across Time (1996) also writer
Titanic (1997) also writer
True Lies 2 (2002) also co-writer

Further reading

Joe Abbott, 'They Came from Beyond the Center: Ideology and Political Textuality in the Radical Science Fiction Films of James Cameron', *Literature Film Quarterly*, vol. 22, no. 1, 1994, pp. 21–8.

Tim Blackmore, ' "Is this going to be another bug hunt?" S-F Tradition Versus Biology-as-destiny in James Cameron's "Aliens" ', *Journal of Popular Culture*, vol. 29, no. 4, 1996, pp. 211–27.

Nancy Griffin, 'James Cameron is the Scariest Man in Hollywood', *Esquire*, vol. 128, no. 6, 1997, pp. 98ff.

Christopher Heard, *Dreaming Aloud: The Life and Films of James Cameron*, New York, Doubleday, 1998.

Constance Penley *et al.* (eds) *Close Encounters: Film, Feminism and Science Fiction*, Minneapolis, University of Minnesota Press, 1991.

Anne Thompson, 'Cameron's Way', *Premiere*, August 1997, pp. 63ff.

ALEXANDRA KELLER

JANE CAMPION

Jane Campion is widely acclaimed as one of the most original and talented directors of her generation, one of the few women, as Lizzie Francke points out, 'to leap the barrier and join the pantheon of great filmmakers'.[1] Her films have won an array of prestigious awards and attract extensive, enthusiastic critical attention. Such achievements appear all the more impressive when it is remembered that Campion has in fact directed only five feature films to date (with a sixth currently in production). Indeed, however one views her remarkable career, Campion's status in contemporary cinema seems rather unusual. Her films are generally regarded as quirky and offbeat. Yet increasingly they command considerable budgets and receive international, mainstream distribution, while boasting high-profile stars such as Kate Winslet, Nicole Kidman and Harvey Keitel. As an Australasian filmmaker, Campion has successfully negotiated the often precarious transition from low-budget, independent cinema to the international mainstream. In so doing, her films have become no less innovative and she appears to have retained an enviable degree of authorial autonomy. As one critic has said, 'Campion really does approach her films oblivious to Hollywood's conventions, and Hollywood doesn't seem to mind.'[2]

It seems fair to claim, then, that Campion's films and her status in the industry have challenged and extended some of the received wisdoms about contemporary commercial cinema and the opportunities it affords women directors. In common with many other women directors, Campion's route into filmmaking was typically circuitous. If she took her time deciding on a career in film, initial success and recognition were comparatively swift. With the support of the Australian Film Commission, three of the short films Campion had made at film school – *Peel*, *Passionless Moments* and *A Girl's Own Story* – were accepted at the 1986 Cannes Film Festival, where *Peel* won the Golden Palm Award for Best Short Film.

With the benefit of hindsight at least, it is easy to trace in *Peel* many of the thematic and stylistic preoccupations that characterize Campion's subsequent work. More specifically, it takes an obliquely ironic look at familial dysfunction – a theme that, in one way or another, would reverberate through all Campion's feature films. The narrative begins as Tim Pye, his sister, Katie, and son, Ben (each playing themselves), take a car journey during which Tim stops the car and insists that his son pick up the orange peel he has been throwing out of the car window. It is a patently ridiculous, even cruel, demand since the roadside is dangerous and already strewn with litter. The boy skulks off and disappears from view while Katie looks on bemused. But as the terse narrative unfolds, it becomes clear that Tim is not the only problem: all three are equally stubborn and belligerent. After Tim retrieves his missing son, they return to find Katie also littering the roadside with peel. Father and son both round on her, refusing to continue the journey unless she picks up the peel. Thus, as the film ends, it is clear that the family, both literally and figuratively, are going nowhere, their petty power struggles leave them hopelessly locked in a three-way stalemate.

Although *Peel* takes a swipe at a family's perverse relationships, it is none the less attenuated by a certain gentle humour. The intransigence of each of the characters seems as much an expression of their intimacy as a family unit bound together by their striking similarities, as it is a critique of their dysfunction. Nor does Campion attempt to moralize or, indeed, to offer any discernible polemic at all. As she was later to comment, 'I'm averse to teaching messages, they're a load of rubbish.'[3] Her refusal to direct our sympathies in any explicit way, her fascination with the absurdities of family life, and an often startling visual style which defamiliarizes and yet accentuates the drabness of the *mise-en-scène*, were all to become characteristic of Campion's authorial signature.

Campion's success at Cannes in 1986 effectively launched her career and helped pave the way for her progression into feature filmmaking. Such was the impact of *Peel* that festival director Gilles Jacob reportedly told the Australian Film Commission, 'you must give her lots of money so she'll be in competition with a feature film in two years'.[4] And, after completing a tele-feature, *Two Friends* (1986), Campion did indeed return to Cannes in 1989 with her first feature film, *Sweetie*. Given the critical acclaim that had accompanied her début, it now seems ironic that the hostility with which *Sweetie* was received at Cannes almost prematurely ended a career the festival had done so much to foster. The film was booed during a press screening, faring little better at a subsequent public screening.

It is difficult to gauge precisely why *Sweetie* should have aroused such animosity. True, it is an uncompromising film, both in terms of its unconventional style and its difficult subject matter. But these were precisely the nascent strengths for which *Peel* had been warmly praised. Like *Peel*, *Sweetie* strikes an edgy balance between moments of broad comedy and disturbing scenes of familial and sexual dysfunction, psychosis and taboo (the film hints at an incestuous relationship between Sweetie (Genevieve Lemon) and her father). The narrative revolves around the central conflict between two sisters whose opposing personalities wreak havoc on the whole family. Kay (Karen Colston) is repressed, rigid and, bizarrely enough, afraid of trees. Early in the film, she visits a fortune-teller who informs her that her destiny lies with a man with a question mark on his forehead (a symbolic touch befitting almost any male character in a Campion film). Kay sets her sights on Louis (Tom Lycos) when she sees that a lock of hair has fallen to form a question mark with a mole on his forehead. But she is unable to settle into her fate and soon begins to retreat into herself, withdrawing from any sexual contact with Louis. In contrast, Sweetie is exuberant, infantile and libidinous; her primary means of relating to the world around her is through her body as she veers between histrionic, noisy tantrums and spontaneous displays of her sexuality.

The sisters' conflict ultimately proves intractable. Sweetie's final assault on her family's fragile dignity is to strip naked and barricade herself in the tree-house at the family's suburban home where, in full view and earshot of the neighbours, she dances around screaming a stream of expletives. The obscenity of Sweetie's exhibition is the final confirmation, if one were needed, of the sisters' polarization. When Sweetie tumbles from the tree to her death, it is difficult to escape the sense that somehow Kay has willed such an end. Yet, although the symbolism of Sweetie's fall from the tree is hard to miss, its precise meaning is rather more ambiguous. On the one hand, it seems to confirm that the sisters cannot coexist, that one must inevitably cancel out the other. On the other hand, the reason for Kay's apparently bizarre phobia of trees is given some logic and a psychic connection between the two sisters is suggested, as Sweetie suffers the fate that Kay has perhaps subconsciously been dreading for herself.

In the light of Campion's subsequent success, *Sweetie* has been critically reclaimed and is now justifiably regarded by many as one of Campion's most innovative and courageous works. Campion's next project was an adaptation of Janet Frame's acclaimed autobiography, *An Angel at My Table*. Although originally made for television, it was subsequently theatrically released and well received by the critics. Thus it went some way towards repairing the damage to Campion's confidence and reputation that *Sweetie*'s mauling at Cannes had inflicted. But the impact of her work had yet to register fully beyond the limited art movie and festival circuits – it took another film to propel Campion to international, mainstream recognition. As breakthrough movies go, *The Piano* constitutes a rare example, a film able to attract large audiences and still be regarded as 'genuine art'.[5] Aside from the occasional dissenting voice, it was more or less universally praised; the overwhelming critical consensus seems to have been that this, at last, was Campion's 'coming of age' film. But if *The Piano* won new audiences for Campion's work, its broader appeal did not come at the expense of her trademark quirkiness. As Barbara Quart observed, what made Campion's success so satisfying for many was that it was 'happening to an uncompromising, idiosyncratic director'.[6] Nor was Campion, despite having a large budget at her disposal, under any pressure to make the necessary ideological or aesthetic concessions to fit her unconventional style to mainstream tastes since, after rejecting Hollywood money, she had the good fortune to be bankrolled by the French company, CiBy 2000, who gave her the freedom to make the film as she wished.[7]

The steady flow of critical attention *The Piano* has consistently received renders it, justifiably, one of the most exhaustively discussed films of the 1990s.[8] Amid the raft of critical discourse that surrounds *The Piano*, one question, crucial to any account of Campion's authorship, has yet to be fully resolved: is Campion a feminist director?

On both a formal and thematic level, it is easy to see why *The Piano* was immediately heralded an explicitly feminist film. The degree to which it foregrounds the theme of voyeurism (as characters continually spy upon one another) and repeatedly confounds the conventions of transparency (the inclusion of extra-diegetic animation or the recurring motif of performance and masquerade, for instance) suggest that Campion's direction is self-consciously informed by some key tenets of feminist film theory and practice. Moreover, the debt *The Piano* owes to female gothic literature and the woman's film genre has meant that it has readily been assimilated into existing feminist debates.

Yet Campion has often expressed reservations about being identified as a feminist filmmaker. For instance, in one interview which she gave at the time of *The Piano*'s release, she asserts: 'I think it's clear in my work that my orientation isn't political or doesn't come out of modern politics.'[9] But on another occasion (again in 1993), she seems more receptive to the idea: 'I thought I wouldn't like to be pigeon-holed as a feminist. Now I think that yes, I really am a strong feminist in the sense that I like women a lot and am curious about women.'[10] Ultimately of course, it is not a matter of trawling through Campion's various commentaries to ascertain whether or not she should be dubbed a 'feminist': her films consistently privilege the point of view of complex, resistive, female protagonists and challenge gender stereotypes and as such are easily open to feminist readings. That Campion shows a certain reticence about explicitly aligning herself with feminist politics may not just be a canny career move (though I very much doubt she would have enjoyed the same level of mainstream success with *The Piano* had she done so). Rather, she is pragmatic about the odd combination of circumstances that have facilitated her career, recognizing that her opportunities have been the product of both a feminist legacy *and* the entrenched sexism of the film industry and her Antipodean culture:

> I feel I'm the child of a strong feminist movement, that I have the freedom it fought for. I also feel that women's work shouldn't be marginalized. In Australia, sexism is out front – it can't be avoided. I think that men in the industry feel so guilty about it that they bend over backwards for me. I've never had any problems working.[11]

The overwhelming success of *The Piano* was, ultimately perhaps, something of a mixed blessing: it forged Campion's high-profile reputation, but it also gave her a tough act to follow. After a break of three years, Campion returned with an adaptation of Henry James' *The Portrait of a Lady*. That she should decide to follow *The Piano* with another costume drama in which the heroine rails against the confinement of a monstrous marriage, made comparisons between the two films all the more inevitable. Thus, while *The Portrait of a Lady* enjoyed reasonable critical and commercial success, it is difficult to escape the impression that many of its reviews were rather more respectful than enthusiastic.

Campion's most recent film, *Holy Smoke*, signals a return to the terrain of her earlier work. Like *Sweetie* and *Peel*, it explores what Campion once described as 'the tragic underbelly' of an apparently ordinary Australian family, while acutely exploiting its comic potential.[12] As has become customary in Campion's work, *Holy Smoke* features a spirited heroine, Ruth Barron (Kate Winslet), who is determined to live her life by her own rules. Indeed, Ruth is perhaps the most self-possessed and least compromised Campion heroine to date: unlike her forerunners, she simply refuses to suffer in confinement. As Kate Pullinger argues, '*Holy Smoke* is a tale of girl power … Ruth Barron is a Campion heroine with the masochism excised'.[13]

Ruth's autonomy is thrown into question, however, at the outset of the film when she joins a Hindu cult while travelling in India. Although Ruth's newly discovered spiritual enlightenment is something of a cliché, the film none the less offers plenty of scope for understanding why she is so desperate to escape the life that awaits her in Australia. Initially at least, her parents are presented as little more than caricatures (a beer-drinking, lecherous father, a neurotic, long-suffering mother), while the Barrons' suburban home, with its miniature picket fence and claustrophobic rooms, seems as surreal and isolated as the outpost in the desert where they eventually send Ruth to be deprogrammed.

Believing that her daughter has been brainwashed, Ruth's mother calls in the services of a middle-aged American 'cult-exiter', P.J. Waters (Harvey Keitel), who confidently predicts he can 'deprogramme' Ruth if he has three days alone with her. Waters subjects her to his regime (confiscating her shoes, burning her sari and bombarding her with antagonistic questions) and by the second night, she concedes she has lost her faith. As she stands in the desert night naked and urinating, it appears that Waters has won their battle of wills. But it is precisely at this moment when Ruth seems completely defenceless that the power dynamics of their relationship reverse and Waters is irrevocably disempowered. Confronted by the spectacle of Ruth's vulnerability, he agrees to sleep with her, only to find that by the morning, far from being pacified, she is as combative as ever, ridiculing his unimaginative sexual techniques and deflating his ego with barbed comments.

From this point, it becomes clear that it is Waters, not Ruth, who is to be 'deprogrammed.' When Waters arrives in Australia, he is dressed in the full garb of an urban cowboy (black jeans and shirt, cowboy boots and sunglasses), an attire which mocks his outdated machismo as explicitly as the Neil Diamond lyrics, 'the frog who dreamt he was a prince', which accompany him as he swaggers through the airport. Towards the end of the film, Ruth realizes that to disempower Waters once and for all, she must take away these clothes. She sets about his 'make-over', dressing him up in a grotesquely tight-fitting red dress and daubing his face with make-up. Waters' method of deprogramming is to strip his subjects of their 'props', but it is ultimately Ruth who strips *him* of his props, his dignity, his identity. If further proof of Campion's iconoclastic style were needed, then one need look no further than the image of Waters (underpinned by the full irony of Keitel's star image) staggering through the Australian desert in search of Ruth, still clad in the red dress, lipstick smeared across his face and, most incongruously of all, wearing one black cowboy boot.

Though this suggests that *Holy Smoke* is an unrelentingly cruel film, it is perhaps Campion's most redemptive film to date; its final message summed up by the words Waters writes across Ruth's forehead – 'be kind'. The film's epilogue (set a year after the events in the desert) demonstrates that both Ruth and Waters have been positively transformed by their encounter. Ruth has returned to India (though not to the cult), escaping the dull, restricted life in the suburbs that otherwise beckons. Waters has become a novelist and a father and there is no trace of his former machismo in the loving letter he sends to Ruth. There is, however, another rite of passage buried just below the surface of the primary narrative, a transformation as profound as Waters' and as emancipating as Ruth's. At the beginning of the film, Ruth's mother is entirely taken for granted by her children and adulterous husband. When she first travels to India to persuade Ruth to return to Australia, she is so terrified by the different world she encounters that she has a severe asthma attack and has to be flown home in an air ambulance. By the end of the film, she has dumped her cheating husband and returned to India to begin a new life with her daughter. The final scene of the film shows mother and daughter together: this time at least, the conflicts of a family relationship appear to have been resolved satisfactorily.

Above all, it seems to me that *Holy Smoke* testifies to Campion's continuing commitment to make challenging, innovative films that make few concessions to mainstream orthodoxies. That *Holy Smoke is* none the less a mainstream film (at the very least, in terms of its budget, cast and distribution) perhaps tells us more about how the parameters of commercial cinema are shifting as it at last finds space for filmmakers such as Campion, than it does about the compromises she might have made as her career developed. At the beginning of this piece, I quoted a critic who claims that Campion approaches her films oblivious to Hollywood's conventions. I would like to modify this slightly by suggesting that Campion is more than aware of those conventions, and it is her ability to test and extend them which makes her contribution to contemporary cinema so significant and distinctive.

Biography

Born Wellington, New Zealand, in 1954, Campion is based in Australia. After graduating with a degree in Anthropology in 1975, she undertook a further stint at art school where she made her first short film, *Tissues*, before eventually enrolling at the Australian Film and Television School in 1981.

Notes

1 Lizzie Francke, 'Jane Campion is Called the Best Female Director in The World. What's Female Got to Do with It?', *Guardian* (Section 2), 21 February 1997, p. 4.

2 L. Marshall, 'Mystery Jane', *Independent on Sunday*, 9 February 1997, p. 4.

3 M. Cantwell, 'Jane Campion's Lunatic Women', *New York Times Magazine*, 19 September 1993; reprinted in V. Wright Wexman (ed.) *Jane Campion Interviews*, Jackson, Mississippi University Press, 1999, p. 158.

4 A. Urban, 'The Contradictions of Jane Campion, Cannes Winner', *The Australian*, 21 May 1986; reprinted in V. Wright Wexman, *op. cit.*, p. 15.

5 B. Quart, '*The Piano*', *Cineaste*, vol. 20, no. 3 (April) 1994, p. 55.

6 *Ibid.*

7 V. Wright Wexman, *op. cit.*, p. x.

8 See, for example, S. Bruzzi, 'Jane Campion: Costume Drama and Reclaiming Women's Past', first published in *Sight and Sound*, vol. 3, no. 10, 1993; reprinted in Pam Cook and Philip Dodd (eds) *Women and Film: A Sight and Sound Reader*, London, Scarlet Press, 1993, pp. 232–43; B. Quart, *ibid.*; P. Mellencamp, *A Fine Romance: Five Ages of Film Feminism*, Philadelphia, PA, Temple University Press, 1995.

9 See V. Wright Wexman, *op. cit.*, p. xv.

10 B. Johnson, 'Rain Forest Rhapsody', *Maclean's*, vol. 106, no. 47, 22 November 1993, p. 73.

11 A. Taubin, 'Notes on Campion', *The Village Voice*, 28 May 1991, p. 62.

12 R. Hessey, 'Campion Goes Out on a Limb – Again', *Sydney Morning Herald*, 5 July 1989; reprinted in V. Wright Wexman, *op. cit.*, p. 28.

13 K. Pullinger, 'Soul Survivor', *Sight and Sound*, October, vol. 9, no. 10, 1999, p. 8.

Filmography

(All Australian productions unless otherwise indicated)

Tissues (1980) short
Peel (1981) short
Passionless Moments (1983) short
A Girl's Own Story (1984) short
Sweetie (1989)
An Angel at My Table (NZ/Australia, 1990)
The Piano (1993)
The Portrait of a Lady (UK/US, 1997)
Holy Smoke (US, 1999)

JUSTINE ASHBY

JACKIE CHAN

More so than even Bruce Lee or John Woo, Jackie Chan has come to represent the global image of 'Hong Kong Cinema'; a hyperkinetic, breathless national cinema fashioned by impossibly limber and fearless performers, and by prodigiously inventive choreographers (Chan, significantly, is both). 'No Fear. No Stuntman. No Equal', proclaimed the English-language posters for *Rumble in the Bronx*, underlining both the supposedly 'universal' aspects of his films and those qualities Hollywood could not deliver. Built into this, however, is the implication that Hollywood once *did* deliver such 'uncomplicated' pleasures, as is evidenced in numerous references to silent cinema (Keaton, Chaplin, Lloyd) or classic Hollywood musicals (those of Gene Kelly, in particular). This casts Chan as Hollywood's 'lost innocence', an alternative to 'high concepts' and (most importantly) special effects – his admirers often portray him as a filmmaking throwback, a cinematic *idiot savant* – 'cliff-hanger, kung fu and Keystone cops all in one'.[1] Certainly, the silent cinema/ Hollywood musical comparisons, while limited, stand as a reminder that there is more to cinematic pleasure than the classical 'well-made film'. In Chan's *œuvre*, with some exceptions, the text is the set-piece – no Chan book, his autobiography included, is complete without a list of his ten best fights or ten best stunts. This suggests a kind of 'cinema of attractions', or what David Bordwell calls an 'ecstatic cinema', which transports spectators 'into a realm of rapt, electric apprehension of sheerly pictorial and auditory momentum'.[2] The danger is, however, that such accounts can easily conspire with a patronizing 'trash aesthetic', celebrating Hong Kong as a 'cinema of mindless pleasures'; never mind the quality, feel the stunts.[3]

Chan's ingenuous persona, vulnerability, and mixture of comedy and action have been celebrated as an antidote to the machismo and heartless irony of western action cinema[4], an anti-Schwarzenegger and Tarantino rolled into one. Although such accounts are well meaning, they are sometimes a little light on considerations of Chinese masculinity and heroism or on the context for Chan's persona. Steve Fore is a bracing exception, seeing Chan's films as a negotiation of 'certain contradictions characteristic of Hong Kong culture', mediating between a need for individual action and 'respect for the value of nurturing a group orientation based on altruism and humility'.[5] This is a considerable part of Chan-fandom, too – magazines like *Screen Power: The Jackie Chan Magazine* emphasize his work for charity, his love for and friendliness towards his fans –

qualities which support rather than contradict his bravery and martial arts skills. There are generic precedents for this – Chan has made two films about the virtuous kung fu legend, Wong Fei-hung (albeit in an early, mischievous, incarnation), the epitome of social responsibility.

References to Keaton, Chaplin and Kelly point to another key aspect of Chan's public persona, namely the star-auteur as performative genius. Chan's filmography encompasses a multiplicity of filmmaking roles – director, producer, choreographer, stuntman, co-head (with Willie Chan) of Golden Way films – and his role is rarely confined to performer alone. Behind-the-scenes projects like *Jackie Chan: My Stunts* explore his 'creative process' (improvisation and brainstorming with his stunt team, a choreographic emphasis on 'rhythm' and tempo) and promote the stuntman as star, choreographer as auteur, self-endangerment as popular art. Chan's reputation hinges on 'control', even over those films which he has not nominally directed; several of his directors have walked off his films, willingly or otherwise. The failure of his early US vehicles, *The Big Brawl* and *The Protector*, is popularly attributed to the precise lack of this 'control', to the blind hubris of B-movie hacks who thought they knew better. Relatively speaking, he is one of Hong Kong's most expensive filmmakers; costly period re-creations, international settings, but more importantly for the legend, fights which take months to film, multiple takes and, of course, lengthy stays in hospital. *Mr. Canton and Lady Rose* (a re-creation of 1930s' Hong Kong, inspired by Capra's *A Pocketful of Miracles*, 1961) and *Operation Condor* (a rambling desert adventure filmed in Morocco and the Sahara), in particular, have taken on the reputation of expensive *follies de grandeur*, not least because Golden Harvest subsequently reigned in his excesses.

Chan's popularity is one of the paradoxes of global popular culture; for most of the last twenty years, he has managed to be a cult figure and an international superstar at the same time. Prior to *Rumble in the Bronx* (released in the US in 1996), he was little more than a cult figure in the West, a cult fostered since the early 1980s by Chinatown cinemas and video rental. Meanwhile, no Chinese New Year would be the same without a new Jackie Chan film. 'In Asia ... I am *Jurassic Park*. I am *E.T.*', Chan claims.[6] But in another sense that is precisely what he *is not* – 'We are very poor ... The only choice I have is dangerous stunts.'[7] However, this statement is not entirely true – as witnessed in the lavish spectacles Tsui Hark and Wong Kar-wai deliver on smaller budgets – but there is something irresistible about the 'real' body pitted against the tyranny of the digital, the Drunken Master versus the *Titanic*. But Chan is no cinematic primitive – his control over camera placement and (largely invisible) editing is as meticulous as his control over bodies in motion, and his multiple takes often function as 'action replays' of jaw-droppingly 'real' (read: dangerous) on-set events. Rather, Chan has astutely gauged those elements of Hong Kong cinema that Hollywood cannot absorb or copy. He is fond of chiding American stars for not doing their own stunts and American stuntmen for being too slow. But he also differentiates himself from other, more stylized, Hong Kong filmmakers, especially those who *do* incorporate technology visibly into action scenes or foreground the artifice of cinema – the invisible wires, MTV-cutting and undercranking of 'new wave' martial arts films such as Tsui Hark's *Once Upon a Time in China* series. For Chan, cinema is in the service of the body. In Renee Witterstaetter's entertaining hagiography, his filmography constitutes an autobiography of his body – its performative achievements and 'a chronological account of every broken bone and crushed head, broken finger and twisted knee'.[8]

Few Hong Kong filmmakers have enjoyed Chan's longevity. His career spans the most significant period in Hong Kong cinema – from the Mandarin-language kung fu films of the 1970s (Hong Kong cinema's first global export) to the 'new' Cantonese cinema of the 1980s and 1990s, which looked to Hong Kong itself for its thematic and narrative content; from the island's 'economic miracle' to the turmoil generated by the 1984 Sino-British Joint Declaration returning sovereignty to China. There is a set-piece in most Chan films where he is attacked from all sides, parrying furiously, receiving as many blows as he successfully blocks or returns – the culture-shock of rapid modernization and urban transformation translated into a flurry of high-impact action. Neither the hand-over of Hong Kong to China nor his belated success in Hollywood has stopped him making successful films in the now depleted Hong Kong cinema; the dust had barely settled on *Rush Hour* before he was making the more locally oriented New Year film, *Gorgeous*. Unlike émigré Hong Kong filmmakers, he continues to work in both industries, a truly transnational figure.

Chan's career grew out of an already dying genre, the kung fu film. His earliest star vehicles were lacklustre period films for former Bruce Lee director Lo Wei, and his breakthrough came in two kung fu comedies directed by Yuen Woo-ping, *Snake in the Eagle's Shadow* and *Drunken Master*. In the latter, he reinvented folk hero

Wong Fei-hung as a pre-legend juvenile delinquent – in one scene, he sees off an opponent by farting in his face. Both films were variations on the 'master–pupil' theme, which had been popular since the mid-1970s and which was being given an increasingly comic twist. His early films as director were essentially reworkings of his breakthrough hits, made with the larger budgets Golden Harvest could provide, but the failure of *Dragon Lord* suggested that even comic martial arts films had run their course for now. Subsequently, he was instrumental in creating a hybridized comedy-action film with hair-raising stunts and meticulous choreography, but Chan never lost sight of the martial arts film's 'difference' from western spectacle, its performative virtuosity and the centrality of the body-in-motion. By the time of *Project A*, the emphasis was equally on the body-in-danger – falls from clocktowers, hanging from a moving bus by an umbrella handle (*Police Story*) or dangling from a helicopter (*Police Story 3*) – all injuries replayed in end credits out-takes. If one looks for evidence of 'maturity', then *Project A* is indisputably Chan's breakthrough film. Not only is it more enjoyable than any film has a right to be, but it displays a penchant for period re-creation and a new interest in Hong Kong rather than the kung fu film's mythical China. The film is set in turn-of-the-century Hong Kong and pits Chan's coastal guard Dragon Ma (aided by Yuen Biao and Sammo Hung) against a conspiracy of pirates and corrupt British officials. This is where the 'silent cinema' comparisons begin – the film includes a virtuoso comic bicycle chase and a Lloyd-inspired clocktower sequence. There is a new variety to the fight choreography, too, ranging from riotous bar-room brawls to an extended fight with the pirate leader full of hyperbolic sound effects, slow-motion leaps and Peking Opera acrobatics. The sequel was equally good, mixing elements of farce and anti-Qing dynasty revolutionaries.

Chan developed another series with *Police Story*, usually seen as his riposte to the 'rogue cop' posturing of *The Protector*. The stunts are as breathtaking as ever – Part 1 is the final word on the pleasures of breaking glass and demolishing shopping malls. However, in some respects, the film only differs from its counter-model in execution, and, notwithstanding the comedy and Chan's vulnerable persona, it is striking how close parts of the film are to being 'Dirty Jackie'. The generosity and 'social responsibility' of Chan's period films only patchily appears in the modern-day ones – what are we to make of his character's destruction of a refugee shantytown during a car chase as Part 1's opening 'spectacle', or the grotesquely stereotyped deaf-mute heavy in Part 2? *The Armour of God*, an Indiana Jones-type adventure filmed in Europe, represents another important development in that Chan's films began to transmute into travelogues with intermittent action scenes. This film almost (literally) killed Chan, but it is almost unwatchable (not least for its racism) until the final twenty minutes. *Operation Condor* was an expensive sequel and one excess too many for Golden Harvest, but Chan was displaying a growing weakness for colourless internationalism with yawning longeurs in between his films' set-pieces.

Although not critically well received, *Rumble in the Bronx* holds an important place in the Chan biography. Fore provides an illuminating account of how it was modified for and promoted to US multiplexes – the new version played down Chan's physical comedy (always a sticking point in his 'crossover') and those self-effacing aspects of his star persona that conflicted with him being a straight action performer.[9] *Rush Hour* seems more comfortable with both the 'nice guy' persona and the comedy, even if the latter is toned down (especially in comparison with Chris Tucker's mugging). Interestingly, the action is the casualty; Chan had to work with American stunt co-ordinator Terry Leonard for reasons of both safety and expense. The film captures the dilemma of absorbing Chan into Hollywood – he is not only a conventional star, but also a filmmaking process. *Rush Hour* displays an 'idea' of Chan – dangerous stunts made safe, choreography slowed down to incorporate western actors – rather than the 'Jackie Chan' exported from Hong Kong. The film's fight scenes largely consist of a series of 'moves' rather than the elaborate compositions of his Chinese films.

Chan's career overlaps significantly with that of Sammo Hung Kam-bo. Hung was the oldest member of the 'Seven Little Fortunes', the Peking Opera troupe in which Chan trained as a child. Hung, like Chan, is a prolific star, director, producer and choreographer, and a key influence on the Hong Kong action film. Chan and Hung appeared together in numerous films including the all-star *Lucky Stars* series, *Dragons Forever* and Chan's own *Project A*, usually accompanied by a third 'Little Fortune', the agile Yuen Biao, and sometimes by a fourth, wiry Yuen Wah, as the villain. Collectively, they represent the last generation of Peking Opera performers to make their mark on popular cinema. Hung is as talented as Chan and their styles have some similarities, but he is even less of a conventional leading man (one film title tells all – *Enter the Fat Dragon*) and has not enjoyed the same level of adulation. Hung, Chan and another important choreographer-director

Yuen Woo-ping represent an intermediary stage in martial arts cinema. Bruce Lee had consolidated a demand for 'real' martial artists, both in front of and behind the camera, and this 'authenticity' was guaranteed by extended takes and wide framing of the action. Hung, Chan and Yuen shifted this 'authenticity' away from the kung fu itself to a new kind of hard physical action, away from recognizable styles (Snake, Tiger, Crane, etc.), and towards a mixture of operatic tumbling, gruelling street fighting (with real contact and impossibly painful landings) and self-effacing comedy. Hung and Yuen, however, have shown more willingness than Chan to adapt their styles, including working with wires and special effects on 'new wave' martial arts films (Yuen even worked on the Hollywood science fiction movie, *The Matrix*, 1999), and Hung has subsequently forged an unexpected Hollywood career in the *Rush Hour*-inspired television series, *Martial Law*.

More recently, Chan's most frequent collaborator has been Stanley Tong, the director hired to make cheaper Jackie Chan films. *Rumble in the Bronx* and *First Strike* are undistinguished – although no worse than Sammo Hung's *Mr. Nice Guy* (1997). However, *Police Story 3: Supercop* stands out for the role it offered to Michelle Yeoh. Women are unreconstructedly 'girlish' in Chan's films and he has under-used such stars as Maggie Cheung and Brigitte Lin in thankless roles. But in *Police Story* Yeoh performs a stunt to match any of Chan's – landing a motorbike on a moving bus – and her tough mainland cop is the best thing about the film. Chan's best 1990s' film was a more fractious collaboration with Shaw Brothers veteran, Lau Kar-leung (Mandarin name: Liu Jialiang). Lau is the epitome of 1970s' style authenticity, and the glorious *Drunken Master II* saw Chan performing genuine southern kung fu moves as well as the eponymous 'Drunken Boxing'. Thematically, the film bore some similarities to the *Once Upon a Time in China* films (which also dealt with Wong Fei-hung) – colonialist villains, Wong Fei-hung's coming of age – but the style was very different. Chan has likened Lau's style to 'classical music' – 'very traditional' – and his own to 'jazz',[10] and Lau reportedly walked off the set before Chan's trademark masochistic finale, walking across hot coals and drinking industrial alcohol to counter the super-kicking skills of villain Ken Lo. But the film is more seamless than Chan might like to think and offered two incongruously old-fashioned figures giving the 'new wave' a run for its money.

Chan's abilities are still formidable, but he is also the most trapped of Hong Kong filmmakers, his transglobal mobility notwithstanding. At best, what Hollywood seems to be able to offer him is a new status as a brand-name for a type of spectacle it cannot actually produce. Even in Hong Kong, it is uncertain where he can now go, beyond jumping off bigger buildings or fighting in new locations. *Who Am I?* is the most ambitious of his recent films, but it is too location-conscious and under-scripted to capitalize on its premise of an amnesiac Chinese secret agent. *Gorgeous* is a more low-key film – a romantic comedy and the first Chan film to acknowledge that he is not getting any younger. None the less, the websites, fan clubs, video and DVD re-releases, and the box-office figures for *Rush Hour*, tell a very different (and equally important) story: Jackie Chan is clearly nowhere near his sell-by date.

Biography

Chan Kong-sang ('Born in Hong Kong') was born in 1954, in Hong Kong. In 1962 he joined the Peking Opera School and studied under teacher Yu Cha Yuen, and subsequently performed (as 'Yuen Lo') in the Seven Little Fortunes opera troupe, which included Sammo Hung, Yuen Biao, Yuen Wah and Yuen Kwai. He played a handful of child roles in Hong Kong films, but his film career began in earnest as a stuntman in the early 1970s. Chan was groomed as a replacement for Bruce Lee by producer-director Lo Wei and renamed Sing Lung ('Becoming a Dragon'). However, his real breakthrough came while on loan to Seasonal films – *Snake in the Eagle's Shadow* and *Drunken Master* (both 1978) made him a star. His signing to Golden Harvest in 1980 made him the biggest star in Asia and he blossomed as a director/choreographer. Chan achieved international success with the dubbed, re-edited version of *Rumble in the Bronx*, a success consolidated by his first Hollywood-produced hit, *Rush Hour*.

Notes

1 Renee Witterstaetter, *Dying For Action: The Life and Films of Jackie Chan*, London, Ebury Press, 1998, p. 5.
2 David Bordwell, 'Aesthetics in Action: Kung Fu, Gunplay, and Cinematic Expressivity', in 21st Hong Kong International Film Festival, *Hong Kong Cinema Retrospective: 50 Years of Electric Shadows*, Hong Kong, Urban Council of Hong Kong, 1997, p. 88.
3 Ackbar Abbas, *Hong Kong: Culture and the Politics of Disappearance*, Minneapolis, University of Minnesota Press, 1997, p. 19.
4 Mark Gallagher, 'Masculinity in Translation: Jackie Chan's Transcultural Star Text', *Velvet Light Trap*, 39, 1997, pp. 23–41.

5 Steve Fore, 'Jackie Chan and the Cultural Dynamics of Global Entertainment', in Sheldon Hsiao-peng Lu (ed.) *Transnational Chinese Cinemas: Identity, Nationhood, Gender*, Honolulu, University of Hawaii Press, 1997, pp. 239–62 and p. 254.

6 Fredric Dannen and Barry Long, *Hong Kong Babylon: An Insider's Guide to the Hollywood of the East*, London, Faber, 1997, p. 3.

7 Renee Witterstaetter, *op. cit.*, p. 53.

8 *Ibid.*, p. vii.

9 Steve Fore, *op. cit.*

10 Jackie Chan and Jeff Yang, *I Am Jackie Chan: My Life in Action*, New York: Ballantine, 1998, p. 361.

Filmography

(All Hong Kong productions unless otherwise indicated)

As stuntman/supporting player/stunt co-ordinator

Fist of Fury (1972)
The Heroine (1971)
Police Woman (1972)
Hapkido (1972)
Not Scared to Die (1973)
Enter the Dragon (1973)
The Young Dragons (1973) as fight arranger only
Golden Lotus (1974)
The Himalayan (1975)
All in the Family (1975)
The Dragon Tamers (1975) as stunt co-ordinator only
Hand of Death (1976)
Dance of Death (1976) as stunt co-ordinator
Iron Fisted Monk (1977) as assistant stunt co-ordinator
The 36 Crazy Fists (1979) as stunt co-ordinator
The Odd Couple (1979) as stunt co-ordinator
Two in a Black Belt (1984)
Pom Pom (1985) cameo role
Outlaw Brothers (1989) as stunt co-ordinator
A Kid from Tibet (1991) cameo role

As producer

Naughty Boys (1986)
I am Sorry (1987)
Rouge (1988)
The Inspector Wears Skirts (1988) also stunt co-ordinator
The Inspector Wears Skirts II (1989) also stunt co-ordinator
Stagedoor Johnny (1990)
Centre Stage (1993)
Project S (1993) also cameo role

As director/performer

Spiritual Kung Fu (1978)
Fearless Hyena (1979)
The Young Master (1980)
Dragon Lord (1982)
Project A (1983)
Police Story (1985)
Armour of God (1986)
Project A II (1987)
Police Story II (1987)
Who Am I? (Benny Chan, Jackie Chan, 1998)

As leading performer/director/choreographer

(Directed by Chan unless indicated otherwise)
The Little Tiger of Canton / Master with Cracked Fingers (Chin Tsin, 1971)
New Fist of Fury (Lo Wei, 1976)
Shaolin Wooden Men (Lo Wei, 1976)
Killer Meteor (Wang Yu, 1977)
To Kill with Intrigue (Lo Wei, 1977)
Snake and Crane Arts of Shaolin (Lo Wei, 1978)
Half a Loaf of Kung Fu (Chen Chi-hwa, 1978)
Magnificent Bodyguards (Lo Wei, 1978)
Dragon Fist (Lo Wei, 1978)
Snake in the Eagle's Shadow (Yuen Woo-ping, 1978)
Drunken Master (Yuen Woo-ping, 1978)
Fearless Hyena II (Lo Wei, 1980)
The Big Brawl / Battlecreek Brawl (Robert Clouse, HK/US 1980)
Cannonball Run (Hal Needham, US 1981; supporting role, intended to break into the US market)
Fantasy Mission Force (Chu Yen Ping, 1982)
Ninja Wars (Mitsumisa Saito, Japan 1982)
Winners and Sinners (Sammo Hung, 1983)
Cannonball Run II (Hal Needham, US 1983)
Wheels on Meals (Sammo Hung, 1984)
My Lucky Stars (Sammo Hung, 1985)
Twinkle, Twinkle, Lucky Stars (Sammo Hung, 1985)
The Protector (James Glickenhaus, HK/US 1985)
Heart of the Dragon / First Mission (Sammo Hung, 1985)
Dragons Forever (Sammo Hung, 1987)
Mr. Canton and Lady Rose / Miracles / Miracle (1989)
Armour of God II: Operation Condor / Operation Condor (1990)
Island of Fire (Chu Yen-ping, 1991)
Twin Dragons (Tsui Hark, Ringo Lam, 1991)
Police Story III: Supercop (Stanley Tong, 1992)
City Hunter (Wong Jing, 1993)
Crime Story (Kirk Wong, 1993)
Drunken Master II (Lau Kar-leung, aka Liu jialiang, 1994)
Rumble in the Bronx (Stanley Tong, 1994)

Thunderbolt (Gordon Chan, 1995)
Police Story IV: First Strike / First Strike (Stanley Tong, 1996)
Mr. Nice Guy (Sammo Hung, 1997)
Burn Hollywood Burn ('an Alan Smithee film' [Arthur Hiller], US 1997)
Rush Hour (Brett Ratner, US 1998)
Gorgeous (Vincent Kok, 1998).

Television/video

Jackie Chan: My Story (1998)
Jackie Chan: My Stunts (1999)

Further reading

Craig Reid, 'An Evening with Jackie Chan' (interview), *Bright Lights Film Journal*, 13, 1994, pp. 18–25.

LEON HUNT

THE COEN BROTHERS

Independence and auteurism

Joel and Ethan Coen – the Coen brothers – have made seven films, yet only two have made money:[1] *Blood Simple*, with a budget of $1.5 million, grossed $3 million for tiny Circle Releasing in 1985, and *Fargo*, released by Grammercy Pictures in 1996, grossed almost $25 million and received two Oscars.[2] The key question with regard to the Coens is not so much how have they managed to stay *independent* – whatever that means these days – but how have they continued to find money to make movies at all?

Independent film, alternative film, has to be understood, as Chuck Kleinhans reminds us, as a relational term.[3] Certain films are made independent of, or provide an alternative to, what might be called the dominant Hollywood cinema. Independence is also a relative term. Independence is never *complete* so long as a feature is screened in commercial theatres or on pay or network television, so long as it is made available on video and laserdisk and DVD, so long as it has an MPAA (or BBFC) rating classification.

'Indie' films, historically, have been defined by the two principal and intersecting characteristics of the movies as a medium. Such a definition regards specific matters of content (plot, style, a 'productive' relationship with the PCA, MPPDA, MPAA, CARA)[4] and by cash, as it is made evident on screen, as it regards the way a film is platformed or presented to the public. Two Hollywood adages are worth considering here. The first is a bastardization of an H.L. Mencken quip: 'When they say it's not about the money, it's about the money' (Mencken's line was about politics: 'When they say it's not about sex, it's about sex' – Mencken was nothing if not prophetic).

The second Hollywoodism seems even more to the point here: 'You take the money, you lose control.' We have come to suspect that independence has something to do with a refusal to make concessions. But such a refusal is bottomed on the relative commercial inconsequence of independent projects. Critics and filmgoers have come to look to independent film as the last refuge of auteurism – films made with a signature style that would have been difficult to make in a studio industry committed to a collaborative, assembly-line mode of production.

Autuerism and independence in the new Hollywood intersect in various and interesting ways, with Joel and Ethan Coen situated at this critical intersection. The Coen brothers produce, direct and write all their films. The amount of real control they exert over *their* films seems fairly extensive. Their ability to finance movies when most of them fail at the box office suggests an auteurist project, a body of work assembled somehow independent of the profit motive.

Is it, dare we surmise, in the consistent commercial failure of their cinema that the term independent is implied? Seven films in fifteen years, only two of which have made money, only one of which has made *real money*. What is it about the Coen brothers that keeps them in the grid? Allows them access to financing? Keeps them interesting? There are two possible answers to these questions, both of which are tied more or less to the old-fashioned notion of the auteur. First, the studios know what to expect from the Coens. The brothers have, in the old-fashioned sense of the term, a signature style. Second, they have, to borrow a term coined by Tim Corrigan, successfully exploited the 'commerce of auteurism'.[5] They have been able, despite the low box-office returns, to maintain an aura of auteur-celebrity.

The Coen brothers 'burst upon the scene' in 1984 with their début film, *Blood Simple*. It premiered at the New York Film Festival where audiences 'cheered themselves hoarse' – or so *Film Comment* columnist Elliot Stein reported at the time. The film's popularity was in Stein's view the result of a kind of knee-jerk anti-elitism. *Blood Simple* was 'considerably less rarefied' than the other titles on the festival programme and the cheering crowd mistook genius for simple difference. The Coen brothers' film seemed unlike the rest of the festival fare, Stein glibly concluded, because it was not (good enough to be) a festival film.

Stein focused on the young auteurs' signature, over-the-top visual style:

> Boy do the Coen brothers have style. Amplified chunks of face are shoved up close to our dumbstruck gaze, prosaic household objects are given the fisheye and magically attain ominous connotations that don't mean anything in particular ... Most of this *vacant virtuosity* is what the American screen can't get enough of and emphatically doesn't need.

American cinema's descent into empty style had already taken shape in studio Hollywood thanks to the popular Spielberg-Lucas cycle of light, commercial adventure films. Though it was produced for a different, more elite audience, *Blood Simple* was nothing more than another 'cynical' film – 'like *Raiders of the Lost Ark* and *Star Wars*'. The Coen brothers' 'virtuosity' (no mean feat given the film's tiny budget and the brothers' relative inexperience) was – as with Spielberg and Lucas – in and of itself, *the problem* with the film.

A second, related problem for Stein was the art-house audience's willingness, anxiousness even, to be *entertained*. Stein's review begged an obvious and important question: Is independent film defined in terms of pleasure? Accessible pleasure? Visceral pleasure? Erotic pleasure? The reason that the Coen brothers are seen as important in contemporary US cinema is in their insistence that an independent film need not be high-brow, need not take itself too seriously, need not require any real sophistication to be appreciated and understood.

Stein's fears concerning the impact of *Blood Simple* were realized soon enough as more widely read critics began to celebrate the film and its auteurs. Richard Corliss, writing for *Time*, commented that:

> *Blood Simple* (the title comes from Dashiell Hammett) works tense, elegant variations on a theme as old as the fall; it subverts the film noir genre in order to revitalize it; it offers the satisfactions and surprises of a conniving visual style. Most important, it displays the whirligig wit of two young men ... in a debut film as scarifyingly assured as any since Orson Welles was just this wide.[6]

David Ansen, Corliss' colleague at *Newsweek*, was no less enthusiastic. He described the film as 'at once a bated breath thriller and a comedy as black as they come – the most inventive and original thriller in many a moon'.[7]

Writing after the *Time* and *Newsweek* reviews, the *New Yorker*'s Pauline Kael, who by this stage was using her 'Current Cinema' column to lament the state of post-renaissance Hollywood, savaged *Blood Simple* and the critics who mistook the film for real art. *Blood Simple* 'is so derivative, it isn't a thriller,' she wrote, 'it's a crude ghoulish comedy on thriller scenes'. Kael, like Stein, damned the Coens for their stylistic audacity, which, she argued, served a small and stupid narrative: 'What is at work here is [nothing more than] a visually sophisticated form of *gross* out humor.'

Kael's objections to the film reveal two parallel concerns, both consistently examined in her film reviews throughout the 1980s. The first regards the content and style of 'third generation auteurs'. Coppola, Altman and Scorsese spearheaded the first wave and their films, according to Kael's scheme, were, in general, terrific, original and modernist. The second generation, comprised of Spielberg and Lucas, pretty much spoiled everything for everybody as the two young men crassly traded on their talent in service of simple and simplistic Hollywood entertainment. The third generation (of which the Coens are a part) had less talent than the first two. These young auteurs, Kael bristled, possessed an encyclopaedic knowledge of cinema and television but little practical or experiential knowledge of anything else. Kael also complained about how these *postmodern* filmmakers pointlessly shattered genre categories. They made films comprised of allusions, not images or themes or plots. Their films were ahistorical and ironic; in-jokes for a new in-crowd. 'What's the glory of making films outside the industry,' Kael mused, 'if they're Hollywood films at heart?'[8]

Fishmongers and big men in tights: the Coen brothers' films

There are two keys to all Coen brothers' films: pace and critical distance. *Blood Simple* is dead slow – a complete reversal on the hectic, urban noir universe. And much the same can be said about *Barton Fink*, *Miller's Crossing* and *Fargo*. *The Hudsucker Proxy* is fast like the screwball films it apes. As are the other two comedies: *Raising Arizona* and *The Big Lebowski*, both of which descend into slapstick and by their mid-point degenerate and/or develop into 'chase films'.

All these films are about stupid people; all, we should remember, were made by university-educated sons of college professors. One need not worry about the Coens 'killing all their darlings'. They are all too willing to see any and all of their characters suffer through most anything for a laugh, for a cool image, for a gross-out effect. In her extended review of *Blood Simple*, Pauline Kael found a formal explanation for this critical distance: '[*Blood Simple*] has the pattern of farce ... a bedroom farce except that the people sneaking into each other's homes have vicious rather than amorous intentions'.[9] Such a subtle tweaking of genre has become the Coen brothers' distinct auteur signature. Their tendency to find farcical the everyday violence of US culture other more mainstream directors glorify, or at the very least sensationalize, forms the foundation of an original social commentary – a commentary that emerges despite the pervasive irony and the cheeky games with style.

The characters in the Coen brothers' films find themselves in familiar genre predicaments but react in crazy, stupid ways. In *Blood Simple*, Ray finds Marty's 'corpse' in the café office and tries to clean up the crime scene. He succeeds only in making a bigger mess, spreading Marty's blood over every surface in the room. Then, like so many other characters in a Coen brothers' film, Ray comically botches an attempt to dispose of the body. The aptly named Snopes brothers in *Raising Arizona* stumble through a bank robbery, then leave behind the baby who they have kidnapped for ransom. Norville Barnes, the proxy in *The Hudsucker Proxy*, is a dupe and a moron from Muncie! The film borrows liberally from Capra's *Meet John Doe* (1941): the promise of a holiday suicide, the exploitation of an innocent by a *dame from the newspaper*. Tim Robbins (who plays Norville) is tall enough for the Gary Cooper role in the Capra film, but seems instead modelled on another 1940s' dupe, the dim-witted Dick Powell character in Preston Sturges' *Christmas in July* (1940).

And then there is Jerry in *Fargo*, whose plot to change the life he has and deserves (as a wimpish moron) ends much as all such plots launched by characters in Coen films end: in butchered bodies and wrecked cars. He resorts to crime (the kidnapping for ransom of his own wife) because his plan to get out of an embezzlement mess – to build a parking lot – goes awry. There are at least four scenes set in parking lots in the film. All four are important set-pieces featuring hundreds of empty parking spaces.

In *The Big Lebowski*, there are the so-called nihilist kidnappers (who are neither nihilist nor are they kidnappers) and the ill-fated Donnie who is told to 'shut the fuck up' all film long and for good reason. When Walter and the Dude locate the Dude's car (and the million dollars supposedly tucked in a briefcase on the back seat), Donnie points out that the car thief's house is near a hamburger joint he really likes. They both tell Donnie to 'shut the fuck up' because he is missing the gravity of the situation: $1 million in lost cash has suddenly been found. But the joke does not end there. All three men sit through a ridiculous one-man dance recital given by the Dude's landlord before they exit to retrieve the money. By this point, they are hungry and decide to stop, as Donnie suggested, for burgers on the way. Donnie dies in a parking lot confrontation that has nothing to do with him or the one thing he seems to care about, bowling. Bowling may be on the rise again in the US, but what, the Coen brothers ask, do we really think about men who bowl and take it seriously?

The Coen brothers are especially unkind to people like themselves: upper-Midwesterners and Jews. Like David Lynch, who grew up for a time in Montana and bitterly satired small-town mean-spiritedness and dumb-wittedness in *Twin Peaks* and *Blue Velvet*, the Coens use 'place' evocatively and satirically. The Coens were brought up in Minnesota, a place they describe as a 'bleak windswept tundra, resembling Siberia except for its Ford dealerships and Hardees restaurants'.[10] The simple folk who try to sort their way through the complex plot of *Fargo* speak in a dialect and at a pace that seems not only foreign but otherworldly. The film is populated by stupid people who are stupid simply because they live in the upper-Midwest.

As to the Jewish question, a more worrisome self-loathing emerges. First and foremost, there is *Barton Fink*, a film which offers caustic stereotypes of a Jewish commie-artiste (Barton), a lunatic Jewish studio boss (Lipnick, who introduces himself as 'bigger and meaner than any other kike in this town'), and a motor-mouthed Jewish studio producer (Geisler). We should recall here that *Barton Fink* won the Grand Prix at Cannes. An American film with anti-Semitic caricatures in France!

Two other prominent Jewish characters appear in Coen films. Bernie Birnbaum, 'the Shmata kid' in *Miller's Crossing*, is, we are told, 'ethically kinda shaky'. Bernie's a *player* with loyalty to no one except himself. He is also gay. Much is made of the fact that gay-ness and Jewishness are taints that are at once related and worse than (just) criminal. Finally, there is Walter in *The Big Lebowski*, a recent convert who has taken to Judaism with a seriousness that makes no sense to the Dude or, apparently, to the Coens. When the

Dude asks Walter to drive on the Sabbath, Walter contemplates the notion of transgressing '3,000 years of beautiful tradition from Moses to Sandy Koufax'. What, we might ask here, is not a joke to the Coens?

The flesh is weak in these films, but sex is seldom at issue. We are treated instead to scene after scene of spurting blood and projected vomit. Marty throws up blood and food several times in *Blood Simple*. The writer Bill Mayhew (based on William Faulkner) is introduced in *Barton Fink* puking in the commissary bathroom. Charlie (whose ears ooze pus) throws up when he sees Audrey dead in Barton's hotel room (though we later discover that Charlie has killed her).

Violence in the Coen brothers' films is pervasive and explicit. As Kael suggests, theirs is a 'splatter art cinema', an alternative film project rooted in exploitation genre pictures. We see a knife stabbed through the detective's hand (*à la The Godfather*) in *Blood Simple*. *Raising Arizona* climaxes with a fifteen-minute fight between Hi and the Snopes – a fight that is capped when the bounty-hunter, Smalls, is blown to bits. Casper murders the Dane with a fireplace shovel in *Miller's Crossing*. Walter bites off the ear of one of the nihilists in *The Big Lebowski*.

Because of the many graphic scenes in their films, the Coen brothers are able to *play* with our expectations. In *Miller's Crossing*, a gangster film filled with sudden, graphic bursts of violence, the narrative pivots on Tom's decision to spare Bernie's life in the woods. The violence in this case is only deferred, as the narrative pay-off has Tom gun down Bernie in cold blood. A second scene in *Miller's Crossing* recalls the closing image of Rainer Fassbinder's *Fox and His Friends* (1974) (like Tarantino, and many other third-wave auteurs, the Coen brothers allude to a wide range of films). After Leo is shot and left for dead in the street, a little boy stops to examine the body, then exits stealing the gangster's toupee.

Violence is a key element even in *The Big Lebowski*, a film played entirely for laughs. The on-screen violence in the film is so outrageous that it is often funny. Two thugs burst into the Dude's apartment and find him in the bathtub. When the Dude cannot answer their questions, they drop a marmot in the water. We watch and laugh and squirm. As Freud suggests – as is self-evident, really – things are funny when they happen to someone else.

Fargo goes the furthest into the splatter tradition and it is far and away the Coen brothers most profitable, and probably their best film. Gaer shoots a cop in the face in the opening scene of the movie.

Carl, Gaer's partner, is then shot in the face by Jerry's father-in-law. Gaer kills Carl and feeds his dead body into a wood-chipper. There is a preoccupation with the disposal of bodies in the Coen brothers' films: in *Fargo*, *Blood Simple*, *Barton Fink* and *Miller's Crossing* the plots turn on the success or, most of the time, failure to dispose of a body properly, completely, finally.

As with many low-budget filmmakers, the Coens' early work makes light of their performers' shortcomings. In *Blood Simple*, with the exception of M. Emmett Walsh (who is slimy and menacing and delivers his lines with a drunken slur), the other actors are dreadful. As Pauline Kael quipped: 'At moments, the awkwardness of the line readings is reminiscent of George Romero's *Night of the Living Dead* ... the actors talk so slowly it's as if the script were written in cement on Hollywood Boulevard'.[11] However, as the money got better so did the performances. Like Spike Lee, Steven Soderbergh and Quentin Tarantino, and frankly unlike the A-list Hollywood players making bigger-budget films, when they have the time and the money, the Coens are superb directors of actors. They frequently use the same actors (which helps): McDormand, Walsh, John Turturro, John Goodman, Steve Buscemi, John Malloy, Peter Storare and Jon Polito.

They use voice-over extensively in four films: *The Hudsucker Proxy*, *Raising Arizona*, *Blood Simple* and *The Big Lebowski* – mostly as a way to set things up. In all but one case it is the voice of a minor, even tangential character, like the all-knowing Moses, who works in the bowels of the Hudsucker building in *The Hudsucker Proxy*.

Dream sequences abound in their films, often to unsettling effect. Abby dreams that Marty is still alive in *Blood Simple*. Tom's dream of 'a foolish man chasing his hat' opens *Miller's Crossing* and foreshadows the film's final scene. Barton Fink hallucinates with some regularity. At one point, while reading the *Book of Daniel*, he finds instead help with his script about 'fishmongers and big men in tights'. Norville in *The Hudsucker Proxy* dreams up a romantic dance number. The set-piece is staged to accompany an aria from Bizet's *Carmen*. But even in his dreams, Norville is just a gangly idiot, the object and subject of someone else's joke. In *The Big Lebowski*, the Dude dreams that he is Superman, flying above the city. Then, like Norville, he finds himself transformed into a performer in a Busby Berkeley production number. The Dude's dream – like the dreams realized on screen by the Coen brothers – is framed by the movies.

The Coens seem prepared to keep us at a distance from the action in their films, so much so that it is difficult to know what, if anything, should be taken seriously. The films are populated less by characters than by comic grotesques. The level of humour is often adolescent, but that is not to say that it is not also funny. The best or worst of such grotesqueries can be found in *The Big Lebowski*. There is the paedophile, bowling-ace Jesus, the scriptwriter in the iron lung, the German techno-nihilists, the crippled millionaire, the loopy cowpoke narrator. At a moment of understandable frustration in the film, the Dude tries to talk some sense to Maud and says: 'I'm sorry your stepmother is a nympho, but what's that got to do with me?' The remark is at once comical and revealing. It is comical because the Dude is accurately summarizing (and satirizing) Maud's motivation as a character. And it is revealing because it makes obvious the adolescent preoccupation of two brothers whose development seems, like so many filmmakers these days, arrested someplace in and at the movies.

Like the Coen brothers, I too am a suburban Jewish white boy. Ethan is my age; Joel three years younger. So I am anxious to believe that the critical, ironic distance that pervades their films and speaks so keenly to my own sense of things adds up to something more than just a refusal to leave adolescence, and the movies of our adolescence, behind. To that end, I defer to Devin McKinney and his revealing, albeit mostly negative, review of *Fargo*:

> The spin which the Coens give our expectation of and need for empathy amounts to an existential reversal, given that empathy as a literary idea is commonly understood as a unifying agent ... At their most original, the Coens have exercised the darker, more difficult impulse to unite characters and audience not in the warmth of common affirmation (which I'd argue is the stuff of most mainstream films), but in the chill of common alienation.

Biography

Joel Coen was born in 1954 and Ethan Coen in 1957, both in Minnesota, USA.

Notes

1   *O Brother, Where Art Thou?* was released in winter 2000, too late for inclusion in this essay. The title of the film was taken from Preston Sturges' *Sullivan's Travels*. In Sturges' film, set during the Great Depression, a Hollywood director famous for making frivolous musical

comedies decides he needs to make a film truer to the human condition. He sets out to meet 'the common man' only to discover that the plight of such folk is hardly the stuff of an interesting motion picture. Sullivan, the director, decides at the end of the Sturges' film to ditch the 'O Brother, Where Art Thou?' project in favour of yet another innocuous comedy. The Coen brothers' *O Brother, Where Art Thou?* seems a similarly ambitious project, an adaptation of Homer's *The Odyssey*, set in the rural American South in the 1930s. But unlike the fictional Sullivan who sets out to make a serious film, it is clear that the Coens have made a movie that resides firmly in the ironic tradition of the rest of their *œuvre*. As of April 2001, the film had grossed just under $40 million in US cinemas, this on a production budget of $26 million and an estimated promotion and advertising cost of $13 million. It is too early to tell whether or not the film will make much money in the various ancillary markets. Taking into account just its theatrical revenues, the film seems at best a moderate box-office failure.

2 The Coen brothers won for Best Original Screenplay. Frances McDormand, who played Marge, the very pregnant policewoman who solves the case, won for Best Actress.

3 Chuck Kleinhans, 'Independent Features: Hopes and Dreams', in Jon Lewis (ed.) *The New American Cinema*, Durham, NC, Duke University Press, 1998, pp. 308–9.

4 PCA stands for the Production Code Administration (which supervised, that is, censored production, from 1930 to 1968); MPPDA stands for the Motion Picture Producers and Distributors Association (the organization which regulated the business of making films in the United States between the two world wars); MPAA stands for the Motion Pictures Association of America which replaced the MPPDA after the Second World War (just in time to institute the blacklist); and CARA stands for the Code and Rating Association or Classification and Rating Association which was formed by the MPAA in 1968 to implement a new film classification system (G, M, R and X – now G, PG, PG-13, R and NC-17).

5 See Timothy Corrigan, *A Cinema without Walls*, New Brunswick, NJ, Rutgers University Press, 1991, pp. 101–36.

6 Richard Corliss, 'Same Old Song', *Time*, 28 January 1985, p. 90.

7 David Ansen, 'The Coens: Partners in Crime', *Newsweek*, 21 January 1985, p. 74.

8 Pauline Kael, 'The Current Cinema', *The New Yorker*, 25 February 1985, pp. 81–3. The critical debate over the Coen brothers' films continues to be heated. After much anticipation and promotion in the USA, *O Brother, Where Art Thou?* opened to an astonishing range of good and bad reviews. Writing for the widely read *Entertainment Weekly*, Owen Gleiberman savaged the film: 'the latest misanthropic flimflam from the Coen brothers is like an extended Three Stooges episode featuring an even stupider version of Hee Haw'. Also writing negative reviews were other such powerful and influential critics as Roger Ebert, J. Hoberman (*The Village Voice*) and Deeson Howe (*Washington Post*). On the positive side, John Anderson (*Newsday*) described the film as 'hilarious … ingenious, literary and looney'.

Jonathan Foreman (*New York Post*) and Todd McCarthy (*Variety*) also wrote extremely positive reviews. The popular website, 'Rotten Tomatoes' (www.rottentomatoes.com), keeps a running scorecard of raves and pans for every film released in the US. *O Brother, Where Art Thou?* received a '78 per cent fresh' rating – a surprisingly good score which at once affirms that many critics liked the film and that a minority of widely read reviewers who hated the picture dramatically skewed the 'critical consensus'.

9 *Ibid.*, p. 81.
10 Ethan Coen and Joel Cohen, *Fargo*, London, Faber and Faber, 1996, p. x.
11 Pauline Kael, *op. cit.*, p. 81.

Filmography

Blood Simple (1985)
Raising Arizona (1987)
Miller's Crossing (1990)
Barton Fink (1991)
The Hudsucker Proxy (1994)
Fargo (1996)
The Big Lebowski (1998)
Oh Brother, Where Art Thou? (2000)

Further reading

Joel Coen and Ethan Coen, *Blood Simple*, London, St Martins Press, 1989.
—— *Raising Arizona*, London, St Martins Press, 1989.
—— *The Hudsucker Proxy*, London, Faber and Faber, 1994.
—— *Barton Fink and Miller's Crossing*, London, Faber and Faber, 1995.
—— *The Big Lebowski*, London, Faber and Faber, 1998.
Emmanuel Levy, *Cinema of Outsiders*, New York, New York University Press, 1999.
R. Barton Palmer, 'Blood Simple: Defining the Commercial/Independent Text', *Persistence of Vision*, no. 6, 1988.
Paul Woods (ed.) *Blood Siblings*, Plexus Books, 2000.

JON LEWIS

FRANCIS FORD COPPOLA

Francis Ford Coppola is, if anything, a paradox. The highs and lows of his career chart the trajectory of the New Hollywood era: the first of the film school directors to make his name as an auteur, the first to show such promise that he was often referred to as a 'genius', and also the first to crash and burn. Coppola has spent close to twenty years making films that, for financial and aesthetic reasons, continuously, and in a very public way, betray his initial promise. The rise and fall of his career can be mapped against the rise and fall of New Hollywood and the auteur cinema of the 1970s. Coppola provides an interesting case study of the twin pull of art and commerce in contemporary Hollywood. Taking his middle name from the 'Ford Sunday Evening Hour', a television series on which his father was musical arranger, he was also one of the first American directors to feel the influence of the emerging post-war European new waves.

From the outset, Coppola demonstrated a drive and audacity to get things done, to take risks. When other film students at UCLA talked of making movies, Coppola went out and shot them. His first film, *The Peeper*, was very much in the tradition of exploitation filmmaker Russ Meyer's first film, *The Immoral Mr. Teas* (1959), whose main character could see through women's clothes. In Coppola's film, the main character tries, in a variety of ways, to see the women in a pin-up photo session. To accomplish this, he comes up with devices that seem to emerge full-blown from a 'Tweety and Sylvester' cartoon. Too short to be a feature, Coppola agreed to cut together his film with another sexploitation film that had a totally unrelated plot: a drunken cowboy gets hit on the head and sees cows as naked women. This improbable combination became his first feature *Tonight for Sure*, which, given the descriptions outlined above, must have lent itself more to surrealism than sexploitation. It goes without saying that this early work was not brilliant, but at least Coppola could claim to have a made a film.

Coppola's drive also landed him a job working for B-movie maestro Roger Corman, who had quite bizarrely bought up the North American rights to a Soviet science fiction film. One of Coppola's first jobs was to re-edit this film and dub on English-language dialogue. The pulpy, low-budget origins that these early career moves demonstrate undercut to some degree the latter-day narrative of Coppola's artistry and singular vision. Furthermore, despite his training in low-budget filmmaking – of which Corman was pretty much the master – Coppola's 'singular vision' often got the best of him in later years, when budgets would, more often than not, go out the window.

Working for Corman gained Coppola his first real chance to direct a 'proper' film. While in Europe working as an assistant on *The Young Racers* (1963), Coppola wrote a quick proposal for Corman, arguing that with the crew already on location, it made sense to shoot a second film, thereby reducing costs. On the basis of only one finished scene, Corman agreed – on condition that the word 'dementia' appear in the title to help sell the film. Coppola's *Dementia 13* is somewhere between Agatha Christie and Hitchcock's *Psycho* (1960). Set in a lush manor house, the story revolves around the murder of various members of the Haloran family. Like many families in the horror-gothic genre, the Halorans harbour a dark past and, after various murders, the killer is revealed as one of the family's own. While a decent exploitation film, *Dementia 13* is predictable, and, except for its reliance on pulpy origins, does not foreshadow the kind of films that Coppola would eventually make. The difference is that, as his career progressed, Coppola stopped relying on pulp and transformed it instead.

Moving away from the Corman stable, Coppola began to make his name in Hollywood as a scriptwriter on such films as *Paris brûte-t-il?* (1966), *This Property is Condemned* (1966) and *Patton* (1970). In the late 1960s, alongside his writing assignments, Coppola directed a series of films that paved the way for his future success. The beginning of the 'mature' Coppola, in many ways these films foreshadow the strengths and weaknesses of his most renowned work. *You're a Big Boy Now*, written while in Paris, is Coppola's first 'personal' film, establishing him as a Young Turk under the influence of the various European new waves. *Finian's Rainbow* was a revival of a Broadway musical starring Fred Astaire. While a box-office failure, the movie demonstrated that Coppola was at home in many different genres – and indeed, for better or worse, the musical was a genre that Coppola would return to again and again. It was on the set of this film at Warner Bros. studio that Coppola met a young intern named George Lucas – his future protégé (Coppola would serve as executive producer on Lucas' 1973 *American Graffiti*) and American Zoetrope (Mach I) partner. *The Rain People*, Coppola's second 'personal' film, is a largely improvised road-trip movie featuring future mainstays James Caan and Robert Duvall. The film was distinctive in that both the crew and the characters within the film itself were on the trip (they all drove a caravan across the US). During shooting for *The Rain People*, Lucas shot one of his earliest films, *Filmmaker* (1968), a portrait of Coppola at work and of the road trip itself.

Until this point, while well respected for his visual flair and for his scripts, none of Coppola's films had been successful. This is one of the many reasons that Paramount producer Robert Evans famously did not want Coppola to direct the film of the best-selling novel to which he had the rights: Mario Puzo's *The Godfather*. Yet it is for the

Godfather trilogy – along with *Apocalypse Now* – that Coppola is best known, and it is the trilogy that lies at the heart of claims for Coppola as the key New Hollywood auteur.

It is at this point in his career that both commentators and Coppola alike begin to refer to his work as to some degree autobiographical. Yet, these autobiographical moments are, more often than not, filtered through pulp fiction and art cinema aesthetics. The three *Godfather* films paint a sweeping portrait of American capitalism in the guise of telling the saga of the life of the Corleone family of *Mafiosi*. Yet, what is most compelling about the trilogy is not the detail that Coppola, Puzo and their collaborators bring to the films, nor the visual richness with which both New York and Sicily are painted; rather, it is the 'operatic' nature of the narrative itself that gives the trilogy its strength. Indeed, it is the way in which the 'operatic' is combined with other generic and aesthetic motifs that makes the *Godfather* trilogy a decisive break with classical Hollywood cinema. Furthermore, the influence of the European new waves can be seen in the narrative structure of *The Godfather Part II*, while Michael Corleone (Al Pacino) is quite self-consciously portrayed in the manner of Shakespeare's Lear in *The Godfather Part III*. Coppola's fusion of Euro-'art' sensibilities with the pulpier aspects of American genre fiction (which had greatly influenced the European new waves in the first place), along with the autobiographical motifs, created what seemed to be a new kind of hybridized Hollywood cinema. The *Godfather* films changed many things: the role and power ascribed to the director as auteur, the kind of films produced by the studios, and the face of Hollywood itself. Indeed, the revenue from the *Godfather* films allowed Coppola for the first of many times to try and set himself up, in this case with Lucas, as an independent producer under the rubric of American Zoetrope.

While the *Godfather* trilogy allowed Coppola the freedom he needed to make the kinds of films he wanted, *The Conversation* consolidated his position at the forefront of 1970s' auteur cinema. *The Conversation* succeeds because Coppola resists giving in to his more 'operatic' tendencies. With the *Godfather* trilogy and *Apocalypse Now* he uses operatic motifs to great effect; in many other films, his grand designs lead him to lose the plot of the film itself – metaphorically, he becomes like *The Conversation*'s Harry Caul (Gene Hackman), trying to find meaning in the cacophony surrounding him. Caul is a specialist in bugging who realizes, to his dismay, that the technology which he uses to carry out surveillance is being used against him. *The Conversation*, followed closely by Alan J. Pakula's *The Parallax View* (1974), provides one of the most claustrophobic analyses of paranoia to be released in the very paranoid America of the 1970s. The strength of Coppola's film lies not only in the way in which he manipulates the cinematic image, but also in the way he manipulates the soundtrack. While sound is most often couched in invisibility in the cinema, Coppola not only successfully foregrounds the key role played by sound in the construction of cinematic 'transparency', but also deconstructs its duplicitous nature, in a manner similar to the way in which Antonioni deconstructs the photographic image in *Blow-Up* (1966).

Coppola's next project left tightly plotted coherence behind, with the script created during shooting. The three-year production of *Apocalypse Now* has acquired near epic status in Hollywood film history. Most famously, Coppola declared at a preview screening at the Cannes Film Festival in 1979 (where it was awarded the Palme d'Or) that his film was not about Vietnam, but that it *was* Vietnam. *Apocalypse Now* offers the most fully realized vision of Coppola's cinematic preoccupations, highlighting both his strengths and weaknesses. His aforementioned comment on the nature of his film points to the extreme autobiographical nature of *Apocalypse Now*, while the film's most infamous scene – helicopter attack set to music by Wagner – again foregrounds Coppola's dual obsessions with the 'operatic' on one hand and technology on the other. With the death of Kurtz (Marlon Brando) at the film's dénouement, Coppola decisively – although perhaps unknowingly – brings an end to one phase of his career, and opens a new one where the family, so omnipresent in his *œuvre* up to this point is overrun, like Kurtz's compound, by technology.

One from the Heart, Coppola's musical, studio-bound follow-up to *Apocalypse Now*, was regarded at the time of its release as an unmitigated failure. Indeed, the film's financial failure led to the bankruptcy of Coppola's fledging independent, American Zoetrope (Mach II). Upon reflection, *One from the Heart* is interesting to the extent that it takes place within an entirely constructed, mediated space which foregrounds the relationship between technology and imagination that Coppola believed, to a greater and greater degree, lay at the heart of the cinema. The plasticity of the film's images continued in Coppola's 'director-for-hire' years, and is visible in the two quickies he shot to make some money: adaptations of S.E. Hinton's *Rumble Fish* – shot in the style of the European avant-garde – and *The Outsiders* – shot in the style of *Gone with the Wind*.

As a 'director-for-hire', Coppola did not have that much control over the production of some of his films. That said, his desire to assert authorship, and to play the role of auteur, was fierce. A case in point is *The Cotton Club*. Called in as a script-doctor by Robert Evans, his old nemesis on *The Godfather*, Coppola eventually became the film's director. He was hampered not only by Evans and the investors' desire for the film to have Richard Gere's role at the centre of the film (even though all the performers in the actual Cotton Club in Harlem were African-American), but also by the fact that Gere stipulated in his contract that he had to play his own cornet solos. Here Coppola's improvisation techniques, and the lack of a solid script, led to a beautiful-looking film that meandered for over two hours. Increasingly, his narrative style was described as postmodern. Yet, in his later films, despite his desire to be seen as an auteur, the weakest link in his control over his films was his inability to deliver narrative cohesion.

Gardens of Stone marked Coppola's return to two of the topics that have reoccurred throughout his work: the role of the family and Vietnam. While not well received upon its release, it is one of Coppola's most controlled, coherent films since the 1970s. Unlike *Apocalypse Now*, *Gardens of Stone* was applauded by the US military, for its portrayal of the soldiers of Arlington cemetery, whose job it was to bury the dead returning from Vietnam. In many ways, *Gardens of Stone* can be seen as a successor not to *Apocalypse Now*, but to *The Godfather* saga, where the bonds of family tie together a group of people even if they dislike the actions of the family. Gruff army-man Clell Hazard (James Caan) echoes the attitudes of Michael Corleone in the first *Godfather* film. Hazard may not want to be a part of his family's actions – in this case the US presence in Vietnam – but he will defend the family from any attacks from the outside.

Tucker: The Man and His Dreams follows the autobiographical strain that comes to dominate Coppola's work to a greater and greater degree. The film tells the story of Preston Tucker, who took on Detroit's 'big three' car producers in an attempt to produce the car of his dreams. The parallels between this vision of Tucker and Coppola's unsuccessful efforts at setting up American Zoetrope as an independent film production company are obvious. Produced by George Lucas' Lucasfilm, Coppola originally wanted to make *Tucker* as a Brechtian musical, incorporating other inventors, such as Thomas Edison and Henry Ford, into the narrative. Lucas, ever-conscious of popular tastes, encouraged Coppola to take a less radical approach to the film's style, and the director, desperate for success, followed his former protégé's advice. Yet, *Tucker* is far from a realist account of the car manufacturer's trials. The film begins in the style of a 1950s' industrial film promoting Tucker's history. Here, Coppola's aesthetic strategy is closer to the parodic tone found in John Paizs' *faux*-industrial film *Springtime in Greenland* (1981) than that of a Hollywood narrative. Throughout, Coppola deploys a hyper-realist aesthetic that captures both the nostalgia and the parodic elements of Tucker's over-the-top American ideals. Again, Coppola foregrounds form as a means of asserting an authorial voice, and in so doing produces a film that seems both sincere (in his belief in Tucker) and self-deprecating (to the extent that the film is a highly self-conscious autobiography).

Coppola returned to prominence with his adaptation of *Bram Stoker's Dracula*, in many ways the highlight of his post-*One from the Heart* career. In Coppola's hands, the story of Dracula and the image of the vampire become an allegory for the origins of the great technology of the undead: the cinema. Combining hand-cranked footage, black and white images, and sets inspired by the magical cinema of Georges Méliès, the film is as much about the pleasures and powers of the cinema itself as it is about the trials and tribulations of a lovestruck vampire.

Yet, despite these successes his career remains uneven. If *Jack* is a work-for-hire embarrassment, then Coppola's adaptation of John Grisham's *The Rainmaker* is, if not a return to the heights of *The Conversation* or the *Godfather* trilogy, then at the very least a tight narrative that takes fairly straightforward source material and turns it into a compelling film. Coppola now seems to swing back and forth between journeyman director and auteur. Increasingly, his guise as the auteur 'godfather' of New Hollywood rests on revisiting past glories, such as the release of *Apocalypse Now Redux*, which restores 'lost' footage to the film. Coppola's career unites two forms of New Hollywood: the filmmaker as artist and the blockbuster film as spectacle. After thirty years, it remains to be seen if Coppola can again amalgamate them.

Biography

Coppola was born in 1939, in Detroit, USA, to a musician father and an actress mother. He graduated in 1967 with an MFA in film from UCLA. Over a long career he has worked extensively as a producer as well as a director and scriptwriter (sharing Oscars for his work on *Patton* and *The Godfather Part II*).

Filmography

Tonight for Sure (expanded and re-edited version of *The Peeper*, both 1961)
Battle Beyond the Sun (1962) Soviet film *Nebo soyot* (1960), re-edited with new footage
The Playgirls and the Bellboy (1962)
Dementia 13 (1963)
You're a Big Boy Now (1966)
Finian's Rainbow (1968)
The Rain People (1969)
The Godfather (1972)
The Godfather Part II (1974)
The Conversation (1974)
Apocalypse Now (1979)
One from the Heart (1982)
The Outsiders (1983)
Rumble Fish (1983)
The Cotton Club (1984)
Peggy Sue Got Married (1986)
Captain Eo (1986) short
Gardens of Stone (1987)
Tucker: The Man and His Dreams (1988)
New York Stories (co-directors: Woody Allen and Martin Scorsese, 1989) segment
The Godfather Part III (1990)
Bram Stoker's Dracula (1992)
Jack (1996)
The Rainmaker (1997)
Apocalypse Now Redux (2001)

Further reading

Ronald Bergan, *Francis Coppola: The Making of His Movies*, London, Orion, 1998.
Peter Biskind, *Easy Riders, Raging Bulls: How the Sex 'n' Drugs 'n' Rock 'n' Roll Generation Saved Hollywood*, London, Bloomsbury, 1998.
Nick Browne (ed.) *Francis Ford Coppola's The Godfather Trilogy*, Cambridge, Cambridge University Press, 2000.
Jeffrey Chown, *Hollywood Auteur: Francis Coppola*, New York, Praeger, 1988.
Paul Coates, 'Coppola, or the Ambiguities of Technology', in P. Coates, *The Story of the Lost Reflection: The Alienation of the Image in Western and Polish Cinema*, London, Verso, 1985, pp. 107–12.
Eleanor Coppola, *Notes on the Making of Apocalypse Now*, London, Faber, 1995.

Roger Corman, with Jim Jerome, *How I Made a Hundred Movies in Hollywood and Never Lost a Dime*, New York, Delta, 1990.

Peter Cowie, *Coppola*, London, Faber, 1990.

—— *The Godfather Book*, London, Faber, 1997.

Robert Evans, *The Kid Stays in the Picture*, New York, Hyperion, 1994.

Howard Hampton, 'Jungle Boogie: *Apocalypse Now Redux*'s Unfinished Legacy', *Film Comment*, vol. 37, no. 3, 2001, pp. 36–42.

Pauline Kael, 'Alchemy: *The Godfather*', in P. Kael, *Deeper Into Movies*, New York, Little, Brown, 1973, pp. 528–34.

Judy Lee Kinney, 'Rituals and Remembrance: *Gardens of Stone, Platoon*, and *Hamburger Hill*', in Michael Anderegg (ed.) *Inventing Viet Nam: The War in Film and Television*, Philadelphia, PA, Temple University Press, 1991, pp. 153–65.

Harlan Lebo, *The Godfather Legacy*, New York, Fireside, 1997.

Jon Lewis, *Whom God Wishes to Destroy: Francis Coppola and the New Hollywood*, Durham, NC, Duke University Press, 1995.

Scott MacKenzie, 'Closing Arias: Operatic Montage in the Closing Sequences of the Trilogies of Coppola and Leone', *P.O.V.: Danish Journal of Film Studies*, 6 1998, pp. 109–24.

Michael Ondaatje, 'Apocalypse Again: An Interview with Walter Murch', *Guardian Weekend*, 12 May 2001, pp. 30–7.

Michael Schumacher, *Francis Ford Coppola: A Film-Maker's Life*, London, Bloomington, 1999.

William Simon, 'An Analysis of the Structure of *The Godfather, Part One*', in R. Barton Palmer (ed.) *The Cinematic Text: Methods and Approaches*, New York, AMS Press, 1989, pp. 101–17.

SCOTT MACKENZIE

DAVID CRONENBERG

Canadian director David Cronenberg is the most challenging and controversial auteur to emerge from the post-1968 horror/science fiction boom. Belonging to a generation of maverick male outsiders who cut their cinematic teeth in the culturally disreputable genre of low-budget horror (among them George Romero, Wes Craven, Tobe Hooper and John Carpenter), he has managed to sustain and develop his career to the point where he is now critically regarded as a major contemporary director: a new Cronenberg movie is a cinematic event. A mild, conformist family man in person – his publicity photos still make him look like an erudite mature Ph.D. student, and in interviews he is serious, attentive, always willing to explicate his view of his work – he has none the less never entirely thrown off the somewhat lurid reputation of Dave 'Deprave' Cronenberg, the 'King of Venereal Horror' and the 'Baron of

Blood', which was quickly established with his early shockers *Shivers*, *Rabid*, *The Brood*, *Scanners* and *Videodrome*. His subsequent move into the commercial mainstream with *The Dead Zone* and *The Fly* and into the more openly arty and character-centred dramas of *Dead Ringers*, *Naked Lunch*, *M. Butterfly* and *Crash*, have increasingly tended to downplay body horror in favour of aesthetic and psychological contemplation, while his most recent movie, *eXistenZ*, is a multifaceted reprise of many of his themes and concerns. In fact, for all their visceral gore, the early films are also intellectual and experimental and the later ones still include a bodily gross-out factor. While avoiding the temptation to press Cronenberg's work into perfect auteurist coherence (any body of work worth its salt resists this), it is nevertheless the case that his *œuvre* to date reveals remarkable consistencies and continuities.

One reason for this is that Cronenberg is an author as well as an auteur, writing or adapting the screenplays for most of his movies. As a child he read voraciously, from the modernists to science fiction, and he cites Vladimir Nabokov and William Burroughs, rather than any filmmakers, as his artistic precursors. He wrote his first, three-page 'novel' at the age of 10, won a short story prize as a college freshman, and intended to become a novelist until he discovered the magic of film through the work of his University of Toronto student peer David Sector. (Cronenberg was thrilled to see his friends and the campus on celluloid and has always preferred to work in and around his home city of Toronto.) As a scriptwriter he has been able (unlike many Hollywood auteurs) to exercise considerable control over his material and it is noticeable that the films which he has had no hand in writing – the little known drag car racing actioner, *Fast Company*, the psychic thriller, *The Dead Zone*, adapted by Jeffrey Boam from a Stephen King novel, and David Hwang's screen version of his play *M. Butterfly* – have most often been labelled 'unCronenbergian'.

A second reason is the clinical gaze which informs the look and style of Cronenberg's films. This may partly stem from his lifelong passion for science in general and biochemistry in particular. No doubt mischievously, Cronenberg has identified himself with the bespectacled Mantle twins in the early scenes of *Dead Ringers*, whose childlike yet ultimately lethal fascination with the mysteries of sex, reproduction and the human (especially female) body is dramatized by their early experiment in 'inter-ovular surgery'. Indeed, he began studying biochemistry at university before switching to English because he found his tutors' academic approach too dry and dull. He is, in a sense, a scientist-artist, whose work has repeatedly been viewed as cool and detached, favouring deadpan acting, distancing the spectator and refusing the consolations of identification. Such apparent coldness and aloofness has sometimes been equated with a reifying and pornographic consciousness, seen as analagous to scientific method. Yet equally discernible in the movies is a complex, if ambiguous, displaced and sometimes repressed range of emotions, from icy fury (*The Brood*) to black comedy (*Shivers*) and even accessible sentimentality (*The Fly*). Promoting *Crash*, Cronenberg expressed his surprise that for him it had become a very emotional movie.

Writing and the clinical/emotional gaze fuse in Cronenberg's conception of cinema as a hotline to the contemporary unconscious. As Michael O'Pray[1] and others have argued, his films give symbolic and narrative shape to primitive unconscious fantasies and fears, centring on the human subject as a traumatized body and/or mind, playing out the horror genre's pervasive themes of separation, ageing, disease, invasion, decay and death in a series of literalized metaphors which unflinchingly detail grotesque and abject bodily and psychic mutation. Early on, critics (notably Wood)[2] noticed that a kind of Cronenbergian Ur-Text or generative formula underlay the movies, based on the trope of the mad scientist so often found in sci-fi/horror: a male scientist figure (usually with a bizarre name), often located in a formal institution (also with a bizarre name), invents or disseminates something which is of potential benefit to humanity but which turns out to have disastrous consequences.

Thus in Cronenberg's first, underground, movie, *Stereo*, the theories of absent parapsychologist Luther Stringfellow concerning the possibilities of telepathic communication are tested at the Canadian Academy for Erotic Inquiry; violence and suicide ensue when the experiment's subjects are isolated from one another. This telepathic theme is reprised in *Scanners*, where the cynical Dr Paul Ruth (Patrick McGoohan), sponsored by the conspiratorial organization ConSec, has invented the pre-natal drug ephemerol which produces telepathic 'scanner' children, the most potent avatars being his own sons, the 'good' Cameron Vale (Stephen Lack) and the 'evil' Darryl Revok (Michael Ironside). A comparable pattern underlies the progression from the underground *Crimes of the Future* to the breakthrough features *Shivers* and *Rabid*. In *Crimes*, the disciple of (once again absent) dermatologist Antoine Rouge, Adrian Tripod (Ronald Mlodzick), seeks a cure for Rouge's malady, a disease caused by cosmetics which has killed all sexually mature women and threatens humanity with extinction; while in

Shivers an aphrodisiac parasite, invented by Dr Emil Hobbes (Fred Doederlin), passes between the denizens of a luxury high-rise block. In the follow-up *Rabid* Dr Dan Keloid (Howard Ryshpan), pioneer of 'neutralized' tissue transplants at the eponymous Keloid Clinic, attempts to save the life of 'girl on a motorcycle' accident victim Rose (Marilyn Chambers), instead transforming her into a naturalized blood-sucking vampire with a sexual neo-organ secreted in her armpit, which resembles an anus when dormant and a penis/knife/syringe when active, who turns her victims into violent zombies, creating an epidemic in the environs of Montreal. This generative formula also fits, to varying degrees, *The Brood*, *Videodrome*, *The Fly*, *Dead Ringers*, *Naked Lunch* (where the sinister Dr Benway (Roy Scheider) controls the supply of the black powder narcotic made from giant centipede meat), *Crash* (where Vaughan (Elias Koteas) fulfils the mad scientist function) and *eXistenZ*. Once again the films which the model does not fit are those which Cronenberg did not script (the scientist figure in *The Dead Zone* is merely a witness to the magnitude of Johnny Smith's (Christopher Walken) newly acquired psychic powers).

Feminist critics have attacked Cronenberg's work for its hostility towards women, and it is certainly the case that patriarchal fantasies and anxieties surrounding gender difference provide its symbolic foundation (as they do for much of the horror genre and mainstream cinema more generally). What Cronenberg's movies offer, however, are especially graphic and literal manifestations of the contemporary patriarchal unconscious which are arguably as critical of as they are collusive with the issues of male desire and control they exhibit. It is also the case that although men and masculine-coded institutions are the source of the mutations in the movies, the effects on individuals' bodies and psyches transform men too, albeit usually through a problematic feminization of male characters.

Shivers (aka *The Parasite Murders* and *They Came from Within*) is a case in point. A limit text in visceral horror, the mutations wrought by Hobbes' parasites, a combination of aphrodisiac and venereal disease shaped like penile turds, affect men, women and children alike, turning them into rapacious Romero-like zombies who gleefully embody the polymorphous perverse. Shot on a shoestring budget of Can$180,000 on location outside Montreal, the fictional luxury Starliner Towers apartment complex is coded as an alienated bourgeois space awaiting (deserving?) sexual apocalypse. Following the title sequence in which publicity stills and an insincere voice-over market the Towers to the accompaniment of wistful, almost fatalistic music, the relentless narrative begins with Hobbes assaulting, cutting open and pouring acid into the belly of the young woman in whom he has implanted the parasite, before slitting his own throat. It looks like a rape and snuff movie, however, it is not nearly that simple. If the film's most memorable instants centre on women's bodies – the parasite swimming between Betts' (Barbara Steele) legs, or passing up her oesophagus and down Janine Tudor's (Susan Petrie) in a hedonistic moment of lesbian seduction – it is nevertheless male birth images played out on the body of Janine's husband, Nick (Allan Migicovsky), which are most consistently developed. Bugs move about under his stomach and ooze disgustingly from his mouth, parody offspring which (or is it whom?) he addresses with affection: 'Come on boy! Come on fella! You and me are going to be good friends.' This is Cronenberg's philosophy entirely; he regards the outcome of *Shivers*, as the inhabitants drive off serenely to infect the world, as a happy one.

Men's anxiety and jealousy concerning women's reproductive powers motivate Cronenberg's best movies to date, *The Brood*, *The Fly* and *Dead Ringers*, which may be termed the 'Womb Trilogy'. As Barbara Creed and Helen W. Robbins have demonstrated, these films offer elaborate womb fantasies, manifesting both horror at women's power to create life and male attempts to destroy, emulate or control it (indeed, this is arguably the power, possessed in religious discourse by God and in aesthetics by the Artist, which all Cronenberg's mad scientists seek to acquire).[3] The outcome, of course, is mayhem and destruction but there is a shift – in terms, at least, of the trilogy's chronology – towards men becoming victims of their own repressed desires.

The Brood is family horror in the evil-children-and-monstrous-births cycle inaugurated by Polanski's *Rosemary's Baby* (1968). Set in and around a bleak, wintry Toronto (images seem cold enough to freeze and cut), its scientist is Dr Hal Raglan (Oliver Reed), opportunist head of the Somafree Institute of Psychoplasmics, where residents are encouraged to externalize their psychic traumas on their own bodies. His star patient, Nola Carveth (Samantha Eggar), is afflicted by childhood parental abuse and estrangement from her husband Frank (Art Hindle), who determines to gain custody of their young daughter Candy (Cindy Hinds) when she returns from a visit to her mother covered in bruises. Howard Shore's dissonant music underscores the brutal murders of those against whom Nola has grievances – her parents, Candy's teacher (guilty only of babysitting) – by the Brood, snow-suit-clad 'children' with an uncanny resemblance to Candy (and to the killer dwarf in Roeg's *Don't Look Now*, 1973). Hermeneutic mystery surrounds their identities, the film's drawn-out climax detailing Raglan's murder by the offspring of his therapy and revealing, in an abject spectacle witnessed by Frank, that the Brood are mutants born from a literally hysterical womb on the outside of Nola's body. The sight of Nola, kneeling in hieratic white robes, biting open the sac and licking her latest 'child' clean, is another landmark in visceral cinema (one trimmed by the censor), not least because of its close proximity to the mess of natural birth. True to 1970s' horror, the nightmare continues (the sequel can be made), as the lumps on Candy's arm in the closing shot reveal her tragic inheritance. Written during his own marital break-up and child custody battle, Cronenberg has called *The Brood* his *Kramer versus Kramer* and acknowledged the rage ('the brood') at its heart as his own.

In *The Brood* the father escapes with the daughter; the scientist and the partner/mother die. *The Fly* and *Dead Ringers* mutate this pattern; the scientists die, the women survive. *The Fly*, Cronenberg's second mainstream movie, made on a (by his standards huge) budget of US$10 million, is by far his most popular film to date. Casting relatively big name stars, Jeff Goldblum and Geena Davis (then romantically involved), in the roles of techno-magician Seth Brundle and science journalist Veronica 'Ronny' Quaife, it combines gross-out horror with a moving love triangle melodrama (the third is Ronny's ex-lover magazine boss Stathis Borans (John Getz)). Inventor of a patently womb-like 'designer phone booth' which can transfer matter, at the outset Seth can only teleport inanimate objects (Ronnie's erotically charged stocking); when he learns about 'the flesh', however, he is able to teleport first a baboon and then, in a fit of drunken pique when he thinks that Ronnie has abandoned him for Borans, himself, unfortunately along with a common housefly with which he becomes genetically spliced. Cue an extraordinarily affecting mutation from charming, naïve geek to repulsive hybrid species, which may be interpreted as a metaphor for AIDS, BSE or other diseases, but which equally (from Ronnie's perspective) shows your loved one ageing rapidly and horribly as you look on helplessly. Seth's hubris infects Ronnie too; in his sexual athlete phase he impregnates her, and the nightmare sequence in which she is delivered of a hideous maggot by none other than the director himself – in due acknowledgement of his own art as a case of rampant womb envy? – is a shocking monstrous birth fantasy. *The Fly*'s brilliance derives from its use of horror coding to articulate melodramatic meaning. Horror iconography serves and develops the tragic love story, as when Brundlefly resembles the Hunchback of Notre Dame claiming his Esmerelda, or (having fused with his own creation, the telepod), in his final, terrible mutant form he pleads for release with still-soulful eyes.

Dead Ringers, for many Cronenberg's masterpiece to date (it won a Genie Award for Best Film and Screenplay and the Los Angeles Film Critic's Award for Best Director), is womb envy cinema *par excellence*. On the surface a sombre tragic drama, charting through its obsessively controlled *mise-en-scène* and pacing the decline of identical gynaecologist twins Elliot and Beverly Mantle (both played by Jeremy Irons), underneath it is a classic of nightmare cinema, the out of genre horror movie which prevailed in the 1980s.[4] Specializing in making women fertile, the Mantles are fascinated by 'trifurcate' actress Claire Niveau (Genevieve Bujold), a 'mutant' woman and expert in promiscuity, masochism and drugs, who destabilizes their lives when she threatens to separate them, being the first thing which they have not been able to share fully. The movie implies that they are two bodies with one soul, its most explicit horror sequence depicting them organically joined at the abdomen like Siamese twins, with Claire biting through the tissue. The narrative's trajectory as a melancholy chronicle of control, torture and loss is traced by the transition from their 1967 prize-winning Mantle Retractor (though even back then, their tutor remarks 'it might be fine for a cadaver but it won't work with a living person') to Bev's invention, twenty years later, of 'gynaecological instruments for operating on mutant women', his use of which finally gets the twins banned from practice (their symbolic importance is signalled through their presence as cruel aesthetic specimens in the title sequence). As Elliot (now feminized as 'Ellie') takes drugs to 'synchronize' himself with Bev, Bev uses these instruments to try and separate them, opening up his own twin where his womb should be and killing him. Their unresolved masochistic desires have re-figured them as the real mutant women, the true objects of their lifelong gynaecological quest.

The closing shot of *Dead Ringers*, the half-naked Bev draped over Ellie, plays as an almost Derek Jarman-like queer tableau and raises the question of the possible gay subtext in Cronenberg's cinema. Though little dwelt upon, there is a strain of homoerotic imagery in the movies, running from the sensibility of his gay friend Ron Mlodzik which suffuses *Stereo* and *Crimes of the Future* through *Dead Ringers* (surely Bev and Ellie are 'really' gay?) to *eXistenZ*

(Willem Dafoe 'plugging' Jude Law). Just where we might expect queer Cronenberg, however, as in his adaptations of Burroughs' *Naked Lunch* and J.G. Ballard's *Crash*, it is the powerful hetero-sexuality of his concerns which is overbearingly stressed. For all the gay erotics of male collaboration that might be read into Cronenberg's *Fly*-like 'fusion' with Burroughs, the movie downplays the homosexuality of its sources, foregrounding Joan Lee's/Frost's (Judy Davis) role as literary muse and offering in its one gay coupling, the ruthless decadent Cloquet (Julian Sands) taking the beautiful boy Kiki (Joseph Scorsiani), the movie's most grotesque horror image. Similarly, while Ballard's circular novel can be read as the love letter of the narrator Ballard to his perverse mentor Vaughan and its sexual encounters peak with their intercourse (admittedly only after they have dropped some acid), Cronenberg marginalizes all this, restructuring the plot to focus on the Ballards' marriage and the quest to initiate the pristine Catherine (Deborah Kara Unger) into the erotic cult of car crash wounds. (See Sinclair for a counter-argument to this.[5]) *M. Butterfly* also, among the least discussed and assimilated of the films, unfolds what is literally a homosexual affair, between a French diplomat (Jeremy Irons, again) and a Beijing Opera male impersonator (John Lone), under the guise of heterosexuality.

Mutations of the gendered subject also underpin *Videodrome* and *eXistenZ*, each concerned with the power of the media to effect transformation. Hailed as the summation of Cronenberg's career to date on its appearance in 1982, *Videodrome*'s special effects – the vaginal opening in Max Renn's (James Woods) abdomen into which cassettes are inserted, the lethal hand/gun which melds the human and the technological – remain startling and arresting and Debbie Harry's presence as the sadomasochistic Nicki Brand perpetuates its cult status. However, the film's 1950s' style conspiracy theories about the dangers of television and its heady confusions of reality and hallucination look strangely dated twenty years on. *eXistenZ*, amazingly Cronenberg's first wholly original screenplay since *Videodrome*, is almost *Videodrome: Part II*, replacing television with semi-organic game pods which jack directly into players' spines via an anal-looking bioport and induce all-too-real hallucinations. Arguably its most memorable effect, the gun constructed by Ted Pikul (Law) from the leftovers of a vile-looking meal, directly recalls its predecessor, suggesting that Cronenberg is currently treading water (as he did, perhaps, throughout the 1990s) in his search for the right new material.

Biography

Cronenberg was born in Toronto, Canada, in 1943. He was educated at the University of Toronto, and gained a BA in Literature in 1967.

Notes

1 Michael O'Pray, 'Primitive Fantasies in Cronenberg's Films', in Wayne Drew (ed.), *BFI Dossier 21: David Cronenberg*, London, BFI Publishing, 1984, pp. 48–53.
2 Robin Wood, 'Cronenberg: A Dissenting View', in Piers Handling (ed.) *The Shape of Rage: The Films of David Cronenberg*, Toronto, Academy of Canadian Cinema, General Publishing Company, 1983, pp. 115–35.
3 Barbara Creed, *The Monstrous Feminine: Film, Feminism, Psychoanalysis*, London, Routledge, 1993, pp. 43–58; Helen W. Robbins, '"More Human Than I Am Alone": Womb Envy in David Cronenberg's *The Fly* and *Dead Ringers*', in Steven Cohan and Ina Rae Hark (eds) *Screening the Male: Exploring Masculinities in Hollywood Cinema*, London, Routledge, 1993, pp. 134–47.
4 See Kim Newman, *Nightmare Movies*, London, Bloomsbury, 1988.
5 Iain Sinclair, *Crash: David Cronenberg's Post-mortem on J. G. Ballard's 'Trajectory of Fate'*, London, BFI Publishing, 1999.

Filmography

Transfer (1966) short
From the Drain (1967) short
Stereo (1969)
Crimes of the Future (1970)
Shivers (1975)
Rabid (1976)
Fast Company (1979)
The Brood (1979)
Scanners (1980)
Videodrome (1982)
The Dead Zone (1983)
The Fly (1986)
Dead Ringers (1988)
Naked Lunch (1991)
M. Butterfly (1993)
Crash (1996)
eXistenZ (1999)

Further reading

Michael Grant (ed.) *The Modern Fantastic: The Films of David Cronenberg*, Trowbridge, Flicks Books, 2000.

Chris Rodley (ed.) *Cronenberg on Cronenberg*, London, Faber and Faber, 1996 (rev. edn).

MARC O'DAY

JULIE DASH

Writer, producer and director of the critically acclaimed *Daughters of the Dust*, Julie Dash was the first African-American female to have a feature-length film in theatrical distribution. Named Film of the Century by the Newark Black Film Festival, *Daughters of the Dust* embodies the radical potential of narrative cinema in its reclamation of African-American history and culture, its negotiation of the intersection of gender and race, and its construction of African-American female subjectivity. It exemplifies what Toni Cade Bambara has called 'oppositional cinema', a re-vision of narrative film from a female-centred, Africentric perspective.[1] In all her work, Dash's desire is to 'redefine images of black women'.[2] She writes:

> We all become who we are through the intersections of histories and personal influences. ... What I accomplish as an independent filmmaker is in line with the legacies of pioneer filmmakers like William Foster, George and Noble Johnson, Zora Neale Hurston, Oscar Micheaux, Spencer Williams, William Alexander, and many names now forgotten in the struggle to create an African American Cinema for this past century.[3]

An homage to this legacy, Dash's breakthrough black-and-white short, *Illusions*, not only explicitly challenges the sexism and racism of mainstream cinema, but also theorizes and exemplifies an 'oppositional' narrative film. Set in Hollywood in 1942, the year the NAACP (National Association for the Advancement of Colored People) met to convince studio moguls that more African-Americans should be positioned on- and off-screen, *Illusions* focuses on Mignon Dupree (Lonette McKee). As an African-American studio executive passing as white, Mignon 'want[s] to use the power of the motion picture'.[4] Dash expresses a similar ambition:

> [*Illusions*] intentionally mimics the form and conventions of Hollywood films of the thirties and forties. But by

embedding certain foreign objects in the form – the protagonist Mignon, for example – I've attempted to throw the form into relief, hopefully making all of the sexist and racist assumptions of that form stick out.[5]

Illusions opens with a quote from Ralph Ellison's 'The Shadow and the Act' in a voice-over juxtaposed with a swirling Oscar, followed by a cut to documentary footage of white soldiers, and shortly thereafter, to an African-American janitor cleaning the glass on the outer door of the white studio executive's office. These four components clearly delineate the extant racial perimeters of mainstream cinema (and US society), as well as the transformative possibility of this cinema that *Illusions* takes as its theme. The voice-over ('to direct an attack upon Hollywood would indeed be to confuse portrayal with action, image with reality. In the beginning was not the shadow, but the act, and the province of Hollywood is not action, but illusion') acknowledges the racism of Hollywood film, but also emphasizes that such depictions mirror the racism of the society which produces such films. The 'reality' of society's racism is depicted by the African-American janitor in a subservient position outside the studio door, excluded from the inner sanctum of Hollywood power. However, this scene immediately suggests that the opposition between 'image' and 'reality' is less clear-cut than Ellison may have presumed since the 'reality' of the janitor's off-screen position in Hollywood simultaneously represents the exclusion of African-Americans from on-screen Hollywood. Just as the twirling Oscar acknowledges the recognition and fame garnered by Hollywood films, implying the power of images, the presence of the documentary footage, snippets from the province of the cinema of the 'real', demonstrates how easily subjective imagery elides into 'objective' reality: no African-American soldiers appear in this footage. But as Mignon later states: 'The real history, the history that most people will remember and believe in, is what they see on the silver screen.'

Thus the film's opening moments acknowledge both the power of cinematic illusion and its exclusionary foundations. *Illusions* is not simply an attack upon racism in Hollywood and US society; it also theorizes the possibility of a transformative narrative cinema which would give voice to the voiceless and make the absent present (making visible the heretofore 'invisible man', the African-American janitor). If, as the passing Mignon observes, her studio cohorts 'see me, but they cannot recognize me', *Illusions* assures that its audience will 'recognize' her. And, in recognizing her, the audience also recognizes the possibility of African-American female subjectivity.

This recognition also comes through Mignon's relationship with an African-American singer, Ester Jeeter (Rosanne Katon). Although Ester dreams of being on-screen, she makes her living dubbing the singing voices of white stars. When the sound on a new musical is out of synch, Ester is hired to dub the blonde star's musical number with Mignon in charge of the process. We see Mignon standing behind the glass of the recording booth, looking out into the studio, but positioned between the reflections of two white male sound engineers. Ambiguity predominates: Mignon towers over them, but is contained by their reflections. Moments afterward, Mignon's gaze frames Ester and the microphone on the left and the dubbing room film screen on the right, blank (and white) at first and later filled with the blonde actress lip-synching. As Judith Mayne has elucidated, while the Hollywood screen functions as a barrier, what Mignon imagines and what the viewer literally sees is a new film with Ester as subject.[6] The subsequent cuts from a close-up of the white star to close-ups of Ester make explicit that what we are watching is a new cinema, born from the relationship between Ester and Mignon, negotiated through African-American female spectatorship, and predicated on making 'real' African-American female subjectivity.

After the dubbing session, Mignon and Ester (who immediately recognizes her as an African-American woman) discuss Mignon's position, sharing their dreams and aspirations about the movies. At one point they stand together at the doorway of a huge sound stage. Shot from the interior of the building, the foreground of the frame is black, with the figures of Mignon and Ester silhouetted in an extreme long shot against the extreme whiteness of the sunlight outside the doorway. Mignon tells Ester, 'There's no joy in the seduction of false images'. However, the composition of the shot implies that they are poised on the threshold of possibility. With their backs to the blinding white state of current cinema, they stare into the blackness of the sound stage and the potentiality of a new Black cinema is foregrounded, just as the promise of a cinema which centres its gaze on Ester and Mignon is affirmed. The Black Filmmaker Foundation's Film of the Decade, *Illusions* is a particularly important film in Dash's career, foregrounding characteristics central to her work: her espousal of narrative, revelry in the pleasure of the visual, embrace of 'Afro-American expressive traditions', and her delight in the representation of the diverse beauty of African-American women.[7]

Dash's first experience with film came as a high school student in the late 1960s when she attended an after-school programme at the Studio Museum in Harlem, New York. Initially fascinated by the 'mechanics' of filmmaking, by her junior year at City College, she had become a film production major.[8] Introduced to the African-American literary tradition, she found inspirational the works of its women writers, especially Toni Cade Bambara, Toni Morrison, Paule Marshall, Alice Walker and Zora Neale Hurston. In particular, she was influenced by Bambara's circular narrative structures and deviation from the 'male Western narrative', and Morrison's 'depth of character'.[9] After producing her first film, *Working Models for Success*, a promotional documentary for the New York Urban Coalition, she discovered that 'people in the community want[ed] to see a *story*', and she resolved to work with narrative film.[10]

Thus, upon graduation, Dash journeyed to Los Angeles and the American Film Institute (AFI). At the AFI, one of her teachers, Slavko Vorkapich, the well-known montagist, greatly influenced her sense of film aesthetics. Also influential, however, were her fellow students, half of whom came from outside the States. She found their 'non-western', non-formulaic work 'bold' and filled with more 'dynamic' shots than typical Hollywood films.[11] The seven-minute experimental dance film, *Four Women*, reflects these concerns in its interpretation of the Nina Simone ballad. In 1978, *Four Women* received the gold medal for Women in Film at the Miami International Film Festival, the first of Dash's many awards.

Dash then moved to UCLA's graduate film school. In the midst of the social and political upheaval of the period, the university was challenged by its students. Out of this struggle, and through the efforts of Haile Gerima, Charles Burnett, Larry Clark, John Reir, Ben Caldwell, Pamela Jones, Abdosh Abdulhafiz and Jam Fanaka, the Black Independent filmmaking movement at UCLA was born. Named the 'L.A. Rebellion' by film scholar Clyde Taylor, it had as its goal the establishment of an 'independent Black film enterprise that was true to their cultural roots and contested the falsification of African American history by Hollywood'.[12] Dash, Alile Sharon Larkin, Bill Woodberry and Bernard Nichols were part of the 'second wave'. A study group 'screened and discussed socially conscious cinema from directors like Satyajit Ray, Yasujiro Ozu, Ousmane Sembene, Humberto Solas, and Sara Gomez'.[13] Their influence is evident in Dash's *Diary of an African Nun*, an adaptation of a short story by Alice Walker. This lyrical film, in which 'the protagonist struggles with the conflict that develops when her adopted Christian beliefs are intruded upon by the traditional African beliefs of her community', gained Dash a Director's Guild Award for student film.[14]

Four Women, *Diary of an African Nun* and *Illusions* exemplify the evolution of Dash's vision. All acknowledge a black female spectator, de-centre the white male gaze, and revel in a story-telling tradition that dates from the first African griot. They are critically important not only in terms of the history of black independent film, but in terms of the history of *all* independent film. *Diary of an African Nun* and *Illusions*, in particular, demonstrated not only the transformative power and radical potential of narrative film, but also posed a challenge to the unacknowledged racism of the feminist film movement. By engaging with the intersection of race and gender (and later, sexual identity) in her films, Dash spurred the creation of an inclusive feminist film movement which now includes such filmmakers as Michelle Parkerson, Trinh T. Minh Ha, Cheryl Dunye and Midi Onodera.

It was Dash's first full-length feature film, *Daughters of the Dust*, which transformed forever the face (literally and figuratively) of filmmaking, both independent and mainstream. Here, her gifts of story-telling and visual aesthetics come to full fruition in a film which Greg Tate has called 'an unparalleled and unprecedented achievement in terms of both world cinema and African aesthetics'.[15] Set in 1902 at Ibo Landing in the Sea Islands, off the coast of Georgia and South Carolina, *Daughters of the Dust* is the story of the Peazant family and the northern migration of some of its members. As a stopping place after the Middle Passage and before slaves were taken to the slave market in Charleston, the Sea Islands, because of their isolation from the mainland, have the 'strongest retention of African culture', as reflected in its Gullah culture's dialect, food and rituals.[16]

Steeped in a history, myth and tradition never before seen in full-length narrative film, *Daughters of the Dust* focuses on the women in the family (characters based on African deities). The camera celebrates the beauty of their diversity by lingering on a broad range of skin tones, hairstyles and body types. The head of the family and its spiritual centre is the elderly Nana Peazant (Cora Lee Day), an ex-slave who worries that in moving away from this land, her family will also move away from the ancestors, and thus, the traditions, histories and other 'scraps of memories' which have given the family the strength to triumph over slavery, Reconstruction, and beyond. Recognizing that her family 'ain't going to no land of milk and honey', Nana calls on the ancestors to help ensure that the family's connection with them is honoured and maintained. The ancestors send the Unborn Child (Kai-Lynn Warren) of Eli and Eula Peazant (Alva Rogers and Adisa Anderson) both to help Nana and to reconcile Eli and Eula, who are in turmoil because the pregnant Eula was raped by a white man. Although the Unborn Child represents the future, it is a future predicated on the necessity of remembering the past.

Neither the Unborn Child, nor Nana Peazant, are able to touch and transform Haagar (Kaycee Moore), who married into the Peazant family and who becomes Nana's nemesis. Haagar, anxious to move away from Nana Peazant and her 'hoodoo mess', is eager to embrace the urban North. Other Peazant women are poised between the beliefs of the two. Viola (Cheryl Lynn Bruce), who has returned from the North with a photographer, Mr Snead (Tommy Hicks), in order to document the Peazant family's leave-taking, is fearful of Nana's beliefs because of the Baptist Christianity she has adopted. She urges a renunciation of the old ways, but, unlike Haagar, her respect for Nana makes it difficult for her to sever her connection. Yellow Mary (Barbara-O), the most urbane of the Peazant women, has also returned from her journeys for this special occasion. Accompanied by her lover, Trula (Trula Hoosier), she is scorned by most of the older women (except Nana) because of her light complexion and because of this 'thing' (Trula) she brought with her, but mostly because she got 'ruint' and is a prostitute. At the end of the film, with the intercession of Nana, the Unborn Child and the ancestors, all of the Peazant family, except Trula and Haagar, maintain their connection to the old ways and 'old souls' and in so doing are given the strength to carry on.

Daughters of the Dust is rich in its diversity, encompassing aspects of African-American culture and history. It refers to the ongoing history of the rape of black women by white men; the anti-lynching movement; the entwined history of Native Americans and African-Americans; the varieties of African-American religions; the importance of myth and oral tradition to African-American culture; the enrichment of US culture through African and African-American traditions, language and philosophy; the attempted infestation of African-American culture with white patriarchal ideology; the depiction of an agrarian African-American history; and so on.

In its depiction of this suppressed history, and bolstered by years of intensive research, the film overflows with ethnographic detail. However, Dash had no desire to make an ethnographic film. Rather, she characterizes the film as 'speculative fiction'.[17] Thus, its ideology, script, structure and cinematography are far removed from both the purview of ethnographic cinema and the conventions of mainstream narrative cinema. The structure is not plot-driven; the story 'unravels [in] much the same way that an African griot would recount a family's history'.[18] In addition to this 'Africentric grounding', Dash uses multiple voice-overs, and, in collaboration with cinematographer Arthur Jafa, and production designer, Kerry Marshall, utilizes 'multiple point-of-view camera work'; 'wide-angled and deep-focus shots in which no one becomes a backdrop to anyone else's drama'; camera placement inside groups, rather than outside looking in; and off-centre framing of characters, as well as deep-focus long shots and extreme long shots, so that the environment seems to become a character, too.[19] The production was shot exclusively in natural light. Jafa, 'question[ing] ... whether the standard of twenty-four frames per second rate is kinesthetically the best for rendering the black experience', frequently slows down certain scenes, emphasizing spirituality and the connection between the present and the future to the past and the ancestors.[20]

Dash's vision was not welcomed with open arms or wallets; as Erhart notes, *Daughters of the Dust* 'is less a product of its time than a product in spite of its time'.[21] Inspired by her own Gullah family and by photos of African-American women taken in the early twentieth century by James Van Der Zee, Dash first conceptualized the film in 1975. In 1986, after eleven years of research, Dash was ready to shoot the film, but could get only enough funding to shoot a sample. Hopeful that actually seeing what the film would look like would generate funds, Dash, even with the sample, a completed script and an award-winning filmography, was unable to secure money from either Hollywood or European sources. Eventually she received $800,000 from the Public Broadcasting System's *American Playhouse* and began shooting late in 1989 – with only twenty-eight days in which to complete the film and no money for post-production. In the following year Dash worked on editing, completing the final cut at the end of 1990 with grants from the Rockefeller Foundation and the National Black Programming Consortium.

Dash encountered the same problems with distributors that she had with investors. She later speculated that since 'role-playing' can be a part of the viewing experience, white men, including distributors, '[did] not want to be a black woman for two hours. That's two hours too long.'[22] Distributors told her that there was no market for such a film, so she took it to film festivals – including Sundance (where it received the award for best cinematography), Munich, London and Toronto. Finally, it was picked up by a small New York distributing company, Kino International, and opened in January 1992.

As with the potential investors and distributors before them, some white reviewers had a problem with the film. B. Ruby Rich, likening it to Isaac Julien's *Looking for Langston* and Lourdes Portillo's and Susana Muñoz's *La Ofrenda: The Days of the Dead*, notes that white critics attacked these films for their beauty. 'People of color are expected to produce films of victimization', she writes, positing that because these films 'look at the richness of their cultures instead of their poverty', the films evoke 'aesthetic envy' from white critics.[23] None the less, upon its release, *Daughters of the Dust* sold out in theatres across the US. Even with non-comprehending white critics and without an expensive advertising campaign or bookings into multiplex theatres, during its first year of release, *Daughters of the Dust* grossed over $1 million.

After its release and its warm reception by the audiences who had an opportunity to see it, there was much speculation that *Daughters of the Dust*, as well as the films of Darnell Martin, Spike Lee, John Singleton, Matty Rich, Bill Duke, Charles Burnett, and so forth, had ushered in a new 'black film wave' which would 'take responsibility for *framing blackness* away from Hollywood'.[24] Dash herself was hopeful, speculating in a 1991 interview that:

> we are going to start seeing a lot of work by Black women independent filmmakers and I think it's going to ... make a lot of young Black women happy and inspire them and address their needs ... it's all going to come together in the '90s.[25]

Near the end of the decade, however, Dash said 'Black women have not ridden in on the wave of the New Black Cinema ... and there haven't been any signs that they will.'[26] Although Hollywood wooed her, she received no offers to direct a theatrical feature film but did direct two feature-length films for the cable network, Black

Entertainment Television: *Incognito* and *Funny Valentines*, as well as a segment of HBO's *Subway Stories*. She also made two shorts in the 1990s, both for the Public Broadcasting System: *Relatives*, a dance film featuring Ishamel Huston Jones, and *Praise House*, performed by Urban Bush Women and directed a number of music videos for African-American artists. Dash also published a novel, *Daughters of the Dust*, revisiting the Peazant family, with the addition of new characters.

While the importance of Dash's cinematic achievements cannot be overestimated, it is telling, and unfortunate, that she has not secured the financial support to write and direct her own films. She 'sees herself as in and out of Hollywood' because she uses its crews and would use its money, but does not want to 'duplicate the Hollywood popcorn fodder'.[27] She explains: 'I want to do the films that *I* want to do', and for this reason, she is 'not locked into features; for [her] it's about making films and showing Black women in ways that have not been seen before. It's about moving people, about disseminating information.'[28] With or without support from Hollywood, but with inspiration from black women filmmakers of the past and present – Kathleen Collins, Jackie Shearer, Sara Gomez, Madeline Anderson, Neema Barnette, Barbara McCullough, Euzhan Palcy, Michelle Parkerson and Darnell Martin – Dash will continue to create a profound and influential cinematic legacy.[29] Mignon and Ester were left poised on the threshold of cinematic possibility, but Julie Dash has taken her camera through that doorway and has shown us the promise of African-American women's cinema.

Biography

Julie Dash was born in New York City, USA, in 1952. In 1969 she attended the Studio Museum of Harlem before undertaking a BA in Film Production at the City College of New York. She then attended the Center for Advanced Film Studies at the American Film Institute and received an MFA from UCLA.

Acknowledgement

Thanks to Mijoung Chang at Women Make Movies, distributor of *Illusions*, *Praise House* and *The Cinematic Jazz of Julie Dash*, for providing me with video copies. Contact information: http://www.wmm.com./

Notes

1 Toni Cade Bambara, 'Preface', in Julie Dash, *Daughters of the Dust: The Making of an African American Woman's Film*, New York, New Press, 1992, p. xiii.

2 J. M. Redding and V. Brownworth, *Film Fatales: Independent Women Directors*, Seattle, Seal Press, 1997, p. 192.

3 Julie Dash (1995) *Daughters of the Dust: Secrets and Whispers*. Online. Available HTTP: < http://www.geechee.com > (accessed 18 November 1999).

4 Julie Dash, *Illusions*, in P. Klotman (ed.) *Screenplays of the African American Experience*, Bloomington, Indiana University Press, 1991, p. 212.

5 K. Harris, 'New Images: An Interview with Julie Dash and Alile Sharon Larkin', *Independent* 9, 10, 1986, p. 18.

6 Judith Mayne, *The Woman at the Keyhole*, Bloomington, Indiana University Press, 1990, p. 64.

7 K. Harris, *op. cit.* p. 18.

8 H. Baker Jr and Julie Dash (1992) 'Not without My Daughters: A Conversation with Julie Dash and Houston Baker, Jr.', *Transition 57*, 1992, p. 153.

9 *Ibid.*, pp. 150–1.

10 *Ibid.*, p. 154.

11 *Ibid.*, p. 158.

12 C. Taylor, 'The L.A. Rebellion: New Spirit in American Film', *Black Film Review*, no. 2, 1986, pp. 11 and 29; N. Masilela, 'The Los Angeles School of Black Filmmakers', in M. Diawara (ed.) *Black American Cinema*, New York, Routledge, 1993, pp. 107–8.

13 Julie Dash, 1995, *op. cit.*

14 Dash, in K. Harris, *op. cit.*, p. 18.

15 Greg Tate, 'Of Homegirl Goddesses and Geechee Women: The Africentric Cinema of Julie Dash', *The Village Voice*, 4 June 1991, pp. 72.

16 Julie Dash, *Daughters of the Dust: The Making of an African American Woman's Film*, New York, New Press, 1992, p. 6.

17 bell hooks calls it 'mythopoetic', bell hooks, *Black Looks: Race and Representation*, Boston, South End Press, 1992, p. 29.

18 Julie Dash and bell hooks, 'Dialogue between bell hooks and Julie Dash', in Julie Dash, *Daughters of the Dust: The Making of an African American Woman's Film*, New York, New Press, 1992, p. 32.

19 Toni Cade Bambara, *op. cit.*, p. xiii.

20 *Ibid.*, p. xv.

21 J. Erhart, 'Picturing *What If*: Julie Dash's Speculative Fiction', *Camera Obscura*, no. 38, 1996, p. 117.

22 See Y. Welbon's film, *The Cinematic Jazz of Julie Dash* (1992) and 'Calling the Shots: Black Women Directors Take the Helm', *Independent*, 15, 2, pp. 18–21.

23 B. Ruby Rich, 'In the Eyes of the Beholder', *The Village Voice*, 28 January 1992, pp. 60 and 65.

24 E. Guerrero, *Framing Blackness: The African American Image in Film*, Philadelphia, PA, Temple University Press, 1993, p. 1.

25 Z.I. Davis, 'An Interview with Julie Dash', *Wide Angle*, 13, 3–4, pp. 110–18.
26 J.M. Redding and V. Brownworth, *op. cit.*, p. 191.
27 Y. Welbon, *op. cit.*; J.M. Redding and V. Brownworth, *op. cit.*, p. 201.
28 Y. Welbon, *op. cit.*; Z.I. Davis, *op. cit.*, p. 115.
29 Julie Dash, 1995, *op. cit.*

Filmography

Working Models of Success (1973)
Four Women (1975) short
Diary of an African Nun (1977)
Illusions (1983) short
Breaking the Silence (1988)
Phyllis Wheatley (1989)
Preventing Cancer (1989)
Relatives (1990)
Praise House (1991)
Daughters of the Dust (1992)
Lost in the Night (1992)
Breaths (1994)
Subway Stories: Tales from the Underground (1997)
Funny Valentines (1999)
Incognito (1999)

Further reading

Toni Cade Bambara, 'Reading the Signs, Empowering the Eye: *Daughters of the Dust* and the Black Independent Cinema Movement', in M. Diawara (ed.) *Black American Cinema*, New York, Routledge, 1993.
J. Bobo, *Black Women as Cultural Readers*, New York, Columbia University Press, 1995.
—— *Daughters of the Dust*, New York, Dutton, 1997.
M. Diawara, *Black American Cinema*, New York, Routledge, 1993.
G.A. Foster, *Women Filmmakers of the African and Asian Diaspora*, Carbondale, Southern Illinois University Press, 1997.
G. Gibson-Hudson, 'Aspects of Black Feminist Cultural Ideology in Films by Black Independent Artists', in D. Carson, L. Dittmar and J.R. Welsch (eds) *Multiple Voices in Feminist Film Criticism*, Minneapolis, University of Minnesota Press, 1994.
S.V. Hartman and F.J. Griffin, 'Are You as Colored as That Negro?: The Politics of Being Seen in Julie Dash's *Illusions*', *Black American Literature Forum*, vol. 25, no. 2, 1991, pp. 361–73.
P. Klotman, *Screenplays of the African American Experience*, Bloomington, Indiana University Press, 1991.
A.S. Larkin, 'Black Women Film-makers Defining Ourselves: Feminism in Our Own Voice', in E.D. Pribram (ed.) *Female Spectators: Looking at Film and Television*, New York, Verso, 1988.

V. Smith, *Representing Blackness: Issues in Film and Video*, New Brunswick, NJ, Rutgers University Press, 1997.

Greg Tate and A. Jafa, 'La Venus Negre', *Artforum*, vol. 30, no. 1, pp. 90–3.

TERRY MOORE

HOMELESS

ATOM EGOYAN IN CANADA

> 'Have you ever noticed that the things you want are the things that slip away?'
>
> *Exotica*

In a disconcerting departure from the novel it is based on, the film of *Felicia's Journey*, written and directed by Canadian Atom Egoyan, leaves off somewhere near home. Not literally, but in the sense of an arrival at a place where everything will finally be all right. Home as safe harbour, the welcoming embrace of closure. Having barely escaped an unspeakable fate at the hands of the fussy serial killer Hilditch (who, in yet another arresting flight from William Trevor's novel, has freed his quarry in a fit of near-evangelical remorse), the Irish runaway Felicia is seen in the film's final moments tending shrubbery and attending to young mothers in a public park. She is a glowing, happy nurturer, earthbound and family-oriented, the embodiment of all that is good in the idea of home. Compare this to the book's final destination, which drops us on the step of madness, that most unhome-like of dwellings, yet the place Trevor insists both Felicia and Hilditch must be left. The finicky killer is driven to suicide as a result of the girl's escape (and not, as the movie suggests, because of a cold splash of spiritual reckoning), while she is left to an even more chilling fate. When we last encounter Felicia in Trevor's book, she is mad, feral and – much to the point of the novel if not the film – homeless. 'She seeks no meaning in the thoughts that occur to her,' Trevor writes of Felicia, 'any more than she searches for one in her purposeless journey, or finds a pattern in the muddle of time and people, but still the thoughts are there.' Felicia's journey has been 'purposeless', bereft of destination and direction. The opposite, one might say, of the journey she takes in Egoyan's film, which leaves her not only safe but wiser. Clearly her experience with the murderer Hilditch has lifted her to a more caring and sensitive station in life: a place where children and shrubbery grow, but only if properly tended. Like Hilditch, who kills himself after recognizing his own evil, Felicia has been transformed by the revelation of horror. She has found serenity and peace, which means her journey has been anything but purposeless.

These matters are worth stressing for the purposes of fixing Atom Egoyan's position as a 'Canadian' artist. Where the Irish novelist Trevor's conception of Felicia's journey leaves the young woman like a vessel adrift on remorseless seas, the Canadian filmmaker sees her safely home to port. Even at the risk of what might be judged, if not the film's failure, at least its dramatic good sense. For while the novel's bleak ending at least follows a certain cold logic – wherein Felicia's fate is the inevitable outcome of a predatory world, as embodied by the epicurean obsessions of the more benignly Hannibal Lecterish killer Hilditch – Egoyan's ultimately upbeat adaptation smacks of an over-determined optimism, an unconvincing attempt to spread a little sunshine in a tomb. But the attempt is revealing, for if it fails to illuminate the darkness surrounding it – and Hilditch's last-minute, pre-suicidal conversion verges on gallows hysteria – it at least sheds some light on the role certain national predilections may play in the worldview of one of the most internationally conspicuous of Canadian artists. (Atom Egoyan is currently the most internationally celebrated English Canadian director since Cronenberg. He is as close as a filmmaker can get to being a household name in Canada; that is, slightly better known than dead prime ministers but not nearly as well known as living hockey players.) Which is to say that, if we are to understand Atom Egoyan as a Canadian artist – with all the self-conscious uncertainties such an enterprise implies – we could do much worse than start with the idea of home. And the determination, in the case of *Felicia's Journey*, even at the expense of dramatic consistency and emotional logic, to get there.

Like many Canadian artists, Egoyan's work has frequently articulated the difficulty of basic human affinities, the almost pathological absence of rootedness which has also been widely described, in the discussion of the Great Northern Cultural Project, as alienation. And in this, if little else on the level of apparent articulation (he is, if nothing else, a highly non-traditional stylist), his work explores and extends one of the most deeply abiding themes in Canadian movies. From the homeland-seeking ethnographic odysseys of Quebecois documentarist Pierre Perrault (*Pour la suite du monde, L'Acadie, L'Acadie!?!*, for example), to the wrenching coming of age experienced by the adolescent protagonist of Claude

Jutra's *Mon oncle Antoine*; and from the lost highway of Donald Shebib's *Goin' Down the Road* to the existential black holes probed in the work of directors as disparate as Cronenberg and Michael Snow, Canadian films have demonstrated a distinctive fascination with the vacuous elusiveness of self and place. (One of the most astute questions ever posed of Canadian experience was asked by Canadian literary scholar Northrop Frye: 'Where,' he famously wondered, 'is here?') And, when self is defined by external parameters – as, in Canadian movies, it so often is – this elusiveness extends to a sense of place. In many movies made by Canadian filmmakers, and in just about every movie made by the Cairo-born, British Columbia-raised Egoyan, there is literally no place like home.

There are many means of accounting for this persistent condition of spiritual drift in Canadian movies, but it may perhaps suffice in this context to suggest that, in their concern with inescapable solitude, Canadian movies (ironically enough) are not alone. Indeed, as the possible consequence of clinging to an expanse of landscape that is as vast as it is unyielding (and where the most significant geological entity is called the 'Canadian Shield'), Canadians have developed a telling tendency to the anxiety of imminent disappearance, as though one must constantly cling for fear of losing purchase and falling off. But losing purchase of what? Falling off what? And clinging to what? It is an existential paradox of the first order: the only greater fear than losing one's grip is not knowing if there is anything to grip in the first place. In *Calendar*, which Egoyan shot in Armenia with Russian money, the director plays a photographer whose lens frames the dissolution of his own marriage. His wife is falling in love with an Armenian tour guide, and her husband feels a frosty nothingness in the face of it. The setting may be a long way from the Canadian Shield, but the sentiment expressed is right at home: 'What I really feel like doing is standing here and watching,' the photographer's narration coldly states. 'Watching while the two of you leave me and disappear into the landscape I'm about to photograph.'

To the extent that something like a mythological undercurrent exists in Canadian culture (and perhaps it is because it does not that these anxieties thrive), it is pretty much stuck on this possibility of drift. To grow up and be educated here in the 1960s and 1970s, as I did, was to be constantly reminded of the tenuousness of one's hold. The country was forever (and remains) on the verge of doing a deconfederating Humpty Dumpty: losing its delicate balance and shattering to miserable little pieces. Seminal Canadian volumes, of the kind anyone passing through the public school system must confront, had titles which prodded constant attentiveness to the danger of what lay just beyond the timberline: Susannah Moodie's pioneer classic *Roughing It in the Bush*, Farley Mowat's school curriculum staple *Lost in the Barrens*, W.O. Mitchell's *Who Has Seen the Wind?*, Pierre Berton's *The National Dream*, Margaret Atwood's *Survival*. Indeed, the latter, a key work of identity-carving literary criticism, merely gave scholarly credence to what many Canadians probably felt in the chill of their bones anyway, that is, that the single most prominent and abiding theme in Canadian literature was the monumental challenge of just getting by – of trying not to let this unforgiving and infinite landscape swallow you up or blow you away.

If the landscape provides a particularly vivid metaphor for the rocky, settler-deflecting uninhabitability of the country (tellingly, there are few more forbidding schools of landscape painting than Canada's renowned 'Group of Seven'), it also expresses the echoey vastness of the role played by alienation in Canadian cultural life. Egoyan is Canadian, of course, which argues for his consideration in the context of certain general tendencies apparent in the country's national culture. But, as an Egyptian-born Armenian, Egoyan also compels us to consider his alienation from an already alienated culture. His films have developed a singular tone of *communicatus interruptus*, in which the primary form of experience defining the relations between characters is what they cannot communicate to each other. (His adaptation of Samuel Beckett's *Krapp's Last Tape* seems ideally suited for Egoyan's fascination with the space between words.)

As a Canadian filmmaker, Egoyan practises a domestic art-form which has never enjoyed much popularity or currency with Canadians, who have historically preferred Hollywood movies to their own, and who thus find Canadian films alienating. (More than one observer has likened the status of Canadian movies to that of a foreign cinema in its own country.) Moreover, he is a Canadian filmmaker whose archly non-naturalistic aesthetic has broken considerably with the so-called 'traditions' of Canadian filmmaking, which have tended toward docu-dramatic realism – a legacy which is partly accounted for by the non-commercial haven provided by the National Film Board, a largely non-fiction-producing institution whose once pervasive influence was in steep decline by the early 1980s when Egoyan began making films. To sum up, he is a non-native Canadian filmmaker working in a marginal medium in a non-traditional way who makes movies which people from other

149

countries tend to get more excited about than Canadians do (as Egoyan's serial invitations to festivals like Cannes, Berlin and Venice attest), all of which leaves his work at the point where alienation disappears over the horizon and becomes something else. Something vaster and more infinite: alienation ad infinitum. And you don't get much more Canadian than that.

Nor does it get you any closer to home, which is not an idea likely to thrive under such circumstances of marauding detachment. Canada is a place to get lost in, the United States a place to call home. Thus, while the root of American mythology (the border-spanning mirror inverse of Canada) ploughs beneath the concept of homesteading, making a garden of civilization from an untamed wilderness, the rootlessness of Canadian mythology springs from the impossibility of laying down stakes. Home on such a landscape is never secure: it can never win against nature, and nature is never less than stubbornly opposed to it. While it is true to say that nations in all parts of the world have felt the cultural influence of America, and perhaps truer to suggest that cinema is one of those areas where this influence has been felt most acutely, no national entity has had – or could have – the experience of English Canada, the only country to live right snug upside the US and speak the same language. Needless to say, this has had its effects – effects which ripple right through the entirety of Canadian culture and history, from the revealing 'settlement' of the Canadian west to the particular tone and form taken by Egoyan's movies.

Which may not be as random a conceptual span as it appears. There is a connection, particularly if you place any significance in the relations between history, culture, nationalism and popular myth. If one accepts western settlement as the key event of American popular mythology – the seed planted in the wilderness from which everything that is essential to America's self-image grew – one must also consider the peculiarly refracted shadow this has cast upon Canada, a country that shares the northern extension of America's continental west but not its western mythology. Or, more to the point perhaps, it shares exactly the same mythology which, unlike the region's weather, tends to blow north. Which is to say that Canada may have a west, but it has no Western. Or not one it can call its own. Fearing an outbreak on the Queen's soil of the kind of unpleasant business that characterized the Indian Wars in America, Canada's first Prime Minister, Sir John A. Macdonald, created a special police force to precede Canadian settlers and pre-empt their mixing it up with the newly established Dominion's aboriginal populations. In so doing, Macdonald not only created Canada's most enduring symbol of tenacious, top-down Canadian dullness – the Mountie: anti-outlaw, anti-cowboy, anti-sex, anti-fun – he pre-empted a northern-style Wild West. Moreover, in the process he also undercut any possibility that Canada might develop a national mythology based on Manifest Destiny, individualism, or ritualistic codes of honour and retributive justice. Instead of cowboys, that is, Canada got cops. Thus a country was born which, to this day, is renowned for its virtues of compromise, diplomacy and politeness. The Nice Guy Next Door of the first world. Not that this is necessarily a bad thing (one John Wayne-producing nation should do for us all), but it has played havoc in the country's development of a sense of national destiny.

In Canada, where no deep mythological roots have been permitted to grow, everything is open for discussion and debate. (And few topics are debated more vigorously or tirelessly than the issue of national identity.) Out of the West, with its blood, lawlessness, genocide and bone-simple code of survival, America drew its most potent and elementary mythological archetypes, and one of these was the raw sentimental poetry of home – what the West was fought and won for. As an idea, America was as inevitable and natural as home, and home was America. Home was where your journey took you, what you risked danger for, the end of all suffering. In narrative terms, Manifest Destiny was the ultimate Happy Ending. Endings were made happy not just by the literal appearance of Home, Sweet, Home, they could be made so by the implication of home: marriage would do, a brilliant sunrise, a clinched embrace on a railway platform. To be delivered to a happy ending was to be dropped safely on the doorstep of home, and the very threshold of a national idea. And, in Canada, we didn't have it. In Winnipeg director Guy Maddin's 1992 movie *Careful* – a truly great Canadian title – an entire social system grows out of the fact that, if anyone belonging to the movie's mythical alpine community makes too much noise, an avalanche could sweep everybody off the mountain and into oblivion: if you speak up too loudly, or surrender to too much raw feeling, you could kill everyone around you. It seems a singularly Canadian theme, as is the subject of one of the totemically Canadian pop band The Tragically Hip's most anthemic songs. Called 'Fifty Mission Cap', it is inspired by the true story of a hockey player who, within days of leading his team to the national championships of the national sport, simply disappeared, fell off the edge of national experience never to be heard from again. It would seem that, for Canadians, no degree of skill or notoriety is insurance against the fear of simply being inhaled one day by the landscape.

With the exception of *The Sweet Hereafter*, in which a school bus full of children is swept off a mountain road and swallowed up by a partially frozen lake, the slipperiness of place in Egoyan's films has been articulated in terms more spiritual and psychological than physical. In fact, it has most often expressed itself as a kind of chronic *ennui*, a vague but crippling condition of terminal disconnectedness. In his first feature, *Next of Kin* (made in 1984, and the first of several to deal with the pregnantly troubled relations between adolescents and adults), the protagonist – the only child of a well-to-do Toronto WASP couple – is so disengaged from his actual family that he seeks (and creates) a surrogate one, in the form of an Armenian family (a reflection on Egoyan's Armenian heritage) to whom he presents himself as a long-lost son. In *Family Viewing* another teenager seeks to avenge a sense of domestic betrayal by taking revenge against the divorced father who has been erasing the archive of family videotapes. (Videotape, and its status as instantly disposable artificial memory, figures prominently in Egoyan's early work.) In *Speaking Parts*, the medium of disengagement is again video, as a number of characters peripherally involved in a film production struggle to establish virtual connections where actual ties are absent. In *The Adjuster*, the protagonist is an insurance adjuster whose own familial displacement is (futilely, as it turns out) compensated by his determination to play surrogate patriarchal saviour to families with whom his business puts him in an inequally dependent relationship. He needs broken homes to feel that he is putting something together.

The 1994 film, *Exotica*, traces a similar cycle of doomed domestic simulation, as a father whose daughter has been kidnapped and murdered establishes a creepy paternal relationship (foreshadowing, in less overtly predatory terms, the Hilditch–Felicia relationship) with a teenage stripper with whom he becomes obsessed. Even *The Sweet Hereafter*, with its more literal evocation of a killing landscape, is ultimately about doomed and tortured patriarchal imperative: unblessed home-building. Based on Russell Banks' melancholy novel, it follows a troubled lawyer's attempts to relieve his own sense of paternal failure (his daughter is a suicidal drug addict) by playing conniving saviour to the families bereaved by the accident.

Indeed, if there is a single dramatic preoccupation to Egoyan's work, it is the desperate attempt to build something like home, usually through the medium of something like family. It is an attempt bound to fail due to the most elementary of engineering oversights: homes without foundations collapse. Sooner or later the weight of their own artifice brings them down. Interestingly however, Egoyan's films have consistently been marked by a kind of melodramatic pose of closure, moments of final punctuation so archly articulated that they seem to mock the very idea of happy endings, and thus the possibility of home itself: the kiss that summons the end credits in *Speaking Parts*, the haunted suburban pastoral that concludes *Exotica*, the hand stretched before the flame (of a burning home) in *The Adjuster*. Even *The Sweet Hereafter*, which carefully wraps up its narrative strands by weaving together moments that suggest a form of peace beyond catastrophe, contains a distant rumble of doubt: the final image, of the young woman we know will be crippled and sexually abused after the flashback we are seeing, undercuts the very notion of an unbitter sweetness hereafter: she has yet to face the horror of that mountain ride. An ending yes, but happy? Not quite.

The ending of *Felicia's Journey*, on the other hand, strikes no mere momentary attitude of contentment. On the contrary, like Hilditch pleading desperately for Felicia to 'let the healing start' before releasing her to the rich soil of a nurturing future, the film seems almost hysterically determined to convince us that everything that we have seen – the systematic cruelty, loneliness, disappointment, heartbreak and alienation – can be swept away in an instant of soul-cleansing clarity. Strangely then, while it would appear to be intended as the least ironic of Egoyan's happy endings, it is the one that most desperately seems so: it registers as if it were a dream of a happy ending, a vision of peace and home that might visit someone for whom such ideas are, and can never be, more than fantasies, momentary and necessary escapes from the oppressive reality bearing down. It seems, that is, the type of fantasy that the mad Felicia at the conclusion of Trevor's book might have before falling asleep in another alley on another hopeless night, or that which a Canadian filmmaker like Egoyan, otherwise so deeply disinclined to believe in such ideas, might have of the impossible dream of a place like home.

Biography

Born in Egypt, in 1960, Egoyan was raised and works in Canada.

Filmography

(All Canadian production unless otherwise indicated)

Next of Kin (1984)
Family Viewing (1987)
Speaking Parts (1989)
The Adjuster (1991)
Calendar (1993)
Exotica (1994)
The Sweet Hereafter (1997)
Felicia's Journey (Canada/UK, 1999)
Krapp's Last Tape (Canada/UK, 2000)

Further reading

Carole Desbarats, Daniele Riviere and Jacinto Lageira, *Atom Egoyan*, Paris, Dis Voir, 1993.
Atom Egoyan, *Exotica: The Screenplay*, Toronto, Coach House Press, 1995.
Geoff Pevere and Greig Dymond, *Mondo Canuck: A Canadian Pop Culture Odyssey*, Toronto, Prentice-Hall Canada, 1996.

GEOFF PEVERE

DAVID FINCHER

David Fincher is something of an anomaly. He is a big-budget, commercial, Hollywood filmmaker whose films are large, high-concept and star-laden. Like Stanley Kubrick before him, however, Fincher manages, from within the system, to make films that are themselves critical not only of 'The System' but of *systems* more generally; his films are especially critical of his generation's apparent desire for stability and structure. Fincher is, in short, Hollywood's latest thinking filmmaker, and the link to Kubrick is not merely a felicitous one. Fincher's own late twentieth-century themes of alienation and discontent, as well as the visual design of his films, descend in marked ways from his predecessor. And, also like Kubrick, Fincher's films, in particular *Fight Club*, have been the subject of much heated debate, especially over the filmmaker's possible contributions to that which he purports to critique. To what degree, critics ask, are his films a celebration of their sometimes violent, anarchistic subjects?

Fincher rose to popular and critical prominence with *Seven*, a film that chronicles an ageing and thoroughly disenchanted Detective Sommerset's (Morgan Freeman) attempts to retire peacefully from the profession that has brought him to the end of his psychological rope. A series of highly structured murders enacted according to the seven deadly sins and the as-yet uncorrupted moral outlook of his younger partner, Detective Mills (Brad Pitt), however, slowly reactivate Sommerset, causing both men to reflect upon their ability to affect change. The film moves well beyond the potential pitfalls of the bi-racial buddy/cop film. Like all of Fincher's films to date, *Seven* is at its best in its critique of late twentieth-century complacency, or as the deadly sins would have it, *apathy*. John Doe (Kevin Spacey), the film's serial murderer, enacts his rage toward a society grown comfortable in its moral bankruptcy upon the bodies of his victims. Sommerset, also repulsed by the city, perhaps even the world, seeks not revenge or punishment, but escape. His own disgust nearly forces him to the ultimate act of complacency: dropping out altogether, leaving the force, the city, and his past behind. The film's visual design, its acute attention to the *mise-en-scène* of the contemporary urban space and its instability and violence, lends significantly to these, Fincher's larger, less generically derived themes.

The Kubrickian notion of man alone in the universe that he has created for himself is a theme to which Fincher's films return repeatedly. In *Seven*, this feeling of isolation finds its visual expression in Fincher's and director of photography Darius Khondji's wide-angle, shallow-focus cinematography. In *Seven* space is engulfing, threatening to absorb the individual and trap him in his anonymity. These same ideas were elegantly and quite literally realized in Kubrick's 1968 exploration of space and the individual's place in it, *2001: A Space Odyssey*. Fincher captures this sense of isolation most palpably in the sequences which depict Sommerset alone in his apartment, contemplating his involvement in the case. Fincher frequently reduces the details of the *mise-en-scène*, transforming them into an all-encompassing, amorphous blanket behind his centrally composed, smaller-than-life protagonists; this idea is foregrounded in Fincher's decision to locate *Seven* in an anonymous city, a stripped down 'any-city' with no defining characteristics (save its constant, sheeting rain). Even the film's historical moment is difficult to determine; characters are not dressed in era-specific clothing; they work at monochromatic computer terminals in offices that seem to have dropped out of a 1940s' film noir. Technically, Fincher's method of reduction is achieved, at least in part, through a careful muting of light and colour so that the discreet 'items' of background interest merge together. More critically, these oppressive, monolithic backgrounds threaten to consume his characters. The individual, Fincher's films repeatedly suggest, is at risk in the contemporary world.

A less commercially successful but equally engaged film, *The Game*, continues *Seven*'s central critique of complacency; it is also a prototype for his 1999 foray into the realm of chaos and hyper-reality, *Fight Club*. *The Game* assigns a class to complacency: the rich. Fincher has arranged the narrative details so that there is satisfaction in watching our hapless protagonist, Nicholas Van Orton (Michael Douglas), shaken, in classic Hitchcockian fashion, to his very foundation; it is no coincidence that Fincher's film, like *Vertigo* (1958), is set in San Francisco. *The Game*, however, shares more in common with Hitchcock's more popular, rollercoaster-ride, comic thriller *North by Northwest* (1959). In the same way that we are introduced to Roger Thornhill (Cary Grant) in *North by Northwest*, our introduction to Nicholas in *The Game* is not an especially favourable one. He is arrogant, aloof, conspicuously wealthy; however, he is also, like his predecessor, redeemable. Nicholas' brother, Conrad (Sean Penn), the younger and more reckless of the two, serves in the film as his redeemer, enlisting Nicholas in a complex game as part of a bizarre and extravagant birthday gift. The game, which to Nicholas is indistinguishable from reality and causes him to question his relationship *to* reality, quite literally forces him to *hit bottom*, an idea at the heart of *Fight Club*. Nicholas emerges, by the end of the game/film, reborn and separate from his comfortable, predictable, safe, and seemingly emotionless existence.

As with *Seven*, *The Game* is muted in both light and colour. It also perpetuates what are clearly the thematic obsessions of its director. Fincher, as critics have been fast to point out, is simultaneously fascinated and repulsed by the American city and it, more than John Doe's false moral superiority in *Seven* or Nicholas' comfortable, classed existence in *The Game*, is the enemy, the destroyer of men. I use the exclusionary term 'men' here quite deliberately, for it begins to hint at what seems to be another emergent theme in Fincher's work: an interest in the psychological and emotional state of the late twentieth-century American male. Fincher's films are remarkably devoid of three-dimensional female characters. Mills' wife Tracy (Gwyneth Paltrow) in *Seven*, is almost a non-presence; in fact, by the film's end she is a severed head wrapped up in a package that Doe bestows upon her husband as part of his plan to complete the sixth and seventh murders in his series. Critic

Amy Taubin rightly compares Tracy's 'saintly domesticity' to the women in John Ford's films.[1] As with Ford's women who gaze upon their men as they engage in activities of mobility, there is a sense that behind this static gaze lies some real knowledge about men, of which the men themselves are not aware.

While Fincher's films tend to marginalize their female characters, they collectively evidence Fincher's related interest in the American family, its dissolution and decay. In *Seven*, Mills' wife is murdered before she has the opportunity to inform her husband of her pregnancy and after tearfully divulging her secret to Sommerset. She discloses a fear that Sommerset himself admits to giving in to many years ago: that of bringing another being into the city. The city, *Seven* suggests, has made Ford's romanticized agrarian domesticity an impossibility. In fact, the family of Fincher's world is about as safe as the lone women in John Ford's *The Searchers* (1956); unable to fend off the murderous element, they are threatened, abducted, slaughtered. John Doe also speaks to this failure in *Seven*, informing Mills that before he murdered Tracy he attempted to 'play husband' with her, though unsuccessfully. In *The Game*, Fincher's interest in the family is focused more squarely on the theme of abandonment. Nicholas is divorced, his bachelor's existence captured in much the same way as Sommerset's (though differently marked by class). His home is a fortress to himself and his obsessive selfhood, characterizations implied by widely composed shots that highlight the vastness of his immediate space. Gated and enormous, like the city, it threatens to swallow its occupant. His housekeeper, Ilsa (Carol Baker), functions more like a mother than a maid. On the evening of his birthday she prepares for him a child's plate (though under a stunning silver lid) of a hamburger and French fries; a cupcake with a candle serves as dessert. Nicholas, in spite of his existence in a seemingly adult world, is trapped in the realm of his own problematic childhood. His father's suicide is presented as a supreme act of familial abandonment, one that forced Nicholas to prematurely assume an adult role. Fatherlessness, then, is at least partly to blame for Nicholas' condition, an idea explored more thoroughly in *Fight Club*.

Fincher's ideas about the state of the individual in contemporary society are most articulately realized in *Fight Club*. Very much in keeping with Fincher's interest in the contemporary state of masculinity, *Fight Club* is reminiscent of Stanley Kubrick's controversial film, *A Clockwork Orange* (1971), both in its theme and in its popular and critical reception. Steeped in critical,

Kubrickian 'ultraviolence', *Fight Club* is about men who, on the surface, seem indifferent to women. It is, finally, a film critical of its own audience. Our unnamed narrator (Edward Norton), who occasionally refers to himself in his voice-over monologues as some organ or another belonging to 'Jack' (an idea gleaned from a stack of similarly narrated magazines he finds), is what Susan Faludi identifies as the personification of 'the modern male predicament: fatherless, trapped in a cubicle in an anonymous job, trying to glean an identity from Ikea brochures, entertainment magazines and self-help gatherings. Jack traverses a barren landscape familiar to many men who must contend with a world stripped of socially useful male roles and saturated with commercial images of masculinity.'[2] Faludi's argument that the film is ultimately 'a quasi-feminist tale' relies upon her reading of the film's seemingly very old-Hollywood ending where our hitherto uninterested narrator joins hands (and forces) with the film's only female character, Marla (Helena Bonham Carter), whose neurotic existence outside of 'the system' has remained invisible to the narrator until the film's end.

The narrator's literalized doppelgänger, Tyler Durden (Brad Pitt), *is* the commercial image of masculinity, one that the narrator buys into in precisely the way he buys into Ikea's vision of personal space. The narrator's myopic and narcissistic obsession with his own alter-ego consumes his life and blinds him to Marla who, the film suggests, is the more appropriate 'object choice'. Tyler (and Fincher's decision to cast Pitt in this role is a stroke of genius) is another commodity in a culture that fetishizes commodities; he is the narrator's media-derived fantasy of independent masculinity. He is Hollywood's version of the individualist; he is pretty, strong, and maintains an animalistically active and emotionless sex life with Marla.

Tyler's connection to the world of film is hinted at in his late-night job as a porn-splicing projectionist. His role as *image*, however, functions more provocatively. His image is introduced in the film one frame at a time, a feature virtually (but not entirely) unnoticeable without viewing the film on DVD and pausing on these single inserted frames. He operates, like the penises he splices into children's films, at the subliminal level. At one point in the film, Tyler's image addresses the audience directly, shaking the cinematic frame containing him as he does so and exposing the sprocket holes at either edge. Tyler is film; film is seductive. And, through much of *Fight Club*, Tyler's warped ideas about hitting bottom are likewise seductive both to our narrator (whose imagination has created Tyler) and to the viewer. There is something appealingly base in Tyler's philosophical stance, at the centre of which are the clubs themselves. Late-night, bare-knuckled, male-exclusive basement brawls, Fight Club contests do not pretend to be anything they are not. They are simple, brutal, and to the contestants, affirming in their ability to reclaim some mythic sense of the masculine individual. Project Mayhem, an anarchistic branch of the clubs, proposes to extend exponentially Tyler's brand of primitivism by levelling the corporate world and balancing the economic playing field. The seductiveness of these ideas, however, spins out of control.

Men, the film suggests, are in a precarious state in contemporary US culture, where even the notion of individuality is a product of consumer culture. Fight Club and Project Mayhem are flawed because their organizational logic descends from the very structures their members seek to escape. Fight Club becomes a franchise and Project Mayhem an exceedingly fascistic and militaristic operation reminiscent of the first half of Kubrick's *Full Metal Jacket* (1987). While the narrator's fight is ultimately an internal one (in a twist on the logic of Vietnam, he must shoot himself in order to save himself), the film is careful not to blame the *individual* for his own unravelling. As with Fincher's other work, it is ultimately the system, in this case, an inescapable, corrupting, capitalist system, that has undone the individual. Even Fincher's début feature film, *Alien 3*, a film the director all but disowns as he did not oversee the final cut, contains remnants of what have come to be Fincher's central themes. *Alien*ation and family (particularly of the maternal sort) are larger than life issues in the entire *Alien* series. The series is also critical of the capitalist system and, Fincher's film perhaps more than any other in the series, focuses on this problem by positing, in microcosmic form, a generation of men abandoned by and alienated from the system which they helped to build. The outpost in *Alien 3* is an extension of Fincher's decaying urban landscape.

Herein, however, lies a fundamental problem. Unlike, for instance, John Cassavetes who acted in Hollywood films in order to finance his strictly non-Hollywood films and thereby managed to maintain his hard-earned status as a Hollywood outsider, Fincher, in spite of his acute critiques of consumer culture, has also participated in it to varying degrees. Fincher made his first forays into visual culture in the early 1980s, working for George Lucas (an acknowledged hero of the young filmmaker-to-be) and Industrial Light and Magic. This largely technical work served as Fincher's education in film (he claims not to see the point of film school). From Industrial Light and Magic, Fincher began a career directing music videos for such pop artists as Paula Abdul, Billy Idol, Madonna and Aerosmith, and making commercials for corporate giants like Coca-Cola, Pepsi and Nike. He started the super-slick production company *Propaganda Pictures*, nomenclature that hints at the director's sense of irony. Fincher's relationship to the image is thus a complicated one. He is not a 'sell out' as that term has traditionally been used. He is, rather, the perfect model of postmodern *image infatuation*. Fincher's almost childlike love for things that look cool, most obviously and endearingly revealed in the director's voice-over comments on the DVD versions of his own work, keeps him working in a more broadly conceived visual realm, and not only in the cinematic realm. Documentary director Errol Morris, who also occasionally makes television advertisements, has referred to them, in what is his typical mix of love and irony, as the haiku of the West. Fincher's relationship to the form might be less poetic. His commercial work, however, like Morris', exhibits a love for the image, disconnected from its possible relationship to products or profits.

Biography

David Fincher was born in Denver, Colorado, USA, in 1962. He has directed four feature films to date and has assisted on an equal number. In the early 1980s he served as optical effects photographer on *Indiana Jones and the Temple of Doom*, *The Never Ending Story* and *Return of the Jedi*. He has also worked in advertising and on music videos. He is currently working on *The Panic Room*, which is due for release in 2001.

Notes

1 Amy Taubin, 'The Allure of Decay', *Sight and Sound*, vol. 6, no.1, 1996, pp. 22–4, p. 23.
2 Susan Faludi, 'It's 'Thelma and Louise' for Guys', *Newsweek*, 25 October 1999, p. 89.

Filmography

Alien 3 (1992)
Seven (1995)
The Game (1997)
Fight Club (1999)

Further reading

Ilsa J. Bick, ' "Well, I Guess I Must Make You Nervous"': Woman and the Space of *Alien 3*', *Post Script: Essays in Film and the Humanities*, vol. 14, nos 1 and 2 (Fall 1994, Winter/Spring 1995), pp. 45–58.
Chris Drake, 'Inside the Light', *Sight and Sound*, vol. 6, no. 4, 1996, pp. 18–20.
Richard Dyer, 'Kill and Kill Again', *Sight and Sound*, vol. 7, no. 9, 1997, pp. 14–17.
—— *Seven*, London, BFI Publishing, 1999.
Steve Macek, 'Places of Horror: Fincher's *Seven* and Fear of the City in Recent Hollywood Film', *College Literature*, Special Issue 26, no. 1, 1999, pp. 81–97.
Amy Taubin, 'So Good it Hurts', *Sight and Sound*, vol. 9, no. 11, 1999, pp. 16–18.
John Wrathall, '*Seven*: A Film Review', *Sight and Sound*, vol. 6, no. 1, 1996, pp. 49–50.

DEVIN ORGERON

HAL HARTLEY

Arguably the most significant cinematic phenomenon in the United States in the 1990s has been the resurgent independent filmmaking movement in which Hal Hartley continues to enjoy a position of prominence. Personifying the association of independent US and European art-house cinemas (in theme and aesthetic as well as budget), Hartley has received critical recognition as an auteur. His key place within American independent cinema is a matter both of his own inheritance of the mantle of his predecessors, and the position of influence which he now enjoys. Benefiting from the path established in the 1970s by such figures as Scorsese and Coppola, and followed in the 1980s by filmmakers like Spike Lee and Jim Jarmusch, 'The New Jim Jarmusch' – as Hartley has been somewhat fatuously described – has, in turn, become a source of inspiration for an even younger generation of independent filmmakers.[1]

As a screenwriter, director, and frequently editor and composer, Hartley has been the creative force behind both feature-length and short films. Hartley's increasing maturity as a filmmaker, and the sense of progression within his work, has inspired the temptation to view his early Long Island films as a trilogy and *Amateur* as a point of departure whose trajectory his subsequent films have followed. Indeed, certain members of Hartley's portfolio of actors (notably

Adrienne Shelley as the troubled teenager in *The Unbelievable Truth* and *Trust*) came to characterize 'types' from which Hartley has departed. Yet Hartley's consistency of style and tendency to return to key thematic concerns, notably that of the marginality which both distinguishes his characters and informs his filmmaking aesthetic, render such a neat approach to his films problematic.

Perhaps because of his status as an American who makes 'European' films, Hartley is a filmmaker whose decidedly minimalist aesthetic has tended to pose difficulties for critics. The restraint in both sound and image in his films owes as much to budgetary constraints as to Hartley's approach to style. His musical compositions (credited under the pseudonym Ned Rifle) recall the work of such 'reductive' or 'minimalist' musicians as Reich and Glass,[2] relying upon the repetition which is key to Hartley's work for effect. Visually, Hartley prefers the subtlety of gesture to ostentation, choreographing and controlling the movements of his repertory of actors with a precise figure placement which occasionally erupts (to great effect in *Surviving Desire*) into a semiotically rich dance sequence.

Given the austerity Hartley exhibits in his visual style, it is inevitable that dialogue provides the most immediate impact. Exaggeratedly non-naturalistic, Hartley's characters speak in aphorisms. His actors recite their lines in a deadpan delivery which, in seeming to avoid affording the characters the complications of real emotional engagement with each other, is emblematic of their distanced, marginal societal positions and troubled relationships, both romantic and familial. Although the setting of Hartley's films has now moved, along with the filmmaker himself, from his native Long Island, to urban locations, and the aphorisms are now spoken by adults rather than angst-ridden, serious youths, it is the consistency of this style which demarcates Hartley's films.

Andrew Sarris, the champion of the American auteur theory, granted Hartley the status of auteur.[3] Indeed, Hartley's auteurism is emblematic of that which European and independent US cinemas have in common, namely a mode of film less driven by narrative than by a concern with interpersonal relationships and self-definition, with an emphasis on personal vision. Thus, although Hartley is notable within this most recent reincarnation of the independent movement in American cinema, receiving much critical recognition (principally within film journals, and on the Internet), his greatest source of inspiration comes from the European art-house aesthetic which Godard embodies and to which Hartley, in his evasion of and ironic play with genre, his use of iconic women, and the degree of control he maintains over his artistic output, aspires.

Having made three shorts – the graduation film *Kid*, *The Cartographer's Girlfriend* and *Dogs* – Hartley funded his first feature with the help of Jerome Brownstein, his boss at a company which made public service announcements. *The Unbelievable Truth*, itself concerned with the negotiation of relationships through fiscal exchange, was the result. A satirical, marginal take on suburbia, *The Unbelievable Truth* is concerned with the character of a young teenage girl, Audrey, whose belief in an impending nuclear explosion causes her estrangement both from her parents and her boyfriend, Emmett. On the brink of college, her father negotiates with her in order to control not only the institution she should attend (not Harvard, which is too expensive) but the subject she should study (his choice: communication, is ironic given their relationship). To their town returns Josh, repeatedly mistaken for a priest because of his austerity in dress and material needs. Josh has spent time in jail for a murder which, it transpires, he did not commit. Audrey's faith in Josh is borne out in a balletic sequence where a host of characters seek each other in deliberate movements through Josh's otherwise empty house.

The film's narrative constitutes a Godardian commentary on the commercialization of the body. Audrey, who spends much of the film involved in a modelling career, was persuaded into it by her father, who is seduced by her potential for earning money, if unprepared for the revealing nature of the results. The girl who both sleeps under the gaze of (there is a large frieze of a dollar bill on her bedroom wall), and reads books on, George Washington is a commodity who has been brought up to believe that people are only as good as the deals they make and keep. It is only by surrendering her total earnings to her father at the end of the film, and accepting the austere Josh's embrace, that she frees herself from relationships dependent upon monetary exchange.

Similarly problematic are the familial relationships within *Trust*, in which damaging patterns of behaviour abound. Its protagonists, Matthew and Maria, are linked in a parallel syntagma of dysfunctional family lives before they meet. Matthew's diminutive expressions of rage in the factory in which he works (punching boxes, putting his boss' head in a vice) release the anger which he cannot express within his home. Both Matthew's father, Jim, and Maria's mother, Jean, exhibit a sort of parenting-by-rote, asking of their respective children whether they have eaten, despite the malevolence of their behaviour towards their children. Jim compulsively inflicts emotional abuse on his son through a repetition of assignment of blame for the failure of their relationship, forcing Matthew to repeatedly clean the bathroom because he blames his son for the loss of his wife, who died in childbirth. Maria, who 'killed' her father by slapping him when, learning of her pregnancy, he called her a slut, is only accepted back into the home of her knife-wielding mother if she promises to act as her slave.

The misfits Matthew and Maria find each other. Maria rescues Matthew from his father's home. Matthew's influence in turn transforms Maria from a lurid stereotype of a teenager ashamed of her ignorance into a young woman (now Oedipally clothed in his mother's plain dress) capable of making mature decisions about her future. The crux of their relationship lies within the trust of the film's title ('Do you trust me?' Maria asks of Matthew, who replies: 'Do you trust me first?'). Yet Maria, tricked by her mother into believing that Matthew has slept with her sister, Peg, has an abortion and decides not to marry Matthew. The possibility of a romantic ending has been displaced into an understanding fostered by mutual recognition and respect, which allows Maria to take a spent grenade from Matthew's hand and toss it away at the end of the film, saving them both.

Equally desirous of security is Miho, the final protagonist of the self-contained trilogy which is *Flirt*. As the title suggests, the film is concerned with the tension between flirtation and the emotional intimacy which commitment entails. Each of the thrice repeated narratives (the film is composed of a short film made three times with essentially identical dialogue) concerns a flirt who is given an ultimatum by an established lover who is about to leave the country. The flirt, having suffered a gunshot wound to the face, goes out to explore other possibilities before making the decision of whether or not to commit. Since the flirts are respectively a heterosexual male (Bill: 'New York'), a gay male (Dwight: 'Berlin') and a female (Miho: 'Tokyo'), it is tempting to suggest that the crux of the film lies in gender. Indeed, the most notable differences between the sections lie in a tendency to lapse into gender stereotypes. Hence it is the destruction of Miho's face that seems most likely to end her promiscuous tendencies: whilst Bill chases after his lover to the airport, and Dwight enjoys the possibilities of a new encounter, Miho (played by Hartley's wife), is the only flirt whose section sees her in comfortable assimilation with her steady companion (played by Hartley himself). It is also highly problematic that it is only the female flirt whose wound is self-inflicted (Miho is holding the gun to her face when it goes off), and who therefore equates her sexual guilt with a peculiarly female mode of masochism.

Yet, despite the importance of *Flirt*'s gender politics, its significance lies in its status as Hartley's most formally experimental film. Although Jarmusch, in *Night on Earth* (1992), similarly placed three distinct narratives within one feature, *Flirt* takes this one step further by repeating a single narrative three times. Partly arising out of the conditions of production (*Flirt* was originally a short, the 'New York' section, which gained funding to be expanded into a feature from Japan and Germany), the decision to repeat the short rather than expand the original demonstrates both Hartley's willingness to play with conventional modes of film narrative, and his increasing concern with the issue of repetition. The culmination of this concern, the degree of repetition in *Flirt*, is at last so great as to draw attention to the differences between the sections rather than the repetition itself, which has become the 'norm'.

The short films *Theory of Achievement* and *Ambition*, made between *Trust* and *Simple Men*, further exemplify Hartley's manipulation of genre and modes of expression, although this time through performance art and Godardian pastiche. Short films generally concentrate the essentials of a filmmaker's style, and *Theory of Achievement* and *Ambition* are no exception. *Ambition*, the briefer and more oblique of the two, concerns an artist who asserts, 'I'm good at what I do', before moving through a brightly coloured *mise-en-scène*, participating in the sort of cartoon violence that was later to appear in *Amateur*. Like *Surviving Desire*, in which Hartley uses choreographed physical movement to express Jude's joy, *Theory of Achievement* exploits another of Hartley's favourite modes of mannered gesture: slaps. It is also the most literal visitation of Godard in Hartley's films: he appears as a character who, unheard by the spectator, talks of sound and image through a translator. The film is populated by a group of people who are not only defined, with a list of increasingly abject embellishments, as 'white', 'middle class', 'college educated', 'unskilled' and 'broke', but who are also too 'drunk' to do anything about it.

The protagonists within these comedies of abstraction are marginalized, whether by their modes of expression (the artist who relies on his self-belief in the face of adversity) or by their social position (it is ironic that a generation whose ideological construction is ostensibly so 'establishment' can be marginalized). In this they represent both Hartley himself (his position as an independent filmmaker operating outside of his dominant national cinema is inherently marginal) and the marginal characters who inhabit his features. It is this position of marginality which allows for the sort of critique of social constructs which occurs across Hartley's films.

Simple Men follows two brothers (one a criminal, the other a student) on a quest to find their father who, jailed for radical bombing activity in the 1960s, has escaped. In their search of Long Island, Bill and Dennis encounter two women, one of whom, it transpires in a neatly Oedipal twist, is their father's girlfriend. The other lives in fear of the return of her ex-husband, who has just been released from prison. Much of the interest of the film lies within its representation of femininity. The quiet strength of Kate moves Bill to surrender to the police when they finally track him down for his own, financially motivated, criminal activity. Elina, in a debate about whether it is a feminist achievement to exploit your own body, asserts that she admires Madonna's self-determination. Like *The Unbelievable Truth*, *Simple Men* asks questions about the definition of criminality: is the father's criminal activity justified by the ideology which inspired it, and redeemed because he continues strongly to hold to his beliefs in maturity? (A nurse proclaims to the brothers: 'He wouldn't have blown up that building if he knew people were in there! He's a great man!') Is Bill's crime, less serious in nature because it concerns robbery rather than death, somehow worse because its motivation is material gain?

A non-generic thriller, *Amateur* is also concerned with criminality and redemption. Thomas, formerly involved in a life of criminality and exploitation of women through pornography, develops amnesia, having been thrown from a window. Isabelle, a former nun who believes that she has a task in the outside world, takes the now 'good' amnesiac under her protection, and guides him through an encounter with Sofia, the wife he once exploited and who is still afraid of him. The first of Hartley's films to be cast with a 'star', albeit of French cinema, *Amateur* is largely concerned with the relationship between Thomas (Hartley regular Martin Donovan) and Isabelle (Isabelle Huppert, who appeared in Godard's 1983 film *Passion*). Critical attention has rightly focused on the surprisingly emotional aspect to this film. Isabelle discovers romantic desire only to find that the object of her love has a terrible past, and yet remains able to trust this man. Her belief that she was destined to save Sofia from Thomas, like the fact that he is killed before their love can be consummated, is curiously emotive, though portrayed with characteristic understatement.

Amateur is a film about transformation, conveyed on Isabelle's part most succinctly through the film's visuals. Isabelle's embodiment of the virgin/whore dichotomy (she is a nun who discovers desire, a virgin who believes she is a nymphomaniac) is demonstrated both through her mode of dress (she starts the film in demure blue and ends it in sexy red and black) and her hair, which appears neatly bobbed until she lets the back down to reveal a haircut of curious duplexity. Thomas' transformation lies within the redemption which Isabelle's willingness to love and trust him affords: he is, significantly, forgiven by her before he dies. Yet the question of whether this redemption is more far-reaching is left unanswered by the film's denial of the return of Thomas' memory. Although amnesia allows him to shed an identity and become good, we are never given the opportunity of discovering whether Thomas is temporarily or permanently redeemed by his amnesia.

In another story of transformation and redemption, the protagonist of *Henry Fool* (which won a screenplay award at Cannes) is given, and refuses, the opportunity of repeating the past seduction of a girl of 13 for which he was jailed. The Shamanic Henry comes into the life of garbage disposal man Simon Grim and, in encouraging Simon to write, gives him the articulation he needs to express the insight he possesses. As one would expect of a Hartley character, this insight is afforded by Simon's position of marginality (he is taunted by others, and observes the human sexuality around him with the air of an anthropologist, curious yet distanced from his subjects). Simon's writing, at once vehemently dismissed as pornography and ardently lauded as a great work, secures him a Nobel Prize.

Henry, on the other hand, takes on Simon's life in a gradual role reversal which sees Henry married to Simon's sister, living in Simon's house and doing Simon's garbage disposal job by the end of the film. Hartley places Henry's criminality in a position of ambiguity, carefully situating the age of the girl with whom he was caught engaged in sexual intercourse at 13: young enough to be prohibitive, old enough to allow for the possibility of precocious consent. Like Simon, Henry occupies a position which allows him insight if not Simon's ability of successful articulation. It is of course the role of the fool to effect a commentary on society, the success of which commentary, analogous to Hartley's work as a filmmaker, relies upon the very marginality of his position.

The exploration of religious dogma implicit in *Henry Fool*'s interrogation of issues of redemption is explicit in Hartley's most recent short, *The Book of Life*. A millennium film set on the eve of the twenty-first century, *The Book of Life* modernizes a key Biblical conceit as Jesus (Martin Donovan) contemplates the fate of man, removing the Fifth Seal from the book with a click of the mouse. The film looks both backwards (reprising Hartley's irreverent treatment of religion, his use of a portfolio of actors, his tendency towards aphoristic dialogue, his concern with marginal characters) and forwards, suggesting a visual style that is looser and more fractured, and a tone more cautiously hopeful.

Hartley's films share a cinematographic and stylistic quirkiness, controlled irony, spontaneous outbursts of choreography and an eye for absurdity. In departing from the dominant Hollywood aesthetic, Hartley is perfectly placed to explore the marginality of the characters who inhabit his films. Consistently concerned with individuals whose search is for self-definition, Hartley alludes both to Godard and to the art-cinema aesthetic Godard exemplifies. This is emblematic of the cross-fertilization, nurtured by a film school education, of independent American and European art cinemas. For it is the nature of Hartley's characters, as much as his style and flouting of the conventions of narrative and genre, that simultaneously marks him as marginal, and secures his status as an important and original filmmaker.

Biography

Hartley was born 3 November 1959, in Lindenhurst, Long Island, USA, into a working-class family. In the late 1970s he attended the Massachusetts College of Art, and upon leaving began making short films on Super-8 before being admitted to the State University of New York (SUNY Purchase) Film School. Here, he made *Kid*, his thesis film, in 1984, and then worked for a time as a freelance Production Assistant before getting a job at Action Productions (which made public service announcements). Company president, Jerome Brownstein, invested $50,000 and Hartley made *The Unbelievable Truth*, his first feature.

Acknowledgement

This chapter was written with support from the UK's Arts and Humanities Research Board.

Notes

1 J. Pierson, *Spike, Mike, Slackers and Dykes: A Guided Tour across a Decade of Independent American Cinema*, London, Faber, 1996, p. 22.
2 J.W. Strubble, *The History of American Classical Music: Macdowell Through Minimalism*, London, Robert Hale, 1995, p. 333.

3 Andrew Sarris, 'The Care and Feeding of Auteurs: Trusting Hal Hartley', *Film Comment*, vol. 29, no. 1, 1993, pp. 66–8.

Filmography

Kid (1984) short
The Cartographer's Girlfriend (1987) short
Dogs (1988) short
The Unbelievable Truth (1989)
Trust (1990)
Theory of Achievement (1991) short
Ambition (1991) short
Surviving Desire (1991) short
Simple Men (1992)
Amateur (1994)
Flirt (1995)
Henry Fool (1997)
The Book of Life (1998) short

Further reading

G. Andrew, *Stranger Than Paradise: Maverick Filmmakers in Recent American Cinema*, London, Prion, 1988.
J. Boorman and Donohue (eds) *Projections: A Forum for Film Makers*, Issue 1, London, Faber, 1992.
P. Bowen, 'In Images We Trust: Hal Hartley Interviews Jean-Luc Godard', *Filmmaker*, vol. 3, no. 1, 1994, pp. 14–18, 55–6.
J. Fried, 'Rise of an Indie: An Interview with Hal Hartley', *Cinéaste*, vol. XIX, no. 4, 1993, pp. 38–40.
Hal Hartley, *Simple Men and Trust*, London, Faber, 1992.
—— *Amateur*, London, Faber, 1994.
—— *Flirt*, London, Faber, 1996.
—— *Henry Fool*, London, Faber, 1998.
K. Jones, 'Hal Hartley: The Book I Read was In Your Eyes', *Film Comment*, vol. 32, no. 4, 1996, pp. 68–72.
http: //www.best.com/ drumz/Hartley/Reviews/index.html.

LESLEY DEER

TODD HAYNES

TO ACT WITH GRANDEUR

> 'A man must dream a long time in order to act with grandeur, and dreaming is nursed in darkness.'

The above quote from Jean Genet, infamous French novelist,

playwright, filmmaker and outlaw, closes Todd Haynes' feature debut *Poison*. The words offer a call to action for those alienated and isolated from mainstream society, the major theme of the film, but even more so they perfectly capture the audacity of this young filmmaker. For Haynes, 'acting with grandeur' is a given through works that challenge, confuse and surprise audiences, even those accustomed to the world of art-house cinema.

Within the popular and academic worlds of film criticism, Haynes enjoys an enthusiastic following, with critics lauding his films as groundbreaking, visionary and bold. Haynes is perhaps most readily tagged as a cult director, beloved by critics, intellectuals and those who appreciate experimental cinema. By 2000, he had yet to direct a 'crossover' work – even *Velvet Goldmine*, an evocation of the glam-rock era and Haynes' most accessible film, failed to attract a wide audience. Secondarily, Haynes has been categorized as one of the most significant forces within the 'New Queer Cinema', a loosely defined group of gay and lesbian filmmakers whose work demonstrates a queer agenda, both politically and aesthetically. Despite his involvement with ACT-UP (AIDS Coalition to Unleash Power) and ACT-UP art collective, Gran Fury, Haynes' films address queer issues only obliquely. His films – from *Poison* to *Dottie Gets Spanked* and *Velvet Goldmine* – are more interested in the historical construction and determinants of gayness than in accounting for contemporary queer life or falling in line with standard genres of gay/lesbian film (e.g., the 'coming out' film). Haynes' work demonstrates a desire to connect gays/lesbians/queers with other marginalized groups and persons. Through this process, the division between dominant and subordinate groups in society is destabilized, disturbing the space allocated for 'others' in the social order.

As the writer and director of all his projects, Haynes has been able to guide each film carefully through all stages of development. His brief career is distinguished, however, by important collaborations with producer Christine Vachon, editor and actor James Lyons, and cinematographer Maryse Alberti. Vachon, in particular, plays a pivotal and continuing role in Haynes' career, producing all his projects from *Poison* onward.

After graduating from Brown University's programme in art/semiotics in 1985, Haynes co-founded Apparatus Productions with Vachon and Barry Ellsworth. Essentially a re-granting organization, Apparatus helped to fund those makers of short films who would not be competitive through the usual granting routes: 'We wanted to preserve the form of short film-making, and make it something really exciting that wasn't just a stepping stone for feature film-making.' After part of his post-graduate film production training at Bard College, Haynes made *Superstar: The Karen Carpenter Story*, a 43-minute mock documentary, acted entirely by Barbie and Ken dolls, telling the rise and fall, due to anorexia, of saccharine pop singer Karen Carpenter. The notoriety of the project – Haynes withdrew the film from distribution due to legal injunctions from the Carpenter family – was matched by Haynes' first feature, *Poison*, inspired by both Jean Genet and the AIDS epidemic. *Poison* moves between three interconnecting stories: 'Hero', a television-style documentary about patricide; 'Horror', a hyperbolic 1950s' style horror/science fiction parody about a scientist who becomes a leper sex killer after ingesting the 'sex drive' in liquid form; and 'Homo', the most direct connection to Genet, a florid examination of power and romantic obsession between two prisoners in 1930s' France. After winning the Grand Jury prize at the Sundance Film Festival, *Poison* was targeted by the religious right, particularly Reverend Donald Wildmon's American Family Association, who objected to the film's small completion grant from the National Endowment for the Arts.

While raising money for his next feature, Haynes wrote and directed the short television film *Dottie Gets Spanked* for the ITVS series, 'Television Families'. Like *Poison*, *Dottie* paints a picture of an outsider; this time, 6-year-old Steven, obsessed almost equally with television sitcom star Dottie Frank and spanking as a form of discipline. Steven's escape through his endless drawings of Dottie and his visit to her television show set represent important moments of happiness in this portrait of a child, already alienated from his father for his 'inappropriate' interests and fascinations. Haynes' heroine, Carol White, in his next feature, *Safe*, is also defined, first and foremost, by alienation. Set in the near past of 1987, the austere and completely restrained *Safe* vividly depicts Carol's disintegration: an upper-middle-class suburban housewife in the San Fernando valley, Carol begins to suffer from amorphous environmental illness, reacting toxically to everyday chemicals and stimulants in her environment. Medical doctors and psychiatrists fail to reverse Carol's deterioration, and she flees to Wrenwood, an alternative healing centre led by a New Age guru supposedly suffering from both chemical sensitivity and HIV-related infections.

Stylistically, *Safe* is distinguished by deliberate pacing, controlled settings and minimalism, parameters that are polar opposite to the cinematic traits of *Velvet Goldmine*. That film's fictional glam-rock world is, by design, excessive, energetic and highly stylized. Haynes' juxtaposition of opulent visuals (including Sandy Powell's Oscar-nominated costume designs), a hip star cast and original soundtrack aided the presentation of this world considerably. *Velvet Goldmine* is structured around reporter Arthur's investigation into a missing figure, fictional British glam-rock star Brian Slade (Jonathan Rhys Meyers). As Arthur (Christian Bale) interviews Slade's previous manager, his ex-wife and others associated with the androgynous star, the film's structural parallels to Welles' *Citizen Kane* (1941) become obvious. As the reporter recreates Slade's meteoric rise and fall, capped by a faked on-stage murder of the star at a London concert, Arthur is forced to confront his own adolescent fascination with glam, his confused sexuality, and his brief liaison with Slade's muse, American rock star Curt Wild (Ewan McGregor). *Velvet Goldmine* follows *Poison* in its interest in gay history, with Haynes locating Oscar Wilde, rather than Genet, as the film's spiritual father. Writing gay history as part of a fictional glam-rock exploration left mainstream audiences and some critics merely perplexed. How much of the audience could appreciate the startling opening with baby Oscar Wilde being delivered to his parents' doorstep by a spaceship? The lineage between Wilde and glam-rock is sketched lightly by Haynes, assuming a certain knowledge of gay history and culture on the part of his audience. This introduction illustrates how Haynes refuses to compromise his own vision, even within the context of a potential crossover production.

Echoing one of his heroes, Rainer Werner Fassbinder, Haynes' work is perhaps most significant for the relationship between formal experimentation and audience reception. Very few American directors of his generation evidence this kind of interest in narration, problematizing audience expectations and orientations. The form of this experimentation varies considerably, but invariably audiences are asked to question their notions about cinematic storytelling and character as part of this exercise. The origins for this may be located in having *Superstar* cast entirely with Barbie and Ken dolls. In some ways, the choice is obvious; tell the story of the most saccharine pop group of the 1970s using plastic figures, a camp gag at first glance. Yet *Superstar* cannot be reduced merely to camp or kitsch. Haynes dramatizes the film following the dictates of the star story and the 'disease-of-the-week' television movie, allowing for some intertitles, voice-over narration and inserted documentary footage. The dramatic force of the genres, our desire to connect with Karen Carpenter and our empathetic response to her battle with anorexia eventually make the film emotionally affecting and moving rather than a camp tale using dolls as its cast. Of course, the immediate response of viewing the family/star drama played with dolls is laughter, particularly given that the tale is depicted in a straightforward manner. Haynes' clear feeling for Karen and her pressures soon becomes evident. Moving from an immediate response of laughter and superiority to the sincere emotional one at Karen's demise is one of the film's most extraordinary accomplishments, forged through realizing that audiences want to identify so much with character and narrative that even plastic dolls will not derail this engagement.

Poison offers a different formal experiment through its interlacing of three stories of social outsiders. Nevertheless, just as *Superstar* shifts between disengaging (through the dolls) and bonding (through the narrative trajectory and genres) with the audience, *Poison* confronts the viewers through the interlacing of its three stories. The editing moves between three starkly different stories ('Horror', 'Homo', 'Hero') told in contrasting styles (black-and-white 'exploitation' in 'Horror'; lush colour and intimate surroundings in 'Homo'; and blank television documentary for 'Hero'). Audiences are forced to make the connections between the stories, some of which are obvious, others much more subtle. Haynes cuts, for example, from Dr Graves mistakenly ingesting the sex drive ('Horror') to a shot of the suburban homes in Richie's neighbourhood ('Hero') with the voice-over narration, 'the quiet community of Glenville was stunned'. While the narration refers to Richie's patricide and disappearance, the statement could just as readily refer to the 'stunned' community reaction to Graves' physical deterioration and disease. Other omnibus films – *Aria*, *Flirt*, *Three Cases of Murder* – tell sequential stories in full, yet Haynes' structure challenges viewers to build connections and to seek meaning. As with all Haynes' work, *Poison* is so dense in its style, structure and themes that multiple viewings are required.

Safe and *Velvet Goldmine* continue the stylistic experiments, but these films also illustrate Haynes' innovation in terms of character and identification. Both withhold traditional information and background on character and the cinematic structures through which we connect to them. For a film centred so squarely on a single character, we learn very little of Carol White's history, and motivation. Except for a single voice-over of Carol narrating one of her letters, Haynes offers almost nothing to anchor Carol as a character. She is defined by her milieu (upper middle class, San Fernando Valley), primary role ('home-maker'), and her frail yet blandly pretty good looks. Carol's identity equals these simple components, nothing more. We are left with a character study without the character – instead, Haynes examines the ways through which cultural and social factors construct Carol as a character. Stylistically, Haynes matches the blank lead with medium or long shots. On occasion, Haynes and cinematographer Alex Nepomniaschy hint at a close shot, such as the scene where Carol faints for the first time outside the kitchen. The camera moves closer, as if a close-up were the ultimate goal, but stops at a medium shot before abruptly cutting to the next scene. The close-up, critical for connecting the audience to the emotions of the character, is withheld.

Velvet Goldmine also revolves around a structuring absence, the missing Brian Slade. Just as *Safe* confounds viewers with a heroine blank, empty and reflective, *Velvet Goldmine*'s glam world is recreated, ten years on, by the boring and staid reporter Arthur. Rather than presenting Slade's stardom directly, Haynes refracts the action through Arthur so that we learn only bits and pieces of Slade's life, with many elements and pieces clearly missing. Slade remains an enigma, even once his 'new identity' has been revealed at the end of the film. While many filmmakers would have foregrounded the glamorous and exotic Slade and Curt Wild, their exploits and liaisons, Haynes is perhaps more interested in Arthur, the reporter and fan whose life has been altered forever by glam-rock.

These experiments in narrative, narration and character are not empty exercises or games on Haynes' part. Indeed, the formal experimentation follows from Haynes' sustained critique of the dominant ideology. This critique centres on the social structures designed to omit and ostracize certain people and groups from the mainstream of society. *Superstar*, for instance, clearly depicts how Karen Carpenter's family and the ingrained desire to be part of a 'perfect family' contribute greatly to her bulimia and anorexia. Haynes dramatizes this brilliantly with the shot of Karen waking up in the hospital after fainting on stage due to her bulimia: from Karen's point of view, the family members hover over the bed creating a spectacle of oppression for the fatigued young woman. Similarly, the shifts in genre and style in *Poison* and the narrative structure of *Velvet Goldmine* are motivated by a desire to avoid the traditional storytelling structures of classical and post-classical cinema and to investigate how these traits are complicit with the dominant society. For Haynes to offer alternatives for those alienated and marginalized, he must forge a new filmmaking language, upsetting the norms of cinematic story-telling.

For many critics, this desire to locate a space for those on the margins would be reduced to Haynes' status as one of the leading 'New Queer Cinema' directors. Identified by critic B. Ruby Rich, the New Queer Cinema united a group of films – by Haynes, Gus Van Sant, Tom Kalin, Gregg Araki, Jennie Livingston, among others – offering bold representations, unbounded by political correctness, of gays and lesbians in the era of right-wing agendas and AIDS stigmatization. After winning the Grand Jury prize at Sundance in 1991 and appearing on a queer filmmaker panel the following year at Sundance, Haynes became a central figure for Rich's argument. Certainly Haynes' work does qualify as queer, but in the traditional sense of the word: unusual, strange, disturbing. Placing Haynes within the New Queer Cinema in terms of identity politics is more problematic.

Tellingly, none of Haynes' films address the contemporary lifestyle of gays, lesbians, queers and others. Haynes completely avoids the form of labelling that limits his own work and the characters contained within it. To label is to limit the possibilities and opportunities for interpretation. Labelling also permits those in power to feel secure with clear boundaries separating those within and those outside the realms of power. Consider Steven from *Dottie Gets Spanked* and the leading characters (Slade, Wild, Arthur, Mandy) in *Velvet Goldmine*; none can be adequately typed or contained through sexual labels. The categories fail as a means to define the characters and their actions. The one openly gay character (self-help Guru Peter in *Safe*) also fails to adhere to a comfortable position for a gay character created by a gay director. Narratively, Peter could be presented as Carol's saviour, the person who potentially can make Carol love herself enough to cure her chemical sensitivity. Haynes deliberately undercuts Peter by suggesting that he is self-involved, manipulative and perhaps a fraud. Consequently, even the 'out' gay character in a Haynes film is typed more by social and economic power than by sexuality as a defining characteristic. Haynes denies the simple affirmative role models dictated by some in gay culture, a refusal that further complicates audience identification.

This emphasis on Haynes playing with audience expectation and cinematic convention may suggest that the films are cool, ironic and detached. Haynes is nevertheless, at the core, a deeply compassionate filmmaker. This can be gauged from the critical moments when outsiders do gain control: Steven burying his naughty drawing of Dottie getting spanked; Richie Beacon killing his father and flying through the bedroom window in *Poison*; and Arthur imagining a bold declaration of his sexuality to his parents in *Velvet Goldmine*. These attempts to empower the disenfranchised often take place in a fantasy world created by the characters apart from their tormentors. Haynes' ability to depict this world so expertly signals his total conviction in reclaiming the boundaries for those pushed to the side by dominant forces. Through presenting this reclamation project in such a formally experimental style, Haynes evokes the Russian Formalists' claim for the function of art in our lives, defamiliarization. In film after film, the director makes the familiar 'unfamiliar' and, in the process, helps to restore our own sense of the unusual, unexpected and beautiful within the everyday.

Biography

Todd Haynes was born 2 January 1961, in Los Angeles, USA.

Filmography

Superstar: The Karen Carpenter Story (co-written with Cynthia Schneider, 1987)
Poison (1991)
Dottie Gets Spanked (1993)
Safe (1995)
Velvet Goldmine (1998)

Further reading

M. Dargis, 'Endangered Zone', *The Village Voice*, 4 July 1995, pp. 38–40.
R. Grundmann, 'How Clean Was My Valley: Todd Haynes' *Safe*', *Cineaste*, 21, 1995, pp. 22–5.
T. Haynes, *Velvet Goldmine*, New York, Hyperion Books, 1998.
N. James, 'American Voyeur', *Sight and Sound*, Sept. 1998, pp. 8–10.
B. Kruger, 'Into Thin Air: Karen Carpenter Superstar', *Artforum*, vol. 26, no. 4, 1987, pp. 107–8.
M. Laskawy, '*Poison* at the Box Office: An Interview with Todd Haynes', *Cineaste*, 18, 1991, pp. 38–9.
E. O'Neill, '*Poison*-ous Queers: Violence and Social Order', *Spectator*, 1994, pp. 9–29.
B. Ruby Rich, 'A Queer Sensation', *The Village Voice*, 24 March 1992, pp. 41–4.
J. Savage, 'Tasteful Tales', *Sight and Sound*, October 1991, pp. 15–17.
C. Vachon and D. Edelstein, *Shooting to Kill*, New York, Avon Books, 1998.
J. Wyatt, 'Cinematic/Sexual Transgression: An Interview with Todd Haynes', *Film Quarterly*, vol. 46, no. 3, 1993, pp. 2–8.
—— *Poison*, Trowbridge, Flicks Books, 1998.

JUSTIN WYATT

STRANGER THAN FICTION

THE RISE AND FALL OF JIM JARMUSCH

'I'm hopeful there can be a new kind of American cinema that can embrace influences from Hollywood and from Europe or Japan or other more pure kinds of cinema.'

Jim Jarmusch, 1984

All hail the resident hipster

Jarmusch is a rarity among American directors in that he actually stands for something – independence. He also stands apart from his compatriots in a stated commitment to the fostering of art cinema, to offering his viewers a global perspective (even if it means delving into an author–pupil relationship). Jarmusch has the persona to make people listen. His status as a walking symbol of 'American independent film' is both a function of his own creation, and a critical consensus nurtured by historical trends. The public perception of Jarmusch has enabled him to get his message across – up to a point.

A prematurely grey mop of hair and a deliberate laconic drawl, combined with Jarmusch's background in the late 1970s' New York art scene as musician, filmmaker and social gadfly, create the image of the worldly hipster. Jarmusch has carefully bolstered his persona through cameo appearances in such films as Alex Cox's *Straight to Hell*, Raúl Ruiz's *The Golden Boat*, and films by Aki (*Leningrad Cowboys Go America*) and Mika (*Tigrero*, appearing alongside Sam Fuller, no less) Kaurismäki; cameos in popular films like *Sling Blade* have ensured wider recognition. Despite hailing from Akron, Ohio, and despite the fact that only two of his films have been entirely set in New York (*Permanent Vacation* and *Ghost Dog*), at the height of his fame a *New York Times* profiler went so far as to call the Bowery 'Planet Jarmusch'. From 1984 through to as late as 1993, a new Jarmusch film was an event. All four of his features premiered at the selective and prestigious New York Film Festival, most after first débuting at Cannes.

Much of this reaction is a factor of Jarmusch's early adoption by the influential members of the US zeitgeist press, many based in his adopted New York, as the great white-haired hope: this reached a high point very early on, with a National Society of Film Critics

Award for his second film, *Stranger Than Paradise*, in 1984.[1] (The film also won the Camera d'Or at the Cannes Film Festival.) A Warholian work born out of the New York avant-garde minimalist scene as much as the Antonioni-influenced strain of European cinema, the black-and-white *Stranger Than Paradise* is the blueprint for Jarmusch's road movies that followed: a foreigner (Estzer Balint) comes to the States (from Hungary) and forces the natives (John Lurie, Richard Edson) to confront their own deeply held ideas about their country, and the American dream. The screenplay and the characters' physical reactions are laced with an absurdist sense of humour.

Though *Stranger Than Paradise* seemed to appear out of nowhere, Jarmusch's first film, *Permanent Vacation*, set the tone for the 'Jarmusch film'. The *Variety* reviewer for this relatively unseen film, made with the help of Nicholas Ray, described it thus: '*Permanent Vacation* is a visually arresting narrative of alienation hailing from the New York underground school of indie filmmaking'[2] (a description which could summarize Jarmusch's next four features). Repeating oneself, whilst one's definition of an auteur, is another's definition of playing up to an audience (and, consequently, mistaking crowd-pleasing for personal artistic expression). Jarmusch's familiar pattern would soon attract the scorn of some of his earliest admirers. As Jarmusch's most perceptive commentator Jonathan Rosenbaum presciently wrote in a 1992 review of *Night on Earth*:

> Jarmusch is mainly honoured and rewarded to the extent that he turns out familiar goods (attitude as style, star as icon, road as the world) rather than assumes any risks. The paradoxical upshot is that our most photogenic representative of artistic independence and freedom is often rewarded for doing the same things over and over again.[3]

Those 'same things' – a reliance on an episodic structure at the expense of the strong narrative characteristic of Hollywood films in particular – could only be tolerated by most American critics up to a point. Some critics had deserted Jarmusch even earlier: writing about *Mystery Train*, David Denby commented that: 'one feels Jarmusch has pushed hipsterism and cool about as far as they can go, and that isn't nearly far enough'.[4] Yet at precisely the moment that Jarmusch turned away from what could be mistaken for an all attitude and style cinema, the critics wanted precisely that which they had begun to criticize.

Dead Man premiered in 1995 to little American acclaim at the Cannes Film Festival. *Variety*'s Todd McCarthy appreciated its 'quirky tone, hipsterish performances and ... highly refined visual style' but found that 'the film's pleasures are simply too elusive and mild to make up for a lack of narrative propulsion'.[5] The irony – and where would Jarmusch be without irony – is that these pleasures (and the lack of a traditional narrative) were precisely those factors fawned over in 1984 – but in the context of a film that was not as openly political. *Dead Man* may have amounted to a paradigm shift in Jarmusch's work insofar as, in a more sober tone than usual, it elucidated the political subtext that had informed his work up to then. Furthermore, most critics who were the first to hail Jarmusch failed to realize that, in fact, in 1984 they were actually watching art films that attacked the myths of prosperity of Reagan's America, and general ideas of ethnocentrism. They were being confronted by their own narrow-mindedness; when this became clear, they unsurprisingly backed off.

(Foreign) influence

A semi-neorealist black comedy in the style of an imaginary Eastern-European film director obsessed with Ozu and familiar with the 1950s American television show *The Honeymooners* ... It's easier to talk about the style of the film than 'what's it about'.[6]

When one lists the number of filmmakers that Jarmusch alludes to, it reads like a dictionary of the cinema. A quick survey: Jarmusch had all of Antonioni's movies screened before shooting *Down by Law* (with its Wim Wender-like images provided by cinematographer Robby Müller) because, he has said, 'Antonioni is so elegant in the way he can let the scene go past its normal length, or the shot even, and the whole weight of the scene changes, the essence'. (Other filmmakers mentioned in the interview include Ray, Kurosawa, Ozu, Godard, Rivette, Eustache, Vertov, Ruiz, Fellini, Lang, Sirk, Ulmer and Vigo.) Why does he use homages? At times it is indeed a wink to his audience, underlining his status as a global filmmaker. More fundamentally, Jarmusch sees something inherently American about this clash (as opposed to integration) of references: 'America's kind of a throwaway culture that's made of this mixture of different cultures. To make a film about America, it seems to me logical to have at least one perspective that's transplanted here from some other culture, because ours is a collection of transplanted influences.'[7] This sense of what it means to be American spawns the educative function of Jarmusch's cinema; his is a kind of model for other Americans who want to make films not based on established Hollywood or television style.[8]

Jarmusch's foreign influences are, for the most part, integrated on a structural level, rather than existing on the surface as postmodern references (though he seems to be moving in that direction). His use of homage is also a mnemonic effect of the process of his writing: 'Rather than finding a story that I want to tell and then adding the details, I collect the details and then try to construct a puzzle or a story.'[9] The idea of putting William Blake at the centre of *Dead Man*, for example, only appeared near completion of the script's first draft.[10]

To give another example, homage is the structural principle of *Night on Earth* – five stories, five different filmmakers and/or national cinemas alluded to: the first episode, starring Gena Rowlands and shot by *The Killing of a Chinese Bookie* cinematographer Frederick Elmes, is an homage to Cassavetes; the New York episode is Jarmusch's nod to Spike Lee; the final episode, set in Finland, is Kaurismäki-laden (the main characters are called Mika and Aki). Again, the purpose is not a wink at the audience so much as a desire to open one's eyes to other ways of seeing and making films. Although not traditionally self-reflexive, Jarmusch's persistent use of homage and the privileging of chance in his storylines has many viewers and critics mistaking him for an empty postmodernist – however, nothing could be further from the truth. Jarmusch's fiction films all adhere to a traditional three-act structure; his road movies are more inspired by Homer than Hope and Crosby. If there is a postmodern strain in his work, it is a sorrowful one. Jarmusch's use of homage has changed over his film career towards one more recognizably postmodern in *Ghost Dog*, where it seems as if the references are directed towards the foreign audience, in a film dedicated to Seijun Suzuki and Samuel Fuller, and loosely based on the Japanese works of the Hagakure and *Rashomon*, plus Jean-Pierre Melville's *Le Samourai*. *Ghost Dog* not only speaks to other cultures, but at times seems to be made for them.[11]

Yet, when the hipsterism, Jarmusch's punk background and ethos, and his personal stylistic choices combine, Jarmusch's films feel like more than just the sum of their parts. In any of his first five films, it takes minutes to establish that one is watching a 'Jim Jarmusch' film – because of the music, the cast, the camera style and, above all, the attitude (which often is, in fact, the style). As J. Hoberman notes:

> With its dislocated travelogue, *Stranger Than Paradise* suggests Wim Wenders' *Kings of the Road*; the transcendently shabby moonscapes evoke Chantal Ackerman's *News from Home* and the absence of reverse angles her *Jeanne Dielman*; while the shaggy-dog narrative and vignette structure are anticipated by Jim Benning's *81.2 X 11* and *11 X 14*. Jarmusch exhibits free-floating affinities to filmmakers as disparate as Ron Rice and Carl Dreyer as well, but ... the film is too strongly imagined and assembled to ever seem derivative. It's never less than wholly and confidently itself.[12]

When he is working at his best, Jarmusch's works are *sui generis*.

Dead Man – American independent filmmaking at a crossroads

> To me, 'independent' means staying independent from your work being dictated to, or formed by, some concept of a marketplace. ... 'Independent' means being artistically free.[13]

Does independent filmmaking matter any more? What does it mean to be an independent in today's American film marketplace? Along with fellow NYU film school graduates Susan Seidelman, the Coen brothers and Spike Lee, Jarmusch became part of a new American independent film movement in the mid-1980s. The reason why Jarmusch and 'independent filmmaker' are synonymous in many viewers' minds may have something to do with style (French New Wave-influenced visuals, minimalism in the age of MTV) and content (a healthily critical attitude to mainstream America and its values, from the American dream in his 1980s' trilogy through to the preoccupation with deglamourizing violence in *Dead Man* and *Ghost Dog*). Yet these same attributes can be found in any number of Hollywood films.

Jarmusch's true independence – as distinct from the other New Yorkers – has to do with a decision to maintain as much control as possible over his means of production, and striking an unprofitable balance between commercial requirements (that is, the need to raise money to make the film and the need to deal with a distributor to have the film seen) and artistic interests. As he has said, 'Independent filmmaking is a lot like gambling, I could make a lot more money by taking directing jobs, or giving away control of my films and selling them to the highest bidder. But if I'm putting up three years of my life and a lot of work, and you put up the money, we can split the profits, but I keep the negative.'[14] Jarmusch is the only American narrative filmmaker to own his own negatives. *Mystery Train* was the first US-directed film to be fully funded by a foreign source, Japan's JVC.

This form of independence has given rise to, as Hoberman puts it, a cool sense of solitude and isolation.[15] The Jarmusch hero is often self-reliant, refusing the help of others. His America is no melting pot of assimilation – rather, it is a multicultural, worldly view of America; what Americans must confront when 'outsiders' are injected into their midst, providing a view that they cannot account for in their own, culturally specific, logic.

A film about death – of a way of life, a culture, and of an individual – the biting conceptual brilliance of *Dead Man* comes in the fact that the outsider is not Johnny Depp's visitor from the industrial East, but Gary Farmer's Nobody, a stranger in his own, increasingly strange land. The reason why Jarmusch is less appreciated at home than abroad is that Americans probably do not care much about how other people see them; they prefer their mythologies home-grown and time-worn. Although *Dead Man* might be the first Western in black and white since *The Man Who Shot Liberty Valance*, it is anything but John Ford-inspired; the landscape, though evocatively photographed, can only be described as ugly.

It is not that this fierce defiance towards commercialism breeds hostility in and of itself; rather, it is clearly out of fashion. The movement in American independent film is away from Jarmusch's definition of freedom, towards one more readily associated with the increasingly artistically irrelevant Sundance Film Festival, where US films without a distributor come to steal their souls and snatch multiple picture deals with Miramax. *Dead Man* appeared as the Sundance phenomenon had become fully accepted as the route for American independent film; the film was produced for and distributed by Miramax, and essentially dumped; Jarmusch refused to allow a recut, and publicly denounced Miramax for the handling of the film at the New York Film Critics Circle Awards.

Yet even with such an accomplishment as *Dead Man*, the few supporters at the time of its release could not stray from their standard comparisons. Hoberman wrote, 'This is the Western that Andrei Tarkovsky wanted to make'.[16] Rosenbaum commented that:

> *Dead Man* can be seen as the fulfillment of a cherished counterculture dream, the acid Western. This ideal has haunted such films as Jim McBride's *Glen and Randa*, Dennis Hopper's *The Last Movie*, Monte Hellman's *The Shooting* and *Two-Lane Blacktop*, Robert Downey's *Greaser's Palace*, and Alex Cox's *Walker* … Yet in some ways *Dead Man* goes beyond all of them in formulating a chilling, savage poetry to justify its hallucinated agenda – a view at once clear-eyed and visionary, exalted and laconic, moral and unsentimental, witty and beautiful, frightening and placid.[17]

In other words, *Dead Man* is, like Jarmusch, *sui generis*.

Postscript: does a director matter?

> Movies are very musical … To me, music is the most pure form of art in that it communicates something immediately and it doesn't necessarily have to be restricted by your understanding of a language. And film is a lot like music in that a film has a rhythm like a piece of music. You start a film and that rhythm takes you through the story that's being told or the length of time the film lasts. The same way with a piece of music. They're closely related with rhythm: the cutting of the film, the way a camera moves, and the way a story is put together.[18]

So Jarmusch may be the inbred bastard of American directors; film, after all, is the bastard of the arts. The signifying elements of a 'Jarmusch film' are the rhythms, often in association with the music: the travelling pans over the opening credits of *Down by Law* to Tom Waits' 'Jockey Full of Bourbon'. John Lurie's evocative, jazzy scores (*Down by Law, Stranger Than Paradise*), Waits' jangly score for the serialist *Night on Earth*, the RZA's hip-hop playing as Forrest

Whittaker practises swinging his sword on the roof in *Ghost Dog*; Neil Young's indispensable solo guitar accompaniment to *Dead Man*.

Jarmusch's most cruelly underrated film is his 1997 concert film of anti-establishment rockers, and the musical equivalent of Sam Fuller, Neil Young and Crazy Horse, *Year of the Horse*. Rather than overlapping attitude and style, *Horse* is a perfect blend of content (here, the music) and style – shot in Super-8, 16mm and Hi-8, in a mix of colour and black and white. The rhythms are perfect. Other commentators ignore it because of the absence of typical Jarmuschian themes and structure in this non-narrative film, but this is the exception that proves the rule. The main character is an outsider who sheds light on American society and values; furthermore, with Jarmusch's definition of independence, it fits in perfectly. Jarmusch listened to Young's music while writing *Dead Man*. Young, a Canadian living and working in the US, whose abrasive modernism and punk ethos must appeal to the director, a former punk musician: they are the warhorses who represent systemic challenge. Young is known for his outspoken anti-digital stance; Jarmusch considers himself 'an analogue man'; Young's contract battles with Geffen Records are legendary, akin to Jarmusch's difficulty with Miramax over *Dead Man*.

Year of the Horse is anomalous in one respect – instead of focusing on a solitary hero, Jarmusch goes through pains to enforce the band's solidarity.[19] For all of Jarmsuch's independence, the subtext of *Year of the Horse* is that he would be nowhere without his collaborators – the musicians, for sure, but also his editor (Jay Rabinowitz), cinematographers and actors. If, as with the most relevant contemporary American directors (e.g. Soderbergh), Jarmusch uses film to explore his anxiety with Hollywood filmmaking, *Year of the Horse*, most of all, is a subtle metaphor for the moviemaking compromise.

Biography

Born in Akron, Ohio, USA, in 1953, Jarmusch studied at New York University Graduate Film School (1976–9) and was a teaching assistant to Nicholas Ray.

Notes

1 *The New Yorker* excluded: Pauline Kael wrote that *Stranger Than Paradise* was full of 'bombed out listlessness'; her acolytes have been

consistent in their disapproval. Pauline Kael, *State of the Art*, New York, E.P. Dutton, 1985, p. 262.

2 *Variety*, 15 October 1982.

3 Jonathan Rosenbaum, 'Five Easy Pieces', *Chicago Reader*, 15 May 1992, p. 12.

4 David Denby, 'The Memphis Blues Again', *New York*, 20 November 1989, p. 120.

5 Todd McCarthy, 'Jarmusch's Mystery Train Goes West', *Variety*, 5 June 1995, p. 36.

6 Jim Jarmusch, 'Some Notes on *Stranger Than Paradise*', Press Kit, p. 1.

7 Tim Holmes, 'Too Cool for Words', *Rolling Stone*, 6 November 1986.

8 As Kevin Smith notoriously quipped: 'I don't feel that I have to go back and view European or other foreign films because I feel like these guys [i.e., Jarmusch] have already done it for me, and I'm getting it filtered through them' (Jonathan Rosenbaum, 'A Gun Up Your Ass: An Interview with Jim Jarmusch', *Cineaste*, vol. 22, no. 2, 1996, p. 20). Yet it is hard to argue that Jarmusch's purpose for most Americans is as a filter and reinterpreter, or as a replacement for seeing foreign films, because so few Americans see Jarmusch's films in the first place. Ironically, it seems that *foreign* filmmakers are the more influenced by Jarmusch now.

9 Harlan Jacobson, 'Three Guys in Three Directions / *Stranger Than Paradise* $120,000', *Film Comment*, vol. 21, no. 1, 1985, p. 54.

10 Jonathan Rosenbaum, *op. cit.*

11 Indeed, Jarmusch's popularity abroad – in France and Japan especially – now far eclipses his notoriety in the US.

12 J. Hoberman, 'Americana, Right and Wrong', *The Village Voice*, 2 October 1984, p. 50.

13 Jim Jarmusch, Filmmaker Focus, 'Sundance Channel' website: www.sundancechannel.com/focus/jarmusch (1996).

14 *Variety*, 27 December 1989.

15 *The Village Voice*, 5 May 1992, p. 59.

16 J. Hoberman, 'Promised Lands', *The Village Voice*, 14 May 1996.

17 Jonathan Rosenbaum, 'Acid Western', *Chicago Reader*, 26 June 1986.

18 Filmmaker Focus, 'Sundance Channel' website, *op. cit.*

19 This is not a documentary about Neil Young, or really about the band Neil Young and Crazy Horse. It is about the results of the creative process – the music. (Truthfully, it is more concert film than documentary.) Compare this to the distorted view of The Band provided by Martin Scorsese in *The Last Waltz*, where 'leader' Robbie Robertson was privileged over the other members.

Filmography

Permanent Vacation (1982)
The New World (1982) short
Stranger Than Paradise (1984)
The Lady Don't Mind (1985) music video for Talking Heads
Down by Law (1986)
Coffee and Cigarettes (1987) short

Sightsee MC! (1987) music video for Big Audio Dynamite
Coffee and Cigarettes (*Memphis Version*) (1989) short
Mystery Train (1989)
It's Alright with Me (1990) music video for Tom Waits
Night on Earth (1991)
I Don't Wanna Grow Up (1992) music video for Tom Waits
Coffee and Cigarettes (*Somewhere in California*) (1993) short
Dead Man (1995)
Big Time (1996) music video for Neil Young
Year of the Horse (1997)
Ghost Dog: The Way of the Samurai (1999)

Further reading

Dan Gribben, 'Gone Fishing: Jim Jarmusch's *Mystery Train*', *Film Comment*, vol. 31, no. 6, 1995, pp. 80–4.
Ludvig Hertzberg (ed.) *Jim Jarmusch: Interviews*, in 'Conversations with Filmmakers' series, Jackson, MS, University Press of Mississippi, 2001.
J. Hoberman, 'Individualists', *The Village Voice*, 5 May 1992, pp. 59–60.
Flo Leibowitz, 'Neither Hollywood nor Godard: The Strange Case of *Stranger Than Paradise*', *Persistence of Vision*, no. 6, 1988, pp. 20–5.
Gregg Rickman, 'The Western under Erasure: *Dead Man*', in Kitses and G. Rickman (eds) *The Western Reader*, New York, Limelight, 1998.
Jonathan Rosenbaum, *Dead Man*, London, BFI Publishing, 2000.
—— 'International Sampler', *Chicago Reader*, 17 March 2000.

MARK PERANSON

NEIL JORDAN

Neil Jordan's work cannot be easily classified, since it ranges across genre (comedy, thriller, horror), location (Ireland, Britain, the United States), era (contemporary, 1920s, 1940s, 1960s) and subject matter (Northern Ireland, vampires, incestuous desire, religion, adolescence). His career has also been erratic, from the outstanding critical and popular success of *The Crying Game* to the lukewarm reception of *We're No Angels*, the hostile response to the ill-conceived *High Spirits*, and the virtual silence surrounding *The Miracle*. The interest in Jordan's work lies in his skill with characterization, the creation of atmospheric locations and the way in which his films are consistently concerned with the crossing of the boundaries of gender, sexuality and the body.

A novelist and short story writer as well as a filmmaker, Jordan's writing abilities are evident in the dialogue, characterization and narratives of his films. He has written the screenplays for ten of the twelve films he has directed so far, in collaboration with the original authors in the case of *Company of Wolves, Interview with the Vampire* and *The Butcher Boy*. Flawed but sympathetic heroes populate Jordan's films, which are concerned principally with the yearning and longing underpinning relationships between lovers, family and friends; the permutations of these relationships are often highlighted by violent situations. Jordan's novels and short stories minutely dissect the emotions of their protagonists, mapping out inner landscapes of thoughts and feelings. These are firmly linked to place; emotional states are placed in the context of physical surroundings, the outer landscapes of sea, beach, or alienating city. A similar juxtaposition of interior emotions and exterior surroundings occurs in the films, but here emotions are conveyed through facial expression and atmospheric locations, resulting in a dream-like feel. The casting of Stephen Rea, whose low-key acting style conveys sadness and thoughtfulness in many of the films, is significant here ('he's got a face that you can project every thought into,' says Jordan).[1] The expression of inner emotions through *mise-en-scène* is particularly pronounced in the gothic/horror films, *Company of Wolves, Interview with the Vampire* and *In Dreams*. Music is also a crucial factor in establishing mood. The protagonist of *Angel*, Jordan's first feature film, is a saxophonist in a showband who exchanges his saxophone for a gun after the murder of a deaf-mute woman; Nat King Cole's 'Mona Lisa' underlines the mystery and inaccessibility of Simone, the black prostitute in *Mona Lisa*; Dil's lip-synching performance of 'The Crying Game' prefigures the difficulties her relationship with Fergus will face, as well as referring back to her relationship with the now-dead Jody. The final scene's inspired use of 'Stand by Your Man' (beginning with the lines 'Sometimes it's hard to be a woman'), takes on an amusingly ironic meaning in the context of Dil's transvestism.

If there is one theme which could be identified across Jordan's work, it is the crossing and blurring of boundaries: between countries (Ireland and the UK in *Angel, The Crying Game* and *Michael Collins*), political factions and ideologies (*Angel, Michael Collins*), black and white (*The Crying Game*, although this aspect of the film is under-developed), male and female (*The Crying Game*), heterosexual and homosexual (*Mona Lisa, The Crying Game, Interview with the Vampire*), animal and human (*Company of Wolves, Interview with the Vampire* and, to a lesser extent, *The Butcher Boy*), mind and body (*In Dreams*) and love and hate (*The End of the Affair*). It is this aspect of Jordan's work which has gained the most critical attention, particularly in relation to *The Crying Game*. The coincidence between this particular theme in Jordan's films and the preoccupation of critical theory and film criticism with the construction and negotiation of identities (particularly gender and sexual identities, and, increasingly, national and racial/ethnic identities) is probably one of the main reasons why Jordan is held in high esteem by critics, and why his work is relevant to the cultural concerns of the late twentieth and early twenty-first centuries. In addition, while his films are, for the most part, art-house, several have had crossover appeal, ensuring popularity with critics and audiences alike. Given the contentious subject matter of some of his films, he is also a figure who has excited controversy, most notably over *The Crying Game* and *Michael Collins*.

Gender and national identities: 'The Crying Game'

The extreme difficulty in acquiring funding for *The Crying Game*, its subsequent success at the box office and at the Academy Awards (nominated in six categories, it won the award for Best Original Screenplay), and the success of its marketing campaign, where reviewers were asked not to reveal the 'twist', ensured enormous publicity for the film, bringing Jordan to international attention. Celebrated and excoriated in equal measure for its portrayal of an ex-IRA man who falls in love with a woman who is later revealed to be a gay male transvestite, *The Crying Game* has received extensive critical attention, mostly focusing on the play with gender identity.

On the one hand, *The Crying Game* addresses the constructedness, performativity and fluidity of identity, particularly gender and sexual identities. Throughout the film, characters are not what they seem. Jody, the black British soldier who is held hostage by the IRA, is initially seen being seduced by Jude, a female IRA recruit, but is then revealed to be in a gay relationship with a transvestite; Fergus is, at the beginning of the film, in a heterosexual relationship with Jude, but later has to come to terms with his attraction to Jody and his feelings for Dil, whom he initially mistakes for a woman. This, of course, is the principal instance of mistaken identity in the film, the 'secret' that reviewers were asked not to reveal as part of the marketing campaign. Dil's performance of femininity is achieved through her clothes and make-up and mannerisms, which are exaggeratedly 'feminine': coy, flirtatious, helpless, needing and desiring male protection. The mostly successful deception of the audience, however, is also achieved by the narrative and visual techniques used on Dil, techniques which are usually used in relation to female characters, constructing them as erotic objects of male desire. Dil is first introduced as an image, a photograph which Jody shows to Fergus, asking him to admire her. Dil is subsequently seen repeatedly from Fergus' point of view; in narrative terms, her character is positioned as the object of his desire. Thus Dil's performance of femininity is aided and underscored by the techniques of classic narrative.

Other characters also adopt different identities: Fergus leaves Ireland and the IRA, reinventing himself in London as Jimmy; at one stage, Fergus compels Dil to dress in Jody's clothes, thus reconstructing her as a man; Jude, too, reinvents herself, exchanging blonde curls and jeans for a sleek black bob and 1940s' style suit. National and racial/ethnic identities are blurred in the bond formed between an IRA man and a black British soldier, and in Dil's assumption that Fergus is Scottish. In this respect, the film appears to be arguing that one is not born a man or a woman, straight or gay, Irish or British, but that these identities are contingent, constantly in flux.

On the other hand, the treatment of Jude is conventional in its demonization and punishment of a woman who crosses the boundaries of traditional femininity, and her re-appearance in London, wearing a suit, carrying a gun and threatening Fergus' relationship with Dil, evokes the *femme fatale* of film noir. Her punishment, where she is viciously and repeatedly shot by Dil, is also reminiscent of the *femme fatale*'s.[2] In addition, some Irish critics have taken issue with the portrayal of the IRA, arguing that the characters of Maguire and Jude merely continue a pattern established by British films about Northern Ireland – one which portrays the IRA as ruthless fanatics and attributes humanity only to the character who attempts to leave the organization.[3] David Lloyd has also castigated *The Crying Game* for its implicit opposition between a rural Ireland mired in atavistic violence and a pluralist, metropolitan London.[4] Interestingly, then, while *The Crying Game* questions notions of fixed and essentialist identities, it simultaneously reinforces female and national stereotypes.

Mysterious, often inaccessible women recur in Jordan's films, idealized and pursued by a troubled male character. It is masculinity and masculine identity, rather than femininity that provides the main focus for Jordan's films. Although female characters are given a voice, interest lies in the films' troubled male characters; female characters serve either as the ostensible cause of the men's anxieties or to highlight them. Like the heroes of film noir, the codes of which

Mona Lisa, particularly, alludes to, Jordan's heroes are often acted upon more than acting, innocents who consistently fail to see or understand either themselves or the people around them. Fergus unwittingly follows through his unexpressed desire for Jody by pursuing Jody's transvestite lover, unaware that Dil is a biological man; in *Mona Lisa*, George fails to see that Simone's search for Cathy is motivated by love rather than friendship; in *The End of the Affair*, Bendix is tortured by his lack of understanding of why Sarah ended their affair. Even in those films containing more dynamic heroes (*Michael Collins, The Butcher Boy*), the protagonists are haunted by the loss of friends.

Although critical attention to the construction of masculinity in cinema is growing, *The Crying Game* and *Michael Collins* are as yet the only of Jordan's films to have received sustained analyses on this point. This is surprising, since the romantic/sexual triangle is a significant and recurrent feature of his work, with the woman frequently functioning as a mediator of homoerotic desire. Although a common dramatic device in cinema and literature (as analysed by Eve Sedgwick's *Between Men*), Jordan's variations of this structure foreground rather than suppress its homoerotic underpinnings. The scenes between Louis and Lestat in *Interview with the Vampire* (as when Louis receives a sensual bite from Lestat), between Fergus and Jody in *The Crying Game*, and, to a lesser extent, between Collins and Boland in *Michael Collins* and Francie and Joe in *The Butcher Boy*, are infused with homoerotic desire, but tend to avoid overt homosexuality.

National filmmaker: 'Michael Collins'

Although several of his earlier films had been set in Ireland (*Angel, The Miracle, High Spirits, The Crying Game*), Jordan's status as a national filmmaker was fully consolidated with the release of his historical epic, *Michael Collins*, covering the life of the guerilla leader from 1916 to his death in 1922, at the age of 31. Prior to this, Jordan's relationship to Irish viewers and critics was an uneasy one. His first feature, *Angel*, caused controversy from the outset, the only film to receive funding from the newly established Irish Film Board.[5] Critically, it had a mixed reception. Richard Kearney praised the film's metaphysical exploration of violence.[6] But John Hill's highly influential 'Images of Violence', which analyses British films about Northern Ireland, argued that the film did not represent any significant break from the narrative patterns already established by British films. For Hill these patterns avoid any sustained analysis of the roots of the conflict in Northern Ireland and thus decontextualize IRA violence.[7]

Michael Collins saw Jordan's first cinematic engagement with Irish history. The events it covers, the War of Independence (1919–1921), the Civil War (1922–1923) and the establishment of the border between Northern Ireland and the Free State (later to become the Republic), still have enormous resonance and significance to contemporary Irish politics. Made and released during the turbulent negotiations around the peace process, *Michael Collins* had extraordinary parallels with contemporary political proceedings in Northern Ireland, parallels which Jordan acknowledged whilst maintaining they were not intentional. Addressing events from the relatively recent past, the repercussions of which are still being felt today, it was inevitable that *Michael Collins* would cause controversy. Heated debates took place in the Irish press, mainly around the historical accuracy of the film, while in Britain, the response was mixed, with several reviewers condemning it for being pro-republican and thus implicitly pro-IRA.[8] Although the first film since *Irish Destiny* (Dewhurst, 1926) and *The Dawn* (Cooper, 1936) to portray its nationalist protagonist in conventionally heroic terms, it is highly unlikely that *Michael Collins* would or could have been made if Collins had not turned from violent resistance to British rule to negotiation with it. Even the first half of the film, where Collins wages guerilla war against the Empire, is ambiguous about the use of violence, and the second half, which covers the Civil War, is imbued with a sense of tragedy and irony.

Michael Collins was rapturously received by the general public in Ireland, and by most of the press, as a national epic. It rapidly took on the status of the Irish equivalent of Griffith's *Birth of a Nation* (notwithstanding that film's controversial treatment of racial issues), a sweeping epic narrating a pivotal moment in a nation's history. The press reported regularly on the production and shooting process; thousands of people took part in the film as unpaid extras in the crowd scenes; a significant number of Irish actors were cast in the main roles (Liam Neeson as Collins, Aidan Quinn as Boland and Stephen Rea as Ned Broy), and, just before its release, the national film censor revised the age certificate from 15 to 12, announcing in a press statement that he had done so in order that as many people as possible would have the opportunity of viewing it.

The intensity of the response to *Michael Collins* in Ireland and its elevation to the status of national epic are due in part to the paucity of films about Ireland's history from an Irish point of view. Yet Jordan's masterly use of the narrative techniques of Hollywood cinema and the gangster genre also lends a dynamic energy and emotional depth to complex historical events. The relationship between Collins and his friend Harry Boland is the film's principal affective drive, functioning to personify the two opposing sides in the Civil War which followed the War of Independence: those who opposed the Treaty and those who supported it. Julia Roberts' role as Collins' fiancée, Kitty Kiernan, was criticized for being under-written, but, as one Irish critic noted, the main function of Kiernan's character is not realist but symbolic:[9] Kiernan, dressed in a green coat in the final scenes which cut between her shopping for her wedding dress and Collins' assassination in Béal na Bláth, symbolizes the Irish nation itself.

Neil Jordan's status as a filmmaker lies in his ability to address issues of contemporary cultural and social significance, such as sexuality, gender and colonialism/postcolonialism. His skilful writing and masterful construction of character, dialogue and narrative allows for an accessible exploration of such issues, one that does not sacrifice complexity. Jordan has increasingly moved towards studio productions with major stars, but although he is now working on a broader canvas, the same themes recur, most notably the placement of characters in atmospheric surroundings which convey their inner emotions. The eclecticism of Jordan's interests, the erratic nature of his career and the wide range of subject matter already treated by his films ensure the continuation of critical and popular interest in his work.

Biography

Neil Jordan was born in Sligo, Ireland, on 25 February 1950. He worked with Jon Boorman on *Excalibur* (1981) and directed his first feature, *Angel*, a year later. Jordan is also a novelist and short story writer. His books are: *Night in Tunisia, The Past, The Dream of a Beast* and *Sunrise with Sea Monster*.

Notes

1 Jane Giles, *The Crying Game*, London, BFI Publishing, 1997, p. 32.
2 Mark Simpson, *Male Impersonators: Men Performing Masculinity*, London, Cassell, 1994; Sarah Edge, ' "Women are Trouble, Did You Know that Fergus?": Neil Jordan's *The Crying Game*', in *Feminist Review*, vol. 50, 1995, pp. 173–86.
3 Sarah Edge, *ibid.*; Conor McCarthy, *Modernisation: Crisis and Culture in Ireland, 1969–1992*, Dublin, Four Courts Press, 2000.

4 David Lloyd, *Ireland After History*, Cork, Cork University Press, 1999.
5 It was on viewing *Angel* at the Scala cinema in London that Stephen Woolley, who went on to produce the majority of Jordan's films, was first introduced to Jordan's work. Jane Giles describes in detail the dedication Woolley put into finding funding for *The Crying Game*, against all odds (see Jane Giles, *op. cit.*, 1997).
6 Richard Kearney, *Transitions: Narratives in Modern Irish Culture*, Manchester, Manchester University Press, 1988.
7 John Hill, 'Images of Violence', in Kevin Rockett, Luke Gibbons and John Hill (eds) *Cinema and Ireland*, Syracuse, New York, Syracuse University Press, 1988.
8 Keith Hopper, ' "Cat-Calls from the Cheap Seats": The Third Meaning of Neil Jordan's *Michael Collins*', *The Irish Review*, vol. 21, 1997, pp. 1–28.
9 Luke Gibbons, 'Engendering the State: Narrative, Allegory and *Michael Collins*', *Éire-Ireland* 31 vols 3–4, 1996, pp. 261–9.

Filmography

(All UK productions unless otherwise indicated)

Angel (Eire, 1982)
The Company of Wolves (1984)
Mona Lisa (1985)
High Spirits (1988)
We're No Angels (US, 1989)
The Miracle (1991)
The Crying Game (1992)
Interview with the Vampire (US, 1995)
Michael Collins (US, 1996)
The Butcher Boy (1997)
In Dreams (Eire/US, 1998)
The End of the Affair (UK/US, 1999)

As script consultant

Excalibur (John Boorman, 1981)

As screenwriter

Traveller (Joe Comerford, 1982)

As executive producer

The Courier (Joe Lee and Frank Deasy, 1987)
The Last September (Deborah Warner, 1999)

Further reading

Maggie Anwell, (1988) 'Lolita Meets the Werewolf: *The Company of Wolves*', in Lorraine Gamman and Margaret Marshment (eds) *The Female Gaze: Women as Viewers of Popular Culture*, London, The Women's Press, 1988.

Vincent Browne, 'Neil Jordan', *Film West*, vol. 20, 1995, pp. 32–4.

Gary Crowdus, 'The Screening of Irish History: Neil Jordan's *Michael Collins*', *Cineaste*, vol. 22, no. 4, 1997, pp. 14–19.

James MacKillop (ed.), *Contemporary Irish Cinema: From The Quiet Man to Dancing at Lughnasa*, Syracuse, New York, Syracuse University Press, 1999.

Martin McLoone, 'The Abused Child of History: Neil Jordan's *The Butcher Boy*', *Cineaste*, vol. 23, no. 4, 1998, pp. 32–6.

Kevin Maher, 'From Angel to Vampire', *Film Ireland*, vol. 45, 1995, pp. 16–18.

Eileen Morgan, 'Ireland's Lost Action Hero: *Michael Collins*, A Secret History of Irish Masculinity', *New Hibernia Review*, vol. 2, no. 1, 1998, pp. 26–62.

Charlotte O'Sullivan, 'Massacre of the Innocents', *Sight and Sound*, vol. 8, no. 3, 1998, pp. 10–13.

Maria Pramaggiore, ' "I Kinda Liked You as a Girl": Masculinity, Postcolonial Queens and the "Nature" of Terrorism in Neil Jordan's *The Crying Game*', in James MacKillop (ed) *Contemporary Irish Cinema: From The Quiet Man to Dancing at Lughnasa*, Syracuse, New York, Syracuse University Press, 1999.

Eve Sedgwick, *Between Men: English Literature and Male Homosexual Desire*, New York, Columbia University Press, 1985.

Ted Sheehy, 'A Look Over Jordan: Interview with Neil Jordan', *Film Ireland*, vol. 74, 2000, pp. 16–17.

Sharon Whooley, *Neil Jordan: In Conversation with Michael Dwyer at the Galway Film Fleadh, Sunday July 13th 1997*, The Fleadh Papers vol. II, Galway, Film West, 1997.

Kathleen Gallagher Winarski, 'Neil Jordan's *Miracle*: From Fiction to Film', in James David Lloyd, *Ireland After History*, Cork, Cork University Press, 1999.

Lola Young, *Fear of the Dark: 'Race', Gender and Sexuality in the Cinema*, London, Routledge, 1996.

Carole Zucker, ' "Sweetest Tongue has Sharpest Tooth": The Dangers of Dreaming in Neil Jordan's *The Company of Wolves*', *Film and Literature Quarterly*, vol. 28, no. 1, 2000, pp. 66–71.

FIDELMA FARLEY

THE FACE OF A SAD RAT

THE CINEMATIC UNIVERSE OF THE KAURISMÄKI BROTHERS

The motor of this essay is 'genealogical curiosity', perhaps against better judgment since I cannot but agree with Mikhail Iampolski's insistence that it is impossible to establish an authentic source behind the choices that result in a work of art.[1] However, confronted with a phenomenon, our curiosity demands an exegesis. As Andrew Sarris put it: 'That was a good movie, who directed it?' Less sophisticated perhaps, but to the point.[2] This essay is posited between a pragmatic quest for an explanation and an acknowledgement of the folly of such an endeavour, i.e. between the questions of *how* and *why bother*, to travesty Sarris. Not least since the Kaurismäki brothers (particularly Aki) have consistently sabotaged any proposal of meaning or intent behind their work. None the less, their films are full of cues that beg for explanation.

Though Aki and Mika Kaurismäki have not made many films together, audiences tend to perceive them as a unit. Aki's work alone has come to signify the phantom notion of 'the Kaurismäki brothers', perhaps since his style is more consistent. Interest in their work was substantial from the beginning. The short, *Valehtelija* (*Liar*) – Mika's exam film, released in 1981 – won a prize at the Tampere film festival. *Saimaa-ilmiö* (*The Saimaa Gesture*), *Jackpot* and *Arvottomat* (*The Worthless*), all immediately hailed as inventive, creative and ingenious confirmed their position in Finland. Here the fashioning of the public persona of the Kaurismäki brothers started – intentionally or not. Giving interviews together, they used a kind of nonsensical jargon mixed with critical remarks about Finnish cultural life, film politics and the film production business: 'American cinema is dead, the European one is dying – and I'm not feeling particularly well either!', said Aki in 1986.[3] The interview strategy is to make a statement on a topic, immediately contradict it and finally finish the sentence with: '... I don't know, who cares?' Few pictures or stories of the Kaurismäki family have circulated in public. Instead, Aki (in particular) has painstakingly worked on creating a public persona in line with his cinematic universe, orchestrating the national, political and gendered values on display in his films.[4]

When the brothers developed their separate careers – quite early in the 1980s, with Aki directing *Rikos ja rangaistus* (*Crime and Punishment*)[5] – their public images also took different directions. Aki continues to elaborate the absurd, whereas Mika seems willing to discuss his work in more accessible terms. Aki talks of the need to provide filmworkers with a steady income, while headlines about Mika offer a more conventional image (such phrases as 'I am a Restless Soul' or 'Rootless Adventurer', preferably next to a photo of him on a motor bike).[6] However, since Aki's public behaviour is identified with the Finnish brand of romantic artist (a heavy-drinking scoundrel), Mika emerges as a fervent intellectual deeply involved in his work.[7]

The production speed was breathtaking from early on. *Arvottomat* was shot in fifty days, a model for the output of their production company, Villealfa.[8] In a field characterized by time-consuming funding applications and 'well-made', literary, prestige productions, the Kaurismäkis proved that it was possible to produce films for relatively little money. Their ethos has been crucial to the revival of Finnish film production. Moreover, the brothers' productivity and industriousness also vindicated their bashing of Finnish cultural politics ('Finnish culture is dead – we are old men'), and the politicians responsible for the administration of state support in particular.[9]

The milieu

Aki Kaurismäki's films are preoccupied with past milieus. Thus for instance, many of his films begin with a description, a montage from a workplace such as a factory, a mine or a truck depot. Obselete settings in Aki's films harmonize with another recurrent milieu (shared with his brother): places of transit, 'spaces-in-between', such as staircases, locker-rooms, supermarkets, jails, cars – even boats (all places where one naturally meets strangers).

In shots of the city, central perspective street sights dominate; while in the countryside, the scenery is characterized by horizontal lines, just like the side-strips on big American cars (another Kaurismäki sign). The flat landscape of Finnish Ostrobothnia with a black ribbon of forest separating the grey fields and equally grey skies from each other – or a sand shore with the layer of rocks behind as in *Ariel* – look equally artificial. The archetypal Aki Kaurismäki landscape is, however, a cafeteria. Understood as a sign, a reminder for post-war Finnish audiences of the shared past, its 1950s' design signals a period of transition from agrarian to city life. Such cafeterias (*baari*) were characteristic of small Finnish communities and working-class quarters of the cities where the Kaurismäki children grew up. Ubiquitous and pleasantly anonymous, they became meeting places for post-war teenagers.

Existing on the borderline between the cultural and political power blocs of East and West, Finns have always defined themselves by exclusion: 'We are not Swedish, we will not become Russian – so let us be Finnish!' Today Finnishness exists in a limbo between the demolished worldview of the former Soviet Union and an onrushing Euro-Americanism. Aki Kaurismäki's films reflect this fact in their condensed image-frames, exposing visual reminiscences from an earlier period of national identity crisis.

Crucially, Aki Kaurismäki's films both derive from and comment on classical melodrama. What may be called the commonsensical mechanisms of melodrama – ritualization, repetition, proverbial sayings, clichés, its employment of history and memory – involve a stylized and naturalized commitment to past actions and behaviour, allowing explorations of the relationship between the past and the present.[10] Classic film melodrama is, then, a part of the public sphere where all kinds of hegemonic struggles take place. In a sense, as Fassbinder's work has shown, modernist films yield similar functions. For Marcia Landy: 'the insertion of a modernist perspective, the notion of increasing self-consciousness, serves to impose a new narrative of progress, replacing action with self-awareness on the part of the auteur and his handling of the genre.'[11]

In Aki Kaurismäki's films, too, the story often holds a secondary position to cinematic space. In fact it is constructed as *critical space* allowing the interrogation of political, social and economic power structures. The orchestration of the narrative, the emphasis on muteness and the excessive use of music (not to mention all the cues and references) refer to the commonsensical functions of the melodramatic though in a heightened, self-conscious way. Thus, for instance, the excess in *Tulitikkutehtaan tyttö* (an Aki film *par excellence*) is *inverted excess*. Instead of an exposure of abundance (of colours, forms, décor), an Aki Kaurismäki film presents a *mise-en-scène* which is highly stylized, archaic and minimalist.

A different kind of perspective on this complex problem of past and present is brought into focus by Mika Kaurismäki's *Tigrero, A Film that Was Never Made*. Kaurismäki takes ageing American film director Samuel Fuller to an Indian village in Mato Grosso to relate his recollections of a film he was unable to finish. The team brings old film stock shot by Fuller forty years earlier, allowing villagers to see long-deceased family members and friends on-screen. Close-ups of the highly attentive faces of the present-day villagers, juxtaposed with the ritual dances performed by their friends and loved ones in the past, show memories literally coming alive. Remembrances of the past alternate with images of ancient rituals, creating an amalgam of time congealed in the images recorded by Kaurismäki's team. This amalgam is corroborated further by the manipulation of film stock: at times it is difficult to distinguish which shots have been taken by Samuel Fuller, which by Jim Jarmusch (who came along on the trip with his video camera), and which by Kaurismäki's own team.

The boundary of Aki Kaurismäki's cinematic realm is Helsinki harbour. Even if, for example, the Leningrad Cowboys do go to America, the milieus they visit bear a striking resemblance to the scenery in his Finnish-based films. Mika Kaurismäki's characters in their turn move from one milieu to another. The rainforests and watercourses of South America (*Tigrero, A Film that Was Never Made*) are just as 'normal' surroundings for Mika Kaurismäki's characters as Hollywood sites (*LA without a Map*), views from Italian hills (*Rosso*) or European cities (*Helsinki-Napoli All Night Long*). As they vary, the settings lose their immediate signifying potential, becoming transparent: the spectator's attention is pulled to characters or to the camerawork.

Actors

Both brothers have stressed that story is the main component of their filmmaking: 'You do not make films about ideas, you make films about stories', Aki has said. And for Mika, human relations rather than narrative is central: 'At the heart of all the stories there is a human being.'[12] In an interview after *Condition Red*, in which a prison guard falls in love with a female inmate, he talked of his special interest in love under impossible conditions. When Aki and Mika Kaurismäki were students, there was widespread interest in the theatre of Bertolt Brecht (from the mid-1960s, every small township theatre played *The Threepenny Opera* and *Caucasian Chalk Circle*). It is likely that Brecht's idea of an epic or dialectic theatre as opposed to a dramatic/illusionist one, influenced the brothers (both men clearly have leftist sympathies). For Brecht, it was important to emphasize human relations, provoking audiences to draw intellectual conclusions instead of becoming emotionally attached to what they saw on the stage.[13] The main responsibility lay, in Brecht's opinion, with the actor who should regard him/herself as a narrator, a person who would only *quote* the character he/she was playing. The Kaurismäki brothers also contest that 'acting' should be avoided in films,[14] that actors should avoid identifying themselves too deeply with the role.[15]

Both brothers obviously like to work with the same actors. Why, asks Aki, replace a good actor just because you are making a new film. What characterizes a good actor seems to be more difficult to establish: when Matti Pellonpää was alive, Aki Kaurismäki said that he liked to work with him because he was the only Finnish male actor who looked like a sad rat. When Pellonpää died , Kaurismäki was working on the script of *Kauas pilvet karkaavat*. Unable to think of another male as the main character, he rewrote the script and cast a woman.

Topics

According to public fantasy, the Finns are a taciturn and lonely people, frozen into numb silence by the arctic chill. 'The myth about Finnish people depicts them as strong witches, intrepid soldiers and beautiful women. Even the export of our cultural products supports these prejudices. Aki himself supports the image of such odd Finns in an excellent manner', writes a journalist, not entirely pleased with this state of affairs.[16] Difficulties with expressing feelings do not indicate their absence: the obvious lack of eloquent verbal expression in the Kaurismäkis' films only proclaims that they are to be found elsewhere. *Desire* is omnipresent. It is sealed in the evasive gazes and in the music: most of all in the tangos. *Tulitikkutehtaan tyttö*, for instance, a film that contains only twenty-four lines of dialogue, presents a well-known Finnish tango from the first bar to the last: Iiris visits a dance hall, the camera is placed in the doorway and registers the band in three steady takes.

Tangos are a crucial part of Finnish popular culture and folklore. The melody sung in this film tells of the singer's yearning for the land beyond the vast sea: the far away land of ever-blooming flowers where warm wind sweeps over sunny beaches. The singer is lamenting because he is 'a prisoner of the earth, without wings'; unable to fly to where love calls him. The words create a stunning discrepancy with the rigidity of the dance-hall. Furthermore, the conflict invades the musical performance: the drummer maintains the flat rhythm with a steady, stiff beat of his sticks and the incompetence of the musical performance stands in conspicuous contrast to the words. The drums are an ancient symbol of male sexuality. It has sometimes been said that the yearning words of a tango are the only means for the Finnish man to express his tender thoughts, his only way to declare what he really feels for his woman as he moves her around the dance-hall floor.[17] In this scene the musical performance becomes an expression for both his feelings and his inability to assert them.

Finnish film critics have called the 1980s to the mid-1990s the age of the 'Male Odyssey', with a succession of films made by young men, describing a young man's search for adulthood (or death). Though the Kaurismäki brothers' films are part of this Odyssey, when we examine how men and all-male groups relate to their environment and to women, it is clear that they portray a bankrupt masculinity. Such films as *Juha* by Aki and *Paperitähti* by Mika Kaurismäki, for example, showcase a corrupt and destructive male image. Both *Calamari Unioni, Leningrad Cowboys* and its sequels adopt a parodic distance to young men. Assembled in tight groups, they wander the streets of Helsinki or Midwestern US towns, fast and heedless. Dressed in white shirts and thin black ties, dark coats and Rayban sunglasses, they resemble penguins on the seashore (perhaps it is coincidence that both have their habitat in the Arctic hemisphere?). Both films can be read as an ironic portrait of a cultural Male Odyssey in contemporary Finland. The hollowness of any such fellowship and its feebly defined goals is demonstrated in a scene where the manager of Leningrad Cowboys, sitting in the front seat of the car, finishes his beer and throws the can over his shoulder; it hits the statue-like face of a band member, producing no reaction. The Cowboys are equated with the empty beercans in the back seat: in fact, their eccentricity – expressed in their clothing and excessive black pompadours – seems to offer the only discernible value.

Male Odyssey films typically feature few women (or any other antithetic pole to relate to), but in a film like *Juha*, the limitations of the male image are exposed precisely in its relation to femininity. In this film a man's relation to a woman is reduced to its two basic patriarchal figures: either an infantile dependency (Juha) – the flip-side of which is uncontrolled aggression – or sexual exploitation (Shemeikka). Both reduce woman to an object, but are also destroyed: Shemeikka dies at Juha's axe – a weapon as primitive as the man himself – whereas Juha is shot by his rival and perishes on the city dump. Marja, in her turn, survives and, embracing her child, boards a train.

Mika Kaurismäki considers such films as *Condition Red* and *Paperitähti* to be feminist, proclaiming his interest in strong women who, when necessary, act like men.[18] *Paperitähti* tells the story of

Anna, a former beauty queen and model whose career is going downhill. In an analogy with her profession's exploitation of a woman's looks, her relationships are founded on exploitation. She has an unhappy love affair with a pimp and drug-dealer, Ulf, while the photographer, Ilja, depletes her sexually and professionally.

Nevertheless, *Paperitähti* is told by the woman herself. Her voice-over begins when she is in jail having killed her persecutors. Analysing and evaluating not only past events but her own conduct and earlier values, she maintains a firm grip on the narrative. Her detached attitude and brutal language create a necessary distance, effectively preventing the film from displaying her body simply for visual pleasure. The *mise-en-scène* also corresponds to Anna's mental state at times. She is repeatedly seen from strange angles (for example, from the corner of the ceiling), or in confined settings (in doorways or narrow corridors). The space around her is ample and light when she is alone, or with someone whose first idea is not to use her. Recurrent black-and-white sequences with the young Anna moving in slow motion among fields and water, signal remembrances of a period of lost innocence, though her harsh voice saves these scenes from sentimentality.

It has been said that the female body in its capacity for erotic spectacle and status as an object of the multiple (male) gaze tends to stop the narrative flow. *Paperitähti* insistently problematizes the act of looking. Every time Anna poses in front of a camera (as a professional model), exposing her face and body to the imaginary looker, the screen-field is covered by the grid that aids the photographer to compose the picture. This detaching and de-naturalizing mechanism controls the gaze of the camera and, by extension, the spectator's. The grid turns the visual field into a number of even squares, making visible the evaluative aspect of the look. Such devices prevent the spectator from falling into pleasurable contemplation at the sight of Anna's body.

Escaping constraint

At the end of her tale, Anna is released from jail. We learn that she has another male friend with whom she has no sexual relationship: Tuukka, who waits for her outside the prison walls. Not a 'deus-ex-machina' but a 'deus-cum-machina', Tuukka's lightweight motor-bike takes them through a never-ending landscape in a montage that lengthens the ride on and on. In the minds of Scandinavian teenagers, especially those who lived in the countryside during the

1950s and 1960s, the moped – 'mopo' (in Finnish) or 'moppe' (Swedish) – was a sign of adulthood and freedom. Drivers' licences or cars for youngsters were unheard of in most homes. But a moped represented wordly possibilities: it was cheap, easy to drive and the moto-cross-variant brought excitement, an air of bravery and flamboyance, into their lives. Not surprising then, that in such different films as *Paperitähti* and *Last Border* (1991) the hero(ine) rides a lightweight motorbike into the big, big world. The bike, the boat (*Ariel*), the train (*Juha*) – all disappear into the horizon. Numerous Kaurismäki films end with the characters leaving, letting loose, moving on to new settings and to a new life. The yearning of the tango singer, the restlessness of a teenager of thirty years ago, the image of a Western hero – all are condensed in that one image.

Biography

Mika Kaurismäki was born in 1955 and Aki Kaurismäki in 1957, both in Finland.

Notes

1 Mikhail Iampolski, *The Memory of Tiresias, Intertextuality and Film*, Berkeley, CA, University of California Press, 1998, p. 15.
2 Andrew Sarris, 'Towards a Theory of Film History', in Bill Nichols (ed.) *Movies and Methods*, Berkeley and Los Angeles, CA, University of California Press, 1976, p. 250.
3 *Jyväskylän ylioppilaslehti*, 13/86.
4 See Marcia Landy, *Cinematic Uses of the Past*, Minneapolis and London, Minnesota University Press, 1996, p. 22.
5 However, Mika was the producer on this film. Aki wrote parts of the dialogue for *Rosso*, and was involved in the script of *Klaani* (*The Clan*).
6 *Satakunnan Kansa*, 900610.
7 *Me Naiset*, 1996.
8 Ville Alfa was the name of the main character of *Valehtelija*, played by Aki Kaurismäki, and, of course, the name comes from Godard's *Alphaville*. *Kauas pilvet karkaavat* was produced by a new company, Sputnik OY, in twenty-six days. In a period of ten years, the company produced twenty features and eight short films. Today Aki and Mika both have production companies of their own: Sputnik OY and Marianna respectively.
9 *Oulu-lehti*, 821014.
10 Marcia Landy, *op. cit.*, pp. 19–23.
11 *Ibid.*, p. 85.
12 *Iltalehti*, 960302.
13 Martin Esslin, *Brecht, the Man and his Work*, New York, Norton and Co., 1971, pp. 140–1.
14 *Etelä-Suomen Sanomat*, 960930.
15 *Lapin Kansa*, 850813.

16 *Turun Sanomat*, 930402.
17 M.A. Numminen, *Tango är min passion*, Stockholm, 1999.
18 *Iltalehti*, 960302.

Filmography

Aki Kaurismäki

Saimaa-ilmiö / Saimaa Gesture (1981)
Rikos ja rangaistus / Crime and Punishment (1983)
Calamari Union (1985)
Varjoja Paratiisissa / Shadows in Paradise (1986)
Hamlet liikemaailmassa / Hamlet Goes Business (1987)
Thru the Wire (1987)
Rich Little Bitch (1987)
Ariel (1988)
Leningrad Cowboys Go America (1989)
Tulitikkutehtaan tyttö / The Match Factory Girl (1990)
I Hired a Contract Killer (1990)
Those Were the Days (1991)
Boheemielämää / La Vie bohéme (1992)
These Boots (1992)
Pidä huivista kiinni, Tatjana /Take Care of Your Scarf, Tatjana (1994)
Leningrad Cowboys Meet Moses (1994)
Total Balalaika Show (1994)
Kauas pilvet karkaavat / Drifting Clouds (1996)
Juha (1999)

Mika Kaurismäki

Valehtelija / The Liar (1981)
Saimaa-ilmiö / The Saimaa Gesture (1981)
Jackpot 2 (1982)
Arvottomat / The Worthless (1982)
Klaani – tarina Sammakoitten suvusta / The Clan – Tale of the Frogs (1984)
Rosso (1985)
Helsinki Napoli All Night Long (1987)
Cha Cha Cha (1989)
Paperitähti / Paper Star (1989)
Amazon (1990)
Zombie ja kummitusjuna / Zombie and the Ghost Train (1991)
The Last Border – Viimeisellä rajalla (1993)
Tigrero – elokuva joka ei valmistunut / Tigrero, a Film that Was Never Made (1994)
Condition Red – Hälytystila / Condition Red (1996)
Sambólico (1996)

LA without a Map (1999)
Highway Society (2000)

TYTTI SOILA

NEW WAVES, AUTHORSHIP, AND THE POLITICS OF THE FESTIVAL CIRCUIT

ABBAS KIAROSTAMI AND THE NEW IRANIAN CINEMA

Abbas Kiarostami is perhaps the most recognizable name associated with contemporary Iranian cinema. The US magazine *Film Comment*, a staunch Kiarostami campaigner, declares that when it comes to art cinema, 'we are living in the Age of Kiarostami, as we once did in the Age of Godard'.[1] In its poll of the top-thirty unreleased foreign-language films of the 1990s, Kiarostami wins hands down as the director who garnered the most number of votes.[2] Similarly, the UK film magazine *Sight and Sound* proclaimed Kiarostami 'standard bearer of the new Iranian cinema'.[3] The attention that popular film critics have bestowed upon Kiarostami, and by extension contemporary Iranian cinema, in the 1990s parallels the sort of attention that the Fifth Generation directors of Chinese cinema received a decade earlier. What these successive national cinemas have in common is the stage on which they are showcased. Bill Nichols notes that the 'usual opening gambit in the discovery of new cinemas is the claim that these works deserve international attention because of their discovery by a festival'.[4] The festival circuit thus provides the immediate context for international reception of these films and of Kiarostami as a filmmaker. There is a balance to be negotiated between his undoubted status as Iranian auteur and as both pawn and player in the art cinema game of keeping a pantheon alive.

International art cinema

When Kiarostami's films, examples of a post-revolution Iranian cinema, travel the art cinema circuit, they move outside the particular national and cultural context in which they are made and into an international realm in which they are received. When films contextualized within a national cinema travel around the world, new questions emerge. For instance, are festival audiences implicated as voyeurs looking into an alien culture? While watching these films of a different culture and way of life, how do festival audiences comprehend their cultural intricacies and infer meaning from them? What gets lost in the process? Perhaps we could consider how a seasoned art cinema auteur such as Kiarostami works the international scene, and possibly, caters to the tastes of festival critics and audiences. In an interview, Kiarostami clearly sees himself as an art cinema director when he compares the aesthetics of his films to painting, especially given his previous vocation as an artist.[5] Art films in general have particular characteristics.[6] The most convenient distinction is perhaps that between art circuit-style films and classic Hollywood cinema, although they are by no means in direct opposition. Historically, the European notion of *cinéma d'art* represented an attempt to legitimize the cinema in the eyes of the middle classes. Within today's frame of reference, art cinema would address issues of cinematic aesthetics and practices; display formal innovations; include social and psychological realism; affirm certain directors as auteurs; disturb classic realist narrative codes and conventions, as well as temporal and spatial constructions.

The almost obsessive self-referentiality that marks Kiarostami's films closely aligns his films to the codes and conventions of art cinema. His films very often directly address cinema practices and aesthetics, as well as question the notion of realism. In general, reflexivity is a stylistic feature of many contemporary Iranian films, attributed by Ahmad Sadri to the historical role of intellectuals in revolutionary Iran who lived to see their utopian visions result in an ultra-conservative regime run by religious leaders, a regime that infringes basic rights and freedoms. Sadri argues that Iranian filmmakers take it upon themselves, as part of the intelligentsia, to meditate 'on the dialogue of the author – not as the writer of an impersonal text, but as an agent in full human flesh – and the society'.[7] While this sort of authorial commentary and distanciation is far from new, Sadri notes that Iranian reflexivity and distanciation are none the less unique in their limpidness due to historical imperatives. The very transparency of Kiarostami's reflexivity begins with foregrounding himself as director within such films as *Homework, Close-up, And Life Goes On, Under the Olive Trees* and *Taste of Cherry*. While *Under the Olive Trees* and *And Life Goes On* use actors playing directors as Kiarostami's proxies in the films, *Taste of Cherry* concludes with footage of the production process in which Kiarostami himself appears. In *Homework*, Kiarostami steps in as interviewer, as he does in *Close-up*. In other words, Kiarostami blurs the boundaries between the filmic, the pro-filmic and the extra-filmic. This self-referentiality points to the 'authorial dialogue' to which Sadri refers and gives Kiarostami, as artist and intellectual, the authority to comment on contemporary Iranian culture and politics, however obliquely. His position as commentator within contemporary Iranian cinema in turn fulfils the requirements for recognition by festival audiences. Nichols notes that international audiences looking into a particular national cinema generally use two reading strategies: the aesthetic and the political. However, 'induction into an international art cinema/film festival aesthetic clearly does not so much uncover a pre-existing meaning as layer on a meaning that did not exist prior to the circuit of exchange that festivals themselves constitute. ... And the political will be refracted not only by our own repertoire of theories, methods, assumptions, and values, but also by our limited knowledge of corresponding concepts in the other cultures to which we attend.'[8]

Social realism

In art cinema terms, Kiarostami's films exhibit strong social-realist characteristics. *Close-up* tells the story of a trickster who masquerades as an acclaimed Iranian filmmaker, Mohsen Makhmalbaf, gaining the trust of a family, the Ahankhans, eager to be involved in a film project. Using a mixture of real and staged footage, *Close-up* shows the fraud being exposed and records the court proceedings (with permission from the rather sympathetic judge) where the trickster, Sabzian, tells his side of the story. According to Sabzian, he impersonates a famous director because it gives him a sense of dignity that he, as a poor unemployed man, would not otherwise have. In addition, he claims a special affinity with the cinema and tells of how Makhmalbaf's *The Cyclist* (1987) speaks to him about the bleakness of his own life. The family finally withdraws all charges, and the film ends with the real Makhmalbaf making an appearance to fetch Sabzian on the former's motorbike to apologize at the Ahankhan residence. In *Close-up*, unemployment is the cause of social malaise. Both the Ahankhan sons are engineers, but a lack of raw materials in the factories means that neither can get the jobs for which they trained. Towards the end of the trial, the duped son himself acknowledges that Sabzian would not have been up to mischief had he been gainfully employed.

An earthquake renders an entire village homeless in *Under the Olive Trees*. A film crew recruits locals for a shoot in the village. In one of the film's most poignant moments, a woman given a ride in the lorry cannot produce an address at which Mrs Shiva, the set director, might locate her daughter for a part in the film. The woman simply says, 'I have no address. Nothing.' While the director in *Under the Olive Trees* counsels Hossein, unsuccessful with his marriage proposal because he does not own a house, Hossein tells the former that, being illiterate himself, he does not want an illiterate wife because such a coupling would help neither of them. Hossein also has the most progressive ideals. He thinks that the rich should marry the poor 'so that everyone can help each other'; he also assures Tahereh, the girl he has set eyes on, that she would be able to continue with her studies after she marries him and that she does not have to serve him. Kiarostami's liberal ideas of social progress are evident in this film. As Kiarostami assures an interviewer before the film's production, the efficient and powerful Mrs Shiva in *Under the Olive Trees* is an alternative representation of women in a cinema that tends to portray women as a marginalized group.[9] Moreover, the director in the film acquiesces to Tahereh's refusal to address Hossein as 'Mister' during filming, on the latter's advise that Tahereh cannot bear to do so because many wives in these parts no longer prefix 'Mister' to their husbands' names when addressing them.

A Cannes Film Festival favourite, *Taste of Cherry* also exhibits social-realist traits. The protagonist, Badii, drives his Range Rover over a desolate landscape looking for someone desperate enough to help him commit suicide in exchange for money. While cruising in the car, he passes various characters: unemployed labourers looking for work, children playing in an abandoned car, a man arguing about a debt over the public phone, a rag-and-bone man who collects waste plastic. Those that consider helping Badii are not well-off either: a poor young farmer-turned-soldier, a seminary student who moon-lights as a labourer, and an old taxidermist who needs money for his child's medical fees. In *Taste of Cherry*, Kiarostami extends his concerns to immigrants ravaged either by war or poverty. The security guard who offers tea, and his seminary friend, are Afghans escaping a war in their country. The young soldier is Kurdish and, it is implied, has suffered much from the wars in Kurdistan. The plastic collector is a migrant who sends his meagre earnings home to help out his family. The taxidermist, Mr Bagheri, tells a Turkish joke after making sure that the protagonist is not Turkish. The people whom Badii meets form the underbelly of Teheran society, and in a way, the prevalent sense of hopelessness culminates in the protagonist's suicidal tendencies.

Kiarostami's commitment to social-realist themes is evident from these brief sketches. His commentary on Iranian politics and society is perceived as necessarily oblique by festival audiences. Nichols notes the importance of 'back region or behind-the-scenes information' in the international reception of Iranian films; how 'Iranian film representatives learn, with experience, what predispositions and doubts loom foremost in the festival-goer's mind'.[10] In terms of Kiarostami's films, such knowledge is also provided by various discourses, popular and scholarly, on Iranian cinema, society and politics. Looking through an assortment of articles on Kiarostami and Iranian cinema, one sees what sort of back region knowledge is supplied. That the Iman Khomeini likened cinema to prostitution in the heydays of the Revolution is well known. Concerns over the infamously strict censorship policies in Iran loom in graver censorship watchdog pieces.[11] Faithful attendees of the Fajr Film Festival in Teheran, *Film Comment* contributors give upbeat reports of how contemporary Iranian cinema is progressing and negotiating the very slowly loosening reins of governmental and religious intrusions.[12] As he tours film societies around the world, Kiarostami also provides back region knowledge of the circumstances surrounding the films' production. For instance, at an opening of *Taste of Cherry* in Ohio, he commented on Iranian society and culture and on the political circumstances surrounding the production of his films whilst discussing *Taste of Cherry* itself at length.[13] Together with a set of aesthetic elements and stylistic trademarks that have come to be defined as Kiarostamian, this sort of circulating information influences the way in which Kiarostami's films have been received internationally.

Stylistic austerity

What sort of cinematic style does Kiarostami employ to complement his social-realist themes? Although his major themes are bleakness and loss, Kiarostami's films seldom sink into despair. Quite the contrary, hope abounds in the meekness, care and concern that characters receive from, and give to, one another. Hope that transcends bleakness is understandably austere, and this austerity is in turn translated into visual sparseness. In *Taste of Cherry*, much screen time is taken up by long shots of the parched yellow landscape. Travelling on dirt tracks, Badii passes by construction materials and debris. However, kindness prevails despite the landscape. When he drives off the track and his car gets stuck, help comes unexpectedly and seemingly from nowhere. A group of workers help to lift his car and set the wheel on the ground. In a similar way, the film shows how kindness may literally change the landscape. Mr Bagheri, in his attempt to talk Badii out of suicide, makes the latter take a prettier route and as the landscape changes, so Badii's resolution to take his own life weakens. Mrs Shiva, in *Under the Olive Trees*, drives through dirt tracks and ruins at the start of the film, although the landscape here is lush with greenery. Still, death and sadness are as close to the heart of *Under the Olive Trees* as they are in *Taste of Cherry*. The film's characters have lost relatives, friends and homes to the earthquake. That anachronistic values and traditions hold the locals back is evident in Tahereh's grandmother's refusal to let her marry Hossein. The earthquake can be read allegorically as the revolution that did not quite succeed in shaking off the problems and ideas of the previous regime. In the same way, Tahereh's grandmother persists in her refusal of Hossein's proposal because he does not have a house, even though the catastrophe has rendered virtually everyone homeless. Hope, in this case, comes in the form of the director in the film. The filming process provides Hossein with opportunities to make contact with Tahereh and the film ends optimistically as he follows her through the olive trees. Despite the social ills identified as propellers of the story, *Close-up* ends with reconciliation and hope. Sabzian and Makhmalbaf ride off to the Ahankhan residence, but not without bringing with them the gift of a plant as the sign of Sabzian's remorse, possibly the only beautiful thing in a film that features relentless city traffic, a long courtroom interrogation scene, prisons, accusations, and the story of a life without hope.

Kiarostami's stylistic austerity functions to serve his social-realist themes. These themes are in turn facilitated by the films' reflexivity to apply in both popular and academic discourses of Iran and its cinema. There is plenty of space for enthusiastic international audiences to infer universal or humanist meaning at the same time that these same audiences are all too aware that they are looking into a vastly different culture and cinema. The reading of Kiarostami's films in terms of an austerity of hope translated into an austere visual style can be taken as testament to the difficulties Kiarostami and other Iranian filmmakers face, but none the less prevail over, given audiences' perception of state repression and censorship. In this way, the construction of Kiarostami as romantic auteur, a key figure of international art cinema in the 1990s, emerges. A figure who, despite all the odds, directs beautifully austere, aesthetically cinematic, humanistically universal, but yet profoundly Iranian films.

Biography

Born 22 June 1940, in Teheran, Iran, Kiarostami studied to be a painter at Teheran University and subsequently worked as an illustrator and designer for advertisements and children's books. In 1969, he set up the cinema department in the Institute for Intellectual Development of Children and Young Adults under the patronage of the Empress Faraah. The following year, he made his first short film, *Bread and Alley*.

Notes

1 Philip Lopate, 'New York', *Film Comment*, November/December 1997, p. 60.
2 'Foreign Affairs: Which Foreign Films Must Be Seen at All Costs?', *Film Comment*, July/August 1997, p. 40.
3 Farah Nayeri, 'Iranian Cinema: What Happened in Between', *Sight and Sound*, 3/12, 1993, p. 26.
4 Bill Nichols, 'Discovering Form, Inferring Meaning: New Cinemas and the Film Festival Circuit', *Film Quarterly*, vol. 47, no. 3, 1994, p. 16
5 Ali Akbar Mahdi (n.d.) *In Dialogue with Kiarostami*. Online. Available HTTP: < http://www.iranian.com/Arts/Aug98/Kiarostami >
6 See Susan Hayward, *Key Concepts in Cinema Studies*, London, Routledge, 1996.
7 Ahmad Sadri (n.d.) *Searchers: The New Iranian Cinema*. Online. Available HTTP: < http://www.iranian.com/Sep96/Arts/New Cinema.html >
8 Bill Nichols, *op. cit.*, p. 19.
9 Farah Nayeri, *op. cit.*, p. 28.
10 Bill Nichols, *op. cit.*, p. 20.
11 See, for example, Reza Allamehzadeh, 'Iran: Islamic Visions and Grand Illusions', in Ruth Petrie (ed.) *Film and Censorship*, London and Washington, Cassell, 1997, pp. 129–32.
12 Richard Peña, 'Being There', and Alissa Simon, 'Tehran Journal', *Film Comment*, May/June 2000, pp. 11–13 and pp. 70–1.
13 Ali Akbar Mahdi, *op. cit.*

Filmography

Bread and Alley (1970) short
Breaktime (1972)
The Experience (1973)
The Traveller (1974)
Two Solutions for One Problem (1975)
So Can I (1975)
The Colours (1976)
The Wedding Suit (1976)
The Report (1977)
Tribute to Teachers (1977)

Solution (1978)
Jahan Nama Palace (1978)
Case No. 1, Case No. 2 (1979)
Toothache (1980)
Regularly or Irregularly (1981)
The Chorus (1982)
Fellow Citizen (1983)
First Graders (1984)
Where is the Friend's Home? (1987)
Homework (1989)
Close-up (1990)
And Life Goes On (1992)
Under the Olive Trees (1994)
Taste of Cherry (1997)
The Wind Will Carry Us (1999)

Further reading

Godfrey Chesire, 'How to Read Kiarostami', *Cineaste*, vol. 25, no. 4, 2000, pp. 8–15.
Abbas Kiarostami, 'With Borrowed Eyes', *Film Comment*, vol. 36, no. 4, 2000, pp. 20–5.

SHARON TAY

KRZYSZTOF KIEŚLOWSKI

WHY KIEŚLOWSKI?

In 1994, the monthly film magazine *Kino*, Poland's *Sight and Sound*, published a special edition entitled 'Why Kieślowski'. No question mark followed the director's name: the implication was that his work had axiomatic force. How might one justify this claim?

One might begin with reference to the Polish context alone, with the manner of Kieślowski's exploitation of the opportunities of co-production indicating how a Polish film industry might continue meaningfully after the series of major shocks inaugurated in 1989: the 'freedom shock' that stripped directors of their prestigious roles as smugglers of Aesopian messages to an eager nation, then the precipitous erosion of state funding. Kieślowski's exemplariness seems to me, however, to go far further than this, as his films – particularly the 'late' ones that yielded his greatest fame, even cult (*The Decalogue, The Double Life of Véronique, Three Colours*) – pose a rippling array of questions. The first ripples might be seen as rocking the boat of many hegemonic contemporary filmmaking practices. Moving out wider, they might also be seen as interrogating a certain definition of 'Europe' and the nature or desirability of a 'European' identity. This interrogation would then overflow into meditation on the degree to which what convenience calls 'western culture' still finds cardinal points of reference in its Judaeo-Christian texts (*The Decalogue*) or Enlightenment watchwords (*Three Colours*). The works' furthest range of reference would ask how dimensions of the spiritual and numinous may be represented, even conceptualized. The simultaneously pungent authority and complexity of the questions' orchestration, of the dialogue the works initiate – both individually and as a quasi-musical sequence – might determine 'why Kieślowski', rendering him arguably as crucial for the 1990s (and, I would say, beyond) as Godard had been for the 1960s, and Fassbinder and Tarkovsky for the 1970s and 1980s. As audiences fragment, perhaps only work as multilayered as Kieślowski's is well equipped for survival, open as it is to various appropriations (aesthetic, sociological, even religious and metaphysical).

First, some of the contemporary filmmaking practices Kieślowski undermines, beginning – as arbitrarily as all beginnings – with the increasingly frequent fusion of documentary and fiction. A glance at his filmography shows a director moving from documentary to fiction. This is, of course, a well-worn path, but in Kieślowski's case it does not reflect conventional low-budget Cinderella dreams of future feature glory, with documentary the perennially bent-backed stooge whose hump one steps up from, but issues from a piercing awareness of the possibly irresolvable ethical dilemmas documentary poses. Should one not fear the real tears, rather than solicit them as markers of authenticity, preferring harmless glycerine instead, as Kieślowski came to say he did? Should one not switch off the camera rather than render otherwise safely anonymous people identifiable by the authorities whose police-forces all too easily impound one's footage (just such an incident during the making of *Station* helped motivate Kieślowski's early 1980s' abandonment of documentary)? And should one not separate documentary from fiction by a caesura as strong as the one that crosses Kieślowski's career, rather than fuse and confuse the two ('freedom' being the freedom to manipulate, with 'postmodernity' as one's alibi)? Kieślowski may not answer these questions, may not even pose them all explicitly – his most characteristic phrase being 'I don't know' (*Nie Wiem* – the title of one of those documentaries) – but the courage and seriousness with which he walked away from the form he had never thought to leave, from one life into another (the greater glamour of the second doing nothing to alleviate the catastrophic experience of its onset) pose them with fierce incisiveness. If reality's scenarios were indeed richer than those of art, as he had maintained in his film school thesis, then the pain of their loss must have stung; and the final announcement of retirement – implicitly challenging another filmmaking habit, the exhausted addict's clutch of the camera's fix – must have included a sweet desire to recover them.

Insofar as hybridity and fusion lie at the heart of contemporary filmmaking practice, another pairing worth reviewing is that of television and film in the production of 'amphibious' works, consumable both in the cinema and on the small screen. The reasons why 'amphibious' practice moved from West German television to achieve normative European status are obvious: often ill-distributed, minority work gains an audience of sorts, while networks acquire material whose 'special event' cachet can be a focal point of programme schedules and an effective advertisement for their aspirations to cultural centrality. Aesthetic issues – the effect of different screen ratios (unwritten proscriptions on full use of the frame), the nature of experience and of audience receptivity and even existence (before or after a watershed? how long after? *how far* into the witching hours?) – are often swept under the carpet in the happy consensus that such 'amphibiousness' meets everybody's needs (more or less ... half a loaf being all one can expect in the new globalized environment). Kieślowski's excursion into the form – *The Decalogue* – is different. Here the amphibian is two animals (the double life of ...). *Dekalog 5* is also *A Short Film About Killing*, and the work advertising its brevity (for a film) is in fact thirty minutes longer than the television one. *Dekalog 6* is also *A Short Film About Love*; had the intensive grind of prolific production not drained him of energy, Kieślowski would probably also have made a feature of *Dekalog 9*. The separation and separate evolution of the various versions recognize that not everything *can* cross the border, slide from water to dry land. *A Short Film About Killing* has more of the extended silence – and hence visuality – so often deemed 'cinematic', and a more drastic and prolonged murder scene, than the television version. Perhaps it was Kieślowski's slight depression *vis-à-vis* the often lukewarm Polish reaction and critical accusations of chronic improbability, or merely a more chronic modesty, that caused him to doubt that he had mastered the television aesthetic (this after a work generally deemed one of the decade's finest pieces of television!).[1]

Could the utopia of the amphibious work in fact be a fudge? Is 'the same' work 'the same' in different situations of reception? During the cinema screenings of *The Decalogue* was the habitual pairing of parts the ideal solution, or would just one – as during the initial terrestrial broadcast – have been preferable? Was the coupling simply a reflex of the desire for a programme of customary 'movie' length? What happens to the amphibian when it first sees the light on a television screen, rather than (as so often) in a cinema? By provoking such questions, Kieślowski's extraordinary amphibians become, I believe, exemplary (quite apart from the small matter of their aesthetic urgency). They also demonstrate the consequences of his modernist editorial passion for the alternative version: an interest in the possible alternatives that could be hewn out of one body of footage would be thematized in the use of parallel lives (*Blind Chance, The Double Life of Véronique*), in starkly existentialist dramatization of the weight of choice rather than any postmodern unbearable lightness of being; it also preserved the use of the series from seeming to depend entirely mechanically on the external factor of, say, the number of statements or keywords to be 'illustrated', or from the demands of a set of slots on television, that homeland of serial production. Kieślowski's two series also raised and furnished their own idiosyncratic answer to the question of how a *cinephilia* (which also means: a regular audience) is to be grown from the discrete experiences of individual art films, whose prioritization of originality may undermine the pleasures of repetition. And insofar as those pleasures are identifiable with genre, it may be argued that the series restores to art cinema its forsworn generic pleasures ('art cinema' itself being too broad a category to function generically, despite some critical attempts to make it do so).

Another contemporary European filmmaking practice that happily guarantees both funding and distribution is that of co-production, which of course overlaps with 'amphibious production', with many works being co-funded by a clutch of television channels. One need not read the small print of credits to discover that *The Double Life of Véronique* is a Polish/French co-production: the story of the Polish singer with a heart ailment whose death during her first concert mysteriously 'instructs' her French double – Véronique – in art's perilousness, clearly bares the bases of its own production in a manner far more explicit and perhaps even 'Brechtian' (Brecht being after all an arch-pragmatist) than its art cinema beauty might lead one to expect, for despite beginning with the two girls paralleled and opposed – the Polish perspective a vertiginous inversion of the wintry city night sky, the French one that of summer close to earth – the asymmetry in their stories' length germinates doubts about the real equality of 'East' and 'West', the relative marketability of different cultures. This foreshadows the inverse asymmetry of *Three Colours: White* (one-third France, two-thirds Poland) and the key theme of that mid-section of the Trilogy: equality. How much equality will there be (has there been so far) in the integrated, enlarged European Union? Will easterners continue to find Orwell relevant even after the fall of the would-be totalitarian regime (all animals are equal *but* ...)? Nevertheless, the uneven fortune at work also in the disparity between the internationally promoted co-produced late films and the virtually non-distributed earlier Polish ones should not be read entirely conspiratorially: the early work's primary (and, worse still, political!) address of a Polish viewer did indeed limit distribution, while later Kieślowski *is* genuinely more accomplished than even the one of *No End*, the first work co-written with Krzysztof Piesiewicz (hence Mirosław Przylipiak rightly observed that further works in that vein would hardly have earned Kieślowski his eventual reputation, tartly adding that he might thus have deemed the Poles' negative reception of *No End* a blessing).[2] If co-production is the superstructural, ideal reflection of the integrated EU base, the reflection must crack to mirror the state of the soil from which it rises – to introduce the material into the ideal. In doing this, Kieślowski's co-productions become exemplary.

The account of *The Double Life of Véronique* given above is reductive, but it can serve for the moment to indicate Kieślowski's awareness of the inevitable costs and unevenness of integration – an end that may only be reached after passage through defiles of contempt and hatred, like the reconciliation of the French Dominique and the Polish barber Karol Karol in *Three Colours: White*. In speaking of such matters as European integration, we are now of course already within the orbit of the question of the 'wider resonance' of Kieślowski's work. The degree to which its material success stems from that 'wider resonance' – from its status as a series of essays on such topics as the viability of European integration or the continued relevance of the Ten Commandments or French revolutionary slogans – probably cannot be determined. If it is safe to say that inept think-pieces would have gained few plaudits and sold few tickets, it is also true that the works' status as discourse on large abstractions (the attempt to grapple with postmodern crises of meaning squarely presented as their main agenda by Kieślowski's co-scenarist, Piesiewicz)[3] rendered them 'cultural events', enhancing the likelihood of their designation as 'must sees'. Nevertheless, since the works are multilayered – allowing viewers to watch *Three Colours*, in part or in total, say, with an eye to abstractions and concretions of colour rather than concept – high seriousness is not the only level on which points of entry are located. One may simply appreciate a set of deftly moulded, terse, tense stories, the performances of Irene Jacob, Grażyna Szapołowska or Jean-Louis Trintignant – among others – or the music of Zbigniew Preisner (whose alias of Van den Budenmeyer permits entry at what is probably the lowest and most trivial level of all, because least integrated into the systematicity of the aesthetic: that of the in-joke).

The potential elevation of the discourse is, of course, greatest in *The Decalogue*, that confrontation of representative samples of behaviour in a modern Polish housing block with the founding maxims of a nominally Judaeo-Christian culture nearing the end of its second millennium. If on one level – that described by the series itself *mise-en-abime* in *Dekalog 8*, whose main Polish protagonist is an ethics professor – the method and issues are ethical, tensely weighing the minute-by-minute morality of modern daily encounters, on another – represented by the mysterious witness played by the same actor but figuring as different people from one section to another, and by the dramatization of questions of God's existence, responsibility and representability in *Dekalog 1* – they are more mysterious, even mystical. Here the ellipses of art cinema become the structuring absences of the spirit. In touching on this area Kieślowski becomes available for appropriation as guru by the young humbly soliciting advice in his many interviews, for condemnation as a mystagogue by the critics of *Cahiers du cinéma*,[4] or as a purveyor of New Age vagueness by various churches (though in fact religious orders, including the Vatican, have taken a broader view and welcomed Kieślowski's dramatizations of religious issues). This is the level addressed by the juxtaposition of his work with the philosophy of Emanuel Levinas: his intense, intimate focus on the face and one-on-one encounters in *The Decalogue* in particular may indeed parallel Levinas' concern with faces and dialogic acceptance of the Other.[5] A concern with Otherness, a settled will to accept *both* sides of any polarity, may indeed be a recurrent feature of Kieślowski's work, both thematically and in terms of his working practices. Their final name may be the one that dominates his final interviews, and the last minutes of *Three Colours: Blue*: that of love. Whether or not the existence of love proves the existence of God is the key question of *Dekalog 1* in particular: Paweł's aunt Irina shows him what God is by hugging him. But will Paweł's father Krzysztof – his first name (significantly?) shared by both Kieślowski and Piesiewicz – ever find out?

To speak of love is of course to name the emotion Kieślowski's co-workers clearly felt for him; the feeling his working practices elicited. Those practices raise the question of authorship and the mode of its renewal Kieślowski proposed, implicitly if not explicitly. For the power and resonance of the late work surely derives as much from the continual and acknowledged co-authorship of Krzysztof Piesiewicz and Zbigniew Preisner, as well as the intermittent co-authorship of many others – for instance, cameraman Sławomir Idziak (who suggested the filters of *Dekalog 5*) or actress Grażyna Szapołowska (who prompted a new ending for *A Short Film About Love*). Kieślowski thus recognized the ease with which the repetitions an auteurist conception of 'art cinema' values as indices of spiritual autobiography and psychological obsession can descend into monotony, or the putative authenticity of the signature signal commodification. Shifts from documentary to fiction or from 'political film' to 'the esoteric' would then be neither futile attempts to overleap one's own shadow nor coolly disengaged postmodern play but indicators of the sublime unpredictability of growth, continuity through discontinuity: the ability to change completely and yet remain the same. Kieślowski renewed art cinema by transforming the auteur autocracy into a democracy, where the director is anomalous on the set only inasmuch as he lacks a clearly defined job and – as he told Danusia Stok[6] – may best be described as 'someone who helps'. That definition of the director may well be the most liberating – the most exemplary – thing about Kieślowski's work, the paradoxical justification of his relevance in an artistic afterlife stretching far beyond the ongoing buzz of fans' websites (use your search-engine to check out Cine-Kieślowski!) and echoing well into the next millennium.

Biography

Krzysztof Kieślowski was born in Warsaw, Poland, on 27 June 1941. He studied at the Lodz Film School, graduating in 1968 and working in the WFD (Documentary Production Unit) before joining the Tor Film Unit in 1974. His feature début was the television film *Personel*. In 1978 he became vice-president of the Association of Polish Filmmakers. Awards include the Felix for *Krótki film o zabijaniu*, the Ecumenical Prize at Cannes for *La Double Vie de*

Véronique, the Golden Lion at the Venice Film Festival for *Trois couleurs: bleu*, and Oscar nominations in 1995 for the script and direction of *Trois couleurs: rouge*. Kieślowski died during a heart operation in Warsaw on 13 March 1996, leaving his wife Maria and daughter Marta.

Notes

1 Danusia Stok (trans. and ed.) *Kieślowski on Kieślowski*, Boston and London, Faber and Faber, 1993, p. 155.
2 Mirosław Przylipiak, 'Monter i studentka, czyli jak to bylo naprawde z niszczeniem Krzysztofa Kieślowskiego przez polska krytyke filmowa', *Kino*, vol. 31, no. 3, 1997, p. 50.
3 Katarzyna Jablońska, 'Jestem sam. Z Krzysztofem Piesiewiczem rozmawia Katarzyna Jablońska', *Wiez*, vol. 39, no. 9, 1996, p. 105.
4 Antoine Baecque, 'Faut-il entrer dans l'eglise de Kieślowski?', *Cahiers du cinéma*, no. 429, 1990, pp. 32–3.
5 Véronique Campan, *Dix breves histoires d'image: le Decalogue de Krzysztof Kieślowski*, Paris, Presses de la Nouvelle Sorbonne, 1993.
6 Danusia Stok, *op. cit.*, p. 199.

Filmography

(All produced in Poland unless otherwise indicated)

Tramwaj / *The Tram* (1966)
Urząd / *The Office* (1966)
Koncert życzeń / *Concert of Requests* (1967)
Zdjęcie / *The Photograph* (1968)
Z miasta Łodzi / *From the City of Lodz* (1969)
Byłem żolnierzem / *I Was a Soldier* (1970)
Fabryka / *Factory* (1970)
Przed rajdem / *Before the Rally* (1971)
Refren / *Refrain* (1972)
Miedzy Wrocławiem a Zieloną Gorą / *Between Wroclaw and Zielona Gora* (1972)
Podstawy BHP w kopalnii miedzi / *The Principles of Safety and Hygiene in a Copper Mine* (1972)
Robotnicy 71: nic o nas bez nas / *Workers '71: Nothing About Us Without Us* (1972)
Murarz / *Bricklayer* (1973)
Przejście podziemne / *Pedestrian Subway* (1973)
Prześwietlenie / *X-ray* (1974)
Pierwsza miłosc / *First Love* (1974)
yciorys / *Curriculum Vitae* (1975)
Personel / *Personnel* (1975)
Szpital / *Hospital* (1976)
Klaps / *Slate* (1976)
Blizna / *The Scar* (1976)

Spokój / *The Calm* (1976)
Z punktu widzenia nocnego portiera / *From the Point of View of a Night Porter* (1977)
Nie wiem / *I Don't Know* (1977)
Siedem kobiet w różnym wieku / *Seven Women of Different Ages* (1978)
Amator / *Camera Buff* (1979)
Dworzec / *Station* (1980)
Gadające głowy / *Talking Heads* (1980)
Przypadek / *Blind Chance* (1981)
Krótki dzień pracy / *Short Working Day* (1981)
Bez końca / *No End* (1984)
Siedem dni w tygodniu / *Seven Days a Week* (Netherlands, 1988) section of a compilation film, *City Life*
Krótki film o zabijaniu / *A Short Film About Killing* (1988)
Kroacute;tki film o miłosci / *A Short Film About Love* (1988)
Dekalog / *The Decalogue* (1988)
La Double vie de Véronique / *The Double Life of Véronique* (France/Poland, 1991)
Trois couleurs: bleu / *Three Colours: Blue* (France/Poland, 1993)
Trois couleurs: blanc / *Three Colours: White* (France/Poland, 1994)
Trois couleurs: rouge / *Three Colours: Red* (France/Switzerland/Poland, 1994)

Further reading

Vincent Amiel, *Kieślowski*, Paris, Payot & Rivages, 1995.
—— (ed.) *Krzysztof Kieślowski*, Paris, Jean Michel Place, 1997.
Geoff Andrew, *The 'Three Colours' Trilogy*, London, BFI Publishing, 1998.
Giulia Carluccio, Sara Giulia and Dario Tomasi (eds) *Krzysztof Kieślowski*, Torino, Scriptorium, 1995.
Paul Coates (ed.) *Lucid Dreams: The Films of Krzysztof Kieślowski*, Trowbridge, Flicks Books, 1999.
Michel Esteve (ed.) *Krzysztof Kieślowski presenté par Michel Esteve avec les textes de Yvette Biro ... (et al.)* , Paris, Lettres modernes, 1994.
Malgorzata Furdal and Roberto Turigliatto (eds) *Kieślowski*, Torino, Museo Nazionale del Cinema, 1989.
Christopher Garbowski, *Kieślowski's Decalogue Series: The Problem of the Protagonists and their Self-transcendence*, New York, Columbia University Press, East European Monographs 452, 1996.
Gina Lagorio (ed.) *'Il Decalogo di Kieślowski.' Ricreazione narrativa*, Casale Monferrato, Piemme, 1992.
Tadeusz Lubelski (ed.) *Kino Krzysztofa Kieślowskiego*, Cracow, Universitas, 1997.
Serafino Murri, *Krzysztof Kieślowski*, Rome, Il Castoro Cinema Press, 1996.
Stanislaw Zawislinski (ed.) *Kieślowski*, Warsaw, Skorpion, 1996.

PAUL COATES

DIANE KURYS

Diane Kurys' status as an auteur is an ambivalent one. Her first film, *Diabolo menthe* (*Peppermint Soda*), which she wrote, directed and co-produced at the age of 29 on a shoestring budget with a cast of unknowns, topped the 1977 box office for French films in France (overtaking George Lucas' *Star Wars*) and enabled her to abandon her career as an actress and become a full-time writer-director. Her third film, *Coup de foudre* (*At First Sight*; *Entre nous* in the US), was another box-office hit, this time made with a relatively large budget, a star cast (including Isabelle Huppert and Miou-Miou) and shot in Cinemascope. *Coup de foudre* received an Oscar nomination for Best Foreign-language Film and Kurys an invitation (which she subsequently turned down) to work in Hollywood. These two films made Kurys one of the best-known and most successful French women directors of her generation. They also gave her a reputation in Britain and North America as a European auteur whose films focused on the bittersweet experiences of girls and women,[1] even though she herself (like other French women) consistently refused the label of 'woman director'.[2] Ginette Vincendeau rates Kurys among 'the good' in her imaginary all-female canon of European directors.[3] In France, however, where there is no call for feminist film criticism, the appeal of Kurys' films to mainstream audiences means that her work has been regularly dismissed in comparison with that of her more obviously 'art-house' contemporaries.

Kurys' career reached its peak in 1987 when her fourth film, *Un Homme amoureux* (*A Man in Love*), was chosen to open the Cannes Film Festival. An ambitious international co-production with a star cast (including Greta Scacchi, Peter Coyote, Claudia Cardinale, John Berry, Vincent Lindon and Jamie Lee Curtis), *Un Homme amoureux* uses the self-reflexive device of the film within the film, in this instance the shooting of an Italian co-production about Communist writer Cesare Pavese, to underpin a melodrama about the passionate affair between Jane, a young European actress playing a bit-part as Pavese's last mistress (Scacchi) and Steve, a famous American actor playing Pavese (Coyote). However, Kurys was heavily criticized for delivering a Europudding, a superficial, glossy love story dependent on glamorous locations (Rome, Tuscany and Paris), which showed little depth of feeling or sensitivity to film as an art form. Her lack of favour within the French critical establishment was confirmed by the recent critical assault on *Les Enfants du siècle*, another big-budget film aimed at a mass audience.

Kurys' reconstruction of the passionate but doomed affair between nineteenth-century writers George Sand and Alfred de Musset, set in 1830s' Paris and Venice, was slated even before it had opened, fuelling director Patrice Leconte's protest in November 1999 at French critics' delight in demolishing their national cinema. In France, then, Kurys' status as an auteur is highly questionable, in particular because her often very personal films nevertheless address a popular audience.

Kurys' work lends itself to an auteurist analysis because her first seven films, to varying degrees, all draw their inspiration from her own life (although following *Diabolo menthe* she collaborated on adaptations of her original screenplays with various male writers, particularly Alain Le Henry, Olivier Schatsky and Antone Lacomblcz). Although Kurys' attitude towards her autobiographical source material is ambivalent (her statements in interviews both acknowledge and deny its significance), her reworking of recognizable characters, incidents, themes and motifs enables the critic to trace disguised autobiographical elements from film to film. Her films do not use first-person, subjective narratives, nor do they reconstruct her life in chronological order, but each one constructs a fictional figure (occasionally doubled, as in the case of the two sisters of *Diabolo menthe*) who can be read as a stand-in for Kurys herself (and who share Jewish-sounding names and physical casting resemblances). This unifying factor produces a unique series of texts which, taken together, document a woman's life history in the latter half of the twentieth century (although Kurys herself has never claimed to have consciously embarked on such a project). At the same time, they can be divided into two groups with rather different preoccupations: those set in the past, drawing their material from memories of childhood and adolescence, and those set in the present, centring on adult desires and anxieties. The first group comprises *Diabolo menthe*, *Cocktail Molotov*, *Coup de foudre* and *La Baule Les Pins*, which chart the passage of the Kurys stand-in figure from childhood in the early 1950s to leaving home in 1968. They rework the same, or similar settings and themes (particularly female rites of passage and the consequences for the daughters of the breakdown of their parents' marriage) and incorporate devices (such as opening or closing dedications or end titles) which explicitly signal to the spectator, if in retrospect, that the fictional children/adolescents are to be understood, at least partially, as representations of Kurys herself. The second group comprises *Un Homme amoureux*, *Après l'amour* (*After Love*) and *A la folie*, which focus on a woman's attempts to combine a successful career and a (heterosexual) love affair, a situation which is reprised in the ostensibly non-autobiographical *Les Enfants du siècle*. The choice in each case of a heroine who acts, writes or paints for a living implicitly signals that the character is a stand-in for writer-director-producer Kurys herself.

The two key films on which Kurys' reputation as an auteur is based, *Diabolo menthe* and *Coup de foudre*, have been taken up by Anglo-American feminist critics because they invest their reconstructions of the post-war years with a proto-feminist sensibility. *Diabolo menthe*, made at the height of the women's movement, addresses female audiences by drawing attention, unusually, to what it is like to grow up female. As Barbara Quart comments: 'one had never before seen a camera focus with this kind of attention, time, care, truth, affection and interest on young girls'.[4] The film charts a year in the lives of two rebellious sisters, Anne (aged 13) and Frédérique (aged 15), and their relationships with each other, their schoolfriends, their separated parents, their teachers and their first boyfriends. It does not hesitate to portray adolescence with all its awkwardness and irritability, and deftly links the girls' struggles against authority figures with a critique of repressive French society in the early 1960s (including the insertion of a schoolgirl's account of the Charonne massacre of 1962).

Coup de foudre was made in the wake of various other French and American independent women's films of the late 1970s and early 1980s, at a time when feminism was starting to wane. Based on Kurys' interviews with her mother, it charts the growing friendship between two young wives and mothers, Léna (Isabelle Huppert) and Madeleine (Miou-Miou), after their meeting at a school concert in 1950s' Lyons. (A long prologue sequence set during the Occupation cross-cuts between Jewish Léna's escape from deportation and Madeleine's loss of her young husband, shot by the Militia, their traumatic experiences indirectly accounting for the strength of their subsequent friendship.) The two women gradually become aware of the limitations of their provincial marriages, embodied by their hapless husbands, loveable but incompetent Costa (Jean-Pierre Bacri), and Michel (Guy Marchand), a doting father who clings to patriarchal notions of gender roles. Léna's investment in her friendship with Madeleine is accompanied by her gradual assertion of economic independence from Michel. However, feminist scholars have focused productively on the film's ambivalent representation of intimacy between women, the absence of an authoritative male gaze, and the use of two-shots, long takes and pregnant silences which allow for readings of their relationship as the expression of lesbian desire.[5]

The women's mutual affection, expressed in particular through their shared love of fashion, contrasts with the increasing violence of Léna's relationship with Michel, which culminates in his destruction of her newly opened fashion boutique. However, the final, poignant sequence, set by the seaside at Cabourg, where Léna dismisses Michel, witnessed by their little daughter, Sophie, uses cross-cutting to emphasize both Michel's pain and the daughter's loss. (An epigraph appearing over the final image confirms that the daughter is Kurys herself.) *Coup de foudre* thus appeals on a variety of levels, combining a narrative of female emancipation with the foregrounding of desire between women, yet also expressing sympathy for the man and the child's nostalgia for the imagined stability of the idealized, traditional couple.

Kurys attempted to recapture the success of *Diabolo menthe* and *Coup de foudre* in her fifth film, *La Baule Les Pins*, which reworks the story of her parents' separation, set this time during a family summer holiday in 1958 and viewed from the point of view of the (slightly older) children. The film's nostalgic, visually pleasurable reconstruction of the seaside resort of La Baule Les Pins is punctured by the mother's determination to go her own way, the father's violence and despair, and the traumatic effect of their behaviour on the young girls. Disappointingly, however, the film attenuates the previous emphasis on girls and women. The two sisters are joined by a family of cousins (mostly boys), and Léna (Nathalie Baye) leaves Michel (Richard Berry) to have a conventional heterosexual affair with aspiring artist Jean-Claude (Vincent Lindon), her friendship with Madeleine being replaced by her more marginalized relationship with her half-sister Bella (Zabou). Nevertheless, the film still privileges female points of view and female narrative agency, focusing on the frustrations of women and the uncertainties of adolescent girls as they struggle to establish their identities, and foregrounding shots of women talking together without being the objects of a voyeuristic gaze. It also allows 13-year-old Frédérique (Julie Bataille), the Kurys stand-in figure, to take on the role of writer-narrator through the use of a (fragmented) voice-over of her diary entries.

Cocktail Molotov, Kurys' less successful second film, bridges the world of youth and adulthood through the figure of 17-year-old Anne (Elise Caron), who has a shockingly violent fight with her divorced middle-class mother, leaves home, makes love for the first time with her working-class boyfriend, Fred (Philippe Lebas), and embarks on a journey, first to Venice, alone (in order to catch a boat to Israel), then back across France with Fred and his best friend Bruno (François Cluzet). The film suffers from a desultory plot in which the trio miss out on the events of May '68 (the boys are arrested as soon as they arrive in Paris), and a gloomy *mise-en-scène* which, rather than recalling the excitement and optimism of the period, instead charts its disappointments (as when the Molotov cocktail of the title fizzles out by the side of the road). Anne's own personal rebellion prefigures (with hindsight) the women's movement to come (challenging her mother's bourgeois values, learning about contraception and sexual pleasure, getting an abortion at a time when abortions were illegal). However, Kurys keeps the central character at a distance, refusing to give the spectator full access to her thoughts and feelings. Furthermore, the recourse to a cyclical ending (Anne leaving home again) and a freeze-frame to immobilize the final image (recalling the freeze-frame ending of *Diabolo menthe* and foreshadowing *A la folie*) is a typical Kurys device which suggests that Anne, like other Kurys stand-in figures, is literally going round in circles, unable to extricate herself from the psychological damage inflicted by her upbringing. What most distinguishes *Cocktail Molotov* from the childhood-based trilogy is the focus on triangular heterosexual relationships, the marginalizing of female friendships, and the introduction of a rival woman (in this instance a beautiful Italian anarchist who steals Anne's belongings).

These elements resurface in the 'adult' films which explore their impact on the heroine's evolution as an artist. In *Un Homme amoureux*, Jane knows that Steve will not leave his (jealous) wife and that the affair will cost her her relationship with Bruno (Vincent Lindon), but she is able to turn her experience into art (the film ends self-reflexively with a zoom-out of her sitting alone at her typewriter writing 'Un homme amoureux'). *Après l'amour* centres on Lola (Isabelle Huppert), a childless thirty-something woman with three books to her name, who is experiencing problems with her relationships and her writing. The film tracks her affair with Tom (Hippolyte Girardot) and her more permanent relationship with David (Bernard Giraudeau), each of whom is involved with another (jealous, hysterical) woman with children. When Lola finds herself unexpectedly pregnant by David, her pregnancy coincides with her new-found independence and renewed creativity. By contrast, *A la folie* focuses on Alice (Anne Parillaud), a young woman on the verge of artistic success, whose life is thwarted by the violent jealousy of her mad, bad sister, Elsa (Béatrice Dalle), and the insensitivity of her working-class lover (Patrick Aurignac). The film ends as it begins, with the threatened reappearance of Elsa, concluding disturbingly on a freeze-frame of Alice, the artist, gazing out of the window, her creativity paralysed.

These 'adult' films are disappointing for a number of reasons. First, Kurys' concern for female rebelliousness and intimate relationships between women seems to have disappeared (except for the mother–daughter bond evoked in *Un Homme amoureux*), and has been replaced by an exploration of women's precarious place within the heterosexual couple, beset by antagonistic relations with other women. Second, Kurys' construction of the woman artist is curiously empty, demonstrated primarily by the image of the (solitary) artist at work rather than through an investigation of the desires which inspire her or the substance of what she is creating (a sign perhaps of Kurys' own anxieties about her inspiration and originality, but also symptomatic of the difficulty of portraying the artist as female in French culture). Third, Kurys refuses to accord her heroines their full subjectivity, keeping them at a distance and weaving in other narrative strands, particularly those of the generally sympathetic but inadequate males with whom they are involved. Finally, the lifestyles of these privileged, semi-bohemian Parisians are not embedded in everyday, contemporary social reality and thus lack the universal appeal of the more ordinary, recognizable protagonists of her 'childhood' films. These observations are also applicable to *Les Enfants du siècle*, which reduces the life of writer, essayist and proto-feminist George Sand (Juliette Binoche) to her relationship with Musset (Benoît Magimel), marginalizes her relationships with women (Marie Dorval turns out to be a perfidious friend), and ends with sorrowful Sand standing alone by Musset's grave before going off to write her own version of their affair.

Kurys' work has been significant within French film production and Anglo-American feminist film criticism for its feminist-influenced articulation of female anxieties and desires and its female-centred appropriation of post-war history.[6] But it is marked on the one hand by the director's personal psychodrama, underlined by repeated images of lonely, abandoned children or disillusioned adults, and on the other hand by the French cultural context, which explains its reluctance to identify fully with its adult female protagonists and its address to a mixed audience. Kurys' refusal of the label 'woman director' is re-inscribed in *Les Enfants du siècle* when Sand declares that she is 'not a woman writer, but a writer who is also a woman'. Despite this ambivalence, however, *Diabolo menthe* and *Coup de foudre* continue to illustrate Kurys' key contribution to women's filmmaking.

Biography

Diane Kurys was born in Lyons, France, in December 1948, the younger of two sisters, and the daughter of Russian Jews who had met and married in a Vichy detention camp during the German Occupation of France (and whose marriage ended in divorce in 1954). After a rebellious childhood, Kurys spent a year in a kibbutz in Israel with Alexandre Arcady, a young Jewish *pied noir* and an activist in a left-wing Zionist youth movement. On her return to France, she became involved in the events of May '68, and left university to take up a career in the theatre, working as an actress for eight years (including a brief appearance in Fellini's *Casanova*). Dissatisfied with acting, she began adapting American plays, and started to write a first-person novel about her schooldays which a friend advised her to turn into a screenplay. After the success of *Diabolo menthe*, both Kurys and Arcady (with whom she set up the production company Alexandre Films) have been able to live from writing, directing and producing, and have a close personal and professional relationship, and a son, Yasha, though, in the spirit of May '68, they have never married.

Notes

1 G.A. Foster, *Women Film Directors: An Introductory Bio-critical Dictionary*, Westport, CT and London, Greenwood Press, 1995, pp. 211–13; B.K. Quart, *Women Directors: The Emergence of a New Cinema*, Westport, CT and London, Praeger, 1988, pp. 145–53.
2 Ginette Vincendeau, 'Like Eating A Lot of Madeleines', *Monthly Film Bulletin*, vol. 58, no. 686, 1991, p. 686.
3 Ginette Vincendeau, 'Issues in European Cinema', in John Hill and Pamela Church Gibson (eds) *The Oxford Guide to Film Studies*, Oxford, Oxford University Press, 1998, pp. 440–8.
4 Barbara Quart, *Women Directors: The Emergence of a New Cinema*, Westport, CN and London, Praeger, 1988, p. 146.
5 C. Holmlund, 'When Is a Lesbian Not a Lesbian?: The Lesbian Continuum and the Mainstream Femme Film', *Camera Obscura*, nos 25/26, 1991, pp. 144–79; C. Straayer, 'Voyage en douce, "Entre Nous"': The Hypothetical Lesbian Heroine', *Jump Cut*, no. 35, 1990, pp. 50–7; P. Powrie *French Cinema in the 1980s*, Oxford, Oxford University Press, 1998, pp. 62–74.
6 Carrie Tarr, 'Heritage, Nostalgia and the Woman's Film: The Cinema of Diane Kurys', in E. Ezra and S. Harris (eds) *France in Focus*, Berg, 2000.

Filmography

Diabolo menthe (1977)
Cocktail Molotov (1980)
Coup de foudre (1983)
Un Homme amoureux (1987)
La Baule Les Pins (1990)
Après l'amour (1992)
A la folie (1994)
Les Enfants du siècle (1999)

Further reading

G. Colvile, 'Mais qu'est-ce qu'elles voient? Regards de Françaises à la caméra', *The French Review*, vol. 67, no. 1, 1993, pp. 73–81.
Pauline Kael, 'The Current Cinema, "Entre nous" ', *New York Times*, 5 March 1984, p. 130 and pp. 133–4.
Judith Mayne, *The Woman at the Keyhole, Feminism and Women's Cinema*, Bloomington and Indianapolis, Indiana University Press, 1990, pp. 124–54.
C. Portuges, 'Seeing Subjects: Women Directors and Cinematic Autobiography', in B. Brodzki and C. Schenk (eds) *Life/Lines: Theorizing Women's Autobiography*, Ithaca, NY and London, Cornell University Press, 1988, pp. 338–50.
Barbara Quart, '*Entre Nous*, A Question of Silence', *Cineaste*, vol. 13, no. 3, 1984, pp. 45–7.
Carrie Tarr, *Diane Kurys*, Manchester and New York, Manchester University Press, 1999.

CARRIE TARR

ANG LEE

At the beginning of Ang Lee's *The Ice Storm*, one of the central characters, Paul Hood, reflects on the nature of the family and its place in the world: 'Your family is the void you emerge from and the place you return to when you die. And that's the paradox. The closer you're drawn back in, the deeper into the void you go.' The paradoxical permanency of the family is a central tenet of Lee's work. He has referred to himself as 'a filmmaker who does family dramas'.[1] With the aid of long-term producer/screenwriter James Schamus, he has proven himself to be one of the most accomplished contemporary practitioners of the melodrama. Critically and commercially successful both in the west and his native Taiwan, he is the only director to have won two Golden Bear awards at the

Berlin Film Festival and is a popular presence at other festivals around the world.[2]

To date, Lee's films can be divided into two seemingly different types. *Pushing Hands, The Wedding Banquet* and *Eat Drink Man Woman*, referred to by the director as his 'Father Knows Best' trilogy, were all Taiwanese co-productions.[3] Combining social comedy and light drama, their success paved the way for his more recent, larger-budget, US films. In contrast to his earlier work, *Sense and Sensibility, The Ice Storm* and *Ride with the Devil*, occupy a territory that Schamus terms the 'cinema of quality', part of 'that body of "classy" Hollywood movies that borrows its middlebrow legitimacy from its literary pedigree'.[4] Seemingly unconnected thematically, although displaying a marked progression in both the complexity of Schamus' writing and Lee's fluid direction, the two periods of Lee's career share an interest in the potentially transgressive situations at the heart of family life, be it the simple act of leaving home, or the emotional ravages of civil war.

Lee's films attempt to analyse the social order of each given society, whether based on ethnicity, sexuality, age or class, within the context of his own distinctive form of family drama. Writing on Chinese family melodramas, Ma Ning has argued that the genre has proven to be 'one of the most dominant forms of expression in Chinese cinema since its beginning in the early years of this century'. The roots of this popularity can be found in the emphasis placed on the family unit in traditional Chinese society, and its role as 'a cultural ideal consisting of a set of norms that motivated the individual in his or her social practices'.[5] For Wimal Dissanayake, the centrality of the family unit in Asian/Chinese melodramas is the antithesis of its western counterpart; western melodrama is typically concerned with the individuals within the family, rather than the unit as a whole.[6] From the consummate chamber pieces that exemplify his early films, through to the more expansive, visually breathtaking later work, Lee appears to offer an interpretation of both forms in order to explore the values and principles of his characters and their place in a constantly changing world. This is markedly visible in Lee's early films.

In interviews, Lee emphasizes the cultural diversity of his background, which has had a profound effect upon his work: 'I talk English and turn around and speak Chinese to someone else. It's hard for us to look at a specific event from an American or a Chinese or even an Asian-American point of view. It's always a mixture.'[7] *Pushing Hands, The Wedding Banquet* and *Eat Drink Man*

Woman use the collision of differing cultural attitudes to sexuality and age to expose the cracks in the veneer of the ostensibly stable family structure. The most complex example of this approach can be found in *Eat Drink Man Woman*. Lee's only film to be set in Taiwan, it centres on the seemingly traditional relationship between a widowed master chef and his three grown-up daughters. Tracing the breakdown of the Chu family as each daughter leaves home to build a life or family of her own, the drama slowly builds up to the climactic final family dinner where Mr Chu reveals a secret that irreversibly changes the future of the family, and each member's relationship with one another. Oscillating between domestic farce and a more serious rumination on the loss of the traditional values held dear by Mr Chu, the film ends with – or resigns itself to – the recognition that each individual and his/her values are as important as those of the family.

Eat Drink Man Woman follows Lee's first two films in using the traditional Chinese archetype of the father-figure as the focal point of the drama; and as Peter Matthews points out, all three films are 'scrupulously poised between celebrating and chastising our modernity for its loosening of the ties that bind'.[8] In *Pushing Hands*, the father travels from Taiwan to live in his son's house, but is eventually forced to find his own accommodation because the family ties which existed in his homeland are considered less important in America. Similarly, in *The Wedding Banquet*, Gao's parents return from New York to their home in Taiwan having reluctantly accepted their son's homosexuality. At the end of both films, there is a note of regret that acknowledges what has been lost in order for modernity, and the new set of values accompanying it, to survive. In *Eat Drink Man Woman*, Lee uses the strained relations between Mr Chu and his middle daughter, Jia-Chien, to explore generational conflict. Unable to accept each other's lifestyles, they avoid all forms of communication with each other. It is only when the two generations recognize, if not accept, each other's way of life that any future happiness, no matter how small, can be guaranteed. As Nigel Andrews observed:

> the film's beauty and witty pathos lie in its perception that life is not about reconciliations. It is about generations eternally programmed to fight each other, with only the meal table as a truce area in which, for a few hours each day or week, common appetite can overcome warring self-concern.[9]

The use of food as a metaphor for domestic strife is a recurrent feature of Lee's work. Its preparation and presentation links values and traditions, both old and new, and is the catalyst that ignites familial differences and generational conflict. In *Pushing Hands*, the contrasting meals of the elderly tai-chi teacher and his American daughter-in-law symbolize the cultural and generational differences between them. For Gao and Simon in *The Wedding Banquet*, any intruder into the domestic intimacy of their immaculately clean kitchen poses a threat to their future happiness together. And for the three daughters in *Eat Drink Man Woman*, the traditional family dinner represents the imposition of their father's patriarchal values. Moreover, Mr Chu's inability to taste the food he eats symbolizes his unwillingness to accept the world around him as it is, and not what he wants it to be. When he tells his friend that 'people today don't appreciate the exquisite art of cooking', he is referring to the disappearance of the values he has always used to make sense of the world. The new values are embodied in his daughters, who work in fast-food restaurants, marry without their father's consent and would rather live alone than with their family. It is only when he accepts the inevitability of change that Mr Chu regains his ability to taste and, as a result, is able to display his affection for Jia-Chien.

Mr Chu's struggle to adapt to the changing world is echoed by Ben Hood, the central patriarchal figure in Lee and Schamus' adaptation of Rick Moody's *The Ice Storm*. The Hoods, a seemingly perfect image of the all-American family, gather together for Thanksgiving dinner, and Ben announces that 'it's great that we can all be together', asking daughter Wendy to say grace. Instead, she offers a petulant criticism of her parents' values. One of the many scenes of domestic strife in the film, Wendy's comments chip away at her family's Rockwellian façade to reveal that the Hoods have not been 'together' for a very long time. Over the course of the weekend, this façade will crumble entirely. Ben's secret affair with his neighbour, Janey Carver, will become public knowledge, his wife will despise him for his dishonesty, his desire for a perfect family life will be shattered forever, and a young boy will die.

The Ice Storm is a caustic account of 1970s' Connecticut society gone awry, focusing on two families, the Hoods and the Carvers. In exploring the generational differences between the characters, it looks back to themes raised in Lee's earlier films. However, the tone is more sombre, particularly in the way the film questions the adults' responsibility both for their own behaviour, and for that of their children. Their apparent unwillingness to assume any responsibility has resulted in the increasing gulf between and within generations. Jim Carver announces his return from a business trip only to be greeted with indifference by his sons who had failed to notice his absence. Even Jim's wife greets him with indifference. Having been emotionally frozen for so long in a relationship where she appears to be little more than a social accessory to her husband, she is concerned that he has disturbed her reading rather than happy at his return. Relations are hardly better in the Hood residence where son Paul would rather be in boarding school and his sister's extra-curricular activities elicit little interest from her parents.

Through its focus on the characters' lack of involvement in each other's lives, the film paints a portrait of the loneliness and suffering they all experience. Ultimately, it takes the death of a family member to rouse these characters from their emotional somnambulism, only to realize that any hope of reconciliation has long passed. As Thomas Elsaesser writes:

> [family melodrama] more often records the failure of the protagonist to act in a way that could shape the events and influence the emotional environment, let alone change the stifling social milieu. The world is closed, and the characters are acted upon. Melodrama confers on them a negative identity through suffering, and the progressive self-immolation and disillusionment generally end in resignation: they emerge lesser human beings for having become wise and acquiescent in the ways of the world.[10]

The 'stifling' closure of this social world is manifested throughout *The Ice Storm* in the pathetic fallacy of the frozen landscape, against which the drama is played out. When the actions of the adults are at their most negative, destroying the social fabric of the New Canaan community, the natural forces reach their most positive with devastating consequences; the aftermath of the ice storm results in the electrocution of Mikey Carver.

The sense of a larger force at work, reflecting and affecting each of these lives is successfully nurtured through the film's distinctive visual style. Unlike the vivid colours on display in Lee's earlier films, *The Ice Storm* uses a muted palette to reinforce the repressed emotions of the characters. Lee and long-term editor Tim Squyres employ a series of snapshots of life in the Stepford-like community, emphasizing the banal activity of its inhabitants; from the train platform crammed with businessmen wearing the same bland, beige trenchcoats, to the archetypal village green where Elena attempts to find a brief respite from her dull existence. Lee also makes good use of editing to interrupt the passionless exchanges between Elena and Ben as they prepare the Thanksgiving meal. Cutting between their conversation, shots of frozen food and the minutiae of objects that populate their household, Lee accentuates the lack of emotion between the couple whose feelings for each other are colder than the outside environment.

A number of critics have highlighted the increasing maturity of Lee's visual style.[11] While the frenetic restaurant scenes in *Eat Drink Man Woman* and the period settings of *Sense and Sensibility* showed Lee to be adept at creating striking images, it is with *The Ice Storm* that he most effectively uses *mise-en-scène* to project the inner turmoil of the characters onto the environment around them. The interiors exhibit a cool, ascetic sheen, influenced as much by the depthless unreality of the photo-realist movement, as by the sterile *bricolage* of 1970s' artefacts that populate the sparse, soulless spaces.[12] Lee defends his stylized approach as a way of creating an atmosphere that his previous mode of directing would not have allowed:

> I think this sort of intense material needs a style, otherwise it won't hold up. Because nature, in its naked structure, is so patchy, you have to make visual parallels and pull the film together carefully. ... In this film you're watching a progression of moments, so it's more artificial – or artsy, if you will – than the others I've made.[13]

Highly praised for its style and the quality of the performances, *The Ice Storm* has, more than any of Lee's previous films, been criticized for an apparent conservatism. Peter Matthews was one of a number of critics who saw Lee's melodramatic tableaux as deeply conservative, accusing Lee and Schamus of blunting the satirical sword with which novelist Rick Moody attacks his characters, and opting instead for an oblique assault upon the liberal values of the previous decade.[14] Openly admitting that he was interested in making a film that was 'both provocative and conservative at the same time',[15] Lee is more disposed to absolve the characters of their actions, preferring to place the blame on society. To borrow from Elsaesser, fault lies at the 'social and existential level, away from the arbitrary and finally obtuse logic of private motives and individualized psychology'.[16]

Julian North has also identified a strong conservative vein running through Lee's *Sense and Sensibility*, claiming that the adaptation capitalizes 'on the subversiveness of [Austen's] work, but more so on the fact that her subversiveness may be so safely contained'.[17] For instance, the glamorization of Colonel Brandon as a romantic hero, comparable with Willoughby himself, renders Marianne's fate more attractive than it appears in the novel. Although she is obliged to marry him for future financial security, the film implies that she commits herself to him out of a deep affection. Much of North's criticism is levelled at Emma Thompson's script, particularly given that Lee was brought in as a 'gun for hire'. Yet the film's preoccupation with patriarchal power and the role of the family certainly echoes the themes of his previous films, in which he had more involvement. The film is also significant for its phenomenal critical and commercial success, earning Thompson an Academy Award for Best Adapted Screenplay in 1996 and paving the way for the funding of Lee's subsequent films, *The Ice Storm* and *Ride with the Devil*.

Based on Daniel Woodrell's *Woe to Live On*, *Ride with the Devil* is an account of the life of a German immigrant, Jake Roedel, as he travels with Southern Bushwackers during the American Civil War, accompanied by Daniel Holt, a freed black slave. Whilst not endorsing their racist attitudes, Lee adopts the perspective of the Confederate supporters, documenting the loss of tradition in the face of modernization, this time enforced by the Unionist government. Although thematically linked to Lee's earlier work, the film differs in its emphasis on the physical, as well as the emotional drama. Moments of intimacy are intercut with epic battle scenes between Bushwackers and Jayhawkers (the bands of Unionist irregulars enlisted to hunt down their Confederate rivals). The world of Roedel and his friends is a microcosm of the larger battle being waged across the fragmented nation. The fight for freedom is reduced to the ambitions and hopes of individual men and women: Jake's dream of a peaceful life; his love's desire for a family; and Daniel's search for his place in the world amidst the ravages of a bloody war.

Crouching Tiger, Hidden Dragon, Lee's most recent film, once again deals with the conflict between freedom of expression and the restrictions enforced upon individuals by societal conventions and traditional values. His first Chinese-language film since *Eat Drink Man Woman*, it tells the story of four warriors whose attempts to achieve happiness in their emotional lives are thwarted by their allegiance to the honour of their craft and the complexities of the moral codes binding them to their social status. Lee interweaves breathtaking fight sequences with scenes of domestic drama, appealing to both mainstream and art-house audiences. A phenomenal international success, it is one of Lee's most accomplished and enjoyable films. With plans to film and direct a big-budget version of Marvel comics' 'The Incredible Hulk' and an English-language remake of Alain Resnais' *On connait la chanson*, it is no surprise that Lee has been referred to as 'the most mysterious talent at large in American cinema'.[18]

Biography

Ang Lee was born in Taiwan in 1954. He received a BFA from the University of Illinois and an MFA in Film Production from New York University, graduating in 1984. Lee won the Best Director and Best Film award at the 1984 NYU student film festival for his graduation short *Fine Time*.

Notes

1 O. Moverman, 'The Angle on Ang Lee', *Interview*, September 1997, p. 65.
2 *The Wedding Banquet* in 1993 and *Sense and Sensibility* in 1996. Lee's films have also opened a number of film festivals; most recently, the 1999 London Film Festival.
3 The films were produced by The Central Motion Picture Corporation and Good Machine, the company owned by Ted Hope and James Schamus.
4 James Schamus, *The Ice Storm*, London, Nick Hern Books, 1997, p. xi.
5 Ma Ning, 'Symbolic Representation and Symbolic Violence: Chinese Family Melodrama of the early 1980s', in Wimal Dissanayake (ed.) *Melodrama and Asian Cinema*, Cambridge, Cambridge University Press, 1993 , p. 29.
6 Wimal Dissanayake, *ibid.*, p. 4.
7 *Filmmaker*, vol. 11, no. 4, 1993, p. 22.
8 P. Matthews, 'Ride with the Devil', *Sight and Sound*, December 1999, p. 35. Lee claims to have used his father as the model for the three father-figures in *Pushing Hands, The Wedding Banquet* and *Eat Drink Man Woman*. More than just a parent, Lee has stated that the father-figure in Chinese society is 'the symbol of how tradition works' (O. Moverman, *op. cit.*, p. 68).
9 Nigel Andrews, 'Eat Drink Man Woman', *The Financial Times*, 12 January 1995, p. 13.
10 Thomas Elsaesser, 'Tales of Sound and Fury: Observations on the Family Melodrama', in B.K. Grant (ed.) *Film Genre Reader II*, Texas, University of Texas Press, 1995, p. 374.

11 P. Matthews, 'The Big Freeze', *Sight and Sound*, February 1998, p. 14.
12 Lee acknowledges the influence of the photo-realist movement on the visual style of *The Ice Storm* (interview with I. Blair, '*The Ice Storm*', *Film and Video*, October 1997).
13 O. Moverman, *op. cit.*, p. 68.
14 P. Matthews, *op. cit.*, 1998, p. 14.
15 I. Blair, *op. cit.*, p. 68.
16 Thomas Elsasser, *op. cit.*, p. 374.
17 J. North, *Conservative Austen, Radical Austen: 'Sense and Sensibility' from Text to Screen*, London, Routledge, 1999, p. 49.
18 P. Matthews, 1999, *op. cit.*, p. 35.

Filmography

Pushing Hands /Tui Shou (Taiwan/US, 1992)
The Wedding Banquet /Xiyan (Taiwan/US, 1993)
Eat Drink Man Woman (Taiwan, 1994)
Sense and Sensibility (US, 1995)
The Ice Storm (US, 1997)
Ride with the Devil (US, 1999)
Crouching Tiger, Hidden Dragon (China/HK/Taiwan/US, 2000)

Further reading

James Schamus, *Ride with the Devil*, London: Faber and Faber, 1999.

IAN HAYDN SMITH

SPIKE LEE

Spike Lee has directed musicals (*School Daze, Mo' Better Blues*), edgy sex comedies (*She's Gotta Have It, Girl 6*), resonant family dramas (*Crooklyn, He's Got Game, Jungle Fever*), documentaries (*Four Little Girls, The Real Kings of Comedy*), slices of larger than life New York (*Do the Right Thing, Summer of Sam*), an intimate road movie (*Get on the Bus*), an urban crime drama (*Clockers*), and the sweeping political biography *Malcolm X*. He has also found the time to work in advertising, executive produce other filmmakers' projects and to run merchandising outlets. Lee has variously written or co-written, performed in and produced many of the films that he has directed. Even while working across such a range of genres, his films typically combine and exceed any one of the labels which I have attached to them here: think of the high-colour musical number in his black-and-white début feature *She's Gotta Have It*, or the charged combination of domestic melodrama and urban life in

Jungle Fever, or the juxtaposition of documentary-style and rites-of-passage road movie that is *Get on the Bus.* Combining political energy, a bold formalist style, perceptive use of music and sound commercial skills, Spike Lee has established himself as a vital figure in contemporary US film culture.

Moroever, Lee is in some ways the most visible symbol of a vibrant and evolving African-American film culture that extends from the mainstream to the experimental. In industry terms, as Reginald Hudlin commented in 1989, 'Spike's films are evidence that you can make quality black films or even art films, and still make money.'[1] Since his breakthrough success with the low-budget, new-wave inspired *She's Gotta Have It,* Lee has not only kept working (hard enough for a filmmaker so explicitly antagonistic to mainstream images and studio culture) but kept up a commentary on Hollywood's representation of African-Americans through interviews, letters to the press and, of course, his movies – most recently *Bamboozled,* a controversial satire on the US television (and film) industry in which writer Pierre Delacroix (Damon Wayons) launches a modern minstrel show. Although he expects a disaster and a release from his contract, the show is a perverse hit. Typically, the ramifications draw together questions of personal identity and wider political concerns.

Produced with New Line, *Bamboozled* is the first of Lee's films to tackle the industry in such direct terms.[2] He had essayed the territory in *Girl 6* (written by Suzan Lori-Parks), a film which was book-ended by two exploitative audition scenes featuring Theresa Randle, the first in New York with director Q.T. (Quentin Tarantino) the second with Ron Silver in Los Angeles. The majority of the film is taken up with Randle's telephone sex-work as Girl 6 – a different (but the film suggests, related) kind of performance – and the crisis of identity that it provokes. *Girl 6* is also punctuated by celebrity cameos and by sequences – just a little bit too sharp to be simply deemed affectionate – in which Lee evokes the stars and genres of the past (Randle as Dorothy Dandrige in *Carmen Jones,* as a Grier-esque action heroine 'Lovely Brown' and as the daughter in sitcom family *The Jeffersons* – Lee plays the father). *Bamboozled's* concern with representation foregrounds a longstanding feature of Lee's work – an awareness of the work performed by stereotypes together with a willingness to mobilize such types to his own ends.

Lee's visibility, indeed his star persona as a filmmaker, is bound up with a commitment to popular filmmaking, or at the very least to getting his films seen. From the start, Lee realized the importance of promotion in terms of gaining an audience for his films and getting them talked about. A New York Film School graduate, Lee appeared on the scene just as the commercial possibilities of the developing independent sector – hip, low-budget films could make significant profits relative to their costs – were beginning to become evident. His thesis film, *Joe's Bed-Stuy Barbershop: We Cut Heads*, won acclaim; however, funding collapsed on his follow-up project. This struggle to secure a budget which would enable him to make the high-profile films he wishes to would be a consistent feature of Lee's career (he established his production company, 40 Acres and a Mule Filmworks, early on).

It is difficult to discuss Spike Lee's significance without thinking about the context of black filmmaking in the United States.[3] Through the latter part of the 1980s and the 1990s, it became clear that certain kinds of black subject matter could find commercial backing. As *Get on the Bus*'s student filmmaker Xavier (Hill Harper) wryly says: 'They sum us up with the four R's: rap, rape, rob and riot.' Lee acknowledges his talent for publicity, presenting it as a necessary counter to the film industry's typical failure to successfully promote the work of African-American filmmakers ('marketing is an integral part of my filmmaking').[4] Distribution and marketing – both theatrical and through video and DVD release – have become areas of contention in a context where executives seem to have fixed ideas about where and, crucially, how well, black-themed films will play. Lee steered clear of drugs until *Jungle Fever* in which Samuel L. Jackson's Gator tears at the illusions of the central family (the end credits of *She's Gotta Have It* proclaim: 'This film contains no Jerri curls!!! and no drugs!!!'). Interviewed about *Clockers*, Lee showed an acute awareness of the limitations of 'the whole gangsta-hip-hop, urban-drug genre film', but also of the daily presence of imagery on the news associating young black men with drugs and criminality: 'I just hope that people will see some of the insights they might not see on the news at 6 and 11.'[5] Thus the film is concerned to explore the psychological complexity of protagonist Strike's (Mekhi Phifer) choices as much as the acute social issues surrounding drug use, to open up familiar media images.

Like fellow New Yorker Martin Scorsese (who served as executive producer on *Clockers*), Lee is independent in spirit, an innovative mainstream filmmaker (questioning and controversial, Lee can also be rather conservative – not least in the portrayal of relationships between men and women). When a three-picture deal with Island collapsed, he quickly signed with Columbia for his second feature,

School Daze, a celebration and interrogation of black college life. Lee wrote at the time that '*School Daze* is my arrival in the big leagues', and that the relationship represented 'an ideal situation for an independent filmmaker working with a studio'.[6] (Later, however, he would criticize Columbia's marketing campaign.) He has subsequently worked with Universal, Warner Bros, 20th Century Fox, even Disney's Touchstone (for the Oedipal father/son basketball fantasy, *He Got Game*). Lee's very public challenges to the industry form an important part of his persona – for instance, securing backing from African-American celebrities when *Malcolm X* (a film he took over from Norman Jewison after extensive lobbying) went over budget and Warners would not back the lengthy epic (it was finally released with a running time of over three hours). And as a credit at the end of Columbia's *Get on the Bus* informs us, the film 'was completely funded by 15 African American Men'.

It was Lee's third feature, still one of his most accomplished, which established him as a major presence. *Do the Right Thing* follows twenty-four hours in the life of a Brooklyn neighbourhood on the hottest day of the year. Shot in bold colour, the film shifts between key locations on the block – Sal's pizzeria, a Korean-owned grocery store, a radio station, the street itself – foregrounding the uneasy relationships, whether romantic, professional or antagonistic, between the block's different ages and ethnic groupings. The film's compelling treatment of racism – institutional on the part of the police, casual or personal in the life of the block – was crafted into an elegant screenplay making effective use of an ensemble cast; the film gained event status in the US. *Do the Right Thing* aims to dramatize the complexity of racism through multiple characters with whom we are invited to sympathize or to judge. Lee's intense involvement in media discussions of the film was crucial in questioning the very terms in which the film was discussed: why was the focus of some white critics on the destruction of property (Sal's pizzeria) rather than people (Radio Raheem's death at the hands of the police); why was the *absence* of drugs an issue – 'do those interviewers ask the people who made *Rain Man* or *Wall Street* why they did not include drugs in their pictures?' asked Lee.[7]

Whilst there is a realist impulse at the heart of Lee's stylized cinema, evident in his evocative portraits of urban life, he is primarily a story-teller and sometimes a rather fantastic one at that. In a 1986 interview, Lee said with typical assurance: 'I wanted to see black stories on the screen and I figured the only way that was going to happen was if I put them there.' By 1991, a similar rhetoric was combined with allusions to art cinema: 'I try to show African-American culture on screen. Every group, every culture and ethnic group needs to see itself on screen. What black filmmakers can do is show our culture on screen the same way Fellini's done for Italians and Kurosawa's done for the Japanese.'[8] As his nod to international art cinema suggests, though popular in style, Lee's films are typically more complex than they have been given credit for. So much attention has been paid to somehow fixing the political meaning of Lee's persona and films that his status as a filmmaker can get sidelined. If one word could describe Lee's style it would be restless: from the mobile camera and dollies to jump cuts and montage sequences. The films are replete with striking visual devices – direct address to camera, canted frames in *Do the Right Thing*, multiple film stocks in *Get on the Bus*, the fragmented flashbacks of *He Got Game*, or those conversations staged with both performers facing the camera.

Thoroughly identified with New York, Lee's work is never less than public and social in its dimensions, even when focused on familial drama. In *Jungle Fever*, for example, Flipper's (Wesley Snipes) and Angie's (Annabella Sciorra) mutual fascination is mapped explicitly through the urban geography of New York. Moreover, their lives are lived in public – watchful, unseen neighbours turn a playful row into a police incident. The later *Crooklyn* – widely reviewed as an autobiographical portrait of 1970s' Brooklyn (the script, co-written by Lee, his sister Joie and brother Cinque, featured a jazz musician father and schoolteacher mother) – maps a process whereby Carolyn's (Alfre Woodard) responsibilities are shouldered by 10-year-old Troy (Zelda Harris). Women with responsibilities are in the background of both *Do the Right Thing* (Mookie's girlfriend Tina and son Hector) and *Jungle Fever*, but at the centre of *Crooklyn*. Yet the film is an uneasy mix of tragedy (Carolyn's death) and comedy (the scenes set in the South where Troy is dispatched during her mother's illness), of cliché and genuine innovation.

After the success of his first five features, Lee embarked on an epic film based on the life of Muslim leader Malcolm X – his biggest studio project to date, featuring Denzel Washington in the title role. Perhaps inevitably, given the political and historical significance of Malcolm X, debate over the way in which Lee presented his story was fierce. The question of how to interpret Malcolm X's life for a mass audience centred on a perception that Lee's popular style could not convey the complexity of the subject. Lee talked of the need for a David Lean-style epic, remaining true to his vision of a popular narrative cinema. Many critics were surprised that he opted for such a conventional format, setting aside many of the formal flourishes associated with his earlier films. Perhaps this was a sign that Lee took his task seriously.[9] Both an historical film and an intervention, Lee's film insists on the contemporary significance of Malcolm X; the opening sequence shows Malcolm speaking over images of a burning American flag intercut with footage of the Rodney King beating, while the closing montage, featuring Nelson Mandela, takes us from Malcolm X's funeral to schoolrooms in the contemporary US and South Africa.

Both the possibilities and the limitations of mainstream production are foregrounded in the contrast between the epic *Malcolm X* and Lee's powerful Oscar-nominated documentary, *Four Little Girls*. Achieving only a limited release, the film uses the 1963 bombing of a Birmingham Baptist church to stage a complex portrait of the Civil Rights movement of the early 1960s. Promoting the film, Lee said:

> I never thought about making a movie as opposed to a documentary because I've seen how similar race [issues] films get distorted. I could have reached a larger audience with a proper movie but I felt that this story was so important and needed to be told.[10]

He Got Game, arguably Lee's most mainstream movie and his first original screenplay since *Jungle Fever*, centres once more on questions of masculinity and responsibility. Prisoner Jake Shuttle-worth (Denzel Washington) has seven days to persuade his estranged son Jesus (Ray Allen) to commit to the Governor's alma mater Big State. This family melodrama touches on yet another aspect of the American entertainment industry, professional sports. Set to Aaron Copeland's music, *He Got Game* offers a commentary on – and at times a hymn to – basketball and the politics of professional sports more generally. In the film's present, almost everybody wants something from Jesus, whilst flashbacks show Jake pushing the young Jesus to his limits, insistent that basketball provides a chance of success (shades of jazzman Bleek's childhood, reproduced once more in relation to his son in the final scenes of *Mo' Better Blues*). Jake's constant pushing leads to a family row in which he accidentally kills his wife Martha (Lonette McKee) – out of prison Jake embraces Martha's headstone and finds redemptive romance with Milla Jovovich's prostitute, Dakota. As this implies, female characters take a backseat to the awkward moves between father and son; the movie ends with a fantasy gesture of reconciliation. Lee followed this film with *Summer of Sam*, a period portrait of a frenzied city under siege during the summer of 1977. Typically, Lee avoids the clichés of contemporary serial-killer cinema, sketching the life, rituals and suspicions of a New York Italian-American neighbourhood; the film culminates in Berkowitz's arrest cross-cut with the communities attack on an outsider within, punk rocker and part-time stripper Ritchie (Adrien Brody).

Writing of what she regards as the missed opportunity of *Malcolm X*, bell hooks comments that Lee too often remains with the familiar:

> No matter how daring his films, how transgressive their subject matter, to have a predictable success he provided viewers with stock images. Uncompromising in his commitment to create images of black males that challenge shallow perceptions and bring the issue of racism to the screen, he conforms to the status quo when it comes to images of females.[11]

The limitations of Lee's broad-brush style have most often been discussed in relation to his female characters, from the controversial rape scene in *She's Gotta Have It* on. As Douglas Kellner notes,[12] Lee's films tend to restrict women to a private rather than a public sphere – from Indigo (Joie Lee) and Clarke (Cynda Williams) competing over star performer Bleek in *Mo' Better Blues* to the mother/daughter narrative of *Crooklyn*. *Girl 6* ultimately turns in on itself, ending with Theresa Randle walking out of her Los Angeles audition (and over Dorothy Dandridge's star on the pavement) before disappearing into the crowds outside a theatre where *Girl 6* is announced on the marquee. Randle's audition monologue – finally recited in full in these closing scenes – is none other than Nola Darling's opening address to camera from *She's Gotta Have It*: a self-referential moment whose circularity points up the limited spaces open to black women in film. For hooks, Lee 'is at his creative best in scenes highlighting black males. Portraying black masculinity through a spectrum of complex and diverse portraits, he does not allow audiences to hold a stereotypical image.'[13] It would certainly be fair to say that Lee's preoccupations are with black masculinity and with communities of men – perhaps the reason why *Get on the Bus* (written by Reggie Rock Bythewood), which follows a diverse group of men as their coach takes them across country to the million man march in Washington, is so effective.

While Lee's characters are boldly sketched, the men typically move beyond stereotype, looking past the easy assumptions of mainstream movies. At a more general level, Lee's films make use of multiple characters. The main protagonists do not bear the sole weight of the narrative since they are firmly grounded in a community – sometimes supportive, sometimes antagonistic, but none the less a space for discourse and exchange. Consider the way that issues are talked out/about across characters in such films as *Do the Right Thing*, *Get On the Bus*, *Jungle Fever* or *Summer of Sam*. In these definitively urban films – even the relationship-oriented, distinctly middle-class world of *Jungle Fever* – exchanges take place in public places from the street itself to social spaces such as bars and restaurants. Lee's own pivotal role as Mookie in *Do the Right Thing* is indicative here; his job takes him through all the film's key spaces. Initially a spectator and occasional commentator, he finally becomes involved in events following Radio Raheem's death.

Lee regularly casts himself as a confidante figure – Giant in *Mo' Better Blues*, Shorty in *Malcolm X*, Cyrus in *Jungle Fever*, Jimmy in *Girl 6*. Though *Jungle Fever* revolves around the relationship between Flipper and Angie, the film as a whole is concerned with the wider impact of this relationship (as in the improvised group scene between the film's black women), with Gator, with the developing relationship between Paulie (John Turturro) and Orin (Tyra Ferrell), with Angie's family, and with Flipper's parents played by Ossie Davies and Ruby Dee. 'The people in this film are constantly talking about identity, where they belong,' says Lee.[14] In Lee's films more generally people are constantly talking, shouting, listening, understanding and misunderstanding – communication (and its failure) is at the centre of his work.

Biography

Born Shelton Jackson Lee, in Atlanta, USA, in 1957, to jazz musician Bill and schoolteacher Jacquelyn. The family moved to Brooklyn, New York within a few years. Lee studied mass communications at Morehouse College and film at New York University.

Notes

1   Thulani Davis, 'Local Hero: Workin' 40 Acres and a Mule in Brooklyn', *American Film*, vol. 14, no. 9, 1989, p. 27.

2 His student film, *The Answer*, was about a black filmmaker who remakes *The Birth of a Nation* (D.W. Griffith's 1915 canonical civil war epic in which the Ku Klux Klan are the heroes). Troy Patterson links this early endeavour to *Bamboozled* ('About Face', *Entertainment Weekly*, 20 October 2000, p. 43).

3 See Ed Guerrero, *Framing Blackness*, Philadelphia, PA, Temple University Press, 1993.

4 Spike Lee, *By Any Means Necessary: The Trials and Tribulations of the Making of 'Malcolm X'* ..., London, Vintage, 1993, p. 21.

5 'Spike', *Premiere*, vol. 9, no. 2, 1995, p. 108.

6 Spike Lee, 'Class Act', *American Film*, vol. 13, no. 4, 1988, p. 59.

7 Mark A. Reid (ed.) *Spike Lee's 'Do the Right Thing'*, Cambridge, Cambridge University Press, 1997, p. 148.

8 Janice Mosier Richolson, 'He's Gotta Have It: An Interview with Spike Lee', *Cineaste*, vol. 18, no. 4, 1991, p. 12.

9 Not that this impressed many of his critics – see the various views collected in the 'Malcolm X Symposium', *Cineaste*, vol. 19, no. 4, 1993, pp. 4–24.

10 Ronke Adeyemi, 'Spike Lee Interview', *Black Film Bulletin*, Spring 1999, p. 5.

11 bell hooks, 'Malcolm X Symposium', *op. cit.*, p. 14.

12 Mark A. Reid, *op. cit.*, p. 94.

13 bell hooks, *op. cit.*, p. 13.

14 In Richolson, *op. cit.*, p. 13.

Filmography

As director/producer

The Answer (1980) student film
Sarah (1981) student film
Joe's Bed-Stuy Barbershop: We Cut Heads (1982) student film
She's Gotta Have It (1986) also writer, editor
School Daze (1988) also writer
Do the Right Thing (1989) also writer
Mo' Better Blues (1990) also writer
Jungle Fever (1991) also writer
Malcolm X (1992) also screenplay
Crooklyn (1994) also co-writer
Clockers (1995) also co-authored screenplay, co-producer
Get on the Bus (1996) also executive producer
Girl 6 (1996)
Four Little Girls (1997)
He Got Game (1998) also writer
Summer of Sam (1999)
The Original Kings of Comedy (2000) documentary
Bamboozled (2000) also writer

Further reading

Manthia Diawara (ed.) *Black American Cinema*, London, Routledge/AFI, 1993.

Ed Guerrero, 'Spike Lee and the Fever in the Racial Jungle', in Jim Collins, Hilary Radner and Ava Preacher Collins (eds) *Film Theory Goes to the Movies*, London, Routledge/AFI, 1993.

bell hooks, *Reel to Real: Race, Sex, and Class at the Movies*, London, Routledge, 1996.

Eric Perkins, 'Renewing the African American Cinema: The Films of Spike Lee', *Cineaste*, vol. 17, no. 4, 1990, pp. 4–8.

John Pierson, *Spike, Mike, Slackers & Dykes: A Guided Tour Across a Decade of Independent American Cinema*, London, Faber and Faber, 1996.

Betsy Sharkey, 'Knocking on Hollywood's Door', *American Film*, vol. 14, no. 9, 1989, pp. 22–7 and pp. 52, 54.

YVONNE TASKER

DAVID LYNCH

David Lynch has arguably been the foremost romantic filmmaker to come out of America in the last thirty years. Love him or loathe him, he is an edge director who has elaborated a distinctive vision of the mythical, wholesome American innocent's encounter with darkness, decay and evil across a range of film and art/media contexts, including not only underground, independent and blockbuster cinema but also television, painting (his first love), photography, animation and popular music. The most famous examples of his style are, of course, *Blue Velvet*, where naïve Jeffrey Beaumont (Kyle MacLachlan) descends into the violent world of sexual perversion and criminality lurking just beneath the surface of Lumberton's bland suburban normality, and its television sibling, *Twin Peaks*, with MacLachlan as FBI Special Agent Dale Cooper investigating the brutal sex murder of Prom Queen Laura Palmer (Sheryl Lee). But the dark romantic encounter between seemingly idyllic innocence and corrupting evil can also be found, with varying emphases and across different genres, in much of Lynch's œuvre, from the low-budget *Eraserhead* and his first commercial success *The Elephant Man*, through the gargantuan flop *Dune*, to the 1990s' movies *Wild at Heart*, *Twin Peaks: Fire Walk with Me* and *Lost Highway*. His most recent film, *The Straight Story*, by contrast, re-vivifies notions of folksy, middle-American goodness more than any Lynch movie to date.

The myth of the lost romantic also underpins Lynch's public persona, in concert with an emphasis on a self-taught, well-nigh Emersonian self-reliance, which may also ultimately be romantic. In interviews he comes across as the charming all-American boy who had an idyllic, if peripatetic, 1950s' childhood, much of it spent accompanying his woodsman scientist father in his work around the forests bounding small towns of the Pacific Northwest (towns which he describes in very similar terms to the surface conformity of Lumberton and Twin Peaks), and who was frightened by the city when he visited his maternal grandparents in Brooklyn. From an early age, he claims that:

> I learned that just beneath the surface there's another world, and still different worlds as you dig deeper. I knew it as a kid, but I couldn't find the proof. It was just a kind of feeling. There is goodness in blue skies and flowers, but another force – a wild pain and decay – also accompanies everything.[1]

This statement glosses the basis of the Lynchian poetic of Weirdness, laying equal stress on upholding the idyll's value – Lynch, it is suggested, really believes the small-town 1950s were great, just as he really believes in American innocence and the transcendence of romantic love – and on the threatening inevitability of the darker worlds which lie beneath it and may inhabit or overtake it. Hence also the significance of the two tags which have most readily circulated Lynch's persona, the self-penned 'Eagle Scout, Missoula, Montana', paean of upright, pragmatic American values and eccentric tall-tale humour, and *Elephant Man* executive producer Stuart Cornfeld's 'Jimmy Stewart from Mars', the homely American who is nevertheless very strange indeed.

Lynch's dark romanticism informs his aesthetic sensibility, his cinematic style, his handling of genres redolent with the romantic mode – European surrealism and art cinema, gothic/horror, noir and melodrama in particular – and the pervasive theme of the Freudian family romance which binds much of his work. It is well known that he distrusts words and formal learning, refuses to psychologize or analyse his work because this may spoil its mystery, gets his ideas from a process which amounts to a form of guided daydreaming – apprehending sensory visual or aural images from the unconscious or, as he sometimes, suggests, 'the ether' – and, whatever state his script is in when he goes to shoot, incorporates chance and accident into the filming process (for example, casting set-dresser Frank Silva as Killer Bob in *Twin Peaks* after he accidentally appeared in a mirror reflection during a take). Lynch's imagination is at once concretely sensuous and self-consciously intuitive and atavistic. Almost the romantic artist as creative seer, he is interested in orchestrating visual and aural effects to evoke a certain mood, aura, atmosphere or association, often one of dis-ease, the uncanny or the sublime, rather than in producing coherent cause-and-effect narratives. The archetypal Lynch scene possesses the quality of a dream/nightmare (sometimes it *is* a dream/nightmare), making strange the familiar, shifting us to an unfamiliar world, or articulating a vision of the strange world, often with a terrible and terrifying beauty. Examples include the birth and death sequences of *The Elephant Man*; Cooper's dream of the dwarf dancing under strobe lights in *Twin Peaks'* Red Room, as Laura's 'cousin' kisses an aged Cooper and whispers her murderer's name in his ear; Laura's journey into the painting on her bedroom wall in *Twin Peaks: Fire Walk with Me*; Fred's (Bill Pullman) foreboding meeting with the Mystery Man (Robert Blake) at the party in *Lost Highway*; and just about all of *Eraserhead*.

Lynch's romantic vision, giving rein to a dissident conservatism, often alights upon the family idyll and its desecration, usually from the son's perspective but also – in the *Twin Peaks* movie – from the daughter's. Drawing on childhood fears and fantasies, his films return repeatedly to parent–child and sibling relations, exploring the ambivalent bonds of love and hate, power and desire which fuel the dynamic of the family and its roles. Once again *Blue Velvet* is the primary exhibit, its Oedipal fantasy scenario so obvious that critics feel duty-bound to comment on it. *Twin Peaks* multiplies plots and supernaturalism around the secret of the incest at the heart of the all-American Palmer family, with the movie, Laura's last days, showing the trauma which the series sought to investigate and reveal. But try these, too. *The Grandmother* is a child's view of birth and his compensatory fantasy – the creation of a special grandmother – against the cruelty of his parents. *Eraserhead* features Henry Spencer's (John Nance) attempts to cope with the monstrous baby which he has allegedly fathered. *The Elephant Man* is suffused with John Merrick's (John Hurt) fantasies of his beautiful mother and his incestuous desire for return to her. *Dune* works to position Paul Atreides (MacLachlan's first outing with Lynch) as the privileged male in an extended family of women. *Wild at Heart's* Sailor

(Nicholas Cage) and Lula (Laura Dern) are more grown up than Lula's wicked mother Marietta (Diane Ladd), who invokes bad fathers to prevent their union. And the baffling *Lost Highway* is, at one level, structured around the bad father-figure, Mr Eddy/Dick Laurant (Robert Loggia), thwarting the heroes' access to the femme fatale Patricia Arquette figure, split as the brunette Renee and blonde Alice.

Lynch's early films comprise a mini monstrous-births-and-deaths cycle within the broader trend which ran from Polanski's *Rosemary's Baby* to Scott's *Alien* and beyond. They also chart his emergence from art-house obscurity to surprising mainstream success. Unlike many of his contemporaries, Lynch was an art school student; he has continued to paint throughout his more illustrious cinematic career, and his love of Edward Hopper and Francis Bacon is discernible in the *mise-en-scène* and ambience of his films. His move into filmmaking came from a desire to bring his paintings to life, to build a world and furnish it with motion and sound, and he learned the mechanics of the trade very much by trial and error.

His first experimental shorts, *The Alphabet* and *The Grandmother*, combine animation and live action to present archetypal Lynchian motifs and themes. In *The Alphabet*, which Lynch has called 'a little nightmare about the fear concerned with learning', a white-faced and white-smocked girl, lying on a bed (the bed is a major prop for Lynch) with a curious plant next to it, is violated by the letters of the alphabet, which partly emanate from the plant, and vomits blood. *The Grandmother*'s elemental and animalistic invocation of family life from a young boy's perspective offers extraordinary birth and death sequences, from the initial autochthonous birth of the Father (Robert Chadwick), the Mother (Virginia Maitland) and the Boy (Richard White, fully suited and bow-tied!) in an Edenic wood and the Grandmother's (Dorothy McGinnis) messy emergence out of a large pod which the Boy has grown from a seed planted in a mound of earth on the attic room bed, to the parents' fantasy murder by the Boy on a stage framed by a proscenium arch (Father executed by a sharp blade, Mother crushed by a heavy weight) and the Grandmother's death in a frenzy of pixilation shots. Both films are crammed with weird symbolism and the model of the life cycle which they imply remains a matter of speculation.

The feature-length *Eraserhead* is the cult underground masterpiece of 1970s' hideous infant cinema. Begun in 1971 with an American Film Institute grant and filmed mainly at night using friends as cast and crew, Lynch worked intermittently for five years to complete the film, taking part-time jobs to support the ongoing work. The result is a black-and-white expressionist nightmare, the grotesque and sexually anxious tale of vacationing printer Henry, whose neurotic girlfriend Mary X (Charlotte Stewart) is delivered of a mutant creature which the couple have to care for in Henry's rundown bedsit. It opens with an elaborate conception fantasy: as Henry floats horizontally in space, a worm-like form – possibly an umbilical cord (they are everywhere in the movie) – issues from his mouth, before plunging into a pool on a planet when the scarred Man in the Planet (Jack Fisk) pulls a lever. What follows is just as surreal. Henry, the innocent with a phallic coiffure, waddles around the desolate landscape (actually Los Angeles factory-lands) like a perplexed silent film comedian. Mary's family are threatening eccentrics. Henry's apartment contains trademark mounds of earth and a hairy-cheeked woman who inhabits a vaudeville stage behind the radiator. When he enters this world, the monstrous baby knocks off his head, which is turned into pencil erasers. And, in the dénouement, when he cuts open the bandages protecting the limbless infant, it expands into a threatening serpent, the world of the opening explodes and, in a flash of blinding white light, Henry is united with the Lady in the Radiator (Laurel Near). The movie's claustrophobic atmosphere is augmented by long-time collaborator Alan Splet's ambient soundtrack, which presses the spectator back into intense solipsistic isolation. Often interpreted as Lynch's Kafkaesque response to his own parental anxieties (daughter Jennifer was born in 1968), *Eraserhead* became a midnight movie favourite, popular both with college students who admired its symbolism and with horror fans for its gore.

Eraserhead's black-and-white aesthetic is continued in its successor, *The Elephant Man*, adapted by Lynch, Christopher de Vore and Eric Bergren from historical accounts of the real John Merrick and shot in London with highbrow British theatrical actors. The contrast in directorial control between hippie cottage industry filmmaking and Hollywood-financed commercial production could scarcely be greater but arguably the film still exhibits a distinctly Lynchian vision. Its narrative, of course, is more readable than its predecessors': eminent surgeon Frederick Treves (Anthony Hopkins) rescues sideshow exhibit John Merrick, afflicted from birth with neurofibromatosis which has caused grotesque physical deformity, from the evil Bytes (Freddie Jones), makes him a home and a family at the London Hospital, and introduces him to London society. Far from being the congenital idiot initially assumed, Merrick turns out to be educated and chivalric in his desire to be a gentleman and a courtly ladies' man. Yet atmosphere is as important as story and reality at any moment can slip away into pure gothic or the uncanny. An initial nightmare sequence matches images of a woman's face, elephants marauding, a hideous rape, smoke and a baby's cry to a garish Splet soundtrack; only later do we realize that this is Merrick's vision of his own monstrous conception. It is answered by the transcendent closure, his pantheistic reunion with his idealized mother after he literally lies down to die, her voice reassuringly intoning that 'nothing will die'. The movie's most surprising aspect is perhaps that it is wonderful melodrama. It is a weepie that works (nominated for no less than eight Oscars, although it landed none).

It is a tribute to Lynch's toughness that, following the commercial failure of the $45-million space opera *Dune* – a sci-fi blockbuster beset with adaptation and technical problems, which Lynch later disowned – he rebuilt his career with the works for which he is best known: the small-town murder mysteries *Blue Velvet* and *Twin Peaks*. *Blue Velvet*, widely regarded as his masterpiece to date (it won the National Society of Film Critics Awards for Best Film, Best Director, Best Supporting Actor (Dennis Hopper) and Best Cinematography), is a cruel romantic fairytale with a postmodern air of pastiche. Jeffrey Beaumont is the archetypal Lynch innocent (MacLachlan is Lynch's most abiding alter-ego), launched on a quest into dark sexual awakening by the discovery of a severed human ear (itself the entrance to another world) and the clue provided by Detective Williams' pure all-American daughter Sandy (Laura Dern) that the ear may be linked to exotic nightclub singer Dorothy Vallens (Isabella Rossellini). The famous opening sequence establishes the bizarre small-town locale of Lumberton with a deft yet surreal economy, shifting us from the shimmering blue curtain (evoking other realms of desire) into an arena counterpointing images of dream-like 1950s' suburban bliss (white picket fences, friendly firemen waving in slow motion, the safe middlebrow house with its neat lawn) with others which are disturbing and threatening (a hand holding a gun on the television screen, Mr Beaumont's mysterious seizure as he waters the garden, the descent into the bug-infested horror beneath that neat lawn). Equally famous is the 'primal scene' sequence where Jeffrey, secreted in Dorothy's closet, voyeuristically spies on the sadomasochistic sexual ritual enacted by psychotic hoodlum Frank Booth (Hopper) and Dorothy, in which the roles of parent and child are fluid and only the sexual fetish of blue velvet (another umbilical cord?) enables Frank's sexual pleasure.

Shocking to many when it was released, the film's perverse sexual violence aroused the wrath of feminists yet caught the 1980s' *Zeitgeist* for mainstreaming psychosexual deviance. It also marked the emergence of allegedly postmodern trends in two distinct but related forms of recycling: first, by using the classic pop standards 'Blue Velvet' and 'In Dreams' in a manner which had thematic resonance but which could also lead to the synergy of soundtrack CDs and promotional tie-ins; and second, by restaging 1950s' iconography with a tone at once naïvely innocent and mockingly self-knowing. The latter led to a view of Lynch as a sophisticated postmodern cynic. But if this is the case, it is surely only the disappointed flip-side of thorough-going romanticism.

The television series *Twin Peaks* crosses and multiplies the small-town murder mystery formula with a compendium of film and television genres, from film noir and supernatural horror to situation comedy and soap opera. The expansiveness of the television format allows for the rich development of the Twin Peaks community, with its Sheriff's department and high school, the Great Northern Hotel and the Packard sawmill, the Double R Diner (site of a mighty fine cup of coffee and delectable cherry pie), the Roadhouse nightclub and the sinister One Eyed Jack's brothel just across the Canadian border, all immersed in fecund nature (the waterfall and the river from which Laura's body is washed up, the evocative forests of Ghostwood where the Black Lodge is located). While the central plot, with its increasingly supernatural twists, grounds the drama in sombre darkness (its lineage leads to *The X Files*), there is also an off-beat humour and magic which is ordinary and accessible (and continues in a series like *Northern Exposure*). Marketed as quality television from a cinematic auteur, *Twin Peaks* arguably works because of – and not in spite of – its soap ingredients and due to the brilliant collaboration between Lynch (who directed only six of the thirty episodes, with a writing credit on four), co-creator Mark Frost and composer Angelo Badalamenti. As Biancamaria Fontana argues, its form most closely resembles the nineteenth-century feuilleton, the lengthy saga published in weekly instalments in the popular press, which drew on stereotypes (the shining knight, the sinning woman) and the exotic intrigues of the romance mode to build multi-genre entertainments with cryptic clues and strong cliffhangers.[2] As such, its delights derive from traditional popular fare as much as from intertextual postmodern cleverness.

Twin Peaks made Lynch a household name but his decision to film the movie prequel, *Twin Peaks: Fire Walk with Me*, proved to be another commercial mistake. He seems to have been motivated by the desire to give screen reality to Laura Palmer's story – to let her live, before she died. Public interest had dwindled, however, by the time the movie was released, and its seriousness was not offset by the charm of everyday Twin Peaks' eccentricity, making it a relentless and increasingly harrowing viewing experience. However, it is a valuable addition to Lynch's œuvre, and ripe for reassessment.

In amongst the *Twin Peaks*' mania and merchandising, Lynch speedily filmed *Wild at Heart*, adapted from Barry Gifford's novel, a brash, episodic, rock'n'roll-fuelled testament to the power of romantic love. Mixing noir, comedy and fantasy within the couple-on-the-run road movie frame tale of Sailor and Lula's flight to the South, pursued by a private detective and gangsters set in motion by Lula's jealous mother, it plays as a pop-video-style tribute to Americana, laced with bravura Lynchian types and motifs. Leopard-skin jacketed Sailor is an Elvis look- and sound-alike; sex-pot Lula is a joyous babe inversion of *Blue Velvet*'s doe-eyed Sandy; Bobby Peru (Willem Dafoe) is a close cousin to Frank Booth; and Sheryl Lee puts in an appearance as the Good Fairy from *The Wizard of Oz*, rescuing Sailor when his conviction momentarily wanders from the course of true love. The night-time sequence where Sailor and Lula, cruising to the sound of Chris Isaak's 'Wicked Game', come upon a beautiful, dying car-wreck victim (Sherilyn Fenn) by the side of the road, is one of the most haunting in Lynch's cinema. Winner of the Golden Palm at Cannes, *Wild at Heart* displays Lynch at the height of his powers but it also drew various attacks: that it was mere style over substance, that it mindlessly glorified sexualized violence, that Lynch had fallen into self-parody. Nevertheless, it was the moment when his star was at its zenith, and around this time he further diversified his activities by collaborating with Badalamenti and singer Julee Cruse on the musical spectacle *Industrial Symphony No. 1* and the albums *Floating Into the Night* (1989) and *The Voice of Love* (1993).

Lynch's recent films exemplify the darker and lighter aspects of his vision in turn. *Lost Highway* is a potent amalgam of horror and film noir, exploring the theme of the double as troubled saxophonist Fred Madison mysteriously transforms into much younger garage worker Pete Dayton (Balthazar Getty) after he has been convicted of savagely murdering his wife Renee (he later transforms back again). Their worlds are held together by metaphorical links and encounters with the same or similar people and situations: Renee and Alice are both played by Patricia Arquette, who may or may not be the same woman; Robert Loggia's demonic gangster goes by two names, Dick Laurant and Mr Eddy, but is the same person; and crucial experiences for both Fred and Pete occur in the luxury house of porn filmmaker Andy (Michael Massee). The initial 'Fred' segment, set largely in his and Renee's Bauhaus-style home (apparently part of Lynch's condominium in LA), is a brooding and threatening distillation of psychic disintegration and the uncanny (its use of shadows and darkness recalls *Eraserhead*). The shift to the familiar suburban landscape when Fred segues into the innocent Pete – an avatar of Jeffrey Beaumont and the high school kids in *Twin Peaks* – is at once a relief and a dissipation. Like much of Lynch, *Lost Highway* is a mood film, and though it performed poorly at the box office, its power to disturb is undeniable.

The Straight Story, by contrast, does what it says in its title, narrating the story of self-reliant 70-something Alvin Straight's (Richard Farnsworth) journey from Iowa to Wisconsin to visit his long-lost brother Lyle (Harry Dean Stanton), who has suffered a stroke, in a remarkably straightforward fashion. Although this is the first Lynch film which he has had no hand in writing – it was scripted by John Roach and Lynch's partner and editor Mary Sweeney – it provides an occasion to indulge his vision of American wholesomeness unencumbered by the perennial darkness found elsewhere in his work. This is not to say that it is not eccentric. Alvin's preferred mode of transport, a motor-driven lawnmower (with trailer), is strange to say the least, and the slow-paced travelogue which ensues affords opportunities aplenty to meet up with off-beat people (including a hysterical woman who loves deer but keeps on running them over). At once a celebration of the middle-American landscape and traditional rural American values – Alvin is, at heart, a cowboy – *The Straight Story* recalls *The Elephant Man* when Alvin contemplates the ineffable mystery of the stars in the night sky with his daughter Rose (Sissy Spacek) and, at the close, in deep silence with Lyle. A delightful film of profound simplicity, it suggests that Lynch may still have plenty of surprises in store.

Biography

David Lynch was born in Missoula, Montana, USA, in 1946. He was educated at Corcoran School of Art (*circa* 1964), Boston Museum School (1965), Pennsylvania Academy of Fine Art

(1965–69) and the American Film Institute Centre for Advanced Studies (1970), studying under Frank Daniel.

Notes

1 Chris Rodley (ed.) *Lynch on Lynch*, London, Faber and Faber, 1997, p. 8.
2 Biancamaria Fontana, 'Kin Peaks', *Guardian*, 14 March 1991, p. 27.

Filmography

The Alphabet (1968) short
The Grandmother (1970) short
Eraserhead (1976)
The Elephant Man (1980)
Dune (1984)
Blue Velvet (1986)
Twin Peaks (1989–1991) television serial, thirty episodes
Wild at Heart (1990)
Twin Peaks: Fire Walk with Me (1992)
Lost Highway (1997)
The Straight Story (1999)

Further reading

John Alexander, *The Films of David Lynch*, London, Letts, 1993.
Michael Atkinson, *Blue Velvet*, London, BFI Publishing, 1997.
Michael Chion, *David Lynch*, trans. Robert Julian, London, BFI Publishing, 1995.
Norman Denzin, 'Wild About Lynch: Beyond *Blue Velvet*', in *Images of Postmodern Society: Social Theory and Contemporary Cinema*, London, Sage, 1991, pp. 65–81.
Kenneth C. Kaleta, *David Lynch*, New York, Twayne, 1993.
David Lavery, *Critical Approaches to Twin Peaks*, Detroit, MI, Wayne State University Press, 1994.
Laura Mulvey, 'Netherworlds and the Unconscious: Oedipus and *Blue Velvet*', in *Fetishism and Curiosity*, London, BFI Publishing, 1996, pp. 137–54.

MARC O'DAY

MICHAEL MANN

ELEGIES ON THE POST-INDUSTRIAL LANDSCAPE

In many respects Michael Mann is the quintessential postmodern director, although in ways unflattering both to him and the whole notion of the postmodern. Traduced for being too entranced with style, Mann is an artist whose sense of the world is manifest precisely in the realization of style. He is perhaps the figure most closely associated with the introduction of 'rock video stylistics' to cinema, especially after his hit 1980s' television crime show *Miami Vice* (he was executive producer) began to have an impact. The show's high-gloss, slick fashions, pounding rock score and hyperkinetic editing showed the increased influence of advertising culture on the commercial entertainment industry during the age of Reagan, and the predominance of business in American life. This facile view places an unfair burden on Mann. The attributes associated with Mann were plentiful on the mediascape before he arrived, and with little of the particular focus and irony that make Mann a chronicler of the postmodern sensibility and a figure with whom to reckon. Mann's sensibility has little in common with morning-in-America Reaganism; episodes of *Miami Vice* and *Crime Story* are often about the failure and contradictions of the justice system, and the tensions within and failure of the male group

I do not intend here to bother the reader with new definitions of postmodernism, the debate about which has persisted to such an extent that I will assume a degree of familiarity with the ways that the new landscape, with its cybernetic culture and highly mediated and commodified environment, constitutes a transition from the relatively industrialized mid-twentieth century to the present moment.[1] Michael Mann is an emblem of postmodern cinema in ways that make him distinct from his contemporaries. While filmmakers such as Lynch and Tarantino focus on the destruction of linear narrative and incessant allusions, Mann's work looks rather straightforward and generic (to the point that many accuse him of merely puffing up old formulas), with few references either to other works or to the cinematic apparatus itself. Instead, Mann's work depends on some of the realist conventions both of the plastic arts and the European cinema to create an elegy for civilization as it enters the realm of postmodernity.

In many respects, Mann's elegies are highly problematical. He seems very much concerned with the fading of the male subject in the climate of post-industrial society, as this subject is swallowed up by a sense of hyperalienation that Mann captures with an eye peculiar to him, a visual style that owes more to the painting and architecture of postmodernity than to cinema. His concern for the eclipse of the male, overwhelmed by a culture showing the effects of a corporatized 'world system'[2] has little in common with Angry

White Male films of the last two decades (for example, *Fatal Attraction*, 1987, and *Falling Down*, 1992), especially given the very European *angoisse* of his films. His sensibility seems to have more affinities with the abrogation of the hero's centrality in the nineteenth-century novel[3] than with the rightist cinematic ideologues of the Reagan-Bush-Clinton era, and yet one comes away wondering if Mann's work is yet another critique of capital from the right,[4] with its sense of a lost era subsumed by a cruel technological present. Mann's nostalgic sense of the eclipse of the male subject is mitigated to a great extent by his questioning of the demarcation of Self and Other (in, for example, the near-disintegration of Will Graham in *Manhunter*; in the notion that inside and outside are interchangeable as the barbarism of the penal system has equivalence with the normal bourgeois world in *Thief*; in the feeling of dissolution at the end of *Heat*; and the dismissal of the all-encompassing corporate world and their compromised democratic institutions at the end of *The Insider*). Mann's films are also notable for their sense of the abject and transgressive penetrating bourgeois life (the photos of a bloody crime scene slipping from Will Graham's file, terrifying a child in *Manhunter*; the photo of a young girl's body stuffed in a trash can in *Heat*); a brutal world is interrupted by something so horrific as to seem out of place even in the context of the world's assumptions. Many of the bloody or otherwise horrific still-lifes and set-pieces have the matter-of-fact preciousness of much postmodern art, suggesting the loss of affect discussed by chroniclers of the new sensibility.

For the most part the films end badly, featuring wretched, largely ineffectual protagonists overwhelmed by circumstance. Mann's bleak vision is shared with, say, the horror films of the 1970s, which saw civilization at a dead end but could not posit any alternative vision.[5] Mann's representation of crisis is not nearly as visceral though; his sense of the postmodern *cul de sac* comes across in the delineation of his cinematic landscape. Like Antonioni – especially *The Eclipse* (1962), *Red Desert* (1964) and *Zabriskie Point* (1969) – Mann sets humdrum stories (rooted very much in genre) against carefully constructed backdrops that emphasize his characters' alienation. Images recall the paintings of David Hockney, Eric Fischl, Robert Longo or Gilbert and George, with lonely subjects framed by cityscapes, industrial wastelands, bodies of water, or large bay windows, the images often photographed with heavy blue or amber casts to convey an icy or autumnal effect.[6] Such carefully composed images are plentiful: Frank seated in front of a deep-blue stockade fence, reading a letter from Okla in *Thief*; Will Graham staring at himself in a restaurant window in *Manhunter*; Neil and Chris talking, framed by a glass wall overlooking the Pacific in *Heat*; Vincent Hanna and his cops standing in an over-lit industrial complex in *Heat*; Jeffrey Wigand seated alone in a nicely appointed but eerie hotel room in *The Insider*. The hyperalienation that forms the emotional context of Mann's eulogies is bolstered by his eclectic use of industrial/techno/ambient/neo-goth music. Tangerine Dream, Einsturzende Neubauten, Lisa Gerard, The Kronos Quartet, Moby, The Reds and others provide an aural correlate to the unrelenting claustrophobia that is Mann's view of postmodernity The music underscores the aridity of the current world (again, *Red Desert* comes to mind), while providing numerous largos and *longeurs* that demonstrate the director's essential romanticism (the prolonged male *pieta* at the end of *Heat* is a notable example). The aura of suffocation that suffuses Mann's work provides a utopian/dystopian dialectic that brackets the struggles of his characters.

Mann's first film, *Thief*, has as its protagonist an ex-con and high-line safecracker, Frank (James Caan), who seeks a normal life by creating, rather irrationally, an impromptu family as if to affirm to the remains of his inner life a sense of utopia. The movie establishes Mann as a poet of the city and the suburbs, which is why I exclude from these remarks *The Keep* and *The Last of the Mohicans*, works which have their successes and identifiable Mann characteristics, yet seem outside the world that Mann has delineated as his own (although I would note that *Mohicans* seems in part about envisioning the lost world implicit in *Thief* and the rest of Mann's output). *Thief* foregrounds men in factories, prisons, bars, suburban living rooms, used car lots, in the bowels and webworks of warehouses and hi-tech office buildings. The film has a strong 'men at work' theme, from the pulsating opening scene of Frank's safecracking (replete with protective goggles and various tools), to the spectacular final heist, with Frank and his partners clad in asbestos, burning through a vault with an 8,000-degree thermal lance filling the image with sparks – the moment evokes socialist-realism. When Leo (Robert Prodsky) holds back Frank's cut from the theft, Frank complains that Leo profits from 'the yield of [my] labour'. When the cops who want a percentage of Frank's action rough him up, he says: 'Have you guys ever heard of working for a living?' Frank's notion of hard work, like the instant family he creates with Jesse (Tuesday Weld), suggests the bankruptcy of the American Dream. The notion of the ex-con trying to enter bourgeois life is deeply entrenched in the crime genre, dating at least to *High Sierra* (1941). But in *High Sierra* the criminal is locked out largely by the consequences of his own decisions; in *Thief* the very desire to mimic normality brings consequences, since the normal world is itself criminal (as Frank tells the still-imprisoned Okla (Willie Nelson), 'It's real fuckin' weird out there'). The cruelty of the everyday bourgeois world is represented everywhere, such as Frank and Jesse's failure to adopt a child (which pushes Frank further into the arms of the Mafia); the police beating; the judge at Okla's parole; Okla's sudden death; the conflation of organized crime with nine-to-five business life. Frank's Last Stand at the end of the film is as much about erasing himself and his bogus vision of a peaceful world as it is about taking revenge on Leo and the mobsters. Frank tells Jesse to leave in an especially unnerving moment given his insistent and rather boyishly naïve courtship of her. He blows up his home and businesses before murdering Leo. The final scene has nothing of the 'apotheosis effect' that allows the gangster a final moment of glory. Frank's burning of his car dealership ('Rocket Used Cars') is a rather surreal moment; the camera tracks past random burning vehicles in a sequence reminiscent of J.G. Ballard, and Frank's explosion of his home and tavern recall *Zabriskie Point*, as the utopia of consumerism becomes the apocalypse of self-abrogation. Frank pauses to throw away the photomontage he carries in his pocket, which he has glanced at earlier and displayed proudly to Jesse. The montage, featuring images of his mentor Okla, a mother and child, dead bodies, and other scraps from his miserable 'state raised' life, is Frank's modernist utopian gesture, his pulling together of the disparate elements of his fractured world. In the film's landscape, Frank's montage looks outdated and naïve, like the jacket art of *Sgt. Pepper's Lonely Hearts Club Band* (perhaps the key appropriation of utopian montage by pop culture). While Frank survives the shoot-out with Leo's thugs, he enjoys no release or vindication, but merely disappears into the night in Mann's most brutal conclusion.

The conclusion to *Manhunter* is not nearly as bleak, but the film conveys, even more so than *Thief*, a sense of entrapment, and of the questionable status of normality. FBI agent Will Graham (William Petersen) is besieged from all sides: his key enemies are less his manipulative boss Jack Crawford (Dennis Farina, a Mann regular), or his serial-killer nemeses Hannibal Lecter (Brian Cox) and Francis Dollarhyde (Tom Noonan), than his own tormented consciousness. Graham's special gift, for which he is dragooned back into active duty by his superiors after suffering a physical and emotional breakdown, is his ability to understand the sensibility (and therefore methods) of the serial-killer. Unlike 'the man who knows Indians' who populates numerous Westerns,[7] Graham's gift is a curse, especially as it blurs his sense of self and other, of difference. *Manhunter* is among the postmodern crime films to have special connections with the horror film, at least in its challenge to the notion of the monstrous.[8] The challenge poses a sense of entrapment to Graham that is figured, as in all of Mann's films, by the association of the protagonist with landscape and architecture. After an upsetting conversation with the wily Hannibal Lecter, Graham literally runs from a bone-white, Panopticon-like prison. One sequence has him descending in an elevator in Atlanta's Peachtree Plaza, a John Portman building very much like the Bonaventure Hotel in Los Angeles, the model *par excellence* of postmodern alienation.[9] As in most of Mann's work, the natural world is figured as ambiguous, photographed in a way that lends it a hyperreal, synthetic quality, suggesting its fusion with industrial civilization. Examples in *Manhunter* include the early meeting of Graham and Crawford by the edge of the sea, each man seated on opposite ends of a piece of driftwood. Similar images appear in *Heat* and *The Insider*, such scenes show the steady sealing-off of nature, as if to suggest the increased suffocation of humanity (the empty, beach-front house of Neil in *Heat*; the grey, windswept beach and rooftops of *The Insider*, from which Lowell Bergman makes his impassioned phone calls). In *Manhunter*, nature is hardly more than a wish-dream fabrication, like Frank's photomontage in *Thief*. Will Graham is regularly engaged in important conversations within the most crass settings, such as his explanation to his son of his psychological problems as the two stand in the cereal aisle of a supermarket.

Graham's pursuit of Francis Dollarhyde is marked by the notion that serial murder, as horrendous as it is, is bracketed by a world out of joint, responsible for the production of monsters. Graham recognizes this when he speaks to Crawford of Dollarhyde: 'This started from an abused child, a battered infant.' Mann shows Dollarhyde as ominous but, through his artifice and Blakean citations, possessing an authentic (if fractured) poetic sensibility. The most evocative moment is Dollarhyde taking the blind Reba (Joan Allen) to a zoo veterinarian, in whose office she pets a sleeping, sickly tiger. Dollarhyde is enraptured by this moment of sensitivity as much as Reba, as the film draws the spectator toward a sense of the murderer's rage at a cruel civilization. The eventual vanquishing of Dollarhyde restores Graham and his family to 'normality' at the coda, but the film's essential definition of the normal has been so unsettling thus far, that the victory seems somewhat tenuous.

Heat, based on the teleplay *L.A. Takedown*, was until *The Insider*, Mann's most ambitious film, even (perhaps especially) considering the aspirations of *The Last of the Mohicans*. The film was subtitled in its advertising copy, 'A Los Angeles Crime Saga', bringing charges of pretension, especially considering the film's roots in a television script. But the film's operatic aspect, with its emphasis on some of the features mentioned earlier (the *longeurs* enhanced by a highly eclectic and atmospheric musical score; the shots of lonely individuals carefully framed within postmodern geometry), suggest Mann's concern for describing a situation and conveying a mood as much as story-telling, features that, as suggested, make his work cinematic in a very European sense. The film's on-screen reunion of 'rival' superstars Robert De Niro and Al Pacino, who had not worked together since *Godfather II* (and then in separate sequences of an elliptical parallel narrative), might be considered rather overstated. However, Mann uses the occasion well. These rather similar, method-informed 'sons of Brando' portray characters who continue Mann's notion of the thin line between self and other. Vincent Hanna (Pacino) is a cop in relentless pursuit of gang leader Neil McCauley (De Niro). Both men lead troubled lives in a postmodern landscape saturated with Prozac, CNN, cybernetic technologies, broken families, even child neglect and murder. Both men are self-absorbed pragmatists who neglect or abuse their mates (and are patently dismissive of women overall), and it this factor that Mann uses to complicate our regard for his otherwise elegiac portrait of the demise of the male group.

Indeed, *Heat* provides Mann's most sustained preoccupation with the fading centrality of the male, conveyed with the usual melancholy but with more than usual influence from the 'men-with-their-backs-to-the-wall' cinema of an earlier epoch (Ford, Hawks, Aldrich, Peckinpah). When Neil's gang recognizes that the police are on to their plans, they decide to proceed anyway, an affirmation of the male self basic to a director like Peckinpah. The gang's Last Stand after the botched bank robbery also harks back to the Western, but perhaps with more attention to the homoerotic subtext of such narratives,[10] especially as we see the close bond between Neil and his young acolyte Chris (played by a blonde, pouty-mouthed Val Kilmer), a relationship basic to the story. Just as basic to this dynamic is Vincent's obsession with Neil. The idea of the dedicated cop pursuing his *dopplegänger* has deep roots in crime fiction, but here the theme looks especially hyperbolic when we observe Vincent's home life. Again, the basic situation looks highly generic – the overly dedicated cop and his neglected wife – until Mann uses it for something of a tirade about the effects of a (feminized) postmodern condition on the male. One of Justine's (Diane Venora) complaints seems Baudrillardian: ('You sift the detritus, you look for signs of passing, the scent of your prey'). She later tells Vincent that although she is 'stoned on grass and Prozac', she has more humanity than her husband, with whom she needs to 'get closure' by her affair. Vincent explodes, complaining to Justine's boyfriend Ralph about the 'dead-tech bullshit postmodern' house (Justine's from her last divorce) he has been forced to live in. He destroys his television – his last emblem of domesticity – as he goes back to the pursuit of Neil. After his brief reunion with Justine following her daughter's near suicide, Justine sets him free, and Vincent literally floats blithely (the soundtrack suddenly silent to emphasize the privileged moment) back to battle. The prolonged trackdown and final shoot-out between Vincent and Neil, culminating in the vaguely homoerotic tableau with Vincent holding the hand of the dead Neil, underscores this rather obsessive elegy for the male and the forms of art that have portrayed his travails (for example, *The Death of Thomas Chatterton*). Moby's apocalyptic, operatic techno composition ('God Moving Over the Face of the Waters') accompanies Neil's death and the end credits.

The Insider is Mann's most accomplished work to date, embodying fully the elegiac, melancholy sensibility informing all of his work, and offering a compelling example of political postmodernism. The film's political aspect derives to some extent from the Capraesque one-man-against-the-system paranoid populism revived in the 1990s primarily by Oliver Stone. While Stone's work is a fairly radical dissent aimed at the Cold War military-industrial state, it is burdened by overwrought nostalgia for an earlier America. Mann's tendencies toward nostalgia have been jettisoned in *The Insider*, his anxieties centred on the very specific power of contemporary global corporatism. The disorienting authority of this new power is perhaps best represented in the film's web page,[11] which downloads with a rapid series of 'flash' pictures showing oblique images of the film's many locales. The images suggest well the film's sense of a disparate simultaneity in the new global system that the individual subject can just barely grasp.

The film is based on the very contemporary real-life story of Jeffrey Wigand, a senior biochemist for Brown and Williamson, one of the biggest of the Big Tobacco corporate conglomerates. In 1995, a disgruntled, recently fired, Wigand gave information to the CBS news magazine *60 Minutes* about the company's attempts to make addicts of consumers, in the process poisoning them. CBS convinced *60 Minutes* to shelve the story due basically to the company's dense entanglements with Big Tobacco. The programme's producer, Lowell Bergman, goes to bat for Wigand, pitting sectors of the media and corporate capital against each other until the show is finally aired. More than in Mann's previous work, the male protagonist is made irrelevant by the dizzying effect of the postmodern transnational corporate state. Bergman (Pacino) wanders nearly blind through the events of the story, a motif prefigured in the Middle East establishing sequence where Bergman is brought blindfolded to Hezbollah headquarters in Lebanon to arrange an interview. At first the immediate establishing of the East as Other (so typical of post-Cold War cinema) seems highly problematical, until the scene suddenly changes and the Other is transmutated into Brown and Williamson CEO Thomas Sandefur (Michael Gambon). As Bergman enters Wigand's (Russell Crowe) life, he seems a mere ancillary appendage to an array of video monitors, cell phones, fax machines, computers and other gadgets that function as metaphors for the corporate arena. East and West become fused, although Mann does not allow the situation to dissolve into some free-floating paranoia in the face of the new mediascape and capitalist structure. The extremely topical story is so familiar as to be almost banal, yet Mann turns it into his grandest opera yet, with a dramatic, near-liturgical score by Lisa Gerard and Pieter Bourke. The impulse in this project flows from the banality of evil in the postmodern, corporatized world, with its features at once benign, impervious, and incomprehensible. The Lebanon opening is accompanied by a percussion-driven composition entitled 'Tempest', which quickly conveys the idea that this establishing sequence is less about the Middle East crisis – one of those constant media field days – than the maelstrom that is the current technological/media/corporate environment. During Wigand's testimony, and later during the appearance of the Big Tobacco giants in Congress (as Wigand loses all), Gerard/Bourke's 'Sacrifice' fills the soundtrack with a dolorous requiem. Although the world eventually hears Wigand's *60 Minutes* story, saving him from total marginalization, the film is by no mean a vindication of the media and the other institutions with which they are interlocked. When the show finally airs, we note that spectators in airports and bars are barely conscious of its import; after a bitter interchange at CBS, Bergman leaves the building, the movement of the scene shifting to slow motion – as it did when Wigand was fired. Mann suggests that the public is inured to the mediascape, and the most good-hearted players within the corporate/media state (the film notes that Bergman was a former radical journalist for *Ramparts*) are fairly insignificant against current capitalist assumptions.

Mann's eulogizing of the male subject raises more than a few questions about his political focus. He cannot seem to posit a world outside of patriarchy, even in its decayed, postmodern moment. Yet this decay seems fairly absolute, making Mann's vision hark back to an earlier (post-Watergate) cinema that encouraged the critical faculties of the audience, and looked beneath the façade of the existing order of things.[12]

Biography

Michael Mann was born in Chicago, USA, on 5 February 1943. He attended the University of Wisconsin and the London International Film School.

Notes

1 See Fredric Jameson, *Postmodernism, or, The Cultural Logic of Late Capitalism*, Durham, NC, Duke University Press, 1991; Steven Connor, *Postmodernist Culture: An Introduction to Theories of the Contemporary*, Oxford and New York, Basil Blackwell, 1989; David Harvey, *The Condition of Postmodernity*, Oxford and Cambridge, Basil Blackwell, 1989.

2 The subject of Fredric Jameson, *The Geopolitical Aesthetic: Cinema and Space in the World System*, Bloomington, Indiana University Press, 1992.

3 Of some relevance is Mario Praz's elegy for the romantic hero in *The Hero in Eclipse in Victorian Fiction*, London, Oxford University Press, 1956.

4 An important discussion of the phenomenon is George Steiner's introduction to Dostoevsky's *The Gambler* and *Notes from the Underground*, New York, The Heritage Press, 1967.

5 See Robin Wood, *Hollywood from Vietnam to Reagan*, New York, Columbia University Press, 1986, pp. 70–135.

6 Compare Mann's compositions to the art featured in, for example, Charles Jencks, *Post-Modernism: The New Classicism in Art and Architecture*, New York: Rizzoli, 1987.

7 See Richard Slotkin, *Gunfighter Nation: The Myth of the Frontier in Twentieth-Century America*, New York, HarperCollins, 1993.

8 The best discussion I have seen on the politics of *Manhunter* and its relation to the horror film is Tony Williams, *Hearths of Darkness: The*

Family in the American Horror Film, New Jersey, Fairleigh Dickinson University Press, 1996, pp. 255–59.

9   See Fredric Jameson, *op. cit.*, 1991, on the Bonaventure and Portman.
10 Last Stand narratives and the ideology underneath them are developed in Slotkin's *Gunfighter Nation*, and in his earlier *The Fatal Environment: The Myth of the Frontier in the Age of Industrialization, 1800–1890*, Middletown, CT, Wesleyan University Press, 1985.
11 www.theinsider-themovie.com
12 Mann's cinema seems to have much in common with the 'incoherent texts' of the 1970s, with their conflicted ideological positions. See Robin Wood, *op. cit.*, pp. 46–70.

Filmography

Thief (1981) also writer
The Keep (1983) also writer
Manhunter (1986) also writer
The Last of the Mohicans (1992)
Heat (1995) also writer
The Insider (1999) also producer

Television

Vega$ (series, 1978)
The Jericho Mile (1979) also writer, producer
Miami Vice (series, 1984) also executive producer
Crime Story (series, 1986) also executive producer
Band of the Hand (1986) also producer
L.A. Takedown (1989) also writer, producer-director
Drug Wars: The Camarena Story (mini-series, 1990) also executive producer
Drug Wars: The Cocaine Cartel (1992) also executive producer

CHRISTOPHER SHARRETT

MIRA NAIR

Mira Nair is a cineaste of uncompromising feminist postcolonial subjectivity in-the-making. Her work explores the nomadic space of postmodern feminism, displacing the essentialism of the idea of 'First' and 'Third' worlds. Recognizing that, as an Indian woman, she has been subject to the essentializing norms of colonialized subjectivity, Nair seeks to challenge and rupture the borders of identities based on class, race, gender and location. Nair's nomadic identity, as an Indian filmmaker living in Africa, has had a liberating and formative impact on her creative choices. In interview Nair sums up her feelings toward the issues of home, displacement and

Nomadism as 'a brown person, between black and white, I could move between these worlds very comfortably because I was neither'.[1]

Nair's goal as a filmmaker is distinctly political, yet she is completely at home when disrupting others' notions of political boundaries of politeness. She has taken criticism, for example, for her bleak portrayals of the lost and disenfranchised subalterns of her India. In *Jama Masjid Street Journal*, a short diary/documentary (shot in black and white), Nair recorded Muslim men's reactions to her presence as a filmmaker in Delhi. This constituted a reversal of the traditional objectification of woman in film and photography as veiled object of gaze, thus claiming a site of an active and subjective female subaltern gaze.

So Far from India follows the grim journey of Ashok, an Indian immigrant to New York, who leaves his homeland to make better money to support his pregnant wife whom he has left in India. Nair records Ashok's grim deculturation. In America, the film tells us, 'You forget everything, who's your brother, who's your wife'. Amit Shah applauded the films *cinéma vérité* qualities, adding that it records 'the duality of the immigrant reality, the slow disintegration of rootedness, the new avenues and roadblocks of assimilation and belonging'.[2]

Nair captures the multifacetedness of nomadic subjectivity, both the joy and pains, and everydayness of exile, here and later in *Mississippi Masala* and *The Perez Family*. 'My job is to provoke',[3] states Nair, and provoke she does with both *Salaam Bombay!* and *India Cabaret*, masterpieces of documentary/narrative noir. *Salaam Bombay!* is a grim narrativist documentary, shot in *cinéma vérité*-style, about the forgotten and destitute children, prostitutes and drug addicts of Bombay. *India Cabaret*, a sobering ethnographical film on the lives of exotic dancers in India, was attacked by some Indian feminists on the basis that it presented the women from the point of view of a 'male gaze'.

Mira Nair suggests that these reactions represent a bias formed by western feminist theoretical opinion. *India Cabaret*, she notes, does not portray women as 'essentially passive'.[4] Nair points out that the class-based and western feminist-based comment locates 'a myopic view because it refuses to confront the dancers and the dance ... Not looking at the situation as it is will not make it disappear.' Perhaps what viewers find the most unsettling, Nair contends, is that 'the women in it don't ask for our help, refuse to be viewed as victims, and do not need our pity'.[5] *India Cabaret* won the award for Best Documentary at the Global Village Film Festival in

New York, the Golden Athena at the Athens International Film Festival and the Blue Ribbon at the American Film Festival in 1986.

Nair's penchant for championing the underprivileged classes and, in particular, economically deprived women, is consistently a centre of her film projects. Her 1985 documentary, *Children of Desired Sex*, looks at the misuse of sex-determination tests that quite often lead to female foeticide in India. The film is another example of Nair's ability to bring controversial subject matter to the public eye. She consistently maps spaces for those who are culturally invisible.

Nair operates from a postcolonial feminist rhetorical space, one that speaks for the dislocated exiles of inequality towards class, gender, race, ability, nationality, age and sexual orientation. Her feminist rhetoric does not only address women's circumstances; her ethos is one of 'empathetic knowing', as described by the feminist philosopher Lorraine Code:

> Responsible, empathetic knowing will start from a recognition that mutuality can never be assumed, but it can sometimes be realized, not just between two people, but by extending a second-person mode into even wider contexts.[6]

Empathetic knowing is an important concept within the context of current debates about who can speak for whom. Empathetic knowledge fosters border crossings and 'resists closure, invites conversation, and fosters and requires second-person relations'.[7] Above all, empathetic knowledge can be a tool for rupturing hegemonically perceived power/knowledge relationships, especially those defined by outmoded terms such as 'Third World' and 'First World', for example. Certainly cultural and historical determiners must be kept in mind when making or talking about films on the 'culturally invisible'; the culturally silenced and politically oppressed subalterns of the world; but cultural/historical knowledge must not be repositioned as a new frontier/border or silencing mechanism itself.

Salaam Bombay! is a narrative fiction film that uses specific tropes of the narrative feature film to voice the marginalized figures who are so often rendered voiceless in colonialist ethnographies. Nair uses elements of *cinéma vérité* to imbue the film with a metanarrative of the real. She shoots in actual locations on Bombay streets, she uses non-actors, her lighting and *mise-en-scène* is naturalistic and stylistically underscored by her documentary background. It is important to remember, however, that the film is a fictional narrative designed to provoke empathy among viewers toward homeless children, prostitutes, drug addicts, and young women from Nepal who are forced into prostitution and commodification through the flesh trade of Bombay.

The narrative of *Salaam Bombay!* is seen through the child's gaze in the form of Chaipau, a young boy who leaves home and goes to the city (Bombay) to make enough money to extricate himself from the trouble he caused by taking his brother's bicycle. The tragedy of Chaipau is that, as the viewer suspects, he will never be able to return home because he is inexorably drawn into a colonial urban nightmare of economic exploitation. The viewer identifies with Chaipau's struggles. More importantly, perhaps, is the fact that Chaipau empathizes with those around him whom he views being pressed into prostitution, drugs and a complex system of capitalist exploitation.

Chaipau's gaze functions as a signifier of those who would ignore or misperceive the suffering and oppression of the homeless, the lost drug-dependent dealers, the women forced into prostitution and bondage. Chaipau's gaze supersedes any question of 'First' versus Third World. He is not only interchangeable with 'any oppressed Third World subject',[8] as Arora concedes, but he is interchangeable with any modern homeless urban figure. Though his story takes place in a 'Third' World city, he is a fictional construct who can essentially be seen as a stand-in for the homeless person in any modern city. His gaze demands a multiplicity of viewing positions and Nair repeatedly cross-identifies him with oppressed women (prostitutes and children) through eye-matches and gazes that lead the viewer (whether from New York City, Bombay or London) to involve themselves in the embodied subjectivities of the fictional constructs.

Salaam Bombay! was made despite almost unprecedented adversity, especially funding problems. Nair initially found support from Britain's Channel 4. She later secured funds from the National Film Development Corporation of India, and, despite the reluctance to support a feature film by an Indian woman director, she made the film for about $450,000, a minuscule budget for such a massive undertaking, with its many set-ups and extensive location shooting. Nair's ability to film *Salaam Bombay!* on such a limited budget, in a limited period of time is truly impressive. The film was received with tremendous international acclaim at the Director's Fortnight at the Cannes Film Festival – Nair won the Camera D'Or for best first feature and the Prix du Publique for most popular film at Cannes – and went on to receive an Academy Award nomination for Best Foreign Language Film.

Hollywood executives courted Mira Nair after the success of *Salaam Bombay!*; however, as Nair notes, she was not happy with the manner in which Hollywood wished to 'whiten' her projects: 'At first everybody wanted me to do white things, and white issues.'[9]. Nevertheless, Nair began pre-production for *Mississippi Masala*, a film about people of colour, particularly exile cultures, and the issues of home, cultural displacement and intercultural romance. Made on a budget of around $6 million, *Mississippi Masala* stars Sarita Choudhury (Mina) and Denzel Washington (Demetrius) as young lovers who cross borders of black and brown communities in a star-crossed love affair that brings a colonial narrative to postcolonial issues. While the dominant narrative of *Mississippi Masala* is centred around Mina and Demetrius, it could be argued that the film employs a superficially constructed Hollywood love story to actually voice a narrative of exiled Indian people who were forced out of Uganda under the regime of Idi Amin. This counter-narrative strategy, in turn, re-situates the film as a contemplation of issues found in Nair's earlier documentary films: exile, difference, and the border crossings of African and Asian diasporic communities.

The first hint that *Mississippi Masala* is not a mere love story is that it opens with a flashback to war-torn Uganda in 1972. Here Jay (Roshan Seth), an Indian lawyer, and his African friend Okelo (Konga Mbandu) are harassed by military police. Their friendship is displaced by Idi Amin's order that all Asians must leave the country. Okelo reiterates the philosophy behind Amin's orders, 'Africa is for Africans: Black Africans.'

The viewer sees this through young Mina's point of view. Mina observes a tragedy of forced exile and the mechanics of militarist regimes which rips apart Asian/African relationships and causes so much pain to her family. As Mina watches, her family is forced onto a bus and a military police officer takes her mother off the bus at gunpoint. After humiliating her and threatening her life, he returns her to the bus. At this point in the film, we see the tragedy of exile through Mina's eyes, but the film rapidly moves us to Greenwood, Mississippi, 1990, where Mina's mother owns a liquor shop in a predominantly black neighbourhood. Mina's mother seems to have largely recovered from the hardships of forced immigration, but Mina's father is obsessed with the past. He continues to seek the return of his land by suing the Ugandan government.

The disharmony between black and brown communities bubbles under the surface until the relationship between Demetrius and Mina is discovered. The Asian and African-American communities know little about one another. For example, Demetrius' partner, Tyrone, insists on referring to Mina as Mexican. Mina's exile status is the object of much questioning at the dinner table when Demetrius brings her home to meet his family. Is she Native American Indian? they wonder. Is she African? Her identity under scrutiny, Mina explains that her family migrated from Africa, but they are Asian. Demetrius' family asks her why there are Indians in Africa, and Mina explains how the British colonists used Asians to build the railways in Africa. Demetrius' brother observes, 'kinda like slaves?' A member of the family observes the parallel with the African-American community: 'We are from Africa, but we have never been there.'

Mina's family reacts with horror when they learn about her relationship with an African-American. Her parents accuse her of bringing shame upon the family. They cannot conceive of integrating Demetrius into the family and the Asian community. Indeed, the Asian and African communities, though they share many common values, are culturally exiled from one another. They are isolated by cultural practice and by an economic system that deprivileges them and discourages them from creating bonds. The white bankers leap at any opportunity to disenfranchise people of colour; they immediately cut off Demetrius' bank loan at the slightest hint of impropriety. Mina's mother fears that she will lose business at her liquor store and Mina's father almost loses his job at the motel. Nair demonstrates exactly how people of colour are objects of routine discrimination and how the Southern white hegemony holds the keys to economic power and free enterprise. Mina and Demetrius flee the South, leaving their families in order to be together, demonstrating the manner in which diasporic cultures are torn apart by the politics of racism.

Nair left India when she was only 19. As an exile, she began to understand the economics of British colonization. Nair observed firsthand the experience of the colonization process, whereby Asians are colonized and forced into poverty and exile. As they move to other countries, Asians and Eurasians tend to do well as merchants, but they serve to uphold the privileged few, and are often resented by the older working-class communities. In the American South, Indians bought many of the hotels, sometimes angering the African-Americans who had lived there for several generations. In an interview in the *New York Times,* Nair told Samuel Freedman that she saw blatant racism when she went to South Carolina to research the phenomenon of Indian motel chains. Nair described the situation:

There's a tension around the issue of alliances. The black folks think, 'All of us people of colour must stick together.' And the Indians cash in on that when it suits them. But the white people are glad the middle class isn't black.[10]

Perhaps even more provocative, however, is Nair's treatment of whites as absent peripheral characters: 'I wanted the white characters to be absent.'[11] The characterization of white as absence has the effect of bringing the African-American and Asian communities into the foreground, reversing Hollywood filmic representation of people of colour as absence, lack, or peripheral stereotypes.

The few times that Nair shows us a glimpse of white presence, she usually cuts to a scene in which white people are harshly criticizing African-Americans or Asians. For example, one scene shows two white shop clerks complaining about the noise of a nearby Asian wedding. Their accents and expressions mark them as ignorant and racist. 'I wish they'd go back to the reservation', says the older man. In another scene, two white women who were apparently supportive toward Demetrius when he needed a bank loan, observe Demetrius and his brother. 'He's the *good* one', one of the women says – demonstrating the white American practice of separating African-Americans into good/bad binarisms based on little more than prejudice and privilege.

Mississippi Masala appeals to black spectators, both through its narrative pleasures and its visual effects and the use of music. Nair worked closely with her cinematographer, Ed Lachman, to find the most pleasing and effective lighting designs to portray black and brown flesh. She became interested in the lack of knowledge around filming black skin, stating, 'No one seemed to question the fact that Hollywood cinematography is designed to flatter one particular group.'[12] Nair's attention to blackness supports her position as a champion of black spectatorial pleasure. The soundtrack of *Mississippi Masala* is a pleasurable melange of African, Indian, African-American and worldbeat music that provides bridges across black and brown cultures. The audience is treated to African chorales and instrumentals, African-American blues and rap music,

Indian wedding songs and reggae music. Nair's choice of actors for the film is also in keeping with the needs and desires of black spectatorial pleasure. Denzel Washington is both an excellent actor and a veritable heartthrob in the African-American female community. Sharmila Tagore is well known to Asian women from her work in Indian musicals. Roshan Seth, who has worked for the Royal Shakespeare Company, is a figure with whom both Asians and blacks of the diaspora can identify. With all these multiple points of audience access in its favour, *Mississippi Masala* garnered a great deal of critical praise and a fairly wide release.

For her next film, *The Perez Family*, Mira Nair moved on to study the lives of immigrant exiles from Cuba. *The Perez Family* is a love story that documents the lives of Cuban refugees who fled to Miami in 1980, seeking political asylum. The film stars Marisa Tomei, Angelica Huston, Chazz Palminteri and Alfred Molina. Like *Mississippi Masala*, *The Perez Family* uses the standard Hollywood romance formula as a tableau to stage political critique and to embody the visual pleasure of people of colour. Nair followed this film with the colourful and sensual *Kama Sutra: A Tale of Love*, starring Indira Varma (Maya) and Sarita Choudhury (Tara). The film takes place in sixteenth-century India, where two girls come of age: Tara, who is brought up as a princess; and Maya, who is born into a servant caste, and must serve Tara's every fickle whim. Maya, however, takes instruction in the ways of the Kama Sutra, the Indian book of love, and eventually seduces Tara's husband on her wedding day to gain her revenge. Beautifully photographed, the film was originally produced by Channel 4 in the UK, and received only a marginal release in the United States. Without a doubt, *Kama Sutra* is one of Nair's most sumptuously visual films, with gorgeous cinematography and appropriately dream-like pacing. In every respect this is one of Nair's most deeply felt and personal films, resounding with her passionate interest in the history of her native country.

Most recently, Nair completed the television movie *My Own Country*, starring Naveen Andrews, Hal Holbrook, Swoosie Kurtz and Marisa Tomei. Shot in Toronto, Ontario, Canada for the Showtime cable television network, *My Own Country* is based on the true story of Dr Abraham Verghese (Andrews), an East Indian physician who came to work in the United States as a young graduate, and wound up battling the nascent AIDS epidemic in Johnson City, Tennessee in the mid-1980s. As in Nair's other films, the white community initially views Verghese and his fellow expatriates with disdain and suspicion, and Verghese is initially assigned menial jobs, despite his medical degree, such as cleaning out latrines. But Verghese's compassion for his patients soon has victims of the AIDS epidemic flocking to him for care, which he provides to the best of his ability, until the pressure overwhelms him. *My Own Country* is unusually experimental in its visual style, mixing highly stylized flashbacks with present-day sequences, despite its rather straightforward narrative, and suggests that Nair is moving into new territory both visually and thematically.

Nair lives with her husband, Mahmood Kampala, and their son Zohran. She continues to commute and work between Hollywood, Africa and India. As she told Janis Cole and Holly Dale, 'I'm one of those hybrids that has a foot in both worlds'.[13] As a documentarist, she has made some of her finest work. As a fiction filmmaker, she is forging a new hybrid aesthetic. As a woman from India and Africa and the black Asian diaspora, Nair comes from an exile discourse that affords her a uniquely privileged space of identity, or, as she herself puts it, 'I come from a place of personal filmmaking.'[14]

Biography

Born in Bhubaneshwar, Orissa, India, on 15 October 1957, Mira Nair is the daughter of a civil servant. Early schooling at the Irish Catholic School in Simla was followed by study at the University of New Delhi. For a time, Nair performed various stage roles as an actor in repertory theatre in India. In 1976, she entered Harvard University, and graduated with a degree in sociology in 1979. After graduating, she took a number of film jobs, most notably for the documentarists Rick Leacock and D.A. Pennebaker, but soon set out on her own as a director.

Notes

1 Janis Cole and Holly Dale (eds) *Calling the Shots: Profiles of Women Filmmakers*, Kingston, Ontario, Quarry Press, 1993, p. 149.
2 Amit Shah, 'A Dweller in Two Lands: Mira Nair, Filmmaker', *Cinéaste* vol. 15, no. 3, 1987, pp. 22–4, p. 22.
3 Janis Cole and Holly Dale, *op. cit.*, p. 151.
4 Mira Nair, '*India Cabaret*: Reflections and Reactions', *Discourse* 8, Fall/Winter 1986/7, pp. 58–72, p. 66.
5 *Ibid.*, p. 67.
6 Lorraine Code, *Rhetorical Spaces: Essays on Gendered Locations*, New York, Routledge, 1995, p. 142.
7 *Ibid.*, p. 126.

8   Poonam Arora, 'The Production of Third World Subjects for First World Consumption: *Salaam Bombay!* and *Parama*', in Diana Carson, Linda Dittmar and Janice Welsch (eds) *Multiple Voices in Feminist Film Criticism*, Minneapolis, University of Minnesota Press, 1994, pp. 293–304, p. 295.
9   Janis Cole and Holly Dale, *op. cit.*, p. 149.
10 Samuel G. Freedman, 'One People in Two Worlds', *New York Times*, 2 February, 1992, pp. 13–14.
11 Andrea Stuart, 'Mira Nair: A New Hybrid Cinema', in Pam Cook and Philip Dodd (eds) *Women and Film: A Sight and Sound Reader*, Philadelphia, PA, Temple University Press, 1993, pp. 210–16.
12 *Ibid.*, p. 215.
13 Janis Cole and Holly Dale, *op. cit.*, p. 153.
14 *Ibid.*, p. 150.

Filmography

Jama Masjid Street Journal (1979) documentary
So Far from India (1983) documentary
Children of a Desired Sex (1985) documentary
India Cabaret (1986) documentary
Salaam Bombay! (1988)
Mississippi Masala (1991)
The Perez Family (1995)
Kama Sutra: A Tale of Love (1996)
My Own Country (1998) television movie

Further reading

Gwendolyn Foster, *Women Filmmakers of the African and Asian Diaspora: Decolonizing the Gaze, Locating Subjectivity*, Carbondale, Southern Illinois University Press, 1997.

GWENDOLYN AUDREY FOSTER

SALLY POTTER

THE MAKING OF A BRITISH WOMAN FILMMAKER

As the foremost woman director to have emerged in the UK in the last twenty years, Sally Potter can be positioned as a British, European and global filmmaker; her work marks a fascinating career trajectory inside and out of Britain, in and around the medium of film. Her first movie of the new millennium, a British/ French co-production entitled *The Man Who Cried*, continues to imagine the feature film as a composite artwork with a strong

emphasis on music, meticulous production design, lavish cinematography (by long-time collaborator Sasha Vierny), original screenwriting by Potter, and with an international cast and characters
(including Hollywood actors Christina Ricci and Johnny Depp). Set
in Europe during the 1930s, the melodrama centres around the story
of a displaced young Jewish woman and her relationships with a
Romany Gypsy man, a Russian dancer and an Italian opera singer.
The Man Who Cried speaks powerfully to questions of racial/ethnic
oppression, exile and diaspora.

Potter's previous feature, *The Tango Lesson*, self-reflexively
addresses issues of internationalization and interdisciplinarity. What
does it mean to be a multi-tasking woman filmmaker in contemporary Britain? A film about making a film, created in the wake of
her breakthrough art-house hit *Orlando*, *The Tango Lesson* is
written, produced and performed (acted/danced/sung) by Potter. It
chronicles the story of a woman director (Potter playing herself)
who, while writing a screenplay for a would-be Hollywood movie,
ends up taking tango lessons and making a very different and
personal film about the process. As the director enacts the
professional and personal dance of an independent contemporary
woman filmmaker, learning to tango becomes an apt metaphor. Shot
in Buenos Aires, Paris and London – with funding from Argentina,
France, Japan, Germany, the Netherlands and the United Kingdom
(including the Arts Council of England and the European Co-
Production Fund) – *The Tango Lesson* is both a British film and a
truly international co-production. Yet at the same time it is also an
exemplar of independent filmmaking by a woman, in an industry
where female film directors are few and far between. The
development of Sally Potter's multifaceted career, spanning three
decades, connects with the experiences of other women filmmakers
in the UK, and the narrative of the emergence of contemporary
'British' cinema.

The history of British cinema as it is currently written illustrates a
dismal lack of women feature filmmakers (with Muriel Box and
Wendy Toye as rare exceptions, both of whom successfully directed
studio feature films in the 1950s and 1960s).[1] Though largely
critically under-recognized, an increasing number of English, Irish,
Welsh and Scottish women directors have emerged in the past two
decades, including: Carine Adler, Lezli-An Barrett, Zelda Barron,
Antonia Bird, Maureen Blackwood, Gurinder Chadha, Christine
Edzard, Martha Fiennes, Mandy Fletcher, Coki Giedroyc, Margo
Harkin, Beeban Kidron, Hettie McDonald, Mary McMurray, Pat

Murphy, Ngozi Onwurah, Angela Pope, Lynne Ramsay, Margaret Tait, Conny Templeton and Jan Worth. British women have had the opportunity to helm films largely as a result of workshops, training programmes and collaborative efforts with other makers; television opportunities for feature film production; advocacy organizations such as Women in Film and Television UK; and new funding and production schemes within the British Film Institute and elsewhere. Contemporary television and filmmaking in Britain remain profoundly interlinked. Women in Britain have traditionally found work within the television industry, although the glass ceiling restricts directorial positions within certain genres and upper-level administration; documentary as a filmic/televisual genre has historically proven to be one space where women have been able to make relative inroads within the industry and stay active as filmmakers.[2]

Sally Potter's career in film, television and dance/music performance has been about claiming the tools of representation and blurring genre boundaries. Potter began her career as a filmmaker after leaving school at the age of 16. Her training-ground was the London Film-makers' Co-op, which provided support for the making of experimental film, distribution and exhibition opportunities for women's films. At the Co-op Potter made what she has called mostly short 'abstract visual poems'.[3]

With initiatives led by women's movements in the 1970s and the Workshop Declaration (made between the trade union ACTT, the British Film Institute and Channel 4 television) in the 1980s, women filmmakers also participated in the creation of production units such as Four Corners Film Workshop, London Women's Centre/WAVES (Women's Audio Visual Education Scheme), WITCH (Women's Independent Cinema House) in Liverpool, the Leeds Animation Workshop, Sheffield Independent Film and Television (formerly the Sheffield Film Co-op), Derry Film and Video, and Women's Media Resource Project (London). Women feature filmmakers also emerged out of the so-called black British collectives such as Ceddo, Sankofa, and Black Audio Film Collective. The workshop movement had its roots in collective practice, and often, feminist politics.[4] These alternative modes of production also allowed for the possibility of expression of diverse, culturally marginalized British voices, and the films which were produced often actively engaged with discourses of hybrid identities, employing new aesthetic models, different from Hollywood and the European art cinema. Throughout the 1970s, more British college and polytechnic film courses were developed, and women have continued to graduate from the

National Film School. British women also established women's film distribution organizations such as London Women's Film Group, Circles, Cinema of Women, and more recently, Cinenova (which, like its sister organization Women make Movies in the US, currently distributes some of Sally Potter's short films and her first feature *Gold Diggers*). Film festival activities also promoted the work of women filmmakers in Britain, and have assisted in the rewriting of the history of British cinema.[5] In 1972, Laura Mulvey, Claire Johnston and Lynda Miles co-organized the landmark Women's Event at the Edinburgh Film Festival, the first time a collection of films by women had been showcased at a major exhibition venue in the UK. The same year, the influential London Women's Film Group, a production and advocacy organization, was formed.

Throughout the 1980s and 1990s, women programmers did important work in exposing audiences to films by British women directors. For example, Sally Potter was represented in Sheila Whitaker's series 'A Century of Women's Film-Making' at the National Film Theatre in London in 1996–7. *Orlando* was also on the roster in a 1995 season of films by women and a documentary film called 'Reel Women' televised on Channel 4. (However, *Orlando* was the only British feature included, and Potter and Gurinder Chadha were the only British directors interviewed in the 'Reel Women' documentary.) Women in Film and Television UK was established in the early 1980s as a non-profit support organization for women in the film and television industry, and Cinewomen was established in 1993 to raise the profile of women working in film, video and television; currently, the organization hosts Britain's longest running annual women's film festival. Sally Potter has been widely celebrated as a model for independent filmmaking at women's film festivals in the UK and internationally.

Potter trained as an interdisciplinary performance artist, dancer and musician. During the 1970s, she toured with the Limited Dance Company and the Feminist Improvisation Group. (There are some interesting parallels between Potter and American avant-garde director Yvonne Rainer *vis-à-vis* the connection between dance performance and film.) With her experimental film *Thriller*, funded by the Arts Council of Great Britain, Potter attempts to subvert the opera *La Bohème*, telling the story from Mimi's point of view – foregrounding issues of gender and race (with Mimi played by black actress Collette Laffont, who stars with dancer Rose English), deconstructing the popular Hollywood genre of film noir (with references to Hitchcock) and positioning the heroine as a detective.

Thriller became a catalytic text for nascent feminist film theory which began to evolve in the 1970s, and which celebrated counter-cinematic/avant-garde/experimental alternatives to the dominant filmmaking paradigm. British theorist and film and video artist Laura Mulvey's influential essay, 'Visual Pleasure and the Narrative Cinema', offered a re-evaluation of the classical Hollywood paradigms of representation of the female body.[6] Potter's film work (and Mulvey's own) extends this deconstruction to the practice of filmmaking. Feminist film theorists – including Doane, Fischer, Kuhn, Kaplan, Cook, Mellencamp and others – have argued that Potter's *Thriller*, together with films like Laura Mulvey and Peter Wollen's *Riddles of the Sphinx*, provides a new model for feminist filmmaking which radically reinscribes the female body.[7] The subsequent feature films written and directed by Potter, while still displaying a feminist politics and commenting on gender roles, are more cohesive, viewer-friendly and 'mainstream' in narrative terms.

All of Potter's films can be seen as meta-commentaries on the role of the female film story-teller, consistently challenging formal narrative strategies and genres, while also aiming for increasingly accessible visual and auditory pleasure in the synthesis – or rather, choreography – of image and sound. Such an evolution is demonstrated in Potter's short fanciful film *The London Story*, a spy story as a dance musical.

Women producers have been instrumental in developing film and television projects and partnerships for women in Britain, as in the film collaborations of Philippa Giles (producer), Beeban Kidroon (director) and Jeannette Winterson (writer), with such projects as the acclaimed *Oranges Are Not the Only Fruit*, a three-part BBC television film, and the less fortunate *Great Moments in Aviation*. Potter has worked as producer/director/writer; she founded and developed a production company with Christopher Sheppard called Adventure Pictures, which produced her features *Orlando* and *The Tango Lesson*. Like many other women filmmakers, Potter has used television as a forum for non-feature work, especially documentary – including the four-part Channel 4 series on emotions and cinematic representations, *Tears, Laughter, Fear, and Rage*, produced by Sara Radcliffe (Working Title Productions). Potter's series uses interviews with a wide range of personalities and film-clips from mostly British films to explore the nature of human affect, and to find a space for emotions in the personal and collective British consciousness. Potter's work has consistently created its own spaces in terms of funding and film form (genre, visual style, modes of performance, etc.). The Channel 4 documentary, *I Am Ox, I Am Horse, I Am Man, I Am Woman*, produced by Adventure Pictures and directed by Potter, examines some of the absent histories of the post-Soviet film industry uncovered by Potter during her attempts to find locations and funds for her epic feature *Orlando* – the director's own struggle to gain industrial support for feature filmmaking and to find her own place within a national cinema. This documentary chronicles the labours of women within the Soviet film industry; images of women on film also become a way to examine the history of women in the Soviet Union.

While her peers Beeban Kidron and Antonia Bird have managed to varying degrees of success to move between commercial Hollywood (*To Wong Foo, Mad Love*) and BBC-funded British films (*Great Moments in Aviation, Priest*), through the 1990s, Potter consistently avoided the lure of Hollywood and the mainstream, and her British/international features found theatrical life in the art-house rather than the multiplex. Potter's first feature, a genre-bending revisionist twist on the musical *The Gold Diggers*, was financed by the British Film Institute, shot in Iceland and London (another multinational production in terms of location), and had an all-woman cast and crew, including star Julie Christie and independent filmmaker Babette Mangote as cinematographer. It was more visually and narratively experimental than her later feature films and was not generally well received. *The Gold Diggers*, an interesting remake and revision of Busby Berkeley's Warner Brothers musical *Gold Diggers of 1933*, reached limited audiences but deserves critical attention for its attempts to bridge the gap between theoretical investigations and artistic practices. During the Thatcher era in Britain (1979–90), women filmmakers such as Lezli-An Barrett (*Business as Usual*, 1987) and Jan Worth (*Doll's Eye*, 1982) made first features informed by overtly feminist sensibilities, highly critical of socio-economic issues which impact upon women's lives and labour. Neither Barrett nor Worth has to date made a follow-up feature, while after *The Gold Diggers* Potter was considered too risky by potential financiers.

Eight years in the making, Potter's second feature, *Orlando*, an adaptation of Virginia Woolf's novel, triumphed on the international art-house circuit. Pam Cook called the film 'a positive way forward for British cinema'[8] and Potter herself has acknowledged that this film enabled her to 'find her feet' as a director.[9] British films of the post-Thatcher 1990s consistently expressed confusion about Britain's status as a nation, and about British identities. Thatcherism resisted European consolidation based on the assertion of cultural and linguistic differences between nations, and an anxiety around the question of sovereignty. However, postmodern geopolitical shifts made the re-imagination of the national cinemas of Europe (and the idea of European Community) a necessity. Potter's adaptation of *Orlando* conducts sophisticated boundary-crossings of nation, gender and genre. In the film, Tilda Swinton plays the title character who changes sex throughout centuries of British history in a wry, winking performance (including moments of direct address to the camera); Quentin Crisp is ironically cast as Queen Elizabeth. The film adaptation of Woolf's fictional biography (itself a *roman-à-clef* of the author's female lover) updates the end of the novel to contemporary England, giving Orlando a daughter who in the film's final scene uses a video camera, a metaphor for a new way of seeing the world in the postmodern electronic age. The lush visual fabric of *Orlando* connects Potter's work with the modernist art films of British contemporaries such as Peter Greenaway and the late Derek Jarman. In production terms, Potter also employs Greenaway's production designers, Jarman's long-time collaborator, actress Tilda Swinton, and costume designer Sandy Powell (who worked with both Jarman and Greenaway). *Orlando* is in dialogue with (bending the rules of) the genre of the British costume/heritage films, which have successfully sold England to the international market.[10] In the introduction to her film script, Potter asks,

> But what of Orlando's change of sex, which provides the most extraordinary narrative twist, and was Virginia Woolf's rich and light way of dealing with issues between men and women? The longer I lived with Orlando and tried to write a character who was both male and female, the more the notion of the essential human being – that a man and woman both are – predominated.[11]

An auteur in the most contemporary sense, Sally Potter has managed to make British feature films as international co-productions which challenge the conventions of narrative cinema and gendered points of view, with a unique artistic vision.

Biography

Born in 1949, in the UK, Sally Potter has worked primarily in Britain for many years. Her recent films exploit the possibilities of international co-production. As well as directing, writing and performing in films, Potter has worked as a dancer, choreographer and composer.

Notes

1   See W. Dixon (ed.) *Reviewing British Cinema, 1990–92: Essays and Interviews*, New York, SUNY, 1994; Justine Ashby, 'Betty Box, "the Lady in Charge": Negotiating Space for a Female Producer in Postwar Cinema', in J. Ashby and A. Higson (eds) *British Cinema: Past and Present*, London, Routledge, 2000, pp. 166–78.

2   A. Muir, *A Woman's Guide to Jobs in Film and Television*, London, Pandora Press, 1987; A. Lant, *Blackout: Reinventing Women for Wartime British Cinema*, Princeton, NJ, Princeton University Press, 1991.

3   S. Potter, *The Tango Lesson*, London, Faber and Faber, 1997, p. viii.

4   M. Auty and N. Roddick, *British Cinema Now*, London, BFI Publishing, 1985; L. Friedman (ed.) *Fires Were Started: British Cinema and Thatcherism*, University of Minnesota Press, 1993; J. Caughie and K. Rockett, *The Companion to British and Irish Cinema*, London, Cassell/BFI Publishing, 1996.

5   S. Whitaker, 'Declarations of Independence', in M. Auty, M. and N. Roddick (eds) *British Cinema Now*, London, BFI Publishing, 1985; S. Harvey, 'The "Other Cinema" in Britain: Unfinished Business in Oppositional and Independent Film, 1929–1984', in C. Barr (ed.) *All Our Yesterdays: 90 Years of British Cinema*, London, BFI Publishing, 1986; C. Brunsdon (ed.) *Films for Women*, London, BFI Publishing, 1986.

6   L. Mulvey, 'Visual Pleasure and Narrative Cinema', *Screen*, vol. 16, no. 3, 1975 (reprinted in L. Mulvey, *Visual and Other Pleasures*, Bloomington, Indiana University Press, 1989).

7   M. Doane, 'Women's Stake: Filming the Female Body', in C. Penley (ed.) *Feminism and Film Theory*, New York, Routledge, 1988; L. Fischer, *Shot/Countershot: Film Tradition and Women's Cinema*, Princeton, NJ, Princeton University Press, 1989; A. Kuhn, *Women's Pictures: Feminism and Cinema*, London, Routledge, 1982; E. Kaplan, *Women and Film: Both Sides of the Camera*, New York, Routledge, 1983; P. Cook and Philip Dodd (eds) *Women and Film: A Sight and Sound Reader*, London, Scarlet Press, 1994; P. Mellencamp, *A Fine Romance: Five Ages of Film Feminism*, Philadelphia, PA, Temple University Press, 1995.

8   P. Cook and Philip Dodd, *op. cit.*, p. xiii.

9   S. Potter, *op. cit.*, p. viii.

10   A. Higson (ed.) *Dissolving Views: Key Writings on British Cinema*, London, Cassell, 1996; A. Higson, *Waving the Flag: Constructing a National Cinema in Britain*, Oxford, Clarendon Press, 1995; S. Street, *British National Cinema*, London, Routledge, 1997.

11   S. Potter, *Orlando*, London, Faber and Faber, 1994, p. xiv.

Filmography

Thriller (1979) short
The Gold Diggers (1983)
London Story (1987) short
Orlando (1992)
The Tango Lesson (1997)
The Man Who Cried (2000)

Documentary (television)

Tears, Laughter, Fear, and Rage (1986)
I Am Ox, I Am Horse, I Am Man, I Am Woman (aka *Soviet Women Filmmakers*, 1990)

Further reading

A. Ciecko, 'Transgender, Transgenre, and the Transnational: Sally Potter's *Orlando*', *Velvet Light Trap*, no. 41, 1998, pp. 19–34.
—— 'Sex, God, Television, Realism and the British Woman Filmmakers', *Journal of Film and Video*, vol. 51, no. 1, 1999, pp. 22–41.
—— 'Representing the Spaces of Diaspora in Contemporary Films by British Women', *Cinema Journal*, vol. 38, no. 3, 1999, pp. 67–90.
—— 'Gender, Genre, and the Politics of Representation in Contemporary British Films by Women', Ph.D. dissertation, University of Pittsburgh, PA, 1997.
P. Florence, 'A Conversation with Sally Potter', *Screen*, vol. 34, no. 3, 1993, pp. 274–85.

ANNE CIECKO

JOHN SAYLES

INTEGRITY AND BORDERS

In his discussion of the author, Michel Foucault stresses that this category is a mode of classification that creates 'a relationship of homogeneity, filiation, authentification of some texts by others'.[1] Rather than identifying some pre-existing essence, it produces that which it purports to identify. The figure of the author is constructed in an attempt to identify 'a point where contradictions are resolved, where incompatible elements are at last tied together or organized around a fundamental original contradiction'.[2] It is this notion of the distinctive and unique signature of the individual creator that connects an otherwise diverse and disparate series of texts, and also acts to distinguish these texts from others. The study of authorship, therefore, not only constructs a sense of identity but also otherness, and more importantly it works to patrol the border between the two.

If ever a filmmaker were apposite for considering the complexities of such border-patrolling, it would be John Sayles. On one level, Sayles is often presented as the epitome of autonomy and creative independence that underpins, ideologically, the figure of the author. Characterized by his distance from the Hollywood mainstream, Sayles appears consistently in profiles and articles as 'the doyen of American independent film-making'.[3] Geoff Andrew refers to him as 'the pioneering indie writer-director [who] is none too bothered about sticking to the safe formulae of the mainstream',[4] whilst Sayles himself has reinforced the sense of the 'extraordinary daring'[5] involved in working repeatedly in a precarious financial situation, stating, in reference to his filmmaking, that 'I'll be lucky to do it again is how I feel. Every movie has been a roll of the dice. So far I've never crapped out.'[6]

Sayles' portrayal of himself as the professional gambler, surviving on skill and nerve, and winning through with grace under pressure, contrasts with the more familiar depiction of him as a 'craftsman'. Sayles is often photographed with his shirtsleeves rolled up, and with a camera in his hands, as if to suggest that his style of filmmaking is a form of hands-on, manual labour. Moreover, Sayles' early experience as a carpenter is frequently invoked, often enabling an easy segue into a description of his films as 'well constructed'[7] and 'authentic': as though they could be distinguished from the 'inauthentic' fabrications of modern mass production. Indeed, in a similar vein, Sayles has remarked that 'there aren't many places left in the US that are different from McDonald's shopping mall America', a situation which is supposed to result in people 'drowning [their] senses in alcohol and soap operas'.[8] As Andreas Huyssen has pointed out, fears about mass culture are often linked to a series of anxieties about 'femininity',[9] and with this in mind, it is not surprising that Sayles' depiction as either a gambler or a craftsman underscores the decidedly masculine nature of his heroic independence.

The gendering of Sayles' independence is also apparent in his depiction as a ' "gun for hire", writing scripts for other people's movies'.[10] Sayles started his career with Roger Corman, scripting low-budget exploitation movies such as *Piranha* (1978), made to cash in on the success of *Jaws*; *The Lady in Red* (1979), a film about the criminal world of the 1930s told from the position of the woman who was with John Dillinger at the Biograph Cinema when he was gunned down by the FBI; *The Howling* (1980), a story of werewolves in contemporary California; and *Battle Beyond the Stars* (1980), a science fiction reworking of *The Magnificent Seven*. These films, rarely seen as significant in themselves, are regarded as activities undertaken to fund Sayles' own projects. As Gavin Smith puts it: 'In the tradition of John Cassavetes, who financed his independent films in the sixties and seventies by acting in mainly minor Hollywood pictures, Sayles works as a journeyman writer for hire, ploughing back his earnings into his own personal projects.'[11]

While this position could be seen as one of dependence, it is rarely presented as such. Rather, Sayles is seen in terms of heroic professional detachment, not only for his time with Corman, but for his work as scriptwriter on such films as *Alligator* (1980), *The Challenge* (1980), *Enormous Changes at the Last Minute* (1982), *The Clan of the Cave Bear* (1986), *Wild Thing* (1987), *Breaking In* (1989), *Men of War* (1994) and *Apollo 13* (1995). Even Sayles has, at times, contributed to this sense of these films: 'You get too much money for writing crummy exploitation movies anyway, and that's how I make my living.'[12]

The result of this critical discourse has been to generate a hierarchy within Sayles' œuvre, with his scriptwriting for other people more often than not relegated to the margins (for example, see Jack Ryan's book *John Sayles, Filmmaker*, which includes a chapter for each of Sayles' directed films, yet collects all his scriptwriting for others in a single chapter). Such script work is often portrayed as raising the films in question above the normal standard and quality: Smith, for example, claims that he brought 'invention and subversive humour to pop genre chores ... His knack for witty dialogue, realistic characters, and playful, intelligent genre revisionism – and his ability to deliver fast – quickly established Sayles as an in-demand rewriter.'[13] However, this work is still carefully distinguished from that which is seen to construct the 'real' or 'true' Sayles – namely his career as a director.

The irony here is that in patrolling the border between the 'real' Sayles, and his 'gun-for-hire' activities, such critics also work to create a secure authorial space within which Sayles is usually portrayed as breaking down a whole series of borders. For example, the claim is often made that characters in Sayles' movies cannot be easily summed up: that they possess a plethora of seemingly contradictory motivations. The character of Otis Payne in *Lone Star* is often taken to be speaking for Sayles, when he says: 'It's not like there's some borderline between the good people and the bad people',[14] reflecting the fact that Sayles' narratives are frequently supposed to concern processes of hybridity, creolization and the problems of drawing and defining both literal and figurative borders (most notably, *Baby, It's You, Matewan, City of Hope, Passion Fish, The Secret of Roan Inish, Lone Star, Men with Guns* and *Limbo*).

The key term used to discuss Sayles' conception of character is 'complexity', and it is for this reason that he has often been seen as 'an actors' director'.[15] Furthermore, his films are often regarded not as 'personal' projects, but as team efforts. Sayles' films are often seen to feature 'rep company regulars'[16] or 'a stock company of regular collaborators [that] has remained constant: producer Maggie Renzi, composer Mason Daring, actors David Strathairn, Joe Morton, Gordon Clapp, and many others'.[17] Indeed, Sayles' films are often supposed to be distinguished by their 'ensemble of characters' rather than the presence of a central individual protagonist.[18] Additionally, Sayles is often presented as rejecting the sense of himself as an 'artist' and his films as 'works of art'. As Sayles himself has commented: 'I don't regard anything I do as art. That's a foreign world to me. I regard it as conversation.'[19] In this way, he is distinguished from the preciousness associated with art and the art film, but also from the terms of the 'auteur theory'. This becomes clear in the frequent denial that his films are in any sense expressions of his personality: 'None of my stuff is really autobiographical. I spend 24 hours a day with myself – I'm not that fascinated in how I think about something. I want to have other voices in the picture.'[20]

Thus Sayles' films work to problematize notions of authorial autonomy, operating according to a kind of identity politics which acknowledges the complex and contradictory nature of social and political investments. Reflecting such concerns in a discussion of the anti-Vietnam campaigns of the 1960s, Sayles has claimed:

There's a belief that if we're all against the war, we should believe in the same things – we should be for the civil rights movement, for sexual liberation. But in the civil rights movement, those guys are not just kidding about being ministers – half of the shit you do as a young college student is stuff they condemn ... There are people who are truly kind, open, and generous but who hate black people ... That complexity of human behaviour makes storytelling much more difficult. That's one of the reasons why my secondary characters tend to be three-dimensional and come close to the foreground. If there're just good guys and bad guys, you can make genre pictures. The minute that the good guys get a little more complicated, your stuff starts to fall in between genres.[21]

This position works to acknowledge that one's identity cannot be reduced to one causal factor such as class, enabling Sayles to explore the interaction of a whole series of different identifications – class, race, gender and sexuality and often many more.

We can also see here that Sayles stakes a claim for his films as distinct from mainstream (particularly genre) films. Interviewing Sayles, Leonard Quart uses genre to make distinctions, and a hierarchy within Sayles' films, suggesting to the director that 'in your scripts for hire ... you do your best to deliver the genre goods, but in your own films you do your best to subvert or at least go against the grain of genre conventions'.[22] Here a distinction is being made between films which, however skilfully, are supposed to have conformed to generic conventions, and others (the supposedly 'real' Sayles films) which are posed against these conventions, as either subverting or refusing them.

Whilst it is possible to stress the use of generic elements in Sayles' films – *Baby, It's You* as teen romance, *Brother from Another Planet* as science fiction, *Matewan* as a Western, *Eight Men Out* as a sports movie, *City of Hope* as family melodrama, and *Lone Star* as either a Western or detective film – critics often present the generic elements as simply a cover used to smuggle in the 'real' materials. Trevor Johnston claims that *Passion Fish* 'cloaks itself, like many of its predecessors, in approachable generic garb. From his earliest commissioned screenplays, Sayles has been nothing if not resourceful in his mastery of sundry genre formulae.'[23] In this way, genre becomes the sugar that helps the medicine of Sayles' films go down better with audiences. As Kemp argues: 'John Sayles has always taken a fruitfully oblique angle on genre, and *Lone Star* turns the conventions and vocabulary of the Western to its own ends.'[24] Genre becomes something from which critics need to distinguish Sayles: he may use it, but the implication is always that genre films are formulaic and conventional and that, in the tradition of the auteur theory, Sayles proves his quality as a filmmaker by transforming those generic features to which others simply conform.

The intent behind Sayles' supposed manipulation of so-called generic formula is usually understood as a form of political motivation – as the desire to create 'a much more politically and emotionally challenging kind of work'.[25] Kemp refers to him as 'a fiercely political film-maker'[26] while, according to Quart, Sayles himself distinguishes himself from other filmmakers, saying that 'American filmmakers tend to be afraid of politics'.[27] However, the precise nature of Sayles' politics is rarely spelled out beyond the claims that he represents 'something different from what Hollywood was offering, something more serious'.[28] Instead, an aura of political commitment is constructed through continual references to his 'integrity'. Smith quotes approvingly David Thomson's claim that there 'is an emphatic integrity to Sayles',[29] while Geoff Andrew claims that with 'his talent, integrity and inquisitive attitude to the world, Sayles is rightly regarded as an inspirational influence in US indie movie-making'.[30]

This sense of 'integrity' is not tied to any straightforward commitment, to any specific political position or programme. On the contrary, it is defined largely through Sayles' rejection of partisan politics. Although he is quoted as claiming that there is 'a whole raft of American film criticism that's anti-content, whether it's political or not, because they feel that it's a betrayal of pure film',[31] Sayles' films are carefully distinguished from mere 'message movies' through an emphasis on their concern with complexity. Andrew Ross has claimed that in Cold War America, many intellectuals came to define the rejection of politics *as* politics.[32] Sayles is the product of a later period – the New Left of the 1960s – but in many ways, the New Left was born out of this legacy.[33] It too rejected the supposed totalitarianism of the old left's idealism, themes also common in commentary upon Sayles. He is reputed to have rejected the ideological purism and sectarianism of left politics[34] and, talking of Kenehan, the labour organizer in *Matewan*, has been quoted as saying:

> The Wobblies were not a very old organization when they were broken apart. He's a guy who had just come to this new religion, who is trying to figure out how to apply it. So he is very likely to get his people killed. Both my novel *Los Gusanos* and the film *City of Hope* are interesting in this regard. They both posit that believers can cause as much trouble as cynics. We might like the believers a little bit more, but whether they're Shi'ites, union men, or pro-lifers, they can cause trouble because they absolutely believe.[35]

It is therefore not surprising to find Kim Newman claim, in his review of *City of Hope*, that 'the most corrupt of Sayles' politicians have some noble motives, while the most apparently honest are potentially crooked'.[36]

Reflecting this duplicity, Sayles can, on occasion, be found to endorse a very different, contradictory relationship to the body of his work. Maltin, for example, quotes him claiming that 'working for Roger [Corman] and with Frances [Doel, Corman's story editor and right-hand woman] was terrific' and that working as a writer for hire does 'not just [support his other films] economically. I think I learned a lot from it. So it helps make me a better filmmaker or better writer when I go back to the fray of my own stuff, but it's something that I would do even if I didn't need to; even if I didn't need the money, because I enjoy it, and you're getting to work for the movies, which is a good deal.'[37]

Sayles has stated that he only takes on assignments he thinks he can do well or that he will enjoy. Thus while he is sometimes shown as contemptuous of genre films, he is also presented as a fan of certain genres – 'I liked Westerns, some science fiction, monster movies like *Them!*'[38] – tastes seen as influential upon his writing: 'About the third grade, eight years old, I started to write stories. They were all rip-offs of *Twilight Zone*.'[39] Nor is it just these genres with which he is associated: 'I have wide taste. I like everything from *Cries and Whispers* to *Enter the Dragon*.'[40]

While he has been opposed to the mainstream, here he is presented as refusing such an opposition, as challenging these hierarchies and oppositions. He is even supposed to have stressed the creative possibilities of refusing to maintain that distinction, and has been quoted as saying, 'On *Battle Beyond the Stars*, Corman said, "If you can make *Seven Samurai* into a western, you can make it into a science fiction film." ' He had another idea to make *Mutiny on the Bounty* in outer space. 'Sometimes there's some hybrid vigour you can get into a genre that way.'[41] Here Sayles emphasizes the creative potential of hybridity and boundary crossing, demonstrating that this playfulness with genre was practised and encouraged by popular film, not a subversive strategy of his own: on the contrary, it was something he learned from Corman.

The 'fundamental, original contradiction' of the figure of Sayles, as constructed by reviews, interviews and profiles is thus the paradox of the director defined by an 'integrity' that is, at its core, a refusal of all that integrity embodies – wholeness, clarity, unity and the simple drawing of lines. For all the fluid and heterogeneous identity politics of Sayles' directed films, discussions of those films serve, more often than not, to make distinctions: to patrol the border of an integral Sayles. Ultimately, it may be the John Sayles whose work refutes the borders between blockbusters, exploitation movies and a myriad other genres – the so-called 'writer for hire' – that makes the straightforward telling of the story of authorship more difficult.

Biography

Born in Schenectady, in New York, USA, in 1950. A psychology graduate, Sayles published two novels (*Pride of the Bimbos*, 1975; *Union Dues*, 1977) before writing film scripts for Roger Corman in the late 1970s. He won a prestigious MacArthur Foundation Fellowship in 1983 and directed the television series *Shannon's Deal* (1990). Sayles has continued to combine script work and fiction writing with his own filmmaking, and is currently working on a collection of short stories and his next film, *Gold Coast*.

Notes

1 Michel Foucault, 'What is an Author', in John Caughie (ed.) *Theories of Authorship*, London, Routledge, 1986, p. 284.
2 *Ibid.*, pp. 287–8.
3 Trevor Johnston, 'Sayles Talk', *Sight and Sound*, September 1993, p. 26.
4 Geoff Andrew, 'Going to Extremes', *Time Out*, 19–26 January 2000, p. 18.
5 Jonathan Romney, 'Out on a Limb', *Guardian*, 14 January 2000, p. 6.
6 Pat Aufderheide, 'Filmmaking as Storytelling: An Interview with John Sayles', *Cineaste*, vol. 15, no. 4, 1987, p. 15.
7 Trevor Johnston, *op. cit.*, p. 28.
8 *Ibid.*, p. 26.
9 A. Huyssen, 'Mass Culture as Woman: Modernism's Other', in Tania Modleski (ed.) *Studies in Entertainment: Critical Approaches to Mass Culture*, Bloomington, Indiana University Press, 1986.
10 Leslie Felperin, 'John Sayles: Walking Alone', *Sight and Sound*, September 1997, p. 22.
11 Gavin Smith, *Sayles on Sayles*, London, Faber and Faber, 1998, p. ix.
12 Pat Aufderheide, *op. cit.*, p. 15.
13 Gavin Smith, *op. cit.*, p. xi.
14 Philip Kemp, 'Review of *Lone Star*', *Sight and Sound*, October 1996, p. 48.
15 Philip Kemp, 'Review of *The Secret of Roan Inish*', *Sight and Sound*, August 1997, p. 63.
16 Philip Kemp, 1996, *op. cit.*, p. 48.
17 Gavin Smith, *op. cit.*, p. 58.
18 Pat Aufderheide, *op. cit.*, p. 12.
19 *Ibid.*, p. 13.

20 Gavin Smith, *op. cit.*, p. 66.
21 *Ibid.*, p. 9.
22 Gary Crowdus and Leonard Quart, 'Where the Hope Is: An Interview with John Sayles', *Cineaste*, vol. 18, no. 4, 1991, p. 7.
23 Trevor Johnston, 1993, *op. cit.*, p. 26.
24 Philip Kemp, 1996, *op. cit.*, p. 48.
25 Gary Crowdus and Leonard Quart, *op. cit.*, p. 7.
26 Philip Kemp, 1997, *op. cit.*, p. 8.
27 Gary Crowdus and Leonard Quart, *op. cit.*, p. 7.
28 Eliot Asinof (n.d.) 'John Sayles', *Directors Guild of America Web Magazine*. Online. Available HTTP: < http://www.dga.org/magazine / v22–5/john_sayles.htm >
29 Gavin Smith, 'John Sayles: "I Don't Want to Blow Anything by People" ', *Film Comment*, vol. 32, no. 3, May/June 1996, p. 57.
30 Geoff Andrew, *op. cit.*, p. 19.
31 Gary Crowdus and Leonard Quart, *op. cit.*, p. 7.
32 Andrew Ross, *No Respect: Intellectuals and Popular Culture*, London, Routledge, 1989.
33 See, for example, Richard Pells, *The Liberal Mind in a Conservative Age*, Middletown, CT, Wesleyan University Press, 1989.
34 See Gavin Smith, 1998, *op. cit.*, p. 21.
35 *Ibid.*, pp. 126–7.
36 Kim Newman, 'Review of *City of Hope*', *Sight and Sound*, August 1991, p. 38.
37 Leonard Maltin (n.d.) 'John Sayles', *Writers Guild of America News*. Online. Available HTTP: < http://www.wga.org/pr/0298/sayles.html >
38 Gavin Smith, 1998, *op. cit.*, p. 4.
39 *Ibid.*, p. 5.
40 Trevor Johnston, 1993, *op. cit.*, p. 29.
41 Jonathan Romney, *op. cit.*, p. 6.

Filmography

Return of the Secaucus 7 (1980)
Lianna (1983)
Baby, It's You (1983)
The Brother from Another Planet (1984)
Matewan (1987)
Eight Men Out (1988)
City of Hope (1991)
Passion Fish (1992)
The Secret of Roan Inish (1994)
Lone Star (1996)
Men with Guns (1997)
Limbo (1999)

Further reading

Philip Kemp, 'Review of *Passion Fish*', *Sight and Sound*, September 1993, pp. 51–2.

Jack Ryan, *John Sayles, Filmmaker*, New York, McFarland, 1998.
Clif Thompson, 'The Brother from Another Planet: Black Characters in the Films of John Sayles', *Cineaste*, vol. 22, no. 3, 1996, pp. 32–3.
Dennis West and Joan M. West, 'Borders and Boundaries: An Interview with John Sayles', *Cineaste*, vol. 22, no. 3, 1996, pp. 14–17.

MARC JANCOVICH AND JAMES LYONS

MARTIN SCORSESE

MOVIES AND RELIGION

More than just a filmmaker, Martin Scorsese is the self-appointed guardian of American cinema history. Since the early 1980s he has campaigned for more durable colour film stock, and the preservation and archiving of old American films, while promoting the cinema of the past to modern audiences. For Scorsese, the cinema of the present is always and necessarily influenced by the past. Scorsese has yet to receive an Oscar (he has been nominated three times for Best Director, twice for Best Screenwriter), but he is nonetheless the 'critical' King of Hollywood. As both a sophisticated East Coast filmmaker and a Hollywood director, he commands immense critical respect; whether juggling big budgets and mainstream connections with large studios (Universal, Warner Brothers), delivering star vehicles and box-office successes (*The Color of Money*, *Cape Fear*), or indulging in more personal projects (*The Last Temptation of Christ*, *Kundun*), Scorsese has retained his reputation as, in Geoff Andrew's words, 'the quintessential maverick auteur'.[1] An independently minded cinephile, Scorsese's relationship to popular cinema (indeed to popular culture – his early films were marked by an innovative use of soundtrack music) has been an extremely productive one.

While best known for the savage but complex exploration of masculinity and violence in films such as the New York-based *Mean Streets* and *Taxi Driver*, the searing biographical boxing picture *Raging Bull* or the epic gangster narrative *GoodFellas*, Scorsese's output has been extremely varied. In his period adaptation of an Edith Wharton novel, *The Age of Innocence*, Scorsese's attention to the rituals of self-contained societies takes on a new dimension. The epic musical *New York, New York* maps post-war musical taste through the failed relationship of jazzman Jimmy Doyle (Robert De Niro) and singer turned movie star Francine Evans (Liza Minnelli). The surreal *King of Comedy*, the yuppie nightmare movie *After*

Hours, or the contemporary woman's picture *Alice Doesn't Live Here Anymore* (for which Ellen Burstyn won an Oscar), all testify both to the diversity of Scorsese's career and to the range of influences.

Religion remains a consistent theme: almost all of Scorsese's primary male characters voice a fascination with religion in some form. *Mean Streets'* Charlie (Harvey Keitel) is fixated with the idea of his own spiritual purpose. The archetypal selective devotee, his desire to do penance is at odds with his actions: 'he acts like he's doing it for the others, but it's a matter of his own pride'.[2] *Taxi Driver's* Travis Bickle (Robert De Niro) believes himself to be acting out God's rage against the lowlife of New York city; *Cape Fear's* Max Cady (De Niro) is similarly obsessive; while *Raging Bull's* Jake LaMotta (De Niro, again, in an Oscar-winning performance) punishes his body both in training and in the boxing ring in an attempt to atone for his sins.

In retrospect, the earlier films seem to be leading towards *Last Temptation's* explicit wrestling with Christianity (like the break-through *Mean Streets*, the film feels like a very personal project). Attracting intense reactions from some religious groups (who picketed cinemas in response to the apparent blasphemy implied by Christ's final temptation), the film, based on Nikos Kazantzakis' novel, has Christ appear to leave the cross and experience married life with Mary Magdalene. Scorsese argued that it was his intention to show Christ as a real man rather than as a faultless spiritual being. Thus, the Bronx accents, Christ's (Willem Dafoe) inner emotional struggle and the consistently female image of sin converge, if we are to accept Scorsese's interviews, in making the film as much a working through of his own identity as the story of Christ: 'Jesus has to put up with everything we go through, all the doubts and fears and anger ... he has to deal with all this double, triple guilt on the cross. That's the way I directed it, and that's what I wanted, because my own religious feelings are the same.'[3]

The Last Temptation of Christ can be interpreted in two distinct ways; either it posits Christ as a human being, or it raises Scorsese's vision of masculine identity to an omnipotent spiritual level. Notions of masculinity, a sense of community and the influence of religion on personal identity are all themes common to Scorsese films. In fact, *Last Temptation* suggests an attempt to universalize masculine experience by having these themes transported from the usual urban, late twentieth-century setting to biblical times. Objections to the film's depiction of Jesus as sexual perhaps served to divert attention away from another more uncomfortable theme; that masculine identity is defined in terms of existential conflict and growing self-awareness, while women remain confined to earth, sexuality and Original Sin. Though Scorsese cannot be simply cast as a misogynist, his personal perspective and belief systems are unashamedly patriarchal, grounded in Catholicism. Women feature mainly on a symbolic level, serving as projections of male spiritual conflicts (even, it might be argued, in *The Age of Innocence*).

Alongside the romance of the gangster and of male ritual that is so much in evidence in Scorsese's work – as Lesley Stern writes 'Cinematic desire, in Scorsese, can't be easily extricated from the desire to be a gangster'[4] – characters like Charlie, Travis, Jake LaMotta and Cady can all be understood in terms of a journey towards salvation through self-knowledge. Such themes chime with the contention of the *Cahiers du cinéma* critics, that an auteur film is dominated by the search for self-awareness: 'the individual is trapped in *solitude morale* and can escape from it – transcend it – if he or she comes to see their condition and then extend themselves to others and then to God'.[5] Scorsese's preoccupations are evident in his work and in his many interviews: 'my whole life has been movies and religion. That's it, nothing else.'[6]

Scorsese's film career began in the 1960s, at the tail end of *Cahiers du cinéma*'s glorification of the auteur. Influenced by the French New Wave and Italian neo-realist cinema, he was briefly associated with the 'Radical Newsreel Movement', but concentrated mainly on making his name as an independent filmmaker. Of course, this begs the question what is an independent filmmaker? In the context of American cinema of the last forty years, two distinct versions offer themselves: on the one hand, those working in commercial filmmaking outside the auspices of the major studios (in what might loosely be termed the field of exploitation), and on the other hand, those working in a festival-fuelled circuit of independent filmmaking (equally loosely, a sort of art cinema). Scorsese is an independent in both senses: one of his first features as director, *Boxcar Bertha*, was produced by Roger Corman for AIP.[7] He followed this film with the landmark *Mean Streets*, energetic and innovative but clearly addressed to a knowing youthful audience ready to engage with the more complex narrative patterns we now associate with the American cinema of the 1970s. Scorsese's early successes (both independent and mainstream) began in the early 1970s when his contemporaries were such filmmakers as Francis Ford Coppola, George Lucas, Robert Altman, Brian De Palma and Steven Spielberg. Part of both a nascent American art cinema and what came to be called the 'New Hollywood', the success of

Scorsese's career has been his ability to operate across both spheres – independent and mainstream, innovative and conservative. Director Allison Anders encapsulates the contradictory nuances of this position: 'I would say that Marty Scorsese, no matter how much money he has, he's still operating in an independent realm.'[8]

Together these filmmakers represented a new generation who took full advantage of the more experimental space that an industry in desperate search of an audience permitted. For Richard Maltby, the film-school-educated, 'movie brat' directors 'found obvious material benefits in the enhanced industrial status of the director, in part because they became marketable commodities, even stars, in their own right'.[9] Scorsese has certainly exploited his reputation and star presence (characterized by an enthusiastic cinephilia), both in relation to his own projects and while serving as producer/executive producer for others.

Scorsese's career has been marked by important collaborative relationships. Thelma Schoonmaker first worked with Scorsese as editor on the 1969 *Who's that Knocking at my Door?*, and has edited all his films since *Raging Bull* (for which she received an Academy Award). Cinematographer Michael Ballhaus, who had previously worked with Fassbinder, has been a regular since *After Hours* (although Scorsese sometimes chooses a specific replacement, such as Freddie Francis whose horror/suspense experience was used on *Cape Fear*). Writer Paul Schrader is one of Scorsese's best-known collaborators, although he has only worked on three films, *Taxi Driver*, *Raging Bull* and *The Last Temptation of Christ*. Nicholas Pileggi has written two screenplays, *Goodfellas* and *Casino*, and could thus be said to constitute the 'Mafia influence'. Robert De Niro has starred in more Scorsese films than anyone else, having a significant input into the later films (Harvey Keitel is also a Scorsese regular).

An early collaboration with Paul Schrader produced one of Scorsese's most controversial works. A story of 'God's lonely man', *Taxi Driver* follows insomniac Vietnam veteran, Travis Bickle, as he dreams of ridding New York of the 'scum and the filth' that populate its streets. The film builds slowly toward a violent climax, wherein Travis, a confused vigilante, acts out his fantasies. While the absence of a satisfactory narrative conclusion (the excess of Travis' violence followed by a coda implying that his actions have given him a perverse notoriety) works against either character motivation or salvation, it is this inconsistency of structure and theme that attracted such strong reactions from audiences and critics alike.

Scorsese was shocked when, on an opening night: 'everyone was yelling and screaming at the shoot-out. When I made it, I didn't intend to have the audience react with that feeling.'[10] Concentrating on the violent gestures and speech that constitute male brotherhood in the film, Patricia Patterson and Manny Farber maintain that 'what's really disgusting about *Taxi Driver* is not the multi-faced loner but the endless propaganda about the magic of guns'.[11] Indeed this association with men and violence as a form of retribution or spiritual awakening has disturbed many feminist critics. Pam Cook describes *Raging Bull* in terms of a masculinity in crisis and *Cape Fear* as a rampage against women, seeing Scorsese as a 'master of the masochistic aesthetic'.[12] His films certainly have an ambiguous attitude to violence, since the audience is invited to gain a perverse pleasure from witnessing acts of brutality. In this sense, Scorsese's vision is less about the search for salvation in self-knowledge, and more about the glorification of man's inherent potential for violence – hence the structuring nostalgia for a masculine community of action in *GoodFellas* in which Tommy (Joe Pesci) functions as a perverse kind of hero.

The attempt to fix the meaning of *Taxi Driver*'s violence has shaped critical responses, and indeed the film's continuing resonance. Lesley Stern accepts Scorsese's contention that the film functions as homage to John Ford's *The Searchers* (1956), suggesting that Scorsese's film 'brings out the psychopathic tendencies within the vigilante impulse'.[13] While Robin Wood's response to *Taxi Driver* concentrates on how the 'incoherent narrative' echoes a general cultural malaise, Robert Kolker describes a symbolic notion of 'New York-ness' traceable through Scorsese's films in the repetition of certain gestures and speech patterns.[14] Although these patterns may have as much to do with the repeated presence of actors like De Niro, Pesci and Keitel, this quality of 'New York-ness' has delivered a traceable identity of urban, working-class, male communities in Scorsese's work. Thus the disciples in *The Last Temptation of Christ* echo the bar friends in *Mean Streets*, when they bicker about respect or friendship.

Whilst isolation and crises of identity are key themes that permeate most of Scorsese's films, they necessarily include explorations of community, or brotherhood against which the isolation, or level of identification for an individual can be measured. As most of Scorsese's main protagonists are male, urban, working class and often Italian-American, this notion of brotherhood has encouraged a perception that his settings and characters possess a kind of docu-realism. Obviously this stems in part from Scorsese's commentary on his personal experiences, his sense of his home community and of the people he has known. In most cases this sense of docu-realism extends only so far as setting. Above all, his films are concerned with spiritual, not political or even social conflicts. Audiences are guided by a commentary that draws attention to the subjective and/or constructed character of the fiction (the use of voice-over narration, most notably in *Taxi Driver*, *GoodFellas* and *Casino*, or the identification of key moments in freeze-frame or on-screen text). In fact, Scorsese excels in juggling the audience's perceptions with regard to what is 'real' and what is a character's imagination. Whether it be the questionable subjectivity of *Taxi Driver*, wherein the ending retrospectively casts doubts on the whole narration, or *The Age of Innocence*, in which Newland Archer's (Daniel Day-Lewis) narration veils its subjectivity behind seemingly objective scenes, Scorsese's films offer an inherently self-conscious exploration of their main characters' inner conflicts. For instance, a clue to Archer's subjectivity is given in Madame Olenska's (Michelle Pfeiffer) reply to one of his letters. Filmed as a direct address to camera, it appears to be an image conjured by his desire.

Scorsese does not attempt to hide the collaborative nature of his work, promoting it as an extension of his love of cinema history against the unthinking cult of the director. He will choose a cinematographer because of a particular style from the classical era he wishes to reproduce, or new techniques he wishes to learn.[15] Recently, Scorsese's collaborations have seen him take the role of producer. He served as executive producer on projects including Spike Lee's *Clockers* (1995), a film he was originally to have directed, Allison Anders' *Grace of My Heart* (1996), and Stephen Frears' award-winning *The Grifters* (1990). In the last few years, Scorsese has taken on the role of elder statesman in the movie industry. Amongst the cinematic souls he has saved is his old friend, director Michael Powell, whose controversial *Peeping Tom* (1960) virtually ended his career. Scorsese has tirelessly campaigned for its re-release and critical recognition, as part of an ongoing project to restore neglected films and filmmakers to present-day audiences. Chaper-oning Elia Kazan onto the Academy stage in March 1999, Scorsese emerges as liberal (or is that conservative) defender of the movies as art. He has the critical credibility of a semi-independent East Coast filmmaker, combined with the box-office draw of a major Hollywood player. His intentions may be focused entirely on saving the soul of cinema, but if this makes him a Messiah in the process, then I doubt if we will hear him complain.

Biography

Born in New York, USA, in 1942, Scorsese studied English and then Film at New York University. He worked with producer Roger Corman, achieving commercial and critical success during the early 1970s. As well as numerous feature films, he has directed music videos and worked for television. In 1995 he made the series *A Personal Journey with Martin Scorsese Through American Movies* for Britain's Channel 4.

Notes

1   Geoff Andrew, *Stranger than Paradise: Maverick Film-makers in Recent American Cinema*, London, Prion, 1998, p. 21.
2   Scorsese, cited in David Thompson and Ian Christie (eds) *Scorsese on Scorsese*, London, Faber and Faber, 1996, p. 48.
3   Richard Corliss, 'Body...and Blood', *Film Comment*, vol. 24, no. 5, 1988, p. 36.
4   Lesley Stern, *The Scorsese Connection*, London, BFI Publishing, p. 10, 1995.
5   John Hess, 'La Politique des auteurs: Pt. I World View as Aesthetic', *Jump Cut*, 1 May/June 1974, p. 20.
6   R.A. Blake, 'Redeemed in Blood', *Journal of Popular Film and Television*, vol. 24, no. 1, 1996, p. 2.
7   Jim Hillier calls it Scorsese's 'first "commercial" picture', in *The New Hollywood*, London, Studio Vista, 1992, p. 40.
8   *Directors Guild of America Magazine*, December 1997/January 1998, p. 52.
9   Richard Maltby, *Hollywood Cinema*, Oxford: Blackwell, 1995, p. 32.
10 David Thompson and Ian Christie, *op. cit.*, p. 63.
11 Patricia Patterson and Manny Farber, 'The Power and the Gory', *Film Comment*, May/June 1976, p. 28.
12 Pam Cook, 'Masculinity in Crisis? Tragedy and Identification in *Raging Bull*', *Screen*, vol. 23, no. 3/4, 1982; '*Cape Fear* and Femininity as Destructive Power', Pam Cook and Philip Dodd (eds) *Women and Film: A Sight and Sound Reader*, London, BFI Publishing, 1993, p. 134.
13 Lesley Stern, *op.cit.*, p. 61.
14 Robin Wood, *Hollywood From Vietnam to Reagan*, New York, Columbia University Press, 1986; Robert Kolker, *A Cinema of Loneliness: Penn, Kubrick, Coppola, Scorsese*, Altman, Oxford University Press, 1980.
15 Elaine and Saul Bass, who designed opening sequences for the likes of Alfred Hitchcock, have worked with Scorsese since their return to the industry in the 1980s.

Filmography

What's a Nice Girl Like You Doing in a Place Like This? (1963) short
It's Not Just You, Murray! (1963) short
The Big Shave (1967) short
Who's That Knocking On My Door? (1969)
Street Scenes (1970)
Boxcar Bertha (1972)
Mean Streets (1973)
Alice Doesn't Live Here Anymore (1974)
Italianamerican (1974)
Taxi Driver (1975)
New York, New York (1977)
The Last Waltz (1978) documentary
American Boy: A Profile of Steven Prince (1978) documentary
Raging Bull (1980)
The King of Comedy (1982)
After Hours (1985)
The Color of Money (1986)
The Last Temptation of Christ (1988)
New York Stories (1989) segment – 'Life Lessons'
GoodFellas (1990)
Cape Fear (1991)
The Age of Innocence (1993)
Casino (1995)
Kundun (1997)
Bringing Out the Dead (1999)

Further reading

Michael Bliss, *Martin Scorsese and Michael Cimino*, London, Scarecrow, 1985.
Peter Brunette (ed.) *Martin Scorsese: Interviews*, Jackson, University of Mississipi Press, 1999.
Leighton Grist, *The Films of Martin Scorsese: 1963–1977*, Basingstoke, Macmillan Press, 2000.
Mary P. Kelly, *Martin Scorsese: A Journey*, London, Secker and Warburg, 1991.
Les Keyser, *Martin Scorsese*, New York, Twayne Publishers, 1992.
Amy Taubin, *Taxi Driver*, London, BFI Publishing, 2000.

GEORGE S. LARKE

COLINE SERREAU

Although it is always difficult to assess the importance of a director within a national cinema and his or her influence over his or her successors, it is none the less obvious that Coline Serreau's cinematographic career has played a significant role in the development and filmmaking practices of women directors in France from the 1970s onwards. For over three decades, she has contributed to the growing visibility and recognition of women directors within a traditionally misogynistic French film industry, achieving commercial as well as critical success. More than any other director, she has indirectly challenged the elitist and romantic notion of the director as an auteur, inherited from New Wave (male) directors in the late 1950s, by consistently inscribing her authorial signature in genre films. Although this aspect is now a major trend among 1990s' women directors in France,[1] she undoubtedly initiated it. (It is worth remembering that despite its supposed 'neutral' status in terms of gender, the word 'auteur' in French rarely refers to a woman.) Moreover, she has developed an approach in her genre films which allows the expression of feminist and socio-political concerns while endorsing what has been recently described as 'popular feminism', in other words 'a type of feminism that does not name itself as such but which none the less takes for granted issues and ideas put on the agenda by feminists'.[2] More than any other contemporary director, she makes films which constantly bear witness to the evolution of French society in the past twenty years, while renewing narrative genres.

A baby-boomer (she was born in 1947), Serreau worked as a performer and writer for the stage from the late 1960s. She made her film-directing début in the decade following the May '68 'events' (as the failed 'revolution' was called at the time) in France. Like many of her contemporaries (Diane Kurys and Josiane Balasko, for instance), Serreau's motivation for directing films mainly came from her growing dissatisfaction with the limited range of roles available to actresses in France. During the 1970s more women than ever gained access to the other side of the camera in France. The decade was also marked by the development of the women's and feminist movements in France, and although the links and collaboration between them and women filmmakers were not as strong and obvious as in Anglo-Saxon countries, many films of the period expressed a similar concern and interest for women's issues. Feminism is a clear influence throughout Serreau's career, as illustrated by her most political film, a feminist documentary entitled *Mais qu'est-ce qu'elles veulent?*, made between 1975 and 1977.

Initially entitled *Utopia*, her film was made on a shoestring budget and was meant, as she described it, 'to give a voice to all the women who wanted to speak out'. The result is a kaleidoscope of testimonies which articulate the double axis of class and gender, Marxism and feminism being key words in Serreau's films. Seen by some as the feminist documentary *par excellence*,[3] *Mais qu'est-ce qu'elles veulent?* loudly says what many knew but refused to acknowledge, namely woman's sexual and social oppression in 1970s' France. From its content to the conditions of its making, the film epitomizes the political mood typical of the activist (and feminist) cinema of the 1970s. Serreau also illustrates the debates within feminist circles at the time over content (documenting women's lives and oppression) versus form (challenging traditional narrative forms), successfully combining both, unlike many feminist documentaries made in France during this period. Her choice of Bach for the soundtrack and the recurrent shot of waves on a shore (used as a punctuation to mark a pause between the testimonies) strongly suggest her desire to achieve more than a political pamphlet. In various interviews, she stressed the fact that her editing is her 'signature' and the only way she interferes in the film. The film is more than just a 'talking-women' film, although it gives a voice to various women from different social and regional backgrounds; Serreau's editing and choice of images during the interviews is typical of propaganda materials, with shots either reinforcing or contradicting what is said on the screen. For example, her use of pornographic materials illustrating women's exploitation in the porn industry efficiently contradicts the views of a male director. The issues of editing and the manipulation of images were an important aspect of feminist film criticism in the 1970s.

When considering her later documentaries, it is clear that the form allows her to express more 'committed' positions than fiction films. Thus, her second (commissioned) film made for French television, *Grand-mères de l'Islam*, was devoted to North African grandmothers, women regularly ignored by mainstream media because of their gender, their age and their ethnic origin. In the 1990s, she contributed to collective documentaries financed by Amnesty International and Handicap International.

It is, however, her comedies which made her famous in France and abroad in the 1980s. This is a major achievement when one considers the specificity of comedy in France. The most successful film genre in France since the early days of French cinema, comedy has long been a male preserve so far as directors, actors, and to a certain extent the audience, were concerned. The 1970s changed this pattern as female comedians started to be more visible on the stages of *café-théâtre* (fringe theatres where they could create and perform one-woman shows), breaking taboos by introducing 'controversial' topics regarding women's sexuality.[4] Although she was not the first French woman director to make comedies,[5] Serreau opened a way that many followed, reappropriating laughter and using it as a powerful weapon for expressing her views. Her success proved that comedy, despite its traditionally misogynist content, could become a useful vehicle to express women's claims.

Although her comedies tend to reproduce the French penchant for safe family subjects, her perception of 'family' seems wider and different from her (male) counterparts. One has to keep in mind France's long-lasting family policies and obsession with natality which pervade all aspects of its culture and society. Another key aspect to consider is France's tradition of 'universalism' inherited from the French Revolution, which is based on the principle of equality between every citizen and therefore does not acknowledge difference between them in terms of gender, class, ethnic origin, etc. Serreau consistently questions the very notion of 'family' while suggesting other definitions of sexual and gender roles. *Pourquoi pas!* presents an alternative family unit (a *ménage à trois*), *Trois hommes et un couffin* creates a multi-parent family where masculinity and paternity are put into question, *Romuald et Juliette*, combines an extended family (single mother, five children from five different fathers), and a socially and ethnically mixed family. Finally, *La Crise* shows all families (extended or not) in crisis, and a rejection of traditional female roles.

Her first fiction film, the bittersweet comedy *Pourquoi pas!*, echoes some concerns of filmmakers of the decade regarding gender and relationships between the sexes. She creates a utopian sexual community of two men and a woman, successfully avoiding caricature (the film was made the same year as Edouard Molinaro's *La Cage aux folles*) while reversing expectations regarding gender roles and identities, a tendency she developed in her later films and plays. Her skill at expressing concerns and issues shared by her contemporaries was even stronger in 1985 when she achieved a success rarely attained by women directors in France with the comedy *Trois hommes et un couffin* (*Three Men and a Cradle*).

Trois hommes et un couffin was made on a small budget after the commercial failure of her second film, *Qu'est-ce qu'on attend pour être heureux!* Despite her difficulty in finding a producer and a limited advertising campaign, the film soon became the success story of the decade. The film earned Serreau fourth position on the list of most successful directors of the Fifth Republic (1958) (the other woman after the top twenty is Josiane Balasko with *Gazon Maudit* [*French Twist*] in 1995). The film also contributed to her reputation abroad (she even started shooting the American remake before quitting following major disagreements with the producer).

Serreau considers *Trois hommes* her most feminist film, a view not shared by American feminists who objected to the absence of women within the narrative. In this film as in others, Serreau chooses to focus on her male characters in order to explore men's position in relation to women's and men's parenting role. She uses the situation of three bachelors having to deal with a baby (girl) to address masculinity and men's role in parenthood, in a way rarely explored before. In *Romuald et Juliette*, Serreau's emphasis is more on social and class issues; she uses the framework of comedy to denounce 1980s' rampant capitalism, white-collar delinquency and social inequalities. The title of the film also suggests the element of the impossible love story. Another typical aspect of Serreau's films and plays is obvious here: that is, her refusal to be constrained within a limited narrative framework. Here, Serreau combines various narrative forms, and she parodies the fairytale, creating an overweight working-class black Cinderella meeting a white yuppie Prince Charming.

Serreau frequently offers a multiplicity of plots and borrows from different narrative genres (thrillers, love story, fairytales, etc.), renewing and adapting them to fit her need to address a wide range of issues. A graduate in French literature, she follows the strong tradition of political satire which can be traced back to the eighteenth century, offering interesting intertextual references to Voltaire 'philosophical tales' of the Enlightenment and to nineteenth-century 'utopian writers'. She endorses the tradition initiated by the eighteenth-century writers whose writing was meant to entertain as well as to enlighten their readers. Indeed, her 'social comedies', while diverting the audience, also suggest alternatives to dominant thoughts and beliefs. Although she reproduces some stereotypes of earlier French comedies regarding gender issues, she forces the audience to reflect on the prejudices on which they are based. Her films use humour as both a catalyst and a trigger. After the utopian *Pourquoi pas!* (regarded by some critics as an influence on and an indirect model for Balasko's *Gazon Maudit*), and the 'revolutionary' *Qu'est-ce qu'on attend pour être heureux?*, Serreau's films continued to bear witness to the changes in French society and culture.

Despite the failure of her latest film *La Belle verte*, Serreau's influence remains strong especially in comedies made by women since the early 1990s. Indeed, the unexpected triumph of *Trois hommes* directly questioned the general view that, on the one hand, women directors could not make genre films, and on the other, that films made by women in France could not reach a mass audience. Serreau's achievement proved otherwise and it is clear today that her success indirectly triggered others. It is worth noting that more women directors than ever are choosing this genre in France, and that comedy has allowed them to reach large audiences (see Josiane Balasko and Tonie Marshall among others). More important perhaps is the fact that all of them use the framework of comedy to address gender-related issues, ranging from female sexuality (including the rare occurrence – in French cinema as a whole and in films made by women in particular – of lesbianism in Balasko's *French Twist*), motherhood, couples and family. Like Serreau, many refuse the textual (and sexual) constraints inherent to the genre by mixing genres and offering pleasurable and unconventional representations of femininity.

Biography

Born in 1947, in France, Serreau is the daughter of Jean-Marie Serreau, one of the most important stage directors of the 1950s (he was the first director to stage the work of Genet, Ionesco and Beckett) and of Geneviève Serreau, a writer and translator (who first translated Berthold Brecht in French). Both were left-wing activists, committed politically to various causes during and after the Second World War. Serreau initially studied music and dance before starting a theatrical career as a writer and performer in the late 1960s.

Notes

1 See B. Rollet and C. Tarr (2001) *Cinema and the Second Sex. Women's Filmmaking in France, 1981–1999*, Cassell (forthcoming).
2 A. Kuhn, *Women's Pictures. Feminism and Cinema*, London and New York, Verso, 2nd edn, 1994, p. 230.
3 G. Colvile, 'On Coline Serreau's *Mais qu'est-ce qu'elles veulent?* and the Problematics of Feminist Documentary', in R. King (ed.) *French Cinema*, Nottingham French Studies, vol. 32, no. 1 (Spring), 1993, pp. 84–9.
4 Serreau herself contributed to this radical renewal of French theatre in the early 1970s.

5   Alice Guy-Blaché in the silent era and Andrée Feix after the Second World War.

Filmography

Mais qu'est-ce qu'elles veulent? (1975–8) documentary
Pourquoi pas! (1977) also writer
Qu'est-ce qu'on attend pour être heureux! (1982) also writer
Trois hommes et un couffin (1985) also writer
Romuald et Juliette (1989) also writer
Contre l'oubli (1991) segment: broadcast on French television, November–December 1991
La Crise (1992) also writer
La Belle verte (1997) also writer
L'Enfant (1998) segment of *Lumieres sur un massacre* short

Television

Le Rendez-vous (1975) short fiction
Grand-mères de l'Islam (1978) documentary

Films as actor

Un peu, beaucoup, passionnément (1970, Robert Enrico)
Dada au coeur (1972, Claude Accursi; not released)
On s'est trompé d'histoire d'amour (1974, Jean-Louis Bertolucci)

Further reading

Avant-scène cinéma, '*Trois hommes et un couffin*', no. 356, January 1987.
CinémAction, '1960–1980. Vingt ans d'utopie au cinéma', no. 24, 1982.
—— 'Le cinéma au féminisme', no. 31, 1985.
—— 'Le documentaire français', no. 41, 1987.
D. Overbey, 'France: The Newest Wave', *Sight and Sound*, Spring 1978, pp. 87–8.
B. Rollet, 'Two Women Filmmakers Speak Out: Serreau and Balasko and the Inheritance of May '68', in S. Perry and M. Cross (eds) *Voices of France*, London and Washington, Pinter, 1997, pp. 100–13.
—— *Coline Serreau*, Manchester and New York, Manchester University Press, 1998.
—— 'Women and Popular Genres in France, 1980s–1990s', in *Sites: The Journal of 20th-Century/Contemporary French Studies*, Connecticut (forthcoming).
M. Rosello, 'Disarming Stereotypes: Coline Serreau's *La Crise*', in *Declining the Stereotype. Ethnicity and Representation in French Cultures*, Hanover and London, University Press of New England, 1998.
D. Sherzer, 'Comedy and Interracial Relationships: *Romuald et Juliette* and *Métisse*', in P. Powrie (ed.) *French Cinema in the 1990s*, Oxford, Oxford University Press, 1999, pp. 148–59.

G. Vincendeau, 'Women's Cinema, Film Theory and Feminism in France', *Screen*, vol. 28, no. 4, 1987, pp. 4–18.
—— 'Coline Serreau: A High Wire Act', *Sight and Sound* vol. 4, no. 3, pp. 26–8, 1994.

BRIGITTE ROLLET

STEVEN SODERBERGH

In 1989 Steven Soderbergh redefined Hollywood's concept of 'independent film'. Previously, the label suggested a renegade, low-budget cinema exemplified by the raw experimentalism of John Cassavetes, the fantastic trash of early John Waters or the bleak irony of Jim Jarmusch – all of which embraced an aesthetic and profit margin that was incompatible with Hollywood's blockbuster model. However, with the success of Soderbergh's début feature, *sex, lies and videotape*, an 'independent' film became something that was profitable, viable and appealing to mainstream audiences. As a result, Soderbergh and his film became the cause célèbre of a renewed swell in US independent filmmaking, one which would eventually spawn Quentin Tarantino, the commercialization of the Sundance Film Festival, and a distinct shift in Hollywood's industrial practices.

After *sex, lies, and videotape* premiered at the 1989 US Film Festival (now known as Sundance), Miramax co-founder Harvey Weinstein won a bidding war for the film's distribution rights. Weinstein then took some significant risks that would prove crucial to the film's ultimate success, such as shrewdly manoeuvring the film into the main competition at the Cannes Film Festival. Remarkably, *sex, lies, and videotape* went on to win Cannes' most prestigious award, the Palme d' Or, beating stiff competition, including Spike Lee's *Do the Right Thing*. When Cannes jury president Wim Wenders announced the winner, he professed that *sex, lies, and videotape* 'gave us confidence in the future of cinema'. Instantly, Soderbergh – at 26, the youngest director ever to win the festival's top honour – found himself at the centre of a hyperbolic celebration that declared him a wunderkind of the order of Orson Welles. Indeed, critics called his film 'the most impressive and significant cinematic début since *Citizen Kane*', and went on to compare him to masters of cinema, from Woody Allen, Cassavetes and Roeg to Rohmer, Truffaut and Godard.

Soderbergh and his film arrived in the marketplace at a time when opportunities were already expanding for filmmakers. With the explosion of home video in the 1980s, there was an increased demand for product beyond the output of the major studios. Moreover, video distributors were now financing lower-budget films in exchange for video rights, creating new sources of accessible production funding (in fact, RCA/Columbia Home Video and Virgin Visions video backed *sex, lies, and videotape* in this manner). In addition, the growing legion of independent distributors – most significantly Miramax – was finally supplying these films with a pipeline to cinemas.

Sex, lies, and videotape was dialogue-heavy and had no special effects, action scenes or big stars. Nonetheless, the film's stylish package of understated sensuality and sage commentary on intimacy and relationships impressed both critics and audiences alike. The film grossed $24.7 million in its initial domestic release, more than twenty times its $1.2 million budget. It also did extremely well internationally – to date (2001) it has earned over $100 million, making the film one of the most profitable of the 1980s, with a better rate of return than even the most successful blockbusters. Soderbergh's commercial triumph served to open the door for other independent filmmakers as well; once the profits from *sex, lies, and videotape* registered on the industry radar, all of Hollywood wanted low-budget, introspective projects added to the production slate, turning to the US Film Festival as a rich supply of such films.

Previously, the festival had been a small affair showcasing American independent cinema. In 1979, there were a mere seventy feature submissions. Ten years later, this number had grown by 100. Once Soderbergh was discovered, and following Tarantino's stunning début, *Reservoir Dogs*, in 1992, the event grew exponentially: there were 250 features submitted in 1993, 500 in 1996 and a record 849 films hoping to be picked for competition in 2000. Sundance became a supermarket for new talent in the 1990s. Agents, executives, lawyers and producers began shopping Park City each year and Sundance was established as the place for independents to secure their credibility and distribution. After *sex, lies, and videotape*, the primary focus of the festival shifted from the art to the art of the deal, dramatically raising the stakes along with the opportunities.

The growing recognition and importance of Sundance that is often directly linked to the debut of *sex, lies, and videotape* in 1989 also conferred the concept of 'independent' film with extraordinary marketing cachet. However, mainstream Hollywood's ensuing exploitation of the term 'independent' has created an identity crisis of sorts: is a film's independence determined by its source of funding or its aesthetic, its craft or its attitude, its politics or its narrative concerns? In negotiating these questions, one answer is clear: the industrial and artistic issues raised by the phenomenal success of Soderbergh's film have complicated any definition of 'independent film'.

Such complexity is also the hallmark of Soderbergh's own career. He has navigated through various genres, financing sectors, visual styles and narrative formulas. At first glance, the only consistency to his output might appear to be its inconsistency. He has directed four studio films and five independently financed features to date. Two are big-budget star vehicles, three pictures are carried by relative unknowns and one film stars Soderbergh himself as both leads. In all, there are three non-linear crime films, one surreal experimental comedy, an impressionistic monologue, an expressionistic thriller, a coming-of-age drama, a true story about corporate corruption and, of course, *sex, lies, and videotape*, which was based on a semi-autobiographical script he wrote in about a week.

Although the *sex, lies, and videotape* screenplay brought Soderbergh an Academy Award nomination, his follow-up film, *Kafka*, was demolished by the critics, who saw it as a pretentious film-school exercise. The much-maligned effort was also a disappointment for audiences, and it failed to gross even $1 million. His next project, *King of the Hill*, remains his most conventional and conservative film so far. Based on the memoirs of A.E. Hotchner, it received rave reviews but was generally ignored by audiences, owing its failure in part to the ten other films with child protagonists released that year and a dismal marketing effort by Gramercy. Soderbergh then fell into a personal and professional slump during the lifeless neo-noir production *The Underneath*. This uninspired 'remake' of *Criss Cross* (1949), based on his adaptation of Don Tracy's crime novel, marked a career low point for the director.

Soderbergh credits the freedom of his next project, the stream of consciousness home-movie *Schizopolis* (made for $250,000), with reviving his passion for directing. That same year, he also completed *Gray's Anatomy*, the third Spalding Gray monologue to be filmed after *Swimming to Cambodia* (Demme, 1987) and *Monster in a Box* (Broomfield, 1992). Soderbergh dug deep into his visual bag of tricks for this manic, hyper-visual interpretation of Gray's panicky crusade for a medical miracle but still came up empty-handed at the box office.

After five flops and one commercial hit in eight years, Soderbergh received a call from previous associates at Universal to direct a slick crime romp based on an Elmore Leonard novel. Soderbergh was 'the beneficiary of being cold', as he put it, since everyone else being considered for the job was either busy or too expensive. With the sexy, energetic *Out of Sight*, Soderbergh's career was resurrected; he found critical and commercial success once again, and the added confidence that comes with a profitable $50 million film. His next effort, *The Limey*, stands as his most haunting and stylistically impressive work to date. This custom-made star vehicle for Terence Stamp matched up two 1960s' icons (Stamp's ex-con Wilson and Peter Fonda as music mogul Terry Valentine) in an unforgettable meditation on revenge and regret. *The Limey* sports a significant amount of cinematic baggage, but wears it well. Soderbergh himself has described the film as both 'Captain America meets Billy Budd' and '*Get Carter* made by Alain Resnais'.

Soderbergh remained true to unpredictable form with his follow-up to *The Limey*. Based on a true story, *Erin Brockovich* presents a high-gloss populist fable about a working-class mother of three turned legal activist for an exploited community. The film was a departure from the uncomfortable, dark recesses of *The Limey* and the off-beat surprises in *Out of Sight*. Instead, Soderbergh crafted a modern-day *Norma Rae* with perfectly polished edges and embraced the mass audience with open arms. The hugely successful star vehicle for Julia Roberts (in the title role) made more money in its opening weekend ($28.2 million) than *sex, lies, and videotape* had in its entire first run. *Erin Brockovich* demonstrated that Soderbergh could downplay his unconventional, independent style while directing a $55 million film starring Hollywood's hottest actress, adding cachet to his career that will surely be leveraged for more artistic freedom on future films. *Erin Brockovich* is also notable for giving Julia Roberts two firsts – a $20 million pay cheque (making her the first female star to earn as much per role as the highest paid men in Hollywood) and an Academy Award for Best Actress.

Soderbergh edited his first three films, wrote or adapted four of the screenplays (*sex, lies and videotape*, *King of the Hill*, *The Underneath* and *Schizopolis*) and usually works closely with his writers. He also has some frequent collaborators who help to sustain his cinematic vision, most notably cinematographers Elliott Davis (*Gray's Anatomy, King of the Hill, The Underneath, Out of Sight*) and Ed Lachman (*The Limey, Erin Brockovich, Traffic*), composer Cliff Martinez (*sex, lies, and videotape, Kafka, King of the Hill, The Underneath, Gray's Anatomy, The Limey*) and screenwriter Lem Dobbs (*Kafka, The Limey*). However, he is quite proud of the fact that his work remains difficult to categorize, and he continues to be, as *Interview* magazine noted in 1998, 'one of the toughest directors to nail'.

While Soderbergh defies expectations with each successive film, his work does maintain a unity of spirit and design. At their most stripped down, his projects are meticulously crafted, character-based films that are steeped in ironic humor and a quiet technical virtuosity rare in Hollywood cinema. The diversity of narrative forms and content in his films is related through Soderbergh's unique manipulations of space and time as well as the recurring issues that burden his protagonists.

Perhaps the most consistent theme that runs through his films is a pervasive sense of isolation and loneliness. Soderbergh's characters are often eerily detached, emotionally frozen and unable to fit in with the world around them. Graham (James Spader) serves as a splendid ambassador of alienation in *sex, lies, and videotape*. Graham, who is impotent, has a 'personal project' of videotaping women discussing their sexual experiences. He is the poster child of disaffection, utilizing the video camera to distance himself from, and provide an alternative to, reality and experience. Wilson in *The Limey* is another of Soderbergh's archetypal loners. In the film, language serves as a significant device to illustrate just how out of place Wilson is in Los Angeles. Recently released from British prison and searching for his daughter's killer, Wilson is literally incapable of communicating much of the time. After one of Wilson's extended soliloquies in his rhyming Cockney slang, someone deadpans, 'There's only one thing I can't understand: every single word you just said.'

Kafka (Jeremy Irons), in the film of the same name, is also alienated from the world around him, living a nightmare Franz might have written himself. The unwieldy bureaucracy of modern life has rendered him a nameless, faceless corporate agent by day, practically invisible in enormous rooms full of files and records. At night, he writes tortured confessionals to his father that he will never send and stories that nobody will publish. While more engaged with her environment, Erin Brockovich (Roberts) is also forever out of place in modern office culture. With her high heels, mini skirts and push-up bras, it is clear that Erin will stand alone among the tongue-clucking receptionists and high-priced corporate attorneys in her path. Yet she seems to relish her status as a loner, snapping 'Bite my ass, Krispy Kreme!' at a frowning co-worker and frequently displaying her talents for flouting conventions and clashing with authority.

In *King of the Hill*, Aaron Kurlander (Jesse Bradford) experiences a loneliness which is perhaps the most tragic of all, that of a child trying to survive without his family. In the end, underneath all of its anarchic hysteria, even *Schizopolis* is a melancholy statement about isolation. Soderbergh has explained that the film is an autobiographical story (starring him and his ex-wife) stemming from his own divorce, detailing a marriage that has decayed to the point where language is meaningless.

There is, then, a certain absence in his characters that makes its presence known in their emptiness, despair and longing. Many appear as if they were nothing more than ghosts, exhibiting an eerie, hollow and serenely self-possessed demeanour. So uncomfortable in this world are these characters, that they often escape into an active fantasy life of their own. Their realities grow multilayered and deceptive and they usually become masters of duplicity in order to cope. As this process unfolds, Soderbergh positions his audience as voyeurs on a bleak and awkward modern existence.

Ultimately, his films are character studies populated with strangers in a strange land. Their environments are always richly and vividly crafted, emphasizing hostility in every detail of Kafka's Prague, Terry Valentine's Los Angeles, Erin Brockovich's small California community and the Miami/Detroit hang-outs of the convicted felons in *Out of Sight*. Even Austin, Texas is devoid of its well-known Southern hospitality in *The Underneath*. Whether they figure as the classic 'Westerner', an intruder coming (back) into town with a purpose (*sex, lies, and videotape, The Underneath, Out of Sight, The Limey*) or are merely out of place in their own surroundings (*Kafka, King of the Hill, Schizopolis, Erin Brockovich*), Soderbergh's heroes are true outsiders.

They are also caught in a prism of sorts, the objects of a crystalline perspective created by Soderbergh's ultra-modernist style. Using dynamic manipulations of space and time, Soderbergh comments on his characters from numerous vantage points without shackling himself to any 'rules' of filmmaking. In fact, he seems to enjoy breaking as many rules as possible, and has crafted a distinct aesthetic by pushing the boundaries of popular cinematic expression. Although some of his films have more traditional linear narratives (*Kafka, King of the Hill, Erin Brockovich*, and to a lesser extent *sex, lies, and videotape*), Soderbergh's most interesting work is that which bears his signature of reconfigured chronology. He has developed a fractured, multi-dimensional structure that was initially quite confusing (*The Underneath, Schizopolis*) but has since been refined into an artful and inventive design (*Out of Sight*, *The Limey*, *Traffic*).

Soderbergh has experimented with many innovative devices to shift and layer time, taking the process far beyond traditional flashbacks. In *The Underneath*, Soderbergh created a labyrinthine, tripartite structure that intercuts past, present and future together to suggest their simultaneity in the mind of Michael Chambers (Peter Gallagher). The cues are primarily shifting tints relative to various time frames, resulting in a type of colour-coded temporal logic. *Out of Sight* also embraces a non-linear approach and additionally toys with the nature of time itself in its use of jump cuts, freeze frames, overlaps and flashbacks. The film's lively, sophisticated editing allows time to stop, start again, and retrace its steps as the narrative unravels. *The Limey* distils this fragmentation yet again, taking the overlapping images and sound of *Out of Sight* to the next level and further complicating our connection to the present. Dialogue is cut to overlap two or three locations. Wilson's haunting memories of his daughter Jenny, disconnected moments in planes and hotels, and various flashes of fantasy splinter the path of his obsessive quest. Consequently, time does not go forward in *The Limey* as much as it moves in ever expanding circles, dragging along the dead weight of the past every step of the way.

Soderbergh's films demonstrate an impressive film literacy, inviting the past into his narratives with numerous cinematic references and a studied reflexivity. Cinema history is recycled throughout his work in the form of source material (*Criss Cross*), characters (Michael Keaton reprising his *Jackie Brown* FBI agent, Ray Nicolet, in *Out of Sight*), direct citations (Wilson's off-camera shoot-out in *The Limey à la Public Enemy*), and even topics of conversation (Robert Redford movies from the 1970s: 'when he was young'). Soderbergh liberally samples stylistic innovations as well, such as the overlapping dialogue reminiscent of *The Graduate*, the editing experiments of the French New Wave, or the spirit of German Expressionism which lurks in every menacing shadow of *Kafka* – even the evil scientist is named Dr Murnau.

Soderbergh's films also feature many indirect references (*Easy Rider*, *The Long Goodbye*), homages (*The Collector*, *Point Blank*, *Teorema*) and parodies of films past (De Mille's pretentious introduction to *The Ten Commandments* mimicked in the opening monologue of *Schizopolis*). Perhaps Soderbergh's most provocative intertextual reference comes in *The Limey*, where he creates flashbacks to Terence Stamp's past by using original clips from

Poor Cow, one of the actor's early films. Both characters are thieves named Wilson, of course. This not only enlivens the ghosts of Wilson/Stamp that occupy the entire film, but it is also a profound realization of the manner in which the past is always present in Soderbergh's films.

Soderbergh refuses to quantify success, instead choosing to interpret it as 'doing the work you want to do'. Based on that definition, he has been remarkably successful. His double Best Director nomination at the 2001 Academy Awards (for *Erin Brockovich* and *Traffic*) and his surprising win for *Traffic*, attest that Soderbergh has finally attained success by Hollywood's definition. Yet he continues to push the medium's boundaries, retaining the spirit – if not always the funding – of a true independent. On the release of *Out of Sight*, Soderbergh joked that he was the 'cinematic equivalent of the locust', making a film once every nine years that people wanted to see. However, that seems to be changing with his recent triumphs. Perhaps the future of cinema is finally catching up with him.

Biography

Steven Soderbergh was born on 14 January 1963, in Georgia, USA, and was raised in Baton Rouge where he started making films at the age of 13. In high school, he made a series of Super-8 films and left for Hollywood promptly after graduation in 1980. Soderbergh became a freelance editor, but returned home to make shorts, write scripts and hone his technical skills. He began editing various Showtime programmes long distance and was eventually put in touch with the rock band Yes. The resulting concert film, *9012 Live*, was nominated for a Grammy in 1986. In 1987 he moved back to Los Angeles. Two of his scripts went into development, one of which was *sex, lies, and videotape*. Production began in 1988 and the film was premiered in January 1989 at the US Film Festival. He is divorced from actress Betsey Brantley, with whom he has a daughter, Sarah.

Filmography

9012 Live (1986) music documentary
sex, lies, and videotape (1989) also screenwriter, editor, uncredited sound editor
Kafka (1991) also editor
King of the Hill (1993) also screenwriter, editor

Fallen Angels (1993) Showtime television anthology series, *The Quiet Room*
The Underneath (1995) also screenwriter, credited as Sam Lowry
Schizopolis (1997) also writer, cinematographer, actor
Gray's Anatomy (1997)
Out of Sight (1998)
The Limey (1999)
Erin Brockovich (2000)
Traffic (2001)
Ocean's Eleven (2001)

As producer

Suture (1993) executive producer
The Daytrippers (1996)
Pleasantville (1998)

Further reading

Emanuel Levy, *Cinema of Outsiders: The Rise of American Independent Film*, New York, New York University Press, 1999.
John Pierson, *Spike, Mike, Slackers and Dykes: A Guided Tour Across a Decade of American Independent Cinema*, New York, Hyperion, 1997.
Steven Soderbergh, *Sex, lies, and videotape*, New York, Harper and Row, 1990.

JENNIFER HOLT

TODD SOLONDZ

In a late scene in writer/director Todd Solondz' *Happiness*, psychiatrist/pederast Bill Maplewood has a frank sexual discussion with his adolescent son, Billy, while awaiting arrest for raping two of the boy's schoolmates. It is an excruciating cinematic moment, where father reveals unspeakable desires and son pleads for affirmation of his own sexual self-worth, and the one most often cited in a heated debate which continues to surround the film. Like all controversial art, the cultural meaning of *Happiness* tends to precede it. Rejected by its original distributor (Universal/October Films) for its unflinching look at such sensitive subjects as paedophilia, rape fantasy, incest and adolescent sexuality, *Happiness* was the subject of polemics concerning art and obscenity long before the public had a chance to see it. When it was finally released by Good Machine, a distribution entity created by the film's producers, most critics had already either hailed it for exposing the dysfunction beneath the veneer of American life, or condemned it as prurient and exploitative. The unfortunate effect of such debates is to obscure the individual merits of artists and their work. With controversy, the substance of Solondz' work has been subsumed into others' causes of liberty and morality.

To understand the controversy surrounding *Happiness*, and the significance of Solondz' work in general, we begin with a question of mode. Film vaults are filled with paedophiles, sex-obsessed adolescents, rapists and suicides, but these figures exist only within accepted narrative boundaries. Child predators are monsters of fantasy (the Kid Catcher in *Chitty-Chitty Bang-Bang*) or fops in comedies of manners (*Lolita*'s Humbert Humbert); emerging sexuality is the stuff of teen comedy (from Andy Hardy to *American Pie*); rapists are the savage 'others' of tragedy (Silas Lynch in *Birth of a Nation*) or the madmen of thrillers (Max Cady in *Cape Fear*); and suicides haunt melodramas (*Ordinary People*). But Solondz mixes and matches these modes. In *Happiness*, a poet renowned for elegising the rape of an adolescent girl fantasizes being raped herself; a rejected lover on the verge of suicide uses words better suited to *The Way of the World* than *As the World Turns* to berate his jiltor; in a perverse revision of a teen sex comedy, Bill Maplewood masturbates in his car with a teenybopper magazine; and young Billy's angst over his sexual prowess plays as tragedy. Characters and scenes confound our expectations of appropriate actions (melodrama criminalizes voyeurism, teen comedy embraces it) and types (the nerdy dad, the feckless loser), compelling us to reconsider their relative merits.

If Solondz' compulsion to deconstruct expectations marks his work as truly independent (the experience of watching a film like *Happiness* is like no other), it also describes the trajectory of his career. Born and raised in the suburbs of Newark, New Jersey, his love of cinema developed while as an undergraduate at Yale University. It would lead him briefly to Los Angeles, where he tried his hand at screenwriting in the early 1980s, then to the film school of New York University. Though the technical aspects of filmmaking eluded Solondz – who claims to have had a dispensation excusing him from handling a camera – he distinguished himself as a writer and director: so much so that one of his comic shorts, *Schatt's Last Shot*, was chosen among NYU student work for an industry screening in 1986. The next day, Solondz found himself in the executive offices of 20th Century Fox. *Schatt's Last Shot*, which mines the familiar territory of dysfunctional relationships and the New York art scene, encouraged Fox, and later Columbia, to believe that they had found a Woody Allen for 'Generation X'. He was soon signed to multi-script writing contracts with both companies, writing and directing a feature for the Samuel Goldwyn Company. But when Goldwyn finally released Solondz' first feature, *Fear, Anxiety and Depression* (1989) – which stars the writer/director as Ira Ellis, a neurotic nebbish rehearsing his romantic failures – critics turned on him, audiences barely noticed, and Fox and Columbia terminated his contracts. The film's self-pitying tone and crude humour play more like a parody of Allen's monologic narcissism, and Solondz' ill-conceived blend of romantic and dark comedy frustrated rather than engaged viewers. In a particularly troubling scene, Ira stands by making desperate jokes while his girlfriend is being raped. Here the filmmaker tries to force an Allenesque theme – the nerdy wit in a world of horror – upon a scene that Allen would never attempt.

For a time, Solondz chose to accept the judgement of his critics and left filmmaking. Rejected by the Peace Corps, he spent several years teaching English to Russian immigrants (as will a character in *Happiness*), and hiding his professional past. But fear that early failure would be his cinematic legacy eventually led him back. In the early 1990s, he convinced backers to support production of a script written some time before: a dark comedy about a gawkish adolescent, Dawn 'Wiener Dog' Wiener (Heather Matarazzo), who attempts to navigate her way through a world of Jobian torments. If *Fear, Anxiety and Depression* strained against the conventions of the romantic comedy, the setting and characters of *Welcome to the Dollhouse* were custom-made to communicate Solondz' sensibilities. Again, he mixes modes. Dawn Wiener's story is the waking nightmare of the social outcast, told not as surreal horror/fantasy but a dark comedy of manners. Her daily tortures are neither exaggerated nor justified: they merely occur as a matter of social course. As Dawn's classmate tells her when she asks why no high school boy would ever touch her, 'Sorry, Dawn, that's just the way it is.' The cruel logic of social order stabilizes the narrative and allows Solondz to amplify issues raised in the earlier film. For example, sexual aggression: Brandon (Brendan Sexton Jr), the only boy to show interest in Dawn, repeatedly threatens to rape her. She first responds to these threats with fear, then resignation, and a brief romance ensues when, meeting no resistance, Brandon admits his affection for her. By combining the hegemony of social order borrowed from the comedy of manners with dark comedy's cynicism,

Solondz is able to resolve the victim/aggressor relationship in one of the film's rare moments of humanity.

Such talents were rewarded when *Dollhouse* won the Grand Jury Prize at the Sundance Film Festival and seven Independent Spirit Awards (including Best Director, Best Feature and Best Debut Performance for Matarazzo and Sexton). Success returned attention to a filmmaker long forgotten and, in words strikingly similar to those used earlier by executives at Fox and Columbia, critics hailed Solondz as a visionary of his generation, a harbinger of what was being called the 'New Geek Cinema': an emerging body of work that would give voice to outsiders and the brutalized. Unlike misfit voices to come before it – from James Dean to Johnny Rotten – these would be sustained not by bravado, but persistence. Like Dawn Wiener in the very last scene of *Dollhouse*, drowning out the gibes of her fellows by insistently repeating a tune to herself, Solondz' rehearsal of geek life would mediate horror by drowning it out. Many critics read the film as an elegiac revision of Solondz' own past (citing physical similarities between the director and young Heather Matarazzo, and the film's suburban New Jersey setting), though the filmmaker admits no more than sympathy with Wiener Dog's plight, describing it as a story of survival and applauding her for resisting the self-destructive impulse.

Challenging *Dollhouse*'s near-universal approbation, Solondz' next film complicates issues of sympathy and advocacy by giving voice to a set of outsiders many of us would rather not hear: paedophiles and rapists, murderers and thieves, the feared and the despised. If Weiner Dog's tune serves to keep her head above water, these are people deeply submerged in their own desperation and ugliness. *Happiness* is much more raw and direct than Solondz' previous works. If *Fear, Anxiety and Depression* is crudely playful (it is, after all, a romantic comedy of sorts) and *Dollhouse* is entangled in the social strata of adolescence, *Happiness* is an uncomfortably intimate look at lineaments of the world we all occupy. Where David Lynch uses the manufactured surface of American life as a springboard into a bizarre alternative, Solondz reveals what exists just below its surface, by carefully peeling it away and compelling us to look in. Unlike the news media, which Solondz accuses of turning criminality into titillation or moral grandstanding, *Happiness* stirs the viewer by revealing rather than reading the subtext. The result is disturbing precisely because it is so little mediated. We applaud honesty and disclosure in principle, but are sickened when it exposes us directly to perversion. He is careful to avoid letting the camera signify too much, showing us neither the many criminal acts that occur during the course of the film (child rape, murder, theft, etc.), nor the condemnation and punishment of the perpetrators. We infer our own judgements from a skeleton of words and impressions. As witnesses, our role vacillates between voyeur and captive audience: we watch from a fixed position. He employs relatively few cuts, and usually figures a conversation with participants framed together. The scene, setting and drama are self-contained, and reveal only as much as the characters will.

This intimacy is further complicated by the comic nature of the film. Comedy is, after all, a matter of spectacle and contrast: the striding confidence of the victim before he slips on the banana peel, and the chaotic motion of his fall. A common objection raised to *Happiness* is that it plays these scenes like a sick joke, where the pretence of familial order contrasts the outrageousness of the discussion. Others describe the film in terms of parody or satire. Parody is, after all, the upending of expectations and accepted models. But unlike parody, which exaggerates the generic discourse by reflecting it through a comic hall of mirrors (John Waters' *Serial Mom*, for example), Solondz' film neutralizes the effects of its discourses – where fantasy equals escapism, tragedy catharsis, and comedy pleasure – by subjecting them to opposing forces. What results is not a mutation-like tragi-comedy, where alternating discourses heighten the effect of each, but a flattened narrative, where the audience is denied the fear, pity and pleasure we normally associate with tragedy and comedy. His is the sort of comedy that rarely compels us to laugh, and a tragedy that pre-empts tears.

Happiness does not lack action, emotion or expressive perfor-mances, but because characters are so isolated and closeted, words and actions effect their local space rather than extending it (dramatic narrative is, in part, catalysation from scene to scene). Solondz' execution of dialogue and action has drawn comparisons to Hal Hartley and David Mamet, but where these writer/directors create rich, ornate, self-involved games with dialogue and action, Solondz' characters attempt to speak plainly and out of their isolation. It is their honesty and self-awareness, not their irony, which makes the words so razing. Similar comparisons have been made to the raw, immediate work of John Cassavetes who, like Solondz, favoured an ensemble approach, intimate settings and uncomfortable subject matter, and to neo-realism, with its halting, fragmentary movement and naturalistic pace and setting. But Solondz' work is far more mannered. Cassavetes relied heavily on improvisation and the neorealists allow reality to reveal its truths and contradictions in fits and starts, while Solondz proceeds with a didactic, if ubiquitous, formalism rooted not in art cinema, but in television.

Dollhouse began as a reaction to the *Wonder Years*, which Solondz describes as a fantastical representation of youth. His version tells the story of a family trapped in an ideal that it will never realize – of an *Ozzie and Harriet* family in a *Brady Bunch* home – and of an adolescent who recognizes the limitations such an ideal imposes. Here all things *must* stay in their place, including scapegoats and victims. The film is about naming the pretensions of our existence: the 'dollhouses' in which some of us live (and from which others are excluded), the values we hold (trust, self-love, talent, family, etc.) and what lies behind them. Primary among these values is the pursuit of 'happiness'. But in a world where such is tangled in a web of necessity and ambition, we locate its model in the cultural simulacra of Andy Taylor's Mayberry and Jerry Seinfeld's Manhattan. To breach this utopia, Solondz populates his films with extreme versions of television types (the *Brady Bunch* family that really *does* scapegoat the middle child, the Ward Cleaver dad who rapes children), casting actors best known for their television roles (Louise Lasser, Jon Lovitz, Molly Shannon, Lara Flynn Boyle, Camryn Manheim, Cynthia Stevenson).

Solondz is not the first director to mine this vein of popular culture. Perhaps the best example is Quentin Tarantino's resurrection of John Travolta. But if Tarantino fetishizes popular icons and forms (gangster myth, pulp novel, blaxploitation film), Solondz transcribes them to exploit and manipulate their functionality. Compare Tarantino's use of Travolta in *Pulp Fiction* to Solondz' of Jon Lovitz in *Happiness*. The first plays very much to type: a cool, sweet, confident tough-guy in danger of losing out to his own self-indulgence. Vincent Vega is a latter-day version of Vinny Barberino from *Welcome Back, Kotter* or Tony Manero from *Saturday Night Fever*. But Lovitz' character, the vengeful suicide spewing words of heartfelt hate and pain, is the ugly, repressed side of Lovitz' glib, self-enclosed liars from countless *Saturday Night Live* sketches. If much of our pleasure in Travolta's *Pulp Fiction* performance depends upon our knowledge of earlier roles (particularly the dancing sequence at Jackrabbit Slim's), what we know about Lovitz complicates our response to this performance. Rather than cutting the bitterness of the scene by playing the false bravado that has made Lovitz famous, he allows associations to sour against his deadpan, making the scene still more bitter. The Lovitz we know from television haunts this version, rather than enlivening it.

More than an interest in and appeal to a television sensibility, Solondz' films exploit specific narrative elements of the form as a way of plugging viewers into an otherwise nebulous narrative order. In the situation comedy, for example, narrative action is merely a structure to support a series of jokes, product placements, and public service announcements about teen sex, racism, drugs, and other topics of the day. Sitcoms are designed to deliver messages, not catharsis or clarification, and are driven by inevitability, not revelation or intrigue. Like sitcoms, Solondz' scenes are episodic and self-contained. Though the intricate web of relations in *Happiness* (each character is in some way connected to all others) has been compared to the multi-narrative work of Robert Altman and Paul Thomas Anderson, Solondz uses it to emphasize how very *dis*connected his characters are from each other. Their deeds and words occur in isolation, in the intimate settings familiar to television viewers: family room, restaurant booth, office. When connected, these scenes reveal not narrative continuity or resolution, but a profound level of misunderstanding or miscommunication (the primary narrative functions of sitcoms). If Altman and Anderson revel in tracking shots and elegant editing sequences to establish a unity of actions and characters, Solondz, by contrast, uses the static staging and framing that are the legacy of the live television audience to atomize and flatten characters and their actions.

Television's ubiquity and flatness allow Solondz to figure grave subjects as forces of gravity. The force that brings a character like Bill Maplewood down is an entropic one: a movement towards self-betrayal, instability and death. Solondz describes Maplewood as one who struggles with, and finally gives into, a desire that he can no longer bury or modulate. He is what the director calls 'a bleeding soul', in a losing battle with a monster living inside of him. And, as with all entropic forces, the inevitable result of this battle is flat, undifferentiated chaos. Solondz is often criticized for being sadistic to his characters, for forcing them to occupy that chaos with no room to navigate, but it is here, ironically, that he discovers the greatest hope. Chaos lacks alterity or 'otherness'. As Solondz explained in a 1998 interview with the *Boston Phoenix*, 'to not dismiss something as other makes us more fully human'. Chaos breeds the desperation that forces a sex offender to reach out to his frustrated son, and the understanding that is only possible through the greatest degree of honesty.

In a world where the bounds of isolation are everyday fortified, where television and information technology mediate our primary contact with the global village and personal revelations are made using electronic aliases, the best and worst truths about ourselves emerge (witness the prevalence of paedophilia on the Internet). Todd Solondz' films attempt to address these truths: not to shock, but to communicate and comprehend all that makes us human. If Bill Maplewood finally does succumb to the monster inside of himself, his confession of weakness is a father's gift to the boy, who imagines his delayed sexual development a measure of personal weakness. In a scene echoing the intimate father–son talks that complete most episodes of *Leave it to Beaver*, Bill Maplewood bears the paternal mantle with a seriousness beyond Ward Cleaver, restoring at highest personal cost his son's self-esteem. In the ultimate mixing of modes, the monster of fantasy attempts to restore the familial order ravaged by tragedy. It is a feat as unlikely as dead Laius restoring blind Oedipus' sight, but what makes *Happiness*, and all of Solondz' work, so controversial is that the film holds out a vague hope that the monster may actually succeed.

Biography

Todd Solondz was born in 1960, in Newark, New Jersey, USA. He graduated from Yale University with a Bachelor of Arts in English (1981), and lived briefly in Los Angeles before enrolling in New York University's film school in 1983 (but dropped out in 1986). He currently lives in New York City.

Filmography

As writer/director

Feelings (1984) student film
Babysitter (1984) student film
Schatt's Last Shot (1985) student film
How I Became a Leading Artistic Figure in New York City's East Village Cultural Landscape (1986) short film for *Saturday Night Live*
Fear, Anxiety and Depression (1989)
Welcome to the Dollhouse (1995; aka *Middle Child*) also producer
Happiness (1998)

Further reading

Sean Axmaker (1998) 'A Chat with Todd Solondz', *Nitrate Online*. Online.

Available HTTP: < http://www.nitrateonline.com/fhappiness.html > (posted 30 October 1998).

Bert Cardullo, 'The Happiness of Your Friends and Neighbors', *Hudson Review*, vol. 52, no. 3, 1999, pp. 455–62.

Chris Chang, 'Cruel to be Kind: A Brief History of Todd Solondz', *Film Comment*, vol. 34, no. 5, 1998, pp. 72–5.

Andrew Lewis Conn, 'The Bad Review *Happiness* Deserves Or: The Tyranny of Critic-Proof Movies', *Film Comment*, vol. 35, no. 1, 1999, pp. 70–2.

Alice Cross, 'Surviving Adolescence with Dignity: An Interview with Todd Solondz', *Cineaste*, vol. 22, no. 3, 1996, pp. 24–8.

Peter Keough (1998) 'Welcome to the Filmmaker', *Boston Phoenix*. Online. Available HTTP: < http://bostonphoenix.com/archive/ movies/98/10/22/ SOLONDZ.html > (posted 22 October 1998).

Adam Pincus (1996) 'In Profile: Todd Solondz', *Sundance Channel Online*. Online. Available HTTP: < http://www.sundancechannel.com/profile/ solondz/ > (posted January 1996).

Randy Pitman, 'Fear, Anxiety and Depression' (video review), *Library Journal*, vol. 115, no. 12, 1990, p. 148.

Scott Roesch (1996) 'Todd Solondz Welcomes the World to His Dollhouse', *Mr. Showbiz*. Online, Available HTTP: < http://mrshowbiz.go.com/ interviews/122 > (posted April 1996).

Todd Solondz, *Happiness*, London, Faber and Faber, 1998.

Welcome to the Dollhouse, website maintained by *Sony Pictures Classics Online* (includes 'Director's Notes' and 'About the Filmmaker' by Todd Solondz). Online. Available HTTP: < http://www.spe.sony.com /classics;/ welcome/index.html > (posted May 1996).

DEAN DEFINO

STEVEN SPIELBERG

Few artists have shaped popular culture since the 1970s as much as Steven Spielberg. When Andrew Sarris wrote that '*E.T.* has emerged as the closest thing we have to a universal religion',[1] he nicely captured the centrality and import of Spielberg's work in modern western culture. Spielberg's work can be divided into two categories: fantastic adventure films for the whole family, such as *E.T.*, and serious adult-oriented dramas about important historical issues (*The Color Purple, Empire of the Sun, Schindler's List, Amistad, Saving Private Ryan*). Spielberg's biggest commercial hits are in the first category, and those that have received the most critical acclaim (including Academy Awards) are in the second. However, his main stylistic and thematic concerns cut across this divide.

For example, the intense and fearful exhilaration created by a freely and rapidly moving camera is central to sequences employing hand-held cameras and aerial shots in *Schindler's List*, *Saving Private Ryan* and *Empire of the Sun*, as well as to the rollercoaster rides depicted in the Indiana Jones films. Soft-focus cinematography, eerie lighting, lush colours and *mise-en-scène* can be found in *The Color Purple* and *Empire of the Sun* as well as in *E.T.* and *Close Encounters of the Third Kind*. Suspense and extreme physical violence are at the heart of *Jaws*, the Indiana Jones trilogy and the Jurassic Park movies as well as all of Spielberg's serious dramas. On a thematic level, problematic father-figures – weak, absent, abusive or irresponsible – can be found in *Jaws*, *Close Encounters of the Third Kind* and *E.T.*, *The Color Purple*, *Indiana Jones and the Last Crusade*, *Empire of the Sun*, *Hook*, *Jurassic Park* and *Schindler's List*. Children's experiences, often presented from a child's point of view, are also central to many of these films. Slavery is the subject of both *Indiana Jones and the Temple of Doom* and *Amistad*. The moral weakness, corruption even, of authority figures due to greed or power lust is as central to *Jaws* and *1941* as it is to *Amistad* and *Schindler's List*. The rise of fascism and/or the Second World War are the focus of *1941*, the first and last Indiana Jones films, *Empire of the Sun*, *Schindler's List* and *Saving Private Ryan*.

Finally, to return to Sarris' comment, while *Schindler's List* is usually perceived as Spielberg's coming to terms with Jewish history and religion, all three Indiana Jones films deal with religious mythology (Jewish, Indian and Christian), and both *Close Encounters* and *E.T.* can be understood as messianic pictures (on the surface, *E.T.* would appear to have a distinctly Christian flavour, with E.T. as a Christ-like figure). In any case, almost all Spielberg films, whether fantasy adventure or serious drama, culminate in scenes of redemption and/or spiritual renewal (which may come in life or in death). There is, for example, the final union of Captain Ahab-like Quint with the 'great white one' in *Jaws*, the ascension of Roy Neary in *Close Encounters*, and of the extra-terrestrial in *E.T.*, the revitalization of the old in Spielberg's segment of *Twilight Zone – The Movie*, the sparing of Indy and Marion during the climactic opening of the ark in *Raiders of the Lost Ark*, Albert's redemptive actions and the lifting of Celie's curse in *The Color Purple*, Pete Sandich's acceptance of his own death in *Always*, and the final cemetery scene cherishing the life, and mourning the death, of a 'righteous' man both in *Schindler's List* and in *Saving Private Ryan*.

Indeed, noting the fundamental similarities between Spielberg's fantasy adventures and serious dramas, one could go so far as to say that, rather than being evidence of the 'maturing' of Spielberg as a person and artist, the 'adult' films he made from 1985 onwards merely isolate one element of his work already present in his previous juvenile and children's films. Consequently, his most complex and fully realized films are not the Academy Award-winning dramas *Schindler's List* and *Saving Private Ryan*, but his biggest hits, the fantasy adventures *E.T.* and *Jaws*. While seemingly simplistic, special effects-driven, all-American and cloyingly senti-mental, Spielberg's most popular fantasy adventures are in fact complexly structured stories and spectacles focusing on child-like or rejuvenated characters, placed in archetypal situations that resonate deeply across cultural, social and political boundaries and provoke experiences which at their best are incredibly exciting, deeply emotional and indeed spiritual.

In other words, Spielberg is a modern myth-maker. Like the *Star Wars* films of friend and collaborator George Lucas, Spielberg's fantasy adventures have brought a contemporary perspective and cutting-edge technology to the fairytales, myths and religious tales which underpin (not only) western civilization, and updated these ancient stories for the late twentieth, and indeed the twenty-first century, with movie theatres (once again) functioning as modern temples and cathedrals. At the same time, of course, Spielberg has also used the movie theatre as a forum for public debate of important issues in western history, ranging from slavery to the Holocaust.

By using the movie theatre as a highly public, yet also deeply mystical site of sensual stimulation, emotional release, spiritual renewal and political debate, Spielberg (together with Lucas) has revitalized Hollywood cinema, returning it to the centre of contemporary culture, from which it had previously been displaced by broadcasting and other cultural industries. Today, Hollywood movies not only generate more money at the American box office than ever before, they also dominate most of the international marketplace. They are the primary products of a range of new media delivery systems (such as cable and satellite television, video and DVD), and their theatrical release serves as the launch-pad for a vast array of product lines and other commercial tie-ins and promotions.

The recent merger between the Internet giant AOL and the world's largest media corporation Time Warner, confirmed that the old Hollywood studios and their theatrical features are at the very centre of the integrated entertainment, communications and computer industry of the twenty-first century. To no small degree, this was made possible by the films Spielberg and Lucas have been making since the mid-1970s, and the media companies that these two filmmakers founded (Lucasfilm, Industrial Light and Magic, Amblin Entertainment and DreamWorks SKG) will be key corporate players in the cutting-edge industries of the new millennium. If confirmation of their important role is needed, it is perhaps provided by the fact that one of the main investors in DreamWorks, formed in 1994 by Spielberg with ex-Disney executive Jeffrey Katzenberg and music mogul David Geffen as the first new major Hollywood studio since the 1930s, is Paul Allen, co-founder (with Bill Gates) of Microsoft. Steven Spielberg moves in influential circles indeed.

The question is: who is Spielberg? And how did he achieve this pre-eminence? We can begin to answer this question by looking at what Spielberg was doing in 1998. The summer of 1998 saw the release of the Second World War combat movie *Saving Private Ryan*, the seventeenth feature film (not counting numerous amateur and television films) to be directed by Spielberg since his début, the tragi-comic road movie *The Sugarland Express*, in 1974. *Saving Private Ryan* won Spielberg the Academy Award for Best Director for the second time (the first was for the Holocaust drama, *Schindler's List*, in 1993).

Saving Private Ryan also became the third highest grossing film of the year, both in the US and abroad, surpassed only by the historical disaster epic *Titanic* and the sci-fi disaster movie *Armageddon*.[2] Further down the list of top grossing movies of 1998, many more films in which Spielberg was involved can be found, for example his asteroid movie, *Deep Impact*, and the historical adventure, *The Mask of Zorro*, both of which he produced, as well as the animated features *Antz*, *Small Soldiers* and *The Prince of Egypt*, which his company DreamWorks produced and distributed.

While Spielberg, through his production company Amblin Entertainment (formed in 1984), continues to make films for other major studios such as Paramount, in 1998 his main focus was on producing films for DreamWorks, his own multi-media corporation which engages in the production and distribution of television programmes, records, computer games and, most importantly, movies. Spielberg's focus on the company paid off, and DreamWorks achieved a 7 per cent share of the US cinema market in 1998.[3] With only seven films on release, it generated US box-office revenues of $475 million, more than quadrupling the revenues of the previous year and closing in on the market leaders Disney, TimeWarner, Paramount, Sony and Fox, which released many more films.

Through the products of his various companies, Spielberg also maintained his presence on television screens around the world. In addition to popular broadcasts of his movies, the DreamWorks sit-com *Spin City* played well in the US and abroad, while the Amblin-produced hospital drama serial *ER*, which came out of discussions with best-selling author Michael Crichton in the early 1990s (the other major result was, of course, the sci-fi adventure film *Jurassic Park*), was well on the way to becoming one of the most popular and influential television series of all time. The most popular series of the first part of the 1998/9 season, *ER* has ranked highly ever since its first season in 1994/5, when it also won several Emmy Awards and paved the way for the revival of the drama series (over sitcoms) on US network television.[4]

The list of all-time US box-office successes, compiled at the end of 1998, also featured Spielberg prominently: two instalments of the Indiana Jones adventure series, *Indiana Jones and the Temple of Doom* and *Indiana Jones and the Last Crusade* (ranked at numbers 35 and 26 respectively); *Saving Private Ryan* (no. 28); *Lost World: Jurassic Park* (no. 18); the first Indiana Jones movie, *Raiders of the Lost Ark* (no. 14); the horror-adventure film *Jaws* (no. 11); *Jurassic Park* (no. 4); and *E.T.* (no. 3).[5] Thus, eight of the seventeen films directed by Spielberg made it into the top 35. George Lucas – who was famously supported by Spielberg when it came to the making of *Star Wars*, and who worked with him on the Indiana Jones trilogy – had his sci-fi trilogy placed at numbers 2, 7 and 9. Spielberg's protégés, Robert Zemeckis and Chris Columbus, whose careers were started with scripts that Spielberg turned into the films *1941*, *Gremlins* and *The Goonies*, were responsible for further entries in this list: the picaresque historical comedy-drama *Forrest Gump* ranked at number 5; the children's comedy *Home Alone* at 10; the family comedy-drama, *Mrs Doubtfire*, at 19; and *Back to the Future* (which Spielberg produced) at 22. Finally, two further Spielberg productions – the sci-fi comedy-adventure, *Men in Black* and the romantic action-adventure, *Twister* – were ranked at numbers 13 and 15 respectively. Thus, almost half of the top 35 all-time hits were made by Spielberg and/or his main collaborators and protégés.

When this list is adjusted for inflation, Spielberg's place in the history of popular Hollywood cinema is even more pronounced, and the historical influences on, and models for, his work come into view. The top 25 includes ten films made since 1975, four of which were by Spielberg, plus Lucas' *Star Wars* trilogy.[6] If only a film's first cinema release were counted, *E.T.* would come out on top. A look at the most popular films of the pre-1975 period reveals the only serious competition for Spielberg (and Lucas) as the most popular filmmaker of all time: Walt Disney. Disney's animated features and the live-action musical comedy *Mary Poppins* account for six of the top 25 films.[7] A look at the top sell-through videos of all time confirms this, with nine Disney films in the top 15 (three made during Walt's reign), and also *Jurassic Park, E.T., Men in Black* and *Forrest Gump*.[8]

Disney films and entrepreneurial activities provide a model for Spielberg's and Lucas' fantastic family films, such as *Star Wars* and *E.T.*, as well as for the links between these films and other sectors of the entertainment industry (for example, the toy industry which was licensed to sell *Star Wars* and *E.T.*-related products, the rides based on such films which were installed at amusement parks, the high-tech special effects and sound companies founded by Lucas, the numerous and often animated television programmes produced by Spielberg). Disney's obsession with incomplete or dysfunctional families and children's emotional traumas as played out in his animated features served as an important inspiration for Spielberg's filmmaking.

Spielberg has acknowledged this debt to Disney in his films. For example, he transformed the scene from Disney's animated classic *Peter Pan*, in which the eternal boy and the Darling children fly across the moon-filled night sky, into the very similar iconic image of Elliot and E.T. riding a bike in the air across the backdrop of a full moon, an image he then adopted as the logo for Amblin. Furthermore, going against the original novel's depiction of billionaire amusement park creator John Hammond as a ruthless, greedy, dehumanized tycoon, Spielberg's *Jurassic Park* presents a touching portrait of Hammond as over-enthusiastic yet kind and gentle, a grandfatherly as well as child-like entertainer, who wants nothing more than to share his enjoyment of technologically created entertainment magic and adventure with all the people in the world, especially children. This is not only Spielberg's self-portrait of the artist-entertainer as an old man, but also a tribute to Uncle Walt. (It is perhaps one of the more painful ironies of twentieth-century popular culture that Walt Disney has been accused of anti-Semitism).

Thus, if Spielberg can be seen, and obviously sees himself, as a kind of reincarnation of Walt Disney, another look at the all-time American top box-office successes reveals a second prominent tradition that Spielberg has drawn on. In addition to Disney films and a few 'New Hollywood' films of the late 1960s and early 1970s, the highest ranked pre-1975 films on this list are the romantic epics

Gone with the Wind, *The Sound of Music* and *Doctor Zhivago*, and the religious epics *The Ten Commandments*, *Ben-Hur* and *The Robe*.[9] These films share a focus on their protagonists' emotional and/or spiritual growth (as well as moving their audiences, often to tears) in times of comprehensive social and political upheaval, which are in fact defining moments in world history (the founding of major world religions, the American Civil War, the Russian Revolution, the rise of fascism and the Second World War). Spielberg is clearly influenced by this grand filmmaking tradition. Not only has he explicitly stated that he admires David Lean probably more than any other filmmaker, Spielberg has also produced a string of historical epics, which depict their central characters' emotional and spiritual growth in turbulent times, most notably during the Second World War (in *Empire of the Sun*, *Schindler's List* and *Saving Private Ryan*).

From the start of his career, Spielberg's filmmaking had been concerned with the Second World War (for example, his 1960 8mm film *Fighter Squad*); he returned to this preoccupation many times before making his 'serious' historical epics. The war is the backdrop or at least an important (future) reference point in *Raiders of the Lost Ark* (and again in *Indiana Jones and the Last Crusade* – in both films the Nazis are seeking the ultimate weapon for the looming war), the slapstick comedy *1941* and, indirectly, in the romantic drama *Always* which, although set in contemporary times, is a remake of the Second World War drama, *A Guy Named Joe*. *Jaws* contains a similarly indirect, yet crucial reference to the war: Quint's Indianapolis speech, which links the events of the summer of 1975 depicted in the film to the delivery of the atom bomb to Japan exactly thirty years earlier, was not included in the novel, and adds important historical resonance to the film's events.

Often in conjunction with his obsession with the war, which in part derives from the stories told to him by his father, many of Spielberg's films are centrally concerned with ethnicity and race. This is most obviously the case in *Schindler's List*, which deals with the Nazis' systematic murder of the Jews, and in *Amistad*, which looks at the international trade in slaves from black Africa in the nineteenth century. Furthermore, the background for the sexual oppression of black women in *The Color Purple* is provided by an extremely oppressive racist society, exemplified by the treatment received by Sophia (Oprah Winfrey). These themes are also central to Spielberg's fantasy films, especially *Close Encounters of the Third Kind* and *E.T.*, both of which deal with truly 'interracial' communication and friendship between human beings and extraterrestrials. Finally, while it took Spielberg a long time to direct a film which explicitly reflected his Jewish background, he collaborated with Lucas on the tale of the lost ark (a cornerstone of Judaism), and selected the story of his immigrant grandparents as the basis for Amblin's animated feature, *An American Tail* (1986). Furthermore, although Richard Dreyfuss – one of Hollywood's most high-profile Jewish performers – has never been cast in an explicitly Jewish role by Spielberg, he is the actor with whom Spielberg throughout his career has most frequently worked (using him as an alter-ego of sorts, in his breakthrough films *Jaws* and *Close Encounters*, as well as in his first romance *Always* in 1989).

Spielberg is both decidedly Jewish and a spiritual universalist, a socially concerned citizen of the world and possibly the greatest entertainer of the last decades of the twentieth century, a great stylist and successful entrepreneur. In his work, Spielberg combines two dominant traditions in Hollywood filmmaking, namely the tradition of family entertainment, which is best exemplified by the work of Walt Disney, and the tradition of historical epics, the last master of which was Spielberg's idol David Lean. While Spielberg, the filmmaker, is thus a cross between Disney and Lean (with a healthy dose of Hitchcockian suspense and Wellesian wunderkind baroque), he is also a movie mogul in the mould of the Jewish founding fathers of Hollywood. He combines the almost unrestricted power of New York-based corporate leaders like Adolph Zukor with the extravagant, yet meticulous, management style of Los Angeles-based studio heads like Louis B. Mayer, and the striving for total artistic control of Hollywood's greatest 'independent' producer, David O. Selznick. Together with George Lucas, Steven Spielberg is indeed the heir of the almighty Hollywood of old.

Biography

Spielberg was born on 18 December 1946, in Cincinnati, USA, to Arnold and Leah Spielberg. He began to make 8mm amateur films in 1957, including the 16mm science fiction feature *Firelight* (1964). He worked as an intern at Universal Studios in the summers of 1964 and 1965, and went on to study film at California State College at Long Beach (from 1965), at the same time continuing his unpaid, informal 'apprenticeship' at Universal. In 1968, he signed a seven-year contract as television director with Universal, and dropped out of college. Spielberg directed his first television programme in 1969.

Notes

1 A. Sarris, 'Is There Life After *E.T.?*', *The Village Voice*, 21 September 1982, p. 47.
2 The Editors of *Variety*: *The Variety Insider*, New York, Perigree, 1999, p. 62.
3 *Variety*, 11 January 1999, p. 9.
4 Editors of *Variety*, *op. cit.*, pp. 263–4 and pp. 292–6.
5 *Ibid.*, pp. 64–5.
6 *Ibid.*, p. 66.
7 *Ibid.*
8 *Screen International*, 26 June 1998, p. 9.
9 Editors of *Variety*, *op. cit.*
10 For details of Spielberg's amateur films and television programmes, as well as extensive producer credits, see J. McBride, *Steven Spielberg: A Biography*, London, Faber and Faber, 1997, pp. 501–8; and P.M. Taylor, *Steven Spielberg*, 3rd edition, London, Batsford, 1999.

Filmography[10]

Duel (1971) made-for-television movie (European theatrical release: 1972/3; US theatrical release: 1983)
The Sugarland Express (1974) also co-writer
Jaws (1975)
Close Encounters of the Third Kind (1977; special edition released in 1980) also writer
1941 (1979)
Raiders of the Lost Ark (1981)
E.T. – The Extra-Terrestrial (1982) original idea by Spielberg, also producer
Twilight Zone – The Movie (1983) 'Segment 2', also producer
Indiana Jones and the Temple of Doom (1984)
The Color Purple (1985) also producer
Empire of the Sun (1987) also producer
Indiana Jones and the Last Crusade (1989)
Always (1989) also producer
Hook (1991)
Jurassic Park (1993)
Schindler's List (1993) also producer
The Lost World: Jurassic Park (1997)
Amistad (1997) also producer
Saving Private Ryan (1998) also producer

Further reading

N. Andrews, *Jaws: Bloomsbury Movie Guide no. 5*, London, Bloomsbury, 1999.
J. Baxter, *Steven Spielberg: The Unauthorized Biography*, London, HarperCollins, 1996.
—— *George Lucas: A Biography*, New York, HarperCollins, 1999.

P. Biskind, *Easy Riders, Raging Bulls: How the Sex-Drugs-and-Rock 'n' Roll Generation Saved Hollywood*, New York, Simon and Schuster, 1998.

D. Brode, *The Films of Steven Spielberg*, New York, Citadel, 1995.

C. Champlin, *George Lucas: The Creative Impulse. Lucasfilm's First Twenty Years*, rev. edn, London, Virgin, 1997.

L.D. Friedman and B. Notbohm (eds) *Steven Spielberg: Interviews*, Jackson, University Press of Mississippi, 2000.

A. Gordon, 'Science-Fiction and Fantasy Film Criticism: The Case of Lucas and Spielberg', *Journal of the Fantastic in the Arts*, vol. 2, no. 2, 1989, pp. 81–94.

C. Green *et al.*, 'Steven Spielberg: A Celebration', *Journal of Popular Film*, vol. 18, no. 4, 1991, pp. 172–8.

G. Jenkins, *Empire Building: The Remarkable, Real-life Story of Star Wars*, London, Simon and Schuster, 1998.

P. Krämer, 'Would You Take Your Child to See This Film? The Cultural and Social Work of the Family-Adventure Movie', in S. Neale and M. Smith (eds) *Contemporary Hollywood Cinema*, London, Routledge, 1998, pp. 294–311.

Y. Loshitzky (ed.) *Spielberg's Holocaust: Critical Perspectives on Schindler's List*, Bloomington, Indiana University Press, 1997.

H. Maxford, *The George Lucas Companion*, London, Batsford, 1999.

F. Palowski, *Witness: The Making of Schindler's List*, trans. Anna and Robert G. Ware, London, Orion, 1998.

D. Pollock, *Skywalking: The Life and Times of George Lucas*, rev. edn, New York, Da Capo, 1999.

G. Perry, *Steven Spielberg: The Making of His Movies*, London, Orion, 1998 (includes unabridged *Variety* reviews and credits).

C. Salewicz, *George Lucas*, London, Orion Media, 1999.

A. Yule, *Steven Spielberg: Father of the Man*, London, Little, Brown, 1996.

PETER KRÄMER

OLIVER STONE

> I don't set out to make movies about big, controversial themes. I just make movies about what has happened to my life ... I have to keep digging into our history to understand what happened to me and my generation.
>
> Oliver Stone[1]

> 'Your lies are old, but you tell them well.'
>
> Jon Voight in *U-Turn*

The archetypal 'Oliver Stone' moment can usefully be located in a key event in recent American history, captured on celluloid by a different filmmaker entirely. In the lengthy courtroom scenes towards the climax of Stone's most controversial film, *JFK*,

Capra-esque everyman Jim Garrison (Kevin Costner) insistently plays and re-plays the infamous Zapruder film for the benefit of both diegetic jury and extra-textual audience. What we see in graphic, fetishistic detail is in many ways a cinematic metonym for the Stone aesthetic of 'enlightenment through visual assault'[2] and the formal *excess* that entails. In a rhetorical effort to awaken his complacent audience(s) to the 'truth' of the Kennedy assassination, Garrison/Stone unveils the visceral, violent reality of 'America' through a glass darkly in the grainy frames of Zapruder's text: 'This is the key *shot*', he intones over the footage, a brutal *cinéma vérité* intended to subvert and dissipate the false consciousness and complacency of America's unwary, delusional subjects.

As youthful product of the baby-boom and Eisenhower's USA, so the story goes, the 1960s were for William Oliver Stone a series of 'holocaustal events', the primal scene of contemporary American social and political history; traumatic episodes which 'cannot simply be forgotten and put out of mind, but neither can they be adequately remembered; which is to say, clearly and ambiguously identified as to their meaning and contextualized in the group memory in such a way as to reduce the shadow they cast over the group's capacities to go into its present and envision a future free of their debilitating effects'.[3] It is principally the compulsive return *to*, and mythopoetic re-imaginings *of*, this volatile period and its aftermath which has ensured Stone's status as Hollywood's leading auteur-*provocateur*. As Robert Kolker suggests, through his portentous quasi-revisionist explorations and invocations of history, power, politics and paranoia in contemporary American culture, 'he has become a more controversial, written about, admired and despised figure than any filmmaker in recent memory'.[4] Yet this notoriety also signifies his position as auteur-*star*, for any discussion of 'the films of Oliver Stone' is unavoidably also a sojourn into the director's star image and its accompanying biography; in other words, an illustration of the processes involved in the construction of a *marketable* auteur discourse.

The quasi-symbiotic relationship between the iconoclastic Stone persona and his films has been perpetuated and reinforced in both popular and critical representations, extending into discussion of his early screenplays and emergence as a major Hollywood player. Here we uncover the bare bones of the Stone *œuvre*: the lone, isolated male protagonist embodying the potential for both good and evil; the mythic *rite-de-passage* narrative structure, typically involving a quasi-spiritual journey from a state of innocence, through suffering and experience, to a state of knowledge and either redemption or destruction; colourful, testosterone-driven and often didactic dialogue; and a preoccupation with extreme violence and death. (The deserts and Symbolic Indians come later.) Typified by *Scarface* (DePalma, 1983) and *Midnight Express* (Parker, 1978) – for which Stone won his first Oscar – these films are also characterized by their racism, casual misogyny, and commitment to visual, thematic and, above all, emotional *excess*. This provocative 'aesthetic of excess' forms a distinct homology with the imposing, bear-like charisma of the Stone-persona, itself exacerbated by anecdotal tales of the writer-director's punishing work-rate and substantial recreational appetites. Boundaries between 'author', text and fictional protagonist(s) are further elided in retrospective analyses and the director's ever present self-commentary: events in *Midnight Express*, for example, mirror Stone's youthful incarceration for drug possession, while *Scarface* becomes his post-rehab 'swan song to cocaine'.[5] The emergent auteur signature thus outlined sketches Stone's love-it-or-loathe-it 'paranoid style': 'overheated, oversuspicious, overaggressive, grandiose and apocalyptic in expression'.[6]

This intertextual relay between biography, star image and filmic text becomes ever more reflexive. Early directorial efforts *Seizure* and *The Hand* are exploitation horror flicks about self-destructive artists, a theme that recurs in the artist-martyrs of the angsty, introverted *Talk Radio* and, conversely, *The Doors'* Dionysian extravagance. *Salvador's* political exposé of American foreign policy in Latin America, meanwhile, is a self-legitimizing meditation on the social and ethical role of the artist, personified here by Jimmy Woods' definitively sleazy photo-journalist. *Nixon*, hilariously, is a cycle of constant deferral, with Tony Hopkins-as-Tricky Dicky-as-Charlie Kane-as-Oliver Stone.

Platoon's promotional campaign was successfully founded on this reflexive auteurist rhetoric. This largely autobiographical film's self-proclaimed 'significance' lay in its unique status as *survivor testimony*; the *storyteller* here granted as much import as the story itself. In the discourses surrounding the film's reception, the presence of the veteran auteur acted as an extratextual guarantee of *Platoon's* verisimilitude, both as an authentic corrective to the philosophical and mythic portent of canonized Vietnam movies *The Deer Hunter* (Cimino, 1978) and *Apocalypse Now* (Coppola, 1979), and in opposition to contemporaneously militaristic Reaganite fantasies exemplified by *Rambo* (Cosmatos, 1985) and *Top Gun* (Scott, 1986).[7] Protagonist Chris Taylor (Charlie Sheen) is a direct stand-in for

Stone himself: a naïve, middle-class university drop-out who volunteers for duty in Vietnam, only to have his patriotic idealism and innocence crushed by the purposeless barbarity of the conflict and the profound social divisions between his fellow soldiers. In the auteur-narrative that is inextricably interwoven with his films, this mythic descent into the abyss of Vietnam is a journey towards manhood and knowledge; the pilgrim-protagonist-auteur's progress recounted in a proto-Blakean quest to cleanse the doors of perception for his audience: 'those of us who did make it have an obligation to build again, to teach others what we know, and try with what's left of our lives to find a goodness and a meaning to this life'.

Close identification with his protagonists and symptomatically paranoid anti-authoritarian ethos form the cornerstones of the Stone persona looming over these films. Betrayed – like *Born on the Fourth of July*'s Kovic – by Uncle Sam and denied the regenerative promises of the 1950s, the impassioned non-conformity of the director/protagonist takes on more than a whiff of Oedipal revolt. These modern-day messiahs – *Salvador*'s Richard Boyle, *Platoon*'s Chris Taylor, *Born on the Fourth of July*'s Ron Kovic, *Talk Radio*'s arch-misanthropist Barry Champlain, *The Doors*' Jim Morrison, *JFK*'s Jim Garrison, *Any Given Sunday*'s Tony D'Amato, perhaps even *Natural Born Killers*' nihilistic lovers Mickey and Mallory – come forth bearing the 'truth' in various guises, only to be met with aggression and/or ridicule by the hypocritical, paternalistic 'establishment'.

This homology between diegetic and extradiegetic narratives was most pronounced during the astonishing furore over *JFK*. Denounced as both 'propaganda masterpiece' *and* 'the cinematic equivalent of rape',[8] criticisms of *JFK* were virtually indistinguishable from personal attacks on Stone himself: critical bullets flew from all directions, with Stone caught in the crossfire as the sacrificial lamb akin to *JFK*'s 'slain father-king'. In a media-driven self-fulfilling prophecy, with life imitating art to an ever greater degree, Stone's narcissistic crusade to expose the 'truth' also formed a distinctly mimetic relationship with *JFK*'s embattled detective-messiah Garrison, the former styling himself as a righteous postmodern Ahab, determined to fulfil his quest regardless of the cost. Stone's media profile soared, the seemingly endless debate over *JFK* intensifying his auteur presence and rhetorically bolstering the credibility of his populist 'radical-oppositional' star image. Stone claimed to be taking on both the establishment and 'official history', and the US box office said he was winning by some $70 million.

Epitomized by *JFK*, Stone's historical 'docu-dramas' have, as I noted above, courted controversy in both popular and academic discourse. Always already highly contentious generic cultural forms, the hybridized modes of 'infotainment' or 'faction' that Stone has favoured from *Salvador* through to *Nixon* have all suggested the over-punned slippage between the real/reel; that is, the fluid protean synergy between historical artefact, popular memory and the Hollywood imaginary.[9] Although Stone inevitably fuelled the fire by claiming that the hostile and prolonged *JFK* discourse was a symptom of his dramatic 'revelations', the hysteria that the film provoked amongst journalists, historians, politicians and the media pundits can perhaps be more usefully located in contemporary anxieties.[10] If the benevolent, paternal President is *JFK*'s mourned lost object, he metonymically represents not only the idealized Camelot of popular mythology (the ideological prop upon which *JFK* depends), but also the assurance of *progress* that underpins the modernist grand narrative. *JFK* demonstrates the fluid relationship between past and present, mobilizing the former to explain the latter, illustrating the causes of what Stone perceives to be the ideological and spiritual entropy of contemporary America's cultural malaise.

Stone's meta-textual audacity particularly provoked the collective ire of media commentators: *JFK*'s montage of history (with obvious Eisensteinean aspirations) sutured together documentary footage, painstakingly accurate reconstructions, monochrome and colour footage, archival television reports, melodrama, Hollywood naturalism, fact, hypothesis, conjecture, rumour and fantasy in a near-seamless collage of cut and paste imagery; as one wily critic put it, '*montage* is the message'.[11] While *JFK*'s narrative trajectory moves irresistibly towards mapping out a coherent explanation, the aggressive polyphony of Stone's formal technique has the effect of relativist distanciation; historical narrative here is provisional and illusory, a kinetic collage of partial truths pieced together in an arbitrary and/or strategic way. While paternalistic critics fretted over whether audiences would be able to tell 'fact' from 'fiction', in so doing they displaced the origins of their anxiety over the simultaneous democratization *and* deconstruction of history: Stone's film 'is a formal investigation of the ways images are manufactured to produce memory and history … It is a film about discourse, process, power and ideology, about speaking things into existence by investigating and demonstrating how events are represented, so that learning is accomplished by understanding process and coming to terms with power … Stone wants his film to change minds. But more important[ly], the film wants to show the ways minds can be changed.'[12]

Stone's engagements with history have also been critiqued on various historiographical grounds: the lack of critical distance and overdetermined identification with his protagonist(s); the strategic creation of 'composite' characters and events; his refusal to adhere to historical 'facts', and the subsequent mobilization of dramatic conjecture, manipulation, reductionism and speculation; the persistent use of mythic archetypes to personify historical events and social forces; the polemical bombast and didacticism; and the displacement of the authentic historian's dispassionate objectivity by the sensationalistic emotionalism of the ideologue. Stone himself has adopted a slippery, strategic indeterminacy in response to these increasingly pedantic accusations: claiming to be a cinematic historian at one juncture, purveyor of 'counter-myth' at another,[13] sometimes adopting a position of extreme relativism, at others self-deprecatingly shrugging his shoulders: 'I see myself as somewhat of a passionate blunderer who puts his foot in the proverbial dog shit now and then.'[14]

For the auteurist, Stone's rejection(s) of legitimized history reflects his Nietzschean commitment to what he terms 'Dionysian politics'; this characteristically dualistic philosophy privileges subjective visceral and emotional truths over the intellectual/rational, forcing 'the pure wash of emotion over the mind to let you see the inner myth, the spirit of the thing. Then, when the cold light of reason hits you as you walk out of the theatre, the sense of truth will remain lodged beyond reason in the depths of your being.'[15] Beyond the philosophical mumbo-jumbo, Stone is more honest, if no less ponderous:

> I admit I like excess. I like grandiosity of style. I like characters like Gordon Gekko and Jim Morrison. I believe in the power of excess because through excess I live a larger life. I inflate my life and by inflating my life I live more of the world. I die a more experienced man.[16]

Like both its subject and its creator, *The Doors* is indulgent, pretentious, overblown, decadent and hugely self-important; at the same time, it is a frantic and entertainingly impressionistic medley of the sights, sounds and, naturally, the excesses of late-1960s' West Coast hippiedom through the noir prism of the Stone imaginary: a kind of *counter*-cultural heritage spectacle. The film is resolutely apolitical, the chaos and upheaval of the period abstractly mapped onto the polymorphous soundtrack-led narrative, hallucinatory imagery, frenzied camerawork and 'shamanic' charisma of its iconic protagonist (Val Kilmer). In one early scene, Morrison is derided by fellow UCLA students for his pretentious *avante-garde* filmmaking; the film professor – played by Stone – attempting to locate the source of meaning turns to the star-to-be: 'Let's ask the filmmaker what *he* thinks.' And what does the filmmaker think? 'I believe in Morrison's incantations. Break on through. Kill the pigs. Destroy. Loot. Fuck your mother. All that shit. Anything goes. Anything.'[17] *Right.*

'Anything goes', however, neatly encapsulates the ethos behind Stone's ever grander formal pyrotechnics. Progressively more ambitious and experimental throughout his career, the director's visual grandiloquence reaches its apogee in the hyper-expressionism of *Natural Born Killers'* sledgehammer media-satire and the supposedly anomalous *U-Turn's* stylistic cartwheels and gleeful hybridity. Knowingly exhibitionist, both films revel in their amphetaminized camera work, *bricolage* of styles and stocks, free-associative imagery, eclectic and inventive use of sound and music, and general MTV-ized hyper-mania. Not insignificantly, these playfully nihilistic fantasies arrived in the wake of their predecessor's profound commercial failure(s); they also epitomize the flamboyant pleasures of Stone's 'cinema of attractions'. Overbearing and overwrought he may be, but Stone's 'relentless courting of the overblown and pretentious remain his saving grace, the talisman that inevitably wards off 'tasteful boredom'.[18]

Nevertheless, Stone's 'operatic tendency' towards 'declamatory spectacle[s] of emotional excess'[19] suggest that these films should be read less as solemn cinematic historicism or docu-drama, but more usefully as *melo*dramas of genericized historical moments.[20] Indeed, Stone's fondness for Oedipal dramatics and foundational excess, archetypal ciphers and moral polarization, the frequent use of distanciation techniques, and his sensationalistic interrogations of the gulf between all-American cultural ideals and the social and historical realities encountered by his protagonists, all point towards a neo-Sirkian ethos 'bubbling under' the mythic foundations of these films. Because they acknowledge 'the desire to know completely the stories of history and ... the role of fantasy in that knowing',[21] their *excess* attempts to (over-)compensate for 'the feeling that there is always more to tell than can be said'.[22]

Moreover, Stone's films are also persistently *homosocial* in focus – melodramas of (white) masculinity which explore the emotional and institutional kinship between men. (There is apparently no place for feminism, and little for women, in the worldview of this allegedly unreconstructed 1960s' radical-leftist.) It is surely indicative of Stone's priorities (and the expectations of his audience) that his sole attempt to counter perennial accusations of androcentrism, misogyny and Orientalism, and his one film to feature a central female protagonist – *Heaven and Earth* – is also his greatest commercial *and* critical failure.

The lure of the homosocial is evident throughout Stone's *œuvre*. Despite the consistent marginalization of women and often banal hetero-masculinist agenda (the 'tragedy' of Kovic's 'dead penis' or Morrison's impotence), in keeping with both Hollywood's melodramatic and paranoid traditions, Stone's films can be read as both symptomatically masochistic dramas *and* as restorative tales of remasculinization. Stone's menfolk may eventually grasp the phallus, but it is their prolonged suffering which dominates narratives in which, invariably, a white man is being beaten. Such fantasies of martyrdom repeatedly eroticize male torment and subjugation, from the overt homoerotics of lurid sadomasochistic fantasy *Midnight Express* and explicit love-object worship in *The Doors*, through *JFK* and *Nixon*'s nightmarish intimations of the phallus-as-bad-object in the fetishized guise of the 'military-industrial' complex, to *U-Turn*'s convoluted noir-isms and the (sado-)masochistic montages of brutalized male bodies and Leone-esque grunts in locker-room fable *Any Given Sunday*. You don't have to look hard to detect the relentless undercurrent of fear/desire projected, in Schreberian fashion, towards the homosexual. Yet the seductive charisma of, say, *Wall Street*'s Gordon Gekko *exceeds* the narrative's simplistic (and ostensibly homophobic) morality play; Michael Douglas' iconic Oscar-winning performance embodies the pleasures of an overabundance of homoerotic allure which the film's ideological project systematically fails to contain. 'Greed' may not be *good*, but it sure is fun.

In his review of *Platoon*, Nigel Floyd points to 'conflicting impulses' and apparent contradictions: 'Perhaps,' muses Floyd, 'it is this unresolved tension that allows *Rambo* fans to relish the violence while concerned liberals ponder the horror'.[23] In his biography (subtitled, with appropriate hyperbole, *The Controversies, Excesses and Exploits of a Radical Filmmaker*), Stone's one-time agent Paula Wagner shrewdly notes: '[Oliver]'s a businessman, he's not a fool. He has a sense of commerce as well as art and to make a movie you have to be in touch with both.'[24] Stone's films continue to inspire extensive, passionate and frequently contradictory interpretation and debate: *Natural Born Killers*' alleged copycat killings were both missing *and* precisely to the point. Stone himself is continually called upon to explain or clarify what his films *mean*, what they are *trying* to 'say'. That he counters media 'misrepresentation' and 'misrecognition' (at length and with astonishing regularity) itself suggests an acute auteur *anxiety*.

To this end, both Oliver Stone the auteur-star and the films that bear his (brand) name adhere to the wilful incoherence of what Richard Maltby terms the multiple logics of Hollywood's commercial aesthetic.[25] 'The Most Dangerous Man in America'[26] is also a multiple Oscar-winner; the wild, chaotic, unpredictable auteur-of-excess rarely goes over either budget or schedule; the po-mo relativist/revisionist directs films based on the eternal truths of classical mythology; a populist right-wing masculinist-individualist who stoically carries the radical-socialist torch of the New Left; the anti-authoritarian *avant-garde* filmmaker who directs star-studded, multi-million dollar genre flicks; the maverick 'outsider' who also manages to be 'the second most powerful creative individual in Hollywood after Steve Spielberg';[27] the political iconoclast who adapts Andrew Lloyd Webber for the screen and makes American football seem interesting and – dare I say it – even *exciting*. 'I wonder how I can be all these people at the end of the day. Who am I? The [media] don't know who Oliver Stone is: they have no fucking idea. Oliver Stone is still a mystery – to me too.'[28] The strategic indeterminacy of Hollywood entertainment, like the evermore opaque riddle of the Zapruder film with which we began, mystifies and conceals as much as it reveals. And the 'auteur', even one with a star image as recognizable and relentlessly foregrounded as Oliver Stone's, is a meaningful presence behind or within the text *only if we choose to see him there*. But which 'Oliver Stone' do we choose to see? Now *that's* (provocative) enfotainment.

Biography

Born New York, USA, in 1946, Stone first achieved prominence as a writer and producer, receiving critical acclaim and an Academy Award for his *Midnight Express* (1978) screenplay.

Notes

1   Quoted in Chris Salewicz, *Oliver Stone: The Making of His Movies*, London, Orion, 1997, p. 77.

2 Michael Rogin, 'Body and Soul Murder: *JFK*', in Marjorie Garber *et al.* (eds) *Media Spectacles*, London, Routledge, 1993, p. 13.

3 Hayden White, 'The Modernist Event', in Vivian Sobchak (ed.) *The Persistence of History: Cinema, Television and the Modern Event*, London, Routledge, 1996, p. 20.

4 Robert Kolker, *A Cinema of Loneliness: Penn, Stone, Kubrick, Scorsese, Spielberg, Altman*, Oxford, Oxford University Press, 2000, p. xvi.

5 James Riordan, *Stone: The Controversies, Excesses and Exploits of a Radical Filmmaker*, London, Aurum Press, 1996, p. 128. *Midnight Express* was adapted from protagonist William Hayes' autobiographical account.

6 Richard Hofstadter, *The Paranoid Style in American Politics and Other Essays*, London, Jonathan Cape, 1966, p. 4.

7 *Platoon*'s publicity campaign read: 'In 1967 a young man named Oliver Stone spent 15 months in Vietnam as an infantryman in the United States Army. He was wounded twice and received a bronze star for gallantry. Ten years later Stone was a screenwriter in Hollywood, author of *Midnight Express*. It made him the only man in Hollywood with both a purple heart and an Oscar' (quoted in Thomas Doherty, 'Witness to War: Oliver Stone, Ron Kovic and *Born on the Fourth of July*', in Michael Anderegg (ed.) *Inventing Vietnam: The War in Film and Television*, Philadelphia, PA, Temple University Press, 1991, p. 252).

8 See James Riordan, *op. cit.*, pp. 423–4.

9 Marita Sturken, 'Reenactment, Fantasy, and the Paranoia of History: Oliver Stone's Docudramas', in *History and Theory* No. 36, 1997, pp. 64–79.

10 For detailed accounts of the critical reception of *JFK*, see James Petras, 'The Discrediting of the Fifth Estate: The Press Attacks on *JFK*ash;17; Frank Beaver, *Oliver Stone: Wakeup Cinema*, New York, Twayne Publishers, 1994; James Riordan, *op. cit.*; Norman Kagan, *The Cinema of Oliver Stone*, New York, Continuum Publishing Co., 2000; Michael L. Kurtz, 'Oliver Stone, *JFK* and History', in Robert Brent Toplin (ed.) *Oliver Stone's USA: Film, History and Controversy*, Lawrence, University Press of Kansas, 2000, pp. 166–77.

11 Pat Dowell, 'Last Year at Nuremberg: The Cinematic Strategies of *JFK*', *Cineaste*, no. 19, 1992, p. 9 (my emphasis).

12 Robert Kolker, *op. cit.*, p. 75.

13 Quoted in Susan Mackey-Willis, *Oliver Stone's America: Dreaming the Myth*, Oxford, Westview Press, 1996, p. 42.

14 Oliver Stone, 'Stone on Stone's image', in Brent Toplin, *op. cit.*, p. 43.

15 Quoted in James L. Farr, 'The Lizard King or Fake Hero: Oliver Stone, Jim Morrison, and History', in Brent Toplin, *op. cit.*, p. 156.

16 Quoted in James Riordan, *op. cit.*, p. 343.

17 Quoted in Kagan, *op. cit.*, p. 181.

18 Godfrey Cheshire, 'The Cemetery of Good Taste', *New York Press*, 24 August 1994.

19 Robert Kolker, *op. cit.*, p. 74.

20 Robert A. Rosenstone, 'Oliver Stone as Historian', in Brent Toplin (ed.) *op. cit.*, pp. 26–39.

21 Sturken, *op. cit.*, p. 65.

22　Thomas Elsaesser, 'Tales of Sound and Fury: Observations on the Family Melodrama', *Monogram* 4, 1974, p. 7.

23　Nigel Floyd, *'Platoon'*, in John Pym (ed.) *Time Out Film Guide 8*, London, Penguin, p. 816.

24　James Riordan, *op. cit.*, p. 302.

25　Richard Maltby, *Hollywood Cinema: An Introduction*, Oxford, Blackwell, 1995. Posters for the Stone-produced *The People vs. Larry Flynt* (Forman, 1996) featured his name prominently, trading on his homologous anti-authoritarian star image and populist reputation as all-American defender of free speech.

26　Robert Scheer, 'The Most Dangerous Man in America', *The Los Angeles Times*, 15 December 1991.

27　Chris Salewicz, *op. cit.*, p. 7.

28　Stone, quoted in Chris Salewicz, *op. cit.*, p. 118.

Filmography

Seizure (1974)
The Hand (1981)
Salvador (1985)
Platoon (1986)
Wall Street (1987)
Talk Radio (1988)
Born on the Fourth of July (1989)
The Doors (1990)
JFK (1991)
Heaven and Earth (1993)
Natural Born Killers (1994)
Nixon (1995)
U-Turn (1997)
Any Given Sunday (1999)

MARTIN FRADLEY

QUENTIN TARANTINO

A director who has achieved popular and critical prominence despite having directed only three feature-length films – *Reservoir Dogs*, *Pulp Fiction* and *Jackie Brown*, each with small or relatively modest budgets – Quentin Tarantino is in many ways the most visible new American filmmaker to have emerged during the 1990s. In industry terms, his reputation stems from screenwriting as much as directing or producing, while he seems to see himself very much as a performer. His direct and indirect influence has splashed widely and his media currency has burgeoned to the extent that a critical consideration of Tarantino, the individual and his work, necessitates some unravelling across three key areas: mythology, personality and, to coin an awkward term, adjectivity.

Mythology

The story goes that Quentin Tarantino was a video-store clerk who got his script to the actor Harvey Keitel whose support got *Reservoir Dogs* made and so catapulted Tarantino to directorial stardom. Although there is a kernel of truth in this, there is also a mythological aspect, recalling studio-generated tales of actresses and actors discovered as waitresses and gas station attendants. Tarantino may indeed be 'the most famous former video-store clerk in America'.[1] He is happy to play up to this aspect of his past, staging a press reception for *Reservoir Dogs* at Video Archives, the place where he had worked.[2] Acknowledging his past as 'a film geek', he has commented that 'I think my biggest appeal amongst young fans is that they look at me as a fan boy who made it.'[3]

Although Tarantino had almost no directorial experience before *Reservoir Dogs*, this is not quite the same as the supposedly seamless transition from video-store clerk to fêted director enacted in publicity and media biographies. Tarantino had trained as an actor and had appeared (as an Elvis impersonator) in an episode of *The Golden Girls*. Indeed, it was his lack of success as an actor that first led him to write. Eventually he quit Video Archives and went on to support himself by selling scripts (*True Romance*), revamping outlines (*From Dusk 'til Dawn*) and polishing the work of others. A partial rewrite of *Past Midnight* (1992), a cable TV premiere with Rutger Hauer and Natasha Richardson, gained him an associate producer credit. Thus Tarantino had already achieved a measure of credibility in the industry by the time his script for *Reservoir Dogs* reached Keitel: not so much a video-store clerk turned director, but an industrious Hollywood hopeful hitting the big time.

Nevertheless, it seems to have been the desire to act which sparked the idea for Tarantino to direct *Reservoir Dogs* himself on 16mm for a budget of $30,000 (the fee for the *True Romance* script).[4] In other words, his connection to writing was as an actor. Unsurprisingly perhaps, sensitivity to the needs and talents of actors remains his significant strength as a director. The care taken in assembling the cast of *Reservoir Dogs* is instructive. Whether seasoned or relatively fresh, each brings a celluloid past like a rap sheet.[5] Of course, such a parallel (the filmmaker setting up 'a job', making a good score) also feeds the myth. If the robbery goes badly wrong, the film itself – very much about 'getting away with it' – does not.

Personality

After the success of Steven Soderbergh's *sex, lies, and videotape* in 1989, distributors were keen to spot another crossover hit at the 1992 Sundance Film Festival. Although it did not win a prize, *Reservoir Dogs* caused controversy and gained attention, gathering critical plaudits across Europe. The film's box-office and critical kudos allowed Tarantino to set up favourable deals, including the opportunity to hand-pick actors for his next project. But, for those who could not wait, other extant Tarantino screenplays went quickly into production. *True Romance*, directed by Tony Scott, was put together with another excellent cast and increased Tarantino's stock. Meanwhile, prior to the success of *Reservoir Dogs*, an associate had been allowed to go fishing for finance with another project, *Natural Born Killers*, and it 'got away' from Tarantino – ultimately against his will – to be adapted in visceral style by Oliver Stone, creating further controversy (and profit). The result was a wave of 'Tarantino' movies appearing, building up expectation for his second directorial project, *Pulp Fiction*, which delivered audiences, acclaim (including the Palme d'Or at Cannes) and an Oscar for Best Script.

In the frenzied media attention that followed, it was clear that Tarantino was good copy, clearly someone who had dreamed of fame, someone who conceived of himself as a performer and had no difficulty putting himself across (in a sense, Tarantino is his own best acting role, nicely performed in his cameo as director Q.T. in Spike Lee's *Girl 6*). Tarantino emerged as garrulous autodidact, enthusing over the power of direction and his enjoyment of on-screen violence, who is not afraid to have an opinion. He is defensive of his films, particularly in discussions of violence (*Reservoir Dogs*' torture scene), racism (use of the 'n' word in *Pulp Fiction*), plagiarism (borrowings from Ringo Lam's *City on Fire* (1987) in *Reservoir Dogs*, or the suggestion that he has taken credit for the work of others in his scripts), and perhaps even more so about his acting and personal conduct. Whether self-aware or narcissistic, there are currently six biographies on Tarantino (and he admits to having read them all).

Tarantino's self-forged personality has provoked considerable irritation, with critics attacking him for a lack of moral compass (his interest in movie violence) or pointing to a lack of life experience (having nothing to say). Ian Penman, for instance, dubs Tarantino

'The Man Who Mistook a Video Collection for his Life'.[6] Yet the logic of this criticism would not even allow Ken Loach to operate. Rather than something new, Tarantino represents the extreme of an existing phenomenon. He was raised by his mother in an ethnically mixed neighbourhood in Los Angeles, dreaming, discussing and obsessing about movies. To some extent, what attaches to him in this type of criticism is a backlash against the video-store clerk 'mythology', suggesting that he is somehow not fit to be a filmmaker without years of struggle or film-school training at the very least.

Luckily, or perhaps shrewdly, when the backlash had reached critical mass it was *Four Rooms*, the disastrous compendium piece for which Tarantino wrote, directed and acted in only one section, that was released. Other young festival-hit directors – Allison Anders, Robert Rodriguez and Alexandre Rockwell – shared culpability and, with the possible exception of Rodriguez, came out worse.

To Tarantino's credit he appeared as promised at the UK Shots in the Dark Crime Film Festival in 1994, despite having just picked up the Palme d'Or in Cannes. Furthermore, Roger Avary, the man most often cited as the talent exploited by Tarantino, shared Tarantino's Oscar for *Pulp Fiction*'s writing and Tarantino produced his Paris-set *Killing Zoe* (1994). The mythology, personal contradictions and critical expectations around Tarantino led interviewer Simon Hattenstone to characterize him as 'the most arrogant, precious, pretentious, unquestioning, solipsistic, self-deluded man I've ever met. So I can't work out why I almost like him. Maybe it's because I don't believe he did shaft his friends. Maybe it's because, however shallow he is, he is also a bit of a genius.'[7] As this statement reminds us, beyond the media phenomenon, Tarantino's films have proved sufficiently distinctive to generate the adjective 'Tarantino-esque'.

Tarantino-esque

This handy adjective has become a 'byword for both pop-culture reference and popular post-modern cinema', that is, the space between *Forrest Gump* and Kieślowski.[8] But it has also become 'critical shorthand for hackneyed, would-be-hip, low-budget crime thrillers'.[9] Tarantino complains that: 'It's so broken down to black suits, hipper-than-thou dialogue and people talking about TV shows.'[10] If the also-rans do not measure up that may be because they are more '-esque' than Tarantino.

Tarantino-esque sometimes functions as film journalist short-hand for the weightier, and considerably more problematic, term 'postmodernism'. For film, the postmodern has two essential aspects: the stylistic and the political. Tarantino's relationship to postmodern style is clear and is manifested in a variety of ways such as the use of self-conscious artifice (*Pulp Fiction*'s use of intertitles, the back projections during cab rides or Mia Wallace's finger-drawing indicated by dotted lines on the screen). Also significant is Tarantino's blurring of cultural boundaries, particularly those between exploitation and mainstream cinema,[11] and between genres, for example *From Dusk 'til Dawn*'s mid-movie switch from crime thriller to horror movie, or 'The Bonnie Situation' in *Pulp Fiction*, characterized by Polan as a noir/sitcom hybrid.[12] A further conspicuous postmodern device is the use of intertextual reference. This can be internal, as when *True Romance*'s Alabama is mentioned in *Reservoir Dogs*, or when parole officer Scagnetti is both mentioned in *Reservoir Dogs* and appears (as a corrupt detective) in *Natural Born Killers*. References can be more explicit, as in the discussion of Sonny Chiba in *True Romance*, of Madonna in *Reservoir Dogs* or of Charles Bronson in both *True Romance* and *Reservoir Dogs*. A third aspect involves references to other films through personnel, situations and props: casting Pam Grier in *Jackie Brown*'s title role clearly recalls her memorable blaxploitation roles (*Foxy Brown* (1974), *Coffy* (1973)), or simply placing John Travolta in a dance contest in *Pulp Fiction* conjures up *Saturday Night Fever* (1978). In the same way the glowing contents of the suitcase in *Pulp Fiction* recall 'the great whatsit' of *Kiss Me Deadly* (1955). When Butch is searching for a weapon in the pawnbroker's after he has decided to return and rescue Marcellus Wallace, he finds a trove of items with film-hero resonances; the baseball bat suggests the American vigilante hero of *Walking Tall* (1973), the chainsaw conjures a more psychotic response as in the *Texas Chainsaw Massacre* (1974) or *The Evil Dead II* (1987), while the *katana* he finally, and significantly, selects identifies him with the honourable Japanese heroes of *The Yakuza* (1975) and Kurosawa's *Seven Samurai* (1954).

Some celebrate these elements (there are numerous Tarantino-based websites) whilst others condemn them as style over substance or, perhaps, spectacle over message. Condemnation usually occurs when the politics, rather than the aesthetics of postmodernism are at issue. Since postmodernism has been defined as the failure of grand narratives, it tends to unite critics from left and right against it, whether their preferred narrative is humanist or Marxist. Thus a hostile attitude towards postmodernism tends to determine critical attitudes to postmodern films. Tarantino's clear commitment to postmodern style draws fire from those objecting to its perceived politics as though one was necessarily evidence of the other. For example, Tarantino's use of intertextual reference to commercial crime cinema could be seen as 'pastiche'. Yet this is not necessarily simply blank parody, to use Jameson's terms.[13] Instead we might regard Tarantino's use of intertextual pastiche as a positive exploration of possibilities within the commercial form. Nevertheless, Tarantino's semblance of art-house independence combined with sustained commercial success remains a goad to his detractors.

The rewrite

Tarantino's interest lies in his revamping of genre scenarios which he accomplishes in three key ways. First, he unapologetically places 'the bad guys' centre stage, while examining the lives of those who would often be peripheral characters. In *Jackie Brown* it is neither the cops nor the gangsters but the 'mule' who is central, while *Pulp Fiction*'s series of skewed genre set-pieces focus on the boss's moll (Uma Thurman), and the hitmen's problems disposing of a body. Second, Tarantino injects elements of realism into the dialogue and narrative. In dialogue this means essentially banal and digressive phatic conversations (about Madonna or burgers in foreign countries) and the inclusion of jokes and casual bad language. Much of this may be seen to come from crime writing, particularly that of Elmore Leonard, whose 1992 *Rum Punch* Tarantino adapted for *Jackie Brown*. Leonard's work focuses on characters across a broad social spectrum, but the criminal characters' voices frequently provide the most interest. Their dialogue – ripe, anecdotal and comic – informs that of Tarantino's criminal protagonists. Here are Ordell Robbie and Louis Gara (played in *Jackie Brown* by Samuel L. Jackson and Robert De Niro) touring Detroit in Leonard's *The Switch* (1978):

> 'You can see it's not your classic ghetto yet, not quite ratty or rotten enough, but it's coming. Over there on the left, first whore of the day. Out for her vitamin C. And there's some more – hot pants with a little ass hanging out, showing the goods.'
> 'How come coloured girls,' Louis said, 'their asses are so high?'
> 'You don't know that?' Ordell glanced at him. 'Same way as the camel.'
> Louis said, 'For humping, uh?'

'No, man, for going without food and water when there was a famine, they stored up what they need in their ass.'

Louis didn't know whether Ordell was putting him on or not.

This exchange exhibits the same combination of trivia, bullshit and uneasy, or at least uncomprehending, interracial interaction that passes between Tarantino's male groups. Further moves towards realism in cinematic narrative mean that Tarantino's characters must make toilet trips – at fatal moments in the cases of Clarence Worley (Christian Slater) in *True Romance* and Vincent Vega (John Travolta) in *Pulp Fiction*. Furthermore, these characters are made out of vulnerable materials – blood and brains: we (almost) see their bodies sliced, injected and buggered.

Third, and perhaps most noticeably, Tarantino uses broken, novelistic structures; *Reservoir Dogs* shows us the scenes around a heist rather than the heist itself, placing the emphasis not on the expected generic narrative question 'will the heist succeed?' but shifting it towards a drawn-out dissection of failure. There is a harking back to literary modernism with an interest in perspectival views that is apparent even in the most linear of his films as director, *Jackie Brown*, in which the key exchange in the shopping mall is shown three times. In film terms, such fragmented structuring refers back to *Citizen Kane* (1941), *The Killers* (1946) or *The Killing* (1956), though there are no inquisitive investigators or documentary-style voice-overs to hold the narrative together.[14]

Such narrative complexity involves a move towards reality and, at the same time, an intertextual acknowledgement of fictionality. Depending on one's point of view, these innovations produce either an awkward bind or an intensification of the cinematic experience. As Polan suggests, these elements are used to take us places we *have not* yet been and, as such are comparable to developments in hypertext, choose-your-own adventure novels and alternative endings to narrative-based computer games. In the cinema at least, we have less control over the temporal progress of the narrative. The type of experience is easily demonstrated if one thinks of one's reaction to the ear-slicing scene in *Reservoir Dogs* as what *we* do rather than what the film did. It is clearly around this issue of audience experience that Tarantino acquires his significance as a filmmaker. Using Tarantino to attack his films and his films to attack the perceived values of postmodernism misses the point. Quentin Tarantino is a filmmaker who works successfully within compromised, commodified, popular culture and has been fortunate enough to be able to write, cast and direct on his own terms. The result, and his chief asset, is that he delivers a distinctive and memorable product.

Biography

Quentin Tarantino was born in 1963, in Tennessee, USA.

Notes

1 Paul A. Woods, *Quentin Tarantino: The Film Geek Files*, London, Plexus, 2000, p. 75.
2 Jeff Dawson, *Tarantino: Inside Story*, London, Cassell, 1995, p. 63.
3 Paul A. Woods, *op. cit.*, pp. 30 and 54.
4 Eventually, through Keitel's involvement, the budget reached $1.5 million.
5 Previous criminal roles for the *Reservoir Dogs* cast: Keitel (*Mean Streets*, 1973; *Taxi Driver*, 1976), Michael Madsen (*Kill Me Again*, 1989), Tim Roth (*The Hit*, 1984), Steve Buscemi (*King of New York*, 1990; *Miller's Crossing*, 1990; *Billy Bathgate*, 1991), Lawrence Tierney (*Dillinger*, 1945; *The Hoodlum*, 1951; *Prizzi's Honour*, 1985), Chris Penn (*At Close Range*, 1986; *Mobsters*, 1991). Apart from Tarantino, untried on film, there was also real ex-criminal, Eddie Bunker, writer of *Straight Time* (1978), on *Runaway Train* (1985) and technical adviser on *American Heart* (1992).
6 Paul A. Woods, *op. cit.*, p. 126.
7 *Ibid.*, p. 156.
8 *Ibid.*, pp. 5 and 124.
9 *Ibid.*, p. 152.
10 *Ibid.*, p. 154. The popular or journalistic characterization of Tarantino-esque probably best applies to *Killing Zoe*, in which Eric Stoltz (admittedly in a beige suit) is stuck in a car full of drugged-up amateur terrorists, including a stoned Gary Kemp babbling about *The Prisoner*.
11 Not between high and low culture though; unlike the Coens, Tarantino has yet to base a script on Homer's *The Odyssey*.
12 Dana Polan, *Pulp Fiction*, London, BFI Publishing, 2000, p. 25.
13 See Hal Foster (ed.) *Postmodern Culture*, London, Pluto, 1985, p. 114.
14 The internal intertexts of different temporally displaced parts of the story are thus emphasized, not to say fetishized.

Filmography

Reservoir Dogs (1992) also writer, performer
Pulp Fiction (1994) also co-writer
Four Rooms (1995) 'The Man from Hollywood' segment; also co-writer, performer
Jackie Brown (1997) also screenplay

Further reading

Geoff Andrew, *Stranger Than Paradise: Maverick Film-makers in Recent American Cinema*, London, Prion, 1998.
Emmanuel Levy, *Cinema of Outsiders: The Rise of American Independent Film*, New York, New York University Press, 1999.

GLYN WHITE

TSUI HARK

If a prize existed for the 'Hardest Working Filmmaker of International Repute', then Tsui Hark would be likely to win it. Originally a central part of Hong Kong cinema's post-1979 New Wave, Tsui has worked consistently since that time on an astonishing range of projects. Commercially savvy, stylistically flamboyant, politically opportunistic, these characteristics have made Tsui Hark's name synonymous with commercial Chinese filmmaking of the 1980s and 1990s. However, while there is no doubting the quantity of his work, critics tend to remain divided in their estimation of the quality. After all, here is a director who appears to oscillate between moments of schlock and moments of genuine inventiveness.

With the release of his early feature films – *The Butterfly Murders, Dangerous Encounter – First Kind* and *We're Going to Eat You* – Tsui Hark earned his reputation as the wunderkind of the Hong Kong New Wave. His subsequent filmography comprises period titles (*Peking Opera Blues, The Lovers, The Blade*) and contemporary dramas (*The Master, Twin Dragons*), martial arts movies (*Once Upon a Time in China*), fantasy (*Zu: Warriors from the Magic Mountain*), gangster movies (*A Better Tomorrow III*) and comedy (*All the Wrong Clues, The Chinese Feast*). At their best, such films epitomize an inventive, dynamic and crowd-pleasing cinema of attractions.

Clearly, the very fact that Tsui Hark has been able to secure the green light for such a large number of projects suggests an uncanny ability to play the commercial system. As he explains:

> We've seen so many of our mentors in the industry from the sixties and the fifties, they are very good in a particular genre, but then when a new genre comes to the industry, they fade out for the reason that the genre is not trendy any more and the people are not going for that kind of film. So for us, for me especially, I try to not label myself in some genre.[1]

In order to think through the implications of his comments, however, it is important to remember that Tsui Hark is more than just a filmmaker in his own right. Aside from directing, he has also acted in features like *Run, Tiger, Run* (John Woo, 1985) and *Final Victory* (Patrick Tam, 1987), and produced such audience favourites as *A Better Tomorrow* (Woo, 1986), *A Chinese Ghost Story* (Ching Siu Tung, 1987) and *The Wicked City* (Peter Mak, 1992). Indeed, such is the extent of his popular reputation that Tsui is often credited as solely responsible for these last two titles.

When it comes to the inscription of authorship, in other words, Tsui Hark needs to be appreciated as something of a Renaissance figure, or at the very least as a director whose public image bleeds over into related fields of artistic practice. One may even go so far as to claim that Tsui represents an Asian manifestation of the phenomenon David James, writing about the activities of Andy Warhol and his circle, once termed 'The Producer as Author'. For James, Warhol's 'genius was to arrange it so that the "creative visionary" and "shrewd businessman" in their joint operations consistently ratified the other's activity'.[2] Such is also the case with Tsui Hark.

Given this frenzy of activity behind the camera as well as in the boardroom, it is worth considering whether the name Tsui Hark is perceived to project any kind of coherent or consistent vision. Certainly, he is often taken to have a distinct directorial style. Tsui's work has a restless, knife-edge quality; scenes are moved along at breakneck speed, rapid editing and an assortment of wacky camera angles accentuating his preference for highly kinetic acting styles. Moreover, dynamic sound/image relations underpin his penchant for narratives that combine action and drama with comedy and romance. (Perhaps acknowledging Tsui's stirring use of Canto-pop in *Peking Opera Blues*, the *Once Upon a Time in China* series, and others, electronic dance band Sparks recorded a tribute song, 'Tsui Hark', on their 1995 CD *Gratuitous Sax and Senseless Violins*.) For many critics and fans, all this is enough to confirm Tsui's status as a 'movie brat' whose film-school sensibilities and aesthetic proclivities are there for all to see. Yet at the other extreme, such a hodgepodge of one-damn-thing-after-another may be viewed as testimony to a failure of nerve on Tsui's part. After all, is not restlessness another word for uncertainty? If so much *effort* goes into attaining all those different moods and camera positions does that not suggest a fundamental anxiety over how the films and their spectators are being conceptualized?

There are two ways of approaching such questions. First, the drive and ambition, the sheer *eager-to-please-ness* of titles like *All the Wrong Clues* and *The Blade*, suggest the shrewd businessman's attempt to retain domestic and foreign moviegoers' interest by any means necessary – usually by offering a little bit of this, then a little bit of that. Consider, for example, Tsui's appropriation of diverse generic tendencies. In the 1980s and 1990s, popular Hong Kong cinema differentiated itself in the international marketplace partly on the basis of its creative utilization of elements from traditional Chinese opera and folklore, Japanese manga and anime, MTV aesthetics, and the future visions of Hollywood-style special effects. Accordingly, Tsui's work has at times been identified with each of these artistic bloodlines. (Fan cultures, on the other hand, have tended to identify him largely through narrower definitions of fantasy and martial arts cinema.)

Second, it is possible to view the effort and energy that goes into Tsui's attempts to resist generic labelling as an indication of political confusion or hesitancy. It is significant that the word customarily used to describe this particular filmmaker's worldview is 'cynical', an indication perhaps of a lack of commitment to a set of core social beliefs. Stephen Teo has pointed out that 'Tsui Hark does not mince images – he munches them. He is a primitive, even brutish film-maker',[3] and as evidence one might point to the lack of faith concerning humanity's sincerity and goodness exhibited by scenes of cannibalism (*We're Going to Eat You*), the torture of a beautiful female revolutionary (*Peking Opera Blues*) or the serving up of rare monkey's brains as illicit culinary delicacies (*The Chinese Feast*). Yet, Tsui's films have an undeniable political edge. For example, in 1980 his engagement with pressing social issues landed him in trouble when the Hong Kong Television and Entertainment Licencing Authority reacted with alarm to *Dangerous Encounter – First Kind*'s critique of neo-colonialism.[4]

Tsui's ambivalent, at times detached political stance should be seen in light of his status as an outsider, a member of the Vietnamese migrant community frequently stigmatized in Hong Kong society (cf. fellow New Wave director Ann Hui's *The Story of Woo Viet* (1981) and *Boat People* (1982)). His own take on this subject, *A Better Tomorrow III*, is representative of his work as a whole in being both shamelessly exploitative and genuinely heartfelt. Going beyond the Triad concerns of John Woo's first two films of the series, this 'prequel' contains one of the most startling depictions of the US pull out of Vietnam ever committed to celluloid. In the intensely melodramatic final scene, Mark (Chow Yun-Fat) is saved by the female hero, Chow Ying-kit (Anita Mui), as the two of them attempt to scramble aboard the last American helicopter out of Saigon. But Mark can only watch helplessly as Kit proceeds to die in his arms

Given the alarmist nature of this particular scene, wherein communist soldiers fire indiscriminately into the crowd and the invading army's flag is raised into an ominous-looking sky, it is hardly surprising that *A Better Tomorrow III*, together with other titles directed or supervised by Tsui Hark, has been read allegorically in terms of Hong Kong's recent return to Chinese sovereignty. However, while such interpretations are completely valid (*A Better Tomorrow III* was produced during the time of the 1989 democracy movement's brutal suppression at Tiananmen Square), and have done much to structure international perception of Tsui's films, his movies are also open to other political readings.

One subject largely ignored by western critics, but very relevant to Tsui's reception in Asia itself, is his relationship to earlier periods of Chinese cinema. To be sure, some of the connections are obvious enough – the series of Huang Feihong films made in Hong Kong throughout the 1950s and 1960s, for example, were gloriously updated for *Once Upon a Time in China* and its sequels. Other links have been less widely appreciated, however. Just as mainland Fifth Generation directors like Chen Kaige and Hu Mei have claimed allegiance with the memory of the pre-1949 leftist Chinese cinema, Tsui's *Shanghai Blues* borrows and transposes elements from the 1937 leftist classic *Crossroads* (Shen Xiling, 1937). Yet Tsui's updated version of this story also resembles the 1940 Hollywood melodrama *Waterloo Bridge*, thus spawning an intriguing set of historical analogies. Mervyn LeRoy shot *Waterloo Bridge* on a Hollywood soundstage meant to simulate the image of an England at war against Nazi Germany; Tsui filmed *Shanghai Blues* on a Hong Kong soundstage meant to approximate events in China at the time of the 1937 war against Japan; *Crossroads* was itself shot in 1937, partly as a response to those same momentous events. Beyond this, it is worth exploring too Tsui's understanding and representations of the moment of his own adolescence, namely 1960s' Hong Kong. As the decade when the Crown Colony's modern cultural identity began to ferment against a background of anti-British riots, the Cultural Revolution, youth insurrection and the Vietnam war, how did the imprint of those compelling social issues mutate over time into Tsui's generically diverse creative visions?

Tsui's habitual interest in questions of identity formation and sexual deviancy appears deeply influenced by the new social movements of the 1960s. This subject has both attracted the attention of several western critics[5] and done much to define his image as a cult filmmaker. Simply put, if you are interested in gender inversion, transsexuality, polymorphous perversity and the like, then Tsui's your man. Tellingly, however, the jury is still out with regard to how radical the sexual politics of titles like *Peking Opera Blues*, *Swordsman*, *Once Upon a Time in China II*, *Green Snake* and *The Lovers* actually are. On one hand, gay Hong Kong director Stanley Kwan has led the case for the prosecution, arguing with great force in his wonderful 1996 documentary, *Yang ± Yin: Gender in Chinese Cinema*, that no Chinese filmmaker 'is more fascinated by cross-dressing and gender-bending than Tsui Hark ... but Tsui's films always end by reaffirming heterosexual norms'.

And the case for the defence? It may be worth nuancing Kwan's charge, made in the context of a discussion of *The Lovers*, that Tsui rewrites the film 'in such a blatantly heterosexual way', or reheterosexualizes it. One important issue that discussion of homosexuality, heterosexuality and the position of women in Tsui Hark's work raises is that of cross-cultural understanding. When such films are circulated globally, Asian and western discourses of reception need to be placed against each other so as to highlight their contingent nature. Arguably, then, Kwan's statement needs to be seen in the wider context of Hong Kong cinema's reworking of diverse populist genres, the global dynamics of queer identity politics in the 1990s, the role of sexual disguise in Asian and western popular comedy, and the potential pleasures of ambiguity and indeterminacy opened up transnationally by the concept of the producer as author. If one wanted to be supportive, one might say that debates on homosexuality in Asian cinema were animated in the 1990s, and that Tsui's important films have a lot to tell us about the issues at stake.

In recent years, Tsui Hark has consolidated his position in international film culture as his films have bridged East and West at the point of production. Tsui once looked to Hollywood for inspiration – inviting some of the technicians who worked on *Star Wars* (1977) over to Hong Kong to generate the special effects for *Zu: Warriors from the Magic Mountain* – but Hollywood has now returned the compliment. Along with fellow Chinese directors Jackie Chan, Peter Pau, Ringo Lam and John Woo, Tsui took up residency in Los Angeles in the 1990s, relocating to Beverly Hills while keeping one eye on the latest developments back home. This influx of Hong Kong talent into the constraints of the Hollywood action cinema is frequently characterized as an 'Asian invasion'. Moreover, it is conceptualized through the rhetoric of assimilation or integration, whereby eastern directors have to learn to play the game the American way, rather than the other way around.

Yet the North American reception of Tsui Hark calls for a crucial modification of this perception. Tsui's work for Hollywood over the past few years (*Double Team, Knock Off*) should be viewed in terms of his *return* to the US. Aside from studying and working in the States during formative periods of his life, Tsui also shot what are ostensibly Hong Kong movies on location in Los Angeles and New York during the 1990s (*The Master, Twin Dragons*). And when Stephen Short of *Time* magazine asked him what it was like to move from Vietnam to Hong Kong when he was 13 years old, Tsui replied: 'Hong Kong was a totally different world. It compared to nothing I'd seen in my life to that point. That's odd too, because when I went to Texas to study, everything was Saigon, Saigon, Saigon, and Vietnam was the word on every American's lips. I felt instantly more at home there than I ever did in Hong Kong.'

In returning to his adopted 'home', Tsui Hark has perhaps re-established a sense of connection to the Asian-American communities politicized by the ongoing legacies of the Vietnam war and racial exclusion. In the 1990s, Asian-American film festivals sprang up all over the country, specialized pop culture magazines began to cater to an enthusiastic fan base, and Asian-American film companies produced an impressive array of innovative shorts and feature-length titles. One independent artist, Kip Fulbeck, made *A Critique of Game of Death* (1996), which posed the question of whether or not 1970s' martial arts star Bruce Lee should be held up as a desirable hero for Asian-Americans (the same could now be asked of one of Tsui's regular actors, Jet Li). The equation between Asian and Asian-American cultural spheres should not be made too casually. However, the presence of Tsui Hark, part creative visionary, part shrewd businessman, in both the US and East Asia may have unforeseen effects on the future of Hollywood cinema, just as it has on Hong Kong movies.

Biography

Born in Canton, China, in 1951, but raised as a youngster in Vietnam, Tsui Hark moved to Hong Kong in 1966. He attended film classes at the Southern Methodist University and the University of Texas at Austin in the USA in the late 1960s and early 1970s. From there, he packed his bags for the East Coast, working alongside celebrated documentarist Christine Choy at a Chinese cable television station in New York, before returning to Hong Kong and making an important television mini-series, *The Gold Dagger Romance*, in 1978.

Notes

1 Quoted in Beth Accomando, 'Army of Harkness', *Giant Robot 8*, 1997, pp. 27–30, p. 29.
2 David James, 'The Producer as Author', in Michael O'Pray (ed.) *Andy Warhol: Film Factory*, London, BFI Publishing, 1989, pp. 136–45, p. 145.
3 Stephen Teo, *Hong Kong Cinema: The Extra Dimensions*, London, BFI Publishing, 1997, p. 162.
4 See Kam Tan, 'Ban(g)! Ban(g)! Dangerous Encounter – 1st Kind: Writing with Censorship', *Asian Cinema*, vol. 8, no. 1, 1996, pp. 83–108.
5 Compare Rolanda Chu, '*Swordsman II* and *The East is Red*: The "Hong Kong Film", Entertainment, and Gender', *Bright Lights Film Journal*, no. 13, 1993, pp. 30–5 and p. 46; Julian Stringer, 'Review of *Peking Opera Blues*', *Film Quarterly*, vol. 48, no. 3, 1995, pp. 34–42.

Filmography

The Butterfly Murders (1979)
Dangerous Encounter – First Kind (1980)
We're Going to Eat You (1980)
All the Wrong Clues (for the Right Solution) (1981)
Zu: Warriors From the Magic Mountain (1983)
Aces Go Places III (1984)
Shanghai Blues (1984)
Working Class (1985)
Peking Opera Blues (1986)
A Better Tomorrow III: Love and Death in Saigon (1989)
Swordsman (1990) as co-director
Once Upon a Time in China (1991)
The Master (1991)
The Banquet (1991)
Once Upon a Time in China II (1992)
King of Chess (1992) as co-director
Once Upon a Time in China III (1992)
Twin Dragons (1992) as co-director
Green Snake (1993)
Once Upon a Time in China V (1994)
The Lovers (1994)

Love in the Time of Twilight (1995)
The Blade (1995)
The Chinese Feast (1995)
Tri-Star (1996)
Double Team (1997)
Knock Off (1998)
Time and Tide (2000)

Further reading

Pat Aufderheide, 'Dynamic Duo', *Film Comment*, vol. 24, no. 3, 1988, pp. 43–5.

Howard Hampton, 'Tsui Hark and Ching Siu-tung', *Film Comment*, vol. 33, no. 4, 1997, pp. 16–19, 24–7.

Ange Hwang, 'The Irresistible: Hong Kong Movie *Once Upon a Time in China* Series – An Extensive Interview with Director/Producer Tsui Hark', *Asian Cinema*, vol. 10, no. 1, 1998, pp. 10–23.

Leo Ou-fan Lee, 'Two Films from Hong Kong: Parody and Allegory', in Nick Browne, Paul G. Pickowicz, Vivian Sobchack and Esther Yau (eds) *New Chinese Cinemas: Forms, Identities, Politics*, New York, Cambridge University Press, 1994, pp. 202–15.

Cheuk-to Li, 'Tsui Hark and Western Interest in Hong Kong Cinema', *Cinemaya*, vol. 21, 1993, pp. 50–1.

Bey Logan, *Hong Kong Action Cinema*, New York, The Overlook Press, 1996.

Stephen Short, 'Tsui Hark: You Have to Touch People with Film', *Time*. Online: http://www.cnn.com/ASIANOW/time/features/interview/int.tsui-hark05032000 (accessed 3 March 2000).

Lisa Odham Stokes and Michael Hoover, *City on Fire: Hong Kong Cinema*, London, Verso, 1999.

JULIAN STRINGER

MAKING MOVIES THAT MATTER

CHRISTINE VACHON, INDEPENDENT FILM PRODUCER

Since the 1950s, when some of the first debates about film authorship were aired in the French journal *Cahiers du cinéma*, filmmakers have been measured against a 'continuity' of stylistic vision associated with a pantheon of almost exclusively male directors. The inclusion of Christine Vachon in this collection about contemporary filmmakers serves to widen debates about the role of the filmmaker beyond that of the director. 'Producers may not be auteurs,' writes Amy Taubin, 'but they are much more essential than our director-worshipping and actor-fetishizing culture suggest.'[1]

Vachon came to notice in connection with some of the first films branded as 'New Queer Cinema' – she produced both Todd Haynes' *Poison* and Tom Kalin's *Swoon*. Her involvement with these projects founded her reputation as the 'Queen of Queer' (a title she loathes). Although such 'royal' status remains uncomfortable for her, her subsequent fame and her key role as the producer of an exciting range of independent and, in the broadest sense, 'queer' films makes Vachon an interesting figure.

Although Vachon wrote and directed three short films in the 1980s (*A Man in Your Room* (1984), *Days are Numbered* (1986) and *The Way of the Wicked* (1989)), her reputation rests on her role as producer of an impressive list of low-budget and cutting-edge features. Over the past ten years, Vachon has become the doyenne of New York's independent filmmakers. She has produced notable and, often controversial, critical successes, including Larry Clark's *Kids*, Mary Harron's *I Shot Andy Warhol* and Todd Solondz'*Happiness*. Vachon herself has described the role of the producer as 'one of the great mysteries of the movie-making process'.[2] In many ways a producer has an all-encompassing and yet an unquantifiable role in the making of a film – one that mediates between both the dictates of the financial marketplace and the 'vision' of the director (and, of course, all places in between). In this essay I shall focus on Vachon's contribution to US independent filmmaking, contrasting public perceptions of her role with an examination of her own views and reflections about the job.

Associated with work typically described as 'provocative' and 'risky', Vachon was very much at the centre of the 'New Queer Cinema' movement which exploded in the early 1990s. Not only Vachon's dismissal of herself as 'queer royalty'[3] but writings by B. Ruby Rich and Amy Taubin[4] attest that the 'queer' film phenomenon has proved to be a hugely problematic site for both women filmmakers and, indeed, for some women viewers. While the bubble of a New Queer Cinema brought with it excitement, mainstream interest and the promise of a wider distribution than previously imagined for films that could not be classified as 'straight' (either structurally or in terms of content), it also foregrounded a series of tensions and debates. Vachon's early vehicles were amongst those important productions that Alexander Doty has seen as fuelling 'much of the queer film and popular culture theory and criticisms developed in the 1990s'.[5] With hindsight, one of the most significant functions of these films was the creation of what might be termed a nexus of transition. New Queer Cinema arguably formed a site for the playing out of critical, theoretical and artistic (and here, I mean specifically practice-based) tensions centred on the replacement of lesbian feminism by queer performativity and the working out of post-AIDS sexualities.

For some, as Jackie Stacey suggests, 'Queer cinema offered a direct challenge to what was seen as the "positive images" trap of lesbian and gay cinema of the 1970s and 1980s.'[6] For others, an evaluation of the relation of lesbian to queer provoked various political debates that suggested the creation of a new lesbian marginalization. In an early response to New Queer Cinema, Taubin suggested that women were 'even more marginalized in "queer" than in heterosexual films; at least in the latter, they function as objects of desire'.[7] The lesbian/queer debate was to detonate in a spirited exchange of views in magazines and journals[8] and briefly haunted Vachon herself. As the successful young woman producer of more than one New Queer 'classic', she was the public face at the intersection of queer artistic practice and concerns about gender and lesbian identities. Thus, Vachon herself became a focus for many of these anxieties. Initially her association with 'boys' films' was so strong that when she did the rounds trying to raise funds for Rose Troche's lesbian love story, *Go Fish* (1994), it was seen as some sort of deliberate strategy to break the connection.[9] Although undoubtedly more interested in talking about her film projects than her sexual identity, Vachon did not shy away from controversy or the queer/lesbian film debate. At one point she felt moved to make a personal intervention by way of an angry letter to *The Village Voice*[10], in which she highlighted the very real experience of homophobia in life as a lesbian negotiating the mundane and the everyday. Vachon can be seen, therefore, to firmly politicize her own sense of the personal in the midst of what has been referred to as the fashionableness and 'trendiness of queer cinema'.[11]

Go Fish, a 'girl gets girl' romantic comedy, shot in black and white on a tiny budget, was not only fêted in a deliriously successful début at the Sundance Festival[12] but was heralded in the lesbian press as a new film for a new generation. It destabilized many of the more rigid lesbian feminist orthodoxies about a unified and/or stable lesbian sexual identity and questioned the need for 'positive images'. By concentrating on lifestyle instead of angst and by making the diversity of lesbian relationships its central focus, it not only countered contemporary worries about lesbian marginalization, but also self-consciously played out a transition from a lesbian to a queer notion of sexuality precisely by, to borrow from Richard

Dyer's formulation of queer sexuality, returning 'control over same-sex sexuality to those who live it'.[13] *Go Fish*, one of the first in a wave of films later dubbed 'lesbian lite', was kept alive after its initial shoot with $5,000 from Vachon's own pocket before she managed to bring Jon Pierson's Good Machine company on board.[14] A series of feelgood romances made by lesbian independent filmmakers emerged in the wake of *Go Fish*'s success. While films such as Cheryl Dunye's *Watermelon Woman* (1996) or Maria Maggenti's *The Incredibly True Adventures of Two Girls in Love* (1995) utilized the expected art-film aesthetics, they provided a parallel and yet more optimistic, upbeat exploration of non-hegemonic sexuality.

For a moment in the early 1990s, the kind of publicity and excitement that surrounded both US independent film production and Vachon suggested that there might be the possibility of thinking about producers as auteurs. While I would not want to argue the position forcefully, it does make a difference who makes a film. In the various critical vacillations concerning film authorship of the last forty years or so, the concept of the single author or auteur has tended to be either reified or trashed. By and large, it has been the director who has received all the attention when questions of authorship have been considered. The director emerges as the source or meaning and the driving artistic vision. As Dyer has argued, in this spirit texts 'were often treated, at worst, as illustrations of the author's biography, at best as the expression of his inner life'.[15] As V.F. Perkins has powerfully argued, what has usually been overlooked in discussions of film authorship has been the most crucial element – what films are actually like.[16] Movies are the culmination of a process of collaboration and in the independent sector this can be a particularly 'hands on' affair for the producer. Making films outside mainstream institutional mechanisms presents many challenges (not least those of budget) but also offers the opportunity to make different kinds of films by different kinds of processes. When discussing *Go Fish*, Vachon acknowledges Troche's role as director but also includes writer/actress Guinevere Turner and and actress V.S. Brodie as the 'team' and driving force behind the project.[17] In the first flush of the exciting new turn of US independent cinema that was New Queer Cinema, along with the director's name (Haynes, Kalin, Troche) came the producer's name, Christine Vachon, as part of the package. After seeing her first few productions, I and other viewers worked on the assumption that Vachon's name held out the promise of an interesting film.

Vachon seems both resigned and dedicated to her position in the independent margins of American filmmaking: 'unless someone gives me forty million dollars to make a picture about bisexual rockers, or a sympathetic pedophile, or a woman who wakes up one day and realizes that modern society is slowly poisoning her to death, it's the world in which I'll stay'.[18] Her conception of the space where she makes films is dominated by the myth (if not always the reality) of the auteur. It is understandable why she would want to continue and maintain this connection. As a graduate in semiotics from Brown University who also spent a year in Paris attending lectures by Michel Foucault and studying with Julia Kristeva and Christian Metz, Vachon possesses an unusual theoretical understanding of representation and the medium of film. She admits to having an underlying conviction that 'the more you know about the history of film, the better you can imagine its possibilities'.[19] It is not surprising, therefore, that Vachon should have sought out certain kinds of film projects and filmmakers. In short, to make what she calls 'movies that matter'.[20] Inspired by the idea of the director as auteur, Vachon has chosen to work with directors who endeavour 'to put their singular visions on the screen'.[21] Reflecting on her relationship with film directors, she admits that she has always shown a preference for the obsessive visionary as opposed to the *metteur-en-scène* who sees filmmaking as just a job.

One of her richest working partnerships has been with fellow Brown alumni Todd Haynes. Although they barely knew each other in their Brown days, in the mid-1980s they were both involved with Apparatus Films – an uncompromising company that had the mandate to make movies by young filmmakers who were just starting out. For Vachon and Haynes, this was very much the start of a commitment to radical film practice founded on sound notions of film theory and film history. Their first collaboration, *Poison* (where Vachon acted as both assistant director and producer), made them stars of the burgeoning independent sector. The paranoid environmental/medical thriller *Safe*, reputedly one of Vachon's favourites, and more recently the wonderfully complex, and relatively bigger-budget, glam-rock epic *Velvet Goldmine* have further consolidated their reputations. Central to the success of their collaboration has been an uncompromising attitude to the possibilities of cinematic pleasure. Throughout her career, Vachon has chosen to support films that engage with 'difficult' subject matters – for instance, paedophilia in Solondz' *Happiness* (a film that surely pushes the audience to boundaries of both discomfort and pleasure). As a producer she has encouraged projects involving 'difficult' stylistic and aesthetic choices that destabilize conventional constructions/ notions of genre, narrative and character identification,[22] as in photographer Cindy Sherman's directorial début, *Office Killer*. By choosing not to fix meanings in the way of mainstream cinemas, the kinds of film that Vachon has produced tend to require creative (if often uncomfortable) audience identifications and readings.

By not looking beyond the figure of director as author, the discipline of film studies has negated the real importance of film audiences in contributing to the meaning of film texts. Indeed, at the same time, this omission disallows the possibility of the audience suggesting their own film authors above and beyond that of the director. While I would not go so far as positing Vachon as the author of the texts that she produces, her close involvement at all levels and at every stage of her filmmaking projects would seem to imply at least the possibility of partial collaborative auteur status, though not quite in the way 'classic' auteurs have usually been conceived of. In *Shooting to Kill*, Christine Vachon offers an experiential account of the role of an independent film producer, on more than one occasion likening the process of bringing a project to fruition to childbirth. It is evident from the way in which she discusses her role as general fixer, facilitator and pragmatist – holding hands, stroking egos and even bailing actors out of jail – that she sees her function as that of both nurturer and leader. The fundraising and marketing aspects of the production task demonstrated her confident abilities in leadership. In her close collaboration with each director she can be seen as instrumental in guiding her directors' visions to the screen. As she explains: 'I match directors with cinematographers, cinematographers with production designers, production designers with location managers ...'.[23] Vachon certainly makes a strong claim to have her creative input recognized as integral to the shaping of the film projects with which she has been involved.

While the immediate success of her early productions gave the impression of a golden touch, Vachon's intelligence and energy, together with the deserved reputation for getting six things done at the same time, suggest that more than luck is involved. In exploiting the possibilities of low-budget filmmaking in terms of taking risks with its subject matter, aesthetics and form, Vachon was able to rise with the swell of a new tide of American art-house filmmaking, spearheaded by New Queer Cinema. In addition, she has demonstrated her awareness of the constantly changing nature of the American mainstream and its relationship with the independent sector. Since her early ventures in the early 1990s, the Sundance Festival at Park City Utah has been transformed from a marginal event to an established and highly influential institution. A combination of her reputation and her obvious ability to deliver the goods at the best possible value for money, together with a hungry market for US independent films, means that she can now sometimes call on the support of mainstream companies like Miramax to bring projects (for example, *Kids*, Larry Clark's hard-hitting film about street kids) to completion. More recently, in her third feature with Haynes, *Velvet Goldmine*, Vachon has rather coyly revealed that she was able to command a budget of between $8 and $10 million. James Shamus of Good Machine, INC (one of Vachon's regular co-producers) has articulated the current economic realities of making independent films in what is an increasingly receptive market but which has seen an erosion of public funding. He sums up the working practices of himself and Vachon (whom he describes as 'post-late-capitalist entrepreneurs who aren't thrilled about capital-ism') as the application of sound small business practices to 'counterculture or subcultural modes of expression'.[24] Such are the everyday and material realities of Vachon's role as a filmmaker.

If there is a defining sense of the work that Vachon is involved in producing, it might involve a repetition of explicitly gay and sexually subversive themes. Her product is therefore marked by a certain consistency of theme, but there is still no real way of defining a Christine Vachon film unless arguments about film authorship move forward to both recognize the work of audiences in this area and to realize, as Perkins has suggested, that the 'authorship of movies may be achieved not despite but in and through collaboration'.[25] Vachon's real importance as a filmmaker may be that she has made entire films for the same money a mainstream filmmaker might spend on dining out.

Biography

Christine Vachon was born in 1962, in New York, USA.

Notes

1 'Art & Industry' (n.d.) Online. Available HTTP: < http://www.village voice.com >
2 Christine Vachon, *Shooting to Kill: How an Independent Producer Blasts through the Barriers to Make the Movies that Matter*, London, Bloomsbury, 1998, p. 2.

3   *Ibid.*, p. 18.

4   B. Ruby Rich, 'Homo Pomo: The New Queer Cinema' and Amy Taubin, 'Queer Male Cinema and Feminism', both in Pam Cook and Philip Dodd (eds) *Women and Film: A Sight and Sound Reader*, Scarlet Press, London, 1993, pp. 164–73 and 176–9.

5   Alexander Doty, 'Queer Theory', in John Hill and Pamela Church Gibson (eds) *The Oxford Guide to Film Studies*, Oxford University Press, Oxford,1998, p. 148.

6   Jackie Stacey, 'Feminist Theory: Capital F, Capital T', in Victoria Robinson and Diane Richardson (eds) *Introducing Women's Studies*, 2nd edn, Macmillan, Basingstoke and London, 1997, p. 61.

7   Amy Taubin, *op. cit.*, p. 178.

8   For instance, see Pratibha Parmar's 'Queer Questions: A Response to B. Ruby Rich', first published in *Sight and Sound*, September 1992; reprinted in Pam Cook and Philip Dodd, *op. cit*, pp. 174–5.

9   Christine Vachon, *ibid.*, p. 19.

10 See Rachel Abramowitz's lively discussion, 'Lesbian Filmmakers are Telling Stories of Wit, Wonder and Wide-eyed Romance', *Premiere*, Online. Available: www.premieremag.com/archieve/Feb-96/girls/

11 Yvonne Tasker, *Working Girls: Gender and Sexuality in Popular Cinema*, Routledge, London, 1998, p. 16.

12 As John Pierson explains in *Spike, Mike, Slackers & Dykes: A Guided Tour Across a Decade of American Independent Cinema* (London, Faber and Faber, 1996), *Go Fish* was the first film ever to be sold at the Sundance Festival.

13 Richard Dyer, 'Believing in Fairies: The Author and the Homosexual', in Diana Fuss (ed.) *Inside/out: Lesbian Theories, Gay Theories*, Routledge, Chapman and Hall, New York, 1991, p. 186.

14 Christine Vachon, *op. cit.*, p. 137.

15 Richard Dyer, *op. cit.*, p. 186.

16 V.F. Perkins, 'Film Authorship: The Premature Burial', *CineAction*, 57–64 (Summer/Fall), 1990, p. 61.

17 Christine Vachon, *op. cit.*, p. 22.

18 *Ibid.*, p. 2.

19 *Ibid.*, p. 6.

20 Hence the title of her memoir/how to be a producer manual.

21 Christine Vachon, *op. cit.*, p. 1.

22 There are some exceptions, however, for example, *Kiss Me Guido* (low budget, gay subject matter that challenges stereotypes but which is not visually challenging) was considered too mainstream at Sundance.

23 Christine Vachon, *op. cit.*, p. 2.

24 *Ibid.*, p. 298.

25 V.F. Perkins, *op. cit.*, p. 61.

Filmography

(All as producer)
Poison (1991)
Swoon (1992)
Dottie Gets Spanked (1993) television short

Safe (1995)
Kids (1995)
Stonewall (1995)
I Shot Andy Warhol (1996)
Plain Pleasures (1996)
Kiss Me Guido (1997)
Office Killer (1997)
Happiness (1998)
Velvet Goldmine (1998)
I'm Losing You (1998)
Boys Don't Cry (1999)
Series 7: The Contenders (2001)

ROS JENNINGS

LARS VON TRIER

The films

Lars von Trier is widely regarded as the most important Danish filmmaker since Carl Theodor Dreyer, not only on account of the highly original quality of his cinematic *œuvre*, but also because his role as an inspirational figure has made him a driving force in the renewal of Danish film. Von Trier's relation to the tradition of Danish film is polemical and largely negative; his first feature films established a clear preference for English-language filmmaking in an internationalized art-cinema vein involving a visual style influenced by, among others, Andrei Tarkovsky. *Element of Crime*, *Epidemic* and *Europa* (US title: *Zentropa*) were framed by von Trier as a trilogy exploring a Europe that, although strangely deterritorialized, somehow ends up being largely synonymous with Germany. The trilogy, claims von Trier, pits nature against culture. Each of the three films develops a story centred around an 'inquiring humanist who leaves his home terrain, ... journeys out into nature' and ends up being destroyed by the very process in question.[1]

Von Trier's view that film can induce states resembling hypnotic trance is evident in the trilogy's insistence on a connection between narrative and hypnosis. The entire story of *Element of Crime*, von Trier's attempt at a modern film noir, is framed as a narrative of serial murder related to a Cairo psychiatrist by his hypnotized patient, the European policeman Fisher (Michael Elphick). The low-budget, black-and-white meta-film *Epidemic* features Lars von Trier as both a sardonic irreverent filmmaker and as the idealistic doctor

Mesmer of his envisaged fiction film. The film concludes with the filmmaker and his co-writer, Niels Vørsel, presenting their project to an actual consultant from the Danish Film Institute, Claes Kastholm Hansen. Part of their presentation involves hypnotizing a young woman with the intent of having her enter their imagined fictional universe. The group is suddenly smitten by plague symptoms – the explanation, it would appear, lies in the woman's hypnotic imaginings. In *Europa*, a melodramatic love story involving a Nazi sympathizer, Katharina Hartmann (Barbara Sukowa), and a young American idealist of German extraction, Leo Kessler (Jean-Marc Barr), von Trier makes use of an intricate form of cinematic narration. More specifically, the disembodied voice of Max von Sydow hypnotically directs both the viewer and the main character through the unfolding narrative. Although these three films are different in many respects, they clearly manifest von Trier's affinity with a German expressionist cinematic style which emphasizes long shots and elaborate camera movements through highly contrived and carefully constructed scenographic spaces. The trilogy was accompanied by a series of provocative manifestos. The first called for 'heterosexual films for, about and by men', the second sang the praises of cinematic trifles, and the third, framed as a confession, characterized von Trier as a mere 'masturbator of the screen'.[2]

A key element in von Trier's *œuvre* is his self-image as provocateur, a stance expressed in the influential Dogme 95 project which von Trier developed together with another young luminary of contemporary Danish cinema, Thomas Vinterberg. In brief, the four participating filmmakers (von Trier, Vinterberg, Søren Kragh-Jacobsen and Kristian Levring) agreed to submit to a vow of chastity involving strict rules designed to foster the essential elements of cinematic art that are particularly at risk in big-budget productions using cutting-edge technology. Thus, for example, 'shooting must be done on location', 'the sound must never be produced apart from the images or vice versa', 'the camera must be hand-held' and 'optical work and filters are forbidden'. Dogme 95 also expresses an interest in collective authorship inasmuch as the relevant directors submit to uniform rules and cannot be individually credited. Initially to have been supported by a special grant from the Danish Ministry of Culture, Dogme 95 was ultimately made possible, following considerable controversy, by support from the Danish Broadcasting Corporation. The first Danish Dogme film, Vinterberg's *Festen* (*The Celebration*, 1998), was co-winner of the Special Jury Prize at Cannes and helped to consolidate a growing international interest in new Danish cinema. Dogme 95 has since become a transnational undertaking: as many as five foreign Dogme films have been released, while the producers of an additional fourteen films have applied for the relevant Dogme certificate.[3]

Von Trier's *Idioterne* (*The Idiots*) is the second of the Danish Dogme films; it explores what the director refers to as the 'distasteful idea of people who are not in fact retarded pretending to be'.[4] Karen (Bodil Jørgensen), an outsider who initially questions the propriety of pretending to be retarded, has a special place in the group. The film concludes with her playing the lunatic where the personal risks are greatest, that is, in front of her husband and other family members who have not seen her since the death of her 1-year-old son. She is accompanied by Susanne (Louise Hassing), who learns of her deep grief for the first time and movingly bears witness to Karen's new-found ability to achieve the authenticity that somehow accompanies the project of idiotic pretence. At the level of both form and content, the film reflects von Trier's romantic investment in some of the ideals of the 1960s.[5] In addition, claims von Trier, the aim was to produce a cocktail consisting of 'sickly self-centred idiocy on the part of the group's members, combined with intense sentimentality and emotionally charged scenes'.[6] This insistence on sentimentality is linked to von Trier's intentions in *Breaking the Waves*, whilst recalling his interest in reviving the much maligned and frequently adapted works by the maudlin popular writer, Morten Korch, as well as his remarkably successful attempt in *Dancer in the Dark* to combine certain sentimental qualities with the highly stylized musical genre.[7]

In the context of an exchange about the Dogme rules, von Trier clearly identifies the central role played by the concept of provocation in his cinematic work:

> Specifying all those things the directors aren't allowed to do is in itself a provocation. But the business of not allowing the directors to be credited was like a punch in the face of all directors. I quite like that. But while there's an externally directed provocation here, there's also an even stronger inwardly directed provocation. What provokes others also provokes me. I've used my name a lot in promoting my films, just as David Bowie – whom I'm a great fan of – has allowed his person to fuse with his work. That's why I decided to provoke myself in this way, just to see what would happen.

The provocation is always initially inwardly directed, and then it becomes other-directed as a side effect.[8]

One of von Trier's earliest works, his graduation film *Befrielses-billeder* (*Images of a Relief*), already manifests those elements of formal and thematic provocation that have become defining features of his work. Set in Denmark in 1945, the film uses a visual style heavily indebted to Tarkovsky to explore the defeat of the German occupiers. The film construes the German Wehrmacht soldier, Leo (Edward Flemming), as a victim, showing his eyes being stabbed out by his Danish lover, Esther (Kirsten Olesen), in a sacrificial scene which has him literally ascending to heaven. If the thematic provocation here is a matter of taking issue with broadly humanist conceptions of the atrocities of the Second World War, the formal provocation takes the form of rule-following. *Images of a Relief*, claims von Trier, is 'incredibly, almost hysterically structured. It's in three parts, and every take refers to a take in the next part.'[9] Referring to *Riget* and *Riget 2* (*The Kingdom* and *The Kingdom 2*), von Trier explains his repeated characterization of the David Lynch-inspired hospital series as 'left-handed work': 'It's not the work of a fine hand, which is also a way of provoking yourself, if you're used to writing with your right hand.'[10] Von Trier's *œuvre* lends credence to the idea, which he himself clearly espouses, that creativity is linked not so much to untrammelled freedom, as it is to precisely defined challenges and clearly articulated constraints.

The erotic melodrama *Breaking the Waves* was 'once again, an attempt to provoke myself. I establish a problematic and take things to their logical conclusion, which involves asking whether a sacrifice could be sexual. We know about the sacrifices of saints, so why couldn't a sexual sacrifice be a saintly sacrifice?'[11] According to von Trier, this melodramatic tale of sexual transgression and self-sacrifice can be traced to a childhood fascination with a character called 'Gold Heart' who responds to the need of others by giving away everything she has while claiming in each instance that she will be fine. In true fairytale fashion, she is ultimately rewarded when one of her beneficiaries returns as a prince and lays claim to her heart, which she readily gives away while uttering her standard refrain. *Breaking the Waves* is set in a remote part of Scotland where severe Presbyterian attitudes are dominant. The film centres around the relationship between Bess (Emily Watson), a young and inexperienced local woman, and her husband Jan (Stellan Skarsgård), who is one of a number of outsiders working on an off-shore oil rig.

When Jan is paralysed following an accident on the rig, Bess, having previously begged God for her husband's return, assumes that she is to blame. Bess becomes convinced that Jan's recovery depends on her willingness to sacrifice herself sexually. And Jan does in fact emerge from a coma as Bess expires as a result of knife wounds inflicted by a sexual sadist (played by Udo Kier). The film concludes with shots of enormous bells ringing in the heavens following Bess' secret burial at sea. Von Trier was raised by strict non-believers, but later converted to Catholicism, influenced no doubt by his first wife, Cæcilia Holbek Trier. While critics have been inclined to interpret the religious dimension of *Breaking the Waves* in terms of the kind of ironic attitudes that are clearly evident in von Trier's earlier work, the filmmaker himself insists that the narrative of self-sacrifice and transcendence is an expression of his own deep-seated religiosity. The film, which won the Grand Jury Prize at Cannes, was praised for its remarkable acting and an effective visual style shaped by hand-held cameras and slowly evolving 'chapter' images produced digitally by the renowned Danish painter, Per Kirkeby.

The person

The significance of a public persona can frequently be traced not only to genuine achievements, but to the complicated dynamics of recognition, gate-keeping and self-staging. In the case of von Trier, the combination of properly relevant cinematic elements and more external sociological or institutional factors is particularly noteworthy. In connection with the success of *Dancer in the Dark*, which won the Palme d'Or at Cannes in 2000, Kragh-Jacobsen, a fellow member of the Dogme 95 film collective, underscored von Trier's creative genius, but also his enviable ability successfully to stage himself and his works. During his years at the National Film School of Denmark, Lars Trier dubbed himself an aristocratic 'von' that he had toyed with as early as 1975.[12] In the context of modern Danish mentalities committed to notions of radical egalitarianism, this politically incorrect gesture was bound to attract attention. The programmatic and polemical nature of von Trier's many manifestos have served to intensify the public attention surrounding his works. And in recent times, von Trier himself has remarked on the highly choreographed nature of the projected image of the dynamic Zentropa duo, which presents the filmmaker as sensitive and a highly phobic artist/intellectual, and his partner, Peter Aalbæk Jensen, as a crass, cigar-smoking producer. Von Trier is widely regarded as a consummate orchestrator, with media events and controversies centred around him perceived as staged in some way. For example, the highly publicised controversy surrounding von Trier's discovery that producers Aalbæk Jensen and Vibeke Windeløv had condoned an optical manipulation (in violation of the Dogme rules) of his film, *The Idiots*, has been thought by some to have been a hoax. The situation of von Trier's filmmaking in the context of a small nation intensifies the national publicity that surrounds his work and person; dramatic conflicts between von Trier and Icelandic pop star/actress Björk, in connection with the production of *Dancer in the Dark,* made front-page news as well as providing comic material for various back-page columns.

Von Trier has chosen to foreground, rather than obscure, some of the more personal details of his life as a filmmaker. Key works here are Stig Björkman's 1997 *Tranceformer: A Portrait of Lars von Trier, De ydmygede* (*The Humiliated,* 1998), a film by Jesper Jargil documenting the production of *The Idiots*, and Katja Forbert Petersen's documentary, *Von Trier's 100 øjne* (*Von Trier's 100 Eyes,* 2000), which focuses on the making of *Dancer in the Dark*. Of equal importance is von Trier's deeply moving film diary (relating to *The Idiots*), which thematizes, among other things, the pathos involved in the filmmaker's changed relation to actors. Whereas von Trier's early career is marked by a somewhat hostile, even fearful attitude towards actors, his more recent films reflect a new-found openness to creating optimal conditions for acting.

A recurrent theme in von Trier's personal narrative concerns his relationship to his parents and childhood home. Particularly revealing is his mother's decision, while dying, to inform von Trier that the Jewish social democrat, Ulf Trier, who had raised him as his son, was not his biological father. Inger Høst's startling claim was that she had single-mindedly sought a mate who would provide the artistic genes she wanted for her offspring. She further claimed that this revelation was meant to spur her son on to further artistic achievements. Von Trier has traced many of his phobias (which impinge on his filmmaking inasmuch as they prohibit travel by air and filming in certain kinds of enclosed spaces), as well as his deep-seated commitment to challenging aesthetic and other conventions, to the free-spirited, radical nature of his childhood home, one which emphasized an unusually high degree of autonomy from the earliest age. Høst's stubborn commitment to fostering an artistic genius also meant that von Trier enjoyed every possible form of support for his artistic undertakings from the earliest age.[13] Von Trier's attempts at crime fiction at the age of 7 were duly recorded by Høst and Trier; camera equipment was readily available when the 10-year-old future filmmaker expressed an interest in the medium. The resultant juvenilia includes a two-minute animated film, *Turen til Squashland* (*The Journey to Squash Land*, 1967), *Nat, skat* (*Goodnight Dear*, 1968) and *En røvsyg oplevelse* (*A Miserable Experience*, 1969).[14]

The national context

Von Trier has transformed the landscape of contemporary Danish film, repeatedly taking issue with the standard institutional arrangements and attitudes associated with filmmaking in the context of a small, state-supported industry. Vinterberg makes the point succinctly: 'My collaboration with Lars von Trier has taught me that he is able to make Denmark big, without leaving Denmark. And this, for me, is the ultimate ideal. The idea is not to go international and become famous, but to think oneself beyond certain Danish mentalities.'[15] Von Trier's vision and powerful presence have been a clear source of inspiration to other filmmakers, particularly in recent years, but his work has also helped to reshape the very definition of Danish film. Whereas the Film Act of 1972 defined a Danish film in terms of utilization of the Danish language, Danish actors and technical personnel, the 1989 Film Act introduced an important disjunction allowing an English-language film such as *The Element of Crime* to automatically qualify as a Danish film. Today a film can count as Danish if it either employs the Danish language or is deemed to make a special artistic or technical contribution that helps to further film art and film culture in Denmark. This shift, it is generally agreed, was motivated to a large extent by a desire not to have to seek a special dispensation from the Ministry of Culture for von Trier's feature films, which, it soon became apparent, would favour English and German over Danish.

In 1992 von Trier founded Zentropa Entertainments, together with Aalbæk Jensen whom he had met during his years at the National Film School. The company currently includes subsidiaries and a number of specialized daughter companies. Von Trier is thus actively involved in initiating a remarkably wide range of film and television projects. *Constance* (1998), directed by Knud Vesterskov and produced by the company Puzzy Power, was the first in what was meant to become a series of Zentropa-produced pornographic films allegedly aimed particularly at female viewers. In the mid-1990s

Zentropa purchased the rights to the complete works of Morten Korch, the basis in the 1950s and 1960s for the many popular Danish comedies that virtually exhaust Denmark's contribution to the heritage genre. Von Trier's stated admiration for the sentimentality and narrative efficiency of Korch's stories – equated with the very essence of kitsch and bad taste by almost every self-respecting Danish filmmaker and intellectual – represents another provocative gesture. Zentropa has to date produced two Korch projects, a television series entitled *Folkene i Dale* (*Quiet Waters*, with TV2) and the feature-length adaptation, *Fruen på Hamre* (*The Lady of Hamre*, 2000), directed by Katrine Wiedemann. Zentropa Real was established in spring 2000. The mandate of this new daughter company is to produce non-fiction films in the spirit of a series of manifestos by Jørgen Leth, Tøger Seidenfaden, Børge Høst and Lars von Trier. The latter's manifesto is called 'Defocus' ('Defokus') and defends the existential significance of all that has been rendered trivial or even invisible by journalistic practices designed to find an angle, make a point or create a compelling story.[16]

Zentropa Entertainments is housed in former army barracks in Avedøre, on the outskirts of Copenhagen. In 1999 von Trier released a document which envisaged this site as an 'Open Film Town' (www.zentropa-film.com). Von Trier emphasizes the extent to which filmmaking has traditionally been an exclusive affair veiled in mystery. He links developments, particularly those associated with computer technology, to the possibility of undermining the exclusive and exclusionary practices of institutional gatekeepers. The Internet, for example, would provide a means of mediating between local and global networks in order to transmit both theoretical and practical knowledge about film. Von Trier's project is a characteristically bold, passionate and generous attempt to break the hold of various conventional and stultifying set-ups, with the aim of fostering the conditions for genuine creative expression and dialogue.

Biography

Lars von Trier was born in Copenhagen, Denmark, on 30 April 1956. A student in the Department of Film and Media Studies at the University of Copenhagen from 1976 to 1979, he attended the National Film School of Denmark between 1979 and 1982.

Notes

1   M. Hjort and I. Bondebjerg (eds) *The Danish Directors: Dialogues on a Contemporary National Cinema*, trans. M. Hjort, Bristol, Intellect Press, 2001.
2   T. Degn Johansen and L.B. Kimergaard (eds) *Sekvens Filmvidenskabelig årbog: Lars von Trier*, University of Copenhagen, Department of Film and Media Studies, 1991, pp. 157–9.
3   L. Michelsen and M. Piil, 'The King is Alive by Kristian Levring in Un certain regard', *Film*, no. 9, 2000, p. 5.
4   Lars von Trier, *Dogme 2: Idioterne, manuskript og dagbog*, Copenhagen, Gyldendal, 1998, p. 173.
5   *Ibid.*, p. 166.
6   *Ibid.*, p. 167.
7   M. Hjort and I. Bondebjerg, *op. cit.*, pp. 214, 218, 233.
8   *Ibid.*, p. 221.
9   P. Schepelern, *Lars von Triers elementer. En filminstruktørs arbejde*, Copenhagen, Rosinante, 1997, p. 63.
10 M. Hjort and I. Bondebjerg, *op. cit.*, p. 219.
11 *Ibid.*, p. 220.
12 S. Björkman, 'Trier on von Trier', *Film*, 9, 2000, p. 11.
13 M. Hjort and I. Bondebjerg, *op. cit.*, p. 211.
14 P. Schepelern, *op. cit.*, pp. 16–17.
15 M. Hjort and I. Bondebjerg, *op. cit.*, p. 275.
16 S. A. Madsen, 'Dokumentarens Dogmebrødre', *Berlingske Tidende*, 6 May 2000, p. 1.

Filmography

Orchidégartneren / The Orchid Gardener (1977) short
Menthe – la bienheureuse / Joyful Menthe (1979) short
Nocturne (1980) short
Den sidste detalje / The Last Detail (1981) short
Befrielsesbilleder / Images of a Relief (1982) graduation film, short
The Element of Crime (1984)
Epidemic (1987)
Europa / Zentropa (1991)
Riget / The Kingdom (1994)
Breaking the Waves (1996)
Riget 2 / The Kingdom 2 (1997)
Idioterne / The Idiots (1998)
Dancer in the Dark (2000)

Television productions

Medea (1988)
Lærerværelset / The Teachers' Room, 1–6 (1994)
Riget / The Kingdom, 1–4 (1994)
Riget 2 / The Kingdom 2, 5–8 (1997)
D-dag / D-Day (2000)

Further reading

Anon., 'Sværtegade', *Berlingske Tidende*, 2 May 2000.
S. Björkman, *Trier om Trier. Samtal med Stig Björkman*, Stockholm, Alfabeta, 1999.
M. Hjort, 'Themes of Nation', in M. Hjort and S. MacKenzie (eds) *Cinema and Nation*, London, Routledge, 2000.
Lars von Trier, *Breaking the Waves*, trans. J. Sydenham, Copenhagen, Peter Kofod, 1996.
—— 'Project Open Film City', *Avedøre*, 27 January 1999. Online. Available: www.zentropafilm.com.
—— and N. Vørsel, *Riget* ('The Kingdom'), Copenhagen, Aschehoug, 1995.
www.dogme95.dk
www.zentropa-film.com

METTE HJORT

WAYNE WANG

If auteur theory can be solely described as the search for common stylistic and thematic tropes in a director's body of work, then Wayne Wang is the *anti-auteur* of contemporary film. Yet, if there is such as thing as postmodern authorship, then Wang's work must qualify as an exemplar. From film to film, Wang's aesthetic shifts in genre, form and style self-consciously critique – while at the same time uphold – the fractious and decentred nature of contemporary world cinema culture.

Wang's influences and intertexts far outstrip those of contemporary American postmodern pastiche artists such as Quentin Tarantino and the Coen brothers. From art cinema, to Hong Kong action film, from film noir to Jean-Luc Godard, from Ozu to Capra, and from pseudo-*cinéma vérité* to Fifth Generation Chinese cinema, Wang's films work in dialogue with the cacophony that is world cinema history. Indeed, if one thing holds his work together at its decentred core, it is its hybridity and an ability to juxtapose apparently incompatible cinematic styles; and in so doing he has developed a postmodern and post-national film language all his own. This language is at times universal (*The Joy Luck Club*), at others opaque (*Life is Cheap ... But Toilet Paper is Expensive*). Through the hybrid nature of his representational strategies, Wang's work foregrounds the diversity that inhabits both his films and the national cultures in which they circulate. The hybridized nature of his films is also reflected in the stories he tells, as crises of identity lie at the heart of many of his movies. One explanation for the hybridization of Hollywood and world cinema in Wang's films can be traced to his name: his Hong Kong father named him Wayne after his favourite movie star, 'The Duke' (aka John Wayne).

Chan is Missing, Wang's first feature film – excluding the co-directed *A Man, a Woman, and a Killer* (a 1970s' drug thriller which, according to Wang, only received distribution in the Netherlands) – in many ways marks, along with the early works of Jim Jarmusch, the beginnings of US independent filmmaking. *Chan is Missing* begins with Jo (Wood Foy), a Chinese-American cabbie, driving through Chinatown while a Chinese version of Bill Haley's all-American song 'Rock Around the Clock' plays on the soundtrack. The dominant aesthetic is that of the wave of filmmakers whose careers began in the early 1980s: black-and-white stock, hand-held camera work, improvised dialogue, and meandering narratives predominate. Yet, if Wang's film is a key early 'indie' text, it is important to consider its antecedents, which are somewhat at odds with the traditional influences on 'indie' cinema. According to Alvin Lu, *Chan is Missing*, as one of the first independent Chinese-American films produced in the US, 'took its imperative from Seventies Third World activist consciousness to record the cinematically invisible, and thus disempowered, lives of the community'.[1] This reading is plausible when one considers the film's focus on character and its pseudo-*cinéma vérité* style; it seems even more plausible when one looks at Wang's experimental shorts such as *Take Out*, which explores the racist stereotypes populating popular cinema. Yet, what lies at the heart of *Chan is Missing* is not a celebration of a cultural identity typically left invisible, but a rumination on the absence of any totalizing Chinese-American identity at all. In a similar vein, *Chan is Missing*'s pastiche of film styles points to the lack of any 'authentic' cinematic language for the representation of Chinese-Americans. The main (missing) character also embodies this lack. The Chan who is missing is the film's Charles Foster Kane; he is everyone and no one, mirroring the question of Chinese-American identity that is the true heart of the film. As Jo and Steve (Marc Hayashi) try to find Chan, who seems to have absconded with $4,000 (the film's MacGuffin, as it were), the narrative unravels so that Chan becomes all aspects of Chinese-American culture, depending on the point of view of the storyteller: Chan is smart, dumb, 'FOB' ('fresh off the boat'), a failure, a success, a PRC (People's Republic of China) supporter, an immigrant, a murderer. The same indeterminacy applies to the film itself; while paying its debts to film noir, art-house cinema, *cinéma vérité* and, through its negation, the Charlie Chan cycle of films (often referred to in inverted commas by the characters, as a self-conscious reflection on what is taking place diegetically), *Chan is Missing* never settles exclusively into any one genre. Peter Feng notes that *Chan is Missing* addresses a number of different issues, all concerned with questions of hybridity and transnationalism. He notes that: 'Just as the identities of its characters are destabilized by the film, so is the identity of *Chan is Missing* destabilized by a multiplicity of interpretations drawing on different aspects of cinematic history. But how many subject positions can one film occupy?'[2] The discourses surrounding the film at the time of its release foreground the fact that a film's position is relational; that different publics use the film, and therefore codify it, in quite different, but at times overlapping, ways. The question the film finally raises, therefore, is not 'where is Chan?,' but 'who is Chan?' The notion of identity in flux guides the rest of Wang's film career, on both formal and thematic levels.

Wang's films break with the irony and pessimism of the indie film; while a sardonic streak exists in his work, melodramatic optimism also holds sway (he is probably the only indie director who is influenced by Capra in an un-ironic manner). Indeed, his second film was the first to show his lighter touch. *Dim Sum: A Little Bit of Heart* is often considered Wang's tribute to the influence of Yasujiro Ozu on his aesthetic. At first this may seem bizarre, as Ozu's films deal quite specifically with the kinds of personal and cultural pressures which Japanese middle-class families face. Yet, as Wim Wenders (another Ozu disciple who produces a hybridized or transnational cinema) notes in his film *Tokyo-ga* (1985): 'Ozu's films always tell the same simple stories, of the same people, in the same city of Tokyo. They are told with extreme economy, reduced to the barest essentials ... Ozu's films show the slow decline of the Japanese family and the collapse of national identity. They don't do it by pointing aghast at the new, American, occidental influences, but by lamenting the losses with a gentle melancholy as they occur.'[3] And, indeed, the winding narrative threads of *Dim Sum* – which question what kinds of stories function as points of contact and identity within the immigrant experience – reflect the ways American and immigrant cultural manifestations intersect and the effects this hybridity has on the personal identities of individuals who live in both worlds. The film focuses on an ageing Chinese mother, Mrs Tam (Kim Chew), and her desire for her daughter, Geraldine (Laureen Chew), to marry before she (Mrs Tam) dies the death predicted by a fortune-teller. The mother represents the unassimilated Chinese-American; her foil in the film is her dead husband's former business partner, an uncle (Victor Wong) who wants the mother to be more in tune with the American way of life. These stories reflect an Ozu-like worldview: both the mother and the uncle live under the influence of American culture, though they cope differently with the effect. Furthermore, the film portrays how their responses to these influences affect their family life. To this extent, the daughter is the ground on which these questions of Chinese-American identity are negotiated. When the mother visits China for what she believes is the last time before her imminent and preordained death, her fortune-teller tells her that she will live longer; she returns and her daughter announces that she does not want to get married, and so the film, after a few digressions, ends up where it begins. Throughout *Dim Sum* it is the exchanges between family members that drive the narrative forward, rather than an attempt at closure and resolution; like Ozu's families, it is the narratives of the changing domestic space which give the film its meaning.

Slamdance, often considered Wang's weakest film and his first foray into more 'traditional' kinds of genre cinema, fits into the cycle of neo-noir films that came into prominence in the mid-1980s, with such films as Lawrence Kasdan's *Body Heat* (1981), Alan Rudolph's *Choose Me* (1984) and Curtis Hanson's *The Bedroom Window* (1987). Indeed, the film is a slight affair, dealing as it does with mistaken identity and the Hitchcockian 'wrong man'. Yet, the film foregrounds perhaps one of the more interesting aspects of Wang's work: the way in which different films, seemingly sharing nothing in common, except for the director, can evince stylistic similarities through the cinematic antecedents that they share. *Chan is Missing* and *Slamdance*, for instance, seem unrelated, except for the role played by film noir as a key intertext for both films. As James Naremore notes: '*Slamdance* is filled with visual references to *noir* classics such as *Rear Window* and *The Lady from Shanghai*, although it has no explicitly Asian themes. ... Wang's earlier, low-budget *Chan is Missing* ... employs an investigative plot structure and a style reminiscent of the early New Wave in order to depict a Chinese-American community from the "inside".[4] The intertext of the New Wave is itself of a reflexive nature, as François Truffaut and Jean-Luc Godard explicitly invoked film noir in a manner similar to that of Wang in *Chan is Missing*; as an intertext between a local, minor cinema and that of the global language of Hollywood. Both are concerned with re-imagining Hollywood, allowing different kinds of representations to emerge from the genres in question. Wang himself personalizes this re-imagining: 'I've always been fascinated with the Hitchcock films in that Hitchcock was trained by Jesuits and I was too and there's something about Catholicism that implants in the back of your brain that if you morally do something wrong, the fear of getting caught with that is very great. To get an innocent man caught in that kind of situation then the momentum of trying to get him out of it is, for me, one of the strongest aspects of thrillers.'[5] Yet, the notion of mistaken identity, which lies at the heart of both film noir and Wang's *œuvre*, seems fairly trite in *Slamdance*, as the questions of identity which arise in the film are solely generic. In essence, *Slamdance* does not probe, in a reflexive manner, the shifting nature of identities; a theme that resonates to such a great degree in Wang's other films.

If *Slamdance* represents a retreat into the mainstream, in many ways Wang's next film, the little-seen *Life is Cheap ... But Toilet Paper is Expensive*, stands, on a formal level, as his most radical film. Combining the Brechtian aesthetic of the mid-1960s' Godard with the postmodernist genre-bending of Hong Kong action cinema, *Life is Cheap*, unlike many of Wang's films, breaks out of the confines of its influences and becomes a reflection on hybridity itself. Combining an improvised narrative about a messenger travelling to Hong Kong with startling and vertiginous *cinéma vérité* sequences, *Life is Cheap* explores the possibilities of capturing city life in all its forms; in essence, a postmodern version of the city films of the 1920s and 1930s, most notably Dziga Vertov's *Man with a Movie Camera* (1929).

Such experimentalism at this stage in Wang's career points to an interesting aesthetic trajectory. Unlike many US indie filmmakers, whose careers can be charted as a sojourn from the margins to the mainstream, Wang's career follows the route of the pendulum, swinging back and forth between experimental and dominant cinema. As such, Wang's first real crossover success, *The Joy Luck Club*, addresses hybridity in a different manner from that of his more experimental and independent work. The film tells the story of two generations of Chinese-American women, and the ways in which they negotiate being both Chinese and American. While the younger generation identifies more with the yuppie culture of the 1980s than with Chinese notions of community and family, the first generation remember the extremely harsh past they faced in China. By comparison, the concerns of the daughters seem trivial and materialistic, but even this is problematized by the way in which China itself is portrayed. The *faux*-Technicolor foregrounds the fact that the first generation's China is an imaginary one, to the extent that time and memory have inflected their visions of the past. While the stories told in flashback are tragic, the melodramatic invocation of Sirkian Technicolor mixed with the Fifth Generation filmmaking of Zhang Yimou, places memory firmly in the role of the imaginary. Similarly, in *Eat a Bowl of Tea*, the Capraesque, screwball nature of the film deflects the viewer away from the potentially depressive and fatalistic nature of the narrative. Here, the intertext of Hollywood – and especially of Capra's own *Meet John Doe* (1941) and *It's a Wonderful Life* (1946) – overshadows all other aspects of the tone of the film.

Many of Wang's later films attempt to hybridize mainstream and art-house cinemas. After *The Joy Luck Club*, Wang is best known for his two collaborations with author Paul Auster: *Smoke* and *Blue in the Face*. These films also represent Wang's return to indie cinema, with cameos by Jim Jarmusch and Lou Reed in the latter film thrown in for good measure. In many ways, the Brooklyn of *Smoke* and *Blue in the Face* crystallizes many of Wang's preoccupations. Both films look at the ways in which cultural diversity leads to tension, affinity and, at times, solidarity. Wang himself notes that: 'When we were scouting in Brooklyn for *Smoke*, I saw so much of this cross-cultural spirit of Brooklyn: the faces, the mixtures, the crossing over of cultures, sometimes not really getting along, sometimes sort of getting along. We just went out with a Hi-8 camera and grabbed a lot of things on the fly.'[6] The coming together of cultures in Brooklyn functions as a microcosmic version of the world that Wang's films delineate: one riddled with intersections and divisions, but also one that gains its identity from these very tensions. The highly structured *Smoke* and the entirely improvised *Blue in the Face* are both built around the dual ideas that one is never really in control of one's destiny and that location and contingency largely shape the structures one's life takes. Both films are centred in a smoke shop run by Auggie Wren (Harvey Keitel). A central trope of *Smoke* is Auggie's daily photo-documentation of his shop, shot from the same angle, at 8.00 am every day. This process superficially documents stasis; but, as Auggie points out to Paul Benjamin (William Hurt), each picture has its own specificity encapsulating one moment in history. *Blue in the Face*'s improvised nature allows for a different kind of reflection on the nature of neighbourhoods. Here, the characters themselves make up the community; they all have their own history, but it is their co-existence which gives the community, and the film, its essence. For Wang, Brooklyn becomes an idealized city space where cultural difference does not solely lead to division – it also leads to new forms of solidarity.

The city, as represented in *Chinese Box*, starring Jeremy Irons, Maggie Cheung and Gong Li, poses another set of problems. Set in Hong Kong during the hand-over of the colony by the British to China, the lives of the main characters reflect the destabilized identity of a national culture in flux. Indeed, the lead actors can be seen as icons representing the countries involved: the United Kingdom (Irons), Hong Kong (Cheung) and China (Li). Alvin Lu remarks: 'As national cinemas crumble and a kind of global neo-Hollywood rises in their wake, Wang's works take on a new context distinct from the ones they've traditionally been stranded in: are these films prototypes for the postnational independent filmmaker?'[7] As if by way of response, in addressing the limiting discourses of 'national cinema' projects, Andrew Higson notes that: 'The "imagined community" argument ... sometimes seems unable to acknowledge the cultural difference and diversity that invariably marks both the inhabitants of a particular nation-state and the members of the more geographically dispersed "national" communities'.[8] Wang's cinema, at times successfully, at others times less so, attempts to bridge the gaps between these two questions. By bringing together diverse cultures, and a dizzying variety of cinematic traditions, Wang foregrounds the need for cinematic representation to speak in multiple voices. If one of the powers of the cinema is the opportunity it provides for travel and for visualizing the 'other', Wang's films allow for a transnational space, both in terms of narrative and style, to be inhabited by his works. Through the cultural hybridity of his characters, and through the stylistic intertextuality of his films, Wang can be seen as being at the forefront of transnational cinema; and this, in the end, is the main thrust of his films.

Biography

Wayne Wang was born in January 1949, in Hong Kong.

Notes

1 Alvin Lu, 'Invisible Cities: Wayne Wang', *Film Comment*, vol. 34, no. 4, July/August 1998, pp. 31–6, p. 33.

2 Peter Feng, 'Being Chinese American, Becoming Asian American: *Chan is Missing*', *Cinema Journal*, vol. 35, no. 4, 1996, pp. 88–118, p. 89.
3 Wim Wenders, '*Tokyo-ga*', in Wim Wenders, *The Logic of Images: Essays and Conversations*, London, Faber and Faber, 1991, pp. 60–5, p. 60.
4 James Naremore, *More Than Night: Film noir in its Contexts*, Berkeley, University of California Press, 1998, p. 228.
5 Allan Hunter, 'Dancing Clever', *Films and Filming*, 398, 1987, pp. 6–7, p. 7.
6 bell hooks, 'The Cultural Mix: An Interview with Wayne Wang', in bell hooks, *Reel to Real: Race, Sex and Class at the Movies*, London, Routledge, 1996, pp. 124–41, p. 133.
7 Alvin Lu, *op. cit.*, p. 32.
8 Andrew Higson, 'The Limiting Imagination of National Cinema', in Mette Hjort and Scott MacKenzie (eds) *Cinema and Nation*, London, Routledge, 2000, pp. 63–74, p. 66.

Filmography

A Man, a Woman, and a Killer (1975)
Chan is Missing (1982)
Dim Sum: A Little Bit of Heart (1984)
Slamdance (1987)
Eat a Bowl of Tea (1989)
Life is Cheap ... But Toilet Paper is Expensive (1990)
The Joy Luck Club (1993)
Smoke (Germany/US, 1995)
Blue in the Face (1995)
Chinese Box (France/Japan/US, 1997)
Anywhere But Here (1999)
Center of the World (2001)

Further reading

Paul Auster, *Smoke and Blue in the Face: Two Films by Paul Auster*, London, Faber and Faber, 1995.
Louis Chu, *Eat a Bowl of Tea*, New York, Carol Publishing, 1993.
Erick Dittus, '*Chan is Missing*, An Interview with Wayne Wang', *Cineaste*, vol. 12, no. 3, 1983, pp. 17–20.
William Galperin, 'Bad for the Glass: Representation and Filmic Deconstruction in *Chinatown* and *Chan is Missing*', *Modern Language Notes*, vol. 102, no. 5, 1987, pp. 1151–70.
Amy Tan, *The Joy Luck Club*, London, Minerva, 1989.
David Thomson, 'Chinese Takeout', *Film Comment*, vol. 21, no. 5, 1985, pp. 23–7.
John C. Tibbets, 'A Delicate Balance: An Interview with Wayne Wang About *The Joy Luck Club*', *Literature-Film Quarterly*, vol. 22, no. 1, 1994, pp. 2–6.

Peter Todd, '*Chan is Missing*: An Interview with Wayne Wang', *Framework*, 20, 1983, pp. 21–2.
Wayne Wang, *Chan is Missing*, Honolulu, Bamboo Ridge Press, 1984.

SCOTT MACKENZIE

PETER WEIR

AUSTRALIAN AUTEUR/HOLLYWOOD DIRECTOR

Over a varied filmmaking career, Peter Weir has been seen as an auteur, an Australian filmmaker and, more recently, a successful Hollywood director. In terms of thinking, writing and, indeed, teaching, it has always been easier to discuss such categories separately. The result has been that, at worst, Weir has been constituted only partially and, at best, portrayed as fragmented to an extreme. More often than not, questions of authorship, national cinema and genre have been viewed as discrete and, as a consequence, examinations have privileged the specificities of text and authorial intention. Contextual issues, whether industrial, cultural, technical or political, have generally been set aside. As well as these more obvious elements of context, I would make special mention of the 'work of audiences'. Such elements snake in and out of narrow, and seemingly distinct, categories to disturb and blur neat classifications. Weir's work and career both foreground an interconnectedness between the auteur, national cinema and Hollywood genre.

In his excellent overview of Weir's work, Jonathan Rayner identifies a paradox at the very heart of the sort of auteur criticism that credits the director as the most important source of meaning for film texts.[1] Historically, the concept of 'la politique des auteurs' emerged as an impassioned polemic from the critics and proto-filmmakers of the French journal, *Cahiers du cinéma*. In essence, 'la politique des auteurs' called for the recognition of both the artistic value of certain film directors and then posited such directors (auteurs) as film authors. What is often overlooked, however, is that this critical stance was developed primarily from studies of directors who made their films in that bastion of genre production, Hollywood (e.g., Ford, Hawks and Hitchcock). This more comprehensive approach to film authorship became quickly obscured and, in subsequent examinations of authorship, the 'true' auteur was categorized more crudely as one whose vision would transcend the 'constraints' of both genre and the industrialized context of production. Notions of genre filmmaking and auteur filmmaking consequently became polarized and viewed as cinematic contradictions.

In the study of national cinemas, there has been an impulse to focus on historical, stylistic, linguistic and thematic concepts of 'the national'. This approach has tended to maintain a notion of 'the national' as separate and distinct from its international/global relationships. Ironically, this distinction has been sustained partly through a reverence for key directors and the establishment of the auteur as signifier of national style. Thus, the national has been constructed in an artistic opposition to Hollywood style. As a director who has been successful in both Australia and Hollywood, Weir provides an interesting case study. Brian McFarlane has called Weir 'the nearest Australian approach to an old-fashioned auteur',[2] and although it has been two decades since Weir has made a film in Australia, he is credited as the pioneer of the 1970s' 'Australian revival'.

Although Australian cinema can claim a long history, it has endured more troughs than peaks. Initially, Australian filmmakers responded quickly to overseas developments in filmmaking and for the first twenty years of the twentieth century established successful local initiatives.[3] The history of Australian filmmaking has always been strongly influenced by its isolated geographical location. After a promising start, however, the potential of an Australian indigenous film industry was quickly eclipsed by British and, more especially, American competition. Australia became a home for British and American imports and, some time later, a cheap location for the filming of foreign productions. Apart from Australian newsreels[4] and the work of Charles Chauvell and Ken G. Hall, it would be true to say that during the 1950s when Weir was growing up in a middle-class neighbourhood near Sydney Harbour, he was exposed primarily to Hollywood film culture and, from 1956, American television culture.

The context of Weir's first work in Australia was, thus, one of huge cultural anxiety bordering on a sense of national inferiority. According to Tom Ryan, when Weir first started his career in the late 1960s and early 1970s (graduating from stagehand to writer and programme-maker for Australian television station, Channel Seven, and then filmmaker for the Commonwealth Film Unit), Australia was to all extents and purposes 'isolated from all but an impression of the rest of the world'.[5] Geographical distance, postcolonial status and an imported film culture produced a climate where, as Tom Weir writes, 'the daydreams we get from celluloid are not Australian daydreams'.[6]

After dropping out of university, Weir joined the procession of other young Australians who travelled to Europe in search of more than just 'an impression' of culture. In the late 1960s and early 1970s, however, Australia witnessed something of a break with its traditional conservative identity. Weir returned from Europe influenced by many of the new 1960s' ways of thinking and as a strong opponent of the Vietnam War (in which Australia had taken a combat role). As Weir has stated, the effect of the growing Australian anti-war movement 'unleashed energy and conflict, passion'.[7]

That youthful energy shaped by '1960s sensibilities', European travel (and most certainly, European cinema) was able to harness new possibilities for filmmaking provided by a government that suddenly valued an Australian national cinema as an important element of a modern national identity. Funding opportunities were made available from government sources in a cultural climate that broke with previous ideas of Australian culture's lack of legitimacy. As Turner explains, a sea change was carried through by 'an increasingly powerful nationalist mythology that came to see film as the most desirable medium for projecting an image of the new confidence and maturity seen to mark contemporary Australian culture and society'.[8] The Australian Film Development Commission (AFDC), later renamed the Australian Film Commission (AFC), and the Australian Film, Television and Radio School (AFTRS) became key institutions in the support of this new filmmaking vision. Released the same year as the AFTRS was officially opened, Weir's *Picnic at Hanging Rock* (1975) blew the fanfare for an Australian film revival while gaining Weir himself international recognition.

A period piece based on a literary adaptation of Joan Lindsay's novel, *Picnic at Hanging Rock*'s reputation rested on its credentials as a 'quality' film. Weir's version, however, left the narrative deliberately open, immediately associating its style with traditions of European art cinema. With director of photography Russell Boyd and cameraman John Seale, Weir transformed the harsh Australian light of its Victoria location into a memorable dream-like setting. The temporal became confused by unusual choices of film speed:

shifts to 32 and 43 frames-per-second (rather than the usual 24), accompanied by strict instructions for the actors not to blink, created strangely slow, atmospheric moments. Sensitive art direction produced exterior shots staged like Pre-Raphaelite compositions bathed in pale light. Such shots are frequently intercut (in a style reminiscent of Nic Roeg's 1970 *Walkabout*) with others which emphasize to maximum effect the antipodean freakishness of the flora and fauna. When I first saw the film in the 1970s, more memorable even than its strong visual impact, was its startling use of sound. Apparently, the inclusion of the unforgettable Zamfir pan-pipes had been a last minute impulse, discovered and then suggested by one of the producers, Jim McElroy. If their use was serendipitous, the low rumblings of white noise and other noise samples of the soundtrack were used with precision, 'reinforcing or undermining the image with conspicuous or incongruous sound'.[9]

In *Picnic at Hanging Rock*, 'Australia was caught in the amber of its history, its present credentials implied by the style and sensibility of its representation of the past',[10] and in this, his fourth film, Weir became a figurehead in a filmic and cultural search for identity. Retrospectively, his individual role has possibly been overemphasized, but he was undoubtedly a key figure. His type of questioning, as opposed to 'straight' narrative cinema, had a distinctive resonance with a special moment of filmmaking and it is perhaps here where some sense of 'Australianness' adds a further layer for consideration. Until Weir and other Australian directors of his generation, such as Gillian Armstrong, Bruce Beresford, Philip Noyce and Fred Schepsi, won their colours, the lack of experience in Australia meant that it was like starting from scratch to find technical and artistic solutions to filmmaking. Drawing on skills acquired while working for Australian television stations and the Commonwealth Film Unit (and later the AFTRS), the small band of people making films in Australia created a fertile nursery drawing on various and varied inspirations. In *The Cars that Ate Paris*, for instance, Weir drew on inspiration and imagery from both television cigarette advertising and art cinema technique while explicitly quoting references from that most American of genres, the Western.

In this creative Australian cradle, Weir made films precociously. In interviews, Weir has since likened this period to running before he learned to walk. The ambition of (what is still after all these years my favourite Weir film) *The Last Wave*, made just after *Picnic at Hanging Rock* in 1977, still screams out its extraordinary class with its beautiful complexity of narrative and imagery and, perhaps more startling still, the compelling performance of Richard Chamberlain. More than any other of Weir's films, *The Last Wave* shudders to a halt leaving the viewer with not just an open-ended resolution but practically none at all. The audience falls victim to a relentless rhythm that allows no release. Thus Weir marks out his cinematic territory as one of atmosphere rather than either rounded characters or resolutions. He creates a powerful textual space in the director/text/audience relationship for the viewer to negotiate meanings, pleasures and, indeed in the case of *The Last Wave*, disappointments

It is generally considered that Weir came of age and ended his filmmaking apprenticeship with *Gallipoli* (1980), a transitional film in more than one sense. Distributed by Paramount, this film precipitated Weir's move to Hollywood. We can see in *Gallipoli*, and also two years later in *The Year of Living Dangerously* (made with some funding by MGM), that Weir set about making films outside America with a clear awareness of their American reception. This is particularly interesting since *Gallipoli* explores key tropes of 'Australianness' more explicitly than his last two Australian features, *Picnic at Hanging Rock* and *The Last Wave*. Two elements are central to this explicit exploration of Australianness: first, the 'mateship' of Archy and Frank, and second, the focus on a dramatic historical moment that has since been seen as foundational to notions of Australian national identity.

When discussing his own work, Weir has referred to making his films in the 'crossfire' between Hollywood and a European tradition. His films can be considered as acts of negotiation and it is interesting, therefore, to note that Weir regards *Gallipoli* as one of his favourite but least personal films. This statement would seem to go against the spirit of traditional auteur criticism as the submersion of the personal points to him as a craftsman and not an artist. Surely, however, a concept of the 'personal' should not exclusively lie with the director. As I have argued, Weir films create powerful polysemic spaces for audiences to seek their meanings. These are, of course, not meanings and understandings that are endlessly open to interpretation but ones that are complex and personal nonetheless because of the subtle and sophisticated interactions between readers and text. In *Gallipoli*, the atmospheric layering of imagery and sound requires an emotional response from the viewer. The emotional register is complex and will resonate with different viewers in ways that will be both consistent and inconsistent. Generally, the film makes a persuasive statement about the futility of war and the waste of youthful potential, but the beauty of that youth is, at times, just so exquisite that it seems inappropriate to the hegemonic macho and heterosexual conventions of armies and war. The underwater swimming sequence that takes place under a heavy bombardment of shells can be interpreted, for example, as one of the most hauntingly erotic/homoerotic moments in cinema.

Though Weir is often criticized for avoiding the subject of sexuality, his films portray an amazing amount of tangible erotic desire. His indirect approach has a way of involving the viewer more explicitly than a direct approach, since there is a freedom to go with or against (or indeed fluctuate between) the rhythms that are generated. In many ways, Weir is a profoundly old-fashioned director, firmly stuck in the guidelines of the Hollywood Hays code. Like vintage Hollywood directors, he offers no vivid sex scenes, just a meticulous manipulation of cinematic rhythms and a deep understanding of the conventions of the cinematic gaze. In *The Year of Living Dangerously*, the viewer has no doubt that Jill Bryant (Sigourney Weaver) will follow Guy Hamilton (Mel Gibson) out of the embassy and get in his car because the erotic tension has been fashioned so deftly, to culminate in their kisses. In what can be considered his first US film, *Witness* (1985), Weir's portrayal of cinematic eroticism is unsurpassed. As Rayner suggests, the exchange of looks that Weir builds up between John Book (Harrison Ford) and Rachel Lapp (Kelly McGillis) – particularly in the context of Amish cultural prohibition – 'appear almost immodest in their personal significance'.[11] Weir skilfully implicates the viewer in the eroticism of this immodesty and in the scene where Book comes upon Rachel bathing, Weir reverses the expectations of the male gaze to render both Book and the viewer as the object of burning female desire. An erotic charge that affects the viewer regardless of gender and sexuality and one which lingers because of its lack of cinematic consummation or climax.

Witness is perhaps Weir's most explicit engagement with the genre film to date, but it is one that remains characteristically hybrid. The film reworks the thematic preoccupations of the detective thriller and the Western, and as Johnson and Poole suggest, uses Maurice Jarre's faux-Aaron Copeland music to 'yoke the Amish co-operative ethic to the frontier mythology, thereby closing the gap between Amish and Mainstream values for cinema audiences'.[12] Rather than 'closing the gap', however, I would argue that part of Weir's importance as a filmmaker is the way he exploits the complexity and instability of the perceived 'gap' between Hollywood, European and the newer (and less formulated) Australian traditions of filmmaking in order to make consistently interesting films. Since *Witness*, all of Weir's films have been made in Hollywood (although he often returns to Australia at the post-production stage). He has made these films under a mixture of circumstances. He was explicitly courted to direct *Witness*, *Dead Poets Society* and *Fearless*, whilst *The Mosquito Coast* and *Green Card* stemmed from very personal projects (he produced, wrote the screenplay and directed *Green Card*).

Weir's Hollywood films are marked by a deep knowledge and love of its style and conventions but this has not precluded him from exploring and problematizing them. In *Green Card*, for example, he cast that most un-Hollywood of actors Gérard Depardieu as the lead in a modern reworking of a 1930s' Hollywood comedy of marriages. More recently, Jim Carrey (currently one of Hollywood's most bankable stars) was cast somewhat against the grain of his usual comedic performances in *The Truman Show*. A consistent feature of Weir's Hollywood films has been the questioning of the place of the hero (*Witness, Dead Poets Society, Fearless*) and his ploy has been to make obvious, and yet simultaneously blur, notions of Hollywood, European and Australian filmmaking. Throughout his career, he has consistently presented viewers with films that are much more than the sum of their parts, offering complex, rich and diverse viewing positions and possibilities.

It is perhaps obvious that I prefer Weir's more explicitly Australian films: I am, however, an unapologetic Australianist and this has had a strong influence on the way in which I read his films. For the viewer, one of the great pleasures of Weir's films is to take up his textual invitation and read them actively and, indeed, even selectively. For both the viewers *and* the central characters of Weir's films alike, there is always a requirement to try and move beyond narrow understandings and definitions of cultures and identities.[13] In *The Last Wave*, the Aboriginal elder, Charlie (Nandjiwarra Amagula), asks the white American male lead of the film, David Burton (Richard Chamberlain), a question that makes little sense outside an Aboriginal sensibility and an Aboriginal context of reality: 'Are you a fish, are you a snake … what are you?' The encounter between this Aboriginal mystical interrogation of identity and a white western male brings into relief not just a cultural and intellectual gap, but also vigorously challenges and problematizes Burton's frameworks of comprehension and reference. I suppose my own discussion has asked of Weir: 'Are you an auteur, are you an Australian filmmaker, are you a director of Hollywood genre films ... what are you?'[14] I would want to argue for the rich fusion of all these elements. Ultimately, however, there cannot be just one answer, but many answers, and these answers must come from each beholder of Weir's work.

Biography

Peter Weir was born on 21 August 1944, in Sydney, Australia.

Notes

1 Jonathan Rayner, *The Films of Peter Weir*, London, Cassell, 1998, p. 3.
2 Brian McFarlane, *Australian Cinema 1970–85*, London, Secker & Warburg, 1987, p. 187.
3 See Graeme Turner, *Film as Social Practice* (third edn), London, Routledge, 1999, pp. 161–70.
4 Television came relatively late to Australia in 1956, and its arrival brought about the demise of the Australian newsreels.
5 See Tom Ryan's Preface to his interview with Weir for *Cinema Papers* (1981). Online. Available HTTP: http://www.10pair.com/crazydv.html
6 Tom Weir, 'No Daydreams of our Own: The Film as National Self-expression', in Albert Moran and Tom O'Regan (eds) *An Australian Film Reader*, Sydney, Currency Press, 1985, p. 144.
7 See the interview with Sue Mathews in her *35mm Dreams: Conversations with Five Directors about the Australian Film Revival*, Melbourne, Penguin, 1984.
8 Graeme Turner, *op. cit.*, p. 162.
9 Jonathan Rayner, *op. cit.*, p. 51.
10 Graeme Turner, *op. cit.*, p. 166.
11 Jonathan Rayner, *op. cit.*, p. 142.
12 Bruce Johnson and Gayle Poole, 'Sound and Author/Auteurship: Music in the films of Peter Weir', in Rebecca Coyle (ed.) *Screen Scores: Studies in Contemporary Australian Film Music*, Sydney, AFTRS/Allen & Unwin, 1998, p. 136.
13 Bruce Johnson and Gayle Poole refer to the 'confrontation between two orders of experience' as a fundamental structure in Weir's work. *Ibid.*, p. 127.
14 I owe a great debt to William D. Routt's article, 'Are You a fish? Are You a snake? An Obvious Lecture and Some Notes on *The Last Wave*', *Continuum: The Australian Journal of Media and Culture*, vol. 8, no. 2, 1994. Online. Available HTTP: http://wwwmcmurdoch.edu.au

Filmography

(All productions are Australian unless otherwise indicated)
Homesdale (1971) short

The Cars that Ate Paris (1974)
Picnic at Hanging Rock (1975)
The Last Wave (1977)
Gallipoli (1981)
The Year of Living Dangerously (1982)
Witness (US, 1985)
The Mosquito Coast (US, 1986)
Dead Poets Society (US, 1989)
Green Card (Australia/France/US, 1990)
Fearless (US, 1993)
The Truman Show (US, 1998)

Further reading

Sue Mathews, *35mm Dreams: Conversations with Five Directors about the Australian Film Revival*, Melbourne, Penguin, 1984.

ROS JENNINGS

WIM WENDERS

There is an image of Wim Wenders in which he resembles James Dean. This advertisement, for American Express, shows the German director lounging elegantly at the wheel of a stationary car, head cocked on one side, and staring moodily into the distance. In Germany it apparently carried the slogan: 'Pay with your good name.'[1] The advert presents Wenders' public identity in terms of its 'star quality', constructing a doubly ironic image. It exploits nostalgia for Dean's star image whilst its German slogan has Faustian overtones, implying that your debts may indeed cost you your 'good name'. Such irony stems from an inevitable tension in Wenders' public persona as a filmmaker operating between the United States and Germany/Europe.

This identity makes him, like Stanley Kubrick, a particularly useful point of orientation in the often fraught interchange between the Hollywood industry and European filmmaking. David Puttnam traces such interchange in *The Undeclared War*, in which he describes the row at GATT in 1993, which was apparently resolved by a phoney truce over the 'cultural exception'.[2] Ongoing tensions between filmmaking as art or commerce, between national cultural identity and the global market, or between 'second cinema'[3] and a conglomerate Hollywood, all mark Wenders' career, inspire his filmmaking and propel his international reputation. In this context, Thomas Elsaesser sees Wenders as an auteur continuing a tradition in post-war cinema, and thus: 'inheriting the ambiguous privilege of epitomizing what a European director is and ought to be'.[4] In the late 1980s, Wenders apparently tired of the ambiguity, declaring himself European:

> 'I am a European filmmaker', I said over there. And after I had given myself that label and had accepted with it the fact that I would never become an 'American filmmaker', and after I once decided to come back BECAUSE of this self-definition but also FOR it, then I said: 'I'm going back to Europe.'[5]

He then adopted the very public profile of founding President of the European Film Academy and, as such, declared in 1993: 'If our images are given away now, then Europe will find itself a third world continent by the year 2000. It is that serious.'[6] His fears, doubtless prompted by the wrangling at GATT, have not come to pass, but such apocalyptic prophecies do reveal a commitment to European filmmaking and its 'cultural exception'. This stance derives from Wenders' oft-avowed, existential belief in cinema. He has commented that:

> cinema has something to do with life ... cinema is a more precise and comprehensive documentation of our times than the theatre, than music or the plastic arts ... cinema can damage people when it alienates them from their fears and desires ... cinema can benefit people by opening up their lives and bringing freedoms before their eyes ... cinema is more than the industry that produces films.[7]

Such idealism has not, however, prevented him from re-engaging with the US and Hollywood in the mid-1990s. *The End of Violence* from 1997, his latest directing effort, *The Million Dollar Hotel*, which led off the Berliniale in February 2000, and his work-in-progress, entitled *In Amerika*, all confirm what *The American Friend* indicated in 1977 – that much of Wenders' work bears out Peter Lev's view of 'the Euro-American Art Film' as ' "working-between" the American entertainment film and the European art film'.[8] Moving between Hollywood and a publicly funded European film 'ecology'[9] means wearing a range of hats.[10] Having begun his professional career as a film critic, Wenders has continued to comment on his filmmaking by publishing personal records and more-or-less theoretical reflections.

He works on commission, as with the early feature *The Scarlet Letter* from 1972–3 and the occasional television advertisement, whilst he has also been his own cameraman, an occasional actor, scriptwriter, editor and producer.[11]

Historically, Wenders' range of auteurial creativity stems from the same self-awareness expressed by one of his contemporaries, Hans W. Geissendörfer. Of his own *Lindenstrasse*, a successful soap opera with social-critical pretensions, Geissendörfer maintains: 'That was the ambition from the beginning, and that's why the series was made by a veteran of '68. That's what we have learned: every thing must have a meaning.'[12] Both filmmakers belong to a post-war generation which has, with the advent in 1998 of Gerhard Schröder as Federal Chancellor, succeeded to the leadership of its country. Through the student unrest and extra-parliamentary opposition of 1968, this generation staged the nearest thing Germany has had to a revolution of the children against the parents – a reckoning with them, among other things, for their complicity in the Third Reich and for the subsequent public refusal in West Germany to confront that terrible legacy.[13] Wenders responded to the legacy by seeking to create meaning beyond – and even in opposition to – the entertainment function of visual media.

His films are, however, so *distant* from Geissendörfer's *Lindenstrasse* that this television staple could define them by contrast. Geissendörfer uses the conventions of television realism to create a successful saga of a German *Heimat* ('homeland'/'town'). Wenders also explores the question of his native identity, but he always avoids simplistic constructions of 'Germanness' and of any sort of nationalism, whether in his films or when stating his opinions.

After some desultory studies in the early 1960s, Wenders went to Paris and became fascinated by the Cinémathèque française, returning to join the first intake of students to the Munich film school in 1967. Despite personal contact with political dissidents, he adopted a radical subjectivity early on, questioning the creative process itself, particularly the way it treats masculinity. With his graduation film *Summer in the City*, Wenders became, alongside Fassbinder, Herzog, Kluge and Schlöndorff, one of the defining auteurs of the New German Cinema. In 1971 he engaged with the commerce and politics of his profession as a founding director of the Filmverlag der Autoren ('The Authors' Film-Publisher'), an independent production company. By 1976 Wenders had his own company, Road Movies, which has operated out of Berlin ever since. One of his partners was the noted Austrian writer Peter Handke, with whom he realized his first major creative collaboration, *The Goalkeeper's Fear of the Penalty Kick*. Handke then wrote the script for Wenders' *The Wrong Move* (US title: *False Movement*) and contributed, however hesitantly, to a screenplay for his *Wings of Desire*.

As his reputation grew at home, Wenders was already gravitating to the source of so many vital influences on his childhood and youth, the United States. His complex relationship with things American inspires *Alice in the Cities* as it traces the return of the film's German hero from disillusion with the US to possible identification with Germany. *The American Friend* offers a complex allegory for the impact of American visual culture on Germany/Europe via an adaptation of the thriller genre. Meanwhile, Wenders cemented his reputation with the success of *Kings of the Road* at Cannes in 1975. As with the progression of *The Wrong Move* from North to South Germany, so the setting of this film, the sad, deserted country just West of the intra-German border, scrutinizes local identity. But *Kings of the Road* famously qualifies that identity when one protagonist declares: 'The Yanks have colonialized our subconscious.' To be a German of Wenders' generation, and above all a filmmaker, implies some sort of arrangement with that truth.

Wenders' next creative phase meant engaging directly with the US via Francis Ford Coppola's invitation to direct *Hammett*. The delays and wrangling over the film convinced Wenders that he had no chance of working in a Hollywood studio, but being in America did mean he could undertake the documentary *Nick's Film: Lightning over Water*, made during and about the final illness of one of the American directors Wenders most reveres, Nicholas Ray. Inherently controversial because it minutely traces the death of the filmmaker whilst ostensibly seeking to realize his own last project, the film forces viewers to confront their own voyeurism.

Subsequently, Wenders became his own subject, as it were. Whilst visiting a colleague's set in Portugal he spontaneously embarked on a film about a German director working for US backers. Using the team already assembled, Wenders shot *The State of Things*. Of all his work, this film is the most programmatic and illustrates his auteurship. As Kolker and Beicken comment:

> Wenders' auteurism shows signs of a particularly intense involvement in his characters as if they were acting out vital concerns of his own, as if the films were somehow long photo albums of the filmmaker's desires in the course of time.[14]

The 'film/album' becomes progressively grimmer and culminates in the death of the German director and his producer at the hands of a vengeful LA mob. Wenders did complete *Hammet* but was already scouting locations for his next major project, *Paris, Texas*. With the help of European finance, he applied his own capacity for extemporizing to the script by the quintessentially American playwright Sam Shepard, producing a reckoning with the US and its culture. The success of *Paris, Texas* confirmed his status as the German auteur of his generation, and he began seeking finance for his most ambitious project, *Until the End of the World*. In the meantime, he took a very personal tangent with *Tokyo-Ga* (1985), his 'pilgrimage' to the Japanese settings used by his acknowledged master, Yasujiro Ozu. Following that documentary, Wenders then reverted to homeground for a crucial effort of fiction, *Wings of Desire*.

Where the final shot of *Alice in the Cities* pulls up and away from the Munich express, *Wings of Desire* relinquishes such detached elevation for Berlin's ground-level and what its main figure, the angel Damiel, calls 'the river of Time'. *Wings of Desire* locates the decision of two lovers to embark on their joint *Geschichte* (meaning both 'history' and 'story' in German) in the enclave that was, in 1987 at least, West Berlin. By contrast, *Until the End of the World* skips through countries and time zones and spans images ranging from its characters' dreams to the Earth seen from orbit. Even in its shortened release version from 1991, it has material for two if not three films, indicating both Wenders' strength as a visual master and his weakness as a narrator. The global odyssey is also ironic for Wenders' personally as it took him away to Australia just as the Wall collapsed in November 1989 and Germany re-formed practically overnight.

Faraway, so Close!, the sequel to *Wings of Desire*, takes a broader view of Berlin post-Wall through the 'grounding' of his second angel, Cassiel. Like *Until the End of the World*, it freights some effective imagery with a complex narrative and reflections on the nature of time, history and of German cinema. It then rounds off its 'legend' by referring to 'Him', presumably the Christian God, as the end and reconciliation of all things. Between this film and *The Million Dollar Hotel* there appeared *Lisbon Story*, *Above the Clouds*, *The End of Violence* and the documentary *Buena Vista Social Club*. The first is a cameo effort inspired by Wenders' obvious affection for that year's European City of Culture and rehearses his familiar self-reflexive concern with filmmaking. The second is an homage to Michelangelo Antonioni, casting John Malkovich as an American director whose scouting for settings in Europe reveals three separate love stories. Apparently, Wenders shot linking sequences in order that Antonioni could direct the stories the American observes. Again Wenders is the filmmaker between Europe and America, in this case as the creator of an allegorical role. A film producer is central to the 'whodunit' plot of *The End of Violence*, but this time he is very much a creature of his own turf, with Los Angeles as the capital of world filmmaking. For *Buena Vista Social Club*, Wenders collaborated with musician Ry Cooder to re-discover and popularize a forgotten generation of Cuban musicians. His 'incidental piece' unexpectedly launched a minor cult around its music and won him the documentary prize at the Federal German Film Awards in 2000.

If *The State of Things* is the programmatic, self-reflexive exemplar, then *Wings of Desire* is simply Wenders' best film thus far. In the former, the key scene shows the director asking his writer why a Hollywood producer would want a European director. The writer responds with the ritual framing gesture, and, with a degree of ironic self-stylization, the two men formulate the answer between them: 'The European way of seeing'. What Kolker and Beicken call the 'desires' in Wenders' work, his 'trademark' as auteur, illustrate how his 'European way' interrogates seeing, being a viewer, a spectator or a voyeur – and even simply recording what's there. *The State of Things* explores not just filmmaking but also everything meant by cinema where it emphasizes the practical, even fatal, implications of financing. The film concentrates on one of Wenders' abiding concerns: the tension between image and narrative. As Norbert Grob puts it: 'The desire for stories. And the mistrust of stories. With Wenders those are two sides of the same coin.'[15] Wenders himself has described a story as a 'Vampire' battening on images which 'don't want to carry and transport anything: neither message nor meaning, neither purpose nor moral'.[16] He can shift between scripts and extemporizing, frequently combining the two, whilst his images often interrogate themselves. *Nick's Film* shows early use of video; *Until the End of the World* has High Definition-TV; his documentary, *Notebooks on Clothes and Cities*, compares video and 35mm film; *The End of Violence* explores satellite imaging; while his latest project, *In Amerika*, exclusively deploys digital recording techniques. Thus, the meaning of Wenders' filmmaking lies not in providing a vehicle for anything outside of itself, but, rather, in growing out of a process that constantly reveals and recreates its own nature.

With his early short films and *Summer in the City*, Wenders seems to record events after a story has happened. And with the protagonist of *Summer in the City* he creates the alienated male, the compulsive wanderer incapable of personal relationships, especially with women. The figure immediately reappears in *The Goalkeeper's Fear of the Penalty Kick*, as a murderer waking up beside the woman he has killed for no reason; in the failed writer, Wilhelm, left contemplating Germany from the top of the Zugspitze at the end of *The Wrong Move*; or in Bruno tearfully rediscovering relics of his childhood at his old home in *Kings of the Road*. The director in *The State of Things* sums up such figures by practically quoting F.W. Murnau: 'Don't forget, I'm not at home anywhere, in no town, in no country.' The film ends with a mainline modernist image: Friedrich pans his ciné-camera across his surroundings in an ironic attempt to record the image of the killers. In *Paris, Texas* a different irony marks Travis, where this mute, wandering male reconstructs enough of a personality to retell events and thereby realize that he has no function as either father or husband in the potential story of his son and wife. His final situation is postmodern: he remains a viewer of the events he orchestrates as if they were no more than fictions in someone else's film.

When Damiel decides to become human in *Wings of Desire*, he relates his anticipation, the 'story' of his first mortal day, to his 'buddy', Cassiel. He replies: 'But none of it will be true', and then grows alarmed as Damiel begins to leave footprints. To become human, Damiel has ironically picked a spot which could well get him killed outright: the East side of the Wall. So he is transported through the impermeable barrier and into a world of colour. Such sequences generate a huge range of symbolic allusion to German history, to Wenders' own work, to simply seeing things and to watching a film.

Once he wakes as a lone male, Damiel sets off on a journey, but one with the goal of finding the woman with whom he will establish their story. He abandons observing and recording Berlin through black-and-white images without any purpose after he experiences Marion. She identifies herself as a spectacle to be watched, and Damiel senses its instinctive and emotional appeal and, above all, its existential importance for her. The meeting of the lovers uses postmodern imagery to suggest a positive meaning. Wenders stages an 'aria' where the woman tells the man that their 'story' will become an epic myth for all humanity. The film would be playing games with the conventions of the melodrama, even of the soap opera, were it not for the way Wenders twice cuts to close-up to reveal the viewpoint of each character as each looks directly into the camera. As the characters affirm their decision, viewers have to decide whether to dismiss the entire scene as game-playing or to credit its fiction with some meaning for their own situation. Wenders provides immediate reinforcement for belief in his images through one of his most memorable sequences: Marion practising on a trapeze rope held by Damiel as he reflects on his own 'amazement' that a relationship is possible between man and woman. As he now knows what no angel could know, he also knows that they can live their story.

Unlike his German contemporaries, Wolfgang Petersen and Roland Emmerich, Wenders has not become a 'regular' director in Hollywood. Instead, he operates through the dialectic identified by Toby Miller in Euro-American filmmaking:

> It may even be that part of the European taste for Hollywood is formed, paradoxically, by exposure to its own production; in other words, the US is an entertainment 'other', alluring precisely because it has the weight of Europe against it, and hence benefiting from competition that would not be present without the subsidized screen. For to be left with a monopoly in inessential items – which is what Hollywood desires – is ultimately to run out of stimulus, difference and appeal.[17]

Wenders' talent cannot be directly exploited by the Hollywood industry – Wenders himself does not want it to be.[18] But then, perhaps Hollywood does not need to. As his *The Million Dollar Hotel* indicates, Wenders is now so adept at drawing on American cinema and media culture that his creative talent can exploit the dynamic tension generated by belonging to the dialectical category of the 'other', the 'cultural exception' or the 'second cinema'. And thus, at the beginning of the twenty-first century, this 'star director' and his work will probably remain for Hollywood a necessary factor in the global cinema market. In his own, more complex way, Wim Wenders is an heir to Sirk, Murnau or Lang, the 'otherness' of whose talent served and enriched the dominant industry and yet, justly so, secured their German/European auteurship.

Biography

Wim Wenders was born on 14 August 1945, in Düsseldorf, Germany. He began his professional career with *The Goalkeeper's Fear of the*

Penalty Kick; *Paris, Texas* won the Palme d'Or at Cannes in 1984; and he gained Best Director award for *Der Himmel über Berlin* (*Wings of Desire*). Since the mid-1990s he has mainly made his movies in the US in English. He is currently shooting *In Amerika* in the US, using digital technology.

Notes

1 All translations by M.S.J.; M. Baier, *Film, Video und HDTV: Die Audiovisionen des Wim Wenders*, Berlin, Köhler, 1996, p. 9.
2 D. Puttnam, *The Undeclared War*, London, HarperCollins, 1997, p. 343.
3 M. Dorland, 'Policy Rhetorics of an Imaginary Cinema', in A. Moran (ed.) *Film Policy*, London, Routledge, 1996, p. 125.
4 T. Elsaesser, 'Spectators of Life: Time, Place and Self in the Films of Wim Wenders', in R.F. Cook and G. Gemünden (eds) *The Cinema of Wim Wenders*, Detroit, MI, Wayne State University Press, 1997, p. 241.
5 W. Wenders, 'Nicht allein in einem grossen Haus', in W. Wenders, *The Act of Seeing*, Frankfurt am Main, Verlag der Autoren, 1992, p. 179.
6 A. Finney, *A Dose of Reality*, London, Screen International, 1992, p. 9.
7 W. Wenders, *Emotion Pictures*, Frankfurt am Main, Verlag der Autoren, 1986, p. 103.
8 P. Lev, *The Euro-American Cinema*, Austin, University of Texas Press, 1993, p. 37.
9 T. Elsaesser, *op. cit.*, p. 3.
10 Wenders has written, directed, produced, performed in and edited movies as well as working as a cinematographer and in the sound department on occasion.
11 Wenders has completed a television documentary on the Cologne rock group, BAP (scheduled to be screened in Germany in late 2000).
12 H.W. Geissendörfer, 'Wir fordern zur Rebellion auf', *Der Spiegel*, 22, 1997, p. 218.
13 The situation in East Germany was superficially simpler as the socialist regime declared itself the heir of German resistance to Fascism and allotted the Nazis' unholy heritage firmly to its Western counterpart.
14 R.P. Kolker and P. Beicken, *The Films of Wim Wenders*, Cambridge, Cambridge University Press, 1993, p. 62.
15 N. Grob, *Wenders*, Berlin, Edition Film, 1991, p. 14.
16 W. Wenders, *Die Logik der Bilder*, Frankfurt am Main, Verlag der Autoren, 1988, p. 71.
17 T. Miller, 'The Crime of Monsieur Lang', in A. Moran (ed.) *Film Policy*, London, Routledge, 1996, p. 80.
18 Hollywood has paid him one of its ultimate compliments by remaking *Wings of Desire* as *City of Angels* (Brad Silberling, 1998).

Filmography

Schauplätze (1967) short
Same Player Shoots Again (1967) short
Silver City (1968) short

Polizeifilm (1968) short
Alabama: 2000 Light Years from Home (1969) short
3 American LP's / Drei amerikanische LP's (1969) short
Summer in the City (1970)
The Goalkeeper's Fear of the Penalty Kick / Die Angst des Tormanns beim Elfmeter (1971)
The Scarlet Letter / Der Scharlachrote buchstabe (1972)
Alice in the Cities / Alice im den Städten (1973)
The Island / From the Family of Reptiles (1974) short
The Wrong Move (US title: *False Movement*) / *Falsche Bewegung* (1975)
Kings of the Road / Im Lauf der Zeit (1976)
The American Friend / Der amerikanische Freund (1977)
Nick's Film: Lightning over Water (1980) documentary
Reverse Angle (1982) short documentary
Chambre 666 / Room 666 (1982) short documentary
Hammett (1982)
The State of Things / Der Stand der Dinge (1982)
Paris, Texas (1984)
Tokyo-Ga (1985) documentary
Wings of Desire / Der Himmel über Berlin (1987)
Notebook on Cities and Clothes (1989) documentary
Until the End of the World / Bis ans Ende der Welt (1991)
Arisha, the Bear and the Stone Ring (1992) short
Faraway, so Close! / In weiter Ferne, so nah (1993)
Lisbon Story (1994)
Beyond the Clouds (with Michelangelo Antonioni, 1995)
A Trick of the Light (1996)
The End of Violence (1997)
Willie Nelson at the Teatro (1998) documentary
Buena Vista Social Club (1998) documentary
The Million Dollar Hotel (2000)

STAN JONES

WONG KAR-WAI

Central to the contemporary Chinese cinema renaissance are the seven feature films made to date by young Hong Kong director Wong Kar-Wai. Attracting both cult and mainstream attention, these titles have established Wong as one of the key names in the West's pantheon of Asian filmmakers. Moreover, with Hong Kong now positioned between its existence as a postcolonial global city and its destiny as part of the Chinese nation-state, Wong's films have come to bear the burden of historical representation. Whenever audiences and commentators seek to account for the meaning of new times in Hong Kong they invariably scour his work looking for clues.

Wong's ascendancy has been dramatic. After writing numerous scripts for TVB and the production company Cinema City in the early and mid-1980s, he made his directorial debut a few years later as a member of Hong Kong's 'second wave' (alongside Jacob Cheung, Clara Law and Alex Law). *As Tears Go By*, one of the best Chinese gangster or Triad movies produced in recent times, showcases Wong's profligate talents by transposing Martin Scorsese's *Mean Streets* to Hong Kong's Mongkok and Lantau Island. While this impressive example of genre revisionism made a few waves in domestic and international waters, Wong started to attract attention in earnest in 1991 for his highly idiosyncratic second feature, the 1960s' youth melodrama *Days of Being Wild*. *Ashes of Time*, a gorgeously shot and edited martial arts epic that combines specifically Asian philosophical wisdoms with a modernist deconstruction of narrative, came next. Before long the trope of comparing Asian filmmakers to western 'models' (specifically, in Wong's case, Jean-Luc Godard) began to surface when the director's fourth and fifth titles became art-house hits in Europe and the US – both the charming *Chungking Express* and darker *Fallen Angels* have been identified as 'Hong Kong noir'. Finally, Wong Kar-Wai won Best Director Award at the 1997 Cannes Film Festival for *Happy Together*, a beautifully acted gay road movie which was shot largely in Argentina.

These highly innovative and enjoyable movies have attracted critical attention primarily on the basis of their extraordinary visual qualities. Each contains intriguing graphic designs, flamboyant colour schemes and a playful manipulation of spatial and temporal relationships. Wong has collaborated productively with Christopher Doyle, the famed Australian cinematographer who has worked in China, Hong Kong, Taiwan and the United States alongside such stellar directors as Chen Kaige, Chen Kunhou, Stanley Kwan, Stan Lai, Edward Yang and Gus Van Sant. Doyle's preferred shooting style, which mixes startling stop-motion effects with predominantly hand-held camerawork, brilliantly complements Wong's plot ambiguities and fragmentary storylines. Indeed, for some western critics, Wong and Doyle have helped revive what Pier Paolo Pasolini once termed 'the cinema of poetry'.[1]

Ackbar Abbas has pushed such claims one step further by suggesting that Wong also assigns visuality a clear political function. Proposing 'disappearance' as a keyword central to any understanding of Hong Kong's unique cultural identity, Ackbar argues that since the signing of the 1984 Sino-British Joint Declaration on the Future of Hong Kong, coming to terms with the politics of disappearance has been the great challenge for the city's cultural workers. In the run-up to Hong Kong's reversion to Chinese sovereignty on 1 July 1997, how could a world forever slipping out of sight be re-sited? One answer to that question is provided by the almost dialectical nature of Wong's artistic concerns. *Days of Being Wild*, for instance, with its aimless central characters and shifts in location between Hong Kong and Manila, implies geographic and emotional dislocation so as to 'challenge the definition of Hong Kong culture itself by questioning and dismantling the way we look at things'.[2]

Such ambivalence ties Wong's preoccupations to those of a global audience as much as to a local one. Building on the Hong Kong experience, his success may be partly attributable to a worldwide fascination with the unforeseen effects of large-scale migration and alienation. Certainly, this is a subject that has been of concern to many other Hong Kong filmmakers of the 1980s and 1990s. For example, Peter Chan (*Comrades, Almost a Love Story*, 1996), Mabel Cheung (*An Autumn's Tale*, 1987), Ann Hui (*Song of the Exile*, 1990), Stanley Kwan (*Full Moon in New York*, 1989) and Clara Law (*Autumn Moon*, 1992) have all won acclaim for their explorations of issues of border-crossing, the forging of connections in lonely and unfamiliar modern cities, and the symbolism associated with places of transit.

At the same time, Wong's reception also illustrates how Asian filmmakers need to offer something new and distinct if they are to penetrate global image markets. The dynamic compositions and editing patterns of *Ashes of Time*, *Fallen Angels* and *Happy Together* are far removed from the bland 'international style' characteristic of so much transnational cinema of the 1990s. Expressing displacement and contradiction through striking visual form has provided Wong Kar-Wai with one of the most easily identifiable trademarks in the business.

Wong's use of music only adds to the structural ambiguity of his films. Musical collaborators Frankie Chan and Roel A. Garcia are architects of some of contemporary cinema's most astonishingly creative sound designs, and they have incorporated elements from a diverse range of Asian and non-Asian musical cultures into their work. Across Wong's seven films, the contents of what may be called this global jukebox have included such artists as Ernesto Lecuona,

Los Indios Tabajaras, Xavia Cugat, the Mamas and the Papas, Massive Attack, the Flying Pickets, Marianne Faithfull, Astor Piazzolla, Caetano Veloso, and the Three Amigos, not to mention Chan and Garcia's own pastiche-like compositions in the styles of raga, techno, new age, ambient and Ennio Morricone. Musical serendipity has proved crucial to the emotional and cognitive appeals of a Wong Kar-Wai movie, just as it has helped the soundtrack CDs become cult objects of desire among collectors in the West.

On the other hand, it is interesting to note that despite Wong's recurrent use of Chinese pop stars as actors (Andy Lau, Jacky Cheung, Leslie Cheung, Tony Leung, Faye Wong, Leon Lai, Karen Mok), not that much actual Hong Kong music, or Cantopop, makes it into his films. This strategy of devaluing local music in relation to other kinds of international music can be seen as a tease – denying fans the expected songs by favourite stars (Wong similarly plays around with the iconography of film and pop star images) – and as a clever marketing strategy. After all, a wide range of music on a soundtrack and accompanying CD provides consumers with diverse points of entry and helps a film travel far and wide. Specifically, Wong's work appears more and more to have one eye on the massively expanding mainland market, and one on the markets created by the various Chinese diasporic communities active throughout the world.

Consider the scene in which Faye Wong's character cleans up Cop no. 663's apartment in *Chungking Express*. For this MTV-like segment, the actress loafs from room to room while her own rendition of the Cranberries' song 'Dreams' (now renamed 'Dream Person') plays on the soundtrack. Faye Wong is a native of Beijing, adored in Hong Kong and Greater China for pop hits like the 1992 song 'An Easily Hurt Woman'. At the same time, however, she has been in the vanguard of Cantonese and Mandarin music's transition to rock during the 1990s (she has covered Sinead O'Connor, collaborated with the Cocteau Twins, and married and separated from mainland rock star Dou Wei). Staging this particular scene around Faye Wong's version of 'Dreams', then, does not just exhibit good taste, but also constitutes shrewd marketing. First, it reinforces the importance of processes of indigenization to popular Hong Kong culture by imaginatively transforming western source music (compare, for example, the use of a cover version of 'Take My Breath Away', Berlin's hit from the Hollywood blockbuster *Top Gun*, during the telephone-booth kissing scene between Andy Lau and

Maggie Cheung in *As Tears Go By*, or Danny Chung's version of the Turtles' eponymous 1967 hit that memorably closes *Happy Together*). Second, as the original version of this song will no doubt be familiar to international fans of English-language pop music, a Chinese interpretation may well be expected to prick up the ears of many curious listeners. In other words, Faye Wong's 'Dreams' is neither one thing nor the other; local but not local to Hong Kong, western but not really western, from the mainland but not of the mainland.

Questions of marketability have been crucial to the establishment of Wong's international profile in other ways as well. As with the work of fellow Asian cult directors Kitano Takeshi and Tsui Hark, an aura of exclusivity, determined by the vagaries of access, has surrounded the reception of his films. While Wong Kar-Wai has certainly been active on the international film festival circuit, his titles have also been widely distributed in the West at a more subterranean level, on bootleg tapes, laser discs and videocassette discs imported from Hong Kong and Japan. As a mark of this simultaneous visibility and invisibility, no less than three of his works were included in a list of the Top 30 Unreleased Foreign-Language films of the 1990s compiled by the US magazine *Film Comment* in 1997, even though all were widely available in America at the time through 'unofficial' sources.

Lately, Wong has used his own production company, Jet Tone, to spread interest in a similar fashion. After the success of *Happy Together*, advertisements promoting glossy colour posters and photo-books of an as-yet-unreleased title, *Summer in Beijing*, were posted on the Internet. (Of course, many unofficial Internet sites are now devoted to the director, his favoured stars, and Hong Kong cinema more generally.) Yet when it comes to the coverage Wong's films received in the abundance of Hong Kong film fanzines that flooded the US and European print markets during the 1990s, such 'art cinema' associations are not so easily retained. The mix of populist and experimental tendencies in Wong Kar-Wai's films has sometimes made it hard for audiences and critics to separate his output from that of other popular Hong Kong filmmakers. Unlike the work of Jackie Chan, Ringo Lam, Tsui Hark and John Woo, for example, Wong's films do not play in western multiplexes, and yet they are often talked about in the same breath as such commercial fare. Wong may cross over between the cult and mainstream, but he has also gained a reputation as a troublesome case, someone who makes life awkward for strait-laced commentators by injecting established genres with a modernist or avant-garde sensibility. Such tactics can easily confuse audiences and critics more comfortable with clear-cut distinctions and categories.

In many respects, this 'problem' of determining how Wong Kar-Wai's films should be categorized reproduces the relationship he appears to have with the Hong Kong film industry in general. While Wong's early days included script work for one of the most daring of the city's original post-1979 'New Wave' directors, Patrick Tam (*Final Victory*, 1987), he has also written standard pot-boilers like the patchy sci-fi title *Saviour of the Soul* (Corey Yuen, 1991). Conversely, while Wong as director is renowned for playing around with genre conventions, local filmmakers have themselves played around with Wong's critical reputation by creating their own new genre – the Wong Kar-Wai parody movie. These parodies have been produced back-to-back with Wong's own titles, as in Jeff Lau's *The Eagle Shooting Heroes* (1991), which was shot by some of the cast and crew of *Ashes of Time* on breaks during the latter's lengthy schedule, or else are signalled by wordplay (Blackie Ko's 1992 *Days of Being Dumb*), and the spoofing of iconic moments from individual movies – comedian Stephen Chow's interpretation of the final scene from *Days of Being Wild* in his self-directed *From Beijing with Love* (1994) is hilarious. Not to be outdone, Wong has himself shown a healthy propensity for self-mockery by inserting numerous intertextual references into his own films, as in Takeshi Kaneshiro's studied mimicry, in *Fallen Angels*, of Faye Wong's ditsy body language from *Chungking Express*.

While the highly episodic *Fallen Angels* was seen by some critics as a virtual non-stop parody of the established Wong Kar-Wai style, no such criticism pertains to the movie that has thoroughly consolidated Wong's international reputation, *Happy Together*. Ostensibly influenced by Latin American magic-realist authors such as Manuel Puig, the film is perhaps of most significance for focusing attention not just on Wong's astonishing formalism, but also on debates about homosexuality in Asian cinema. At the very least, *Happy Together* should be placed in the company of other titles that bravely explored such subject matter in the months leading up to and after the 1997 handover, namely Stanley Kwan's *Hold You Tight* (1998) and Shu Kei's *A Queer Story* (1996). Wong's contribution to this progressive artistic tendency won praise for its frank portrayal of a gay relationship between two Chinese men (played by Leslie Cheung and Tony Leung) stranded in Argentina. According to some reports, the original plan was to have one of the young gay protagonists discover that his recently deceased father was also homosexual, but that ambitious-sounding storyline was dismissed upon touchdown in South America.

On the other hand, for all the film's success at Cannes and other exhibition sites, *Happy Together* has had an occasionally chequered reception career. In Korea, for example, it was banned from exhibition at the first Seoul Queer Film and Video Festival on the grounds that it was 'not relevant to the emotional life of the Korean people'.[3] Moreover, in a generally sympathetic piece on the film, Denise Tang points out that the choice of Argentina as the film's location may actually serve to 'reinforce the stereotypical Asian response to homosexuality as a foreign concept'. Because we largely see images of the two central characters in a foreign culture, audiences may be encouraged to view them as ' "cultural exiles", gay Asian men who are traitors of their own ethnicity by the nature of their sexual identity as gay men'.[4] (For his part, Chris Doyle indirectly entered the political fray by 'outing' megastar Leslie Cheung in the written commentary accompanying his photographic record of the shoot, *Don't Cry For Me Argentina*.)[5]

Overall, though, *Happy Together*'s provocative convergence of sexual and geographic politics bodes well for Wong Kar-Wai's future career. While the sight of two Chinese homosexuals cruising and being cruised by white and South American males provides an interesting take on questions of East–West relations, the film also presents a rare Asian variant of the hustler figure identified by Robert Lang as a key icon of contemporary queer road movies.[6] Yet *Happy Together* could just as easily demonstrate how Wong Kar-Wai needs to find new directions in which to travel. Positively, it is a stunning vindication of contemporary Chinese cinema, a work full of exciting possibilities for transnational filmmaking at the turn of the century. Negatively, it occasionally becomes trapped in the same problems that plagued Clara Law's *Farewell, China* (1990) and Stanley Kwan's *Full Moon in New York*, two earlier movies about Hong Kong people living overseas. All three titles arguably get bogged down in the question of how you can express geographic and emotional dislocation without treating other cultures as the mere backdrop to transplanted local issues. In the rush to re-site a world forever slipping out of sight, *Happy Together* risks making Argentina disappear altogether.

Wong's Kar-Wai's most recent film, *In the Mood for Love*, moves away from the politics of displacement and travel to return to questions concerning the meaning of 'home' in a climate of change.

As with *Days of Being Wild*, it is set in 1960s' Hong Kong, and depicts an intense, and at time tortuous relationship between a couple (played by Wong stalwarts Maggie Cheung and Tony Leung Chiu-Wai) who never quite connect with one another during the course of their extra-marital 'affair'. *In the Mood for Love*'s astonishingly vivid images – comprising period sets, sumptuous colours, and clothing designs you cannot help but be fascinated by – almost overwhelm the twists and turns of an already complex and enigmatic narrative structure. Well-chosen musical interludes re-confirm the director's ability to construct highly evocative sound-tracks. The critical and commercial success of *In the Mood for Love* shows that Wong and his collaborators have once again offered something new and distinct in the global marketplace. On the basis of the seven feature films to date, one can be assured that Wong Kar-Wai will continue to excite the eyes and ears of the audiences who are fortunate enough to be exposed to his prodigious imagination.

Biography

Wong Kar-Wai was born in Shanghai, China, in 1958. He trained in graphic design at Hong Kong Polytechnic and in television drama at TVB. In the 1980s he worked as a scriptwriter at Cinema City.

Notes

1 John Orr, *Contemporary Cinema*, Edinburgh, Edinburgh University Press, 1998.
2 Ackbar Abbas, *Hong Kong: Culture and the Politics of Disappearance*, Minneapolis, University of Minnesota Press, 1997, p. 62.
3 'Plug Pulled on 1st Seoul Queer Film and Video Festival'. Online: 20 September 1997.
4 Denise Tang, 'Popular Dialogues of a "Discreet" Nature', *Asian Cinema*, vol. 10, no. 1, 1998, p. 201.
5 Christopher Doyle, *Don't Cry For Me Argentina: Happy Together Photographic Journal*, ed. Law Wai Ming, Hong Kong, City Entertainment Books, 1997.
6 Robert Lang, '*My Own Private Idaho* and the New Queer Road Movies', in Steven Cohan and Ina Rae Hark (eds) *The Road Movie Book*, London, Routledge, 1997, pp. 330–48.

Filmography

(All Hong Kong productions unless indicated)

As Tears Go By (1988)
Days of Being Wild (1991)

Ashes of Time (Hong Kong/Taiwan, 1994)
Chungking Express (1994)
Fallen Angels (1995)
Happy Together (1997)
In the Mood for Love (Hong Kong/France, 2000)

Further reading

Christopher Doyle, *Backlit By the Moon*, Tokyo, Masakazu Takei, 1996.
Don't Cry For Me Argentina: Happy Together Photographic Journal, ed. Law Wai Ming, Hong Kong, City Entertainment Books, 1997.
Jean-Marc Lalanne *et al.*, *Wong Kar-Wai*, Paris, Editions Dis Voir, 1997.
Tony Rayns (ed.) *Wong Kar-Wai on Wong Kar-Wai*, London, Faber and Faber, 2000.
Lisa Odham Stokes and Michael Hoover, *City on Fire: Hong Kong Cinema*, London, Verso, 1999.
Curtis K. Tsui, 'Subjective Culture and History: The Ethnographic Cinema of Wong Kar-Wai', *Asian Cinema*, vol. 7, no. 2, 1995, pp. 93–124.

JULIAN STRINGER

JOHN WOO

Currently, John Woo is the one example of a Hong Kong film director who has successfully managed to transfer his talents from his original national industry to the big-budget domains of Hollywood cinema. Unlike several of his Hong Kong contemporaries, such as Ringo Lam, Kirk Wong and Ronny Yu, Woo's place as a mainstream film director is currently assured within the Hollywood industry (so long as box-office returns continue). As such, his significance represents a fascinating case study in the realm of recent explorations of transnational cinemas, especially the Chinese connection. Woo's films aptly embody Sheldon Hsiao-peng Lu's observations concerning transnational Chinese cinemas. Lu comments that 'Film has always been a transnational entity'.[1] However, in an era where the very idea of a nation-state is both debatable and multifaceted, all national cinemas are affected by new patterns of global distribution and international co-productions which render previous definitions of authorship and genre highly unstable. Thus, as well as deserving study as a director in his own right, Woo represents a fertile area for investigating the various transnational dynamics involving issues of gender, genre and authorship. Both past and present, his films illustrate these issues as well as problematic questions of creative transformation.

Woo is generally characterized as an 'action director', a successor to Sam Peckinpah's equally misleading label of 'master of violence'. However, a closer examination of Woo's major films from *A Better Tomorrow* onwards (as well as some early works) reveals a director whose vision is definitely at odds with the supposed celebration of violence beloved by certain fan audiences and lesser talents such as Quentin Tarantino. After such films as *The Killer* and *Hard Boiled* came to the attention of Hollywood executives, the director joined the ranks of those foreign talents (both past and present) invited to the tempting world of a big-budget industry promising freedom, technological expertise and lavish finance. Championed by several film directors, including Oliver Stone and Tarantino, Woo's transfer to Hollywood appeared to offer the possibility of rejuvenating an already jaded action genre in the same manner as the Italian Westerns influenced the declining Hollywood Western a generation before. However, as Woo's experiences on *Hard Target* and *Broken Arrow* revealed, the studios eagerly exploited him as an 'action director' by constraining his role on the film set without understanding the complexity of his creative vision. It was not until *Face/Off* that Woo was finally allowed the freedom of a director's cut. This gave him the opportunity to display a creative synthesis of talents he had perfected in Hong Kong cinema since 1986 as well as demonstrate his intuitive understanding of a Hitchcockian tradition often misinterpreted by the industry.

Woo's role in contemporary Hollywood not only illustrates the hybrid type of authorship now common in transnational cinema but also evokes memories of previous influences within the industry. Although his style differs from key representatives of the Germanic tradition such as Fritz Lang and Douglas Sirk, Woo's Hollywood work does reveal the presence of similar tensions affecting those of his predecessors, namely the competing dialogue between influential national cinematic tropes and the challenging world of a different cultural environment. However, even in his own national film industry, Woo was already experimenting with such fusions which would reach their creative peaks after 1986 and result in his move to Hollywood.

Despite the mixed nature of Woo's pre-1986 work, an understanding of their shared premises is necessary to really appreciate the nature of his innovative creative breakthrough in 1986. Woo began his film apprenticeship in several Hong Kong film studios in the late 1960s and 1970s. However, one formative influence remains constant throughout his Hong Kong and Hollywood periods, namely the work of Zhang Che. Although Bruce Lee's films have overshadowed other Hong Kong films released to western audiences during the first Hong Kong New Wave, Zhang Che's work is more important. Films such as *One Armed Swordsman* (1967), *Golden Swallow* (1968), *The New One Armed Swordsman* (1971) and *Four Riders* (1972) revealed Chinese cultural issues of friendship, betrayal and a melancholy depiction of violence which Stephen Prince sees as characteristic of Peckinpah's cinema. This latter factor has also influenced Woo. Before beginning his directing career in 1973, Woo worked with Zhang Che as assistant director on *Boxer from Shantung* (1972) and *Blood Brothers* (1973). Woo developed these themes within his mentor's cinema by both elaborating borrowed styles and placing themes within a new cultural context in his post-1986 films. *A Better Tomorrow, A Better Tomorrow 2, The Killer, A Bullet in the Head* and *Hard Boiled* all situate the already threatened heroic values of Che's films within a corrupt, post-capitalist, hybrid world of a colony undergoing a crisis scenario as it moves towards a feared apocalyptic climax in 1997. Although Che's films usually recognized the vulnerability of traditional Chinese heroic codes in a changing world, Woo developed this theme to more explicit and stylistic levels. In his period action drama, *Last Hurrah for Chivalry*, the heroes are already becoming redundant in their own time, as Mark, Ken Ho, Mr Lung, and John will be in the more brutal twentieth-century worlds of *A Better Tomorrow 1* and *2*, and *The Killer*. Woo's apocalyptic nightmarish world of Vietnam in *A Bullet in the Head* witnesses a similar betrayal of friendship affecting the characters in Chang's Ching Dynasty drama *Blood Brothers*. It was not accidental that Woo later directed 60 per cent of the Zhang Che reunion film (featuring former stars such as Ti Lung, David Chiang, Chen Kwan-tai and Danny Lee), *Just Heroes*. Furthermore, despite the influences of Jean-Pierre Melville, Kubrick and Scorsese on *The Killer*, Woo's acclaimed film sees a spiritual and symbiotic kinship developing between investigative cop Inspector Li (Danny Lee) and assassin John (Chow Yun-fat) paralleling motifs seen in early films such as *The Young Dragons, The Dragon Tamers* and *Last Hurrah for Chivalry*. In addition, the literal title of *The Killer*, 'A Pair of Blood-Splattering Heroes', expresses not just the film's duality but its implicit themes of heroic reincarnation in a modern world – another theme fascinating Hong Kong cinema.

Woo's pre-1986 comedy films appear to bear little relation to his acknowledged achievements. But, despite their mixed nature, several contain significant features anticipating his later work. At this stage, the problem involves lack of creative synthesis. References to other traditions occur, but they remain at the level of an incoherent 'referitis'. In *Money Crazy* and *From Riches to Rags*, Woo directed Ricky Hui. Although little-known to western audiences, Ricky Hui is part of a talented team of brothers (the others being Michael and Cantonese pop star Samuel) who have a permanent place in Hong Kong film history for comedy films satirizing various aspects of the colony's crass materialism, class and politics during the 1970s and 1980s. John Woo aided Michael Hui by helping him direct his first acclaimed feature, *Games Gamblers Play* (1974), which parodied the Chinese obsession with gambling. He later acted as associate director on Hui's *The Private Eyes* and *The Contract* (1978). Woo has mentioned his fascination with cartoon-style comedy and the work of Jerry Lewis, influences which appear in his Ricky Hui films. However, despite their incoherent nature, they do attempt to satirize Hong Kong's fascination with materialism and also expose serious issues of class exploitation and poverty. In *From Riches to Rags*, the climactic scenes show mental asylum patients representing the worst materialistic attributes of their saner counterparts outside. Woo inserts a parodic homage to Kubrick's *2001: A Space Odyssey*, embling a block of gold. Later, the patients make Ricky Hui undergo a Russian roulette game borrowed from Michael Cimino's *The Deer Hunter* (1978), a motif Woo used again in *A Bullet in the Head*. Woo has described *From Riches to Rags* as a 'satire on avarice', thereby revealing his intuitive understanding of the Hui comedy tradition. However, Woo's early comedic experiments in cartoon style appear more creatively in the non-comedy *Better Tomorrow* films and *The Killer* while his keen eye for social injustice also characterize *A Bullet in the Head* and *Hard Target*. Similarly, *A Bullet in the Head* treats the issue of greed more seriously in the case of Paul (Waise Lee) who betrays his friends for gold. Finally, Woo's first Cinema City production, *Laughing Times*, sees Charlie Chaplin's Little Tramp reincarnated in Dean Shek's performance. Together with a reconstituted Flower Girl and Cantonese Jackie Coogan version of *The Kid*, Shek's homeless Little Tramp successfully battles both poverty and a child prostitution racket headed by Karl Maka. Again, Woo's sympathy for street people seen in a few significant montages during *Hard Target* is thus not without precedent. The role of cinematic excess characteristic of Woo's later stylistic gangster films also appears in these early comedy films in an experimental manner awaiting perfect realization. This did not occur until Woo's association with Tsui Hark's Film Workshop Company.

Before then, Woo had attempted to make a Vietnam film, *Heroes Shed No Tears*, modelled on a number of sources such as the Japanese 'Lone Wolf and Child' series, stylistic traits borrowed from Jean-Pierre Melville, and an action genre cinema he was steadily moving towards. Unfortunately, Golden Harvest disagreed with Woo's concentration on character relationships and a bleak climax so they only released the film after the success of *A Better Tomorrow*. Produced by Hark and starring former Shaw Brothers hero and Zhang Che discovery Ti Lung in the leading role, *A Better Tomorrow* depicted tensions affecting the Confucian traditions of family and personal relations within an increasingly ruthless corporate world of post-capitalism. Although concentrating on the tortured odyssey of Ho (Ti Lung), the film rocketed Chow Yun-fat into Hong Kong stardom in the role of Mark Gor, a character modelled on both Alain Delon's Melville roles and the heroic traditions depicted in the Shaw Brothers' films of Zhang Che. Stylistically, *A Better Tomorrow* also represented a creative breakthrough for Woo in terms of not only action cinema but also his appropriation of dynamic and tonal montage reminiscent of the cinema of Sergei Eisenstein. Despite some elaborate action sequences, *A Better Tomorrow 2* suffered from a growing rift between Hark and Woo. Under Hark's influence, the theme of Lung's (Dean Shek) betrayal by his partners became a dominant motif in a film Woo intended as a 'comic book' serialization of themes already treated in the previous film. However, *A Better Tomorrow 2* revealed Woo finally succeeding with the stylistic experiments seen in his comedies *Follow the Star, From Riches to Rags, To Hell with the Devil, Laughing Times* and *Run Tiger Run*.

After leaving the Film Workshop, Woo began *The Killer*. Starring Chow Yun-fat and Danny Lee, the film was a co-production of both Golden Princess and Magnum Films, a company owned by Danny Lee. As his most poetic film to date, *The Killer* brought Woo to international attention. Synthesizing eastern and western cinematic traditions, *The Killer* reworked a Takakura-Ken *yakuza-eiga* gangster film, *Narazumono* (1964), directed by Ishii Teruo. As Ken Hall demonstrates, *The Killer* represents the best example of Woo's creative interweaving of the cinematic traditions of Martin Scorsese, Francis Ford Coppola, Stanley Kubrick, Don Siegel, Robert Aldrich, Jean-Pierre Melville, Alfred Hitchcock, David Lean, Akira Kurosawa, Sergio Leone, Zhang Che and Masaki Kobayashi.[2] It also reveals Woo's development of aesthetic elements within Eisenstein's later overtonal montage theories. Woo's methodology represents neither copying nor reductive parody but rather explorations of the creative usages of textual appropriation, which Linda Hutcheon regards as characteristic of certain twentieth-century progressive practices.[3] Hall also points out the influence of not only *Narazumono* but also *Le Samourai* (1966) and Michael Mann's underrated *Manhunter* (1986) on Woo's film, especially the last two's strong emphasis on the kinship between two different protagonists.[4]

Despite *The Killer*'s undoubted achievement, Woo's cinematic masterpiece is definitely *A Bullet in the Head*, a dark romantic treatment of friendship, betrayal and social chaos characterized by apocalyptic feelings following the Tiananmen Square massacre and its consequences for Hong Kong in 1997. Creatively reworking themes from Sergio Leone's *Once Upon a Time in America* (1984), Cimino's *The Deer Hunter* and Sam Peckinpah's *Bring Me the Head of Alfredo Garcia* (1974), Woo directed an epic masterpiece dealing with the corruption of human values by two political systems dominating twentieth-century societies. Although critical of the brutal aspects of communism, Woo also sees it tarnished by the greed and violence characterizing its political alter-ego – capitalism. Frank's (Jackie Cheung) cry to the corrupted Paul, 'Do you measure your friendship in gold?', serves not only as the *leitmotif* for this particular film but echoes throughout most of Woo's cinema. Articulating the social justice tenets of western Christianity and eastern Confucianism, Woo's cinema often displays a spiritual vision many critics neglect in their desire to claim Woo as the heir to Sam Peckinpah's supposedly ultra-violent cinema. Like Peckinpah, Woo's work often contains a critique of violence and a sense of mournful melancholia existing well beneath a supposedly attractive veneer of screen violence.

After seeking some light relief by directing *Once a Thief*, (or '*Jules et Jim* in Hong Kong'), Woo directed the work which would lead to Hollywood offers. *Hard Boiled* was not only as technically accomplished as its Hollywood competitors but also attacked human greed and mourned the loss of old heroic knightly traditions seen in the films of Che and Woo. Like John and Inspector Li in *The Killer*, Tequila (Chow Yun-fat) and undercover agent Tony (Tony Leung Chi-wai) are symbiotic 'secret sharers' in a quest against the new ruthless Triad culture represented by Johnny Wong (Anthony Wong). Brutally taking over from a kindly older Triad boss, Wong's violent methods appal even his most efficient hitman 'Mad Dog' (played by Shaw Brothers stalwart Philip Kwok) who refuses to participate in a massacre of innocent civilians in a hospital.

Eventually relocating to America and assisted by business partner, Terence Chang, Woo found his first Hollywood film riddled by studio compromises and the interference of its star Jean-Claude Van Damme. Despite these problems and the dilution of his creative style, Woo's *Hard Target* does succeed in its aim of being a modern version of Richard Connell's oft-filmed short story, *The Most Dangerous Game*. Casting a sympathetic eye on the plight of homeless people in the land of the free, a perspective obviously influenced by Woo's own early personal life and the scenes depicted in *Laughing Times*, the director attempted to cast Van Damme in the mould of his Chinese knightly heroes battling the forces of corporate capitalist evil represented by Lance Henriksen and Arnold Voslo. Despite studio interference and drastic censorship, *Hard Target*'s concerns revealed the director as more than just an action specialist.

Following an abortive project in the Amazon with Brad Pitt, Woo and Chang returned to America realizing the need to play the studio game and continue working in the industry. They both decided to show Hollywood that they could make as dumb an action film as any American: the result was *Broken Arrow*. Apart from the opening boxing scene between the two protagonists, the film was as empty and formulaic as any Bruce Willis or Mel Gibson vehicle. However, *Broken Arrow* did represent Woo's first collaboration with John Travolta, whose influence resulted in the director finally obtaining a director's cut on their next film together.

The Paramount production *Face/Off* represents Woo's creative synthesis of his Hollywood and eastern traditions. Although the script had been in development since 1990, the final version came to resemble an action film influenced by Hitchcock's *Strangers on a Train* (1951), as well as drawing on the duality motif seen in Zhang Che films such as *Blood Brothers* and Woo's *The Killer* and *Hard Boiled*. Though neither Woo nor his scenarists were consciously aware of it at the time, the pre-credits sequence resembled the carousel sequence of *Strangers on a Train*. Such references reveal the film as a key example of both recent transnational cinema as well as defining Woo's status as a transcultural bridge between Hollywood and Hong Kong. Possibly also indebted to Georges Franju's *Eyes without a Face* (1959), *Face/Off* again presents two characters who become blood brothers with different faces existing within a world of corporate dehumanization and contempt for individual lives. An earlier version of the script included a scene where Archer as Castor Troy visits Castor's mother and sees the squalid environment which influenced his antagonist's upbringing. Had the scene survived, it would have added an extra social dimension to the film similar to Woo's view of the street people in *Laughing Times* and *Hard Target*.

To date, the box-office successes of Woo's American films guarantees both his position in Hollywood cinema as well as offering the possibility of further attempts at the creative synthesis of traditions peculiar to both western and eastern cinema. Woo's involvement on *Mission Impossible 2*, his Hollywood reunion with Chow Yun-fat in *King's Ransom*, and ambition to direct a David Lean epic about a western mercenary in the Ching Dynasty (*The Devil Soldier* with Tom Cruise) suggest greater possibilities for him in the future.

Biography

Born in Guangzhou, the capital of Guangdong Province of South China, in 1946, Wu Yusen and his family moved to Hong Kong when he was young. At Matteo Ricci College in 1967 he joined a student drama group and began making 8mm short films. In 1969, he joined Cathay Film Studios as a production assistant. After moving to Shaw Brothers in 1971, he acted as assistant director to Zhang Che on *Ma Yongzhen* (*Boxer from Shantung*, 1972) and *Ci Ma* (*Blood Brothers*, 1973). In 1973, he went to Golden Harvest as a director. Woo has been resident in Hollywood since 1992.

Notes

1 Sheldon Hsiao-peng Lu, *Transnational Chinese Cinemas*, Honolulu, University of Hawaii Press, 1997, p. 25.
2 See Ken Hall, *John Woo: The Films*, Jefferson, NC, McFarland and Co, 1999.
3 Linda Hutcheon, *A Theory of Parody: The Teachings of Twentieth Century Art Forms*, Stanford, CA, Stanford University Press, 1975.
4 Ken Hall, *op. cit.*

Filmography

(Cantonese titles precede English translations)

As director

Tit hon yau chang / The Young Dragons (1973/1975)
Nui ji toi kuen kwan yong wooi / The Dragon Tamers, aka *Belles of Taekwondo* (1974)
Siu lam moon / The Hand of Death, aka *Countdown in Kung Fu* (1976)
Dai Nui Fa / Princess Chang Ping (1976)
Daai saat sing yue siu mooi tau / Follow the Star (1977)
Faat chin hon / Money Crazy (1978)
Ho hap / Last Hurrah for Chivalry (1978)

Haluo yeguiren / *Hello, Late Homecomers* (1978)
Chin jok gwaai / *From Riches to Rags* (1979)
Waat kai si doi / *Laughing Times* (1981)
Moh dang tin si / *To Hell with the Devil* (1982)
Baat choi Lam A Jan / *Plain Jane to the Rescue* (1982)
Ying hung mo lui / *Heroes Shed No Tears*, aka *The Sunset Warrior* (1983; released 1986)
Siu jeung / *The Time You Need a Friend* (1984)
Leung ji lo foo / *Run Tiger Run* (1985)
Ying hung boon sik / *A Better Tomorrow* (1986)
Ying hung boon sik 2 / *A Better Tomorrow 2 (1987)*
Dip huet seung hung / *The Killer* (1989)
Yi daam kwan ying / *Just Heroes*, aka *Tragic Heroes* (1990)
Dip huet gaai tau / *A Bullet in the Head* (1990)
Jung waang sei hoi / *Once a Thief* (1991)
Laat sau san taam / *Hard Boiled* (1992)
Hard Target (1993)
Broken Arrow (1996)
Once a Thief (1996)
Face/Off (1997)
Black Jack (1998) television pilot
Mission Impossible 2 (2000)

Further reading

Anne T. Ciecko, 'Transnational Action: John Woo, Hong Kong, Hollywood', *Transnational Chinese Cinemas: Identity, Nationhood, Gender*, Honolulu, University of Hawaii Press, 1997, pp. 221–39.

Stephen Prince, *Savage Cinema: Sam Peckinpah and the Rise of Ultraviolent Movies*, Austin, University of Texas Press, 1998.

Tony Rayns, 'Chivalry's Last Hurrah – John Woo', *Monthly Film Bulletin*, vol. 57, no. 680, 1990, p. 276.

Julian Stringer, ' "Your Tender Smiles Give Me Strength": Paradigms of Masculinity in John Woo's *A Better Tomorrow* and *The Killer*', *Screen*, vol. 38, no. 1, 1997, pp. 25–41.

Tony Williams, 'To Live and Die in Hong Kong: The Crisis Cinema of John Woo', *cineACTION*, no. 36, 1995, pp. 42–52.

—— 'Space, Place, and Spectacle: The Crisis Cinema of John Woo', *Cinema Journal*, vol. 36, no. 2, 1997, pp. 67–84.

—— 'From Hong Kong to Hollywood: John Woo and His Discontents', *cineACTION*, no. 42, 1997, pp. 4–45.

TONY WILLIAMS

ZHANG YIMOU

Zhang Yimou is the best-known contemporary Chinese filmmaker both inside and outside China. He is at once the personification of Chinese national cinema, an important figure and frequent award-winner in the international film festival circuits, a director of cutting-edge art-house film, a commercial genius, a political spokesperson through film, an artist and a performer. The way in which he has come to embody these many roles echoes the trajectory of Chinese cinema itself from the mid-1980s to the present day, partly as a result of the international response to the generation of Chinese film artists represented by figures like Zhang. He emerged on the Chinese and international film scene as a key member of the so-called 'Fifth Generation' and more broadly of the New Cinema or New Wave. A graduate of the class of 1982 from the Beijing Film Academy, he and his classmates have forever changed the course of Chinese film history. In the international arena, no other filmmaker has won and been nominated for so many prizes at numerous international film festivals in such a short period of time, including the Berlin Film Festival, the Venice Festival, the Tokyo Film Festival, the Cannes Film Festival and the Academy Awards. In China he has been nicknamed the 'award-winning specialist' (*huo jiang zhuanye hu*).

After graduating from the Department of Cinematography at the Beijing Film Academy, Zhang first worked as a cinematographer in the early stage of his career. He was the cinematographer of the first Fifth Generation film *One and Eight*; of *Yellow Earth*, directed by his classmate Chen Kaige, a landmark film that established the international reputation of the Fifth Generation; and of other classics of the New Cinema such as *The Big Parade* and *Old Well*. If a distinctive visual style has defined much of the essence of the New Cinema from the early phase to the present, Zhang Yimou is undoubtedly a key figure from the very beginning. His extraordinary camerawork in *Yellow Earth* – long shots of the northern Chinese landscape, the grafting of traditional Chinese landscape painting onto modern film technology, and the evocation of Taoist aesthetics in the service of a contemporary cultural critique – amounted to a revolution in Chinese film language. Striking visual images are also a recurrent feature of his work as a director. The symmetries, close-ups, long shots and perfectly framed images, buildings, faces, and figures in *Raise the Red Lantern* are textbook examples of the art of cinematography. The exuberant colours in *Red Sorghum* and *Ju Dou* evoke either a sense of exhilaration and liberation, or a mood of confinement and imprisonment. He is also a gifted story-teller in otherwise convoluted melodramas of modern Chinese history, for example *To Live*. Further, he is able to create dramatic tension in otherwise simple tales of contemporary peasant life, for example in *The Story of Qiu Ju* and *Not One Less*.

His first film, *Red Sorghum*, narrates the legend of peasants in a northern Chinese brewery in the 1930s. The exuberance, excesses, raw energy and psychical and sexual liberation as exhibited by the peasants and the narrator's 'grandpa' and 'grandma' in the film caught the attention of both domestic and international audiences. It was not only a huge box-office hit in China, but also the winner of the Golden Bear Award at the Berlin Film Festival in 1988. Since then, Zhang has become the most popular Chinese filmmaker in China and abroad. Because of the commercial success of the film, Zhang was obliged to make a popular entertainment film for the Xi'an Film Studio. *Code Name Puma*, a detective thriller set in contemporary urban China, was well received by Chinese audiences, but critics and Zhang himself regarded it as a temporary aberration in his career.

Zhang's next two films, *Ju Dou* and *Raise the Red Lantern*, firmly secured his reputation as a master filmmaker. These films also set the paradigm and expectations for what art-house Chinese cinema is supposed to be for a vast number of viewers in the West. These movies represent what might be called the classical stage of Zhang's film art. Both are allegories of physical confinement, sexual oppression and psychical oppression of individuals in China's past (set in the 1920s and 1930s). They are powerful critiques of China's patriarchal social order which silences and suppresses the desire of women and youth. The films enact an all too familiar drama about what is known as China, but in more vivid details – how the Chinese were imprisoned within an inescapable walled space. Although both films were nominated for Academy Awards and won major international prizes, they were banned in China for some time.

The compelling visual images, the consummate narration and the superb acting by the lead actresses and actors in Zhang's films place him at the forefront of international art cinema. The exotic spectacles and rituals staged in *Ju Dou* and *Raise the Red Lantern* satiate the curiosity of the international audience and its desire to know the 'Other' – the 'Orient' in the case of China. For the same reason, Zhang has been severely criticized by many indigenous Chinese critics as a classic example of 'Orientalism' fabricated by the 'Orientals' themselves. They conclude that Zhang makes films primarily for the gaze of the western audience in order to gain recognition and to win prizes at international film festivals. The argument is that, here, the Third-World artist willingly succumbs to the power structure of the global film circuits dominated by the taste and standards of the First World. It should be noted at this juncture that Zhang has also taken the lead in setting in motion a new mechanism of film production, exhibition and consumption. Since *Ju Dou*, many of his films have been joint productions funded by foreign capital where the target audience was not Chinese. The emergent category of transnational Chinese cinema exemplified by Zhang's films problematizes the traditional paradigm of national cinema in the condition of global capitalism. Such films force us to rethink issues pertaining to film markets, audiences and film production at both the national and the transnational levels.

After *Ju Dou* and *Raise the Red Lantern*, Zhang's work branched out in new directions. He began to take on contemporary subjects, setting his films in the 1990s rather than the mythical past. *The Story of Qiu Ju* and *Not One Less* are both tales of a stubborn, single-minded peasant woman who is determined to pursue her goal against overwhelming odds. Whether criticizing the inefficient, bureaucratic judicial system or the primitive, inexcusable condition of the country's primary education, the films offer a glimmer of triumph and hope for China's women and children. Above all, the blockhead yet loveable characters of Qiu Ju and Wei Minzhi have endeared themselves to audiences in China and abroad. Both films were well received by viewers, critics and the media in China. Equally significant, Zhang won the Golden Lion Prize at the Venice Film Festival in 1993 with *The Story of Qiu Ju*, and won the same prize once again in 1999 with *Not One Less*. Departing from sensational legends about a remote past, these stories capture the sight, sound, scene and mood of contemporary China. In fact, Zhang intended to achieve the effects of documentary realism in these fictional films. His crew used hidden cameras to shoot many scenes in *The Story of Qiu Ju*. He went even further with *Not One Less*, in which there was not a single professional actor – the entire cast consists of ordinary people and schoolchildren. Zhang demonstrates that he is not only an expert in visualizing highly stylized images of the past, but also a master story-teller of contemporary life in all its authentic details.

Zhang continues to experiment with new styles and broaden his subject matter. *To Live* marks another direction in which, instead of focusing on a short time-span from the past or a vignette of life from the present, Zhang draws a broad picture of decades of modern

Chinese history from the 1940s to the 1970s. The absurdities of modern Chinese political history as seen through the losses and sufferings of an ordinary family gives the film an epic sweep as well as a sense of intimacy. Although it was temporarily banned in China, the film won the Jury's Prize, and Ge You, its lead actor, won Best Actor Award, at the Cannes Film Festival. This film, together with Chen Kaige's *Farewell My Concubine* (1993) and Tian Zhuangzhuang's *The Blue Kite* (1993), successfully marketed a new brand of Chinese cinema to the international audience – modern political history. An unrelenting, humanist, critical overview of the personal and collective tragedies of socialist China, albeit enlivened by moments of comic relief as in *To Live*, it has opened the eyes of the international audience about the nature of Chinese society and the talent of Chinese filmmakers. What further distinguishes Zhang from many of his fellow Fifth Generation filmmakers is his tendency to inject humour and comic effects in the midst of rather gloomy and tragic events while engaging in serious 'cultural critique' and 'historical reflection' (*lishi fansi*). As a result, his films seem to be richer and more nuanced in meaning and sensibility.

Zhang is a master narrator of China's mythical past, an artful historian of modern Chinese history and an ingenious story-teller of rural China. However, an unturned stone in his films was Chinese urban life. To this end, Zhang wanted to prove that he could also be a skilful ethnographer of urban China in his films *Shanghai Triad* and *Keep Cool*. A gangster film, *Shanghai Triad* describes the underworld of mobsters, the 'triad', in 1930s' Shanghai, while *Keep Cool* is a comedy about the quarrels and noises of Beijing in the 1990s. By ordinary standards, these are competent films, and there are extraordinary moments of masterful filmmaking. But Zhang's domestic and international audiences tend to measure him by the milestones he has erected for himself in the past, and find that his urban films pale in comparison to his earlier achievements. If life and personal experience matter, the Fifth Generation directors, Zhang Yimou included, have yet to create convincing portraits of China's city life to equal their rural films. The Sixth Generation, which is not burdened by political movements such as the Cultural Revolution and did not have the experience of being sent down to the countryside, has been able to fashion more intriguing stories about life in contemporary urban China. It remains to be seen if Zhang, who turned 50 in 2000, is able to capture the feelings of existential malaise and urban alienation, which are sometimes well depicted by the younger graduates of the Beijing Film Academy, the 'post-Fifth Generation'.

Apart from being an acclaimed cinematographer and director, Zhang is also an accomplished actor. He has appeared in several films (for example, a minor character in *Keep Cool*), but is best remembered for his lead role as Wangquan in *Old Well*, for which he was also the cinematographer. The film was directed by Wu Tianming, head of the Xi'an Film Studio, under whose leadership many Fifth Generation directors launched their careers. Zhang won Best Actor Award, and the film itself won Best Film Award at the Tokyo Film Festival. In the film, Zhang vividly portrays a Chinese peasant's life in a poor village in northern China, and his determination to change the living condition of the villagers by finding a new source of life – a well. The figure of the stubborn, comic, yet loveable peasant also appears in films he has directed, such as *The Story of Qiu Ju* and *Not One Less*, as mentioned earlier. These fictional characters seem to have a basis in the real-life story of Zhang Yimou. Since childhood, Zhang lived with the burden of his family – his father was labelled a 'historical counter-revolutionary' (*lishi fan geming*) for once being an army officer in the Nationalist government (Guomindang). Persevering under unfavourable circumstances, Zhang developed an interest and excelled in photography, music, art, and even basketball. After many years of life as a peasant and a factory worker, the doors of opportunity were opened to Zhang and Chinese youth in general with the ending of the Mao era in the late 1970s. At the relatively late age of 28, Zhang took the entrance exam for admission to the Beijing Film Academy. Although he passed the exam, he was initially refused admission for being too old. After a long process of petitioning to the Ministry of Culture, he finally enrolled in the school. He was 32 years old when he graduated from 'college' in 1982. The life story of his difficult personal odyssey in moving up the social ladder, or simply getting things done in China, parallels the fate and endeavour of his characters (Wangquan, Qiu Ju, Wei Minzhi). The steely determination and persistence to break out of a hopeless situation and to escape from patterns of repetition on the part of low, comic, poor, peasant characters is not only Zhang's personal story, but it also speaks to the collective unconscious of a backward Third World country on its way to modernization – hence his films' appeal to the general Chinese populace.

Zhang's name has been intimately tied to an actress discovered and championed by him – Gong Li. She had been his lead actress from his first film *Red Sorghum* to *Shanghai Triad*. Because of her memorable performances in various roles in Zhang's films, she has come to signify the image of the Chinese woman internationally. Their collaboration on screen and love affair off screen ended after the shooting of *Shanghai Triad*, and Zhang has not as yet found a new female star who can replace the presence, prestige and box-office value of Gong Li for audiences around the world.

Between 1987 and 1999, Zhang Yimou directed ten feature films, some of which set the standard of both Chinese and world cinema. He raised the level of film as an art form. Domestically, his films came out at a time when Chinese audiences, having lived through the Mao era and been flooded with the trite formula of socialist-realism, desperately wanted to see scathing works of art that would cross-examine the entrenched patterns of Chinese culture and society and probe the depths of the Chinese psyche. Internationally, his engaging narratives and powerful images allow viewers to witness at close range the rituals, mysteries, dramas, politics, tragedies, struggles and passions of the Chinese people in the twentieth century. As Zhang's experimentation with new themes and new ways of filmmaking continues, we can only hope that even more outstanding films are yet to come.

Biography

Born in Xi'an, Shaanxi Province, in China, in 1950, Zhang entered the Department of Cinematography of the Beijing Film Academy in 1978, and graduated in 1982.

Filmography

Red Sorghum / *Hong gaoliang* (1987)
Code Name Puma / *Daihao Meizhoubao* (1988)
Ju Dou / *Ju Dou* (1990)
Raise the Red Lantern / *Da hong denglong gaogao gua* (1991)
The Story of Qiu Ju / *Qiu Ju da guansi* (1993)
To Live / *Huozhe* (1994)
Shanghai Triad / *Yao a yao, yao dao waipoqiao* (1995)
Keep Cool / *Youhua haohao shuo* (1997)
Not One Less / *Yige dou buneng shao* (1999)
My Father and Mother / *Wo de fuqin muqin* (1999)

As cinematographer

One and Eight / *Yige he bage* (1984)
Yellow Earth / *Huang tudi* (1984)

The Big Parade / *Da yuebing* (1985)
Old Well / *Lao jing* (1987) also performer

Further reading

Rey Chow, 'The Force of Surfaces: Defiance in Zhang Yimou's Films', *Primitive Passions: Visuality, Sexuality, Ethnography, and Contemporary Chinese Cinema*, New York, Columbia University Press, 1995, pp. 142–72.

Shuqing Cui, 'Gendered Perspective: The Construction and Representation of Subjectivity and Sexuality in *Ju Dou*', in Sheldon H. Lu. (ed.) *Transnational Chinese Cinemas: Identity, Nationhood, Gender*, Honolulu, University of Hawaii Press, 1997, pp. 303–29.

Qing Dai, 'Raised Eyebrows for *Raise the Red Lantern*', *Public Culture*, vol. 5, no. 2, 1993, pp. 333–6.

Jenny Kwok Wah Lau, '*Ju Dou*: A Hermeneutical Reading of Cross-Cultural Cinema', *Film Quarterly*, vol. 45, no. 2, 1991, pp. 2–10.

Sheldon H. Lu, 'National Cinema, Cultural Critique, Transnational Capital: The Films of Zhang Yimou', in Sheldon H. Lu, *op. cit.*, pp. 105–36.

Yuejin Wang, '*Red Sorghum*: Mixing Memory and Desire', in Chris Berry (ed.) *Perspectives on Chinese Cinema*, London, BFI Publishing, 1991, pp. 80–103.

Mayfair Yang, 'Of Gender, State Censorship, and Overseas Capital: An Interview with Director Zhang Yimou', *Public Culture*, vol. 5, no. 2, 1993, pp. 297–316.

Ming-Bao Yue, 'Visual Agency and Ideological Fantasy in Three Films by Zhang Yimou', in Wimal Dissanayake (ed.) *Narratives of Agency: Self-making in China, India, and Japan*, Minneapolis, University of Minnesota Press, 1996, pp. 56–73.

Yingjin Zhang, 'Ideology of the Body in *Red Sorghum*: National Allegory, National Roots, and Third Cinema', *East-West Film Journal*, vol. 4, no. 2, 1990, pp. 38–53.

SHELDON H. LU

ZHANG YUAN

After winning the Best Director award for his *Seventeen Years* at the Venice International Film Festival in 1999, Zhang Yuan, the *enfant terrible* of the post-1989 young Chinese cinema, was finally accepted by the mainstream Chinese cinema under the aegis of the government. Unlike his earlier underground (and therefore banned) films such as *Beijing Bastards*, featuring a look at the anarchic rock scene in Beijing, and *East Palace, West Palace*, allegedly the first 'gay film' in China, *Seventeen Years* was officially released in Beijing to considerable critical and popular acclaim in early 2000. A decade after Zhang Yuan made his début with the low-budget independent feature *Mama*, and despite the difficult conditions in which he clandestinely and intermittently had to work, he now has seven feature-length fictional and documentary films and numerous shorts and MTV films to his credit. Not only is this famous independent filmmaker finally on his way to the centre stage of Chinese film culture, but the so-called 'Sixth Generation' as a whole (to which he belongs and for which he has served as a main spokesperson) can no longer be seen as a small group of maverick underground filmmakers. The Sixth Generation has expanded and transformed itself into a broadly defined movement of young urban cinema, its avant-garde spirit infused with a deep concern for contemporary social life as well as the desire to reach mainstream audiences and attain commercial success.

Zhang Yuan graduated from the Beijing Film Academy in 1989, a watershed year in China. 1989 was marked by the student democracy movement, the ensuing Tiananmen Square massacre, and a deepening disillusionment with the communist regime and its ideology among Chinese people, particularly the young, following the fall of the Berlin Wall. In terms of contemporary film history, 1989 also divides the 'Fifth Generation' – the first class to graduate from the Beijing Film Academy after the Cultural Revolution in the early 1980s – and the Sixth or even younger generations, who began to make their first films in the early and mid-1990s under the compounded pressures of political censorship and new commercial constraints.

The difference between the two generations is more than genealogical. By the early 1990s, the Fifth Generation had consolidated its place both on the international scene and in the Chinese national film industry with several representative works, notably *Yellow Earth*, *Red Sorghum* and *Farewell My Concubine*. Despite its profile as art cinema and the political controversy surrounding some of their productions, the Fifth Generation directors worked by and large within the state-sponsored studio system. Many of the younger filmmakers, however, identified themselves as independent, both institutionally and financially, from the outset. In this sense, the key difference between the Fifth and Sixth Generation is their distinct social and professional identities as well as aesthetic outlooks.

After graduating from the Beijing Film Academy, Zhang Yuan declined an assigned post at the August First Film Studio (a studio charged with producing military and propaganda films under the aegis of the People's Liberation Army), and instead embarked upon a precarious independent career. Working on a shoestring budget –

the equivalent of $1,300 from his and friends' savings – he produced, directed and co-wrote his first feature, *Mama* (aka *The Tree of the Sun*). The film is about a Beijing librarian who singlehandedly cares for her autistic son while confronting social prejudices towards the disabled. In addition, it focuses on her deteriorating relationship with an unsupportive, long-distance commuting husband. The minimal plot and small cast of characters are characteristic of Zhang Yuan's films. Shot mostly in black and white, *Mama* also prefigures the documentary sensibility and urban themes that have become more pronounced in his recent works. The story is based on the life experiences of Qin Yan, the actress who plays the mother in the film. Zhang Yuan interweaves the narrative with a series of video interviews with parents of autistic children. The result is an unusual work, treading a thin line between fiction and documentary, lyricism and realism. The film was hailed as 'audacious' and its creator the 'new face of Chinese cinema' by one French critic.[1] *Mama* received the Special Jury Prize at the 1991 Nantes Film Festival, the first of many international awards for the emerging young filmmaker.

Mama demonstrated that it was possible to make a 35mm feature film entirely outside the studio system. Although registered with the Xi'an Studio (which provided no financial support), the film was not widely distributed in China.[2] It was screened at the Human Rights Film Festival in New York and at the Asian American Film Festival in Washington, DC. The film's exhibition at such politically significant rather than glamorous venues initiated a practice associated with Zhang Yuan in particular, and with the Sixth Generation in general. Without sponsorship and evading the restrictions set by the Chinese government, Zhang Yuan and other independent filmmakers have actively sought to connect with an alternative, international film culture centred around festivals and art-house theatres. Indeed, such conscious connection with this international circuit, together with the promotion, albeit with mixed motives, by foreign critics and cinephiles fascinated with contemporary Chinese cinema, has contributed to the critical success of Sixth Generation cinema abroad.

Zhang Yuan's second feature, the controversial *Beijing Bastards*, created quite a stir when it was spirited out of China and shown at several festivals overseas. It was seen as a radical departure from the Fifth Generation cinema, also labelling Zhang Yuan a 'trouble-maker', and thus an emblematic figure of an emergent independent movement, in the eyes of the Chinese censors. Significantly, the film was co-produced by Zhang Yuan and China's foremost rock musician, Cui Jian. Their partnership goes back to Zhang Yuan's filming of Cui Jian's music videos. As with *Days* (1993) and *Dirt* (1994) by Zhang Yuan's classmates Wang Xiaoshuai and Guan Hu respectively, *Beijing Bastards* portrays the bohemian scene in Beijing and the struggle of artists (rock musicians and experimental artists in particular) to create art and seek answers to existential dilemmas in a suffocating environment. The rock 'n' roll spirit is, to an extent, also the spirit of the Sixth Generation, its iconoclastic and restless rhythm the rhythm of the young urban cinema. The film's slender narrative concerns a rock band driven out of its rehearsal space. The problem with space would become a leitmotif of many Sixth Generation films, especially those that explicitly tackle the widespread phenomenon of urban reconstruction and dislocation. Indeed, the film strongly evokes a sense of place, a milieu, and a troubled or 'mixed' (as the title suggests) one at that.[3] The atmospheric, documentary-style look of the film is accentuated with footage of Cui Jian's live performance.

The sense of place becomes the central focus of *The Square*, a documentary about Tiananmen Square. The monumental space in the heart of the capital becomes the protagonist rather than the backdrop of a ceaselessly unfolding history and an everyday drama. Zhang Yuan began this project as a defiant gesture after the government blacklisted him (and several other independent film-makers) as punishment for unsanctioned participation in festivals abroad. The film is essentially a 'documentary on the political and social economy' of the Square.[4] Zhang Yuan let his camera quietly observe the Square and its various occupants and visitors during a 24-hour period. The finished film intercuts political rituals (the raising and lowering of the national flag) with everyday life (children flying kites, tourists posing for photos). The Square emerges as a multifaceted space filled with state-sanctioned symbolic meanings as well as public memory and leisure activities.

If the Fifth Generation and their representative works remained 'idealistic', preoccupied with creating cultural 'myths' rooted in rural China and the past, Zhang Yuan is motivated by a strong concern with contemporary 'social problems and social reality' as experienced or witnessed by the filmmaker.[5] This concern with the 'social', particularly issues concerning relations between public and private, between family ethics and cultural norms, and between the state and marginal social subjects, can be discerned across his work. It is often articulated through a self-conscious deployment of the documentary or docu-dramatic method, which also generally distinguishes the Sixth Generation filmmakers.

Zhang Yuan is not content with merely recording reality; he strives to create new modes of observation and involvement. As an unconventional documentarian, Zhang Yuan is obsessed with, in his own words, the 'dialectical relation between subjective consciousness and objective reality'.[6] His next film, *Sons*, initiated by downstairs neighbours who asked him to make a film about their dysfunctional family, pushes that dialectic to its breaking point. The family, torn apart by alcoholism and insanity, stages its past and present for the camera.[7] A retired couple, formerly dancers, and their two sons live in a typical Beijing apartment complex, surrounded by neighbours with watchful eyes. The father's love of the bottle and the resultant violence nearly destroys the family. The film's impact comes from its unflinching examination of the institution of (the patriarchal) family and the problem of social reproduction. It also probes questions of representation and performance. The characters play themselves with both restraint and abandon. The mother, who suffers most abuse and shoulders the heaviest burden (emotionally and financially), is particularly moving when we learn that she has hidden the certificate of divorce in a drawer, staying on to hold the family together. The film's sense of 'authenticity' is achieved, according to the director, 'through the process of forgetting it rather than its [deliberate] attainment' – as when family members forget their lines and 'perform' as the situation dictates.[8]

Such a blend of performative spontaneity and directorial design, reality and fiction continues in Zhang Yuan's more recent documentaries. Both *Crazy English* and *Miss Jing Xing* (a video film made for the Internet) are in each instance about a unique individual whose action and convictions create sensations and controversies in contemporary Chinese society, albeit in very different ways. In documenting the journey of both protagonists as they realize dreams, Zhang Yuan's camera and editing are constantly foregrounded, suggesting the tenuous relation between subject and object, liveness and construction.

Crazy English is a *tour de force* portrayal of Li Yang, the self-made English teacher and motivational speaker who invented an idiosyncratic pedagogy called 'Crazy English'. In the fashion of collective gymnastics, Li Yang delivers speeches and gives demonstrations with animated body language in front of mass assemblies (his company also publishes textbooks, cassettes and CD-ROMs) at various public venues, including the Forbidden Palace and the Great Wall. His students range from PLA soldiers to primary school pupils. The film opens with Zhang's 'crew' filming while jogging and shouting out loud English phrases together with Li Yang and his followers. Amidst the 'crazy' sound, the 'cameraman' trips and falls, causing chaos. The film captures the 'crazy' spirit of Li Yang's enterprise and the chaotic messages he transmits through his linguistic aerobics. He at once promotes a fierce patriotism (that the Chinese will conquer the world market once they master English) and expresses a strange fascination with the West and the modernity it represents (Li confesses that he has never been abroad). The film is hardly judgmental – there is no voice-over – on Li Yang's crusade to modernize or Anglo-Saxonize, both mentally and physically, the Chinese through mastery of the English language. Yet through the direct investigation of Li Yang's method, the film exposes the ideological confusion shared by him and many other Chinese people in the era of reform.

Miss Jing Xing is a candid yet artful treatment of the sex change undergone by Jing Xing, a gay dancer who, after returning to China from several years of study and work in New York, decided that he was meant to be a woman. The one-hour video film, made for the Hong Kong-based website Tom.com, portrays the outspoken Jing Xing as a cosmopolitan Chinese artist with unconventional cultural and sexual identities. Instead of sensationalizing the sex change, Zhang Yuan interweaves the vaguely re-enacted surgery, shot through a blue filter, with Jing Xing's own narration and reconstructions of other significant episodes in her past and present life. The multilayered montage technique creates a polysemic text suggesting that the significance of Jing Xing's choice is both biological and social. By the end of the film, the crew films Jing Xing in Shanghai where she leads local dancers rehearsing for a modern dance show, the first of its kind in China's largest metropolis. The final images capture Jing Xing leaping in the air, looking both beautiful and strong.

Zhang Yuan treats the theme of marginal sexual identity and the relation between art and erotic desire earlier in a different mode, in perhaps his most stylized film, *East Palace, West Palace*. The minimal yet sophisticated narrative takes place within the walls of a public park where local gay men cruise. A police officer 'picks up' and interrogates A Lan at the police station inside the park throughout the night. Although the result is a theatrical 'chamber piece',[9] the inspiration for the film came from a news report about the way in which a research institute conducts research into AIDS. Unable to access the underground gay circle for study, the institute solicits the help of police to haul gay men in for forced interviews, or questioning. Flabbergasted by what he believes to be 'one of the most absurd things' in Chinese society, Zhang Yuan decided to interview gay people himself and 'find out what is different about them'.[10] However, extensive interviews and research led him to make a very different film. Perhaps in an attempt to get at the core of the absurdity that first inspired the film, Zhang Yuan, with the collaboration of the late writer Wang Xiaobo, crafted a script that delivers a philosophical and aesthetic intensity rarely seen in Chinese cinema from the mainland. The film goes beyond the showing of the gay underworld in Beijing; in Zhang Yuan's words, it 'introduces how the system works'.[11]

The politics of homosexuality is intimately intertwined with the politics of representation in *East Palace, West Palace*. The film is rich with sumptuous images and subtle in its critique of a repressed society. It is significant that A Lan (played by Si Han, a former radio reporter) is a writer who 'confesses' to the officer the formation of his sexual identity. These tales are not so much forced testimony as active (self-)representation which explore the erotic and intersubjective nature of language and communication. It soon becomes apparent that the two engage in a sadomasochistic play (or struggle) of power and desire. The allegorical meaning of the narrative proper is given more complexity by the deliberate insertion of two mini-narratives from traditional opera and theatrical performance. One is an ancient tale about the ambivalent relationship between a palace guard and a female thief, the other that between an executioner and a prisoner. Through the juxtaposition of these theatrical *gestalts* of archetypal power relations, Zhang Yuan's modern tale of sexual and political dominance takes on a symbolic significance.

Paradoxically, the question of homosexual rights that first inspired Zhang Yuan, though never displaced, became overshadowed by the elaborate allegory. *East Palace, West Palace* was again banned in China. And in early 1997, the authorities confiscated Zhang Yuan's passport to prevent him from travelling to the Cannes Film Festival to present the film. Ironically, the prohibition had more to do with the way the film was made than its content. Financed in part by an award from the French Ministry of Culture, as soon as shooting was completed, the film was smuggled out of China for post-production in France, ready for Cannes.

The issue of censorship has been an integral part of Zhang Yuan's international fame in a decade-long career as an independent filmmaker in China. In 1993, after confrontations between official delegates and festival organizers at several international festivals (Tokyo and Hong Kong in particular), Zhang Yuan and six other independent filmmakers (including He Jianjun, Wang Xiaoshuai, Wu Wenguang and Ning Dai, Zhang Yuan's wife) met with harsh punishment from the government. Official directives forbidding any collaboration with or sponsorship of the banned filmmakers were sent to sixteen state-owned studios, processing labs and equipment rental services nationwide.[12] Consequently, Zhang Yuan was forced to discontinue the shooting of his third feature, *Chicken Feathers on the Ground*.[13] The director went back to making music videos with Cui Jian.

The erratic pattern of government repression and relaxation continued while Zhang Yuan and other young filmmakers persisted in working. Over the years, they have learned that it is not possible to make entirely independent films in a country where the state film apparatus controls most means of production and distribution. At the same time they discovered that, thanks in part to the new market economy, there is a substantial margin 'within' the system itself where they could carve out a limited creative space, leasing editing room and equipment from official studios when the political atmosphere is relatively relaxed. After strenuous negotiations, Zhang Yuan was given back his passport and, eventually, permission to resume filmmaking as a reinstated director in 1998. The result was *Crazy English* and *Seventeen Years*, both produced and released through official channels.

Zhang Yuan, who has struggled under the censors' watchful eyes, seems obsessed with forms of institutional imprisonment and possible liberation from it. *Seventeen Years*, his most recent feature which has both solidified his international stature and won him official acceptance at home, centres on a female prisoner getting her New Year's parole after seventeen years. The source of inspiration for this film once more came from real life. Touched by a television programme about prisoners meeting their relatives, Zhang Yuan began to visit a number of prisons and interview the inmates. The extensive preparation obviously contributed to the docu-drama quality of the finished film, accentuated by a mixture of documentary techniques such as hand-held and hidden camera during location shooting, on the one hand, and the melodramatic handling of the family reunion, on the other.[14]

The narrative structure of the film is characteristically simple yet inventive. As with *Sons*, the plot mainly involves a broken family; but unlike the earlier docu-drama, *Seventeen Years* incorporates a female prison warden who accompanies the prisoner Tao Lan home, and who, over the course of the film, gets more involved in the life of her subject despite her initial reluctance and indifference. The seemingly linear narrative unfolds in a decidedly historical time and social space. The period of 'seventeen years' refers not only to youth lost behind bars, but also overlaps with the 'new era' of reform since China re-opened its doors in 1979. 'Going home' (as the Chinese title indicates) proves to be an ordeal across an alien and ruthlessly changing urban landscape. The childhood neighbourhood where Tao Lan killed her stepsister in the heat of a trivial argument is nowhere to be found. Her mother and stepfather have moved to the suburbs, as have thousands of urban Chinese dwellers following the dismantling of inner cities and old neighbourhoods to make way for department stores, office buildings and expressways. We find Tao Lan utterly confused and lost, for instance, in front of huge advertising bulletin boards displaying half-naked women. The middle part of the film takes place entirely on the street, in the urban maze from which Tao Lan wants to flee back to the prison, now more like a home to her after years of insulation. Here the film is perhaps at its most poignant (more so than with the melodramatic happy ending), as it touches on the merits of reform and a market economy, and on a more complex level, the very nature and possibility of freedom in a mainland Chinese society undergoing tremendous, and at times violent, transformation.

Seen mainly as a sensitive portrayal of the Chinese prison system, *Seventeen Years* has been received favourably in China. Chinese critics seem to have overlooked (maybe purposely so) the film's more complex dimensions. One critic writes in the officially sponsored *Popular Cinema*: 'With the success of *Seventeen Years*, the Sixth Generation has reached the summit of the international film world, and has now its representative work.' During the Beijing premiere, Zhang Yuan reportedly went on stage with his cast to greet the audience and answer questions. The distance between the *enfant terrible* of Chinese cinema, who had previously only made films to provoke conventional viewing habits of the Chinese audience, and an audience who had very little knowledge of this baby-faced director with a head of intractable curly hair, seems to have shortened significantly within a couple of years.

The official government film apparatus, perhaps realizing the inevitability of change ahead, is also playing the card of patronizing, or even seducing, young filmmakers by hiring them for productions at major studios, with the possibility of distributing their works in China. Pained by the fact that his earlier films have hardly been seen by the domestic audience, Zhang Yuan seems also inclined to negotiate, if not compromise, his relationship with both the film bureau and the market. Last-minute cuts were needed for both *Crazy English* and *Seventeen Years* to pass for domestic release. There are speculations as to whether or not Zhang Yuan, and for that matter, the Sixth Generation as a whole, has gone mainstream. At the same time, the mainstream is also being redefined in a rapidly transforming China/Chinese film culture. The acute concern for the changing society, an increased awareness of the importance of domestic audiences, and the desire to reinvent the cinematic language and revive Chinese cinema in the face of emerging media such as the Internet have forced young filmmakers to adjust both their outlook and their tactics. As long ago as 1994, *Time* magazine selected Zhang Yuan as one of the one hundred young leading figures of the world for the new century. Zhang Yuan does not care much about that title; what he cares about most is that Chinese people see his films in cinemas, and perhaps eventually in virtual cinemas. He has plans to create more theatrical works, and to move into the world of the Internet.[15] Zhang Yuan will no doubt continue to make films, but his work, as well as the practice of filmmaking itself, is heading in new directions in the twenty-first century.

Biography

Zhang Yuan was born in Nanjing, Jiangsu Province, China, in 1963. He graduated with a Bachelor of Arts degree in cinematography from the Beijing Film Academy in 1989. In addition to feature and documentary filmmaking, Zhang Yuan is an active music video producer and director. His direction of Cui Jian's 'Wild in the Snow' won the Best Asian MTV Award at the American MTV Awards in 1991; 'A Piece of Red Cloth' won a Special Mention at the San Francisco's Golden Gate millennium. He has also adapted his film *East Palace, West Place* for the stage, with productions mounted in Belgium, Brazil, the UK and France.

Acknowledgment

I would like to thank the Humanities Council at New York University for a grant-in-aid that enabled the research and writing of this essay. I am also grateful to Zhang Yuan, Wu Lala, Jia Zhijie and *Time* magazine (Beijing bureau) for providing valuable material.

Notes

1 Ange-Dominique Bouzet, 'Un chonois pour trois continents', *Liberation*, 20 December 1991.
2 The film was reportedly released in China in 1994 and broadcast on cable television. Steven Schwankert, 'Director's Cut', *Far Eastern Economic Review*, 30 November 1995, p. 82. It now also exists on VCD.
3 David Chute, 'Beyond the Law', *Film Comment*, vol. 30, no. 1, 1994, p. 62.
4 Tony Rayns, 'Provoking Desire', *Sight and Sound*, July 1996, p. 26.
5 Ma Li Ya, ' "Hou diwudai" zhenzhi luxian "cuowu" de dianying daoyan–Zhang Yuan' ('The "post-Fifth Generation", politically "incorrect" director – Zhang Yuan'), *Zhong* ('The Chinese'), July 1996, pp. 96–100.
6 *Ibid.*, p. 98.
7 Zhang Yuan had to get special permission for the father to be temporarily released from the mental hospital where he was undergoing treatment.
8 Zhang Yuan, comments made at the Chinese Cultural Studies Workshop, Harvard University, 4 November 1999.
9 Tony Rayns, *op. cit.*, p. 28.
10 *Ibid.*
11 Steven Schwankert, *op. cit.*, p. 82.
12 Godfrey Cheshire, 'Chinese Checkers', *Film Comment*, vol. 30, no. 4, 1994, p. 65.
13 The intense discussion among the crew and other independent filmmakers is the subject of Ning Dai's video documentary, *Discussions Caused by a Film Being Stopped* (1994).
14 Zhang Yuan and his crew obtained special permission to film inside the Tianjin First Prison where the real-life woman was jailed.
15 Conversations with Zhang Yuan, Beijing, June 2000.

Filmography

(All produced in China unless otherwise indicated)
Mama / *Beijing zazhong* (China/Hong Kong, 1993)
The Square / *Guangchang* (co-director: Duan Jingchuang; 1994)
Sons / *Erzi* (1995)
East Palace, West Place / *Donggong Xigong* (China/France, 1996)
Demolition and Relocation / *Dingfzi hu* (1998)
Crazy English / *Fengkuang Yingyu* (1999)
Seventeen Years / *Guonian huijia* (1999)
Miss Jing Xing / *Jing Xing Xiaojie* (2000) documentary made with DV, the first Chinese work of the 'Eighth Art' exhibited on the Internet

Further reading

Chris Berry, 'Staging Gay Life in China: Zhang Yuan and *East Palace, West Palace*', *Jump Cut*, no. 41, 1998, pp. 84–9.

Eric Holm, 'Feted Abroad, and No Longer Banned in Beijing', *New York Times*, 26 December 1999.

Harry H. Koshu, '*Beijing Bastards*, The Sixth Generation Directors, and "Generation-X" in China', *Asian Cinema*, Spring/Summer 1999, pp. 18–28.

Zhiliang Li, 'Toushi aiguo Yingyu feng' ('Looking through the craze of patriotic English'), *Ming Bao*, 8 October 1999.

Jifang Wang, *Zuohoude langman–Beijing ziyou yishujia shilu* (*The last romance – a reportage on the independent artists in Beijing*), Ha'erbin, Beifan wenyi chubanshe, 1999.

Yingjing Zhang, and Zhiwei Xiao (eds) *Chinese Film Encyclopedia*, London, Routledge, 1998.

ZHANG ZHEN

INDEX

Coen
Hartley
Jarmusch
Kaurismaki
A. Lee
Lynch

Sayles

Solondz

von Trier

Yimou